Postcolonial Thought
in the French-speaking World

Postcolonialism across the Disciplines 4

Postcolonialism across the Disciplines

Series Editors
Graham Huggan, University of Leeds
Andrew Thompson, University of Leeds

Postcolonialism across the Disciplines showcases alternative directions for postcolonial studies. It is in part an attempt to counteract the dominance in colonial and postcolonial studies of one particular discipline – English literary/ cultural studies – and to make the case for a combination of disciplinary knowledges as the basis for contemporary postcolonial critique. Edited by leading scholars, the series aims to be a seminal contribution to the field, spanning the traditional range of disciplines represented in postcolonial studies but also those less acknowledged. It will also embrace new critical paradigms and examine the relationship between the transnational/cultural, the global and the postcolonial.

Postcolonial Thought in the French-speaking World

Edited by
Charles Forsdick
and David Murphy

Liverpool University Press

First published 2009 by
Liverpool University Press
4 Cambridge Street
Liverpool L69 7ZU

British Library Cataloguing-in-Publication data
A British Library CIP record is available

ISBN 978-1-84631-054-6 cased
     978-1-84631-055-3 limp

Typeset in Amerigo by Koinonia, Manchester
Printed and bound by CPI Group (UK) Ltd, Croydon, CR0 4YY

Contents

Contents

Acknowledgements

The editors would like to thank the following people for the ideas and assistance they contributed to the preparation of this volume: ACHAC, Christine Dutton, Elizabeth Ezra, Kate Marsh, Aedín Ní Loingsigh. Alec Hargreaves deserves special thanks for providing various forums in which we were able to develop the ideas that inform our introduction. Even more importantly, his comments on an original draft of this volume were a model of academic rigour, and we are very grateful for his constructive engagement with our project, which allowed us to clarify our thinking still further. We take responsibility for any remaining flaws in the volume.

We are particularly grateful to Anthony Cond, our commissioning editor at Liverpool University Press, as well as Graham Huggan, the series editor, for championing this project. Charles Forsdick completed his contribution to this collection while he was in receipt of a Philip Leverhulme Prize; the support of the Leverhulme Trust is gratefully acknowledged. We also acknowledge the support of our friends and colleagues in Stirling, Liverpool and elsewhere, and would like to extend a warm tribute to our contributors, whose innovative and scholarly work made it such a pleasure to prepare this volume. Neil Lazarus and Benita Parry also provided invaluable support and encouragement in the early stages of the project. Finally, we would like to thank Aisling Campbell and Aedín Ní Loingsigh for their translation of Chapter 24.

A note on translations

In cases where a French-language text exists in a readily available translation, contributors have endeavoured to provide the title and other quoted material from this; in order to preserve a sense of the time period in which these texts were initially published, the date of publication of the French original is provided when a text is cited for the first time in each chapter. In all other cases, quotations are printed in the original French, with a translation provided by the author of each individual chapter.

INTRODUCTION

Situating Francophone Postcolonial Thought

Charles Forsdick and David Murphy

On 26 July 2007, less than three months after his election to the French presidency and on his first post-election trip to Africa, Nicolas Sarkozy stood before an invited audience of students, scholars, dignitaries and political leaders at the Université Cheikh Anta Diop de Dakar in Senegal, and delivered a speech that was directed at 'la jeunesse africaine' [African youth].[1] The speech was awaited with a mixture of expectation and trepidation, for Sarkozy had adopted a strangely dualistic discourse on France's colonial past and postcolonial relationships during the preceding campaign: on the one hand, he had expressed a desire to break with the corrupt practices of the previous fifty years, frequently dubbed *la Françafrique*, a netherworld of corrupt oil, arms and trade deals designed to maintain France's global 'sphere of influence', a process charted as early as the 1970s in texts such as Mongo Beti's scathing polemic *Main basse sur le Cameroun* (1972), or Ousmane Sembene's witheringly satirical film, *Xala* (1974);[2] yet on the other hand, he had emphasized in several pre-election speeches the positive effects of French colonialism and had evoked his desire for a vision of history that French people could celebrate rather than one for which they were obliged to repent (see Liauzu, 2007a). If the call to break with the practices of *la Françafrique* was cautiously welcomed in Africa, the attempt to move away from the gradual acknowledgement of certain 'crimes' of the colonial past (a process begun by the previous president Jacques Chirac) created deep disquiet; this anxiety was compounded by the creation of a highly contentious Ministry for Immigration, Integration, National Identity and Co-development by the Sarkozy

---

1   The full text of Sarkozy's speech can be found at http://www.elysee.fr/elysee/elysee. fr/francais/interventions/2007/juillet/allocution_a_l_universite_de_dakar.79184.html (consulted 3 October 2008). One of the few informed and immediate responses to the speech came in a special dossier in the magazine *Jeune Afrique* (see Colette, 2007).

2   One of the most vocal critics of *la Françafrique* is the investigative journalist Xavier Verschave (2003).

government, a development that inherently posited immigrants as a 'problem' for national identity.[3] (For eloquent critiques of this new ministry, see Glissant and Chamoiseau, 2007; Liauzu, 2007a; Noiriel, 2007; Todorov, 2007.)

Sarkozy began his speech with an unexpected acknowledgement of the negative aspects of the French colonial project: 'Le colonisateur est venu, il a pris, il s'est servi, il a exploité, il a pillé des resources, des richesses qui ne lui appartenaient pas' [the colonizer came, he appropriated, he took what he wanted, he exploited, he pillaged resources, riches that did not belong to him]. However, as Pascal Blanchard, among others, has argued, the recognition of colonialism's exceptional 'errors' is designed primarily to underline more clearly the overall positive effect of France's colonial 'mission' (Blanchard, 2007); as *bavures* [unfortunate errors], they are the result of individual incidents of wrongdoing and thus do not constitute a systematic policy of oppression. Following this logic, the subsequent lines of Sarkozy's speech absolved French colonialism of any malicious intent, and he detailed the benefits of France's civilizing mission:

> Il a pris mais je veux dire avec respect qu'il a aussi donné. Il a construit des ponts, des routes, des hôpitaux, des dispensaires, des écoles. Il a rendu fécondes des terres vierges, il a donné sa peine, son travail, son savoir. Je veux le dire ici, tous les colons n'étaient pas des voleurs, tous les colons n'étaient pas des exploiteurs.

> He took but I would respectfully submit that he also gave. He built bridges, roads, hospitals, dispensaries, schools. He made fertile land that had been barren, he gave his effort, his work, his knowledge. I want to say this here today that not all colonizers were thieves, not all colonizers were exploiters.

Albert Memmi had denounced, over fifty years previously, the bad faith that underpinned any such notion of the 'good colonizer', but Sarkozy also refused any responsibility on the part of France for Africa's current social, economic and political predicament.[4] Instead, and to the dismay of his audience, he proceeded to lay the blame at the feet of Africans themselves – and in particular the mythical figure of the peasant – who were denied coevalness with the West and deemed to be living outside history, guided by an innate sense of time and space that made it impossible for them to develop modern societies:

> Le drame de l'Afrique, c'est que l'homme africain n'est pas assez entré dans l'Histoire. Le paysan africain qui, depuis des millénaires, vit avec les saisons, dont l'idéal de vie est d'être en harmonie avec la nature, ne connaît que

---

3 Similar moves towards a strict legislative framework for national identity have been witnessed in many European countries over the past decade: see Huggan (2008). For a discussion of France's position in a wider 'postcolonial Europe', see Forsdick and Murphy (2007).

4 The British historian Niall Ferguson has similarly attempted through a series of publications to present the British Empire in an almost uniquely positive light (Ferguson, 2003).

l'éternel recommencement du temps rythmé pas la répétition sans fin des mêmes gestes et des mêmes paroles.

Dans cet imaginaire où tout recommence toujours, il n'y a de place ni pour l'aventure humaine, ni pour l'idée de progrès.

Africa's tragedy is that the African has largely remained outside History. The African peasant, who has lived by the seasons for several millennia, and whose ideal is to be in harmony with nature, only knows the eternal cycle of time, which is marked by the endless repetition of the same gestures and the same words.

In this imaginary where everything is always repeated, there is no place for human adventure nor for the idea of progress.

This recycling of some of the worst racialized tropes and myths of the colonial era brought about an immediate response from Africanist scholars: within just over a year of the speech, three books had been published in response to it (Mbem, 2007; Gassama, 2008; Chrétien, 2008). However, despite widespread condemnation of the speech in African newspapers, the subject has met with almost total silence in the French press: Achille Mbembe's opinion piece in *Jeune Afrique* is one of the few that appeared in the immediate aftermath of the speech (Mbembe, 2007).

This episode reveals much of the complexity of the 'afterlives' of French colonialism: the persistence of modes of thought from the colonial era; metropolitan blindness to and disregard for France's actions overseas; the asymmetrical relations between the former colonial power and its former colonies; but also the possibility for new axes and alliances to develop between intellectuals from former colonized cultures (as in the response to Sarkozy's speech). It is to this complexity that the current volume responds, attempting to draw out many of the interwoven strands that, taken together, constitute what we have termed 'Postcolonial Thought in the French-Speaking World'. In the following sections of this introduction, we aim to situate this thought in relation to some of the intellectual, social, cultural and political contexts from which it has emerged: we will begin by examining the 'evolving contexts' that have marked the field of postcolonial studies over the past few years; we will then seek to examine the precise nature of academic and intellectual debates on the 'postcolonial' in France, before moving on to analyse some of the specific incidents that have shaped the evolution of this debate; finally, we will discuss the structure and aims of the present volume, and the ways in which it seeks to encourage the development of the field. As is illustrated by the image on the front cover of this volume, intellectual and revolutionary challenges to empire emanating from the colonies (or indeed from within the imperial centre) have often been caricatured in France as 'alien', simplistic and unjustified challenges to the integrity of the (imperial) nation: the essays collected here demonstrate on the contrary that the development of anti- and postcolonial thought in the French-speaking world has been a rigorous, enlightening and highly complex process that warrants much greater critical attention.

Evolving contexts

Several years ago, we edited a volume of essays (Forsdick and Murphy, 2003) that mapped out the contours of a domain that had – via journal articles, conference papers and monographs on discrete topics or authors – increasingly been signalling its existence, but that had yet to be named explicitly as a distinct area of inquiry. Our intentions in formally naming this field 'Francophone postcolonial studies' were twofold: first, to offer consolidation of, and a certain coherence to, the diverse lines of enquiry that had come to constitute this research area; and, secondly, to explore how a Francophone postcolonial debate might challenge and interrogate what was then the primarily English-language field of postcolonial studies. Such taxonomical manoeuvres are, of course, fraught with danger, and may be seen to encourage a degree of self-congratulation that impedes self-reflexivity: however, drawing together 'Francophone' and 'postcolonial' in this way is not to shy away from the deeply problematic nature of these terms, which has been signalled by countless critics (e.g. d'Almeida, 2003; Harrison, 2003b; Rosello, 2003). As we have consistently acknowledged in joint and individual publications over the past few years, the yoking together of these terms in the constructive fashion we have suggested is part of a 'critical strategy' that is fundamentally enabling:

> The persistent assertion of Francophone Postcolonial Studies as a field of enquiry in its own right reflects a constructively critical strategy emerging from dissatisfaction with both the monolingual emphases of postcolonial criticism […] and the monocultural, essentially metropolitan biases of French Studies. (Forsdick, 2003: 36)

> The emergence of Francophone postcolonial studies should not be envisaged as the creation of a mere 'sub-specialisation' of either French studies or postcolonial studies. Rather, it is a challenge to any exclusive definition of the postcolonial, and is an acknowledgement of the necessity of opening the field to comparative 'transcolonial' approaches. (Murphy, 2006: 139)

Essentially, then, our aim might be seen as the prising open – or even the active 'decolonization' – of the terms 'Francophone' and 'postcolonial': using 'Francophone' in a fashion that encompasses France itself seeks to underline the complex, intertwined nature of the relationship between the former empire and its former colonies; equally, to underline the existence of a 'Francophone' postcolonial field is to seek to wrench the field away from its previous, almost exclusive Anglophone focus. Nonetheless, we are neither sufficiently naïve nor sufficiently arrogant to believe that our own understanding of these terms has altered the broader scholarly (and public) understanding of them: in particular, 'Francophone' is still widely perceived to designate locations and contexts outside metropolitan France (including France's overseas departments and territories, which remain constitutionally and economically part of the French state). Consequently, we have used the rather circuitous term 'French-speaking' in the title of the current volume, so as to make clear to the reader approaching the text that our focus encompasses a wide spectrum of Francophone (or, as key cases such as Haiti make clear, partially Francophone) locations, including but not necessarily privileging France itself. Also, at certain points in this introduction as well as in the chapters by our contributors, the term 'Francophone' is used in its 'traditional' sense to designate non-French locations. Despite these pragmatic concessions to the reality of current usage, within our introduction we still use the term 'Francophone postcolonial thought' to refer to a body of ideas emanating from a wide variety of French-language contexts, including France itself, for the 'decolonization' of the terms we use remains a crucial scholarly project. Our conception of Francophone postcolonial studies is thus of a field that is both language- and context-specific, but that also actively seeks to engage in wider and often comparative debates that extend beyond French-language locations and contexts. In essence, then, this volume aims simultaneously to explore further what Françoise Lionnet has described as the 'becoming-transnational' of French studies (Lionnet, 2003: 784), and to promote a dialogue within, and inevitably beyond, postcolonial studies that will continue to move the field away from its foundational Anglophone focus.

While our previous volume attempted to sketch a broad overview of the various contexts, figures and ideas that might constitute the focus of the field of which we were seeking to delineate the contours, the current volume focuses specifically on Francophone postcolonial thought, as developed by key authors and theorists, and as it emerges from debates on key themes, approaches and theories. Our aim here is thus not simply to provide a more recent update on the field (although we do address recent developments below) but rather to identify key ideas within Francophone postcolonial research and, equally importantly, to open up debate to include scholars from as wide a range of disciplinary backgrounds as possible. Our previous volume focused primarily on creative works (literature and film) with other disciplines relegated to the margins; the current volume, however, reverses these emphases, situating what we have dubbed 'postcolonial thought' – by which we imply a broad range of theories and ideas, articulated explicitly as such or emerging more indirectly from various situations and movements, associated directly with the postcolonial or otherwise linked to the genealogies of its emergence – as the unifying factor informing a wide range of disciplinary interventions, among which those of a literary nature retain a prominent but non-exclusive role.

In the period since the publication of our first volume, the field has been the site of frenetic activity and debate, which attests both to its intellectual vitality and to the bitter opposition that it still provokes in certain circles (particularly in France). We are not claiming of course that our volume somehow spawned this activity; we were simply fortunate enough to have drawn together some of the different strands of a field that was expanding rapidly and about to reach a new stage in its consolidation and visibility, and we were able to build on the pioneering work of others (Lionnet and Scharfman, 1993; Britton and Syrotinski, 2001) who had already begun the type of meta-reflection on the field that we were keen to develop. In retrospect, 2003 now appears as something of a landmark date in the development of Francophone postcolonial studies, especially in the Anglophone world: alongside our own book, there were significant special issues of prominent journals, such as *Yale French Studies* (Laroussi and Miller, 2003) and *Modern Language Notes* (Lionnet and Thomas, 2003), as well as the inaugural issues of *Francophone Postcolonial Studies* (2003–04), all three of which were devoted to opinion pieces on the state of the field by over 40 leading scholars; also published in 2003, Nicholas Harrison's *Postcolonial Criticism* is an outstanding contribution to theoretical debates on postcolonial literature with a corpus straddling both English- and French-language texts.[5] Two years later, a specifically North American counterpart to our edited collection, with a specific emphasis on postcolonial approaches to literature and cinema in French, was edited by Adlai Murdoch and Anne Donadey (2005); and this has been complemented by recent volumes, such as Margaret Majumdar's *Postcoloniality: The French Dimension* (2007). This largely (but not exclusively) literary-cultural work was accompanied by the ongoing interrogation of France's colonial empire and its legacy by US historians such as Herman Lebovics (2004), Gary Wilder (2005) and Todd Shepard (2006). This focus on the French Empire does not signify that its Belgian counterpart has been unworthy of attention (see Fraiture, 2007; Spaas, 2008); however, the Belgian colonial project remains a marginal presence within Francophone postcolonial studies (a marginalization we acknowledge that this volume risks replicating, while suggesting at the same time that its content might encourage a shift of the Francophone postcolonial project in this direction – and in other directions).

A major new development has been the emergence of book series on both sides of the Atlantic that span the literary, cultural and historical fields, either specifically conceived of as 'postcolonial' or devoting a large space to 'postcolonial' titles in their catalogues. For example, Lexington Books' series 'After the Empire: The Francophone World and Postcolonial France' has developed a very impressive postcolonial catalogue (e.g. Stovall and Van Den Abbeele, 2003; Hargreaves, 2005; Watts, 2005; Rice, 2006; McCormack, 2007), as has the less specialized series 'Contemporary French and Francophone Cultures' at Liverpool University Press (e.g. Kelly, 2005; Hiddleston, 2006; Hitchcott, 2006; McCusker, 2007; Munro, 2007; Britton, 2008). These new developments complement the work published primarily by North American university presses such as Duke, Chicago, Indiana and Nebraska, all of which have long fostered research in this area and continue to do so (e.g. Thomas, 2007; Miller, 2008). When taken together, this represents an extremely dynamic body of research, attesting to the significance that is attached to the academic project of charting the legacies of French (and to a lesser extent Belgian) imperialism.

This is not to say that all scholars in the English-speaking world have

---

5   A further indication of these shifts may be seen in the 2002 relaunch of the Association for the Study of Caribbean and African Literature in French (ASCALF) as the Society for Francophone Postcolonial Studies (SFPS).

welcomed these developments. The very title of Richard Serrano's monograph, *Against the Postcolonial* (2005), for instance, underlines the polemical nature of his attack on postcolonial studies, a field that is deemed to produce a homogenizing discourse that attempts to fit all literary texts into a restrictive framework. Although Serrano is a sensitive and intelligent reader of *works produced by authors from France's former colonies* – a formula that avoids the terms 'Francophone' and 'postcolonial', which he critiques with such vehemence – his depiction of postcolonial analysis is itself very reductive, with the field serving in his text almost uniquely as a 'straw man' designed to illustrate the richness of his own approach. This hostile position is then betrayed in his somewhat curious conclusion in which he belatedly discovers existing evidence of the potential complexity of a postcolonial studies approach to comparatism in the final stages of preparing his own volume.

More informed and more constructive critical engagement with the development of a field of Francophone postcolonial research is evident in many of the opinion pieces in the first three issues of the journal *Francophone Postcolonial Studies* mentioned above: Mary Gallagher (2003) and Jean Jonaissant (2003) both warn of the dangers of a self-congratulatory view of postcolonial studies presented as the sole source of wisdom in debates on Francophone literatures; Celia Britton (2003), Nicholas Harrison (2003b) and Lorna Milne (2003) view the emergence of this new field as the occasion to elaborate a more concerted and more subtly conceived analysis of postcolonial literary texts as 'texts', permitting a shift away from primarily anthropological or sociological readings; Patrick Crowley (2003) calls for greater attention to local histories while Winifred Woodhull (2004) celebrates the 'deterritorialization' of French studies and the development of transnational approaches. Other contributors warn of the dangers of replicating an Anglophone model that may already be on the wane: Alec Hargreaves evokes the tragic-comic image of Francophone studies and postcolonial studies as 'ships passing in the night' (2003), while Chris Bongie (2003a) stresses the pitfalls of a 'belated liaison' between these two fields.

One of the most insistent critiques of Francophone postcolonial studies has been the charge that it constitutes an Anglophone preoccupation that has neither received nor solicited any input from French-language scholars. This position is articulated by Lieve Spaas in her review article on three recent 'Francophone postcolonial' works, including our previous edited volume – the other texts analysed are by Chafer (2002), and Stovall and Van Den Abbeele (2003) – in which she asks 'does such a book have to come from the anglophone world?' (Spaas, 2007: 136). While Spaas is right to assert that a 'radical change in French Studies is [...] developing outside the hexagon and progressing through channels that circumvent France' (141), we would question the notion that this somehow constitutes the imposition of an alien, 'Anglophone' framework on 'Francophone' realities. For a start, such an analysis risks presenting an overly simplified account of the position of postcolonial studies in France (which we will discuss at length below), but more importantly, it seems to suggest that the primary role of scholars of 'French studies' in the Anglophone world is

7

simply to follow the lead of their French-language counterparts, borrowing paradigms of intellectual enquiry little suited to the implicitly 'ethnographic' imperatives of French studies research.[6] On the contrary, we would suggest that Anglophone scholars working on France and its colonies play a crucial role as *passeurs* who permit the flow of ideas between different language contexts and suggest the ways in which we might contribute to the genuine internationaliza-tion of research practices; indeed, much work in the Francophone postcolonial field is directed towards postcolonial studies colleagues in English – as well as in other modern language departments – and is designed to signal to them the importance of work being written in French. Equally, French-language scholars working in the Anglophone world – particularly, but not exclusively, in North America – have constituted an even more vital conduit for ideas to flow in both directions (e.g. Michel Laronde, Françoise Lionnet, Achille Mbembe, Lydie Moudileno, Françoise Vergès). As was argued above, Francophone postcolo-nial studies is essentially a project rooted in French-language contexts but also involved in a series of transnational dialogues, and such *passeur* figures play a crucial role in this field. (For illuminating analysis of the intersections between Francophone studies and postcolonial theory, and the complex flows of ideas outlined here, see Coursil and Perret, 2005, and Thomas, 2005.)

Attempts at promoting dialogue on postcolonial issues between scholars in France and their counterparts in Anglophone countries have often generated far more heat than light, particularly in the field of literary studies – witness, for example, the articles in the special issue of the journal *Francophone Postcolonial Studies* on 'Francophone Literary Studies and the notion of the "Postcolonial"' (2006), which emerged from a rather rancorous symposium at the Sorbonne in 2005.[7] However, to posit the absence of postcolonial studies from French academia on the basis of the situation in French or comparative literature depart-ments would be an error. It is now something of a commonplace in Anglophone circles – and indeed even among many of those in France who would like the postcolonial debate to prosper – to view the French as lagging behind in their engagement with the issues raised by postcolonial studies. However, we would suggest that it is misguided to dismiss embryonic postcolonial debates in France as pale imitations of their Anglophone counterparts. For postcolonial studies in France, without often designating itself in such terms, has in fact developed in ways that differ significantly from English-language debates. When the term 'postcolonial' is deployed in France, it is usually done so in relation to historical or sociological rather than literary or cultural debates.[8] A telling

---

6   The implication that postcolonial approaches to the field of French studies constitute an act of virtual treason against France and against the field is explored from very different perspectives in Petrey (2003) and Kritzman (2003).

7   The situation in other European countries has sometimes been more receptive to postcolonial studies: see the work of Theo D'Haen (1998) and Kathleen Gyssels (Gyssels, Hoving and Bowers, 2002).

8   In 2003 Jim House was one of the first critics to attempt to qualify the notion that opposition to postcolonial studies was shared across the board in France, and he pointed

example of this transformation/translation of the postcolonial in its voyage from Anglophone to Francophone contexts is the translation of Neil Lazarus's *Companion to Postcolonial Literary Studies* (2004) under the more general title *Penser le postcolonial* [Thinking the postcolonial] (2006): the fact that the book has often wound up on the history shelves of French bookshops reinforces this implicit shift. As Edward Said has taught us, the ability of ideas to travel and take on new meanings in new contexts is a recurring feature of intellectual life (Said, 1983), and French debates on the value (or otherwise) of postcolonial theory have certainly travelled in complex and unpredictable ways.

The contribution to this volume by Nicolas Bancel and Pascal Blanchard (Chapter 24), two of the key members of the postcolonial studies-inspired research group ACHAC (Association Connaissance de l'Histoire de l'Afrique Contemporaine), clearly illustrates the grasp of postcolonial theory that has developed among certain contributors to postcolonial debates in France. It also illustrates that these debates have been highly controversial and have often descended into vitriolic polemics. Despite this negative reaction, it is indisputable that colonialism and its legacy have over the past few years come to occupy a central position in both the academic and the public spheres. Even when there is not outright hostility, there often remains a marked uncertainty as to what postcolonial thought might signify in and for France and the wider French-speaking world. For instance, the confused, even alarmed, tone of the title of the conference at Sciences-Po, in Paris, in May 2006 – 'Que faire des *postcolonial studies?*' [What should be done with postcolonial studies?] – seems to imply that this alien, untranslated, perhaps even untranslatable body of thought is somehow a wayward child requiring the benefits of firm disciplining. The polemical attacks of Pascal Bruckner (2006), Daniel Lefeuvre (2006) or Claude Liauzu (2007b) even suggest that such firm disciplining is at hand; however, the fact that the published proceedings of the Sciences-Po conference adopted the title *La Situation postcoloniale* (Smouts, 2007) indicates that, in certain quarters at least, it is now accepted that the postcolonial might in fact be less alien than was at first feared. In general, then, it seems fair to claim that postcolonial studies has progressively gained a foothold in French intellectual life, and we will examine in further detail below the specifics of the debates that have been conducted in France (and in French), and the circumstances in which they have unfolded.

One of the most significant and original developments of these past few years has been the elaboration of a genuinely transcolonial, comparative awareness across the postcolonial field, a shift that is evidenced by some major recent publications.[9] Certain of these initiatives have been the product of scholars working on non-Anglophone contexts: for example, the editors of a new *Historical Companion to Postcolonial Literatures: Continental Europe and its*

---

to the substantial and growing body of work by historians, sociologists and activists within civil society on the legacy of the French (and Belgian) empires (House, 2003).

9 As we signalled in our previous volume, historians have led the way in developing comparative work of this nature: see Cooper and Stoler (1997), and Clancy-Smith and Gouda (1998).

Empires (Poddar, Patke and Jensen, 2008) deliberately shift the focus away, as the title suggests, from the British to continental European empires (including Belgium, Denmark, France, Portugal, Spain and the Netherlands). Equally, the 2004 American Comparative Literature Association (ACLA) Report on the state of the discipline remarks upon the significance of a comparative postcolonial project that has emerged recently from activity in the Francophone postcolonial studies field (Saussy, 2006; see, in particular, Apter, 2006: 55–56).

However, scholars of English-language material are now also increasingly aware of the need to engage with other colonial trajectories: far from the image of Francophone postcolonial studies constituting the wholesale importation of ideas from various Anglophone spheres, there is now clear evidence that scholars of English-language material are keen to open their field to other contexts. Leading Anglophone postcolonial studies scholars, such as Graham Huggan (2002), have been calling for some time for greater comparative, transcolonial and transdisciplinary work within the field, and the existence of Huggan's new Liverpool University Press series, 'Postcolonialism across the Disciplines', in which this present volume is published, is concrete evidence of the desire to move the area in new directions; see also Ashgate's *Comparing Postcolonial Diasporas* (Keown, Murphy and Procter, 2009), which includes highly innovative work on Dutch postcolonial studies by Elleke Boehmer, the renowned scholar of Anglophone material (Boehmer and Gouda, 2009). In the introduction to his groundbreaking *Companion to Postcolonial Literatures*, which examines the British, French, Spanish and Portuguese empires, John McLeod argues that '[t]he field's centre of gravity is shifting, so that postcolonial studies is now generally more alert to the *different European empires*, and their legacies' (2007: 11; emphasis in original). If, as McLeod persuasively argues, postcolonial studies has largely evolved as a 'hinged concept' (2007: 5–10), which seeks to explore the complex connections between the colonial period and its aftermath, between the colonizer and the colonized, and between the material facts of colonialism and its modes of representation, then it is now also serving as a 'hinge' in explorations of the relationships between the different European imperial projects and their various aftermaths. We are aware that this refocusing of the postcolonial field on a 'hinged' understanding of various European empires itself offers merely a partial response to Harish Trivedi's well-known rebuke that 'the postcolonial has ears only for English' (1999: 272). For promoting the study of material in French, Spanish, Dutch – yet more European and former colonial languages – at the expense of widely used 'indigenous' languages (the true object of Trivedi's comment) perpetuates the focus on certain types of cultural production only. Trivedi's position acts as a welcome reminder that we must avoid premature self-congratulation at recent developments in the field. A more comprehensively comparative and interdisciplinary postcolonial field will require yet further evolution and engagement across disciplinary boundaries. Underlining the limitations of the comparative work that has already been carried out is not to deny its major significance, for, as John McLeod argues, postcolonial studies is a field in which critics are often forced to confront the limits of their own knowledge. This can be a frustrating experience, '[b]ut happening upon our limits can [also] be a fertile, transformative experience' (2007: 17). The ongoing development of the postcolonial field will further test the limits of the critic's knowledge in ways that will continue to be both frustrating and transformative.

Travelling home? The postcolonial studies debate in France

Through the generalizing manoeuvres of postcolonial criticism and the generalized obfuscation of processes of translation in the English-speaking world, it is at times forgotten that many of the texts that have become central points of reference in postcolonial criticism – works by key anti-colonial authors such as Aimé Césaire, Frantz Fanon and Albert Memmi – were originally published in France in the 1950s and 1960s. The publishing history of works such as *The Wretched of the Earth* (1961) or *The Colonizer and the Colonized* (1957) reveals the complex processes of emergence of anti-colonial (and then postcolonial) thought in French, mediated via the metropolitan centre (and more particularly Paris), but disseminated thanks to the commitment of specialist and radical publishing houses such as Présence Africaine and Maspero (and, more recently, its successor La Découverte). In the wake of decolonization, outside an activist readership or one concerned with the disciplinary histories in which, for instance, Fanon as a psychiatrist was engaged, this material was often lost from view. In the late 1960s and early 1970s activists in various contexts around the French-speaking world, in search of the structures and vocabularies of independence struggle, turned to this corpus: nationalists in Brittany engaged with the discourse of Algerian liberation, for instance, while those in Corsica claimed affiliations with the tradition of Toussaint Louverture; the self-definition of Quebec nationalism was assisted by constructive dialogues with Memmi and his work (see Chapters 9, 20 and 21 for a discussion of these processes). A sustained recovery of this anti-colonial critique began, however, elsewhere, outside French-speaking contexts, not least in the Anglophone academies of Australia, North America, and Great Britain and Ireland, where postcolonial criticism emerged in the late 1980s as a sustained but fragmented body of thought with its own set of dominant (if widely contested) methodologies, theorists and canons.

As has been suggested above, it is thus becoming increasingly commonplace to present postcolonialism as a 'travelling theory', the result of the expatriation of two bodies of thought – the anti-colonialism of figures such as Fanon; the poststructuralism of intellectuals such as Derrida and Foucault – and their subsequent fusion in the critical practices emerging from the (largely) Anglophone campuses alluded to elsewhere in this introduction. There is no denying that such a narrative, with its emphasis on distinctly modernist vectors of transfer and influence, ignores what James Clifford – countering Said's conception of a 'travelling theory' – describes as the 'feedback loops, the ambivalent appropriations and resistances that characterize the travels of theories, and theorists, between places in the "First" and "Third" worlds' (1989: 184). At the same time, as Robert Young has made clear (2001a), there is a risk that any such monolingual and largely teleological emphases disqualify the existence of a wider set of anti-colonial and postcolonial practices, including, for instance, the work in the 1980s of Édouard Glissant's Institut martiniquais d'études, evident in the journal *Acoma* and Glissant's own *Caribbean Discourse* (1981), or the more recent elaboration among Latin American scholars of what Walter Mignolo and others have dubbed a 'decolonial' option, refusing the intellectual underpinnings of postcolonial criticism and proposing a thorough epistemological critique.

Much of the taxonomic anxiety surrounding postcolonialism centres on a policing of the field's boundaries, a process that exists in clear tension with the more catholic understanding of a 'postcolonial turn' reshaping, since the late 1980s, humanities and social science research. Whichever understanding is more appropriate – and, given the ways in which the assumptions of postcolonial criticism have permeated such a wide range of fields, the latter seems increasingly helpful – the identification of an abstract, monolithic 'postcolonialism' persists, either as a point of self-identification for those active in the field that the term attempts to designate, or as a straw man for those hostile to it (see comments above on Serrano, 2005). Nowhere is this more apparent perhaps than in France, where terms such as 'le postcolonialisme' or 'les postcolonial studies' have recently served as shorthand for a set of critical practices presented as alien to traditions of French thought (see Chapter 24 in this volume), imposing a divisive 'communitarianism' where the identitarian 'universalism' of French republican ideology is still seen as the only valid social and intellectual rationale. The antagonisms in which this situation can result has led to an urgent need to explore what happens when the transatlantic crossings of postcolonial thought are reversed, i.e. when, according to a logic of progressive iteration, the body of thought known as postcolonialism is projected back into the Francophone world, and most notably into France itself.

As with French feminism, unrecognized (and, for many French readers, unrecognizable) when, freighted via North American academia, it was translated back to France (Célestin, DalMolin and de Courtivron, 2002), the reception of postcolonial thought was slow and uneven. Edward Said's *Orientalism* was made available in translation soon after its original publication, but the ambivalent preface provided by Tzvetan Todorov (see Chapter 14 in this volume) is characteristic of the lukewarm reception it received. Even with the publication in 2000 of the French version of *Culture and Imperialism* (by Le Monde diplomatique and La Découverte), Said's reputation in France remained primarily that of a Palestinian activist (whose essays were regularly translated in the left-wing press), rather than that of a scholar whose work was considered to have inspired the above-mentioned 'postcolonial turn' in much humanities and social science scholarship. James Clifford's collection of essays on postcolonial anthropology, *The Predicament of Culture* (1988), containing important essays on French-language authors such as Aimé Césaire, Michel Leiris, Claude Lévi-Strauss and Victor Segalen, appeared in French translation in 1996, but did so within the disciplinary context of the history of art. It has only been in more recent years that the increasingly rich body of postcolonial criticism produced in English has progressively and somewhat erratically appeared in French translation.

The emergence of what Emily Apter calls 'postcolonial studies *à la française*' (1995: 171) has therefore been a slow and complex process, characterized by periods of relative silence as well as by moments of seemingly frenzied publishing activity. Some early endeavours – such as Jean-Marc Moura and Jacqueline Bardolph's pioneering attempts (Moura, 2007 [1999]; Bardolph, 2002) to intro-duce the central tenets of postcolonial thought (most notably as manifested in the work of Bhabha, Said and Spivak) – may be seen as the attempted wholesale importation of a set of theories and concepts to an often reluctant French-language readership.[10] The catalytic implications of such activity should not, however, be underestimated, for, since the beginning of the present decade, the impact of postcolonial criticism in France has become increasingly apparent. Not only have several key postcolonial-inflected texts originally published in English been translated into French (Lazarus, 2006; Bhabha, 2007; Hall, 2007); but also often forgotten key texts – such as Fanon's *Wretched of the Earth* and *Toward the African Revolution* (1964), republished in their original French by La Découverte in 2004 and 2006 respectively, or the early volumes of Glissant's 'poétique', re-released by Gallimard in 1998 – have re-entered circulation. (See Chapter 6 for analysis of the recent publishing strategies that have attempted to repackage Glissant's work.) At the same time, previous scholarship on topics as diverse as colonialism, ethnicity, immigration and cultural hybridization – produced by an eclectic range of writers and intellectuals, including figures such as Jean-Loup Amselle, Gérard Noiriel, Pierre-André Taguieff and Michel Wieviorka – has been re-evaluated in a postcolonial light, with its divergences from and convergences with a wider postcolonial project made apparent. The risk remains that the selective and delayed nature of translation – the French version of Bhabha's *Location of Culture* appeared, for instance, thirteen years after its initial publication – projects a version of postcolonial criticism that does not at all reflect the current state of the field elsewhere, and illustrates the fact that French debates on such matters are at times 'en retard d'une guerre' [fighting an old war], to use Françoise Lionnet's mischievous phrase (2005: 260). The result is that a certain French style of commentary on such work (e.g. Mouralis, 2006), however valid it might seem, belatedly risks reinventing pre-existing and now widely acknowledged critiques *within* the postcolonial field regarding neo-exoticism and the commodification of difference (Huggan, 2001), the distinction between universality and singularity (Hallward, 2001), or the pitfalls of a politicized critical practice that fails to distinguish between decolonization and postcoloniality (Harrison, 2003a; Scott, 1999; 2004).

10 The fact that a new edition of Moura's volume was published in 2007 suggests that the current situation may be somewhat more receptive to his ideas. Moura's incisive intro-duction to this new edition is a model of the type of informed critical engagement with postcolonial studies that scholars in France might bring to the field. The best account of French literary-critical resistance to postcolonial studies is provided by Delas (2003).

Hostile French reactions to postcolonial thought – epitomized perhaps in the quizzical title of the Sciences-Po conference in 2006 mentioned above – tend to ignore key issues of provenance, ownership and (in)coherent disciplinary identity. There is no denying that the genealogies (as opposed to more reductive teleologies) of postcolonial thought reveal, as has been suggested already, a set of explicitly French-language roots, many of which are associated with reactions against specifically French colonial phenomena such as the universalist foundations of republican ideology, the practice of assimilation, and the propagandist alibi of the civilizing mission. It is arguable – and it is indeed one of the key arguments of this volume – that such material has continuously informed, to a lesser or greater extent, certain modes of reflection on colonialism and its afterlives throughout the French-speaking world. In themselves, the implications and underpinnings of 'les postcolonial studies' are not as unfamiliar or alien as they might appear. The antagonistic relationship between such a body of thought and French republicanism remains apparent, but as the post-9/11 clampdown on postcolonial-inflected Area Studies programmes in the US makes abundantly clear, such political tensions already exist elsewhere. It is possible that the perceived incompatibility is more a matter of institutional context than actual methodological and conceptual antipathy. It is feasible at the same time, as both editors of this volume have argued elsewhere (Forsdick, 2003; 2005; Murphy, 2003; 2006), that a rigorous engagement with postcolonial criticism from within French-speaking cultures will constitute a thorough challenge to the residually monolingual emphases of postcolonialism itself. Such a diversification is already perhaps evident in the rise to prominence of contemporary Francophone postcolonial intellectuals such as Achille Mbembe, whose work (e.g. Mbembe, 2001) is increasingly central to the reconfiguration of the postcolonial field.

It is arguable that any assessment of the emergence in France of a mode of criticism explicitly identifiable with postcolonialism should begin with a consideration of ACHAC (see Chapter 24 in this volume), the collective of historians and other scholars who, since 1989, have perhaps been most active in France in situating debates on colonial history and its afterlives in a postcolonial frame. Through the study of (chronologically) colonial and postcolonial phenomena and contexts covering a period from 1871 to 2006, their recent trilogy of edited volumes – *Culture coloniale* (Blanchard and Lemaire, 2003), *Culture impériale* (Blanchard and Lemaire, 2004) and *Culture post-coloniale* (Blanchard and Bancel, 2006) – sketches out an ambitious research project, the aim of which is to reveal the constitutive role of colonial expansion in the making of modern France. As such, ACHAC seeks to counter two dominant strands of French republican historiography, the first continuing to present overseas expansion in the light of a civilizing mission that admittedly gave rise to certain unfortunate 'errors' (see the essays collected in Droz, 2007), or the second, through the adoption of Eurocentric or even Gallocentric emphases, which projects the 1962 Evian Accords as a clean break with the colonial past, after which it is possible to study the nation in isolation. The ACHAC project has three principal strands. First, in publications such as *Zoos humains* (Bancel et al., 2002) and in associated activity concerning the 1931 *Exposition coloniale*, there has been an effort to salvage evidence of France's colonial past – seen in mass cultural phenomena such as the 'human zoo' of the late nineteenth and early twentieth centuries – and to underline the centrality of empire to the experience of modernity in French culture. Focused on particular locations within metropolitan France, a series of other volumes, drawing on a wide range of contemporary iconography, has challenged observations regarding a recent hybridization of culture in France by presenting evidence of a historical France that was always-already multi-ethnic (Blanchard and Deroo, 2004; Bancel, Bencherif and Blanchard, 2007). Secondly, a commitment to historical excavation has been accompanied by a rigorous theorization, in studies such as *La République coloniale* (Bancel, Blanchard and Vergès, 2003), of the constitutive role of colonial ideology in the formation of French republican identity. The loss of Saint-Domingue and the French delay in recognizing the independent state of Haiti is seen as one of the historical reflections of this process (Benot, 1992), with the Haitian Revolution operating – along the lines suggested by C. L. R. James in *The Black Jacobins* (1938) – as a reminder of the grave limitations of a French Revolution, the founding principles of which were interpreted in a way that remained blind to their applicability in terms of race. In the light of such an analysis, the systematic and dehumanizing violence on which colonial expansion depended (Benot, 1994; Le Cour Grandmaison, 2005) has been seen in much recent critical work to be engrained within republican ideology, revealing the limitations of the universalism on which the justification of this ideology long depended. This interpretation is to be distinguished from a view of republicanism that posits a differential application of the values of the French Revolution inside and outside France (Manceron, 2003). A recognition of the more fundamental, symbiotic interrelationship of republicanism and empire informs the third strand of the ACHAC project, concerning what has been dubbed 'la fracture coloniale' (Blanchard, Bancel and Lemaire, 2005), the notion that the 'silencing of the [colonial] past' (Trouillot, 1995) has generated a series of dislocations apparent in the upheavals and crises of contemporary French society, especially in relation to the role that communities 'of immigrant origin' will be permitted to play in shaping the future of French culture and society.

It is also striking that the collective publications edited by ACHAC have customarily included contributions from leading scholars in the English-speaking academy committed to a postcolonial exploration of France and the wider Francophone world (e.g. Robert Aldrich, Herman Lebovics and Steve Ungar). Their work may be seen not only, therefore, as a place of preliminary dialoguing between scholarly traditions and across national boundaries, but also, more importantly perhaps for the purposes of the present volume, as constituting one of the initial sites of the emergence in contemporary France of debates recognizable as 'postcolonial'. It is perhaps for this latter reason that scholars associated with ACHAC have been the object of criticism from those opposed to a project of postcolonial criticism, whether it be Claude Liauzu reducing the study of 'human zoos' to 'Barnum history' (Liauzu, 2007b: 54), or Bruckner (2006) and Lefeuvre (2006) dismissing a critical engagement with the colonial past and with evidence of its present legacies as, respectively, 'penitence' and 'repentance', or the essays collected in a special issue of *L'Histoire*, which emphasize an 'impartial' scholarly attention to historical 'fact' in the face of demands for 'falsified' communal memories (Droz, 2007).

The backlash represented by the work of Bruckner and Lefeuvre (as well as the latter's website, www.etudescoloniales.fr) constituted a rapid counter-response to the sudden emergence of postcolonialism as a subject of debate in France. From the mid-1990s onwards, a series of disparate volumes began to engage with the postcolonial paradigm in a variety of fields, including literature (Moura, 2007; Bardolph, 2002; Diop, 2002), visual arts (Busca, 2000), sociology (Haubert and Rey, 2000) and politics (Mwayila, 1990). Special issues of the journals *Dédale* (Meddeb, 1997) and *Africultures* (Mongo Mboussa, 2000) outlined the implications of a postcolonial critique for intellectual activity across a range of disciplines. It was only, however, in 2005 – in a France divided by the *loi du 23 février 2005* [23 February 2005 law] (whose revisionist fourth clause obliged educators to teach about the positive aspects of colonialism), and shaken by the social movements in the *banlieues* [suburbs] in November of the same year triggered by the deaths during a police chase of Zyed Benna and Bouna Traoré, two teenagers resident in the Parisian suburb of Clichy-sous-Bois – that the term 'postcolonial' became an item of common critical currency in French. Previously seen as a chronological marker, betokening a straightforward posteriority, in its new usages 'postcolonial' began to suggest the forms of continuity with and rupture from the colonial past that characterized the word's meaning in the Anglophone world. Even publications that insisted on retaining the term 'Francophone', such as *Vocabulaire des études francophones* (Beniamino and Gauvin, 2005), appeared increasingly to converge with comparable publications produced in the Anglophone academy (in this case Ashcroft, Griffiths and Tiffin, 1998); indeed, one might even read these connections as clear evidence that 'Francophone' and 'postcolonial' had betokened all along different taxonomic labels for the same realities.

In this flurry of publishing activity, books engaging with the implications of the postcolonial in French-language contexts continued to appear (e.g. Hajjat, 2005; Gehrmann and Gronemann, 2006), but it was journals that inevitably played a key role as a rapid means of exchanging information and new ideas in the field. To cite only the most notable examples: a special issue of *Hérodote* (120 [2006]) was dedicated to 'La question postcoloniale' [The Postcolonial Question]; *Labyrinthe* (24 [2006]) devoted an issue to addressing the question 'Faut-il être postcolonial?' [Do we need to be postcolonial?]; *Multitudes* (26 [2006]) explored 'postcolonial et politique de l'histoire' [the postcolonial and the politics of history]; *Contretemps* (16 [2006]) looked at 'postcolonialisme et immigration'; *Esprit* (330 [2006]) contained a dossier entitled 'Pour comprendre la pensée coloniale' [Understanding postcolonial thought]; an issue of *Nouvelles questions féministes* (25.3 [2006]), entitled 'Sexisme, racisme, et postcolonialisme', contained a series of articles on the ramifications of postcolonialism for questions of gender; *Mouvements* (51 [2007]) asked 'Faut-il avoir peur du postcolonial?' [Should we fear the postcolonial?]; and finally the journal *Cultures Sud* (Bancel, 2007) collected a range of articles around the theme 'Retours sur la question coloniale' [Revisiting the colonial question]. This rapid generation of a substantial body of material debating the status, feasibility and implications of postcolonial debates in France – in themselves, the special issues above contained over 50 articles, effectively published over a period of only several months – reveals the tensions and ambiguities triggered by the sudden realization that postcolonial criticism deserved serious consideration in relation to France and its former colonies. Moreover, as was mentioned above, a body of thought that had primarily concerned literary scholars in its Anglophone manifestations seemed in France to generate from the outset interest and debate among those active in the fields of the social sciences and history, an aspect that is not surprising – for reasons that will be discussed below – given the political and sociocultural context of these unfolding debates.

The impact of this body of material has been twofold: on the one hand, it has firmly introduced postcolonial criticism into debates in France, while encouraging anxious reflection on the implications of such an importation; on the other hand, in a positive process of self-reflexivity, it has permitted searching debate on the adaptation of a postcolonial critical paradigm to Francophone contexts (with that epithet understood, as outlined above, in its most inclusive senses), with close attention paid for instance to works such as *La Fracture coloniale*. (On reactions to this collection, see Bancel and Blanchard, 2007.) At the same time, there has been evidence of an almost simultaneous reaction against this incipient 'postcolonial turn', with historians and essayists such as Bruckner (2006) and Lefeuvre (2006) warning against, in the case of the former, a decline of the West associated with penitence for the colonial past, and, in the case of the latter, historiographic falsifications linked to processes of postcolonial repentance. In neither case is convincing evidence provided for this 'penitence' or 'repentance', both of which are loosely conflated with the emergence of new critical and intellectual practices that aim to explore the constitutive role of colonialism in the making of modern and contemporary France, that is, to analyse the implications of what Herman Lebovics has suggestively called 'bringing the Empire back home' (2004). This backlash is reminiscent of early reactions to Edward Said's *Orientalism*, which was itself dismissed by some critics as a symptom of expiation for empire. It is a clear indication of the interests at stake in discussions of postcoloniality in both twenty-first-century France and other French-speaking spaces, and also of the progress yet to be made in establishing grounds for discussing the complex, interconnected legacies and afterlives of empire in the Francophone world as a whole.

Francophone postcoloniality:
political, historical and socio-cultural contexts

In a special 1995 issue of *SubStance* devoted to 'France's Identity Crises', Emily Apter reflected on the implications of a rigorous new engagement with postcolonial thought in French and Francophone cultures along the lines of that we have described above:

> it could reform the myopia of French cultural vision by posing a healthy challenge to ideological universalism, metropolitan narcissism, cultural 'pasteurization', and the critically underexamined institutional tenets of national language and literature. It could shift the focus of national identity to points of contact between a 'new Europe' of the future and the 'old Europe' of the colonial aftermath. [...] French postcolonial criticism could reinvigorate the links between political philosophy and literary/cultural analysis. It could broaden the parameters of translation to encompass a polyglot identity in the arts [...]. Finally, postcolonial criticism could foster the inclusion of Francophone studies within a framework other than that of 'enlightened' assimilationism. (1995: 171–72)

As earlier comments have already suggested and as Apter's reflections make clear, the controversies surrounding postcolonialism in France are far from being abstract squabbles regarding scholarly paradigms with minimal implications beyond the academy. Indeed, as has been made apparent, the rapid engagement in France with the possibilities and pitfalls of a mode of criticism dubbed 'postcolonial' cannot be understood outside the socio-political context in which this has occurred and in which it continues to unfold. The series of publications in late 2005 and early 2006 exploring the postcoloniality of contemporary France, some of the most prominent of which have been discussed above, is to be closely associated with a set of key events that preceded it, most notably the *loi du 23 février 2005* (see Bertrand, 2006; Liauzu and Manceron, 2006) and the November 2005 *banlieue* riots (see Cole, 2007).

Historian Henry Rousso (1986) famously described the ways in which France, in the period following the Second World War, became increasingly obsessed with the years of Occupation, with the result that the so-called 'Vichy syndrome' eclipsed attention to other significant aspects of contemporary history, most notably colonialism and its aftermath. The legacies of empire had emerged violently and for many French people unexpectedly in the 1980s, in the islands of Kanaky/New Caledonia, when the independence movement plunged the region into political turmoil, culminating in the killing of FLNKS *indépendantistes* and their hostages by French security forces at Ouvéa in 1988. The Matignon Accords in the same year, followed by the Nouméa Accords a decade later, set the former colony on the road to progressive independence. It was, however, the high-profile trial in 1997–98 of Maurice Papon that signalled (or at least reflected) a shift in the situation analysed by Rousso. Charges against the former Paris police chief and former budget minister focused specifically on his role in the deportation and murder of French Jews resident in Bordeaux and its region, where he served as a civil servant during the war years (see Golsan, 2000). The prosecution, in exploring the character of the accused and in highlighting his complicity in other acts of extreme violence, presented details of the massacre of North African demonstrators in Paris in October 1961 carried out by police officers serving directly under Papon's orders (see House and MacMaster, 2006; see also Chapter 23 of this volume). The implications of this judicial manoeuvre were twofold. On the one hand, there was increasing public awareness of the links between the Second World War and colonialism itself, a connection perhaps best symbolized by the direct coincidence on 8 May 1945 of VE Day and the Sétif massacres in Algeria, understood by many as a forewarning of the imminent Algerian War of Independence (see Planche, 2006). Links between the Second World War and the French colonial empire have also been increasingly apparent in memorial traces of the contribution of colonial troops to the French war effort (Jennings, 1998; Mann, 2006; Schalk, 2002). On the other hand, memories of empire and more particularly of decolonization were no longer subject to systematic disavowal, with the result that some commentators began to foresee an alternative syndrome, related on this occasion to Algeria (Donadey, 1996). The reliance of the French colonial empire on the systematic use of violence has, as was mentioned above, been demonstrated by a number of French historians (most notably Benot, 1994, and Le Cour Grandmaison, 2005). Despite the efforts of certain historians to deflect attention away from such analyses with an emphasis on old-style economic analyses of empire (e.g. Lefeuvre, 2006), or a focus on the 'exaggeration' of the scale of colonial massacres by communitarian pressure groups (e.g. Droz, 2007), the traumatic and formative role of Algeria in French colonial memory became rapidly apparent, perhaps not surprisingly since close to two million Frenchmen (including over a million conscripts) served in the conflict. Indochina – and more particularly the French defeat at Dien Bien Phu – received public attention on its fiftieth anniversary, further developing the ambiguous and at times nostalgic attitudes to the first war of decolonization seen in films such as Pierre Schoendoerffer's 1992 docu-drama *Dien Bien Phu*. It was Algeria, however, a politically and socially sensitive subject given the rise of Islamism in the country in the 1990s as well as the increasingly vocal presence in France itself of those of Algerian origin (not least the *Harkis* and the *pieds-noirs*), that attracted increasing attention. In 1999 the French state for the first time acknowledged that the 1954–62 conflict had been a war, a recognition that coincided with confirmation by the former French commander in Algeria that torture had been deployed systematically throughout the conflict as a means of control (MacMaster, 2002). A subject that had remained largely taboo, at least in the mainstream media, for over three decades was suddenly open to scrutiny, a development accompanied by a rapid proliferation of histories of the Algerian War. At around the same time, similar debates emerged in Belgium, focused not least on state complicity in the murder of Patrice Lumumba, the first Prime Minister of the Republic of Congo, who was killed in 1961 (de Witte, 2002 [1999]). There was also a growing awareness of the place of the Belgian Congo in Belgium's national memory, and an assessment of the implications for contemporary attitudes towards race of the brutal ways in which the colony was acquired and subsequently controlled (Spaas, 2008).

In France, legislation in relation to the Algerian War of Independence inaugurated a number of legal developments regarding colonial memory, relating not least to legacies of the Atlantic slave trade (Vergès, 2006). The ambivalent celebrations of the sesquicentenary of the abolition of slavery in 1998 led to a growing awareness of the role of slavery in the formation of modern France (Chaulet-Achour and Fonkoua, 2001; Reinhardt, 2006), one of the most striking reflections of which was the 2001 Taubira Law, prescribing slavery as a crime against humanity. A further pair of commemorations – the bicentenary of the death of Toussaint Louverture (2003), and that of Haitian independence (2004) – brought to the fore a key aspect of France's Atlantic history, i.e. the loss of Saint-Domingue and the associated collapse of the *ancien régime* empire. (See Chapter 15 on the fall of the *ancien régime* empire.) Marcel Dorigny has claimed that France's sublimation of memories of its defeat in Haiti is central to its ongoing sense of 'fracture coloniale' (Dorigny, 2005), and although such a claim may appear to 'leapfrog legacies' (Cooper, 2005: 17–18), it nevertheless reflects a sense of the troubled afterlives of slavery in contemporary France. Jean-Bertrand Aristide's request, in April 2003, for reparations from the French to balance the economically crippling compensation paid by Haiti in return for recognition by France clearly touched a raw nerve, and is presented by some commentators as an element in Jacques Chirac's decision, in association with the USA and Canada, to play a key role in the overthrow of the Haitian president in February 2004 (Hallward, 2008), instantly overriding the philanthropic intentions of Régis Debray's report on the country to the then Foreign Secretary de Villepin, which appears to have been in press at the very moment of the *coup* (Debray, 2004).

Elsewhere in the Caribbean, the Martiniquan activist Claude Ribbe, author of a polemical attack on Napoleon written to challenge the celebratory overtones of the bicentenary of the Battle of Austerlitz (Ribbe, 2005), used the Taubira law to bring a flawed legal action against the historian Olivier Pétré-Grenouilleau, accusing him of denying the status of Atlantic slavery as a genocide. The case soon collapsed, but it ensured that slavery remained at the heart of public debate, a development made official by the launch in 2004 of the Comité pour la Mémoire de l'Esclavage, under the initial presidency of Maryse Condé. In its annual reports, the Commission has made a series of recommendations about slavery and the school curriculum in France, advising also on the inauguration of a centre for the study of slavery (Glissant, 2007). A new museum of slavery is under development in Nantes, and a substantial portion of the Maison des civilisations et de l'unité réunionnaise in Reunion will be devoted to the exploration of this aspect of colonial history.

Legislative activity – not least the 23 February 2005 law discussed above – and other formal manifestations of the rapid emergence of colonial memory have been reflected more generally in contemporary culture. The site since the French Revolution of debates and conflicts regarding national identity, museology once again became a key element of these processes. In the quest for a 'postcolonial' museum, the collections of the Musée de l'Homme were, in the face of fierce opposition and criticism, dispersed and developed to form the basis of a new institution at the Quai Branly, designed to house the 'arts premiers' ['first' arts] of African, Asian and Native American peoples (Price, 2007; for two very different critiques of the new museum's 'exoticism', see the comments by Laroui [2007], and Thomas [cited in Bancel, 2007: 36–41]). The terminology was carefully chosen to avoid any colonial tropes, but the building's architecture, the clear abstraction of its artefacts from the contexts of their production and collection, and the decision to devote a museum to non-Western art as opposed to integrating these works into the collections of the Louvre suggest a residual exoticism, as well as France's persistently uneasy relationship with the artistic production of many of its former colonies. Similar controversies surrounded the opening of the Cité nationale de l'histoire de l'immigration (Stevens, 2008), controversially located in the former Museum of the Colonies (inaugurated for the 1931 *Exposition coloniale* at Vincennes, in the east of Paris). Cinema also become a site for memory debates. The colonial nostalgia of the 1980s and early 1990s, epitomized by films such as Régis Wargnier's *Indochine* (1992), was replaced by a new anxiety regarding issues of race and ethnicity on screen. Key to these shifts were controversies surrounding Jean-Pierre Jeunet's *Le Fabuleux Destin d'Amélie Poulain* (2001), a film initially greeted with almost unanimous critical approval until an article in *Libération*, commenting on the apparent nostalgia and homogeneity of the Paris it portrayed, led to polemical exchanges about the film's purported 'ethnic cleansing' of contemporary France (see Ezra, 2008: 88–91). The diversity of contemporary France had already been the subject of a series of films by *beur* directors in the 1990s (Tarr, 2005), but there were several hugely important films released in 2005 that created links between the multi-ethnicity of contemporary France and the recent colonial past. For instance, Alain Tasma's *Nuit noire, 17 octobre 1961*, offered a fictional account, grounded in historical detail, of the October 1961 massacres discussed above. It was, however, Michael Haneke's ambiguous and troubling *Caché*, in which memories of this brutally suppressed demonstration play a key role, that brought the 1961 events back to public attention in a way that Didier Daeninckx's detective novel, *Meurtres pour mémoire* (1984), had done two decades previously. One reading of Haneke's film suggests that the dysfunction of contemporary French society has its roots in the disavowal of the violence of the colonial past, a reading developed multi-directionally by scholars in order to link colonialism with memories of the Holocaust (Silverman, 2007). Another key film, Rachid Bouchareb's *Indigènes* (2006), similarly used cinematic devices to link the colonial past to the postcolonial present, presenting in a dramatic fashion the role of colonial troops in the liberation of France in 1944 and suggesting the betrayal of universal republican values inherent in the subsequent failure of the French government to pay equitable pensions to its colonial troops. The film remains problematic, not least because its exploration of Frenchness fails to address directly questions of decolonization and postcoloniality, but – like Mathieu Kassovitz's *La Haine* a decade earlier – it was screened for government ministers and had a direct impact on public policy since pensions for former *tirailleurs* were immediately increased. Films such as *Indigènes* were box-office successes, and reveal not only the power of popular culture to shape knowledge of the colonial past but also, reciprocally, the emphatically public presence of national debates of a postcolonial nature that were until recently the preserve of narrow interest groups.

Tracing the contours of Francophone postcolonial thought

This collection of essays responds to the events, debates and contexts outlined in previous sections of this introduction, and attempts to place them within a wider historical, geographical and intellectual context. It examines the work of individual thinkers – writers, critics, theorists, philosophers, activists – who have operated within the geographical and intellectual context that has emerged in the wake of French and, to a lesser extent, Belgian colonial activity. It also examines, in a heuristic fashion, essential themes, approaches and theories, thereby providing an exploration of the specificity of key Francophone postcolonial debates. A collection of this type cannot pretend to offer the exhaustive or even comprehensive coverage that a glossary or encyclopaedia might provide. Underpinning the volume, however, and linking the contributions is a coherent effort to establish an attenuated narrative of Francophone postcolonial thought that goes beyond a factual account of the field to create connections between individuals, and links between cultural, historical and geographical contexts.

In Section One, contributors explore the work of twelve key Francophone thinkers, some of whom have already substantially influenced or made a major contribution to postcolonial thought, while others are relatively unknown to scholars working within the predominantly Anglophone field of postcolonial studies. The work and activity of these 12 figures – Aimé Césaire, Maryse Condé, Jacques Derrida, Assia Djebar, Frantz Fanon, Édouard Glissant, Ho Chi Minh, Abdelkébir Khatibi, Albert Memmi, V. Y. Mudimbe, Jean-Paul Sartre, Léopold Sédar Senghor (listed purely in alphabetical order rather than in any sort of hierarchy) – represent a diverse and eclectic range of intellectual approaches dealing with various spaces of the Francophone world, including metropolitan France itself. As was already argued above, the decision to open this category to white, metropolitan French writers is a constitutive element of the project of breaking down the reductive taxonomic manoeuvring that often positions 'French' and 'Francophone' as straightforward binary opposites. For, as we have argued elsewhere, 'it is not the place of birth of these writers but rather the content of their thought that interests us' (Forsdick and Murphy, 2009: 164).

Although in our selection of these twelve figures, we have consciously sought to address a variety of 'representative' demands – e.g. gender, period, location, genre, politics – we fully acknowledge that this can only represent a partial overview of the field that the reader must complement by further reading. Certain of the figures we have chosen may already have received sustained critical attention, but many of our contributors have actively sought to interrogate received ideas about them in order to question their often unchallenged canonical status (see, in particular, the chapters on Fanon, Glissant, Memmi and Senghor). Other contributors have explored the factors surrounding the critical neglect of certain thinkers and the difficulties involved in teasing out and 'rescuing' their ideas (Ho Chi Minh), or have extended the consideration of critical thought to include (semi-)fictional work (Condé and Djebar). Certain commentators will lament the focus on writers from the literary-cultural sphere at the expense of political figures or the absence of figures from Francophone Canada – which, as Mary Jean Green argues in Chapter 20 of this volume, retains an oblique relationship to the postcolonial paradigm (see also Desroches, 2003a) – but we stand by our selection as a deliberately productive, inevitably provocative and (for some) undoubtedly surprising mix of both established and neglected thinkers. None of the chapters claims to provide a systematic and comprehensive account of an entire career; they all offer 'takes' on these thinkers, which are written from specific critical and theoretical standpoints. The aim is firmly not to create a new canon of postcolonial thinkers, but rather to promote a greater critical reflection both on established thinkers and certain figures who are currently peripheral to Francophone postcolonial debates.

Section Two is constituted of 12 chapters analysing the ways in which Francophone postcolonial thought has been formulated in many different situations. It includes an appraisal of the body of reflection that emerged, in response to the revolutionary activity of the late eighteenth and early nineteenth centuries, relating to the decolonization of France's *ancien régime* empire, suggesting how the complex terrain of thought and representation of that period represents an important foundation for later forms of colonial racism and anti-racism. Other chapters seek to extend the range of the discussion further by exploring a wide variety of contexts (Canada, Pacific), periods (the *ancien régime* empire, nineteenth-century thought), forms and fields (film, anthropology, history). As was stated above, the aim is to explore Francophone postcolonial thought heuristically, an approach that stresses the diverse forms in which this thought is given expression: fiction, poetry, film, historiography. Equally, it is hoped that the contributors' rigorous approach to context – geographical, cultural, historical, ideological – will allow the field to avoid some of the 'flattening' tendencies that have marked Anglophone postcolonial debates in the past. It is by making this overview available to scholars working in Anglophone postcolonial studies that the book hopes to provide the much-needed analyses that will allow critics to avoid the abstract and decontextualized instrumentalization of postcolonial cultures and literatures inherent in Graham Huggan's notion of 'the postcolonial exotic' (Huggan, 2001).

As we have stated throughout this introduction, while providing a French-language emphasis, we wish to avoid ultimately futile debates about the disciplinary ownership of postcolonial theory, conducted as if its ideas were static and incapable of travelling. In titling our collection *Postcolonial Thought in the French-Speaking World*, we are not seeking to posit a uniquely French-language version of postcoloniality: indeed, we are highly conscious of the risk of fetishizing the 'Francophone postcolonial' as a discrete category to the detriment of charting the transcultural exchanges inherent in the elaboration of this discursive formation. The aim is to consolidate and focus this activity, not by engaging in often partisan and superficial arguments that privilege reading the 'original' French over study of texts in translation, but instead by recognizing that reasserting the significance of French-language contexts allows a twofold, two-way process that is in part self-critical, in part re-invigorating. The book challenges the often cited if less frequently analysed Italian adage, 'traduttore-traditore', and accordingly presents Francophone postcolonial thought as a dynamic body of ideas that is transformed and re-created as it is translated (both literally and figuratively) between contexts.

Above all, the essays in this book are designed to move forward debates from our previous volume in a variety of ways. As was stated above, *Francophone Postcolonial Studies: A Critical Introduction* endeavoured to map out a field, and acted primarily as a general guide to its historical, geographical and a small number of key, thematic dimensions. The sharper focus in the present volume on key thinkers and key debates is a product, we believe, of a more confident assertion of the existence of a field of postcolonial research centred on French-language contexts; although the monolingualism of postcolonial studies and the monoculturalism of French studies are yet to be fully addressed, there is a clear sense that both fields are moving towards the pluralization and decolonization that these critiques imply. This volume attempts to develop the Francophone postcolonial agenda in ways that we could only signal in our introduction back in 2003. Chapters 13, 14 and 15 all contribute to the necessary development of more complex genealogies of the postcolonial, which has been such a prominent feature of recent scholarship: see for example, Roger Little's outstanding 'Autrement Mêmes' series, which 'rescues' from obscurity key texts from the colonial era; or important texts that have explored the 'French Atlantic' (Miller, 2008; Marshall, 2009). Equally, the inclusion of neglected 'Francophone' spaces/thinkers from Asia and the Pacific (see Chapters 7 and 19) is part of a desire to prevent certain paradigmatic locations from dominating the field, while the chapters on culture in France signal the need to improve our understanding of the ways in which empire has travelled 'back home' to the metropolitan centre. Finally, the essays by scholars based in English (Richards, Williams) or history departments (Dubois, Stovall) or working in France (Bancel and Blanchard) signal our commitment to a postcolonial debate that refuses to retreat into repeated literary discussions of the same key figures.

Conclusion

Since the events of 9/11 and the subsequent US-led invasions of Afghanistan and Iraq, talk of a crisis in postcolonial studies, rumblings of which had already begun in the 1990s, reached a new crescendo: witness for example the title – 'The End of Postcolonial Theory?' – of the recent dossier in the leading US journal *PMLA* (Yaeger, 2007). At the very moment when postcolonial studies seemed to have become well established and even enshrined within the academy, the ground was quickly laid by an extreme right-wing US government for a blatant act of imperial aggression. It suddenly dawned on many scholars that their ideas had little purchase on the 'real' world beyond the field of academic debate, i.e. that postcolonial scholarship risked playing a constative rather than a performative function. Jennifer Wenzel's account of her sense of despair that 'our critiques have proved inadequate to obstruct or reroute the imperialist, racist logic of fighting over there to maintain power over here' (cited in Yaeger, 2007: 634) is symptomatic of the realization on the part of many scholars that they had been excessively optimistic (or perhaps even naïve) to believe that postcolonial studies might somehow have produced a sea change in global relations: dominated by literary scholars producing radical, postcolonial re-readings of *Jane Eyre* or *L'Étranger*, postcolonial studies was always unlikely to trouble the conservative ideologues of the Bush administration. We are not seeking here to elaborate a critique of literary-cultural work as somehow apolitical or ineffective; rather, it is a case of understanding more clearly the relationship between academia and the political field. If there is a crisis, then it lies in the transmission of ideas from the academy to the wider world, which as Nicholas Harrison has demonstrated is a far more complex process than many critics admit (Harrison, 2003a).

Despite the talk of crisis, the ideas in this volume are predicated on the assumption that postcolonial studies remains a vibrant field of intellectual inquiry. Far from being on its death bed, postcolonial studies is, in our view, merely in its infancy: promoting dialogue across languages and empires, or across disciplinary boundaries, developing a more complex genealogy of the colonial past, as well as a better understanding of imperial legacies and structures in the present, are all projects that have barely begun. Many critics of postcolonial studies have – with some justification – accused the field of enclosing formerly colonized societies within a framework that ties them eternally to their former colonizers (e.g. Ahmad, 1992; 1995). However, the past decade has provided ample evidence that 'imperial desires' still prevail in many aspects of global affairs. In this context, Priya Gopal and Neil Lazarus have argued that the primary lesson of the war in Iraq is that the world remains deeply marked by imperialism: 'What we are proposing is that "after Iraq", postcolonial studies must change not because the world has changed but because "Iraq" shows that, in quite substantial ways, *it has not changed*' (2006: 7, emphasis in original). This is not simply a case of decrying US imperialism; France's recent military and political interventions in the internal affairs of the Ivory Coast, Haiti and Chad, as well as its implication in the Rwandan genocide of 1994, are all indications that we are still living through the afterlives of the French colonial project (see Hallward, 2008, on French involvement in Haiti). This does not mean – as the activity of groups such as the *Indigènes de la République* may be seen to imply – that all life in France and its former colonies can be traced to some vague colonial origin; however, as Nicholas Ostler (2005) has shown in his impressive account of language and empire across world history, the afterlives of colonial projects can be both long and very unexpected indeed.[11] It is in such a context that Jean-Marc Moura has recently noted, specifically in relation to the literary sphere in France: 'En réalité, on devrait moins s'interroger sur la légitimité des études postcoloniales que sur l'étonnante légèreté d'approches de la littérature qui prétendent ne pas tenir compte de cette histoire' [In reality, it is not so much the legitimacy of postcolonial studies that we should be questioning but rather the astonishing frivolity of approaches to this literature that claim not to take account of this history] (2007: 3).

Fundamentally, what is important is not the coherent institutional existence of something called 'postcolonial studies' but rather the existence of the set of practices that it draws together, for the 'postcolonial' has always been much more of a federating concept than a specific set of prescriptive theories or approaches. Our view of the field is one in which different but complementary disciplinary approaches can work either in parallel or in collaboration with one another. Although we ourselves seek to foster comparative and collaborative interdisciplinary work, we have no desire to push all scholars in this direction, nor we firmly believe would such a programmatic call be effective. Mireille Rosello's account of the strategic usefulness of the term 'Francophone' – 'Francophone studies is a performative statement that may or may not be useful ten years from now' (Rosello, 2003: 124) – is one that we would extend to our use of 'Francophone postcolonial studies', understood as a way of naming the broad field within which all the contributors to this volume work. For Rosello, scholars must continue to question their disciplinary values and taxonomies by holding them in tension with other approaches, and the intellectual practices in which we are variously engaged might best be explored within a series of overlapping frameworks (postcolonial, transnational, global) that provide complementary approaches and insights rather than seeking to displace their 'rivals' as 'obsolete': e.g. Bill Marshall's work on the 'French Atlantic' (mentioned above) opens up the study of France's *ancien régime* empire; Françoise Lionnet and Shu-mei Shih explore the concept of 'minor transnationalism' (Lionnet and Shih, 2005), which traces various axes that bypass former colonial centres; recent historical work, such as the edited volume *Imperial Formations* (Stoler, McGranahan and Purdue, 2007), seeks to extend the comparative study of empire beyond the Western European imperial powers. In his contribution to the special dossier in *PMLA*

---

11   See in particular, chapter 11, 'In the Train of Empire: Europe's Languages Abroad' (Ostler, 2005: 380–455). For such an informed student of language and empire, Ostler produces a curiously benign overview of French colonialism.

alluded to above, Fernando Coronil summarizes the potential for comparative work across Europe's empires:

> Horizontal exchanges between sites of imperial domination would change the field of postcolonial studies not just by including new partners in its discussion but also by transforming its terms and references. A view of colonialism as starting from the fifteenth century would offer a different understanding of modern colonialism and colonial modernity. (cited in Yaeger, 2007: 637)

There is of course a danger that such an approach will contribute still further to the universalizing tendencies that have marked many strands of postcolonial critique, but we would argue that situating Francophone postcolonial thought within the contexts from which it has emerged – as this volume consistently endeavours to do – grounds the process of comparative analysis within a specificity that refuses excessive generalization. Consequently, we share Coronil's vision of the transformative potential of this broad comparative approach, as we do his hope that the 'arrival of [postcolonial studies] signals not its end but creative departures' (637) towards new forms of what Edward Said dubbed non-dominative knowledge.

Further reading

Blanchard, Pascal, Nicolas Bancel and Sandrine Lemaire (eds), 2005. *La Fracture coloniale: la société francaise au prisme de l'héritage colonial* (Paris: La Découverte). A very important and controversial intervention in postcolonial debates in France. The editors, who belong to the ACHAC research group, draw together a wide range of experts (from France and beyond) on the colonial and postcolonial periods in order to trace the impact of French colonialism on the metropolitan 'centre' of empire, a process that has resulted in what they dub a 'fracture coloniale'.

McLeod, John, 2007. *The Routledge Companion to Postcolonial Studies* (London and New York: Routledge). A highly innovative volume by a leading figure in Anglophone postcolonialism, which draws together historical and cultural work on the British, French, Portuguese and Spanish empires. An invaluable book for scholars and students seeking to develop a comparative postcolonial approach.

Poddar, Prem, Rajeev Patke and Lars Jensen (eds), 2008. *A Historical Companion to Postcolonial Literatures: Continental Europe and its Empires* (Edinburgh: Edinburgh University Press). A comprehensive, encyclopaedic resource, providing material relating to the historical contexts of works from a range of postcolonial literary traditions in languages other than English. There are useful essays on geographical areas, as well as thematic entries – on subjects such as historiography, religion and women's histories – that permit comparison between different postcolonial literatures.

SECTION I

Twelve Key Thinkers

CHAPTER 1

Aimé Césaire and Francophone Postcolonial Thought

Mary Gallagher

Aimé Césaire was born in 1913 in Basse-Pointe in Martinique and, like so many members of the educated elite of the colonies, in his late teens he was was drawn to Europe, where he studied at the Lycée Louis-le-Grand in Paris from 1932, and later, from 1935, at the even more prestigious École Normale Supérieure (ENS). It was during these years in Paris that his reputation was sealed as co-founder, along with the Senegalese poet-politician Léopold Sédar Senghor (see Chapter 12) and the Guyanese poet, Léon Gontran Damas, of the *négritude* movement, which could be said to have been launched by this small catalyst group of expatriate writers (see Chapter 18). For in 1935, Césaire, Damas and Senghor founded the review *L'Étudiant noir,* and it was in this journal that Césaire first used the term *négritude*. Suzanne Roussy, also from Martinique, who would marry Césaire in 1937, contributed to this review as well. It was towards 1938 that Aimé Césaire finished writing his epic poem entitled *Cahier d'un retour au pays natal* (begun during a brief holiday in former Yugoslavia in 1935) and completed his studies at the ENS, studies crowned by a thesis on the theme of the South in the 'littérature négro-américaine' of the United States. The review *Volontés* published the *Cahier* in 1939, and Césaire returned in the same year to Martinique, where he and his wife became schoolteachers at the Lycée Victor Schoelcher in Fort-de-France (Césaire's pupils there would include Édouard Glissant and Frantz Fanon).

A double vocation

The highly developed political consciousness and the acute linguistic, poetic and ethical sensibility demonstrated in Césaire's *Cahier* blossomed into a variegated life of writing and politics. Indeed, one is immediately struck by the constancy of the double orientation of Césaire's life and work, divided as they were between his political activity and engagement on the one hand, and his literary work on the other. More specifically, from the mid-1940s onwards, Césaire's writing was shadowed, but not over-shadowed, by his considerable political commitments. In 1945, after an approach from Martiniquan Communists, he was elected mayor of Fort-de-France, the capital of Martinique, and also the small colony's deputy to the French parliament. Not only did Césaire's political involvement stretch to joining the French Communist Party but it was also in his capacity as parliamentary deputy that he was associated as *rapporteur* with the 1946 law that decreed the status of 'département d'outre mer' for Martinique, in other words, its greater assimilation as an overseas part of France rather than as an overseas colony. Césaire (and also those whom their political opponents would disparagingly call the local '*mulâtre* bourgeoisie') saw this change as an opportunity to break the stranglehold of the *békés*, or colonial landowner caste. However, these two political choices cast a long shadow over Césaire's anti-colonialist reputation, and local criticism of his dismissal of the option of outright – or at least greater – independence for the Caribbean colonies was at times extremely harsh.

Césaire resigned from the French Communist Party in 1956, a move prompted essentially by the invasion of Hungary, but also fuelled by his disillusionient with the reality of DOM status for Martinique and, indeed, by his perception of the party's inadequate recognition of the equality, but difference, of the French Caribbean citizen. His *Lettre à Maurice Thorez*, a letter of resignation addressed to the then leader of the French Communist Party, rejects the Communist priority of the proletarian revolution, indicating a conflict between Communist universalism and Césaire's particular priorities as a Martiniquan conscious, above all, of his colonial legacy of solidarity with the other Caribbean islands, with the African diaspora, and with the anti-imperial struggle more generally. Césaire was instrumental in setting up the *Parti progressiste martiniquais* in 1957, a party whose watchword was not political independence but, rather, political autonomy for France's Caribbean ex-colonies. Césaire himself argues forcefully for the *right* to independence from France, rather than for independence itself. For him, 'départementalisation' would replace assimilation with autonomy – i.e. with the right to self-determination, a right exercised by the pragmatic option in favour of belonging to 'un grand ensemble'. His most vociferous local opposition would take issue, of course, with the 'grand ensemble' to which Césaire sees Martinique as opting to belong, namely France and the European Union rather than the Caribbean and the Americas. Césaire withdrew from active political life in 1993, when he gave up his position as deputy in the French parliament, although he only relinquished his role as deputy mayor of Fort-de-France in 2001. He died in Martinique in April 2008.

The late 1940s were a most productive period for Césaire in literary terms: the poetry collection *Les Armes miraculeuses* and the play *Et les Chiens se taisaient* both appeared in 1946; the poetry collections *Soleil cou coupé* and *Corps perdu* followed in 1948 and in 1949 respectively. (Revised versions of these two works appeared in 1961 under the new title *Cadastre*.) A second literary flowering occurred at the end of the 1950s and in the early 1960s with the writing of three plays about the psychology of colonialism and decolonization (*La Tragédie du roi Christophe* in 1963, *Une saison au Congo* in 1965 and *Une tempête* in 1969), and with the publication of a new book of poems, *Ferrements*, in 1960. However, with the exception of one collection of poems, *Noria*, which is included in the *Oeuvres complètes* published in Martinique in 1976, and a final collection, *Moi, laminaire*, which appeared in 1982, Césaire's literary voice gradually fell silent.

Césaire's first and best-known published work remains the *Cahier*, which was 'discovered' by André Breton in 1941 during the latter's wartime stopover in Martinique. Its author was indeed hailed as 'un grand poète noir' by the 'high priest' of surrealism in his work *Martinique, charmeuse de serpents*. While Césaire's literary work clearly straddles the two genres of poetry and drama (his poetry collections just outnumber the four dramas), he also made a significant intellectual and critical contribution in his anti-colonial treatise, *Discours sur le colonialisme* (1955 [1950]), in his historical study on the Haitian leader Toussaint Louverture (1961c [1960]), and in his role as founder of literary journals. In 1941, just a few short years after his return to Martinique, he set up the review *Tropiques,* along with Suzanne Césaire, René Ménil, Aristide Maugée and Georges Gratiant, and himself contributed poetry and also articles on topics such as Martiniquan folklore (Césaire and Ménil, 1942). Later on, in 1947, he would co-found the journal (and, ultimately, publishing house) *Présence africaine* with the Senegalese writer, Alioune Diop.

Critical reception

The critical impact of Césaire's thinking is undoubtedly inflected by the fact that his intellectual reputation has been, not just initially but right up to the present, primarily a literary reputation. Moreoever, this literary profile has been based in the first instance on his epic *Cahier* and on his association as a poet with the foundation (by three poets) of the Negritude movement. As we have noted, André Breton was instrumental in bringing Césaire's poem to the attention of the wider French-reading public. Certainly, that legendary refraction and its rather dramatic circumstances served the dissemination of Césaire's reputation throughout the wider world. Breton's agency presented Césaire's contribution as not only essentially poetic, though with revolutionary political overtones, but also as perfectly aligned in this sense with the (self-proclaimed subversive) literary preoccupations of metropolitan France, notably, of course, with surrealism. Jean-Paul Sartre is another metropolitan figure who served Césaire's poetic reputation, more indirectly, in his preface 'Orphée noir' (Sartre 1988 [1948]) to Senghor's 1948 *Anthologie de la nouvelle poésie nègre et malgache de langue française*.

Among the first literary criticism devoting substantial studies to Césaire's writing, there was an influential European 'first wave' of critics, the most significant of whom are Lilyan Kesteloot, who wrote the volume on Césaire for the

Seghers 'Poètes d'aujourd'hui' series (Kesteloot, 1979), and two French critics (working or influential mainly outside France, however): Jacqueline Leiner, whose interview with Césaire appeared in the first issue of *Tropiques*, and Bernadette Cailler. Important studies were also devoted to Césaire's work by African critics, Georges Ngal and Clément Mbom, the latter concentrating more particularly (and quite exceptionally) on the dramas. Césaire as a writer and thinker, but primarily as a poet, has never lacked critical recognition, especially (but not exclusively) in Europe,[1] Africa and, of course, the Caribbean, where his work received favourable recognition from critics such as Roger Toumson. He has attracted many admirers and imitators in the French Caribbean especially, but has also been the object of some rather polemical criticism from within Martinique, from the pen of Raphaël Confiant in particular, criticism that has been countered by his most vociferous contemporary French champion, Annie Lebrun, who defends Césaire from an unapologetically literary point of view.

Césaire's discourse on Negritude has consistently stressed the need to recover the suppressed (and oppressed and repressed) self: 'C'est le nègre qu'il fallait chercher en nous' [What we needed to look for within ourselves was the Black] (Césaire, 2005: 27). His most recent *apologia pro vita sua*, in the form of published interviews with Françoise Vergès, confirms the constancy of his convictions in relation to the dangers of alienation (or self-dispossession) whether through colonial assimilation, particularism and ghettoization, or dilution in a nameless universalism. This explains why, as a poet, he espoused surrealism in opposition to (French) classicism and (local Caribbean) *doudou-isme* (a slavish and exoticist internalization or imitation of metropolitan literary trends). Paradoxically, however, assimilation is precisely the charge levelled by Raphaël Confiant against Césaire and against his use of the French language in particular, critiqued as being overly 'pure' or *recherché*, not creolized enough.

It is fair to say that Césaire's literary reputation has been primarily founded on his poetic oeuvre. Significantly less critical attention has been paid to his drama, which is, however, to a much greater extent than the poetry, *littérature engagée*, more historically and culturally referential, more politically charged. Indeed, Césaire's poetic work and his poetic reputation could be read as defusing, if not mitigating the message communicated by the dramatic oeuvre. It was, after all, the poetic work exclusively that was 'incorporated' or recuperated by the metropolitan poetic establishment in the person of Breton. However, given the revolutionary political pretensions and associations of the French surrealist movement, this metropolitan mediation of Césaire's poetics cannot, *pace* his most severe critics, be convincingly read in an entirely recuperative light.

The overtaking from 1950 to 1970 of Césaire's poetic writing by his drama

---

1   Although some authors such as James Clifford (1988), who like to refer to Césaire as a means of underwriting their references to 'hybridity' or 'creoleness', do not seem as well informed as others (e.g. Paul Gilroy [1993]) about distinctions between the multiple Caribbean approaches to intercultural relation or encounter, one could certainly say that Césaire's thought has travelled into contemporary cultural theory as exemplified by the writing of these two postcolonial thinkers.

and discursive work suggests that Césaire's orientation as a writer underwent a steady political radicalization corresponding to the disillusionment that accompanied the realities (some might say the fundamentally postcolonial realities) of decolonization. If, however, one takes into account the inward turn apparent in the poetics of his literary swansong, the collection *Moi, laminaire*, such a teleology is disproved. To what extent, then, is it legitimate to associate Césaire with postcolonial thought? Given that his literary oeuvre was complete by 1982, did the specifically postcolonial politicization of literature and of literary criticism, perhaps more outside France than within, register perhaps less on Césaire's writing than on its critical mediation?

Intellectual focus

Césaire's political thought is expressed most clearly and most directly in his *Discours sur le colonialisme* and in his other expositional writing, including his history of Toussaint Louverture. And yet the quasi-pedagogical role of public intellectual with which both Senghor and Césaire credited the writing of drama – 'parler aux gens' [to speak to the people] (Césaire, 2005: 63) – means that his plays also serve as a fairly direct exposition of his thinking. The subject explored in the first play, *Et les Chiens se taisaient,* is revolt against oppression, racism and colonialism: the central figure is the Rebel who faces various figures whom he had sacrificed to his cause, and who, at the end of the play, in a final test, faces Death itself. The anonymous figure of the *rebelle* and the presence of a chorus situate the play on a mythical level: it is without doubt Césaire's least (historically and geopolitically) referential drama and indeed the text of the play started life as part of the poetry collection *Les Armes miraculeuses. Une saison au Congo*, like the *Tragédie du Roi Christophe* is, by contrast, much more clearly situated, and is historically based. In the latter play, Haiti's disastrous post-revolution history is dramatized in the figure of Christophe (Christophe's tragedy is precisely that he replaces one tyranny with another), while *Une saison* turns to the figure of Patrice Lumumba in post-independence Congo. There is little ambiguity in either play about the roles and positions, or about the ideas and politics, of the two historical figures represented.

In the title of *Une tempête*, a rewriting of Shakespeare's classic, the definite article qualifying Shakespeare's *Tempest* is replaced by an indefinite article that makes of Césaire's play a hyponymic variant. The work could thus be regarded as explicitly writing back, and the tenor of this relation between classic and variant, between a text of empire and a text of the post-colony could be seen as fundamentally postcolonial. Moreover, the fact that the play is situated on a tropical island and that slavery, racial difference and miscegenation are its main topics underlines the Caribbean reference. The play's thesis underlines the imprisonment of all of the characters, including the master, within rigid hierarchical positions. Each of these plays is based, then, on Césaire's reflection not just on colonialism, but on the post-independence challenges faced by the ex-colonies. They are, in that sense, profoundly anchored in a critical reflection on both historical reality (Haiti or the Congo, for example) and the recent past and present of the former European colonies (the dictatorship of François Duvalier, the democratic deficit in several sub-Saharan African countries).

If Césaire's most explicit anti-colonial work is his *Discours sur le colonialisme*, the 1960s plays moderate the militant certainties of this tract, substituting for them the deconstructive play of power characteristic of the postcolonial dynamic. The *Discours* is strenuous and graphic in its denunciation of colonial violence, which it compares to the barbarity of Nazism. Césaire, who was living in Martinique when the collaborationist Vichy régime took power, witnessed the particularly overt racism of the pro-Nazi variant of colonialism in the Caribbean. Both horrors are based, in Césaire's view, on the refusal to recognize the humanity of the other, and both inevitably result in the cancellation of the oppressor's own humanity. If Césaire's Hegelian message anticipates current postcolonial thought it is undoubtedly via this notion that colonialism acts as much on the colonizing power as on the colonized. Thus the *mission civilisatrice* that is presented as legitimizing the colonial project in fact de-civilizes the missionaries themselves and their masters. The parallel highlighted by Césaire between Nazi and colonial outrages (including slavery) is particularly significant in the contemporary context of bitter polemical competition between those who speak for the victims of imperial slavery on the one hand, and those who speak for the victims of the Holocaust on the other.

Françoise Vergès's own contribution to her recent book of interviews with Césaire consists largely of an analysis of the value of Césaire's anti-colonialism in the context of the hegemony of postcolonial discourse, a discourse that has been, as Vergès acknowledges, somewhat slow to establish itself in metropolitan France. Vergès implies that Césaire's discourse is of most value when it approximates to the postcolonial orthodoxy. The Vergès interviews accord much space to the controversial question of compensation for the crime of colonial slavery. In May 2001, the French parliament voted into law a statement declaring that the slave trade and slavery were crimes against humanity. It is Césaire's view that the questions of compensation or reparation are not pertinent in that context and that the priority should be, rather, the development of a greater awareness of history and a greater willingness to proffer help for proper development of the former colonies. Césaire presents this as a moral duty for the West, in terms of the incalculable harm that its imperial expansion did to the rest of the world. He argues, moreover, that victimization discourse is disempowering for victims and their descendants.

History has a way of intervening in the play of all such ideological evaluations and reevaluations, however, and it took a most spectacular turn in February 2005, probably just as Vergès's book went in print, when the French parliament passed a law declaring that colonialism had not been exclusively negative for the colonized, but had also been of benefit to them. Some sort of pendulum effect might perhaps have been expected in response to the unambiguously anti-colonial tenor of the May 2001 law, but the 2005 initiative was an unexpectedly rude retort to those who had settled into anti-colonialism as the necessary foundation of the contemporary episteme. The *loi du 23 février 2005* claimed the positive role of the French presence overseas, especially in North Africa. In direct response to protests from overseas leaders of the stature of Césaire (who stated that he would not meet Nicolas Sarkozy during the latter's visit to Martinique) and to Algerian President Bouteflika's charges of negationism and revisionism, the offending claim was expunged in 2006 from article 4 of the law. On the face of it, a pro-colonialist statement was thus retracted and negationism faced down. Yet the broadly revisionist thrust of the law (largely concentrated on the invidious situation of the *Harkis*) remains, and that historical revisionism strikes me – here as in other contexts (Irish historiography, for example) – as being structurally and substantively in harmony with the supposedly more evolved ideological orthodoxies of postcolonial thought. It chimes, that is, with the general postcolonialist undermining of the moral clarity associated with binary distinctions: e.g. victime/*bourreau,* pro-colonial/anti-colonial.

Poetics and postcolonial thought

One of the more striking aspects of the contribution made by Aimé Césaire to Francophone postcolonial thought is precisely the limited theoretical tenor of his work. When Césaire is at his most 'theoretical' his thinking is very clearly humanist and anti-colonial, even if he allows, in a postcolonial spirit, that colonialism was not entirely positive for the colonizer. His strictly theoretical or philosophical work is disseminated across a handful of journal articles and interviews, his short *Discours sur le colonialisme,* and his studies on Toussaint Louverture and on Schoelcher. This theoretical discretion is most uncharacteristic of other prominent, late twentieth-century Martiniquan writers. For the programmatic compulsion is extraordinarily strong in the work of Édouard Glissant, Patrick Chamoiseau and Raphaël Confiant.

Césaire effectively allows his literary and his political work to speak for themselves and, indeed, to speak for him to a certain extent, that is, to represent or mediate his thinking. This is in contrast to his most prominent Martiniquan heirs, who have been at pains to state not just their cultural vision or theory, but also the manner in which their writing itself mediates, performs, realizes and enacts that vision or theory. Glissant and the *créolité* writers represent the cultural movement that they espouse (creolization or *créolité*) as being actualized in a poetics or a style of writing, a representation that blurs the separation between theory and practice, between metadiscourse and discourse.[2] One might be tempted to see this blurring as a camouflaging of a discourse of mastery,

2   The *créolité* manifesto, *Éloge de la créolité* (Bernabé et al., 1993 [1989]) has the status of a *mode d'emploi* for most of the writings of the two novelists who co-signed it, along with the linguist Jean Bernabé. In the case of Édouard Glissant, following three other highly substantial works of literary and cultural theory, his *Traité du Tout-Monde* (1997b) is the theoretical sister-text to his novel *Tout-Monde* (1993), published four years before the treatise.

or as a means of rendering the theory performative and thus incontrovertible. Césaire, however, does not suggest that his poetics or writing style actualizes any particular (theory of) culture or cultural identity. For him, writing (poetry) does not seem to be aimed at illustrating a particular culture, or at constructing a collective cultural identity: rather, 'la poésie révèle l'homme à lui-même. Ce qui est au plus profond de moi-même se trouve certainement dans ma poésie. Parce que ce "moi-même", je ne le connais pas. C'est le poème qui me le révèle et même l'image poétique' [Poetry reveals us to ourselves. What lies at the very heart of myself is certainly there in my poetry. Because I don't in fact know this 'self'. It is the poem, or even the poetic image, that reveals it to me] (Césaire, 2005: 47).

The corollary of this non-programmatic aspect of Césaire's work is, logically, a greater semantic, hermeneutic openness. If the author avoids joining the dots, so to speak, for the reader, if his intention is not fully parsed in accompanying or in parallel theoretical treatises or polemical, even didactic discourses, then readers should be – theoretically at least – freer to interpret the thinking 'behind' or 'beneath' the words that they read. One could argue that metadiscursive mastery of a given author's literary work is not in the interests of creative freedom either for the author or for the reader, not merely because there is often a prescriptive or dogmatic edge to the metadiscourse, but also because of the subordination of the writing subject to a pre-existing vision of collective identity. In any event, Césaire could be expected to avoid one of the deepest pitfalls that awaits the more theoretically prolific writer, whose theory will be pitilessly compared to his or her practice, and whose writing will often be found to fall short of the political, ethical and literary effects to which the writer aspires. This is the trap into which the writers of the *créolité* movement have fallen. In Césaire's case, however, it is the writer's political choices and commitments that have been scrutinized for their congruency with the tenor of the writing, as though the author's political activity constituted the praxis which either did or did not live up to the 'message' of the writing.

The contrast is striking between the enthusiastic assessment elsewhere in the postcolonial French-speaking world (and beyond) of Césaire's work on the one hand, and its undermining by at least one of the most prominent Martiniquan authors of recent times on the other. It is important, of course, to distinguish between the mild and not fundamentally oppositional tenor of the assessments provided by Édouard Glissant and even by Patrick Chamoiseau, or the explicitly tempering comments of the linguist and co-signatory of the movement's manifesto, Jean Bernabé, on the one hand, and the forthright criticisms articulated by Raphaël Confiant on the other, centred as they are on Césaire's fidelity to the French language, his repression of the Creole language and the oral culture associated with it, and his paradoxical political choices, allegedly contradicted by his anti-assimilation discourse. Certainly, Césaire never acknowledged the poetic or liberatory potential of Creole,[3] and so what really distinguishes

---

3   See the interview given by Césaire (1978) to Jacqueline Leiner for the preface to the first volume in the two-volume edition of all fourteen issues of *Tropiques*.

Césaire and Confiant is their poetics. Césaire preferred drama and poetry to prose narrative; he never forsook the exploration of self and of subjectivity for the ideology of collective identity; and he never succumbed to the temptation to write to a programme. In comparison, the writing of Raphaël Confiant, and even, although to a lesser degree, the work of Patrick Chamoiseau, is exceptionally monotonous in terms of style. This is inevitable, given that it is intended to constitute, above all, an 'illustration' of Creole culture or of 'créolité'. In stark contrast, Césaire's language, register, tone and style show an extraordinary variety between and within various genres.

Certainly, Césaire's *stated* political thought may appear more Manichean, less complex than that of Glissant, but it is not so much simplistic as limpid and direct: he does not idealize, as Glissant does, detour and opaqueness. The political strength of Césaire's work lies much less in its subtlety, in its poetic enunciation, or in its embeddedness in a web of intertextual, intratextual, intercultural, interlinguistic associations, than in his steadfast refusal to exchange one oppression for another. It is oppression *qua* oppression, wherever and however it operates, that Césaire combats in his thinking on Negritude, for example, and one would have to agree that his writing reflects that primordial insistence on freedom, and to begin with, on creative freedom. If the proof of the programme is in the writing, then Césaire's writing is, in a number of respects, true to his definition of Negritude as a rejection of all types of alienation, subjection and assimilation. Resisting linguistic, ideological, stylistic and generic bondage, Césaire's protean poetics – from the anti-colonial epic of the *Cahier* via the surrealist shards of the *Armes miraculeuses* to the postsubjective questioning of *Moi, laminaire* and the polyphonic drama – claims full creative licence for his work, refusing to shackle it to a specific drumbeat. In this way, his poetics shows an openness to the heterogeneity of register, tone and tenor that might seem far more convincing than the 'diversalité' preached and claimed by his heirs in writing of a rather unvaried style.

The genres that Césaire favoured are those in which the great writers of the French Enlightenment felt obliged to excel (epic poetry, drama and history), genres disdained by his most severe Caribbean critics. In an article that examines the poetics and politics of the relation between Césaire and his Martiniquan heirs, I have elsewhere suggested (Gallagher, 2007) that the factor of literary genre and the issue of the self (its constitution, definition, authenticity and expression) are central to this relation. More specifically, Césaire is concerned, in his drama as much as in his poetry, to articulate the tentative coming to self-awareness of an individual, singular selfhood. Even if the poet aspires to give voice to an oppressed collectivity, even if, according to J. Michael Dash (1992: 76), a strong 'demiurgic impulse is [...] clearly seen in the dogma of the Negritude movement', and even if, in the words of Édouard Glissant, Caribbean writing is characterized by the fact that 'le Nous devient le lieu du système génératif, et le vrai sujet' [the We becomes the locus of meaning-generation, and the true subject] (1981: 258), Césaire himself expressed a need to defend himself from the social and from the material, to protect the blossoming of the 'fleur inouïe du je':

Se défendre du social par la création d'une zone d'incandescence en deça de laquelle, à l'intérieur de laquelle fleurit dans une sécurité terrible la fleur inouïe du 'Je'; dépouiller toute l'existence matérielle dans le silence et les hauts feux de l'humour: que ce soit par la création d'une zone de feu; que ce soit par la création d'une zone de silence gelé, conquérir par la révolte la part fraîche où se susciter soi-même, intégral. (1943: 7)

To defend oneself from the social by the creation of an incandescent aura beyond or within which the unheard-of flower of the 'I' can blossom in terrible safety; to shed one's material existence in the silence and flames of humour, whether by the creation of a zone of fire or of frozen silence, so as to gain access to that fresh dimension in which to arouse one's integral self.

This singular need is affirmed as much in the surrealist tenor of *Les Armes miraculeuses* as in the postmodern tenor of the final collection, *Moi, laminaire.* Clearly, from the epic *Cahier* to the surrealism of *Les Armes miraculeuses* to the postmodern deconstructive subjectivity of *Moi, laminaire*, the relation of that self to a collective entity – humanity in general, the oppressed, the black race and the (French) Caribbean psyche – is variable and unstable. Moreover, a synecdochic relation between self and collective cultural identity is never, ever a given for Césaire. Indeed, as he himself indicated in *Tropiques*, he often deliberately fled from such an equation.

If one were to characterize Césaire's position reductively on the ideological stock exchange that fixes the market value of writing, one would have to situate it in relation to the extraordinarily bullish trajectory of postcolonial stock. Both Patrick Chamoiseau, in *Écrire en pays dominé* (1997), and Raphaël Confiant, in *Aimé Césaire: une traversée paradoxale du siècle* (1993), explain that Césaire's stances do not correspond to the postcolonial complexity of the contemporary world. Césaire's work, insofar as it concerns the colonial plot writ large (neo-colonial, anti-colonial, postcolonial), is certainly quite resolutely anti-colonial. Yet, even if – as Françoise Vergès suggests – some of his views or positions testify to an awareness of the types of multipolarity, feedback and complexity that the postcolonial turn of mind is adept at recognizing and promoting, the question is not so much how 'postcolonial' is Césaire's work, but rather how adequate or how questionable, in political and epistemological terms, is the 'postcolonial turn' itself (in particular in the manner in which it has been embraced by Césaire's heirs). Certainly, against the background of the recent French legislative attempt to rehabilitate colonialism, Césaire's doggedly anti-colonial stance appears neither anachronistic nor irrelevant. Moreover, his final, unambiguous literary salute, *Moi, laminaire...* , which favours the singular subject over the imperative of collective cultural identity, seems less quixotic than salutary in its focus on creative freedom. If the 'hybrid conditions that the colonial enterprise inevitably promoted [were] always already in the process of eroding its Manichean world view' (Bongie, 1998: 14), if there is indeed an 'epistemic complicity' (Watts, 2005: 6) between the colonial and postcolonial paradigms, then Césaire's anti-colonial thinking is not just difficult to dismiss, but it may well be logically linked to his marked fidelity to creative freedom. Both stances could even perhaps pass as legitimately sceptical and freely questioning with regard to a postcolonialist orthodoxy which, in saturating and overdetermining contemporary cultural thought, production and critique, has risen to a position of apparent global mastery that could, all too easily, itself become oppressive and uncreative.

Further reading

It has not been possible to include in the bibliography the most significant works of all: namely all those works of (chiefly) Caribbean literature (chiefly) in French, written either against Césaire or in the manner of Césaire, or leaning on the Césairean intertext, and in all these cases bearing witness to his influence on postcolonial writing. The three related studies listed below by Raphaël Confiant, Annie Lebrun, and Françoise Vergès are particularly valuable because of their intensely stimulating, if overly polemical effect on the discussion about the contribution made by Césaire's work to the postcolonial debate. Whereas the other studies listed in the general bibliography pay careful attention to Césaire's texts and bear witness as such to the truly protean generic and stylistic richness of his writing, and whereas A. James Arnold's study (1981) gives an excellent account of the working out of Negritude in Césaire's writing, these three volumes, in evaluating the political stakes of Césaire's work, directly or indirectly reference postcolonialism.

Cesaire, Aimé. 2005. *Nègre je suis, nègre je resterai. Entretiens avec Françoise Vergès* (Paris: Albin Michel). The recent analysis provided by Françoise Vergès in her postface to this interview with Césaire suggests that the latter's critique of colonialism is subtle enough to have integrated, *avant la lettre*, postcolonial perspectives on complexity and reciprocity. The interview itself concentrates on political issues, and reference to Césaire's literary works is chiefly to the drama. Nearly thirty years separate the publication of the Vergès interview, on the one hand, from Jacqueline Leiner's interview with Césaire (1978), on the other. The political emphasis of the former contrasts with the literary emphasis of the conversation with Leiner, a conversation that dwells above all on Césaire's aesthetic, especially his views on Creole versus French, on the unconscious and on the imagination.

Confiant, Raphaël, 1993. *Aimé Césairé: une traversée paradoxale du siècle* (Paris: Stock). This frontal critique highlights putative contradictions between Césaire's 'assimilated' language, style and politics, on the one hand, and his anti-colonial stances, on the other.

Lebrun, Annie, 1996. *Statue cou coupé* (Paris: Jean-Michel Place). Defending Césaire against the *créolité* movement, Annie Lebrun emphasizes the gap between the inventive freedom of Césaire's poetics and the totalitarianism of the *créolité* programme, arguing that Césaire's work enables a 'libre circulation du sens' [free flow of meaning].

CHAPTER 2

Maryse Condé: Post-Postcolonial?

Typhaine Leservot

How does one introduce Maryse Condé to the uninitiated reader? Condé's centrality to Francophone studies and her popularity outside academic circles make this question more than merely rhetorical. Indeed, her fame has spread beyond the academic circle of scholars and students in Francophone studies – far beyond, in fact. English, German, Dutch, Italian, Japanese, Portuguese and Spanish translations of her work testify to her growing global audience. Her oeuvre has earned her a number of accolades that reflect her widespread appeal: the French government named her Commandeur de l'Ordre des Arts et des Lettres in 2001 and Chevalier de la Légion d'Honneur in 2004; the Québec government made her an honorary member of the Académie des Lettres du Québec in 1998; and Guadeloupeans acknowledged her importance in a four-day conference on her work in Pointe-à-Pitre in March 1995. In spite of her widespread popularity, however, her creative work has been analysed in a largely fragmented fashion, and her critical work is little known within postcolonial studies in the English-speaking world.

Maryse Condé, née Boucolon, was born in Guadeloupe in 1937, before the island's status changed (nominally) from that of colony to that of Département d'Outre Mer in 1946. She grew up in Guadeloupe until her parents sent her to pursue her studies in France at the age of 16. After receiving her BA in English and Classical Literatures from the Sorbonne in Paris, she married African actor Mamadou Condé in 1959. In 1960, she moved to Africa, where she spent twelve years as a university lecturer in Guinea, Ghana and Senegal. She remained there long after her marriage came to an end around 1964. She returned to France in 1973, completed her doctorate in comparative literature at the Sorbonne in 1975 with a study of stereotypes of blacks in West Indian literature, and continued her extremely varied career as a university lecturer, literary critic and fiction writer. In the late 1980s, after a brief stay in Guadeloupe, she moved to the United States, where she taught Francophone literatures at various universities, including the University of California at Berkeley, and later, in 1995, at Columbia University. Retired since 2002, Condé currently spends half the year in Guadeloupe and half the year in the US, while continuing to write and participate in conferences.

Ever since writing her first play while living in Africa in 1970, Condé has remained a prolific writer, whose highly esteemed oeuvre now spans almost four decades and includes novels, short stories, plays and critical essays. She remains, however, more famous for her novels, among the most famous of which are: *Segu* (originally published in 2 volumes, 1984-85, awarded the German Liberatur Prize); *I, Tituba, Black Witch of Salem* (1986, awarded the Grand Prix Littéraire de la Femme); *Tree of Life* (1987, awarded the Prix de l'Académie Française); *Crossing the Mangrove* (1989), *Desirada* (1997, awarded the Prix Carbet de la Caraïbe); *Tales from the Heart* (1999, awarded the Prix Marguerite Yourcenar); and *Who Slashed Celanire's Throat?* (2000, awarded the Hurston/Wright Legacy Award). Now in her early 70s, Condé continues to write and publish, long after becoming the first Francophone Caribbean writer to receive the Puterbaugh Prize for her work in 1993.[1]

Neither Negritude, nor *antillanité*, nor *créolité*: Condé's fiction and essays

Given the richness of Condé's fiction and her own complexity as a thinker and critic, any overview of her work is necessarily reductive. Keeping this in mind, it seems safe, however, to define Condé's work as a sustained and insightful exploration of Caribbean identity and, in particular, of the three major theories that attempt to define it: namely Negritude, *antillanité*, and *créolité*. From the 1930s onwards, Negritude encouraged Antilleans to find their roots in Africa. In response, Édouard Glissant's concept of *antillanité* in the 1970s encouraged Antilleans to find their identity within the Caribbean and within the Creole language. (See Chapter 6 for more in-depth analysis of Glissant's work.) In 1989, however, Jean Bernabé, Patrick Chamoiseau and Raphaël Confiant once again redefined Caribbean identity by offering another concept: *créolité*. Although the creolists borrowed from Glissant's *antillanité* its linguistic focus on Creole, their definition of *créolité* goes beyond Glissant's exclusive focus on Caribbean Creole culture and includes any people across the world born out of the violent mixing of European, African and Asian cultures.

The quest to define Caribbean identity is not particular to writers from the French Caribbean islands of Martinique and Guadeloupe, but is characteristic of twentieth-century Caribbean literature in general, be it from Anglophone, Hispanophone, Francophone or Dutch-speaking islands. Marked by the tragic crossing of the Atlantic from Africa and Asia during the era of the slave trade and

---

1   For a complete list of Condé's work, see the regularly updated page about her on the website on Francophone postcolonial writers from the City University of New York: http://www.lehman.cuny.edu/ile.en.ile/paroles/conde.html

indentured labour, and by the massive emigration of Caribbeans today towards Europe and North America, the Caribbean is an emblematic site of forced migration. The uncertainties that arise from past, present, and future migrations mean that any identity politics within the Caribbean is imbued with a sense of rootlessness that several generations of Caribbean writers attempted to analyse throughout the twentieth century. In addressing this phenomenon, Condé's work analyses the pitfalls of previous theories of French Caribbean identity and offers original alternatives.

In this vein, Condé's early novels tackle the issue of Negritude, which still resonates among late twentieth-century Caribbean writers. The 1930s Negritude movement led by Aimé Césaire (Martinique), Léon Gontran Damas (French Guyana) and Léopold Sédar Senghor (Senegal) was a direct response to the Eurocentric notion that Africa and its diaspora had no culture. Negritude proclaimed instead that the identity of all descendants of the black diaspora was firmly rooted in the African continent, just as that of whites across the world was rooted in Europe. (See Chapter 18 for a more in-depth discussion of Negritude.) This meant, for Antilleans in search of their origins, the need to go back to Africa. Condé's first novel, *Hérémakhonon* (1976), illustrates the return to Africa encouraged by Césaire as a necessary process in order to understand Caribbean identity. The novel is narrated by Véronica, a young Guadeloupean woman who leaves the island in search of her identity in Africa. Once in Africa, however, she discovers how political corruption prevents African nations from moving forward and decides to leave the continent altogether, admitting to herself at the end of the novel that she looked for the wrong ancestors in the wrong places. Condé's subsequent novels, *A Season in Rihata* (1981) and the two volumes of *Segu* (1984–85), are also located in Africa and also attempt to look at the continent without embellishing either its pre-colonial past or its postcolonial present. Condé's early fiction was sharply criticized for offering what some saw as a reactionary attitude towards Africa. Condé first replied to this severe criticism by explaining that in her 'novel of protest', *Hérémakhonon*, she sought to demystify the superficial and 'devout faith in African socialism that was in the air in many of the newly independent nations of Africa in the 1960s' (Pfaff, 1996 [1993]: 40). After *A Season* and *Segu* also became the focus of similar controversies, Condé decided temporarily not to use Africa as the site of her narrative fiction.

After discovering the limitations of a Césairian return to a mythical Africa, Condé's later characters return resolutely to the Americas, exploring issues of ancestry, rootlessness, migration and identity within the Caribbean, as well as in relation to the other Americas: northern, southern, central and insular. Her short story 'Three women in Manhattan' (1985) is set in New York, *I, Tituba* in Barbados and the US, *Tree of Life* between Guadeloupe, Panama and the US, *The Last of the African Kings* (1992) in the southern US, *La Colonie du nouveau monde* (1993a) between Guadeloupe and South America, *Windward Heights* (1995) on several Caribbean islands, *Desirada* between Guadeloupe, Paris, and Boston, *Who Slashed Celanire's Throat?* in Africa, South America, and Guadeloupe, and

The Cannibal Woman (2003) in South Africa. In her only novel where the setting is restricted to one island – *Crossing the Mangrove* – the multicultural origins of Condé's characters evoke the past migrations that gave birth to the Caribbean. In *Crossing the Mangrove*, the inhabitants of the little Guadeloupean community of Rivière-au-Sel all claim origins beyond the island.

Condé's characters inhabit and often traverse the wide circle of islands and continental locations around the Caribbean, and in so doing they explore the difficulties of being diasporic subjects born out of past and contemporary migrations. It is only in *Desirada*, however, that the main character, Marie-Noëlle, makes peace with her nomadic identity resulting from her unknown origins. Throughout the novel, Marie-Noëlle wanders between Guadeloupe, France and the US in search of her father, until she realizes the need to conclude her search for origins and accept the biological and symbolic unknown that forms her identity. In fact, although Marie-Noëlle does not know her father, she belongs to a line of strong women who do, eventually, help her to accept a female, instead of the more traditional male, genealogy. In the end, she settles in the Boston area to teach Francophone literatures in the very region that rejected Caribbean-born Tituba in the seventeenth century, and where the famous Boston Tea Party initiated the rejection of Europe a century later. The actions taken by Condé's character confirm the need to explore the indelible link between insular and continental America.

These repeated migrations between northern, southern, central and insular Americas allow Condé's Caribbean characters to explore their identity in relation to their closest neighbours in the United States, rather than in isolation from them, or, as was most common among Francophone Caribbean writers, in relation to Africa, France or Europe. This link forged between the various Americas places Condé at odds with both Glissant and the creolist thinkers. Although their respective theories of *antillanité* and *créolité* seek to free the Caribbean from ambiguous and difficult links with Europe, Africa or Asia (the respective ancestral lands of the Caribbean whites, blacks, Hindus, Chinese and Syro-Lebanese), both theories also neglect the strong link between continental and insular Americas. Indeed, according to the creolists:

> It is necessary [...] to make a distinction between Americanness, Caribbeanness, and Creoleness, all concepts which might at first seem to cover the same realities. [...] *Americanness is* [...] *in many respects, a migrant culture*, in a splendid isolation. Altogether different is the process of Creolization [...] which refers to the brutal interaction [...] of culturally different populations [...] *resulting in a mixed culture called Creole*. (Bernabé et al., 1993 [1989]: 91–93; emphasis in original)

The creolists' definition of Americanness as the result of both the United States' self-imposed isolation and of the imposition of Anglo-Saxon culture may well evoke the cultural experience of some of the early Anglo-Saxon settlers, who imagined America as a barren land. Such a definition, however, cannot apply to the experiences of Native Americans or African Americans, both transplanted populations, who experienced an undeniably 'brutal interaction' between their culture and that of another, which is the very definition of creoleness, according to the creolists.

Condé's critical work in the 1990s focuses almost exclusively on the debate surrounding Creole identity and literature following the creolists' 1989 manifesto. In 'Order, Disorder, Freedom, and the West Indian Writer' (1993b), 'Chercher nos vérités' [Finding our Truths] (1995a), and 'Créolité without the Creole Language?' (1998b), she openly engages with this debate by explicitly refusing the creolists' theory that Caribbean literature should be situated primarily in the Caribbean, or that Caribbean identity is rooted in the Creole language. After Chamoiseau, as the first reader of her book *Crossing the Mangrove*, faulted her for not always using proper Creole terms (1991), Condé launched a critique of the trio's concept of creoleness. Although she acknowledges that 'Créolité [...] has many good points' (Pfaff, 1996: 114), she considers its impact minor. Among its good points, Condé appreciates its literary urge not to restrict its characters to the trio white planter/black man/mulatto, its desire to break taboos about sexuality and to portray modest heroes instead of supermen (Condé, 1993b: 129) and, as in Glissant's work, the value it places on the Creole language. However, she also notes how this theory preserves a masculinist and heterosexual world view by omitting issues relating to women, female sexuality and homosexuality (all themes present in her own fiction). She further criticizes the creolists for their refusal to take into consideration the new diasporic Caribbean subjects who live outside of the Caribbean and speak languages other than Creole or French: Haitians and Cubans in the US, Canada and Europe; Jamaicans and Surinamese in England; French Antilleans in France, Dutch Caribbeans in the Netherlands (1998b: 108–09). Finally, Condé forcefully criticizes the creolists' dogmatic tendencies: 'Créolité should not be transformed into a cultural terrorism within which writers are confined. [...] To each his or her own Créolité' (Pfaff, 1996: 114).

Postcolonial icon and iconoclast: Condé's contribution to postcolonial theory

Although Condé's anti-creolist stance may have marginalized her as a rebel within French Caribbean literature, it has certainly not done so within Francophone postcolonial studies or Caribbean studies. Given the centrality of questions of identity and migration in Caribbean Studies and in Condé's fiction and essays, Condé the writer has come to fascinate as much as her fiction, and they both now occupy a central place in Francophone postcolonial studies. The number of interviews with her, and of studies of those interviews, probably equals that of critical readings of her work. Although Condé herself has always refused labels, her work is read as a form of postcolonial fiction that explores issues of race, gender and culture before, during and after European imperialism in Africa and the Americas. Studies, theses, dissertations and books on Condé abound in

Anglo-American universities, where her readership and appeal continue to grow. In a recent volume edited by Emily Williams and Melvin Rahming (2006), which seeks to explore the transnational nature of Caribbean literatures (Anglophone, Hispanophone, and Francophone), four out of the fifteen essays are focused on Condé's work. By contrast, none focuses on creolist writers Raphaël Confiant and Patrick Chamoiseau. Such a selection, it seems, further confirms that, unlike the work of the creolists, Condé's writing deals with more than just the French Caribbean. By refusing to confine her characters to the French islands or pursue the Creole-versus-French debate that is so central to creolist theorization, she avoids the ghettoization of her Caribbean world within the confines of its French heritage and opens it instead to the rest of the Americas. Furthermore, in her work, the questions of race, migration, identity, and gender as they are traditionally explored in Francophone postcolonial studies lose their geographical specificity (i.e. the Francophone Caribbean) and acquire transnational significance. As Condé's postcolonial subjects migrate from the Caribbean to Europe, Africa and/or the Americas, and are shaped by their multicultural experiences, so are the postcolonial issues and identities they carry with them. This Condéan network of geographical and national locations of identity formation should be of particular interest on the one hand to postcolonial studies in the English-speaking world, as it emphasizes the multicultural over the bicultural and, on the other hand, to Francophone postcolonial studies, as it negates the centre/periphery relationship between France and the French Caribbean. Thus, when Condé reveals in an interview that for her the Caribbean 'universe [...] extends throughout the Caribbean region and Latin America, the whole American continent, in fact' (Pfaff, 1996: 125), one understands why her work might be deemed central to postcolonial studies in general, whether Anglophone or Francophone in focus. This being said, when we talk about Condé's 'postcolonial narratives', we should keep in mind the fact that Condé herself does not categorize them in these terms, but, in fact, finds the category of the 'postcolonial' troubling and at times inadequate. So if these are 'postcolonial narratives', then they are narratives that are implicitly self-conscious of the postcolonial category itself and re-inscribe it rather than ones that fall easily within its traditional boundaries.

Condé's perceived irreverence towards postcolonial theory is perhaps the thread that runs through all critical work about her. In the five collections of essays on her writing published within the last decade or so, she is consistently seen as a 'politically incorrect writer' (Araujo, 1996), an 'inconvenient nomad' (Cottenet-Hage and Moudileno, 2002), or 'a writer of her own' (Barbour and Herndon, 2006). In her 1995 article, 'Condé's Critical Seesaw', Leah Hewitt aptly summarizes Condé's contribution to theory as a constant questioning of 'dogmatic positions [...], political assumptions and cultural identities, what is taken for granted on *all* sides of cultural, racial, and sexual divides' (1995: 641). For Hewitt, 'Condé is an iconoclast who picks apart the clichés of the communities she has lived in [...]. [S]he beckons us [...] to recognize the potential conflicts among oppressed groups' (641). As a result, Hewitt believes, along with other scholars, that 'Condé's critical trademark places her at the forefront of contemporary debates about the racial, ethnic and gender markings of literature' (642).

Condé's work indeed contributes to postcolonial theory by consistently criticizing its dogmatic approach to race, gender, culture and history. In other words, she constantly seeks to nuance or even revamp any theory. Regarding theoretical approaches to race and ethnicity, for example, Condé severely criticizes any homogeneous and uncritical vision of the black diaspora. In *Mixing Race, Mixing Culture* (2002), editors Monika Kaup and Debra J. Rosenthal place Condé among the writers from the other (Latin and Caribbean) America who help challenge the tendency, in the United States mostly, to limit questions of race and ethnicity to one's own immigrant origins or to one's biracial/bicultural background. Instead, Kaup and Rosenthal believe that writers, like Condé, from the Caribbean and Latin America offer US writers and scholars a means of exploring the multiracial/multicultural dimension of race and ethnicity born out of the various 'cultural crossroads' that gave birth to the Americas (Kaup and Rosenthal, 2002: xiv).

Condé's criticism of dogmatic approaches to race is particularly evident in her short story 'Three Women in Manhattan' and her novel *The Last of the African Kings*. In these two narratives, Condé mocks what she sees as a militant approach to race, an uncritical rendering of black people as victims, and an uncritical support for Africa, all the while criticizing the opposite attitude of ignoring race altogether. In 'Three Women', the African-American writer Elinor, whose books are shunned by the African-American community for ignoring the issue of slavery, is also criticized for catering to a white audience's thirst for exoticism. In *The Last of the African Kings*, Debbie's racial militancy is mocked throughout the novel for its political correctness, yet Condé, like her protagonist, subtly militates to change the canon by 'peppering her writing with the names and beliefs of black culture from all over the world' (Hewitt, 1995: 649).

Caribbeans fare no better in Condé's work, with regard to their views about race or gender. Although Condé repeatedly says that race is no longer important in the Caribbean – even if money is – she is, nevertheless, aware that Guadeloupeans and Martiniquans think they are 'better than other Antilleans' because they carry a French passport, an attitude that angers Condé deeply (Morris and Reece, 1998). Regarding the issue of gender, Condé confronts the silence of French Caribbean theorists (who all happen to be men) regarding issues such as Caribbean machismo and philandering. When Condé recounts, in *Victoire*, that politician and philanderer Dernier Argilius is transformed, after his death, into a hero who had defended the oppressed and the illiterate, she ponders:

> Qu'est-ce qu'un homme exemplaire? Ne comptent que les écrits, les discours et les gesticulations en public? Quel poids la vie personnelle, le comportement intime? Dernier Argilius a profité dont on ne sait combien de femmes, gâché la vie d'au moins une d'entre elles, planté je ne sais combien de bâtards poussés sans père. Cela n'importe pas? (Condé, 2006b: 50)

What is an exemplary man? Do only the writings, the speeches and public gesticulations count? How much weight should be placed upon their personal life and their actions behind closed doors? Dernier Argilius used countless women, spoiled the life of at least one of them, and seeded an unknown number of bastards raised without a father. Doesn't this matter?

Condé's fiction helps raise further gender issues by ignoring the traditional silence over female sexuality within French Caribbean literature, another choice that links her work to that of Caribbean and American writers. Her independent female protagonists talk openly about sex, female heterosexual desires (Véronica, Tituba, Marie-Noëlle) and even, at times, homoerotic desires (Tituba). However, Condé refuses to depict her female protagonists as flawless heroines. In fact, male or female, there is no hero in Condé's fiction, nor anti-heroes, simply human beings offering a mixture of faults and virtues. It is precisely such a nuanced approach to humanity that Condé expects from theory. She refuses to see the black diaspora as a homogeneous community of victims, united racially and culturally by a history of oppression. She prefers, instead, to explore the conflicts and differences within the black diaspora, in the same fashion as Zora Neale Hurston in relation to the US canon.

By refusing to stand on any one side of the postcolonial issues of race or gender, Condé appears to have become, like Plato's philosopher, the gadfly of postcolonial theory, a role that she seems both aware of and comfortable with: 'I write for myself but also to provoke people, to force them [...] to see things they don't want to see. I think this need to upset people prevails in all my books' (Pfaff, 1996: 30). Although she is resolutely Caribbean in terms of the themes she explores, Condé's unusual transnational settings and characters transform her fiction into the ultimate test against which postcolonial theory must be measured. Even though Condé does not consider herself engaged in an overtly postcolonial discourse and rejects the label 'postcolonial writer', the works she has produced promise to impact upon and perhaps even change the direction of postcolonial studies. Whereas Anglophone postcolonial studies has led the way, resolutely turning postcolonial studies towards history, and whereas Francophone postcolonial studies has added much-needed nuances to Anglophone postcolonial concerns, Condé's work further challenges these two approaches by making her postcolonial characters deal not only with issues inherited from history but also with issues born out of today's globalization.

Towards post-postcolonialism? New suggestions for reading Condé

Condé's contributions to the postcolonial issues of race, ethnicity and gender may seem ironic given that most critics also agree that 'her characters have no fixed identity based on race or gender, even though they may make that the object of their quest' (Barbour and Herndon, 2006: 47). In fact, Condé herself explains that for her, 'race and color questions have become secondary' when considered in relation to 'cultural encounters and the conflicts and changes that come from them' (Pfaff, 1996: 20; 29). Perhaps it is precisely *because* she makes issues of race and ethnicity secondary in her fiction – and not in spite of it – that she adds to postcolonial criticism. Because her narratives do not primarily focus on the issue of racial tensions in the postcolonial world and successfully direct attention to individuals who are less victims of that world than agents in it, Condé's fiction prompts postcolonial theorists and critics to explore other themes and not to confine her writing to a prescribed list of postcolonial issues.

In fact, Condé's 2002 autobiographical essay gives us a strong clue as to what else her fiction explores when she explains that 'without knowing it, [she] had adopted Glissant's theory of the rhizome identity' (see Glissant, 1997a [1990]). The concept of rhizome identity is opposed to the Eurocentric understanding of identity as rooted in one history, one geography and one ethnicity. Instead, a rhizome identity has multiple roots that feed on (multi)cultural encounters. Since the 1990s, Glissant's understanding of rhizome identity frames his own redefinition of creoleness as creolization, and it is this very concept that appears particularly relevant to Condé's exploration of diasporic Caribbean subjects. Glissant's concept of creolization elaborates on his own concept of *antillanité* and on the creolists' concept of creoleness as *créolité*. Following the creolists' criticism that *antillanité* was too Caribbean-centred, Glissant built on the creolists' work and transformed their own understanding of *creoleness*. Whereas the creolists see creoleness as the (fixed) result of traumatic multicultural encounters marking the identity of Creoles across the world, Glissant redefines it as a *creolization*, that is, as an ongoing process, leaving Creole identity resolutely open-ended.

In *Postcolonial Paradoxes in French Caribbean Writing* (2001), Jeannie Suk sees Condé as a writer who explores the dynamics of Glissant's concept of creolization. However, she focuses exclusively on the literary consequences of reading Condé as Glissantian. A more holistic recontextualization of Condé's use of Glissant's creolization needs to be undertaken, however, if one wants to understand the complexities of Condé's diasporic subjects. The concept of creolization at work in Condé's writing appears to be an exploration of globalization and transnational movements rather than an exploration of boundaries within Caribbean literatures (as Suk suggests), Caribbeanness, and/or the postcolonial condition. In fact, Condé genuinely explores the notion of creolization as 'a global phenomenon' (Dash, 1998: 6), and more studies are needed to understand fully the creolized/globalized subjectivities she depicts in her fiction.

Understanding that postcolonial subjects are, like non-postcolonial subjects, part of a globalized world permits us to analyse another major theoretical claim of Condé's fiction that has gone unnoticed: namely, that postcolonial subjects are not defined solely by their postcolonial condition. If one turns to those Condé stories involving the murder of a white individual, for example, one is hard-pressed to find a postcolonial rationale that would explain these violent deaths. In spite of suggestions to the contrary, Francis Sancher's death in *Crossing the Mangrove*, Lorraine's death in *La Belle Créole* (2001b), and Stephen's death in *The Story of the Cannibal Woman* are not the result of postcolonial crimes motivated by race. They are, instead, the result of accidents. By inserting the idea of chance/accident into the deeds of postcolonial subjects, Condé suggests that their lives are not absolutely determined by their colonial past. One is not, in other words, a constant postcolonial subject. What is more, by suggesting, as she does in *Crossing the Mangrove*, that Francis Sancher may have died to expiate his white ancestors' sins, Condé introduces the theme of guilt as an area of postcolonial investigation. Just as postcolonial subjects are not constantly postcolonial, it should not be assumed either that they cannot be of European origin. The concept of (white) guilt in Condé's fiction underlines the fact that certain aspects of European culture itself must be analysed as postcolonial.

Maryse Condé's contribution to postcolonial theory takes on myriad forms. Firstly, her fiction traverses geographical frontiers and breaks through theoretical barriers between Anglophone and Francophone literatures. As she creates a literary world in which her French Caribbean characters travel back and forth between Anglophone and Francophone areas of the globe, Condé offers a critique of the national and linguistic frontiers that separate Anglophone and Francophone theories and cultures. If she urges scholars to nuance their approach to race and to allow for a more realistic depiction of the black diaspora, she also sharply criticizes male Francophone writers for neglecting Caribbean gender issues and the issue of transnational diasporic Caribbean subjects. Secondly, Condé further challenges postcolonial theory by opening it up to its *post-postcolonial* possibilities. As her subjects explore issues of identity in a resolutely globalized world, she uses the theoretical reflection born out of Glissant's concept of creolization to show the relevance of the transnational Caribbean experience to globalization and transnational studies. At the same time, she also suggests that postcolonial subjectivity should never be theorized in such a way as to become dogmatic.

And that is perhaps Condé's single most important contribution to postcolonial studies: in her fiction, postcolonial subjects are subjects first, and postcolonial second. As such, her characters are only partially indebted to the colonial history that preceded them and they remain free, to a certain extent, to make choices based on the present-day reality that surrounds them. Although Condé runs the risk of sounding reactionary, a criticism she faced after her first novel in 1976, she intelligently raises a question that transcends as well as widens postcolonial studies: at what point does the colonial history of a people diminish in importance as new conditions arise?

Further reading

Barbour, Sarah, and Gerise Herndon (eds.), 2006. *Emerging Perspectives on Maryse Condé: A Writer of Her Own* (Trenton, NJ: Africa World Press). The most recent collection of essays in English on Condé's work.

Condé, Maryse, 1995 [1989]. *Crossing the Mangrove*, tr. Richard Philcox (New York: Anchor-Doubleday). [First published as *Traversée de la mangrove*.] The only novel by Condé set solely in Guadeloupe. As 19 characters attend the wake of Francis Sancher, they confess their most intimate thoughts about him. This novel explores the complexities of Caribbean racial tensions and multicultural identity.

Condé, Maryse, 2000 [1997]. *Desirada*, tr. Richard Philcox (New York: Soho Press). [First published as *Desirada*.] This novel follows Marie-Noëlle's quest for her identity from Guadeloupe, to France, to the US. It perhaps best exemplifies the complexities of the new diasporic Caribbean subject in Condé's fictional work.

Pfaff, Françoise, 1996 [1993]. *Conversations with Maryse Condé*, tr. Françoise Pfaff (Lincoln, NE: University of Nebraska Press). [First published as *Entretiens avec Maryse Condé*.] A series of interviews with Maryse Condé conducted over several years. First published in French in 1993 and supplemented by an additional chapter for the English edition, this is a key text that offers a multiplicity of insights into Condé as a writer and a critic.

World Literature Today, 1993: 67.4: 693–768. [Special issue: *Focus on Maryse Condé*.] An important collection of essays in English. It contains, in particular, excellent articles on gender issues in Condé's work by Marie-Denise Shelton, Gerise Herndon and Lillian Manzor-Coats, among others.

CHAPTER 3

Jacques Derrida: Colonialism, Philosophy and Autobiography

Jane Hiddleston

Derrida's influence on, and intervention in, postcolonial criticism has always been provocative and highly controversial. One of the major philosophers of the twentieth century, Derrida invented a new and radical mode of reading that set out to unravel the metaphysical premises of 'Western' or Eurocentric thought, yet his resonance for the criticism of specific colonial systems remains a subject of dispute. His deconstruction of philosophical and political hierarchies, his scepticism towards the concept of 'the West', and, according to thinkers such as Bhabha and Spivak, his persistent interest in marginality and eccentricity have defined the very tools of postcolonial criticism. Yet others, such as Ahmad and Parry, continue to dismiss his methodology as abstract and complicit in the European structures it set out to challenge. While his entire corpus is devoted to decentring apparently grounded, stable and institutionalized systems of thought, his perspective is still frequently construed as metropolitan and insufficiently attuned to the specificities of non-European cultures to be able truly to offer a strategy for anti-colonial resistance. Derrida's reception in postcolonial circles has consequently been somewhat ambivalent, despite the undoubted importance and extent of his influence. He is responsible for the creation of a mode of criticism that serves precisely to overturn apparent, accepted hierarchies, but some readers complain that this philosophical inquiry ought to engage more closely with the everyday mechanics of the colonial system. This chapter will explore the postcolonial angle in Derrida's work, as well as the controversy it has generated, in order to suggest that his contribution relates to his questioning of the very form of philosophical thought. Derrida's work on postcoloniality is idiosyncratic, difficult to read and frequently dehistoricized, but it is precisely this troubled and self-conscious texture of his writing that reveals some of the loopholes and difficulties of postcolonial inquiry. Although he has been criticized for his introspection, Derrida's eclectic writing voice, flitting in his later works between the universal, the specific and the autobiographical, dramatically performs the dilemmas of the attempt to theorize postcolonial eccentricity and Otherness.

Derrida was born in 1930 in El Biar, near Algiers, into a family of Algerian Jews. He went to school at the local *collège* and then *lycée*, though he was traumatically excluded for two years when the Vichy government deprived Algerian Jews of their French citizenship during the Second World War. Eventually returning to school in 1944, he read widely on French philosophy, and passed his baccalaureate in 1948. He then went to the Lycée Louis le Grand in Paris, on to the École Normale Supérieure, and passed the *agrégation* in 1956. He visited Harvard University, completed his military service, began teaching at a *lycée* in Le Mans, and then taught at the Sorbonne. Here, his career began in earnest, as he published his first work on Husserl's *The Origin of Geometry*, and his seminars became increasingly famous. His scholarship became even better known after he visited Johns Hopkins University in 1966, and it is after this that the major works, *Writing and Difference* (1967), *Of Grammatology* (1967) and *Margins of Philosophy* (1972) appeared. His uncovering of the contradictions and uncertainties in the works of major philosophers and writers such as Rousseau, Saussure and Lévi-Strauss was recognized as radical and highly controversial, serving to reinvent philosophical criticism as a strategy of undermining itself from within. Derrida went on to contribute to the founding of the Collège International de Philosophie in Paris, and in 1984 he began the series of seminars at the École des Hautes Études en Sciences Sociales that continued until his death in 2004. His work also became increasingly politicized as it developed, and his philosophical engagements became more and more interspersed with reflections on political institutions. The celebrated and notorious *Specters of Marx* (1993) clarified Derrida's engagement with Marxism and invented the notion of 'hauntology', although it was also vilified for depoliticizing Marx. *The Politics of Friendship* (1994) offered an extended investigation of democracy and totalitarianism, and *Du droit à la philosophie* (1990) threw into question the politics of the university and academic writing themselves. Explicit comments on Algeria and on his own background as an Algerian Jew also started to appear in his work during the 1990s and, despite his success and popularity, he claimed a sort of marginal status. He was awarded an honorary doctorate by Cambridge University in 1992, but not without fierce controversy, and he tended to position himself outside the mainstream of traditional philosophy. This curious eccentricity, this pursuit of marginality despite the breadth of his influence, constitutes a large part of his interest for postcolonial criticism.

Derrida's origins in Algeria and his liminal position in relation to what might be seen as metropolitan French culture have not been widely discussed until recently, and he himself only started writing explicitly and at length about his background in the last ten or fifteen years of his life. His obituaries attempted to weave some reflection on his origins into their summaries of his corpus, but such passing comments were ultimately difficult to square with the broader celebration, and mythologization, of his work in Europe and the United States. Indeed, the obituaries showed that he had become a leading philosophical institution, a position that remained at odds with his musings on his sense of his own Otherness, his non-belonging in the metropolitan culture and language. Jean Birnbaum evoked the importance of the journey in Derrida's work in his obituary in *Le Monde*, asserting: 'c'est toute l'oeuvre derridienne qui peut être lue sous ce même motif du voyage, et de ce que Heidegger appelait "*la mise en chemin*"' [All of Derrida's work can be read according to this same motif of the journey, and of what Heidegger called '*setting on its way*'] (Birnbaum, 2004). Yet although the metaphor is apt, Birnbaum's discussion does not pursue the implications of this questioning, of this movement outwards, for a more focused conceptualization of 'postcolonial' thinking.

I want to begin this investigation, then, by interrogating the extent to which notions of eccentricity and decentring have been 'central' to Derrida's thought from the beginning. Derrida's work has always been concerned with alterity, with the supplementary traces accompanying the main thrust of philosophical discourses, and the decentring of those discourses through attention to 'Other' traces. This gesture is itself associated with the dismantling of the hegemony of 'Western' philosophy, its self-deluding ethnocentrism, and with a demand for increased attention to the Other that 'the West' ignores or omits. 'The West' is, as a result, itself a concept that must be undermined and denounced for its false self-presence and assumed security. I shall then turn to Derrida's more recent, partially autobiographical, writing, where he theorizes the difficulty of writing about his own experience of eccentricity in a language that is always and necessarily 'colonial'. The incursion of a tentative, uncertain autobiographical 'je' itself also undermines the discourse of philosophical neutrality that claims to know and master its objects of investigation.

Deconstructing ethnocentrism

Before embarking on a reading of Derrida's postcolonial resonances it is worth recalling Robert Young's arguments broadly establishing the link between deconstruction and the questioning of both empire and ethnocentrism in the latter half of the twentieth century. Young's own work, *White Mythologies* (1990), aptly dissects the connotations of Derrida's essay, 'White Mythology', printed in *Margins of Philosophy* (1972), for the critique of colonial ideology, since the term designates 'Western' philosophy's assumption of its universality. Young boldly states that, if there is such a thing as a founding moment for poststructuralism, it is not May 1968 but the Algerian War of Independence (Young, 1990). It is this latter event that disabled, in the mind of many French intellectuals, the conflation of historical narrative with 'Western knowledge', and that displayed unequivocally the limited resonance of 'Western' discourse when confronted with its non-Western Other. Poststructuralist scepticism towards apparent hierarchies and institutional divisions was in this sense already rooted in postcoloniality, in the collapse of colonial ideology as announced by the atrocities of the Algerian war. Deconstruction is, as a result, not just an unravelling of 'philosophical thought' in general, but precisely an overturning of 'Western thought', its denial of its hidden supplements, its conceptual and cultural alterity.

Of Grammatology is one of Derrida's first works to offer a critique that could be conceived as 'postcolonial'. Here, Derrida explores the 'Western' concept of language as associated with the voice, with self-presence and immediacy, and he reveals this as deluded and, importantly, ethnocentric. Logocentrism is the affirmation of presence in language; it names the privileging of phonetic writing, in which meaning is apparently unmediated and perfectly captured. This phonetic writing assumes that speech is primary, since it depends on the controlling presence of the speaker, and writing then mimics or follows speech, claiming, in turn, to signify presence. Derrida locates this privileging of the logos in philosophers from Plato to Hegel, and goes on to trace its development in Saussure, Lévi-Strauss and Rousseau. His purpose, however, is not only to unravel a certain myth of language as the signifier of presence but also to show that this is an ideology that predominates specifically in 'the West', and that excludes and denies the cultural Others that it cannot contain. For Derrida, 'phonetic writing, the medium of the great metaphysical, scientific, technological and economic adventure of the West, is limited in space and time and limits itself even as it is in the process of importing its laws upon the cultural areas that escaped it' (Derrida, 1976: 10). Logocentrism offers an illusion of presence, as if to signify control over meaning, but Derrida argues that this ideology fails to admit its own situatedness and the intractable, inassimilable meanings that lie beyond its reach. Derrida argues that in Saussure's work, for example, the spoken language is coupled with phonetic writing, but any traces of the non-phonetic are seen as interruptions, moments of disturbance that unsettle the transparency of the logos, but do not upset his privileging of its rule. These interruptions are unruly traces of an Otherness that resides beyond the reach of a clearly 'Western' desire for presence, but that Saussure is at pains to relegate to the margins.

Derrida's next example is Lévi-Strauss's *Tristes tropiques*, in which he similarly sees a privileging of a specifically 'Western' conception of writing. Lévi-Strauss analyses the 'society without writing' of the Nambikwara Indians of Brazil, but Derrida argues that this analysis relies on a separation of speech and writing that is ethnocentric. Lévi-Strauss refuses to conceive of 'drawing lines' as a form of writing, and also conserves the immediacy and self-presence of speech by naively distinguishing it from the supplementary structure of writing. Derrida's conclusion is that 'to recognize writing in speech, that is to say the différance and the absence of speech, is to begin to think the lure. There is no ethics without the presence *of the other*, and consequently, without absence, dissemination, detour, différance, writing' (Derrida, 1976: 139–40; emphasis in the original). An adherence to a narrow, restricted conception of speech constitutes a denial of the trace, the alterity, that structures all writing. This ties in with the 'Western' myth of the certainty and hegemony of the logos.

Derrida's other important reading of Lévi-Strauss, 'Structure, Sign and Play in the Discourse of the Human Sciences', develops this charge of ethnocentrism and broadens it out even further to deconstruct the very structures that shape and define 'Western' thought. Derrida begins by identifying the persistent 'centre' that structures the 'Western' episteme. This centre serves to give thought a point of presence, a fixed origin, and though it grounds thought, it also remains outside the structure it creates. Paradoxically, 'the concept of centred structure is in fact the concept of a play based on a fundamental ground, a play constituted on the basis of a fundamental immobility and a reassuring certitude, which is itself beyond the reach of play' (Derrida, 1978 [1967]: 279). Up to a point, Lévi-Strauss also relies on this concept of a centre as he persists in seeking to systematize his investigations of other cultures. In the course of his research, however, Lévi-Strauss later finds that this mythical 'centre' is necessarily an illusion, and that his practice as an anthropologist instead resembles 'bricolage' – the use of various instruments of analysis without the positing of an originary ground or centre. This process is then itself subject to mythologization, but the analysis allows Derrida to show that anthropology, while devoted to the study of the Other, has relied on the 'Western' construction of a centre, though this centre is always in tension with the 'play' that escapes it. Interpretation as a result can proceed in two ways: it can continue to pursue its own centre, or relinquish that search entirely in favour of an embrace of the play of signs. Once again, Derrida's implication here is that anthropology, the very science of the Other, has difficulty in remaining open to that Other, its intricacies and singularities, and has repeatedly relied on foundations conceived by the ethnocentric anthropologist and not the object of inquiry.

In addition to this philosophical decentring of 'the West' through the 1960s and 1970s, during the 1980s Derrida began to write more specifically on racism and colonial ideology, though the reception of this work was contentious. Following his own philosophical interest in mythology and semiology, he wrote a short piece on the significatory power of 'apartheid' in the notorious 'Racism's Last Word', at the time of the exhibition 'Art against Apartheid', held in Paris in November 1983. Derrida's argument is that the word itself posits and acts out a myth; it designates separation, but in setting this up as an abstract essence, it promotes a segregation that is also ontological. The irate critique of the essay by Anne McClintock and Robert Nixon points out that its reading of the essentializing power of 'apartheid' effaces the historical conditions of South African racism, but it might be argued in response that this was not at all the point. Derrida's achievement was precisely to dissect the 'white mythology' of the term, its naming of an absolute metaphysics of separation, rather than the empirical practice of apartheid in South Africa.

The highly specific exploration of the term 'apartheid' is later followed by broader 'deconstructions' of some of the other political terms underpinning 'Western' political, and indeed colonial or neocolonial, institutions. *The Politics of Friendship* explores a history of discourses of friendship from Aristotle to Montaigne, in order to reveal both the prevalence of metaphors of fraternity and the difficulty of combining an ethics of equality with the selection necessary for the creation of friendship. The work also unravels the aporia of democracy, and poses the challenge that we conceive a broad, cohesive, democratic community while also remaining attentive to the singularity of the Other. Derrida argues that 'there is no democracy without respect for irreducible singularity or alterity, but there is no democracy without the "community of friends" (*koina ta philon*), without the calculation of majorities, without identifiable, stabilizable, representable subjects, all equal' (Derrida, 1997a: 22). Subsequent writing on hospitality develops this aporia, and theorizes the dual requirement that the host remains open to the radical difference of the guest, while adhering to political norms of hospitality, of frontier controls and asylum. While these works are not explicitly concerned with colonialism, they all shed light on the intricacies and contradictions of political ideologies: of apartheid, of democracy, and of the laws of hospitality. This attention to the loopholes of such political concepts is resonant for postcolonialism, because it encourages attention to singular Others and marginalized subjects hidden by, or subsumed in, the lures of political mythology.

Postcolonial singularity

Derrida's contribution to postcolonial thought in the texts mentioned so far consists, above all, in his evolving conception of the singular. Though he has scarcely mentioned colonial ideology, his interrogation of the subject's self-differentiation outside the framework of the political institution provides a starting point for a theorization of postcoloniality as the trace that resists circumscription by an ideology imposed upon it from the outside. It is in this sense that his notorious *Specters of Marx* is informative, since by unravelling metaphors of haunting in Marx, it encourages a reflection, not specifically on postcolonial identity, but on traces or 'ghostly' supplements forgotten by, but inherent in, the very political vocabulary we rely on. As Spivak points out, the writing on the New International in *Specters of Marx* enables a conception of the modern migrant, frequently postcolonial, as the supplement of global capitalism and, even more, advocates a form of reading that attends to the Others, the phantoms, that history has sought to repress (Spivak, 1995). This attention to half-presences and singularities is contentious as a political strategy, but it is nevertheless precisely this exploration beyond the conventional boundaries of political concepts that defines Derrida's impact on postcolonial philosophy and thought. He analyses not the specific historical conditions of postcolonialism, nor the particular experiences of a given postcolonial community. Rather, his exploration of the traps and limits of philosophical and political discourses helps to conceptualize a certain thought of 'postcolonial' resistance: not so much a proposal for action as a reconfiguration of the assumptions of 'Western' metaphysics.

It is in some of Derrida's more recent writing that he turns most explicitly to French colonialism in Algeria and to his own pursuit of singularity within the colonial language in which he writes. The call for attention to the singular that pervades all his work here becomes a reflection on his own disjunction from any sense of origin or belonging, a disjunction linked to his experience of growing up as a French-speaking Jew in Algeria. This is not a demand for singularity as Peter Hallward understands it, that is, as an absolute, self-sustaining force, but rather a turning away from the determinations of place and context even as he engages with such determinants. The emergence of an autobiographical 'je' is not itself new in Derrida's work; it was theorized explicitly in his exegesis of Rousseau in *Of Grammatology*, and actively dramatized both in *Glas* and in the letters of *The Postcard*. In *Glas*, for example, the exploration of the signature in Genet's autobiographical writing subverts the apparent philosophical neutrality of the Hegel column while also displaying the signature's opacity, its inevitable function as a mask. The universalizing pretensions of conventional philosophical discourse are undermined by the disruptive incursion of a singular voice that resists philosophical gestures of generalization.

With 'Circumfession', Derrida's parallel contribution to *Jacques Derrida* (Bennington and Derrida, 1991), *The Other Heading* (1991) and *The Monolingualism of the Other* (1996), this anxiety towards the universalization of 'Western', ethno-centric philosophical discourse is expressed precisely through exploration of the writer's own sense of exclusion and liminality when growing up in a colonial culture and language that he did not feel were properly his. Derrida's scepti-cism towards the ethnocentrism of 'Western' philosophy becomes here a highly fraught reflection on the exclusion of *all* others from the sovereign language and, paradoxically, at the same time on his own singular sense of marginalization by an oppressive colonial culture. 'Circumfession', printed as a sort of footnote text to Geoffrey Bennington's exegesis, tackles Jewish tradition through the intertext of Augustine's confessions, and starkly juxtaposes partial memories of circumcision and reflections on Judaism in Algeria with Bennington's attempted systematization of Derridean thought. *The Other Heading*, less formally playful, frames an interrogation of the hegemony of Europe, of Valéry's figure of Europe as a 'cap' or head, with passing anxieties concerning the writer's sense of marginalization from the Europe that he is also showing to be different from itself. *The Monolingualism of the Other* is Derrida's most detailed engagement with 'postcolonial' thinking, and focuses on the exclusion of the colonized from the colonial language, on the alienation of all subjects in language and, finally, on the traps hindering the expression of the singular experience of liminality by means of autobiography.

Derrida's contribution to postcolonial inquiry in *The Monolingualism of the Other* involves, on the one hand, the deconstruction of the ethnocentric, or sovereign, language and a call for attention to the singular Other. On the other hand, however, Derrida's intervention also includes an interrogation of the very theoretical language it uses: it is self-conscious about its own production of an anti-colonial critique. First, Derrida argues that all subjects are alienated in language, and he therefore undermines the colonizer's assumed possession of his language and his deliberate exclusion of a subordinate Other: 'the master is nothing. And he does not have exclusive possession of anything' (1998 [1996]:

23). Communities such as the Jews of Algeria in this way become doubly alienated, because the colonizer denied them any sense of cultural belonging in the language that he nevertheless imposed. This was in turn concretized when the Algerian Jews were deprived of their French citizenship during the Second World War. Secondly, however, Derrida undermines the gesture of philosophical neutralization by incorporating the intermittent anxieties of a fragmented, ghostly 'Je', which in turn theorizes its own evacuation from the exegesis. The text is haunted by singular traces of the writer's 'self', but which the writer can never catch up with and encapsulate. The turn to autobiography is an anxious expression of resistance to the universalization of postcolonial critique, but the text also never fully encapsulates the singular 'Je' of the enunciation. It is 'an account of what will have placed an obstacle in the way of this auto-exposition for me' (1998: 70).

In a further twist, moreover, the work begins with the confession 'I only have one language', but the first person is already distinguished from any authorial voice because the quotation is set up as a hypothetical statement, analysed and unravelled in turn by a second apparently authorial voice. On one level, this further troubles the notion that the singular 'Je' of Derrida's persona can be pinned down in language, but the 'Je' also, at the same time, acquires a certain philosophical generality, and the statement suggests once more that all speakers fail to possess their language. What might have been read as an autobiographical narrative of Derrida's own experience of dispossession turns out to fall back into the universalist structure that the fleeting autobiographical references set out to problematize. The analysis of colonialism requires a resistance to the universal, but Derrida also refuses the identification of an authorial subject position that would over-determine him. The text is condemned to a constant and paradoxical movement against each stance it adopts.

In its curious and irresolute shifting between the universal, the specific and the singular, *The Monolingualism of the Other* provocatively questions the practice of postcolonial philosophy and self-consciously signals its traps. Derrida's postcolonialism undermines the colonizer's erroneous claim to possess his language and either to assimilate or reject the marginalized but culturally diverse speakers of that language, and reveals instead the master's hidden contingency and alienation. Having signalled this universal dispossession, however, Derrida pinpoints the particular experience of the Algerian Jews dispossessed of their citizenship and of a sense of belonging in language, though he uncovers at the same time the aporia between the need to present that experience as unique and its exemplification and concretization of the broader law. In drawing attention to the alienation brought about at a specific historical moment, moreover, Derrida also refuses to accord the Algerian Jewish community a false determinism that would once again tyrannize and totalize the singular differences of distinct Jews. Finally, Derrida subverts both the gesture of philosophical generalization and the examination of a historical specificity further in his pursuit of a form of individuation that refuses positionality or the location of a theoretical norm. The singular 'Je' of Derrida's own autobiographical project, and his endeavours at self-exploration, 'let all my specters loose' (1998: 73). *The Monolingualism of the Other* stages the tension between 'theory' itself and the necessity for a form of writing that does not fall into the same traps of totalization and determinism that colonial discourse set for the colonized. Derrida's singularity, however, is necessarily depersonalized, with the result that that singularity once again, paradoxically, attains a quasi-universal status. The text demonstrates in this way the contradictory demands of postcolonialism and the tensions inherent in the philosophical contemplation of the limits of colonial or totalizing thought.

Critical reception

The use of Derridean thinking in postcolonial studies has been both widespread and contentious. Many postcolonial critics choose actively to deploy the tools of deconstruction to undermine discourses of colonial mastery, while others see such strategies as hopelessly abstract and ahistorical. Some readers seek too facile a connection between philosophy and politics, and expect Derrida's deliberately abstract thought to impact on political action, even though his work evidently constitutes a specifically philosophical investigation with no particular claim to change the material conditions of postcolonalism. Those who champion the importance of key Derridean notions such as dissemination in postcolonial criticism include Homi Bhabha, whose work on 'DissemiNation' applies Derrida's conception of proliferating meanings and chains of wordplay to the falsely unifying language of the nation state. Bhabha's premise is that the narrative of the nation is a symbolic or textual apparatus, and the nation's actual heterogeneous cultures are the hidden supplement that the discourse can never catch up with and include. His argument is also that this disjunction is temporal, or, using Derridean language, subject to 'différance'. Migrant and marginalized peoples are also temporally out of joint with the hegemonic discourse of the nation; their own stories are precisely what that dominant narrative defers. In Bhabha's words:

> the nation's people must be thought in double-time; the people are the histor-
> ical 'objects' of a nationalist pedagogy, giving the discourse an authority that
> is based on the pre-given or constituted historical origin *in the past*; the people
> are also the 'subjects' of a process of signification that must erase any prior or
> originary presence of the nation-people to demonstrate the prodigious, living
> principles of the people as contemporaneity. (Bhabha, 1994: 145)

Bhabha's contribution to postcolonial debate has been to emphasize this ambivalence within hegemonic, nationalist and colonial discourses, and to stress these discourses' lack of control over the subjects they set out to 'place' and determine. His language has, like Derrida's, been criticized for being excessively abstract, and his undermining of the colonizer's *text* has been seen as unhelpful at moments of actual political struggle. Yet again, like Derrida, Bhabha's purpose was never activist, and though his prose is certainly looser and more convoluted than that of the rigorously philosophical Derrida, his work can be seen as a thought-provoking supplement to the latter.

The other major postcolonial critic to have used Derrida's work is Gayatri Spivak, though her attitude towards the influence of deconstruction in postcolonial criticism vacillates. Most famously, Spivak translated Derrida's *Of Grammatology*, and she also goes on in her critical writing to emphasize, above all, his unique attention to his own position as a philosophical writing subject (Spivak, 1990: 6–7). Derrida should be read, argues Spivak, because he discusses not only discursive hegemony in general, but also the politics of the academic institution, and his at once marginal and mainstream status within it. At the same time, however, she also points out that deconstruction must be limited in its resonance, since it assumes that there is a clear subject position to be questioned. This self-assertion is precisely, for Spivak, what marginalized peoples lack. As a result of this double response, however, Spivak's writing on Derrida is somewhat contradictory, shifting between an emphasis on the inaccessible, singular trace of the subaltern's voice, oppressed by hegemonic discourse, and more concrete demands for an identity politics. She discusses at once the impossible requirement that we attend to the endless singulariza-tion of the marginalized other, and the necessity that we offer a practical form of engagement. In 'Can the Subaltern Speak?', Spivak uses Derrida's work to conceptualize the 'inaccessible blankness' of the subaltern and to understand the mechanics of the constitution of the Other in discourse (Spivak, 1988: 294). At the end of the *Critique of Postcolonial Reason*, however, she admits that his discourse remains within the academic institution and, though she is at pains to trace the 'setting-to-work' of deconstruction, she concludes in somewhat lukewarm terms that 'it gives rise to restricted but useful debates' (Spivak, 1999: 429).

Spivak undoubtedly modifies her stance towards deconstruction, but her thinking is highly informative in this context because it distinguishes two strands in postcolonial critics' responses to Derrida's work. On the one hand, with Bhabha, Spivak productively develops Derrida's attention to the singular as a means of undermining the hidden ambivalences of colonial discourse, and associates deconstruction with this questioning of power structures. Abdelkébir Khatibi is another thinker who pursues this association, as he amalgamates deconstruction and decolonization, arguing that both require 'une pensée autre' [other thought], and that this would constitute 'l'achèvement silencieux de la métaphysique occidentale' [the silent ending of Western metaphysics] (Khatibi, 1983: 51). On the other hand, another school of postcolonial critics follows the more sceptical strand in Spivak and denounces the application of apparently abstruse textualism to the critique of a system that is empirically, economically and politically oppressive. Aijaz Ahmad broadly dismisses the poststructuralist project of undermining the symbolic apparatus of power because it is appar-ently divorced from history, becoming itself a free-floating commodity in the market-place of ideas (Ahmad, 1992). Benita Parry complains that the use of poststructuralism in postcolonial criticism finishes by eradicating the notion of conflict, which is at the heart of the colonial project (Parry, 1994). She also points out that Derrida's New International, a globalized network of interactions operating above and below the nation, puts under erasure notions of class agency, power and struggle (Parry, 2004). Finally, Azzedine Haddour goes so far as to ally Derridean notions of dissemination with the French colonial policy of assimilation in Algeria. He claims that reducing difference to an ongoing play of differentiation neutralizes and attenuates the agency and subjectivity of the other, effectively reducing it to a homogeneous category of sameness (Haddour, 2000). What these critics all have in common is a perception of the disjunction between Derrida's focus on language and its obfuscations on the one hand, and the demands of an active political critique on the other.

Finally, criticism of Derrida's intervention in, and influence upon, postcolonial criticism has certainly been both abundant and virulent. Positive or negative, however, the response to his work testifies to the extent to which he has helped to shape the evolution of the field. Moreover, while on some level it is undoubtedly true that Derrida's writing on ethnocentrism, sovereignty and singularity is highly self-conscious and does not offer an immediate strategy for resistance, this was never his aim, and his innovation lies precisely in the subtlety of his philosophical and textual musings. Derrida's manner of meticulously unravelling the lures of hegemonic discourse, and his attention to the traces and supplements that slip beyond its reach, display the limits of the colonial project and provide a language in which to theorize the resistance of the colonized other to categorization. More recently, the intense anxiety and self-consciousness of his reflections on his own experience of colonialism and eccentricity help to conceptualize not only the limits of colonial discourses of mastery but also the very difficulties associated with writing about the project of resistance. Derrida constantly stresses the endless self-singularization of the subject in language, but he is also frustrated in his attempts to explore that process in his own past and returns to a quasi-universalism. A sense of unease with the sovereignty of language, then, and with the myth of linguistic belonging and possession, is inscribed and performed in the structure of Derrida's text. This astonishing dramatization of the interpenetration of philosophy with autobiography, of the universal with the singular, constitutes one of the most innovative features of his writing, and displays the frailty, as well as the necessary continuation, of the practice of generalized and neutral theorization undertaken by postcolonial philosophers and thinkers.

Further reading

Hiddleston, Jane, 2005. 'Derrida, Autobiography, and Postcoloniality', *French Cultural Studies*, 16.3: 291–304. This article explains more fully the current argument about the tensions of Derrida's use of autobiography in his writing on postcolonialism.

Spivak, Gayatri, 1999. *A Critique of Postcolonial Reason* (Cambridge, MA: Harvard University Press). This is Spivak's most extensive treatise on postcolonialism, and frequently her angle is Derridean. The text contains an appendix entitled 'The Setting to Work of Deconstruction', which explicitly demonstrates the use of Derrida's thought as political critique. A volume of Spivak's interviews (1990) contains frequent references to the resonance, and the risks, of deconstruction for postcolonial thought.

Syrotinski, Michael, 2007. *Deconstruction and the Postcolonial: At the Limits of Theory* (Liverpool: Liverpool University Press). This text contains a chapter on Derrida's intervention in postcolonialism, while the rest of the work examines his influence on thinkers such as Bhabha, Spivak, Mudimbe and Mbembe.

Young, Robert, 1990. *White Mythologies: Writing History and the West* (London: Routledge). Young charts the contributions of various philosophers and poststructuralist thinkers to postcolonial thought, but the main argument of the book is that the deconstructive thinking of philosophers such as Derrida has its very roots in decolonization. Young (2001) includes a section on Derrida, addressing him in the second person as if to mimic the philosopher's own use of an intimate, subjective perspective, and outlining more specifically his relationship with Algeria.

CHAPTER 4

Assia Djebar:
'Fiction as a way of "thinking"'

Nicholas Harrison

Readers of a book called *Postcolonial Thought in the French-speaking World* will expect it to contain chapters on Fanon, Glissant, Césaire and Senghor. The reasons for including or resituating other figures as postcolonial thinkers will be clear enough. Assia Djebar, however, has written only one book that might be labelled theoretical, *Ces voix qui m'assiègent ... en marge de ma francophonie* (Djebar, 1999b).[1] That collection, not yet translated into English, deserves to be better known, but it is primarily as a novelist that Djebar is a significant figure. To some readers, her place in the present volume may appear anomalous, even tokenistic. My aim is to show that she has engaged deeply with questions around the postcolonial and the francophone that are central to the volume and, ultimately, to argue for the pertinence, in this context, of the distinctive literary *form* of her thought.

Djebar and the postcolonial

Djebar's engagement with 'postcolonial' issues is manifest on several levels, starting with her very focus on a colonial history whose significance Europe has often underplayed or underrated. This theme featured prominently in her speech at the Académie française in June 2006.[2] Djebar recalled the long years

---

1 The title is symptomatically difficult to translate; it is derived from Beckett's *The Unnamable* and is something like *The Voices Assailing Me*. (See also Harrison, 2003a.) In the subtitle, 'en marge de' suggests that Djebar is on (or outside) the periphery of the French-speaking world and the French language itself.

2 The Académie française was founded early in the seventeenth century. Its mission is to maintain literary and linguistic standards in France; it is a generally conservative body, and Djebar is the first North African, and one of very few women, to have been elected to it. There are never more than 40 *académiciens*; a new member is elected only when a member dies. On the occasion of their induction, new members customarily speak about their predecessor.

her predecessor, a lawyer named Georges Vedel, spent in a prison camp during the Second World War, and his deep shock when he found out, after his release, about the extermination camps that had operated nearby. These Djebar describes as 'une Barbarie au cœur même de l'Europe' (Djebar, 2006: 11). *Barbarie* means barbarity or barbarism as well as Barbary ('in the very heart of Europe') and it brings into play the history of conflict between Europeans and North Africans and the persistent European denial of Europe's own record of brutality. This leads Djebar towards an account of 'une autre Histoire' [another History] (2006: 13), that of colonialism and anti-colonialism, emphasized (without belittling the horror of the Second World War) as central to twentieth-century history – even in Europe.

Djebar's writing is 'postcolonial' in various other senses, too. First, it is a classic instance of how 'the empire writes back': for example, *L'Amour, la fantasia* of 1985 (translated as *Fantasia, An Algerian Cavalcade*, Djebar, 1989), one of her best works, in the view of many critics, casts light on a long post-contact history and offers a supplement and a challenge to history books written mainly from the perspective of the colonizer. Djebar interweaves an (apparently) autobiographical narrative and an account of the conquest, at once capturing Algerian perspectives and reminding us how hard it can be to recover the perspectives of the colonized.

Furthermore, Djebar has written repeatedly about a post-independence Algeria that remains deeply influenced by its colonial history, not least in relation to its own traditions. In some sections of Algerian society, according to Djebar's portraits, customs appear to have ossified, partly because of the threat posed to them by colonialism/neocolonialism, while other sections, in which Djebar herself and/or her work may be situated, appear post-traditional in Tony Giddens's sense (1996): that is to say, traditions (including religious traditions) still make themselves felt, but adherence to them can no longer be automatic or unquestioned, and tradition's ability to lend meaning to quotidian activities is correspondingly diminished.

In other ways, Djebar extends and exceeds the classic postcolonial paradigm. Her subject matter reaches back in time to encompass topics and narratives – from classical antiquity, say, or Berber mythology – outside the modern colonial/anti-colonial/postcolonial framework. In this way she challenges, on the one hand, a certain Eurocentricity (and the privileging of French colonialism, not least by postcolonial critics, as the key to North African identities), and on the other, some of the dominant narratives in post-independence Algeria pertaining to religious and ethnic identity. These, she suggests, also remain too concerned with colonialism and anti-colonialism; some still hanker for a mythical pre-colonial culture, their dreams of independence skewing into dreams of purity. North Africa, Djebar reminds us, has seen wave after wave of conquests, has been home to many different ethnic, religious and linguistic groups, and has never been monocultural or monolingual.

Increasingly, Djebar's implied interlocutors and opponents within Algeria have included Islamists. The rise of Islamism in the late 1980s in Algeria led to another

Algerian war, whose victims included several of Djebar's friends. The historical and political context for this turn of events is complex. Djebar suggests that colonial and neocolonial pressures were among those pushing some Algerians towards fetishized and caricatural versions of tradition, a process in which the FLN government has been implicated, perhaps through its own contributions to an ongoing history of violence, and certainly through its failure to commit Algeria to *laïcité* [secularism], a long-term problem greatly exacerbated by its retrograde religio-patriarchal revision of the Algerian 'family code' in 1984.[3]

Djebar's responses included *Loin de Médine* of 1991 (translated as *Far from Madina*, 1994), which returns to the Koran and restores a neglected female dimension to the history of Islam – 'filling in the gaps in the collective memory', as she puts it (Djebar, 1994: xv). She believes this exercise could not have been carried out in Arabic, which she sees as too closely associated with, and too deeply infused with, Islamic formulae. All the same, she makes a point of expressing her attachment to the language of the Koran, noting, in the final words of the preface: 'The variegated richness of the original text, its rhythm, its nuances and ambiguities, its very patina, in a word its poetry, the only true reflection of an epoch, spurred on my efforts in this *ijtihad*' (Djebar, 1994: xvi). In this way she implies that the Koran must be understood as an historical object, but also indicates that her book is true to Islamic principles. The word *ijtihad* is used again in the Académie speech (and was also used by Edward Said to describe his work; Djebar, 2006: 17; Said, 2004: 68–69; 75); it suggests an openness to critique and the play of interpretation, and is glossed by Djebar in a footnote in *Loin de Médine*: '*Ijtihad:* effort intellectuel pour la recherche de la vérité – venant de *djihad*, lutte intérieure, recommandée à tout croyant' [intellectual effort involved in the search for the truth – derives from *jihad*, interior struggle, in which all believers are advised to engage] (page 6 in the original; in the translation [Djebar, 1994], the term *ijtihad* appears not in a footnote but in the glossary).

Two other works deal more directly with the Algeria of the 1990s, experimenting with the varied narrative and affective capacities of different genres of writing. The first, *Le Blanc de l'Algérie* of 1995 (*Algerian White*, 2000), describes the deaths of a long succession of Algerian writers, including francophone friends who have been assassinated. On its title page that work is labelled a 'Récit' [A Narrative] where others, including *Far from Madina* and the more autobiographical texts, are termed 'Roman' [Novel]; like them, it mixes history and fiction, the political and the personal, but the 'I' here – as in the opening sentence: 'I wanted, in this account [récit], to respond to an immediate demand of memory [une exigence de mémoire immédiate]' (Djebar, 2000: 13) – is more straightforwardly Djebar's own.

---

3   The wider context for Djebar also included the Iranian revolution and the *Satanic Verses* affair (see Djebar, 1993). FLN refers to the Front de Libération Nationale, the organization that came to spearhead the independence movement and eventually took power. On the family code and *laïcité*, see Hélie-Lucas, 1987, and Ruedy, 1994.

An attentiveness to memory has been a constant in Djebar's writing, but her most recent work conveys a sharper awareness of, and perhaps greater pessimism about, the gulf between, on the one hand, Djebar's personal memories and/or the work of commemoration carried out in her writing, and, on the other hand, anything one might call a collective memory, especially within Algeria. Like many postcolonial writers, Djebar was always sceptical, of course, about 'official' memories, French or Algerian, but previously seemed quite hopeful that the always troubled process of 'filling the gaps' and bringing to light lost voices – not, then, wholly lost after all – was invariably a beneficial one. That hope may remain in *Le Blanc de l'Algérie*, but in relation to that broadly benign conception of memory, Djebar's other great work on the Algeria of the 1990s, *La Disparition de la langue française* (2003), marks a startling departure. The male protagonist and sometime narrator, Berkane, a writer who has been living in France, returns to Algeria in the hope of drawing productively on his Algerian past, but as buried memories emerge he, like his country, appears to be devastated by a 'passé qui ne passe pas' [a past that will not pass] (a phrase used by Djebar, 2006: 5; borrowed from Conan and Rousso, 1994). This novel suggests that remembering may not always bring personal and social benefits; if the duty to memory persists, that duty now seems more austere.

Djebar's approach to Algerian politics must be understood, above all, in terms of her focus on women's lives and feminine perspectives, which are deeply affected by and involved in all aspects of national/anti-colonial/religious identity. The emphasis on Algerian women was present from her earliest novels; the first, *La Soif*, was published in 1957 (and promptly translated into English, as *The Mischief*, Djebar, 1958), the second in 1958, and both were criticized in nationalist circles for being insufficiently relevant to, and supportive of, the cause. The hostile reception clearly affected her writing; two further novels, more engaged with colonial politics, and works of drama and poetry, appeared in the 1960s, but after this a decade passed before she published again. In the meantime she made two films. These won some acclaim outside Algeria but were again criticized within it, on comparable political grounds. Djebar has repeatedly spoken of her experiences as a filmmaker as fundamental to her mature work, as they convinced her of the importance of capturing and conveying the diverse aspects of women's daily lives, and a history of distinctly feminine memories (including memories of the War of Independence) and ways of looking at the world.

It was with a deepened commitment to feminism and with greater confidence in the legitimacy of her own long-standing preoccupations that she published *Femmes d'Alger dans leur appartement* in 1980 (*Women of Algiers in their Apartment*, 1992) with des femmes, a Parisian feminist publishing house that had emerged from the French MLF (Women's Liberation Movement). In this sense, too, her work is postcolonial (or post-postcolonial):[4] decolonization – political

---

4   Djebar's later work is also marked by its self-conscious engagement with its own fields of
     reception, which must include postcolonial studies. In a 1998 speech, for instance, Djebar
     used (in inverted commas) the terms 'exotisme' [exoticism] and 'orientaliste' [orientalist]

and cultural – may not be complete, but she does not accept that it should continue always to take precedence over, and hold in abeyance, other political projects and frameworks, in particular, women's liberation. The latter emerges as a project whose importance is equal to that of anti-colonial nationalism 'as such', even as Djebar suggests that from the perspective of a wider conception of freedom, and of the history of women's place in colonial and anti-colonial history, the distinction between national liberation and women's liberation is crude and misleading.

Francophonie and feminine voices

The renewal from 1980 onwards of Djebar's desire to publish her work involved, as we have seen, a renewal of her themes and her political consciousness, and a departure into more adventurous forms of writing (about which I will say more below). All of this was tied to a reimagined relation to the French language. For some anti-colonialists, nationalists and Islamists, any Algerian's decision to write in French must be seen as compromising or even traitorous. Throughout her fiction and in the numerous essays on this topic in *Ces Voix*, Djebar comes to offer several overlapping defences of her *francophonie*. (For a rather different understanding of *la francophonie*, see Chapter 12 on Léopold Sédar Senghor.) First, like other postcolonial writers, she appropriates and reinvents the colonizer's language, studding it with untranslatable vocabulary (mainly from Arabic) and reusing familiar terms in contexts where their meanings are changed: *maquis*, for instance, a term for French armed resistance against the Nazis, becomes a term for Algerian armed resistance against the French.

Second, her remouldings of French call into question any simple alignment of language, nationality and identity. Her language underpins her themes in offering reminders that the notion of *francophonie* yokes together cultures that are highly diverse, and that are radically separated, as well as inextricably linked, by their 'shared' history. I mentioned earlier that she reaches back to precolonial history and in doing so she counts figures such as Saint Augustine and Tertullian among her North African ancestors and predecessors. Of course, she also draws on a wide range of writers with no particular link to North Africa. In these ways she calls into question various conventional attitudes towards 'her' history, including Eurocentric views of classical culture, and any restrictive definition of North African culture as Arabo-Islamic. Language and location are both sources of identity for Djebar, but partial ones, sometimes mutually interfering, with a complex relation to 'national' literary traditions and politics and to a putative Republic of Letters. Djebar can thus describe Camus as 'mon

---

and remarked that her writing was, in effect, 'déterritorialisée' [deterritorialized] (Djebar, 1999b: 233, 234), invoking a notion from Deleuze and Guattari that has been widely used in the postcolonial field. Her most recent novel is dedicated 'À Gayatri, avec mon affection' (Djebar, 2007), referring to the postcolonial critic, Gayatri Chakravorty Spivak.

presque compatriote ou moitié compatriote par la terre et l'espace d'enfance, plutôt que par l'histoire...' [my near compatriot or semi-compatriot, by virtue of the land and the space in which we grew up, rather than through history...] (Djebar, 1999b: 226), or write, tentatively, about Camus and Fromentin: 'Je suis tentée de les appeler "frères", mes frères en langue en tout cas' [I am tempted to call them my 'brothers', brothers in language, anyway] (Djebar, 1999b: 218).

Third, it is clear from Djebar's stories that for her, as for many other postcolonial writers, the 'decision' to write in the colonizer's language was not really a decision, but the product of a particular (French/colonial) education. More controversially, it is clear, too, that she considers her experience of education – and her access not just to literacy and literature in general, but to the French language in particular – to have been of enormous benefit to her, partly, as I have already suggested, because of its distance from the language of the Koran. Her speech at the Académie française offered an implicit but very powerful defence of the sometimes uncomfortable linguistic situation in which she has thrived. Georges Vedel, she noted, had remarked on the profound personal impact and significant side-benefits of his wartime experiences; more specifically, he acknowledged that certain pleasures and accomplishments had been made possible for him by his mastery of Spanish and German, acquired during his years as a prisoner of war. Djebar did not point out explicitly the possible parallels with her own situation, and did not need to point out that no one would ever have mistaken such remarks by Vedel for a defence of the Nazis or of his own imprisonment.

Many of the issues mentioned so far in connection with *francophonie* were already familiar to, and from, 'Francophone' writers of the colonial era,[5] but the reaffirmed importance of gender to the post-1980 Djebar allows her to bring newer considerations to the fore. Her preface to *Women of Algiers* suggests that she 'translated' the stories, but she indicates that there was no direct original from which to translate; rather, she tried to evoke a 'subterranean' language that was never written. She explains, 'I could have listened to these voices in no matter what language, nonwritten, nonrecorded, transmitted only by chains of echoes and sighs', and goes on: 'Son arabe, iranien, afghan, berbère ou bengali, pourquoi pas, mais toujours avec timbre féminin et lèvres proférant sous le masque' [Arabic sounds, Iranian sounds, Afghan, Berber, or Bengali – why not? – but always in feminine tones, uttered from lips beneath a mask] (Djebar, 1992: 1; translation adapted). Beyond the question of the historical and religious baggage accompanying particular languages, she has come to feel that as a woman (as well as a postcolonial subject) she cannot be fully at home in any written language available to her. Accordingly Djebar's French, from 1980 onwards, must also be understood as the almost arbitrary vehicle

---

5 In using 'Francophone' in inverted commas I am citing the usual loaded usage of the term, designating writers whose perceived ethnic/cultural characteristics have separated them (unlike non-French 'white' writers such as Rousseau) from the mainstream of French literature.

for a perhaps impossible quest, her attempt to register and communicate in writing distinctly oral rhythms, notably from dialectal and feminine Berber and Arabic, and to make her texts more accommodating of feminine corporeality and experience.[6]

On one level, a text such as *Women of Algiers* thus constitutes an attempt to speak for women who cannot speak for themselves. In this way Djebar takes on a role, as the spokesperson for a culture, that has often been sought by postcolonial writers and even more often ascribed to them. On another level, however, she remains wary of that role.[7] For one thing, it is usually played in relation to a (putative) national community, but Djebar, as we have seen, is interested in communities beneath and beyond national categories and the colonizer/colonized opposition, especially those that may arise from a transnational and translinguistic feminine or feminist solidarity. For another, the educational background that has equipped Djebar to represent other women, including illiterate Algerian women, also distances her from them, as she is fully aware. The very personal tone of much of Djebar's work makes it hard to mistake it for an objective account of other women's lives; the texts' autobiographical dimensions are legitimated in implying both a bold departure from traditions of female self-effacement, and a cautious recognition of her position of personal privilege.

The grounds for caution are not only that the distance between Djebar and the other women she writes about creates, contingently, space for possible misperceptions and misunderstandings between the author and those other women. If one takes seriously the idea of a link between language and thought – that is, between particular languages (dominant, perhaps masculine, laden with cultural bequests and presuppositions) and particular forms of thought – then one must assume that a degree of translation and misrepresentation is inevitable across that gap. Djebar instructs herself: 'Don't claim to "speak for", or, worse, to "speak on", barely speaking next to, and if possible *very close to*: these are the first of the solidarities to be taken on by the few Arab women who obtain or acquire freedom of movement, of body and of mind' (Djebar, 1992: 2). And she speaks of her desire for 'une langue en mouvement, une langue rythmée par moi pour me dire ou pour dire que je ne savais pas me dire, sinon hélas dans parfois la blessure' [a language in motion, a language to which I would give my own rhythm in order to say who I am or to say that I couldn't say who I was, except sometimes, I'm afraid, through a kind of wounding] (Djebar, 2006: 14). All of this

---

6   Djebar must have been influenced in this regard by the theories about masculine/feminine language developed in the 1970s by feminists, including Hélène Cixous, whom she has cited on occasion, and who was also published by des femmes. Cixous, like Derrida, was born an Algerian Jew, and her work has important postcolonial aspects.

7   In another early publication, *Women of Islam* (1961), an essay accompanying a collection of Magnum photographs, Djebar begins by expressing her ambivalence, and her sense of her own limitations, when it comes to speaking about Muslim women in general terms. It remains an interesting text but is a relatively conventional one, not least in its willingness, finally, to generalize.

implies that Djebar's caution must also be linked to her sense that in its search for a feminine, polyphonic mode of writing, her work approaches (and translates for her readership) not only the unfamiliar but the 'unrepresentable'.[8]

Postcolonial aesthetics and literary thinking

As we have just seen, when Djebar describes her own writing practice, relatively clear programmatic statements are juxtaposed with, and to a degree disrupted and modified by, self-reflexive hesitations and flights of metaphorical language. This leads me towards my final concern: the sense in which Djebar's Francophone (or 'francographic') postcolonial work is distinctly literary, and logically takes a stylistic form, somewhat outside logic, which explores and calls into question the relations between writing and thought to which I have just alluded. As responses to a bloody colonial, anti-colonial and postcolonial history, and to pressing questions about democracy, secularism and postcolonial identities, Djebar's texts are at once bold and oblique. If this 'obliqueness' is a problem from a certain (perhaps 'postcolonial') political perspective, it is one of which Djebar has long been conscious. In a 1995 speech, she remarked on:

> la nécessité d'affronter les problèmes d'identité, d'élaboration de valeurs nouvelles par la contestation intérieure, par la revisitation critique de l'héritage de la culture religieuse, surtout par la laïcisation de la langue qui conditionne celle des pratiques sociales, cette nécessité d'affronter les crises de sa propre société [...], cette nécessité-là est, bien sûr, la tâche de tout intellectuel: nous ne pouvons y répondre, nous, écrivains, que dans notre propre langage. (Djebar, 1999b: 246)

> We need to tackle issues of identity and how to build up new values by challenging them from the inside, by returning critically to everything we have inherited from our religious traditions, and above all by secularizing the language that shapes our social practices; each of us needs to face up to the crises in his or her own society [...] clearly, that is the task of any intellectual: as writers, we can only respond in our own language.

The whole question is what it means to respond in this particular 'language', a 'literary' language that seems at once to offer peculiar resources for conjuring up and confronting aspects of reality (including political reality) that may otherwise be lost or neglected, and to carry the reader/writer away into some alternative, less concrete dimension. Djebar herself expresses this tension eloquently when she remarks:

> La violence de l'histoire quand on l'écrit, on l'écrit comme une mise en scène et c'est contradictoire. J'avais pensé à Delacroix. Lorsque Delacroix peint les

---

8   Djebar's scruples on this point are reminiscent of Spivak's famous article 'Can the Subaltern speak?' (1988).

massacres de Sion [sic], il n'est pas dans la douleur des massacres, il est dans ce problème du rouge, il est dans le problème de l'épaule de la dame, il est dans ces détails, pourtant la motivation est de dénoncer cette violence. Mais à partir du moment où vous l'écrivez, où vous l'inscrivez en couleurs ou en mots, c'est une violence au ralenti, c'est une violence anesthésiée par le style ou la forme que vous allez donner. (Cited in Hornung and Ruhe, 1998: 183)

When one is writing the violence of history, one writes it as a mise en scène and that is a contradiction. I thought of Delacroix. When Delacroix paints the Chios massacres, he is not caught up in the pain of the massacres, he's caught up in his problem with the colour red, or with the woman's shoulder, he is caught up in these details, yet the motivation is to denounce the violence. But as soon as you start writing it, or inscribing it in colour or in words, the violence takes place in slow motion, it is anaesthetized by the style or the form that you impart to it.

Delacroix, in many respects a classic orientalist and sexist, is an important figure for Djebar, and not only because he, like Beethoven (another point of reference), forms part of a global, or potentially global, artistic inheritance that may be linked to colonial and other histories in innumerable ways. The point is also that if Delacroix's work is still worthy of attention and praise, it must be irreducible to those histories, the circumstances of its production or the limited political outlook of the painter as an individual. In other words, Delacroix's work must possess a fundamental degree of artistic specificity and autonomy. That 'autonomy' may be less obvious (and in a sense, is lesser) in Delacroix's painting than in Beethoven's music, but it is understood by Djebar, I would argue, as a foundational aspect of art in general. Literary prose is arguably less autonomous again, or more worldly, but it can draw on an array of devices prompting readers to recognize its distinctiveness; in Djebar's case these include the sometimes opaque images to which I have already alluded, a constant switching and blending of narratorial perspectives, and a disorienting disparity of registers stretched across an elaborate framework of textual subdivisions, variously numbered and named –sections, chapters, italicized interludes, and quasi-symphonic 'movements'.

Djebar's remark about the anaesthetizing dimension of aesthetic form may imply misgivings about the way in which art's partial autonomy distances it from politics and in a sense (even in literature) from representation. Nevertheless, Djebar appears to endorse some such autonomy as one of art's great strengths and attractions, seeing it as constitutive of the freedom she finds in writing as writer and reader. As we have already seen, for her this freedom is linked, by analogy and through personal history, to the freedom she obtained as a girl by attending school and going out, unveiled, in public.[9] Writing allows her, even in her more autobiographical texts, both to 'be herself' and to become someone new. Passages when she speaks her mind lead to positions that may not be

---

9 This theme is central to her latest book, *Nulle part dans la maison de mon père* (Paris: Fayard, 2007).

her own; she does not always write, and does not wish always to be read, 'as a woman' (or 'as an Algerian', and so on); she can use her writing to evade certain political demands even as she responds to them. Meanings proliferate and refuse to settle; when she describes writing as a kind of veil (e.g. Djebar, 1999b: 97), that image, self-reflexive and unstable, both prolongs and challenges the orientalist stereotypes with which the writer flirts: she shows that veils can be worn in many different ways, and so, at least sometimes, used as a means of self-expression; she suggests the ways in which, for her, French culture, rather than having displaced Berber, Arab and Islamic cultures, is layered on top of them; and she reminds those critics who turn to postcolonial/'Francophone' literature, especially by women, (only) for autobiography, ethnography and political testimony, that her literary language is one in which she can – and perhaps can only – disguise as well as reveal herself.

There are some more general points I would draw from this. First, I would argue that anyone who thinks it valid to approach political issues through literature, as writer or critic, must have some faith that literature has a specific capacity to re-present or 'suspend' the familiar, to reframe the social, the historical and the religious as the fields of representation and reinterpretation that they always are, to encourage us to think again.[10] They must have some faith in what Djebar calls 'La fiction comme moyen de "penser"' [fiction as a way of 'thinking'] (Djebar, 1999b: 233–34) and as a space for experiment and exploration, a project radicalized in much modern poetry and by writers such as Kafka, Beckett and Blanchot, with whose work Djebar wishes to associate her own (see e.g. Djebar, 1999b: 194–95). If literature is understood in such terms, some peculiar dimension of thinking must be ascribed also to more conventional literary texts, but there will be an argument, at least, for seeing successfully experimental texts – where we cannot assume too quickly that we have understood, and where our usual ways of making sense are given the fiercest jolt – as the most political, too.[11]

However, taking such ideas seriously leaves one in a state of radical uncertainty. If the literary text is held capable of calling into question all points of view, these will include the true as well as the false and the revolutionary as well as the reactionary; the literary text will be unable to offer reliable guidance about how to discriminate between competing versions of events. Of course, historical texts also offer room for interpretation (and as works of writing, they have a certain autonomy of their own, as one sees when Djebar uses colonial historiography for her own ends[12]) but they are under an obligation to aim for accuracy and truth in a way that literary texts are not. This need not mean that literature must work to relativize fundamentally the notion of truth (and I do not think this is the aim or effect of Djebar's work) but it does disrupt the

---

10   I draw this conception of literature's 'suspension' of reference from Derrida (1992b: 48).
11   See Harrison (2005) for a fuller version of this argument.
12   A striking example is her use of Colonel Pélissier's (uncritical) reports of 1845 on the slaughter by his troops of 1,500 members of the Ouled Riah tribe (Djebar, 1989: 64–79).

grounds on which one might pin down the political 'message' of a literary text. Furthermore a text's political impact cannot be confidently predicted on the basis of textual information alone. Correspondingly, while close textual analysis tends to originate in and sustain a text's literary status (such that work like Djebar's appears to *merit* critical attention of that order), revealing and fostering its polysemy and 'suspension' of reference, it is only in a very restricted sense that such analysis can support a claim about the text's 'politics' (when a critic seeks to 'show', for instance, on the basis of textual evidence, that a given text that appears conservative is 'actually' revolutionary, or vice versa).

The uncertainty here concerns not only the scale of a text's political impact, or the vagaries of reception that may reverse a text's putative message, but also the very relation of cultural and political work. When Djebar comments on Delacroix's absorption, so to speak, in his red paint, or uses the phrase 'la main a à dire' [the hand has things to say] in a recent poem about the experience of writing (in Harrison, 2005: 119), she suggests that artistic forms and the extra-linguistic body have their own momentum, so to speak, and their own designs. This may imply that the attractions and pleasures of art (as a practice, or as a set of artefacts) are partly or sometimes apolitical, in a sense that postcolonial studies often struggles to acknowledge, let alone view positively. Moreover, one must recognize – as does Djebar, tacitly, when she uses inverted commas in the phrase 'fiction as a way of "thinking"' – that one cannot pin down in rational discourse the nature of the extraordinary thinking that may take place in artistic responses to the world (or in audiences' responses to art). Indeed, one cannot determine to what extent such thinking is taking place, or to what extent the term 'thinking' is apt.

The 'faith' in literature of which I have spoken is difficult to sustain, then. As we have seen, Djebar keeps this faith partly because her commitment to her art is tied to her commitment to feminine memories, stories, identities and freedoms. But these ties are equivocal, are themselves a source of self-doubt, and are insufficiently supported by conventional political and theoretical vocab-ularies. It is characteristic that when Djebar uses the term *écrivaine*, a recently coined feminine version of *écrivain* [writer], she draws attention to the risks of being confined, as a 'woman writer', to 'un harem pseudo-littéraire' [a pseudo-literary harem] (Djebar 1999b: 85), and also brings out the word's resonance (via *vaine*) with notions of vanity and futility (see also Djebar 2007: 406). Anxieties about the limitations of literary representation, about the bridges and gulfs between the literary and the political, and about the writer's motives and justi-fications emerge repeatedly in her self-reflexive musings and more theoretical pieces, many of them responses to academic invitations and their attendant pressures. One could see a defensive urge towards self-justification in the very presence of the forewords and afterwords with which many of her texts have been cushioned. It is on such texts in particular – those that seem closest to the sphere of 'thought' as an area and object of academic work – that I have drawn in this summary, but one of my aims has been to indicate that in the case of a writer like Djebar, there is something paradoxical and unsatisfactory about this approach. I hope it is clear, finally, that Djebar's 'theoretical' interventions are also poetic, exploratory and sometimes opaque, and that all her mature writing, mobile and multi-faceted, is drawn to the divisions – and hierarchies – separating 'literature' from 'thought' and from history, divisions that it cease-lessly both relies upon and puts under pressure. All this work, in its complex textuality, channels and embodies peculiarly literary ambitions to extend world views and patterns of thought, and so is singularly resistant to summary.[13]

Further reading

Djebar, Assia, 1989 [1985]. *Fantasia, An Algerian Cavalcade*, tr. Dorothy Blair (London: Quartet). [First published as *L'Amour, la fantasia*.] A virtuoso combination of 'self-writing', the evocation of diverse female voices, and a retelling of Algerian colonial history.

— 1992 [1980]. *Women of Algiers in Their Apartment*, tr. Marjolijn de Jager (Charlottesville and London: Caraf Books). [First published as *Femmes d'Alger dans leur appartement*; expanded edition 2002.] Short stories and an essay; one of Djebar's best-known texts. The English edition contains an interview with and an afterword by Clarisse Zimra, one of the major Djebar critics.

— 1999. *Ces voix qui m'assiègent ... en marge de ma francophonie* (Paris: Albin Michel). Her main collection of 'theoretical' writings.

— 2000 [1995]. *Algerian White*, tr. David Kelley and Marjolijn de Jager (New York: Seven Stories Press). [First published as *Le Blanc de l'Algérie*.] Reflections on writing and memory within a generically hybrid narrative that recalls the deaths of a succession of Algerian writers, from Camus to the friends of Djebar who were assassinated in the 1990s.

Hiddleston, Jane, 2006. *Assia Djebar: Out of Algeria* (Liverpool: Liverpool University Press). A comprehensive, theoretically informed survey of Djebar's major texts up to *La Disparition de la langue française,* and their changing relation to her homeland.

---

13 My thanks go to Jane Hiddleston for her helpful comments on a draft version of this chapter.

CHAPTER 5

Frantz Fanon: Colonialism and Violence

Max Silverman

Little more than twenty years ago, Homi Bhabha could justifiably write 'in Britain today Fanon's ideas are effectively "out of print"' (Bhabha, 1986: viii). This demonstrates the extent to which Fanon's current status as probably the most influential thinker in the field of postcolonial studies is a relatively recent phenomenon. In this chapter, following a brief overview of Fanon's life and career, I will outline the major stages of his thought in three sections. In the opening section, I will discuss his first major work, *Black Skin, White Masks* (1952); in the second section, I will deal with Fanon's political writings, which consisted of *A Dying Colonialism* (1959), the assorted articles that were collected and published posthumously as *Toward the African Revolution* (1964), and *The Wretched of the Earth* (1961); and in the final section, I will trace the legacy of Fanon's thought, and outline its continuing significance for a contemporary audience.

Frantz Fanon was born in Martinique in 1925 to relatively prosperous parents and grew up in the capital, Fort-de-France. Martinique was then one of France's colonies, but its status changed in 1946 when it became one of the French overseas departments (Départements d'Outre-Mer). His parents discouraged him from speaking Creole and generally promoted the values of French culture. In his later teens Fanon attended the Lycée Schoelcher, where he was taught by the young Aimé Césaire, who was later to become Martinique's greatest literary and political figure and an important influence on Fanon's thinking on race. (See Chapter 1 for an analysis of Césaire's career.)

Following the defeat of France in 1940, Martinique, like other overseas possessions, found itself under the rule of the Vichy state. In 1943 Fanon joined the Free French forces to fight Fascism and collaboration and was posted in Morocco and France. However, he had become disillusioned with the 'obsolete ideal' (cited in Macey, 2000: 103) of universal freedom that had initially motivated him. After the war he returned to Martinique to complete his education, but in

1946 returned to France to study medicine and then to specialize in psychiatry in Lyons. During this period, he read widely and immersed himself in French post-war intellectual debates, especially concerning Hegel, phenomenology, existentialism and surrealism. While he was in Lyons he also experienced French racism at close quarters and became more interested in the myth of the Negro. The use of contemporary French philosophy to understand the 'lived experience' of a black man in a white world would form the basis of *Black Skin, White Masks*.

Fanon's psychiatric training continued under François Tosquelles at Saint-Alban psychiatric hospital in the Lozère region of France. In 1952, Fanon married Marie-Josephe (Josie) Dublé, a white French woman. When he qualified as a psychiatrist in 1953 he worked for a brief spell in a hospital in Normandy before being appointed as 'médecin-chef' at the Blida-Joinville psychiatric hospital in Algeria. Although he had gained some experience of treating North African patients while he was training in Lyons, had published 'The "North African Syndrome"' in the journal *Esprit* in 1952 (collected in Fanon, 1970b: 13–26), and had been to Oran in Algeria when he was in the French army, this was Fanon's first sustained experience of dealing with alienation in a colonial context. Fanon was soon convinced that the colonial system was at the root of his patients' mental disorders. This understanding, coupled with the beginning of the Algerian War of Independence in 1954, would significantly shape the remaining years of his political and intellectual life.

Fanon's increasing politicization in Algeria led to him joining (probably in early 1955) the Front de Libération Nationale (FLN), the Algerian revolutionary movement for independence from French colonial rule. The following year, unable any longer to maintain the contradiction between working for the French state and witnessing daily the effects of torture and oppression by the state on his patients, he resigned his position in Blida (see 'Letter to the Resident Minister' in 1970b: 62–64) and left Algeria for Tunisia. While in Tunis he continued to practise as a psychiatrist while writing articles for *El Moudjahid*, the newspaper of the FLN. During this time, his writings progressively made the link between the growing movement for national liberation in Algeria (resulting in *A Dying Colonialism*) and the same revolutionary movement in Africa as a whole (see the collected articles in *Toward the African Revolution*). In 1960 the provisional Algerian government appointed Fanon ambassador to Ghana in Accra, from where he made trips to other African countries to extend the call for pan-African unity (see 'This Africa to come' in 1970b: 187–200). Fanon contracted leukaemia and completed *The Wretched of the Earth* shortly before his death in Maryland, in the United States, in December 1961 at the age of 36. The following year, Algeria achieved the national independence that Fanon had predicted as the inevitable outcome of colonial rule. (For full biographical details, see Cherki, 2000; Geismar, 1971; Gendzier, 1973; Macey, 2000.)

Black Skin

Though by no means the first example of 'the empire writing back' in the Francophone world (see especially Aimé Césaire's *Cahier d'un retour au pays natal*, first published in 1939), *Black Skin, White Masks* marks a significant moment in the critique of European colonialism. Fanon is concerned less with the way colonialism deforms the socio-economic infrastructure of colonized lands than with its assault on the minds and bodies of colonized peoples, even to the extent of disfiguring sexual desire and penetrating the recesses of the psyche. The originality of Fanon's project lies in the way he explores how the European imposition of a 'white mask' on the colonized black body is a profoundly traumatic experience for the victim. Fanon adopts the master's conceptual tools for this analysis – the Hegelian view of history, the phenomenological view of being, the psychoanalytic view of desire – and rewrites them from the point of view of a colonized, traumatized and angry young black man. The effect is an explosive, lyrical, problematic but always fascinating exploration of the conscious and unconscious effects of the colonial situation and a profound denunciation of the Western concept of Man.

Fanon presents a number of allegorical scenarios, some taken from his own experience, others taken from literary and scientific texts, to depict the traumatic relationship between colonizer and colonized. The most famous of these is an incident on a train in France when a young white boy, on seeing the black Fanon, says to his mother, 'Mama, see the Negro! I'm frightened' (1986: 112). This moment dramatizes the process by which blackness is objectified and demonized in a white world, producing fear and anxiety on the part of the white boy (Negrophobia) and a devastation of a sense of self on the part of the black man as he sees himself (and especially his own body) through the phobic gaze of the Other.

Fanon's scenario transfers Jean-Paul Sartre's depiction of the Manichean social construction of the Jew by the anti-Semite in his *Anti-Semite and Jew* (1946) to the site of the colonial encounter. Where Sartre maintains that '[i]t is the anti-Semite who *makes* the Jew', Fanon says '*[i]t is the racist who creates his inferior*' (1986: 93; emphasis in original). And just as Sartre shows how the Jew, caught in an ideological web of sameness and difference from which there is no obvious escape route without bad faith ('mauvaise foi'), unconsciously internalizes the look of the anti-Semite, thus converting him into an obsessional neurotic, so Fanon uncovers the 'infernal circle' (116) of the pathological domain of the black person in a white world, which takes the form of what he terms a 'manicheism delirium' (183). Fanon's original analysis of colonial racism is therefore heavily indebted to Sartre's version of French Third Republic anti-Semitism (Maurassian, not genocidal) in which the self is socially constructed as 'an object in the midst of other objects' (109; see also Kruks, 1996).

Fanon blends Sartre's portrait of the alienated self in a racialized society with an idiosyncratic use of psychoanalytical theory (learned during his studies of medicine and psychiatry in Lyons) to provide other allegorical instances of this pathology of colonial racism. He discusses Mayotte Capécia's *Je Suis Martiniquaise* (Chapter 2) to show how the black woman's internalization of Negrophobia results in her desire to 'whiten the race' (47). His analysis of René Maran's hero Jean Veneuse in his semi-autobiographical novel *Un homme pareil aux autres* (Chapter 3) similarly shows the black man in thrall to white beauty. The colonized are simultaneously subjected to, mimics of, and alienated by Europe's Manichean racialized order (Bhabha, 1986; 1994; Fuss, 1999). But the reason Fanon chooses fictional works for his case-studies of colonial alienation is unclear. He consistently confuses the protagonists of these novels with their authors and the analyses themselves are fairly crude – Maran's text is read in terms of the abandonment theory of the little-known Swiss analyst Germaine Guex (see Marriott, 2005) – and by no means even-handed (he castigates Capécia for her desire for 'lactification' while sympathizing with Maran as a victim of European racialized ideology). *Black Skin, White Masks* often lacks consistency and coherence, yet never interest, as Fanon attempts to unmask the deepest effects of colonialism through an eclectic use of theory.

At times this method produces a fascinating rewrite of the Western intellectual tradition, as Fanon slips between adoption of his mentors' formulations and distance from them. He acknowledges his debt to Sartre, describing how 'certain pages of *Anti-Semite and Jew* are the finest that I have ever read' (1986: 181), yet is critical of Sartre's devaluing of blackness in his essay *Orphée noir* (132–34; see also Bernasconi, 2005; Silverman, 2005: 112–27). He pays homage to Aimé Césaire throughout, yet is critical of his and the other Negritude writers' celebration of blackness, which he sees as a simple inversion of the negative image constructed by white society (Chapter 5). He embraces Jung's idea of a collective unconscious, but demands that we historicize rather than essentialize it (188–93), a line of attack he also employs most effectively in his stinging critique of Octave Mannoni's *Psychologie de la colonisation* (Chapter 4). He uses Freudian theory, but shows its European bias when applied to the Caribbean, leading him to make the controversial and unsubstantiated claims that the Oedipus complex and homosexuality are absent from the islands (152, 180). He uses Hegel's Master–Slave dialectic, but reveals its shortcomings by showing that Hegel's version of recognition of the Other and reciprocity is implicitly part of an Enlightenment teleological reading of history (Chapter 7; see also Turner, 1996). In this way, Fanon reverses the colonial gaze and, by demystifying the intellectual and ideological means by which a Manichean system is constructed and maintained, shows how the colonizer's version of Man (and its accompanying rationalizations) is nothing other than European hubris.

However, the inconsistencies in Fanon's approach raise more questions than answers. The text lurches between different concepts of blackness, as a social/racial construct imposed from outside, but also as existential 'lived experience' by the colonized (see Parry, 2004: 37–54). It places black and Jew in the same camp as stereotyped victim, yet expresses at the same time uncertainty as to 'whether Jews should be regarded as "black" or "white"' (Cheyette, 2005: 81), and reproduces uncritically some tired stereotypes of Jews themselves (Chapter 6). It adapts Freudian theory to the colonial context, but is itself driven unconsciously by problematical views on women's sexuality, and is idiosyncratic, to say the least, about that of men. As Diana Fuss remarks, 'Fanon's analysis of colonial mimesis repeatedly runs aground on the question of sexual difference' (Fuss, 1999: 309; see also Lebeau, 2005). It exposes the historical determinism of colonialism and announces the existential freedom of the colonized, but offers no explanation as to how one progresses from one to the other. Hence, the solution in the final chapter of a 'new humanism' to replace Europe's racist version (casting off the white mask) is a rallying cry to the colonized to change the course of history, with no analysis of the political means to bring this about. Ultimately, *Black Skin, White Masks* slides between particularist and universalist formulations and between a dualistic and anti-dualistic method throughout. It talks the language of the victim, yet the master's formulations are often unconsciously present.

Yet the real value of *Black Skin, White Masks* may lie in its slippages and inconsistencies and in the fact that the method never offers a coherent position for analysis. This ambivalence is itself a sign of the trauma of colonization. It is the expression of a restless and haunted mind out of joint with its own body, split between a European education and training and opposition to Europe's values, and between the constraints of an alienating Negrophobic world and the desire for freedom and authenticity.

Politicization

Fanon's writings after *Black Skin, White Masks* reflect his increasing commitment to the struggle for Algerian independence and the cause of Third World liberation politics. In *A Dying Colonialism* he takes 'a few aspects of the Algerian Revolution' (1970a: 159) and uses them to explore the awakening of a national consciousness and the struggle for national independence. The common theme tying together essays on the disparate topics of the veil, the radio, the Algerian family, Western medical science and Algeria's European minority is the way in which forces of tradition and tools of colonial oppression are shown to be progressively transformed by the Algerian people in the course of their movement for independence. Fanon's aim is to show how the social, institutional and ideological structures of colonialism – what he terms 'the mental sedimentation and [...] the emotional and intellectual handicaps which resulted from 130 years of oppression' (159) – are not immutable, but are subject to a 'historical dynamism' (49) when incorporated into the collective struggle for national liberation.

The essay on the veil ('Algeria unveiled') is indicative of Fanon's method in the text. Long before Edward Said's celebrated work, *Orientalism*, Fanon considers the colonial history of the veil not in terms of what it tells us about the wearing of the veil itself, but what it reveals about the violent and sexualized fantasies of the colonizer. The controlling gaze of the colonizer is frustrated by not being able to see the face of the Algerian woman hidden beneath the veil. This frustration leads to aggression as the colonizer forcibly desires to solve the mystery. Fanon talks of a 'double deflowering', as the desire to rend the veil of the Algerian woman mingles with the European man's dreams of rape (1970a: 31). This is a sexualized metaphor for the colonial project as a whole, as 'the occupier *was bent on unveiling Algeria*' (49; emphasis in original). But Fanon's purpose is to show how this attempt at mastery becomes the starting point for resistance. By using the veil strategically and by switching between veiling and unveiling to deny the occupier's control, the Algerian woman assumes her role in the national struggle for liberation and finds her own liberation in the process. (See Chapter 4 on Assia Djebar for a discussion of the veil; for a cinematic portrayal of the process described by Fanon, see Gillo Pontecorvo's film *The Battle of Algiers*, 1965.) This is the 'historical dynamism' of the liberation movement, by which human action transforms oppressive practices.

In *A Dying Colonialism*, Fanon again blends Sartrean existentialism, in which the meaning one gives to the world and the self is transformed through human action, with a loosely Marxist approach to demystification, the creation of a historical consciousness and the emergence of a revolutionary culture through collective action. This method produces a heady blend of ideology, in which individuals cast off the chains of oppression through their collective struggle and discover their true selves in the process: 'Old values, sterile and infantile phobias disappeared' (1970a: 91); 'The Algerian couple has become considerably more closely knit in the course of this Revolution' (95); '*The mingling of fighting experience with conjugal life deepens the relations between husband and wife and cements their union. There is a simultaneous and effervescent emergence of the citizen, the patriot and the modern spouse*' (96; emphasis in original). Is this simply revolutionary wishful thinking? Fanon provides little evidence for statements of this kind and it is clear to see why his fellow anti-colonial writer Albert Memmi (1971b) described Fanon's thinking as utopian.

Moreover, Fanon offers a rather confusing vision of liberation and progress. Forces of tradition in Algerian society, like the institutions of oppression imposed from outside, are seen as impediments to independence and unity. Fanon talks of Algerians' 'infantile patterns of behaviour' (1970a: 97) and notes that the adoption of 'modern forms of existence [...] confers on the human person his maximum independence' (98). With regard to medicine, '[t]he notions about "native psychology" or of the "basic personality" are shown to be vain' (126). This preference for modernity over tradition betrays an implicit appreciation of Western secular values, although Neil Lazarus argues that Fanon's stance was, in fact, born of the mistaken, but genuine, belief that colonialism had, in effect, wiped out 'authentic' cultures in the colonies (Lazarus, 1999: 68–143). Fanon's Western secularism fits uneasily with his advocacy of a clean break with Western structures, which are deemed to alienate colonized people. His belief that '[t]he freedom of the Algerian people [...] became identified with woman's liberation, with her entry into history' (89) is symptomatic more of his own secular idealism than anything that was to be reinforced in concrete terms after independence (Macey, 2000: 406).

Fanon's views on the culpability of the West seem to vary depending on his audience. In his essay on 'Algeria's European minority' (1970a: Chapter 5), which includes a discussion of the position of left-leaning intellectuals in France, Fanon welcomes the support of Europeans who are in favour of the end of colonial rule. He states that 'Algeria's European minority is far from being the monolithic block that one imagines' (128) and that 'another myth to be destroyed is that Algeria's settlers were unanimously opposed to the end of colonial domination' (137). But in his essay 'French intellectuals and democrats and the Algerian Revolution' (1970b: 86–101), published in *El Moudjahid* just over a year before, he maintains that '[t]he whole French nation finds itself involved in the crime against a people and is today an accomplice in the murders and the tortures that characterize the Algerian war' (93) and that 'the Left unconsciously obeys the myth of French Algeria' (99). Similar slippages characterize his views on Algeria's Jews (1970a: 133–37). As a propagandist, Fanon's statements conformed more to the rule of expediency than of consistency. These contradictions are also apparent in his final work, *The Wretched of the Earth*.

The Wretched of the Earth captures that post-war moment of armed struggle by colonized people for national liberation more profoundly than any other text and is the culmination of Fanon's thinking and writing over the previous few years (see his articles from *El Moudjahid* between 1957–60, collected in *Toward the African Revolution*). The Algerian revolution was at its height and Fanon's involvement in that struggle led him to identify so totally with the cause that he proclaims 'We Algerians' on a number of occasions (1967: 151–52, 158) and calls Algerians 'our own people' (1970b: 154; see also the same references in a number of his articles in *El Moudjahid*). The Algerian revolution is Fanon's model for Third World liberation struggles. As he says elsewhere, '[t]he process of liberation of colonial peoples is indeed inevitable. But the form given to the struggle of the Algerian people is such, in its violence and in its total character, that it will have a decisive influence on the future struggles of the other colonies' ('Decolonization and independence', 1970b: 115; see also 'The Algerian War and Man's liberation', 1970b: 154–59). His theory of the compartmentalization of colonialism is based largely on the city of Algiers, while his thesis of violence is based specifically on the armed struggle of the FLN (Macey, 2000: 471, 476).

The Wretched of the Earth is a testament to 'national liberation, national renaissance' (1967: 29) through the creation of a revolutionary culture. Having consistently shown how the Manichean world is a colonial construction (the settler and the native, the master and the slave, man and the animal), here he confirms that it is only by adopting and subverting the rules of Manicheism through 'an ironic turning of the tables' (65) that this oppressive dichotomy can be destroyed. 'On the logical plane', he writes, 'the Manicheism of the settler produces a Manicheism of the native' (72), and as the Manichean colonial regime owes its existence to violence, it will be violence that removes it (67). Fanon sees this moment as 'a murderous and decisive struggle between the two protagonists' (30), 'the single combat between native and settler' (65). As Sartre says in his bold preface to the book, 'it is the moment of the boomerang' (17). The passions of the colonized, formerly channelled into mythical and supersti-tious practices, will be redirected into violent revolution towards the goal of freedom and national liberation (46). There is no place left, then, for modera-tion or 'friendly understanding' (29); only violence will produce the unity of the people, a violence that will act as 'a cleansing force' to rid the shame of past indignity and restore self-respect (73).

As a manifesto for the creation of national unity and successful decoloniza-tion, *The Wretched of the Earth* enumerates the 'tragic mishaps' (121) that must be avoided in order for true national consciousness to emerge. The revolution must beware the 'native intellectual', whose mentality has not been completely decolonized; the reformist compromises of the 'national bourgeoisie'; the decolonizing tactics of the colonizers, which simply aim to conserve their colonial gains by other means; the Cold War conflict between capitalism and socialism, which distorts the true and original mission of Third World liberation, although Fanon's vision of the 'Third World' is itself, as David Macey remarks, 'a composite image' (2000: 470). The success of the revolution can also be threat-ened by tribalism, religion and other internal divisions, such as the division between those who live in the country (more rooted in traditional, communal and sometimes feudal practices) and those who live in the towns (influenced by Western individualism). The colonizer will exploit these tensions and turn them to his advantage.

Fanon warns against the cult of the leader and the party, 'to prevent the party ever becoming a willing tool in the hands of a leader' (148), and the 'blind alley' of national consciousness, unless it is 'enriched and deepened by a very rapid transformation into a consciousness of social and political needs' (162). Fanon's national project of decolonization is, thus, also a social project for the future. It is underpinned by a modern rejection of the nostalgia for roots and for a pre-colonial culture founded on essentialist (and frequently exoticized) positive images of the Negro. 'A national culture is not a folklore', he proclaims (188; see especially the chapter 'On national culture'). In the chapter on 'Colonial War and mental disorders' (201–51) he demonstrates once again how neuroses and other disorders should not be essentialized as part of native character but historicized as a result of the colonial situation (and their faulty diagnosis seen as the result of European racialized science). But the enumeration of 'tragic mishaps' to avoid in the creation of a genuine national consciousness does not include the return of women to their oppressed status, despite his predic-tion in the essay 'Algeria unveiled' in *A Dying Colonialism* (discussed above) that women's liberation and national liberation were part of the same process. Anne McClintock (1999) sees this blind spot as indicative of Fanon's patriarchal views on liberation (although, for a more supportive reading of Fanon's 'feminist consciousness', see Sharpley-Whiting, 1998).

The Wretched of the Earth is an anti-colonial manifesto, which proclaims that revolutionary violence will destroy the compartmentalized mental and physical spaces – the 'two zones' (31) – of the Manichean colonial order. Marxist analysis must be 'stretched' (32) in the colonial context, for here it is a racial-ized Manicheism that determines the compartmentalization rather than, prima-rily, class divisions (or, rather, the latter follow from the former). Revolutionary violence will give the 'natives' back their land, their nation and their unity. The universal awaits but it can only be attained by grasping the particular and using it to torch the earth that gave rise to these terms in the first place. This calls for 'new men [...], a new language and a new humanity' (30), the creation of 'the whole man, whom Europe has been incapable of bringing to triumphant birth' (253).

Like Fanon's previous works, *The Wretched of the Earth* is a wide-ranging, idealistic and idiosyncratic portrait of the anti-colonial moment, a strange but powerful blend of political analysis, philosophical statement, psychiatric diagnosis and literary criticism. The same discursive amalgam that characterizes *Black Skin, White Masks* is both the source of the limitations of Fanon's approach and the fascination of his insights (see Macey, 2000: 473–74). Like *Black Skin, White Masks*, it is full of contradictions, not the least of which is the advocacy of a 'new' version of humanity which, in many respects, resembles the 'old' utopian model of the French revolutionary tradition. He proclaims, for example: 'In undertaking this onward march, the people legislates, finds itself and wills itself to sovereignty' (1967: 106); and 'The living expression of the nation is the moving consciousness of the whole of the people; it is the coherent, enlightened action of men and women' (163). Decrying the Manichean world of colonialism, he also rejects the inverted Manicheism of the 'Negro-ism' of the Negritude writers, with their mythical yearnings for roots, 'the great black mirage', as he calls it in his 1955 essay 'West Indians and Africans' (1970b: 37). But, ironically, he erects 'a binary code almost as pernicious as the Manichean dualism that he sought to supplant' (Gilroy, 2000: 248). His desire to make a clean break with Europe is, therefore, betrayed unconsciously by the inverted European dualistic model he adopts and by the European discourse of nation, people and sovereignty that he employs. His vision is premised on a 'tabula rasa' (1967: 29) and the creation of a new humanity. Yet history refuses to be dealt with in such a summary way, as the more complex ideas of hybridity that inform the works of the creolist writers of a more recent generation would later illustrate (see Bernabé et al., 1993 [1989]; Vergès, 2005). Ultimately, Fanon's vision is based on what appears to be blind faith in the inevitable emergence of the truth (1967: 159; see also 'A continued crisis', 1970b: 117–23), but it is so fixated on the catastrophe of European colonialism that it is a 'truth' inevitably distorted by that history. (Lazarus's arguments regarding Fanon's belief in the tabula rasa necessitated by European colonialism, cited above, prove useful in thinking through Fanon's ideas in this area.)

However, the contradictions are, once again, indications of Fanon's restless spirit of enquiry, or even, as Ato Sekyi-Otu (1996) argues, symptomatic of a narra-tive strategy of dialectics rather than a confused series of absolute pronounce-ments. Some of the contradictions (or dialectical tensions) are echoes of *Black*

Skin, White Masks, but here transposed to the site of the forging of a new radical national consciousness and a new man. As Gibson (2003: 2) observes, it is therefore a response to a different moment in French colonialism. Hegel's Master/ Slave relationship and account of the ineluctable unfolding of history are again reworked to avoid a European synthesis of the dialectic by realizing the 'coming into being' of the colonized. The Sartre of *Being and Nothingness* again appears to provide the existential template for this emergence of being ('être-pour-soi'/Being-for-itself, in Sartre's terms) from its imprisonment as object of the colonizer's gaze. Yet the extent to which Fanon successfully reworks Hegel and Sartre within a colonial context or is still caught within the structures of their thought is one of the fascinations of Fanon's entire career (see for example Sekyi-Otu, 1996: 60–72; Gibson, 1999a). There is an ambivalence in Fanon's work which emerges from the challenge he poses to his intellectual interlocutors and desire for a clean break in tension with the unconscious traces of those same voices in his own formulations. To what extent does Fanon manage to go 'from manicheanism to dialectics' (Gibson, 1999a: 414)? To what extent does *The Wretched of the Earth* differ significantly, in theoretical terms, from the 'solution' proposed by Sartre at the end of *Anti-Semite and Jew*, in which the alienating stratifications of race (like those of class) will dissolve into the ether of a new humanism?

Afterlife

It could be said that Fanon's legacy has been more important than the achievements of his own lifetime. During his life he played no real part in the political or intellectual life of Martinique, had very little impact on that in France outside those few intellectuals who identified with Third World struggles of national liberation, and then played only a bit part in the Algerian revolution. Following his death, however, he became, first, the revolutionary voice of Third World liberation politics and an important influence on the American Black Power movement in the 1960s; and then, more recently, a core theorist in the development of cultural studies and postcolonial theory in the American and British academies. But even his legacy is uneven. There is no commemoration of Fanon in his home town, Fort-de-France, very little recognition of his work even now in France – see, however, Cherki (2000), and the special issue 'Pour Frantz Fanon' in *Les Temps Modernes* (Khalfa, 2005–06) – and his reputation in Africa is mixed, to say the least. Ironically, the 'postcolonial' Fanon constructed in the contemporary Anglo-American academy is a Western celebration of a man who spent most of his adult life fighting the iniquities of Western thought and practice.

Postmodern and postcolonial readings of Fanon have concentrated on questions of identity (especially race, gender and sexuality), textuality and post-humanism and have, on the whole, overlooked those elements of his thought that advocated violent revolution, or have even discounted it as part of the totalizing framework of the era of grand narratives of emancipation. Not surprisingly, therefore, *Black Skin, White Masks*, with its emphasis on split identity and its use of psychoanalysis, has been elevated to the status formerly occupied by *The Wretched of the Earth*, the manifesto of violent revolution for Third World movements of national liberation. This tells us much about the evolution of ideas in the Anglophone academy over the last half century. There have been important attempts to counter this recent appropriation of Fanon's thought and resituate it within the contexts of his day. Macey's biography (2000) rediscovers the Francophone heritage of his work, in Martinique, in metropolitan France and in Algeria; Gibson highlights the 'pitfalls' of the cultural studies version of Fanon (1999b) and sees his thought as an evolving dialectical response to different historical moments (2003); Sekyi-Otu posits an 'African-situationist reading' (1996: 3) in an attempt to place Fanon within the historical situation of colonialism and challenge the 'self-indulgent hybridism of certain "postcolonial critics"' (1996: 22). In this concluding section, I do not wish to comment on the rights or wrongs of particular interpretations, except to say that there might be a place for seeing him as 'very much a product of his time and place' (Gibson, 2003: 12) and for understanding how, since then, his thought has 'travelled' to different times and places (for a discussion of 'travelling' theory, see Clifford, 1997, and McLeod, 2003). I will outline, instead, some important aspects of Fanon's work (by no means an exhaustive list) that demonstrate why Fanon is a major thinker of our time.

First, Fanon's views on the ways in which Western racial (and Manichean) thinking permeates the individual's unconscious and the institutional structures of society have helped to redefine Marxism and have profoundly influenced current thinking on race. Fanon is relevant to the 'cultural' turn in contemporary neo-Marxist analysis because he shows us that race is present in even the most banal aspects of everyday life:

> We must tirelessly look for the repercussions of racism at all levels of socia-
> bility. The importance of the racist problem in contemporary American litera-
> ture is significant. The Negro in motion pictures, the Negro and folklore,
> the Jew and children's stories, the Jew in the café, are inexhaustible themes.
> ('Racism and Culture', 1970b: 46)

This way of reading the unconscious ideological structures of race in popular culture challenges a classic Marxist belief in the primacy of class, and places Fanon alongside neo-Gramscian cultural theorists such as Roland Barthes, Michel Foucault, Edward Said and others, who redefined our approach to culture and ideology in the post-war period.

Second, Fanon was one of the first theorists to realize that race is always inflected by gender and intricately related to sexual desire and the question of power. Although this aspect of his thinking is more prominent in *Black Skin, White Masks* (see Bergner, 1995), it nevertheless informs his later writings too (for example, 'Algeria unveiled' in *A Dying Colonialism*). His analyses of the articulations between race, gender, desire and power may be idiosyncratic, confused and often betray his own patriarchal point of view; but at least he attempts to explain some of the more profound fears and fantasies that invariably accompany racial classifications. Here, too, Fanon's lead has been invaluable for subsequent formulations.

Third, Fanon is not only conscious of the connections between race, gender and power but also of those between different types of racism. It is significant that *Black Skin, White Masks* is so heavily dependent on Sartre's analysis of the situation of the Jew, which Fanon adapts to the colonial situation. Fanon never lost sight of the overlaps between anti-Semitism and anti-black racism or between Fascism in Europe and European colonialism outside its frontiers. He describes Nazism as 'the apparition of "European colonies", in other words, the institution of a colonial system in the very heart of Europe' ('Racism and Culture', 1970b: 43), and states elsewhere '[n]ot long ago Nazism transformed the whole of Europe into a veritable colony' (1967: 79; see also 'Unity and effective solidarity are the conditions for an African liberation', 1970b: 181). Fanon is clearly influenced by Césaire, who claimed that: 'What he (the twentieth-century humanist) does not forgive Hitler is not the crime in itself, the crime against the white man, it is the inflicting on Europeans of European colonialist procedures which until now were reserved for the Arabs of Algeria, the coolies of India, and the Negroes of Africa' (cited by Fanon in 'Racist fury in France', 1970b: 176). The connections between processes of racialization inside and outside Europe are also central to Hannah Arendt's argument in *The Origins of Totalitarianism*. Although Fanon demonstrates a degree of ambivalence regarding these connections, and especially over the similarities or differences between blacks and Jews (see Cheyette, 2005), his views are nevertheless indicative of that post-war attempt to provide a common framework for the analysis of systems of racialized violence, which have, more recently, too often been viewed in discreet terms (for an exception to this and a renewal of the approach adopted by Arendt and Fanon, see Gilroy, 2000).

Fourth, a major fascination of Fanon's work clearly lies in his attempt to find a new language for colonized peoples, to develop a new society and create a new 'man', while being tied profoundly (if unconsciously) to the structures that he challenges. The contradictions that arise from this project mean that he cannot be recruited unproblematically to the post-humanist cause of a certain strand of Western critical thought in the post-war period. But the struggle to break with history while being trapped within it does highlight crucial problems for any definition of a new, non-Eurocentric humanism, for the languages available to voices previously silenced, and for the direction of countries in the developing world after independence from colonial rule. Fanon's struggle with the Manichean binary oppositions of black and white and universalism and particularism is still being waged today.

Finally, as Jean Khalfa reminds us, Fanon's work is founded on 'l'articulation du politique et de l'individuel' [the articulation of the political and the individual] (2005–06: 60). Fanon embodied the Marxist approach to thought and action, whereby the function of philosophy is to change the world. Like Sartre's depiction of the committed intellectual who defines the self and the world through an engagement in specific 'situations', Fanon allied his thought to the project of emancipation in the 'tragic' situation of colonialism (Gordon, 1995). And just as thought shifts with a changing environment, so were Fanon's ideas an evolving and experimental response to that environment, rather than ever constituting a fixed and coherent body of thought (Gibson, 2003). At a time when the committed intellectual is in retreat, Fanon's work is a timely reminder of the duty of the writer to question structures of power and define strategies of resistance. As Fanon writes in the closing line of *Black Skin, White Masks*, 'O my body, make of me always a man who questions!' (1986: 232).

Further reading

Gibson, Nigel C. (ed.), 1999. *Rethinking Fanon: The Continuing Dialogue* (New York: Humanity Books). A wide-ranging collection of some of the most interesting articles on Fanon written in the last two decades, with an excellent introduction by the editor.

—— 2003. *Fanon: The Postcolonial Imagination* (Cambridge: Polity). A comprehensive and detailed analysis of Fanon's works in Polity's 'Key Contemporary Thinkers' series, which presents Fanon as a 'dialectical' thinker writing in and of his time.

Macey, David, 2000. *Frantz Fanon: A Life* (London: Granta). The most thorough biography of Fanon to date, which seeks to resituate Fanon within a Francophone context in order to challenge the Anglo-American postcolonial 'appropriation' of his work.

CHAPTER 6

Édouard Glissant: Dealing in Globality

Chris Bongie

It is over half a century now since Martinique's Édouard Glissant arrived on the literary scene in Paris, publishing his first volumes of poetry in the early 1950s, and his first novel, *La Lézarde*, in 1958. Since that time he has produced eight stylistically demanding novels (the latest being *Ormerod* in 2003), a good many collections of poetry, and one influential play about the Haitian Revolution.[1] Arguably, though, it is not as a novelist or poet that Glissant has proved most influential at the international level, but as a theorist. With his unflagging advocacy of a creolizing world of Diversity and Relation, he has become one of the few French-language writers, after Césaire and Fanon, to have made a major impact on postcolonial theory in the Anglo-American academy. No less a luminary than Gayatri Spivak has, for instance, stressed her 'affinity with Glissant's thinking' (2006, 108), championing his vision of 'creolity' on the grounds that it 'assumes imperfection, even as it assures the survival of a rough future' (109). In the first half of this chapter I provide an overview of this vision, basing my account on his recent collection of essays, *La Cohée du Lamentin* (2005).[2] In the second half, by contrast, I adopt a diachronic approach, arguing that notwithstanding the remarkable consistency of Glissant's vision over the past five decades when it comes to 'creolity', his later work is characterized by a turn away from the political and its necessarily partisan commitments. This shift, which I examine in relation to an important watershed in the marketing of his oeuvre, cannot but

---

1 As of 2007, only Glissant's first two novels had been translated into English: *La Lézarde* as *The Ripening* (1985) and *Le Quatrième siècle* (1964) as *The Fourth Century* (2001). The most recent translations of Glissant into English are his *Collected Poems* (2004) and a new version of his 1961 play, *Monsieur Toussaint* (2005).

2 Glissant's other works of theory are: *Soleil de la conscience* (1956); *L'Intention poétique* (1969); *Le Discours antillais* (1981, trans. 1989); *Poétique de la Relation* (1990, trans. 1997); *Faulkner, Mississippi* (1995, trans. 1999); *Introduction à une Poétique du Divers* (1996); *Traité du Tout-Monde* (1997); *Une nouvelle région du monde* (2006); and *Mémoires des esclavages* (2007).

provoke a certain reconsideration of his work as a whole, and the possible uses to which it can (and cannot) be put by practitioners of 'postcolonial thought'.

Relating poetics: the trembling thought of *La Cohée du Lamentin*

The recently published *Cohée* is an excellent text to focus on when surveying the key ideas upon which Glissant's theoretical edifice has been built, because like his earlier works, only more so, it is self-consciously preoccupied with reiterating so many of those ideas. The opening epigraph introduces repetition as the book's theme (2005: 7), and Glissant time and again stresses his appreciation for it, on both cognitive (51) and aesthetic (67) grounds. As is typical of his non-fictional prose works, *Cohée* is not a unified text pursuing one argument in a linear fashion; it is a diffuse gathering of texts, many of them previously published or delivered, that in characteristic fashion mixes together a wide array of genres: art criticism, autobiography, book reviews, poetry, along with more recognizably 'postcolonial' interventions (e.g. theoretical reflections on Caribbean landscape or the notion of universal Empire). Some new material supplements these 'finished' pieces, notably, transitional passages that provide the book with an evident, if evidently enigmatic, structure. (The structural complexities of Glissant's essay collections often get overlooked by those who read them solely with an eye to singling out his ideas – a pattern of reading that any summary such as mine necessarily replicates.) The almost random-seeming coming-together of these many discursive threads serves to materialize for the reader the 'unity-diversity' privileged by his relativizing 'poetics of Relation', that never-completed 'synthesis-genesis' (1997a: 174) for which Glissant is best known as a theorist.

Over the years, Glissant has come up with a great many different words and phrases to convey this 'Relation [qui] relie, relaie, relate' [Relation that relinks, relays, recounts] (2005: 37). For our introductory purposes, it will be useful at this point to cite a number of the 'master' signifiers of his decidedly 'minor' (in the Deleuzian sense) thought that make a repeat appearance in *Cohée*. First and foremost of these terms is *creolization*, defined as an unstoppable and *unpredictable* process of hybridization (50), as the most human and most intense form of metamorphosis (74); unlike 'arithmetical' conceptions of hybridity (e.g. black + white = mulatto), it is a *métissage* that produces unexpected results (84). Creolization has as its privileged site the *Archipelago* (74), as opposed to the *Territory* (137); the 'unity-diversity' of archipelagic thinking contrasts starkly with *continental* systems of thought (137), which are driven by a passion for the One (72), by a desire for measure (*mesure*) and *transparency* that the West has exported to the rest of the world. This resolute *One-thinking* ('pensée de l'Un') must give way to the irresolutions of *Diverse-thinking* ('pensée du Divers') (245), which thrives on excess (*démesure*) and acknowledges the *opacity* of that which it interrogates. One of Glissant's perennial examples of such Diverse-thinking is the work of French philosophers Deleuze and Guattari, whose concept of the horizontally expanding *rhizome* is yet again invoked in *Cohée* (e.g. 232) as an ethical alternative to the vertically descending *root* and the *atavistic* desire for *filiation* to which *root-identities* testify. The *composite* world of Relation has no one point of origin but springs, rather, from a *digenèse* (179), a double, indeed multiple, beginning. Always-already at a founding distance from Africa or Europe, the Caribbean exemplifies such a world of repeated beginnings: part of *neo-America* (78), it is a place of *baroque* complexity (49), the site of innumerable *traces* (84) that cannot simply be understood and ordered according to 'universal', *classical* criteria (of the sort embraced by *euro-America*).

The above is just a smattering of basic Glissantian terminology. In one way or another, the positive pole of each of his binary oppositions stresses the virtues of *Relation*, which breaks down our too rigidly conceived (ideologized, racialized) identities, exchanging them for more fluid ones, in a process of contamination without dilution (136) that relies upon, and is creative of, 'différences consenties' [accepted differences] (87). Even in its most local instances, this relational process is virtually global, an immanent manifestation of what Glissant calls the *Tout-Monde*, 'la totalité réalisée des données connues et inconnues de nos univers' [the realized totality of the data, known and unknown, of our universes] (87). The spreading of colonial empires across the world first rendered the *Tout-Monde* visible, forging the global links through which it could eventually be discerned in its totality, although in their triumphant particularism these empires could do no more than misrecognize and devalue it (151). By contrast, for Glissant, the challenge facing those living in the *Tout-Monde* today (that is to say, each and every one of us) is to take cognizance of the incessant and unpredictable *translations*, the global rhizome of relaying imaginaries (143), through which it repeatedly comes into being. In this *Chaos-monde* (36) of unceasing metamorphosis, even the binary oppositions through which Glissant makes it provisionally thinkable for us will ultimately be harmonized in a *mesure démesurée*: even continental and archipelagic thinking, he assures us, have an alliance to come (231).

Glissant's essay collections are like archeological sites, where the reader familiar with his resolutely self-referential work can identify the terminological and conceptual debris from earlier texts: a key term such as 'Relation', first introduced in the 1969 *Intention*, jostles against one initially put forward in the 1997 *Traité*, its meaning thereby transformed by this reiteration, advanced by this 'imperceptible deviation' (20). As usual, in *Cohée* Glissant supplements the old 'master' signifiers with a few unfamiliar ones, which set the metaphorical and conceptual agenda for the new collection. His new guiding terms here are *Tremblement* (Trembling) and *Mondialité* (Globality). The image of trembling functions throughout the text as a poetic metaphor for understanding the contingent nature of life in the *Tout-Monde*, while the idea of globality conveys that same understanding of the planetary potential of Relation in a more recognizably theoretical language.

Glissant's new (dis)organizing metaphor, trembling, which picks up on passing mentions in the *Traité* (1997b, 15; 231), is identified explicitly in *Cohée* with

archipelagic thought (2005: 84). The 'pensée du Tremblement' diverts systematic thinking (75); it is in harmony with the world's *errance* [errantry] and its
inexprimable [inexpressibility] (25). Glissant asks that we attend to the trembling
of the world, which is synonymous with its creolization ('le Monde tremble,
se créolise' [75]) and opposed to the brutal, univocal, inflexible thinking of
the *self without the Other* (76). That something trembles puts the fixity of its
identity into question (180), and yet this very putting-into-question – in a typical
Glissantian 'dialectic' – is how identity (as relation) affirms and enriches itself.
The trembling of our identity is thus not a sign of weakness, lack or clumsiness
(180), but of our energizing capacity for *approximation*, the most generous form
of Relation there is (219). Although this trembling conjures up the spectre of
other, more powerful (and destructive) transformations, like that of the earth-
quake, invoked and warded off at the very beginning of the book (13–14), such
calamitous scenarios, the unfortunate products of an *apocalyptic* thinking, are
precisely what the inhabitants of the *Tout-Monde* most need to resist ('résistons
à la pensée d'Apocalypse' [23]).

The metaphor of trembling is doubled, in more sociological language, by the
concept of *Mondialité*, a way of seeing and living the *Tout-Monde* that Glissant
differentiates from *Mondialisation* (Globalization) – a distinction that he had yet
to refine in his previous collection of essays, where words like *globalité* (1997b:
22), *mondialité* (176), *mondialisation* (192) and *globalisation* (211) were used more
or less interchangeably. The reader should by now be familiar enough with the
workings of Glissant's binaries to foresee how these two counterpointed ways of
responding to the *Tout-Monde* function. On the one hand, *Mondialisation* involves
uniformization, the reign of multinationals, standardization, neo-liberalism, the
panoply of commonplaces with which we are all familiar (15). (Just because these
are commonplaces, to be sure, does not make them any less true or useful: as in
the past, Glissant here repeatedly stresses the need to revalue seeming banalities [*lieux-communs*], envisaging them as the common places [*lieux communs*]
in which relational complicity can be established.) *Mondialisation*, however, is
but the negative flipside of a positive and prodigious reality, *Mondialité*, which
he defines as the planetary consciousness of a world of inextricable relations
in which it is necessary for all of us to change our ways of conceiving, living
and reacting (15). *Mondialité* is a poetics of 'la diversité solidaire' [solidarity-in-
diversity] (144). If you cultivate this poetics, if you *live globality*, then you are,
he insists, on the point of truly combating the inequities of globalization (139).

Like all of Glissant's binary oppositions, that between globalization and
globality is suspiciously neat, strangely systematic for such an enemy of 'systematic thinking' (on this contradiction, see Burton, 1997: 99). Even more to the
point, though, there would appear to be no practical implications to be drawn
from this absolute opposition. What does it mean to be *au point de combattre
vraiment la mondialisation* [on the point of truly combating the inequities of
globalization]? Glissant is disarmingly forthright when it comes to insisting
that this combat cannot happen until we have learned how to *sense* the ever-
present positive flipside of globalization, *Mondialité*. To gain a sense of planetary

consciousness, to see what is already right there before our very eyes, is the precondition for social change, and that is why Glissant consistently refers to an *aesthetics* or *poetics*, as opposed to a *politics*, of Relation. He is adamant that *no* solution to the problems of the world will be lasting, or even beneficial for any length of time, without being preceded by an enormous insurrection of the imaginary, one that will prompt *les humanités* to wish to be and to create themselves as what they are in reality: namely, 'un changement qui ne finit pas, dans une pérénnité qui ne se fige pas' [an altering that never ends, in a perennial state of unsettling] (24–25).

The call for *cette énorme insurrection de l'imaginaire* is an avowedly utopian one; indeed, Glissant associates *Mondialité* with a Poetics of Utopia (138), carefully distinguishing his own thinking of Utopia from all those discredited *systems of thought* with which the word is usually associated, and that had as their 'project' the reforming of a given state of affairs or human society through a calculating of norms (224–25). Normative 'utopian' thinking necessarily involves the exercise of power whereas, as Glissant asserted in the *Traité*, 'nos vérités ne conjoignent pas à la puissance' [our truths have no relation to power] (1997b: 28), and are thus *absolutely ineffective* when it comes to 'les oppressions concrètes qui stupéfient le monde' [concrete, world-staggering oppressions] (1997b: 18). Utopia, he proclaims, is 'notre seul Acte, notre seul Art' [our only Act, our only Art] (2005: 27).

It is at this most utopian point of my overview of Glissant's poetics of Relation, where Art and Act become virtual synonyms, that a synthetic account of his ideas must give way to a diachronic argument, for it is by no means the case that Glissant has always held himself and his truths at such an insuperable distance from the principles of action (and thus the exercising of norms) that *political* combat requires. As commentators have begun remarking over the last decade, Glissant's work, from the 1990 *Poétique de la Relation* onward, seems to have declined from (indeed, to have actively declined) the sort of partisan (notably, nationalist) engagement that characterized a good many of his writings from the late 1960s and 1970s, written in Martinique and collected in 1981 as *Le Discours antillais*. It is only after this point – when he left for Paris to work at UNESCO and then in 1988 moved to the United States (teaching, since 1994, at City University of New York) – that Glissant's gregarious vision of an incessantly transforming world of Relation, a constant of his work since the 1950s, began to dominate both his theoretical and fictional work, at the expense of the robust political commitments that he had so often voiced in the *Discours*.

In the words of Peter Hallward, the most vocal and philosophically rigorous critic of this anti-political utopian turn, if there was 'no *sudden* break in Glissant's work, no sharply defined before and after' (2001: 100), there has nonetheless been 'a major shift in his priorities' since the publication of the *Discours*, most notably involving his abandonment of 'the pursuit of a *national* specificity' (2001: 67, 100; on this shift, see also Bongie 1998: 126–86). After the *Discours*, Hallward argues, Glissant has been content to affirm 'an incorporation into the univocity of a new world order based on nothing other than constant internal metamorphosis, dislocation and exchange' (2001: 68); his turn away from the project of nation-building in Martinique marks 'the refusal of worldly complexity, not the reverse' (70). Glissant's apparent embracing of a serene postmodernism whose intentions are purely poetic and whose real-world implications are precisely nil (or, rather, can only serve to perpetuate the status quo) is, for Hallward, exemplary of 'postcolonial theory' as a whole, which has privileged 'the interminable "negotiations" of culture and psychology' over the 'collective principles' without which 'the political pursuit of justice' is quite simply unthinkable (2001: xx).

Is Hallward correct in his assessment? For a critic such as Michael Dash, who has consistently praised Glissant as 'a natural deconstructionist who celebrates latency, opacity, infinite metamorphosis' and who sees this celebration as having 'always been at the heart of his creative enterprise' (Glissant, 1989: xii), Hallward's acerbic critique might be adjudged more a source of pride than of worry. An increasing number of academic readers of Glissant, however, have registered a certain unease, and even distress, when it comes to his later writings: Shalini Puri, for instance, citing Hallward, laments the disintegration in the 1990 *Poétique* of 'the careful equilibrium' of 'art and politics' that was struck in *Le Discours antillais* (2004: 238), and explicitly sidelines that influential text from her enthusiastic account of Glissant's 'critically engaged relationship to oppositional nationalist politics' (75). Nick Nesbitt, who offers an incisive description of the critical abyss that has opened up between Hallward's iconoclastic and Dash's celebratory readings of Glissant's poetics of Relation (2003: 170–74), acknowledges 'the more facile dimensions of Glissant's writings on totality and immanence in the 1980s and 1990s' (173), but nonetheless attempts, somewhat desperately, to rescue a late collection like the *Traité* from Hallward's accusations regarding 'an increasing disengagement and aestheticism in Glissant's work' (184).

One suspects that, faced with a text like *Cohée* – far and away the most 'aestheticizing' of his essay collections – most advocates of Glissantian thinking would react with even greater defensiveness or disavowal. Indeed, as one such established advocate, I myself feel compelled, when faced with his artfully serene translations of Globalization into Globality, to wonder what his work still has to offer a 'postcolonial thought' that surely must, if it is to be of any help in understanding how the wretched of the earth might become less so, pursue the emancipatory project of changing the inequitable power structures of the world. The second half of this chapter addresses that sceptical question, abandoning deferent summary for a more argumentative account of 'late Glissant' and his poetics of Relation.

Marketing poetics: late Glissant and the bastion of literature

Glissant's high profile over the past two decades as 'the major writer and theorist from the French West Indies' (Dash, 1995: 3) is not an 'innocent' phenomenon. Like that of any contemporary thinker, the successful dissemination of Glissant's ideas is inseparable from their marketing, and I will take this obvious – if often anxiously repressed – fact as my point of departure here. My reflections on one key moment in Glissant's marketing history will provide the conceptual base for this second half of the chapter, which sketches out an argument addressing the ideological question of exactly why his vision of a ceaselessly hybridizing 'Chaos-World' of Relation should have proved so attractive to an Anglo-American academic audience, to say nothing of influential French politicians (see, e.g. Villepin, 2004: 146). The current visibility (one might even say, *popularization*) of Glissant-as-francophone/postcolonial-theorist-of-cultural-Diversity needs, I argue, to be understood in relation to his changing attitude toward 'oppositional nationalist politics'. Glissant's parting of ways with such partisan politics after the *Discours*, combined with his strong claims for the global crossing of cultures, meshed well with the belief in that alternative-(to)-politics known as 'cultural politics', which has been so fundamental to dominant versions of postcolonial theory (and that gets expressed, for instance, in Homi Bhabha's enthusiasm for hybrid alliances 'whose struggle for fairness and justice emphasizes the deep collaboration between aesthetics, ethics and activism' [2003: 31]).

The marketing event in question occurred in 1997, a climactic moment in the ongoing transfer (begun at the end of the previous decade) of Glissant's literary properties from one publishing house to another, from Seuil to Gallimard, 'the bastion of pure literature', as Pierre Bourdieu once called it (1996 [1992]: 210). In 1997, Gallimard republished much of Glissant's back catalogue, including his first five novels as well as three earlier works of theory, *Soleil de la conscience* (1956), *L'Intention poétique* (1969), and *Poétique de la Relation* (1990). A mere glance at the cover of these three texts would have surprised any reader familiar with their previous incarnations, for each of the books now sported a new subtitle – respectively, *Poétique I, II* and *III*. When *Traité du Tout-Monde* came out later that year, it bore the subtitle *Poétique IV*, becoming the first of Glissant's works to have as its initial framework of reading the now established 'fact' that his theoretical oeuvre, or at least a significant part of it, must be understood as part of an overarching project spanning half a century. Likewise, when *La Cohée du Lamentin* was published in 2005, its integral place in that project was assured through its subtitle: *Poétique V*. (The next year, this enumerative strategy would be given a new twist with the follow-up to *Cohée*, *Une nouvelle région du monde*, which is subtitled *Esthétique I*.)

One could certainly argue that this retrospective ordering is somehow immanent to Glissant's theoretical approach, which places such a high premium on repetition-with-difference, on recomposing the already composed (see Fonkoua, 2002: 273–74; Biondi and Pessini 2004: 25–26). A less attractive reading, however, would stress the commercial dimensions of Glissant/Gallimard's pouring of old wine into new bottles. I say less 'attractive', because as Bourdieu reminds us, the literary field is 'protected by the veneration of all those who were raised, often from their earliest youth, to perform sacramental

rites of cultural devotion' (1996: 184), rites that actively exclude any consideration of the 'profane' origins of the literary text. Nowhere are such archaic rites
more attended to, paradoxical as it might seem, than in the ostensibly progressive field of postcolonial studies – a field that (to put it in Bourdieusian terms)
has as its fundamental law (*nomos*) the separation of legitimate (politically/
aesthetically 'resistant') from illegitimate ('commodified') cultural production,
and that belatedly grounds itself in a belief (*illusio*) in literary value, and in the
creative power of the artist, that sociologically-minded critics such as Bourdieu
have so ably interrogated. (For an extended version of this argument about the
'foundational bias' of postcolonial studies, see Bongie, 2003b.)

Gallimard's relaunching of most of Glissant's back catalogue in 1997, and
the related publicity campaign, is an evident (if, within the framework of the
postcolonial ideology, virtually unreadable) sign of the upward trajectory of
his 'stock' as a writer of distinction, a watershed in Glissant's 'social ageing'
(Bourdieu, 1996: 240). This imposition of a retrospective unity on Glissant's
earlier works of theory must ultimately be ascribed not to any one individual
or entity (author or publishing house) but to the tactical conglomeration of
singular writer and the ensemble of forces without which he would not exist
as such: as Bourdieu argues, 'the artist who makes the work is himself made,
at the core of the field of production, by the whole ensemble of those who
help to "discover" him and to consecrate him as an artist who is "known" and
recognized – critics, writers of prefaces, dealers etc.' (1996: 167). No less than
with best-selling novelists of pulp fiction, a consecrated highbrow writer such
as Glissant – perennial contender for consideration as Nobel Laureate, and since
2002 himself namesake of a Prix Édouard Glissant – needs to be situated within
this collective framework, in which his authorship (and his cultural authority) is
secured and promoted by a wide range of cultural mediators who deal in him
and his ideas, often to the exclusion of other, less prestigious writers from the
French Antilles lacking access to the nodal points (e.g. Paris, New York) of the
global publishing market.

To speak of 'Glissant' (or 'late Glissant') is, then, necessarily to invoke this
collective author who has dealt him(self) into the mix, and whose dealings in the
market force us to question 'the charismatic ideology of "creator"' (Bourdieu,
1996: 215) that continues to play such a formative, if repressed, role in postcolonial studies. To acknowledge this entangled authorship complicates any discussion of the singular writer's 'expressive drive', his status as intentional agent
(see Bourdieu, 1996: 270–74), but it does not foreclose upon such a discussion,
and if there is no good reason to read the retrospective unification and linear-
ization of certain of Glissant's theoretical works under the *Poétique* rubric as
purely immanent to his writerly project, this reconfiguration can nonetheless
legitimately be interpreted as an act of 'intellectual self-fashioning'. All talk of
marketing and the rituals of consecration associated with social ageing aside,
the creation of a multi-volume *Poétique* manifestly enforced a certain way of
reading Glissant's oeuvre, for while including some theoretical works it also
excluded others, most notably *Le Discours antillais*.

The *Discours*, while not the only one of his theoretical works excluded from the linear order of the *Poétique*,[3] was certainly the most obvious omission. Glissant's most vital contribution to Caribbean studies and 'the most politically combative of his theoretical works' (Britton, 1999: 8), this magisterial book was also republished in 1997, but on its own, as part of Gallimard's Folio Essais series (no. 313). If the *Discours* pursues many of the same relational insights already put forward in *L'Intention poétique* and anticipates a great deal of the global vision that would be given fuller expression in *Poétique de la Relation*, it clearly differs from them in its far greater attention to Martiniquan specificities, containing a wide array of materials written in situ during the late 1960s and throughout the 1970s that bear directly on the future of his native land, in which, for example, he critiques the mimetic symptoms that 'détournent la vie politique martinquaise de son sens réel' [divert Martiniquan political life from its true sense] (1981: 178), and affirms his belief that the temporary traumatic drives of its people and its elites can be 'transformées ou continuées en projets politiques élucidés' [transformed or elaborated into elucidated political projects] (172).[4] The absence of the *Discours* from the belatedly defined, post-nationalist world of the multi-volume *Poétique* is symptomatic of a new position-taking with regard to the place of the *political*, in both Glissant's oeuvre and a now (according to him) fully relational *Tout-Monde*. After 1997, the *Discours* and its commitment to holding on to, and holding forth from, that place necessarily stands apart from that of which it might once have been thought a part.

One instance of this new apartness must suffice here. In his 1990 *Poétique de la Relation* Glissant identified his new book as 'the reconstituted echo or a spiral retelling' of *both L'Intention poétique* and *Le Discours antillais*: there he argued that each of these texts was grounded in a double affirmation, one of 'political strength [*rigueur*], but simultaneously, the rhizome of a multiple relationship with the Other' (1997a: 16). It is precisely such a connection that the direct link forged in 1997 from *Poétique II* to *Poétique III* renders questionable, as does the virtual disappearance in *Poétiques IV* and *V* of any appeals to *la rigueur politique*, amidst countless invocations of rhizomatic multiplicity. Indeed, the very word 'politics' itself vanishes from Glissant's vocabulary: a word that comes up time and again in the *Discours*, and that still makes occasional appearances in *Poétique* and even *Traité*, it is used exactly once, and very much in passing, in *Cohée* (149).

---

3   The two other excluded texts were his lengthy meditation on William Faulkner, *Faulkner, Mississippi* (1995); and the 1996 primer, *Introduction à une Poétique du Divers*, a main function of which, one can now see in retrospect, was to whet the public's appetite, in anticipation of the 1997 marketing campaign.

4   Parts of the *Discours* have been translated as *Caribbean Discourse* by J. Michael Dash (Glissant, 1989). Dash's selection privileges the 'cultural' dimensions of the *Discours*, excluding many of Glissant's more explicit reflections on social and political transformation, such as the essay from which these quotations are taken. The fact that Dash translates 'le drame planétaire de la Relation' (1981: 11) as 'the universal drama of cultural transformation' (1989: 2) gives a good idea of his priorities.

If, until 1997, Glissant's theoretical works could be read as the site of a productive conjuncture of 'political vanguardism and avant-gardism in matters of art and the art of living' (to cite Bourdieu's account of the pleasant dream, 'based on a mere *homology*', that gave shape to modernism as a whole [1996: 387]), the repackaging of Glissant's oeuvre undoes this confusion, policing the distance between a poetics/aesthetics that late Glissant increasingly valorizes and a political commitment without which the *Discours* (and the decolonization movement as a whole) would have been unthinkable. For late Glissant, this commitment now appears not only to have run out of steam but also to have been steeped in an exclusionary, identitarian conception of the world deeply at odds with the relativizing consciousness of *Mondialité* and the ethical emphasis on 'multiple relations to the Other' it demands. As he put it in a round table discussion during a 1998 international colloquium on his work, 'Je ne crois pas que le politique gouverne les mouvements du monde à l'heure actuelle' [I don't believe that politics governs the world's movements at the present time] (Chevrier, 1999: 324). Increasingly insistent on the need to go beyond politics and its inescapably partisan commitments, to invent new manners of resisting because 'it is very evident that the old ones are no longer of any use' (Glissant, 1996: 107), late Glissant is no longer even concerned, as in the 1990 *Poétique*, to reassure readers that his errant-thought is not apolitical (1997a: 20).

Glissant's belated act of intellectual self-fashioning clearly lends itself to being read as exemplary of the shift 'from Third World nationalism to postmodernism' identified (and denounced) by Aijaz Ahmad as among the historical prerequisites of the constitution of the field of postcolonial studies in the 1980s (1995: 1). Less evidently, but even more to the point, given the Bourdieusian approach taken here, this position-taking with regard to the political is a prerequisite for the claiming of poetic *autonomy* that has, ever since the constitution of the literary field in the nineteenth century, been the habitual possession of that 'unprecedented social personage who is the modern writer or artist', 'a full-time professional, dedicated to one's work in a total and exclusive manner, indifferent to the exigencies of politics and to the injunctions of morality, and not recognizing any jurisdiction other than the norms specific to one's art' (Bourdieu, 1996: 76–77). Late Glissant styles (and markets) himself as precisely such a personage, one whose identity as cultural producer is defined, among other things, by his indifference, or even outright hostility, to 'the exigencies of politics'. Hence all the claims in *Cohée* for the work of the 'cultural imaginary' as a far preferable alternative to principled, armed resistance to the universal Empire that the United States is threatening to become (2005: 157); hence the aggrandizing onus placed on poetry as the most unremitting 'guarantor' of 'la connaissance tremblante' (96), and on the Poet's special role in predicting the earth's imminent refusal of the standardizing impositions of globalization (162).

The 1997 marketing campaign is, in short, symptomatic of a fundamental repositioning of Glissant's theoretical oeuvre. Poetics takes the fore, once and for all, accompanied by a proliferation of debunking assertions regarding the

degraded realm of the political and its contingent and compromised engagements, its failed and fallacious commitments, which are increasingly the
subject of dire assessments (the sort of assessments to which, significantly,
the Caribbean's two recent Nobel Laureates, Walcott and Naipaul, have always
subscribed). What are we to make of this drawing of a line between the *poetics*
of Relation and whatever *politics* one might, by way of homology, once have
been tempted to associate with it? In drawing this line, has late Glissant simply
produced a 'mistaken' (Ahmad would say 'postmodern') interpretation of an idea
that he once dealt with in a more effective, counter-hegemonic manner? Has he,
in late texts like *Cohée*, with their insistence on global poetics over trans-local
politics, produced the same faulty reading of his earlier work that, according to
Mimi Sheller, has facilitated its consumption in the Anglo-American academy,
where the theory of creolization tends to get 'displaced from its Caribbean
context' and in that dislocation thereby 'emptied of its resonance as a project of
subaltern resistance' (2003: 203)?

The easy, and by no means incorrect, response to this question is simply
'Yes!' But I would venture, in closing, that while the existence of this line most
certainly does testify to an aestheticizing, post-political turn in Glissant's work,
the 'mistake' does not necessarily lie in the *drawing* of this line. For its drawing
has the signal value of forcing us to question the legitimacy of conflating any
cultural theory, such as that of creolization, with 'the exigencies of politics'. Might
not the popularity of such theories with academic audiences be (and always
have been) based on a confusion between what, in the retrospective creation of
a multi-volume *Poétique*, are clearly identified as two separate spheres?

Symptomatic of his increasingly hard-to-ignore position-taking in 'the bastion
of pure literature', the marketing ploy/self-fashioning act of 1997, in other words,
confronts us with the sobering possibility that, as Hallward (following Alain
Badiou) claims, 'the idea of a "cultural politics" is a disastrous confusion of
spheres' (2001: xix); that however necessary a 'careful equilibrium' of 'art and
politics' may be, it cannot assume the hybrid guise of a *politics* of Relation that
would somehow give substance and direction to Glissant's poetic translations
of the staggering abuses of Globalization into the trembling premonitions of
Globality. Late Glissant's insistence on literary autonomy – his drawing of the line
that extends from *Soleil de la conscience* to *La Cohée du Lamentin*, and that separates
his multi-volume *Poétique* from the more mixed messages of his earlier work –
provides an antidote to the confused enterprise of cultural politics, enforcing,
ironically enough, exactly the 'principled distinction of culture and politics' that
his critic Hallward advocates (2001: xx), albeit for radically different ends. The
value of his otherwise banal and hyperbolic claims regarding the desirability of
a global insurrection of the cultural imaginary and the privileged role of Poets in
promoting it lies, I would suggest, in the rigour with which the author of *Cohée*
distances his utopian claims about culture from politics and its 'militant assertion
of universal principles that brook no qualification' (Hallward, 2001: xx).

Whether this particular value can be profitably exchanged in the academic
marketplace is, of course, quite another matter. Uneasy with straightforward,

partisan politics and its necessarily antagonistic, exclusionary demands (Žižek, 2004: 88–102), many postcolonial producers and consumers remain, as Hallward has demonstrated, reluctant to 'make and preserve a sharp conceptual *break between culture and politics*' (2001: xix). By so visibly making and preserving this break, late Glissant unsettles the hopes for 'deep collaboration' upon which the 'politics' of so much postcolonial theory depends, and that accounted in no small part for the ready consumption of him in the Anglo-American academy as a theorist of cultural diversity. If the field of elite cultural production, as Bourdieu once suggested, shares an economy of practices with 'the game of *loser takes all*' (1996: 217), then late Glissant's unsettling of the 'disastrous' assumptions upon which the popularity of his hybrid theory rested, no less than his artful disengagement from the 'real politics of transformation' once so forcefully advocated in the *Discours* (1981: 210), may yet prove an eminently winning strategy.

Further reading

Britton, Celia, 1999. *Édouard Glissant and Postcolonial Theory: Strategies of Language and Resistance* (Charlottesville: University Press of Virginia). The first book explicitly to situate Glissant's work in relation to Anglophone postcolonial theory (notably, Bhabha and Spivak). It provides compelling close-readings of Glissant's novels. In her examination of Glissant's 'strategies of language and resistance', the author relies primarily on *Le Discours antillais*, and is evidently puzzled at the waning of those 'anti-imperialist' strategies in his later writings.

Dash, J. Michael, 1995. *Édouard Glissant* (Cambridge: Cambridge University Press). The first book-length study of Glissant in English, and still the best point of departure for studying his work (as long as one keeps in mind the book's postmodern investment in Glissant's 'vision of inexhaustible hybridity'). It provides a very satisfying overview of all his writings up to and including *Poétique de la Relation* (1990).

Fonkoua, Romuald, 2002. *Essai sur la mesure du monde au XXe siècle: Édouard Glissant* (Paris: Honoré Champion). A solid example of the recent scholarship on Glissant being produced in France. Isolates three main themes in Glissant's work (travel, knowledge, writing) and provides many useful literary, historical and philosophical contexts for reading him.

Hallward, Peter, 2001. *Absolutely Postcolonial: Writing between the Singular and the Specific* (Manchester: Manchester University Press). Chapter 2 of this important contribution to (and critique of) postcolonial studies offers a refreshingly sceptical, and philosophically rigorous, account of Glissant's gradual shift away from political engagement. Whether one agrees with this radical intervention or not, it is an essential point of departure for future studies of his work.

CHAPTER 7

Tangled History and Photographic (In)Visibility: Ho Chi Minh on the Edge of French Political Culture

Panivong Norindr

Culture becomes as much an uncomfortable disturbing practice of survival and supplementarity between arts and politics, past and present, the public and the private.

(Bhabha, 1994: 175)

On photography

In a letter dated 6 July 1920, L. Josselme, the head of the Indochinese Postal Control in Marseilles, complains in the following terms about the photograph of Nguyên Ai Quôc he has just received from the Résident Supérieur: 'elle est absolument invisible, ayant jauni par progression depuis son arrivée' [it is entirely invisible, having progressively yellowed since its arrival], adding that this deterioration 'm'oblige à vous demander de vouloir bien m'en adresser un autre exemplaire mieux fixé' [forces me to ask you kindly to send another more permanent, better fixed copy] (Gaspard, 1992: 101–02). Nguyên Ai Quôc was suspected of being none other than the Nguyên That Tanh who had taken part in a popular uprising against the French in Annam in 1908. The photograph was eagerly awaited to verify and prove his identity. Photography, very early on, had become an integral part of the panoptic apparatus of surveillance deployed by the French *Sûreté*, both in the colonies and at home, to keep track of potentially dangerous natives. By becoming invisible, the photograph became the failed site of an authoritative marking of the subject's identity. Focusing on the period when Ho Chi Minh was still known as Nguyên Ai Quôc, I want to use this 'invisible photograph', and the very notion of '(in)visibility', to introduce and problematize this process of subjectification, and to reassess not simply Ho's place in history (i.e. his pivotal role in the decolonization of Vietnam from France), but also, as I will argue here, his importance for Francophone postcolonial theory

– and, in illuminating the work of a number of subsequent critics and theorists, for postcolonial thought more generally.

Although Ho Chi Minh has been the subject of recent biographical studies written by such distinguished historians as Pierre Brocheux (2000), William Duiker (2000), Thu Trang Gaspard (1992), Daniel Hémery (1990) and many others, postcolonial critics have yet to turn their scholarly attention to his work, perhaps because they have too readily accepted the common wisdom that Ho was 'more a pragmatist than a theoretician' who 'obviously had relatively little interest in theoretical questions' (Duiker, 2000: 94, 137). Ho Chi Minh's work is not seen to be as compelling as those written by such seminal writers/theorists of decolonization as Albert Memmi, Aimé Césaire or Frantz Fanon. Inviting more active engagement with Ho, this chapter is an initial and consequently modest attempt to provide a point of entry into his work by resituating him in a more dynamic and complex intellectual landscape.

But before we do this, let us return, for a brief moment, to that blank photograph, which, I argue, functions as a screen onto which our fantasies of Ho Chi Minh are projected. I contend that it is against this very 'whiteness' [yellowness], against this blank space or 'void', that we write and reconstruct his story, and narrate his history. This void or space also delimits, somewhat paradoxically, the scene of our engagement, whether these are graphic marks on the white page, silver nitrate traces left on the photographic image or film strip, or noise and sound on the analogue tape-recording. Ho's supporters as well as his detractors, from the West as well as the East, fulfil their desires by filling in this void with composite portraits in his likeness. These personal fantasies constitute the imaginary scaffolding on which public myths and sanctioned truths have been erected. It seems timely to scrutinize these truth-claims and the texts used by scholars and official biographers who have offered their own narratives as transparent (re)presentation, because they all share the same problematic tendency to wallow in the plenitude of narrative signification. Kateb Yacine's evocative political play *L'Homme aux sandales de caoutchouc* (1970) does not share that ethos. Kateb Yacine's play dramatizes and rearticulates Ho's dynamic insertion into French, Russian, Chinese and, of course, Vietnamese cultural and political space. It foregrounds, at the same time, the transnational nature of Ho's engagement against French colonialism and his place on the French political scene. It renders visible without attempting to 'fix' him as an agent of cultural and political change, not as some coherent, unified, undivided subject, but as a wandering individual, a deterritorialized subject on the frontiers between cultures and nations.[1]

---

1 The gradual disappearance of Ho's physical features from the photographic print can be seen allegorically as the paradoxical capture of the essence of Ho's elusiveness, made all the more manifest by the reports of his wanderings from one European capital to the other: London, Paris, Moscow, Berlin and, finally, the Far East (Canton) and Southeast Asia (Thailand), before slipping surreptitiously back to Vietnam, thirty years after he had left in 1911.

Tracing the visibility of Nguyên Ai Quôc/Ho Chi Minh

Let us trace a genealogy of Nguyên Ai Quôc's increased visibility in France. It begins with a name, the name found at the bottom of the 'Revendications du Peuple Annamite' [Demands of the Annamite People]. These demands were presented to the Versailles Peace Treaty delegations in mid-June 1919, and distributed in the following months to Indochinese students and workers living in France. They even made their way to Indochina through the network of Vietnamese hands working for the Compagnie des Messageries Maritimes in Marseilles, inaugurating, in a sense, a new circuit of knowledge. Although Western scholars all claim that Nguyên Ai Quôc was not the sole author of the eight-point demand – Phan Van Truong, Phan Chau Trinh, Nguyên The Truyen and Nguyên An Ninh also contributed to its drafting – it was his name, in effect his 'signature' ('Pour le Groupe des Patriotes Annamites', on behalf of a reformist group of Annamite patriots led by the two Phan), that was affixed to the demands. His 'signature', so to speak, not only rendered him visible but also brought him undue attention. From that point on, he would be closely monitored by agents of the *Sûreté*, who recorded his movements during his entire stay in France, first to ascertain his true identity and, later, to monitor his contacts in France, Indochina and the Soviet Union.

The text of the demands was inspired by, if not modelled after, many such demands made by members of Irish, Indian and Korean nationalist groups, with whom members of the 'Groupe Annamite Patriote' were in close contact. In addition to the plea for a general amnesty for all political prisoners (Demand 1), it called for a complete overhaul of the judicial system in Indochina (Demand 2), freedom of the press and free speech (Demand 3), freedom of assembly (Demand 4), freedom to travel and emigrate (Demand 5), and the creation of technical schools in every part of the colonized territory (Demand 6). Most importantly, Demand 7 stipulates that the freedom and laws that apply in France be extended to French Indochina. In other words, the ideals of French democracy should constitute the basis for a new 'régime des lois', i.e. governance by law and no longer by arbitrary and abusive decrees, a democratic model that would protect the so-called native 'protégés' in French Indochina. The tone is conciliatory, more in keeping with the beliefs of moderate nationalists, i.e. the reformists who were not yet radicalized. It makes modest demands, entertaining the idea of change through parliamentary representation (Demand 8). But such conciliatory tone and reformist inflection ultimately mask more radical ideas, for it also introduces the key idea of self-determination, if not outright independence.

A 1919 'document' shows the remarkable transformation of Nguyên That Thanh (the would-be-student/immigrant who left Indochina in 1911 for Marseilles, with the intention of pursuing his studies at the École Coloniale in France) into Nguyên Ai Quôc (the Socialist militant and student of modern politics). This manuscript-letter, written in French, reveals the extent to which

Nguyên Ai Quôc had changed in a relatively short time. It may also shed light on the 'association'/'assimilation' debate: 'Je suis entièrement dénué de ressources et avide de m'instruire. Je désirerais devenir utile à la France vis-à-vis de mes compatriotes et pouvoir en même temps les faire profiter des bienfaits de l'instruction' [I am penniless and eager to learn. I would like to become useful to France in relation to my compatriots and to be able at the same time to permit them to take advantage of the benefits of education], he writes on 15 September 1911, from Marseilles. His avowed aim, then, was to be useful to France, to act as a 'bridge' and go-between between France and his people.[2] 'Paris, Capital of the Nineteenth Century', as Walter Benjamin put it so aptly, exerted quite a lure for young, privileged Vietnamese subjects who had been conquered by modernist ideas. Nguyên That Thanh's candidacy, however, was rejected. His entanglement with French culture would take him on a very different path from the one followed by members of the native bourgeoisie, i.e. those Vietnamese writers who came to France and wrote about it in the 1920s, and enjoyed the support of and were empowered by the colonial regime.

Quôc acknowledges the lure that France and French culture exerted on him in an interview he gave in French to Ossip Mendelstam, the great Russian modernist 'imagist' poet, in Moscow in 1923:

> Je suis originaire d'une famille annamite privilégiée. Chez nous, ces familles ne travaillent pas. Les jeunes gens étudient le confucianisme. Comme vous le savez, le confucianisme n'est pas une religion, mais plutôt une pratique basée sur l'expérience morale et sur les convenances. A sa base est la notion de paix sociale. Alors que je n'étais qu'un jeune garçon, à treize ans, j'ai, pour la première fois, entendu les mots français: Liberté, Egalité et Fraternité. J'ai eu envie de connaître la civilisation française, de sonder ce qui se cachait derrière ces mots. Mais, dans les écoles indigènes, les Français forment des perroquets. On nous cache les livres et les journaux, on nous interdit non seulement les écrivains contemporains, mais aussi Rousseau, Montesquieu Que pouvais-je faire? Je décidai de partir. […] J'avais dix-neuf ans. Lorsque je suis arrivé en France, il y avait des élections. Les politiciens bourgeois se couvraient mutuellement de boue. (Ruscio, 1990: 55).

I am from a privileged Annamite family. Where I come from, these families do not work. Young people study Confucianism. As you know, Confucianism is not a religion, but rather a practice based on moral experience and conventions. Underpinning it is the notion of social stability. When I was a young boy, at the age of thirteen, I heard for the first time the French words: Liberty,

---

2 See Quinn-Judge, 1993: 69 – 'Hô's linguistic skills made him a useful link between Asians and Europeans. He could communicate easily in French (although in written French he sometimes ignored verb conjugations), in haywire but expressive English, in passable Russian, and in Mandarin and Cantonese. His post [as the representative of the Comintern's Southern Bureau, in Hong Kong in 1929] gave him responsibility for liaising with the party branches in Malaya and Singapore, as well as in Thailand and Viêt Nam. (As the French had condemned him to death in 1929, he could not afford the risk of travelling to Viêt Nam).'

Equality and Fraternity. I wanted to know French civilization, to probe what was hidden behind these words. But, in indigenous schools, the French train parrots. Books and newspapers are hidden from us; we are forbidden access not only to contemporary authors but also to Rousseau, Montesquieu... What could I do? I decided to leave. [...] I was nineteen. When I arrived in France, elections were being held. Bourgeois politicians were slinging mud at each other.

His desire to know and question 'French civilization', to probe what is hidden behind the abstract concepts of 'liberty', 'equality' and 'fraternity', resembles the deconstructive strategies used by (post)colonial critics today. His critique of French colonial education and its debilitating effect on the natives also brings to the fore the question of modernity and the Enlightenment. Rousseau and Montesquieu, in the colonial logic of school administrators, were absent from the curriculum of the indigenous school. The colonial authorities feared, with good reason, that such potentially subversive literature could contaminate the natives' 'world view' and prompt them to action.

Image and mimcry

Let us now turn to a photograph of Nguyên That Thanh taken in France, capturing an Asian man dressed in Western fashion. This photograph elicited the following commentary from the French historian Daniel Hémery: 'Cette photographie montre le changement d'horizon mental de Nguyen Tat Thanh. Distance prise par rapport à sa propre culture, adoption des normes vestimentaires européennes, choix, en 1912, d'un prénom français: le regard assuré, affichant l'apparente aisance d'un élégant occidentalisé, Paul Tat Thanh flâne sur le pont Alexandre III' [This photograph reveals Nguyên That Thanh's complete mental transformation. Distance taken vis-à-vis his own culture, adoption of European dress codes, selection, in 1912, of a French first name: assured gaze, displaying the apparent ease of a Westernized elegant man, Paul That Thanh strolls on the Pont Alexandre] (1990: 40). Are we to believe, following Hémery's suggestion, that Nguyên That Thanh, now known as Paul, is a sophisticated *flâneur*, a francophile who has unproblematically adopted French culture – the assimilationist thesis – or, rather, is he masquerading as a colonial mimic (or camouflaging as a transcultural subject)? Mimicry, as Lacan has shown us, operates in very complex ways. Lacan, building on Roger Caillois's *Méduse et compagnie*, writes that:

[T]he major dimensions in which the mimetic activity is deployed [are] travesty, camouflage, intimidation.
　　Indeed it is in this domain that the dimension by which the subject is to be inserted in the picture is presented. Mimicry reveals something in so far as it is distinct from what might be called an *itself* that is behind. The effect of mimicry is camouflage, in the strictly technical sense. It is not a question

of harmonizing with the background but, against a mottled background, of becoming mottled – exactly like the technique of camouflage practised in human warfare.

In the case of travesty, a certain sexual finality is intended. Nature shows us that this sexual aim is produced by all kinds of effects that are essentially disguise, masquerade. [...]

Finally, the phenomenon known as intimidation also involves this over-valuation [sur-value] that the subject always tries to attain in his appearance. Here too, we should not be too hasty in introducing some kind of inter-subjectivity. Whenever we are dealing with imitation, we should be very careful not to think too quickly of the other who is being imitated. To imitate is no doubt to reproduce an image. But at bottom, it is, for the subject, to be inserted in a function whose exercise grasps it [s'insérer dans une fonction dont l'exercice le saisit]. (Lacan, 1981 [1973]: 99–100)

Building on Lacan's theories, Homi Bhabha describes the 'ambivalence of colonial mimicry' as 'a problematic of colonial subjection' (Bhabha, 1994: 85–92). Nguyên Ai Quôc, very early on, was keenly aware of the pitfalls of mimicry. His remark that indigenous schools merely trained 'parrots' makes this eminently clear. Nguyên Ai Quôc reveals this process in an acerbic fashion: in the second issue of *Le Paria* (1922), the journal he founded with Gaston Monnerville, Lamine Senghor and Messali Hadj, for instance, he wrote a very curious satirical piece under the title 'Zoology'. Composed in the manner of Buffon, and incorporating quotations from Darwin, it describes a strange animal endowed with a measure of 'imitative intelligence'. What really distinguishes the animal, however, is its 'fascinabilité extrême' [extreme fascinatability], which Quôc defines as follows: 'If you take the largest and strongest member of the herd and fasten a bright substance to its neck, a gold coin or a cross, it becomes completely docile This weird and wonderful animal goes by the name of *colonis indigeniae*, but depending on its habitat it is referred to as Annamese, Madagascan, Algerian, Indian...' The author observes in a postscript: 'In the near future we shall be introducing you to a closely related species, the proletarian' (Lacouture, 1968 [1967]: 38).

As I have tried to suggest, the 'subject that gives consistency to the picture' (Lacan, 1981: 97) cannot be understood in terms of the 'assimilation/integration' binary. And yet, this flawed conceptual framework continues to be the privileged mode of analysis. Duiker, for instance, describes Quôc's insertion into French space thus:

Nguyen Ai Quoc's straitened circumstances did not appreciably affect his life. He continued to attend political meetings regularly, to attend art shows, and to frequent the Bibliothèque Nationale. In the course of his activities, he met such celebrities as the singer-actor Maurice Chevalier and the short story writer Colette. According to police reports, he often entertained visitors, cooking dinners of green vegetables mixed with soy sauce, accompanied by jasmine tea, at a small stove on a table in the corner of his apartment. Although his salary left him with little excess after paying his monthly rent,

> he still managed to travel to various meetings around the country, suggesting
> that he was receiving a subsidy from the Communist Party. (Duiker, 2000: 77)

Such an account, whose apparent intent is to demystify Ho, on the contrary, mystifies. Duiker's glib description of Nguyên Ai Quôc's life and activities in France should be confronted with a number of sources to understand how social experience is narrativized and rearticulated in order to probe, in Bhabha's terms, 'the unequal and uneven forces of cultural representation involved in the contest for political and social authority within the modern world order' (Bhabha, 1994: 171). Let us begin with Ho Chi Minh's autobiographical re-presentation of his own life and activities in France. Of course, its reliability is in question in part because of its self-avowed propagandist aim:

> Usually he only worked half a day, earning some money in the morning and
> going to the library in the afternoon or attending political conferences. In
> the evening he attended the meetings which in Paris were fairly numerous.
> Here he made the acquaintance of such people as Léon Blum, Bracke, Vaillant-
> Couturier, Professor Marcel Cachin, Deputy Mac Saugnier, the novelist Colette
> etc. (Tran Dan Tien, 1967: 19; translated from the Vietnamese)

The testimonials written by his comrades – such as the one offered by Michel Zecchini, a former typographer working for *L'Humanité* and a member of the Socialist Party, who had become, after the end of the First World War, the representative of colonial revolutionaries to the Socialist Party – are also revealing. The very real material difficulties Nguyên Ai Quôc faced, and the many challenges he encountered during his six-year stay in France, are reinserted in Zecchini's account. The same details of Nguyên Ai Quôc's life in France have also been reported by police informants and Nguyên Ai Quôc's own original comrades. They differ markedly from Duiker's account of Quôc's life:

> En ce dur hiver de l'après-guerre Nguyên Ai Quôc se consacrait à travailler
> dans son logement du 9 de l'impasse Compoint qu'il avait transformé en
> atelier. Il avait installé un grand poêle à coke dans une alcôve minuscule qui
> lui servait de laboratoire, et nous le priions souvent de nous préparer des
> repas qu'il agrémentait de légumes verts arrosés de sirop de soja. Dans cet
> atelier, où nous venions le soir prendre le thé au jasmin, Nguyên Ai Quôc
> faisait des enseignes pour les commerçants du quartier et il enseignait aussi la
> calligraphie chinoise à des compatriotes qui travaillaient aux Halles. (Gaspard,
> 1992: 74)

> During this harsh post-war winter, Nguyên Ai Quôc devoted himself to
> working in his dwelling at 9, impasse Compoint, which he had turned into a
> workshop. He had installed a big coke stove in a tiny recess that he used as
> a laboratory, and we often asked him to make us meals, which he garnished
> with green vegetables sprinkled with soya sauce. In this workshop, where we
> came in the evening to drink jasmine tea, Nguyên Ai Quôc made signs for local
> shopkeepers and also taught Chinese calligraphy to his fellow countrymen
> who worked in the Halles.

In Duiker's account cited above, the cramped dwelling [logement] that also served as a workshop [atelier] has transformed itself, magically, into a comfortable 'apartment'; worker solidarity, in the form of the sharing of modest meals 'agrémenté de légumes verts', is described as the culinary art of 'entertain[ing] visitors'; and Nguyên Ai Quôc's insertion into French cultural and political life is seamlessly narrated as the activities of a dilettante who attends indiscriminately political meetings and art shows, and studies in the French national library; and of course, he enjoys meeting famous French 'celebrities', such as Colette and Maurice Chevalier. In brief, Nguyên Ai Quôc now seems to be enjoying the 'vie mondaine' of the French bourgeois who dabbles in politics, and entertains and travels for pleasure. I do not want to belabour my point. It suffices to say that Hayden White's lessons on the tropological nature of historical writing, which he compares to fictional writing, do not seem to have been heeded. Reports of police informants tell a very different story, and confirm Zecchini's account. An informant reports in February 1920: 'La vie matérielle de M. Quoc est lamentable; j'ai vu de mes propres yeux qu'il n'a pour dîner et souper qu'un morceau de pain, quelques tranches de saucisson et du lait' [Quôc's material conditions are atrocious; I have seen with my own eyes that for lunch and dinner he only has a piece of bread, a few slices of sausage and milk] (Gaspard, 1992: 88; Hémery, 1990: 48).

What Duiker seems to have completely elided in his representation of Nguyên Ai Quôc's encounter with modern France is the very notion of labour in all of its complex and multifaceted forms. Cheap labour was, undoubtedly, one of the primary reasons for bringing thousands of Vietnamese workers to France, these anonymous workers and nameless soldiers who were conscripted for the war effort. During the period 1914–18, of the 887,400 colonial subjects who had been enlisted to defend the 'mother country', 80,000 were Indochinese men. A further 350,000 colonial subjects worked in armament factories. A 1918 census report reveals that of the 36,715 Indochinese workers, 25,236 were illiterate. By 1 July 1919, only 60,000 Indochinese men remained in France. By 1 June 1920, that number had fallen to 19,000. Some 41,000 had been repatriated. Many scholars have underestimated these men's radical transformation after four years in France, and failed to recognize their role in the decolonization of Vietnam. *Tirailleurs*, workers, as well as students who were known as 'the returned', were indeed vectors of modernity. Their predicament illustrates perfectly what Bhabha has called the 'ambivalence of colonial mimicry'. Over the years, they undermined the power of the traditional mandarinate that collaborated with the French and their colonial order. I do not want, however, to minimize the deleterious role they also played. Nguyên Ai Quôc, long before Frantz Fanon, pointed to the fact that native troops had 'aidé le militarisme français à massacrer leurs frères du Congo, du Soudan, du Dahomey, de Madagascar. Les Algériens ont fait la guerre en Indochine. Les Annamites sont en garnison en Afrique. Et ainsi de suite' [aided French militarism in massacring their brothers from the Congo, the Sudan, from Dahomey, from Madagascar. Algerians fought in Indochina. Annamites are garrisoned in Africa. And on it goes] (Ruscio, 1990: 19).

Labour may take on myriad forms: the forced labour of workers in French ammunition factories or in the open-air Hongay mine; the toiling of the peasant in the fields, and so on. I contend that we need to reconsider Nguyên Ai Quôc's multifaceted French 'experience' in terms of this important concept of labour, and regard his writing as a transformative form of cultural labour: the colonial subject appropriates the master's language, and uses it very effectively as an instrument of cultural and political emancipation. Rather than see his inscription in French cultural space as a crowning achievement of the assimilated native, it would be more productive to regard it as a form of transculturation (Pratt, 1992), or as an ambivalent process of gathering cultural capital, to assert his place and engage forcefully with the issues of the time, aiming to transform and radicalize, for instance, the French Socialist Party's position on the colonial question, and in the long run, to embrace fully the Socialist political and cultural revolution.

On Nguyên Ai Quôc's political thought

By 12 October 1920, the French were getting closer as to who Nguyên Ai Quôc was, deploying all the resources available to them. Pierre Guesde, directeur adjoint du Cabinet du Ministre des Colonies, wrote the following report summarizing Quôc's political activities in France, 'recapitulant les principaux griefs des autorités françaises à l'encontre de Nguyên Ai Quôc, et retraçant les lignes maîtresses de son action' [summing up the main grievances of the French authorities regarding Nguyên Ai Quôc, and recounting the principal strands of his activity] (Gaspard, 1992: 107). He was particularly incensed by the fact that 'Il se mêle à notre politique, fait partie de groupements politiques, prend la parole dans des réunions révolutionnaires, et nous ne savons même pas en présence de qui nous nous trouvons!' [He meddles with our politics, belongs to political groups, speaks in revolutionary meetings, and we do not even know in whose presence we find ourselves!] (Gaspard, 1992: 108). French officials were irritated by Nguyên Ai Quôc's intervention in French public discourse, especially in the light of the fact that an Indochinese could not make such public pronouncements in his native land for fear of being condemned to a long prison sentence, or, more likely, of being summarily executed. Nguyên Ai Quôc illustrates how emergent histories may be written – a subaltern history *avant la lettre* that rewrites and provincializes French colonial history. In short, he intervenes in those ideological discourses of modernity from the margins.

This sketchy account should give a better sense of how Nguyên Ai Quôc penetrated French culture, and acquired a political culture. Duiker comments on the evolution of this twin movement:

> In 1920, Monsieur Nguyen began to attend regular meetings of the FSP and the General Confederation of Labor, as well as the Ligue des Droits de l'Homme, and to take an even more active role in political discussions. There are ample

signs, however, that he began to find the attitude of many of his colleagues exasperating. [The French Communist Party would not have a party line on the colonial question before 1924.] To Nguyên Ai Quôc, the central problem of the age was the exploitation of the colonial peoples by Western imperialism. He discovered that for most of his French acquaintances, colonialism was viewed as only a peripheral aspect of a broader problem – the issue of world capitalism. Marx had been inclined toward Eurocentrism, and most of his progeny in Europe had followed his lead. (2000: 63).

In his 'Rapport sur le Tonkin, l'Annam et la Cochinchine' (Moscow, 1924), Nguyên Ai Quôc writes: 'Marx a bâti sa doctrine sur une certaine philosophie de l'histoire, mais quelle histoire? Celle de l'Europe. Mais qu'est-ce que l'Europe? Ce n'est pas toute l'humanité' [Marx constructed his doctrine on a certain philosophy of history, but which history? That of Europe. But what is Europe? It is not the whole of humanity] (Ruscio, 1990: 70), adding his ongoing intention to '[r]éviser le marxisme, quant à ses assises historiques, l'affermir par l'ethnologie orientale' [overhaul Marxism, as far as its historical foundations are concerned, consolidate it with Oriental ethnology] (71). In a similar move to that of many left-leaning colonized intellectuals who would follow him, Nguyên Ai Quôc decided that Western-inspired communism was of limited use to him in passing through the necessary stage of anticolonial nationalism that would pave the way for independence.

The afterlives of Nguyên Ai Quôc/Ho Chi Minh

I began this essay with a blank photograph. I want to conclude with two further images of Nguyên Ai Quôc/Ho Chi Minh. The first is another photograph of Ho Chi Minh, displayed in the window of a video store in the city of Westminster, California, which caused quite an uproar, triggering massive demonstrations in 1999. Leaders of the Vietnamese community and their followers, distressed by the presence of the portrait of the Communist leader, demonstrated in large numbers, demanding that it be removed from the storefront. Boycotts, sit-ins and threats did not intimidate the Vietnamese owner who refused to comply. Even when threatening colour placards of Eddie Adams's 1968 photograph of Nguyên Ngoc Loan, South Vietnam's national police chief, executing a Viet Cong guerrilla, were pasted on walls of the city, and as far away as Los Angeles some 20 miles distant, the owner still would not submit to their demands. After weeks of confrontation, costing the city of Westminster an estimated $1 million in indirect costs (police, firefighters, etc.), the store was eventually closed down by the local police under the pretext that the owner had illegal, pirated copies of films that he rented to his customers, which constituted a major infringement on strict copyright laws. My aim in relating this incident is not to measure the degree of political maturity of the Vietnamese diasporic community (its members resolved the difference using legal means, albeit intimidating ones, rather than resorting to bodily harm and fatal violence). More importantly, it allows me to introduce and interrogate the logic by which the mere presence of a photographic portrait of Ho Chi Minh, in the largest Vietnamese community living outside Vietnam, can become the catalyst for massive demonstrations. Thirty years after Ho's death and a quarter of a century after the fall of Saigon, his 'image' still haunted the diasporic Vietnamese community in Southern California. It had the power to mobilize thousands of exiles who still regard him as the incarnation of communist evil, the icon of a brutal regime. The response of those who were displaced by force and suffered real hardship cannot be underestimated. For some, his portrait provoked recollection of traumatic events long suppressed, brought back into consciousness and to the fore. For others, his 'ghostly presence' caused a tempestuous emotional discharge that needed to be worked through and reveal that the work of mourning was still incomplete. But what are we to make of the reactions of young Vietnamese Americans, who were not even born when Ho died in 1969, and have, in fact, very little knowledge of who Ho was. It is therefore legitimate to ask who is the subject of this photograph? What aura surrounds the photograph, which may tell us as much about how Vietnamese Americans see the world? A series of questions beg to be asked: who is being represented on the photograph? Is it Uncle Ho, the fierce nationalist who liberated Vietnam from French colonialism and American imperialism, or Ho, the Communist leader who helped impose the dictatorship of the proletariat on a reunified Vietnam? Who is the man behind the mask of benevolence and humility?

Another 'image' of Ho might allow us to develop ways of answering these questions. His embalmed body is displayed in a mausoleum in Ba Dinh Square, the very site where he declared Vietnamese independence on 2 September 1945. Like Ho's embalmed body, the various photographs and texts (memoirs, drama, reportage and police reports that have been analysed in this chapter) produce a 'cultural image' of Ho Chi Minh. They memorialize it, and at the same time fix the image of a great patriot who devoted his entire life to the liberation of his nation, first from French colonialism, then from American imperialism. These texts strive to 'embody', i.e. make concrete and perceptible, his thoughts and ideas, to incarnate and personify the idealism of Vietnamese life, which Ho previously incarnated. I would argue that it is this very desire to 'fix' the man within an official nationalist discourse, a teleological sense of history, that betrays the intelligence of his thoughts and actions, a betrayal made all the more evident when Ho's desire to be cremated and his ashes dispersed, rather than be embalmed, is brought to the fore. My aim is to produce another (hi)story, a different and more dynamic representation of Ho that relies less on concepts such as mimesis and transparency and more on those of border-crossing, transgression and opacity. To put it more simply, my aim is to unravel the process of 'embalming' with all of its poetic and political resonances by privileging the notion of incineration (and trace).

The embalming process, treating a (dead) body so as to protect it from decay and decomposition, is a complicated one that involves filling a cadaver with balsamic, dessicative and antiseptic substances, which are applied to assure its preservation. The effects of the treatment are not permanent and it must be repeated annually. That expert technique remains the monopoly of the Russians, who jealously guard the secret of this process. And hence, once a year, Ho's body is flown to Russia to undergo extensive treatment and rehabilitation, so-called 'maintenance'. We can measure the irony of having built a monumental mausoleum as a place for entombment, as Ho's final resting place, and the yearly flight taken by Ho Chi Minh's corpse to Moscow. Once a year, Ho Chi Minh's mausoleum thus becomes a cenotaph, a tomb erected in his honour while his remains are elsewhere: Ho would certainly appreciate this irony.

In a figural sense, to embalm also means to safeguard and protect against oblivion and forgetting, dangers to which Ho Chi Minh is unlikely to fall victim in the near future, in Vietnam or in the rest of the world. But although his place in the pantheon of twentieth-century world historical figures is quite secure – albeit contested – his place and role as a seminal theorist of decolonization still need to be determined. This study forms an initial contribution to this process, highlighting the ways in which the anti-colonial critique that emerges from Ho's often polemical writings is constantly complemented by his impact as a dynamic political actor, the implications of whose actions have far-reaching consequences – as this chapter has suggested – for subsequent postcolonial thought. To embalm also means to lavish compliments, heap or shower (undeserved) praises upon someone. The physical preservation of Ho's fragile remains not only requires an enormous expenditure of state money, which would be better put to use elsewhere, but it also goes against his desire to be cremated. Furthermore, it facilitates and cultivates so great a devotion to Ho's person that it that borders on the cult of personality. Such blind devotion and naïve allegiance, although perhaps not unfounded or undeserved, nevertheless once again contradict Ho's desires and obscure his dynamic accomplishments. The main concern is to preserve the bodily integrity at all costs, in order that it retains its recognizable shape, but in the end it is legitimate to ask what has been lost in that refusal to incinerate, to disperse his ashes as he requested in his last will. It is also fair to ask to what extent the traces of his legacies are visible on his body. Lastly, I would also argue that this refusal to incinerate is also a refusal of the difficult and laborious work of mourning, a necessary step for moving forward.

Ho Chi Minh's mausoleum provides 'some stable, geometric, solid form [...] that guards the trace of death' (Derrida, 1991: 44), but it also 'guards life – the dead – in order to give rise to the for-itself of adoration' (46). Uncompromising adoration, stable knowledge, these mask the very essence of being of a man whose will to power relied on constant movement, border-crossings, and masquerade, and striving to overcome difficult challenges. Ho Chi Minh was a consummate 'homme de ce monde', whose hybridity illustrates, in even more complex ways, Bhabha's definition. Let us therefore continue to go on Ho Chi Minh's trail, on the many paths that have preserved his worldly traces.

Further reading

Duiker, William, 2000. *Ho Chi Minh: A Life* (New York: Hyperion). The author dedicated his nearly 700-page biography of Ho Chi Minh to the 'Vietnamese People'. This well-researched and readable epic biography dispels many myths of the man who was both a nationalist and a communist, and secures Ho Chi Minh's place as one of the most important political figures of the twentieth century.

Hémery, Daniel, 1990. *Ho Chi Minh: de l'Indochine au Vietnam* (Paris: Gallimard). This concise and highly informative book, by one of France's most perceptive historians of Vietnam, is essential reading for all those interested in French colonial Indochina. The last section of the book, entitled 'Témoignages et documents', provides a fascinating historical record of the emergence of modern Vietnam. Amply illustrated with archival photographs, maps, political cartoons, propaganda posters, autographed letters and so on, Hémery's text places Ho Chi Minh in a complex and rich visual culture.

Quinn-Judge, Sophie (2002). *Ho Chi Minh: The Missing Years 1919–1941* (Berkeley: University of California Press). Sophie Quinn-Judge's book fills an important gap in Ho Chi Minh scholarship. Using previously inaccessible documents from the Comintern archive in Moscow and French intelligence archives in Paris and Aix-en-Provence, the author not only traces Ho Chi Minh's physical journey from France to the Soviet Union, China, Germany, Siam and Singapore but also his activities as a Comintern agent and a staunch anti-colonialist, who played such a vital role in shaping early Vietnamese communism.

CHAPTER 8

Translating Plurality: Abdelkébir Khatibi and Postcolonial Writing in French from the Maghreb

Alison Rice

Born in El Jadida, Morocco in 1938, Abdelkébir Khatibi is the author of a diverse and complex oeuvre that creatively engages with the thought of European philosophers to address the specific challenges facing postcolonial subjects from the French-speaking world. After receiving a French education in his native country while it was still a protectorate of France,[1] Khatibi pursued university studies in sociology at the Sorbonne in Paris. When questioned about this period, the writer affirmed that the years he spent in the French capital, from 1958 to 1964, were characterized by 'great intellectual and political effervescence' (1999: 74). Unlike other French-speaking Moroccan writers of his generation who took up permanent residence in France, Khatibi returned to his native land, where he taught at the University of Rabat.[2] He published his doctoral dissertation on the Maghrebian novel, *Le Roman maghrébin* (1969), followed by the first of his fictional creations, an autobiographical novel titled *La Mémoire tatouée* (1971). In this early text, Khatibi delves into key themes that recur in his work, topics ranging from decolonization to the proper name, from religion to translation.

Khatibi's initial publications reveal leanings he held in common with other Moroccan writers of the period. He collaborated with prominent intellectuals such as Tahar Ben Jelloun, Driss Chraïbi and editor Abdellatif Laâbi on the foremost journal of Maghrebian culture, *Souffles*, a post-independence periodical in circulation from 1966 until 1972, when the Moroccan government shut it down. This collective publication provided a forum for these writers to grapple with crucial questions of language, acculturation, anti-imperialism and national belonging in the wake of French domination in their homeland. The desire to

---

1 The French protectorate lasted from 30 March 1912 until 2 March 1956, when France recognized the independence of the Kingdom of Morocco.
2 Abdelkébir Khatibi died in Rabat in March 2009 while this book was in the final stages of production.

break free from French cultural hegemony while still using the French tongue as a means of expression led many of them to adopt a particular strategy of 'violence' in their writing. They paradoxically sought at once to disrupt, or deconstruct, European and Moroccan traditions *and* remain faithful to them. Each writer employed different techniques, often combining various genres in the same text, in the hope of dismantling the colonial structures that had weighed upon them for so long.

Theoretical conceptions

One of the greatest contributions to postcolonial reflections on Algeria, Morocco and Tunisia – the three countries that make up the North African region referred to as the Maghreb – can be found in Khatibi's collection of essays, *Maghreb pluriel* (1983). The essays reflect the diversity of Khatibi's interests, with titles ranging from 'Orientalism' to 'sexuality' to 'bilingualism and literature' to 'art', topics Khatibi addresses from the particular standpoint of the Maghrebian thinker whose background (linguistic, cultural, political) is indeed 'plural'. The work opens with chapters devoted to two concepts that have become indispensable to critics concerned with this part of the French-speaking world: *pensée-autre* [other-thought] and *double critique*.

In order to introduce his understanding of 'other-thought', Khatibi quotes Martiniquan-born anti-colonial theorist Frantz Fanon and seizes upon his call to find 'something else', now that the 'European game' has come to a close (1983: 11). Khatibi seconds this call and clamours for another 'thought', an unprecedented way of conceiving difference. But he is careful to insist that the ambiguous 'European game' cannot be immediately eliminated from this quest for another way of thinking. In his view, the 'Occident' has come to inhabit the Maghrebian thinker, the 'West' has become a part of the Maghrebian's inner being (1983: 14), and all new thought must be placed in conversation with this world view. The 'other-thought' he promotes is therefore not a return to the 'inertie des fondements de notre être' [inertia of the foundations of our being] (1983: 12–13), but rather a questioning of the bases of Maghrebian societies that makes possible an engagement with the larger questions that make up our contemporary world. This 'other-thought' can only occur alongside a 'double critique' that critically examines the dual inheritance of Maghrebian intellectuals: that of the 'West' and that of 'notre patrimoine, si théologique, si charismatique, si patriarchal' [our heritage, so theological, so charismatic, so patriarchal] (1983: 12). Khatibi refuses to fall into a 'hégélianisme simplifié' [simplified Hegelianism], as he puts it. He avoids binary oppositions and advocates instead what he calls 'le risque de la pensée plurielle' [the risk of plural thought], the only appropriate disposition at 'le tournant de ce siècle sur la scène planétaire' [the turn of the century on the planetary stage] (1983: 14).

Khatibi's writing seems most influenced by those he terms 'our close contemporaries', such as Maurice Blanchot and Jacques Derrida (1983: 20), whose thought has provided the groundwork for Khatibi's own elaborations on crucial concepts such as identity and difference in a postcolonial context. Indeed, much of Khatibi's theoretical and poetic publications are not only influenced by but are also in dialogue with Jacques Derrida. This is evident in *Maghreb pluriel* when Khatibi draws inspiration from Derrida's conception of the deconstruction of Western metaphysics in his formulation of 'une décolonisation qui serait en même temps une déconstruction des discours qui participent [...] à la domination impériale' [a decolonization that would be at the same time a deconstruction of the discourses that participate [...] in imperial domination] (1983: 47–48). Khatibi points out that deconstruction 'a accompagné la décolonisation dans son événement historique' [accompanied decolonization in its historical event] (1983: 47–48, n. 1) and further underscores the similarities between the two movements in that they both deconstruct logocentrism and ethnocentrism. Khatibi reiterates this alliance between the terms in *La Langue de l'Autre*: 'J'ai toujours pensé que ce qui porte le nom de "déconstruction" est une forme radicale de "décolonisation" de la pensée dite occidentale' [I have always thought that that which carries the name 'deconstruction' is a radical form of 'decolonization' of so-called Western thought] (1999: 24).

It is worthy of note that Derrida also likens decolonization to deconstruction in his comments on teaching philosophy:

> Si elle est, comme la philosophie et la déconstruction philosophique, interminable, c'est que la décolonisation ne peut être effective ni sur le simple mode de la réappropriation ni sur le simple mode de l'opposition et du renversement. (1997: 161)

> If decolonization is unending, like philosophy and philosophical deconstruction, it is because it can be effective neither according to the simple mode of reappropriation nor according to the simple mode of opposition or reversal.

Khatibi's promotion of a 'double critique' that criticizes both 'la parole' [the word] of the Western world (1983: 48) and 'des discours élaborés par les différentes sociétés du monde arabe' [the discourses elaborated by different societies of the Arab world] (1983: 49) is indebted to the work of Derrida, especially *Writing and Difference*.

The foremost example of this long-standing conversation between Khatibi and Derrida can be found in the latter's oft-quoted *Monolingualism of the Other* (1998), a text originally composed for a conference on 'Francophonie' in 1992. In his comments, Derrida draws from Khatibi's innovative book-length prose poem, *Love in Two Languages* (1983), to address the historical and linguistic circumstances that characterized their respective childhoods in the Maghrebian countries of their birth. The son of Jewish parents in Algeria, Derrida knew no other language than French, yet he could hardly embrace this idiom from the far-off *métropole* as his 'mother tongue' (Derrida, 1998: 34); he places his situation in contrast to that of fellow 'Franco-Maghrebian' Khatibi, whose knowledge of Arabic (as well as Berber) made it possible for him to distinguish between the language of writing, French, and his native language, which he could refer to without hesitation as his 'mother tongue'. In this striking text on the particular challenges related to language and identity for the 'Franco-Maghrebian' whose childhood and adolescence precede decolonization, it is significant that Derrida should focus on *Love in Two Languages*: this is the only work of Khatibi to be translated into English to date.

What might prove particularly daunting to would-be translators of Khatibi's oeuvre could be the very plurality of his writing, evidenced by the insertion, or the irruption, of terms from a variety of languages in the French-language text. *Love in Two Languages* abounds with words and phrases from Arabic, Berber, Spanish and even Swedish, and repeatedly evokes a seemingly untranslatable concept, the *bi-langue*: 'Bi-langue? My luck, my own individual abyss and my lovely amnesiac energy. An energy I don't experience as a deficiency, curiously enough. Rather, it's my third ear' (1990a [1983]: 5). While no explanation is given for this hyphenated word that constitutes a stroke of luck and a source of energy for the first-person narrator in this quotation, other passages add to a composite understanding of the term: 'I baptised you: *bi-langue*. And now *pluri-langue*. To sum up, a question of translation' (1990a: 101); 'Love eliminates chance, obliterates time and eternity and, for a splendid finish, asks for a *pluri-langue*, mad thought and unmeasurable desire. This is how I translate you in my various transports' (1990a: 81). It seems that the bilingual lover who addresses his beloved in this book is completely caught up in, indeed, carried away by a *multilingualism* that is encompassed in these verbal creations, *bi-langue* and *pluri-langue*.

These coined words are often accompanied by declarations on *translation*, on the necessary linguistic transfers that characterize international travel, a theme that is present from the outset of Khatibi's writing career, but that emerges with great frequency in his later publications, beginning with *Un été à Stockholm* (1990b), continuing with *Pèlerinage d'un artiste amoureux* (2003) and culminating in *Féerie d'un mutant* (2005). In these kaleidoscopic works situated on the boundary between essay and fiction, Khatibi explores the multiple possibilities for travel thanks to modern technology and develops his conception of the 'professional foreigner' whose perpetual transnational movement is not a profession per se, but rather 'une position mobile dans le monde' [a mobile position in the world], characterized by continual border-crossings between 'langues, civilisations, marchés' [languages, civilizations and markets] (2005: 38–39). The principal protagonists in these rather recent books are inevitably proficient in a number of languages and their familiarity with a variety of tongues makes its way into the literary work. This linguistic plurality is what sets apart Khatibi's work from other texts that seem to adhere to a more limited bilingual, or even a monolingual model for postcolonial writing in French.

Language and criticism

Language is arguably at the centre of all of Khatibi's texts, even though his publications demonstrate a variety of interests ranging from calligraphy and Islamic art (*L'Art calligraphique de l'Islam*; *Du Signe à l'image*; *L'Art contemporain arabe*; *Le Corps oriental*) to poetry (*Le Lutteur de classe à la manière taoïste*; *Dédicace à l'année qui vient*), from religion (*Vomito Blanco*; *Le Même Livre*) to theatre (*Le Prophète voilé*), from literary criticism (*Figures de l'étranger dans la littérature française*) to sociology (*La Civilisation marocaine*). Khatibi begins all of his analyses from a linguistic standpoint and inevitably brings everything back to language, whether he is reflecting on sexuality, politics or religion. Even the body is conceived in linguistic terms: Khatibi refers repeatedly to the 'syntax of the body' that provides the rhythm for amorous interactions in *Love in Two Languages* (1990a: 19).[3]

His eloquent statements on language have attracted the attention of French-speaking literary critics such as Françoise Lionnet, who has drawn inspiration from Khatibi's oeuvre to make important statements about the 'appropriation' of French as 'a means of translating into the colonizer's language a different sensibility, a different vision of the world, a means, therefore, of transforming the dominant conceptions circulated by the more standard idiom' (1995: 13). Critics are not unanimous in their praise for Khatibi's work. While many have been eager to compliment *Maghreb pluriel* for its insights into the pluralities of the North African region, Winifred Woodhull laments that 'few of Khatibi's texts are historically and geographically grounded' (1993: xviii). John Erickson notes that 'the love object, the woman' in *Amour bilingue* 'is often confounded with language' (1998: 123), a point that Mireille Rosello agrees with when she elaborates on Khatibi's 'idealization' of 'the mother and the mother's tongue'; she argues that the writer thereby 'feminizes' the 'mother's tongue and forces us to envisage the encounter between the subject and his language as a heterosexual love affair between the man-speaker and the woman-language' (2005: 100). While this model is problematic, it can nonetheless be argued that the underlying concept of the *bi-langue* is so significant that it is the very example of the eponymous 'performative encounter' of Rosello's perceptive study: '*Bilingua* is an unstable and elusive nonspace, the tension between two languages. It is another name for a performative encounter' (2005: 78). Khatibi's formulations of the complex relationships between two, or among several, languages in postcolonial French-language texts from the Maghreb are his most compelling contribution to our present understanding of plurivocality and polyphony, of the 'traduction en marche' (1983: 201), the translation under way in contemporary Francophone postcolonial works.

3   In this text as in others, most notably *Le Livre du sang* (1979a), the writer introduces an androgynous figure, a being Khatibi describes as 'the other name of passion' (1999: 79). This figure might be interpreted as emblematic of Khatibi's ongoing effort to question binary oppositions and think outside categories such as male/female, man/woman to explore other identities, sexualities and expressions of love.

Translating tradition

In his textual explorations of love relationships between men and women in texts such as *Par-dessus l'épaule* (1988), Khatibi revived a French word that had fallen out of use: *aimance*, a term evoking 'affinités actives entre les aimants. Chaque aimant désire l'autre. [...] Au-delà des passions' [active affinities between those in love. Each lover desires the other. [...] Beyond passion] (1999: 80). This word recalls the great tradition of courtly love, according to the writer, and the dignified goal of transforming violent desire into a 'jeu mutuel du corps et de l'esprit' [mutual game of the body and mind] (1999: 81). The explanation Khatibi provides for his use of *aimance* could serve as a condensed elucidation of his written work in general. His attraction to the French language is often coloured by a violent colonial history, but the written game in which he engages aims to respect both the writer and the tongue of composition. A brief, in-depth exploration of the treatment of the proper name, language and religion in Khatibi's *La Mémoire tatouée* (1971) will reveal how Khatibi conceives of restoring dignity to potential cultural confrontations through an effective textual translation of his Islamic tradition.

In the opening passage of *La Mémoire tatouée*, the first-person narrator reveals that his first name, the name he acquired at birth, was determined by the religion of his people: 'Né le jour de l'Aïd el Kébir, mon nom suggère un rite millénaire et il m'arrive, à l'occasion, d'imaginer le geste d'Abraham égorgeant son fils' [Born the day of Aïd el Kébir, my name suggests a millenary rite and I happen, on occasion, to imagine the gesture of Abraham cutting his son's throat] (1971: 17). The importance of his name is underscored only a few pages earlier in the preface penned by the author: 'de là mon prénom Abdelkébir, serf du Grand, esclave de Dieu. Le Patriarche a doublement signé mon enfance, par le nom et la circoncision' [whence my first name Abdelkébir, serf of the Great One, slave to God. The Patriarch signed my childhood twice: by my name and by circumcision] (1971: 10). The emphasis in this passage on the double manifestation of what he calls his 'metaphysical destiny' is essential to the translation project of Khatibi's autobiographical novel. His entry into the world consisted of an entry into a *specific context*: his appellation and his body were determined according to religious tradition. Both require contextualization in the written work, but Khatibi chooses to present them in a very 'untraditional' manner.

The narrator's name reveals his ties to a specific system of belief, a system that must be translated for French-speaking readers who come from the other side of the 'déchirure nominale' [nominal tear] that characterizes Khatibi's relation to 'Orient' and 'Occident' (1971: 17). In the preface to *La Mémoire tatouée*, the author maintains in retrospect that this is one of the crucial philosophical themes that inspired and guided his autobiographical writing in this work: 'Comment ai-je délimité le champ autobiographique?... en dirigeant mon regard vers les thèmes (philosophiques) de ma prédilection: identité et différence..., simulacre de l'origine, blessure destinale entre l'Orient et l'Occident'

[How did I delimit the autobiographical field?... by directing my gaze to the (philosophical) themes of my predilection: identity and difference..., simulacra of origin, the wound between Orient and Occident] (1971: 11). The use of the word 'wound' in this reference to the division between East and West recalls Khatibi's theoretical text, *La Blessure du nom propre* (1974), a title which returns to the initial tearing: 'Je fus sacrifié en venant au monde, et ma tête fut, en quelque sorte, offerte à Dieu' [I was sacrificed in coming into the world, and my head was, in some way, offered to God] (10). This decapitation, this crucial 'cutting off' of an essential, indeed *the* essential body part from the rest, finds its corporeal parallel in the rite of passage known as circumcision.

Circumcision marks the second great instance of the 'Patriarch's signing' of the protagonist's childhood, according to the opening passage. As in the case of the name, very little formal explanation is given. The narrator does not take time to 'set up' the scene and does not give any commentary on the preparations for the momentous event. Instead, the action occurs suddenly and unexpectedly with the following words: 'Regarde les fleurs au plafond; je regardai et mon prépuce tomba' [Look at the flowers on the ceiling; I looked and my prepuce fell] (1971: 36). The 'wounding' of the proper name that occurred at birth has now manifested itself physically in the parallel 'wounding' of the body through circumcision. This ritual is not explained or justified for a foreign readership; it is simply *transposed* in all its vertiginous fury into the French language. The translation in this text takes place not only on a *semantic* level, but also, and more importantly, on the level of *syntax*. Exclamation and question marks pepper this passage, connoting the excitement of the scene and creating a rhythm that communicates the whirlwind of emotions behind the action.

Perhaps the most fruitful translation of Islamic tradition in *La Mémoire tatouée* occurs in passages that juxtapose the colonizers and the colonized in Morocco. The life of the French varied noticeably from the life of the Moroccan 'natives' under the protectorate. The narrator underscores the ways Sundays were different for the French in North Africa: 'Un dimanche pied-noir était un autre dimanche: tangos, valses grognantes, puanteur douce, alcools trop agressifs pour mon débordement' [A pied-noir Sunday was a different type of Sunday: tangos, groaning waltzes, sweet stench, alcoholic beverages too strong for my excesses] (1971: 43). The debauchery of the French is clearest in the consumption of products off-limits to those who adhere to the teachings of the Muslim tradition: 'Scintille une belle femme, donnée à un militaire français, tout rouge et tout rond. A cause du porc et du vin, me disait-on. Dieu engraisse-t-il les mécréants pour les mieux rôtir?' [A beautiful woman sparkles, given to a French military man who is all red and round. Because of the pork and the wine, they tell me. Does God fatten up the unbelievers to roast them all the better?] (1971: 43). This humorous reflection intimates the interdict on pork and alcoholic beverages in Islam without stating it outright, in line with the fashion of the writing throughout this text. The differences in appearance between the French and the Moroccans are attributed to dietary variants that translate disparate lifestyles and points of view.

The clear contrasts between the French and the Moroccans come to a head in the different educational systems the narrator describes in *La Mémoire tatouée*. The young protagonist attends Koranic school for a certain length of time: 'On me demanda de m'exercer à la calligraphie, parce qu'elle mène, nous répétait le fiqh, droit au paradis' [I was asked to practice calligraphy, because it leads, the *fiqh* repeatedly told me, straight to paradise] (1971: 39). References to 'paradise' are nowhere to be found, however, in the secular institution to which the boy's father sends him in 1945: 'A l'école, un enseignement laïc, imposé à ma religion... Où, dans ce chassé-croisé, la cohérence et la continuité?' [At school, a secular teaching imposed on my religion... Where, in this criss-cross, were coherence and continuity?] (64). The continuity between the initial education in the Qur'an and French secular instruction is to be found in the *language* of his writing, the narrator concludes (67). The music and the rhythm of Khatibi's work is the first echo of the writer's early exposure to the Book: 'Arbre de mon enfance, le Coran dominait ma parole alors que l'école, c'était une bibliothèque sans le Livre. Chant d'abord, le Coran s'apprend par Coeur' [Tree of my childhood, the Qur'an dominated my word while school was a library without the Book. Initially conceived of as song, the Qur'an is to be learned by heart] (1971: 67).

As a student in a secular French school system, the boy sought at first to 'annihilate' himself; he deliberately dissimulated his background in order to assimilate to his surroundings. This effort at what Khatibi terms 'pâle décolonisation' was effective: 'On m'acceptait parce que j'étais semblable, annihilant d'avance toute mon enfance, toute ma culture' [They accepted me because I was similar, annihilating in advance my entire childhood, my entire culture] (124). But this self-effacement did not last long, for the culture of the Qur'an ultimately commanded respect and emerged in the writing, even in the adopted French tongue: 'car le Coran se faisait respecter; là où il gisait, il se chantait à l'intérieur et à l'extérieur. La parabole, le proverbe et la bonne nouvelle arrangeaient... notre culture' [for the Qur'an made itself respected; there where it lay, it sang inside and outside. The parable, the proverb and the good news made up... our culture] (1971: 77). Multiple mentions of the Qur'an and other founding texts in Arabic like *The Thousand and One Nights* reveal a *conscious* indebtedness to this literary and cultural tradition; the insertion of parables, proverbs, poetry and anecdotal passages demonstrates indebtedness to this tradition *on another level*. The inclusion of these elements in the French text may not always be 'conscious' but may instead manifest a deep inner attachment to what has been imprinted on the heart.

The narrator makes reference to a 'double identity' throughout *La Mémoire tatouée*. From the very beginning, the young protagonist is marked by a 'dédoublement' (17), a 'dividing' or 'splitting' epitomized through the division of his life into Orient and Occident. In his analysis, this 'double' influence and temporal scission are a source of wealth in writing: 'la parabole coranique... figure la mémoire d'une identité, que le savoir peut redoubler dans quelque rhétorique contemporaine' [the parable of the Qur'an... figures the memory of an identity, that knowledge can redouble in some contemporary rhetoric] (198–99). The insertion of the new verb, *redoubler,* in this passage is very significant, for it marks an evolution in the conception of the 'double identity' mentioned throughout the book. Instead of focusing on a 'splitting in two', with negative connotations of division between different cultures and traditions, the import of *'redoubler'* is entirely other, carrying with it the ideas of 'increasing', 'intensifying', 'redoubling' and 'reduplication'. Instead of conceiving of his cultures as divided neatly in two, the narrator embraces the pluralities of *both* Orient and Occident in the following reflection: 'je lutte contre tous les occidents et orients qui m'oppriment ou me désenchantent' [I struggle against all the occidents and orients that oppress or disenchant me] (118). Engaging in a struggle against the oppressive aspects of his tradition *and* Western thought is an enterprise Khatibi undertakes in *La Mémoire tatouée* by subtly translating the positive and negative aspects of his 'native' culture into the French text. He does not take sides, or aim to assert the supremacy of one culture and accompanying world view over another; he does not seek to expose *only* the pejorative aspects of his Moroccan homeland for the French reader. His project is more complicated, because it begins with and returns to a complicated subject: the self.

The narrator of *La Mémoire tatouée* ultimately shows that he cannot simply be labelled as *split*: 'Certes, Occident, je me scinde, mais mon identité est une infinité de jeux, de roses de sable' [Indeed, Occident, I split myself, but my identity is an infinity of games, of roses of sand] (187). Characterized not by *two* competing factions, but by a *multitude* of orients and occidents, the individual evoked in Khatibi's autobiographical fiction is multiple and varied, just like the written text. The person, like the book, is marked by an 'infinity of games' that incorporate Arabic language (and) practice into written French. Ultimately faithful to *both* cultures, the Francophone Moroccan wordsmith 'literally' makes his mark, permanently inscribing Islamic custom and tradition on the Occident: 'Je tatoue sur ton sexe, Occident, le graphe de notre infidélité' [I tattoo on your sex, Occident, the graph of our infidelity] (189). A common theme in Khatibi's work, the tattoo brings together the *body* and *writing* in evocative, provocative ways. In his essay on 'The Oriental Body', Khatibi describes the tattoo as an 'indelible trace' (2002: 67). This form of corporeal inscription infuses the French-language written work with an 'oriental' practice, placing a potentially lasting imprint of this 'Orient' on the 'Western' literary text.

Postcolonial *Francophonie* and intercontinental quest

In his collection of essays, *La Langue de l'Autre* (1999), the title of which constitutes an obvious reply to Derrida's aforementioned publication, Khatibi maintains that the French language *adopted* him, just as he adopted *it* (66). He takes advantage of the opportunity to translate what he has already argued about the Maghreb in particular to embrace a much larger entity: '[L]e monde francophone est métissage, mixité avec des bilinguismes et des multilinguismes divers. C'est une loi de la langue, de s'entretenir avec une autre ou d'autres, de se brouiller avec, de se confondre avec' [The French-speaking world is characterized by *métissage*, by a mixing with diverse bilingualisms and multilingualisms. It is a law of language to engage with and become mixed up with, even confused with, other languages] (1971: 66). Khatibi explains that it seems that he has greater freedom than writers of French origin, since this tongue is not his 'property', not his direct inheritance but rather was 'imposed' upon him. But he claims that he has left behind a 'submissive' relationship to this language he loves. It is evident in his final texts that he was forever pushing the limits, proving himself to be a truly 'decolonized' writer in the fullest sense of the term, a world traveller whose concerns extend far beyond a bilateral relationship between the homeland and the former *métropole* to the pursuit of an 'intercontinental quest' (1990a: 98). Khatibi's latest work proves open to the future of writing and its dissemination in an increasingly technological world, as is evidenced by passages such as this: 'Je brancherai ce livre sur une chaîne *intermédia* avec un jeu d'interfaces; journaux, radios, photos, télés, chansons et traductions stratégiquement lancées sur le marché international' [I will plug this book into an *intermedia* system that is connected to a whole range of communications: newspapers, radios, photos, televisions, songs and translations strategically thrown into the international market] (1990b: 101). Khatibi continually created new impressions of the 'professional foreigner' (1990b: 84) whose transcribed, transported body signs an innovative oeuvre that made a meaningful mark, perhaps even leaving an indelible trace, in the contemporary literary realm. For Khatibi obeyed the injunction articulated in his novel *Un été à Stockholm*: 'Pour chaque moyen de transport, il faudrait inventer un genre littéraire' [For each mode of transportation, we must invent a literary genre] (1990b: 100).

Further reading

Bensmaïa, Réda, (2003). *Experimental Nations: Or, the Invention of the Maghreb* (Princeton, NJ, and Oxford: Princeton University Press). This work places Khatibi's writing in historical perspective. *Love in Two Languages* divides the 'history and thinking of North African writing into a before and after', by creating a textual space in which Arabic and French can 'meet without merging', forming an unusual translation and breaking free from a 'Manichean vision' of language and identity.

Erickson, John, 1998. *Islam and Postcolonial Narrative* (Cambridge: Cambridge University Press). This study considers language 'at the threshold of the untranslatable' in Khatibi's work, focusing on *Love in Two Languages* to demonstrate how this text 'replaces' 'master narratives' with 'games of dialogical invention' and 'glossophilic verbal play', resulting in a postcolonial 'narrative marked by indeterminacy, variability, and endless permutation' that 'rewrites the language of power'.

Rice, Alison, 2006. *Time Signatures: Contextualizing Contemporary Francophone Autobiographical Writing from the Maghreb* (Lanham, MD: Lexington Books). This work examines translation, movement and multilingualism in Khatibi's oeuvre in an effort to discern the *musical* underpinnings of his various texts. It maintains that, in harmony with Khatibi's own comments on 'identity' and 'linguistic hospitality', the 'status of the

Francophone postcolonial subject is not limited or limiting', but, rather, is 'only a starting point' from which to explore 'multiple horizons'.

Rosello, Mireille, 2005. *France and the Maghreb: Performative Encounters* (Gainesville: University Press of Florida). This book fluidly incorporates into its arguments the concepts of 'Khatibian "love in two languages"', 'the Khatibian third ear', and the plurality of the Maghreb, claiming that 'contemporary authors' have 'internalized the possibilities and difficulties' of Khatibi's *bi-langue* and are now 'moving on and providing us with new models' in their writing.

Woodhull, Winifred, 1993. *Transfigurations of the Maghreb: Feminism, Decolonization, and Literatures* (Minneapolis: University of Minnesota Press). The Introduction concentrates predominantly on Khatibi and his conceptions of pluralizing, or decolonizing, the Maghreb. This analysis identifies 'his notion of the *bi-langue*' as 'indispensable' to 'the interpretation of Maghrebian literary texts written in French', because many of these texts exemplify 'what Khatibi calls *identités folles*, mad identities that resist the constraints of a dualistic sex-gender system, as well as those of other bounded systems such as language, nation and culture'.

CHAPTER 9

Albert Memmi:
The Conflict of Legacies

Patrick Crowley

The necessity of self-renewal is as obvious as the ambiguity involved. While the colonized's revolt is a clear attitude in itself, its contents may be muddled; for it is the result of an unclear situation – the colonial situation.
(Memmi, 2003 [1957]: 180)

Since the publication of his first novel, *The Pillar of Salt* (1953), Albert Memmi has offered textual portraits that bring the discomforting perspective of his *vécu* [lived experience] to bear upon discourses, practices and legacies of domination. In particular, and not surprisingly, Memmi's name often appears alongside those of critics of colonization such as Aimé Césaire, Frantz Fanon and Jean-Paul Sartre (for discussion of these writers, see Chapters 1, 5 and 11 of this volume). Jean-Marc Moura provides a typical example of this when he writes that the work of Memmi, Césaire and Fanon constitute 'les essais de combat' [the essays of struggle] (2007 [1999]: 69) of Francophone anti-colonial writing. In terms of intellectual legacy, Robert Young argues that since 'Sartre, Fanon and Memmi, postcolonial criticism has constructed two antithetical groups, the colonizer and colonized [...], a false Manichean division that threatens to reproduce the static, essentialist categories it seeks to undo' (1995a: 5). Yet even as Memmi's work is acknowledged, it is more often than not largely unread or summarily read. For though Memmi's work offers a trenchant critique of colonialism, far from constructing a simple binary opposition between colonizer and colonized it has consistently brought attention to the cultural imbrications that result from the colonial situation.

Memmi has sought to interrogate issues of domination and difference through his critiques of colonial society, his anatomy of racism and his treatment of issues such as displacement and alienation, nationalism and freedom, cultural assimilation and its limits. His work gestures towards reconciliation (at the very least, self-reconciliation) and social justice, but it also points to, and is symptomatic of, the impossibility of complete assimilation and the difficulties of acculturation. Though much of Memmi's work has commented on the erasure of cultural differences within Western humanist claims, more recently he has argued that immigrant communities in France need to integrate, even at the cost of their 'difference'. In all of this, Memmi's work bears witness to ambivalence: his early work analyses its manifestations within colonial society but his critique, then and since, betrays its own ambivalence.

Portraits and self-portraits

Memmi's literary work and psycho-sociological essays draw upon autobiographical experience and work it into ideal types or portraits. Given his emphasis on the *vécu*, commentators on his work tend to focus on its autobiographical dimension (Dugas, 2001; Strike, 2003). Memmi encourages such readings in his texts and in his use of paratextual commentaries such as prefaces and postscripts. Indeed, any extensive treatment of Memmi's work involves, or results in, a familiarity with the context of Memmi's life, or rather that part of it that he chooses to refract within essays and fictional forms.

It is the *vécu* of his childhood and early adulthood that form the principal matter of his explorations. Memmi was born in 1920 and lived, initially, on the edge of the Jewish quarter (the *hara*) in French colonial Tunis. His father was an artisan, a saddler, and his mother, who was illiterate, spoke only Judeo-Arabic, a dialect of Arabic spoken within the Jewish community. Memmi's early education began in a traditional Jewish school (a *kouttab*) and continued in the Alliance Israelite school, which combined Jewish studies and elements of the French curriculum. He received a scholarship from a benefactor to attend the Lycée Carnot, before taking up university studies in Algiers, which were interrupted by the Second World War. During the war he was interned by the German army and sent to a work camp for Tunisian Jews. After the war he went to Paris to continue his studies at the Sorbonne, where he took classes in philosophy. In 1951 Memmi married, and he and his French wife returned to Tunis, where he taught philosophy and literature. In 1952 Memmi helped found the Centre de Psychopédagogie de Tunis (Tunis Centre for Psychopedagogy), and his work there played a role in his understanding of the psychic effects of oppression. Memmi supported the cause of Tunisian nationalism, but he left Tunisia to return to France in 1956, after the country received full independence, and affirmed a distinctly Arabic-Muslim identity. In France he held a number of academic positions, teaching in prestigious third-level institutes such as the École des Hautes Études Commerciales and the École Pratique des Hautes Études, before being appointed to the University of Paris X as Professor of Sociology in 1970 (Roumani, 1987: 14–17). Since then, Memmi has continued to write sociological essays and literary works that draw upon his store of experience, always already culturally mediated, which he examines with the kind of rational scruple he admired in the French *philosophes*.

127

His first novel, *The Pillar of Salt*, is semi-autobiographical and has attracted much attention in France for exploring the perspective of an acculturated *indigène* [native]. The narrator of this *bildungsroman*, Alexandre Mordekhai Benillouche, offers an insight into the experience of living and growing up in the Jewish *hara*, of being drawn to French thought and values within a colonial context. This intellectual identification with French culture brings the youth into conflict with his father's traditional Judeo-Arabic values and the novel is marked by a sense of disenchantment. The protagonist leaves for Argentina, yet throughout the novel acknowledges the impossibility of himself fleeing: 'In the long run, I would always be forced to return to Alexandre Mordekhai Benillouche, a native in a colonial country, a Jew in an anti-Semitic universe, an African in a world dominated by Europe' (2001: 95–96).

This passage comes at the end of a lengthy consideration of the protagonist's attempt to negotiate between different cultures from a position of apparent weakness. Memmi's Jewish upbringing in Tunisia has largely determined his sense of difference and his unsettled notion of identity, torn as he was between traditions (Jewish and Arabic) and modernity, between identifying with the colonizer or with the colonized. The result is an entanglement of cultures, rather than a clear binary opposition that demands the exclusion of one over the other. As he writes in his 1965 preface to *The Colonizer and the Colonized*: 'I was a sort of half-breed of colonization, understanding everyone because I belonged completely to no one' (2003 [1965]: 12). The tensions inherent in such an identity were confirmed when he returned to Tunisia with his French wife in the 1950s, and the difficulties of a mixed marriage inform his second novel, *Strangers* (1955).

Memmi's capacity for rational critique is brought to the fore in *The Colonizer and the Colonized*. Its forensic analysis of the colonial situation remains pertinent, fresh and acute today. Memmi offers portraits of the colonized and colonizer and analyses their relationship as one based on maintaining the illegitimately acquired economic privilege of the colonizer. Memmi demonstrates the contradictions of colonial practice and thought and delineates the ways in which the structure of colonization ties colonizer and colonized together, even as it deforms both parties.

The function of Memmi's portraits is to provide a rational critique of the mythological portraits of the colonized and the racial stereotypes that emerged from the colonial situation. In this way his work emphasizes the role of cultural analysis in undermining colonial ideology (see Gearhart, 1998). Memmi's portraits steer a course between assessing the economic conditions of colonization and the psychological impact on the individual. He draws on the notion of interiorization in his depiction of the psychic effects of colonization on both colonizer and colonized. Interiorization is important to what he calls the 'Nero Complex', that is, the colonizer's sense of guilt and anxiety, which results from having usurped the rights of others. It leads the colonizer to perform acts that seek, in vain, to justify or reinforce the illegitimate. The colonizer needs to salve his conscience by praising the *oeuvre coloniale* [colonial endeavours] and denigrating the colonial subject, whose gaze is, nevertheless, a constant reminder of the colonizer's illegitimacy and cannot be eradicated but only kept at a distance. Turning his attention to the colonized, Memmi argues that there is no hope of integration into colonial society, for assimilation is perceived by the colonizer as imitation: 'the shrewder the ape, the better he imitates, and the more the colonizer becomes irritated' (2003: 168). Ultimately, the colonizer requires difference in order to sustain the logic of colonial domination. Cultural assimilation cannot succeed and the cost, for the colonized person who attempts this, is guilt and self-alienation.

Memmi's analysis makes it clear that the contradictions of colonial society can only be resolved through revolt and the collapse of colonialism. Change, argues Memmi, will not be brought about by left-wing colonizers who reject colonization because their choice is 'not between good and evil, but between evil and uneasiness' (2003: 87). For Memmi, the socialist activist in the colony cannot reconcile the need for struggle with the means of struggle: terrorism and the galvanizing discourses of nationalism and religion. Memmi espouses the nationalist struggle, but sees it as a stepping stone along the path to a deeper cultural transformation. Sartre, in his introduction to *The Colonizer and the Colonized*, optimistically highlighted how colonial repression could be transformed into anti-colonial revolt: 'A people's misfortune will become its courage; it will make, of its endless rejection by colonialism, the absolute rejection of colonization' (2003: 25). Memmi's position is more nuanced. His attention to the psychological dimensions of colonization convinced him of the impossibility of a clean break with the past and of the dangers inherent in identitarian approaches to liberation that emphasized nationalism and religion, once independence had been achieved. He looks beyond the end of colonization: 'The liquidation of colonization is nothing but a prelude to complete liberation, to self-recovery' (2003: 195). Indeed, Memmi makes it clear that the negative legacy of colonization would have an afterlife beyond the demise of empire.

The Colonizer and the Colonized had an important impact beyond Tunisia. Published during the Algerian War of Independence (1954–62), Memmi's text was among the first to present the French reader with the viewpoint of the colonized. It also attracted attention beyond North Africa. Québecois writers, such as Gaston Miron and Hubert Aquin, drew from Memmi's analysis of culture and colonialism to advance Québécois claims for independence. Marilyn Randall contends that 'most critics would situate the postcolonial moment in French Canada during the period of the Quiet Revolution (1960–70), when young intellectuals in Quebec discovered and circulated the writings of Albert Memmi' (2003: 77). However, in a lecture given at the Université de Montréal in 1967, Memmi avoided using the word 'colonialism' and emphasized instead the issue of domination with regard to relations between Canada's Anglophone majority and the Francophone settler minority. (See Chapter 20 for discussion of this incident from the Quebec perspective.)

During this period Memmi pursued his literary path by once more returning to the dilemmas of his youth. *The Scorpion or the Imaginary Confession* (1969) departs from the linear forms of his earlier novels. The narrator, Marcel, is a Tunisian eye specialist, who is trying to sort out the mix of literary papers belonging to his brother, Emile/Imilio, who has disappeared. The novel is made up of sections of the narrator's brother's novel, diary entries and the fragments of an unfinished chronicle. The narrator's commentaries add a further layer of complication to the novel's interweaving of generic forms: 'Come on Narcissus, let's get back to our puzzle: where does this passage belong? With the Journal, or the Novel?' (1971a [1969]: 9). Memmi's play with generic boundaries is experimental, but the contents and themes are familiar: conflict between father and son, the attractions and deceptions of European thought, the richness of oriental cultures and the disappointment with a decolonized Tunisia that offers little space for the Tunisian Jew. *The Scorpion* dramatizes the attempt to overcome domination – here associated with a violent and traditional father – and the trauma of modernity's passage beyond metropolitan France, as well as the traces of that passage. Like much of Memmi's fiction, *The Scorpion* is saturated with autobiographical allusions. The work contains a number of photographs of Tunis and one of a Roman medal that bears the name 'Memmi'. The narrator, here and elsewhere in Memmi's fictions, makes reference to this medal and pursues possible genealogies and histories of the name. Yet even as the content draws us towards the referent of the author, the text pursues its liberty within generic play and obvious fictions. And though Memmi's own history, real and imaginary, remains intratextually present in his later, more conventional novels *Le Désert* (1977) and *Le Pharaon* (1988), here again, Memmi refuses to allow the autobiographical to be the only ground for interpretations of his work.[1]

The mark of difference

Memmi's novels are also almost always primarily concerned with the mediation of difference. The narrator of *The Scorpion*, for example, offers the initial brush-strokes of a portrait of Uncle Maklouf who seeks wisdom within the 'Cabala, from the Mishna, from the Sages, but always linking everything together perfectly' (1971a: 47). Indeed, the question of interpretation and adjudication between different forms of knowledge is often brought to the fore. The narrator wonders 'How can these degrees [of truth] and these differences be expressed in a common language? [...] Always the need to have a key' (1971a: 51). The novel can be read as a further attempt by Memmi to grapple with the experience of negotiating between differences and of affirming one's own. At one point we read: 'Cultivate your difference if you can, it's all you have left... Ah, if you only can!' (1971a: 201).

This issue of difference is as important to Memmi's work as his critique of

---

1   *Le Désert* is the story of Jubaïr Ouali El-Mammi, a distant, if fictional, ancestor of the author who travels across North Africa at the beginning of the fifteenth century in search of his kingdom, only to find his real kingdom lies within. *Le Pharaon* is set in Tunis in the years preceding independence.

oppression (whether colonial, racist or anti-Semitic) and it offers an insight into the evolution of his thought. In *Le Nomade immobile*, published some 30 years after *The Scorpion*, Memmi recalls what he had written in *Portrait of a Jew*: 'Être, c'est être différent' [To be is to be different] (2000b: 165). Memmi subsequently offered his own hermeneutic key. At a conference in Cologne in 1991 he commented that: 'La clé de toute mon oeuvre c'est l'humanisme. Il faut respecter la vie comme elle est et les hommes comme ils sont' [The key to my entire work is humanism. One must respect life as it is and men as they are] (cited in Strike, 2003: 137). Much of Memmi's work appears to advocate a humanism that engages with and foregrounds difference, rather than effacing it. In challenging an abstract universalism Memmi reminds us that humanism is a project grounded in its own specific tradition despite its attempts to erase the force of traditions beyond itself.

In this respect, Memmi's views on Fanon's relationship to the particularities of his Martiniquan *vécu* are illuminating and have attracted the attention of postcolonial critics such as Ania Loomba. Loomba favourably cites Memmi's view that Fanon's radical universalist humanism and identification with the Algerian cause was a function of his cultural alienation, in short, his rejection of Martiniquan culture and his failure to assimilate into French society (Loomba, 1998: 147). Memmi, in his reading of Fanon's life, privileges the life over the work and critiques what he describes as Fanon's false universalism and abstract humanism on the grounds that they 'reposent sur une négligence de toutes les spécificités, de toutes les particularités sociales intermédiaires' [rely upon a neglect of all specificities, of all intermediate social particularities] (1971b: 269). Memmi sees no way round particularity: 'Car, enfin, l'homme universel et la culture universelle sont faits d'hommes particuliers et de cultures particulières' [For, in the end, universal man and universal culture are made of particular men and particular cultures] (1971b: 269). Memmi's position on Fanon is unequivocal: any aspiration towards the universal (and humanism) must first involve an acceptance of the particularities of one's own *vécu*. Memmi insists on the importance of coming to terms with a *vécu* informed by cultural differences that cannot always be reconciled. He rejects Fanon's belief in violence, seeing it as a refusal to mediate with the past and as a misguided hope in revolution. Instead Memmi works with what is at hand; for him there is neither tabula rasa nor utopian horizon but a rational consideration of the state of things as they are. Memmi refuses to translate his version of a colonial *vécu* into a justification for a practice of rupture and radical transformation. One cannot escape the particularity of one's past just as one cannot escape the circumcized mark that links him to what he calls 'the Orient'.

The protagonist of *The Pillar of Salt* remarks 'Can I ever forget the Orient? It is deeply rooted in my flesh and blood, and I need but touch my own body to feel how I have been marked for all time by it. As though it was all a mere matter of cultures and of elective affinities!' (2001: 169).[2] The critical importance of

---

2 As he makes clear in the autobiographical work *Le Nomade immobile* (2000b), Memmi

this affiliation to Memmi's thought cannot be understated; his Jewish heritage was central to his upbringing and the Arab-Israeli wars of 1948–49, 1956, 1967 and 1973–74 informed his work and led him to adopt a clear position on the question of Israel. In his *Portrait of a Jew* (1962) and *The Liberation of the Jew* (1966), Memmi returns to his Jewish legacy through the heuristic device of the portrait and makes the case for a Jewish state. In portraying the Jew, Memmi emphasizes unhappiness and humiliation: 'Only the territorial solution, a free people on a free territory – a nation – is an adequate solution to the fundamental and specific deficiencies in the Jewish condition' (1966: 294). Memmi's position on Israel chimes with his early espousal of Arab nationalism and his rejection of what he would see as the utopian, internationalist vision of Marxism. It should be added that Memmi's unambiguous Zionism has always insisted on the need for Israel to attend to the rights of Palestinians and, further, he has written that 'sooner or later the *national dimension* of the Palestinians will have to be taken into consideration' (1975 [1974]: 139). Memmi's recurring theme is that of justice and the need to counter practices of domination, yet, though he raises the issue of a Palestinian 'national dimension', there is no deep engagement with the issues involved, such as territorial limits and the return of Palestinian refugees. For Memmi, the nation allows the former subject of colonization to rebuild and consolidate an identity deformed by a colonial situation that fostered racism.

The aim of Memmi's sociological essay *Racism* (1982) is to define racism and to debunk its assertions by examining it as both a psychological and historical phenomenon. Memmi notes the role racism plays in underpinning objective conditions of exclusionary practices, and reads it as symptomatic of subjective forms of hate and domination that are characteristic of a more general drive – which he terms 'heterophobia' – to dominate others, based on differences (both real and imaginary). Memmi recognizes the importance of difference to self-affirmation, but continues: 'to be is to be different, yes, but to be different is to be other. Therefore, everyone is different and everyone is other. In short, all self-affirmation must be by definition relative. Whatever its importance in one's voyage of recovery, difference cannot be considered an end in and of itself' (2000a [1982]: 51). The thrust of Memmi's argument is that anti-racism should dispute the instrumentalization of difference for racist ends rather than affirm it through identitarian politics. Memmi's point that 'everyone is different and everyone is other', subordinates difference to a broader humanist project. Indeed, it indicates the extent to which Memmi's view on humanism's efface-ment of difference in the interests of the universal requires careful reading. If, as we read earlier, Memmi claims that the key to his work is a humanism that respects 'men' for what they are, then clearly, the universal claim of the principle

---

remains deeply conflicted on the issue of circumcision. He rails against his father's insis-tence upon the ritual, yet visits the same upon his own son (2000b: 27–39). Recent articles by Laurence R. Schehr (2003) and Jarrod Hayes (2007) draw attention to Memmi's treatment of circumcision and its function within his writing.

of respect is, in his view, greater than the assertion of identity that demands respect or refuses to grant it to others.

In *Le Nomade immobile,* Memmi reasserts his view of the individual as being grounded in 'des attaches particulières' [particular attachments] (2000b: 165) but goes on to declare that in a society organized more reasonably – if not one more rational, tolerant and secular – each individual 'pourra conserver le droit de pratiquer sa religion s'il y tient, chacun sera libre d'entretenir sa culture, mais tous devront renoncer à ce qui pourrait entraver notre commune et universelle solidarité' [will be able to retain the right to practise his religion if he so wishes, each individual will be free to maintain his culture, but everyone will have to renounce whatever impedes our common and universal solidarity] (2000b: 166). Memmi's emphasis on humanism, secularism and rationalist thought throughout *Le Nomade immobile* serves only to bring to the fore a position informed by an unproblematized version of Enlightenment thought. It is not surprising that this accretion of the thought of the *philosophes* brings Memmi's later work into conflict with postcolonial perspectives.

The absence of leverage

Memmi's writing is realist to the extent that he sees it as providing a mirror, however clouded or cracked, of the world. In the preface to *The Colonizer and the Colonized* he writes that 'these two portraits are faithful to their models'; together, he writes, they constitute 'my mirror', an image he offers to both colonizer and colonized (2003: 13). Memmi seeks to re-present the *vécu* of his world through his portraits. Thus, Memmi's *vécu* has primacy over the possible domination of any one theoretical position (such as Marxism or Freudianism) that might deform, in his view, his analysis of the colonial *vécu* (2003: 9). Against a single theory, the colonial *vécu* is considered in the light of philosophical positions indebted to the universalist presumption that we have a shared experiential core. This position is rational. However, though he refuses the base of a single determinant of human behaviour, Memmi reads experience from a humanist perspective grounded in a version of French Enlightenment thought that is never adequately evaluated.

Throughout much of his career, Memmi's insistence upon reasoned positions derived from reflecting on everyday experience has resulted in illuminating critiques of discourses of oppression. *Decolonization and the Decolonized* (2004), however, exhibits a collapse of reasoned reflection, and the views expressed by Memmi in this volume reflect the kind of doxa that he has long sought to challenge. In short, where *The Colonizer and the Colonized* is an incisive critique of racial and colonial stereotypes, Memmi's sequel, *Decolonization and the Decolonized*, is replete with jaded doxa and shaped by contemporary stereotypes of Arab nations and of African and North African immigrants in France.

This confusion of thought and cliché could be a result of his questionable methodology. A characteristic of Memmi's sociological essays has been a lack of engagement with other thinkers in the field of sociology and a habit of making vague references to anonymous interlocutors, rather than cite names and works. The methodology of his co-authored work, *Les Français et le racisme* (Maucorps, Memmi and Held, 1965), also raises questions, even if the results are laudatory. It was based on 200 questionnaires returned by members of the 'Mouvement contre le racisme, l'antisémitisme et pour la paix' [Movement against Racism, Anti-Semitism and for Peace], the very group that commissioned the work. And, though the touchstone of Memmi's work has been the *vécu*, he consistently neglects detailed analyses of specific historical and social contexts. Thus, Memmi's *vécu* appears to be Memmi's opinion, his version of a familiar doxa.

The methodological weaknesses of Memmi's approach (the lack of real engagement with a corpus of critical work in the field and poor use of empirical data) and his evolving views on difference may explain his suspect portraits of the immigrant Other in *Decolonization and the Decolonized*. He raises, for example, the concern that clandestine immigration denies 'the concept of territory and national borders' and contributes to the 'decline of an already threatened Christian civilization' (2006: 80). Although Memmi voices these fears, he does not advocate a reactionary response. Instead, he maintains the importance of what he sees as those Enlightenment values whose origins coincide with the emergence of the nation-state. However, Memmi's treatment of these issues trades in, and reinforces, racial stereotypes. He writes that 'the son of the immigrant is a kind of zombie, lacking any profound attachment to the land in which he was born' (2006: 119) and that 'because of their color young blacks in France experience additional complexity; they are unstable, agitated, dissatisfied with themselves and the entire world' (2006: 116). In the end, it is Memmi's work, among others, that can be used to critique Memmi. In *Decolonization and the Decolonized* Memmi writes that '[l]ike the decolonized, as long as blacks have not freed themselves of dolorism, they will be unable to correctly analyze their condition and act accordingly' (2006: 19). In *The Colonizer and the Colonized* Memmi had already critiqued those mythical portraits that drew from and reinforced racial stereotypes: 'Another sign of the colonized's depersonalization is what one might call the mark of the plural. The colonized is never characterized in an individual manner; he is entitled only to drown in an anonymous collectivity ("They are this." "They are all the same.")' (2003: 129). Memmi's writing on decolonization in Arab countries and recent immigration into France commits the same errors that he once so cogently critiqued.

Memmi's work deserves its place within the postcolonial pantheon because of the continuing freshness of its early critiques and the overall evolution of an oeuvre that offers an insight into the struggle, not always successful, to negotiate difference. His work is marked by a continuous return to the cultural dissonances of his childhood and the attempt to reconcile them within humanism. However, Memmi's portrait of the decolonized in *Decolonization and the Decolonized* offers a case study in the way the colonial myths we seek to eradicate can return to haunt thought through 'the little strains of daily life' once so acutely observed by a younger Memmi (2003: 69). Analysis is not always a prelude to cure or liberation. Memmi himself constantly points to the limits of analysis, to the 'muddled' contents of the colonial situation (2003: 180) and to the atavistic knots that remain within us and that withstand the sharpest blades of reasoned thought. His work complicates colonial and postcolonial relations, and demonstrates the need for a humble vigilance in the exercise of a form of reason that draws too heavily on experience.

Further reading

Roumani, Judith, 1987. *Albert Memmi* (Philadelphia: Celfan Edition Monographs). A very brief, scholarly and considered introduction. Written in English, it covers Memmi's biography and his bibliographic output up to 1986. It offers little in the way of critique, but expertly brings Memmi's strengths to the fore.

Dugas, Guy, 2001. *Albert Memmi: du malheur d'être juif au bonheur sépharade* (Paris: Nadir). This monograph emphasizes biography and inscribes Memmi within a Jewish identity. Dugas notes the role of Memmi's fiction, the importance of which has grown with time, and the gradual dissolution of the *je* in favour of a more general and collective *nous*.

Strike, Joëlle, 2003. *Albert Memmi: autobiographie et autographie* (Paris: L'Harmattan). The author argues that Memmi writes his life to make sense of it but also to continue the work of constructing an identity. A faithful reading of Memmi's work from the perspective of autobiographical theories that take the autobiographical referent largely for granted.

CHAPTER 10

V. Y. Mudimbe's 'long nineteenth century'

Pierre-Philippe Fraiture

The concept of cultural conversion, understood in terms of its multifaceted intellectual significance but also in its concrete manifestations, lies at the heart of Valentin Yves (or Vumbi Yoka) Mudimbe's oeuvre. Whether as a novelist, a poet, or an essayist (see Coulon, 2003), Mudimbe has dedicated a major part of his creative energy to tracing the emergence of Western modernity in sub-Saharan Africa and to the factors, epistemological and otherwise, responsible for the gradual transformation of the Congo where he was born on 8 December 1941 (in Jadotville, which became Likasi after independence). His critical reflection, conducted in French and in English, is marked by a distinctive penchant for erudition and intertextual resonances. This intellectual brilliance – and 'libido sciendi' (Mouralis, 1988: 9) – is informed and enriched by Mudimbe's own biographical trajectory, first as a so-called *évolué* in the former Belgian Congo, then as a Benedictine monk in Rwanda (1959–61) and, finally, as an acclaimed creative writer and scholar at Louvain, Nanterre, Lubumbashi and, since 1980, in the United States (where he has held professorial positions at Duke University and Stanford University) and Latin America.

These experiences, and the various locations or institutional frameworks in which they have taken place, have understandably fashioned Mudimbe's thought, style of writing, intellectual allegiances and ideological positions. Mudimbe is an unorthodox thinker. In the same way as Edward Said or Abdelkébir Khatibi (see Chapter 8 of this volume), his production sits at the crossroads of various disciplines: African philosophy, critical theory, historiography, anthropology (and its critique) and the social sciences. Although Mudimbe does not identify his writing as part of something called postcolonial theory, the versatility displayed in his work bears clear similarities with key aspects of postcolonial thought. Postcolonial theory does not profess any systematic methodology, but is, rather, characterized by the study, through a variety of textual strategies – poststructuralist and deconstructionist for the most part – of colonialism (in the widest sense of the word) and its many contemporary traces, avatars and resurgences. Mudimbe grew up in what is often regarded as the 'golden age' of Belgian colonialism. In spite of the many concrete signs of the imminent demise of European imperialism – India, Indo-China, Algeria, Bandung – it was widely believed in Belgium that the civilizing mission was still in its infancy and that many more decades would be needed to 'elevate' (the French verb *élever* is interestingly ambiguous) the locals to the European level of development.

Although it would be wrong to assume that the Congolese population was a silent and passive entity, deprived of any ability to act upon and conceptualize its own world and culture (MacGaffey, 1983; Ndaywel è Nziem, 1998), the Congo was a predominantly European construct. Two concomitant and mutually reinforcing objectives (which were also colonizing tools) contributed to this phenomenon. First, the conquest of the Congo in the late 1870s and early 1880s was accompanied by a formidable archival effort on the part of military personnel, missionaries and scientists. This intense activity led to the gradual emergence of a 'colonial library' and to the publication of the first comprehensive bibliographical inventories about the young colony (Wauters, 1895). There was also an attempt to centralize and catalogue colonial knowledge through institutions, publications networks and agencies, which, throughout the colonial period, remained key to what Mudimbe famously called 'the invention of Africa' (Mudimbe, 1988): the 'Musée du Congo' (which became the 'Musée du Congo belge', but has since decolonization been renamed 'Musée Royal de l'Afrique Centrale'), and 'Institut Royal Colonial Belge' (subsequently relabelled 'Académie Royale des Sciences Coloniales' and now known as 'Académie Royale des Sciences d'Outre-mer').

Secondly, Belgian colonization – the same is true of all imperial ventures of the last third of the nineteenth century – aimed at (or, at least, professed to aim at) transforming the newly conquered domain and at implementing its gradual Westernization. The Catholic Church became the major symbol, but also the most effective instrument, of a conversion that went far beyond the religious remit of the missionaries on the ground, and slowly brought the local populations into a new capitalist order. Knowledge (the archival enterprise mentioned above) and faith were therefore also deployed in part (although not uniquely, as is sometimes suggested by reductive analyses of colonialism) to reach very pragmatic objectives. The archive and religion were, as a consequence, both the ends – knowledge and faith as ultimate (progressive) human ideals – and the favoured means of securing Belgian control over the Congo. Unsurprisingly, Mudimbe's work on sub-Saharan Africa focuses 'genealogically', that is, in a method reminiscent of Foucault's analysis of power, on the very agencies that facilitated the gradual conversion and invention of the region: anthropology and the Christian faith.

A colonial library

Anthropology, as an object of study, occupies a prominent position in Mudimbe's writing. (See Chapter 13 for a discussion of anthropological thought.) As European imperialism came to an end, it became customary to question the ability of the discipline to represent other cultures. This critique was expressed not only within the field itself (Lévi-Strauss, 1976 [1955]; Balandier, 1966 [1957]) but also by external figures (Fanon, 1967 [1961]), and by the beginning of the 1970s the ambiguous relationship between anthropology and imperialism was increasingly denounced (Jaulin, 1970; Leclerc, 1972; Gough, 2002 [1967]). Mudimbe embraced the underlying anti-colonial principle of this assessment, but his position needs also to be understood as a rupture with Negritude. From a socio-political standpoint, he belongs to a generation of writers, such as Sony Labou Tansi, Tierno Monénembo or Alioum Fantouré, who became (sometimes in Africa, but often in exile) very disillusioned with the process of decolonizing the continent.

In this respect the Congolese example is particularly edifying. Mobutu's dictatorial hold over Congo/Zaire from 1965 to 1997 could not have been achieved without the support of influential allies in the United States, France and Belgium. Congolese independence – this applies particularly to the Zairian period – was, paradoxically, presented as a return to Bantu authenticity. The term 'zaïrianization' was coined to qualify the political and cultural process whereby the dictator aimed at ridding the country of all its Western and colonial vestiges. Mobutu's main ideologue, Kangafu, evoked in his writings (as did Mobutu himself in interviews and speeches) Senghor's concepts of 'participation' and 'force vitale' to legitimize the country's new direction and the leader's divine status. In his appraisal of Negritude, Mudimbe (1994a), on the other hand, remains Sartrean inasmuch as he, too, considers that the movement took shape in order to fulfil an historical need, that of black emancipation. For Sartre (1988 [1948]), Negritude is the antithetical moment of a dialectical process that will be surmounted (in the Marxist meaning of the word) by the emergence of a raceless society. Mudimbe praises the founding figures of the movement: Damas (1994a: 156) and, above all, Senghor (153–54), but he is, however, extremely critical of Negritude's underlying and persistent (and, therefore, anachronistic) tendency to essentialize Africanness. (For a discussion of Senghor, see Chapter 12; for a discussion of Negritude, see Chapter 18.)

This anachronism was borne out of the movement's inability to break away from tenets and world views developed by European anthropology. In the 1930s, Senghor and Césaire paid tribute to Leo Frobenius's attempt to rehabilitate Africa (Mudimbe, 1982: 133); later, in 1949, Alioune Diop, the founder of Présence Africaine, gave an unreserved accolade to Placide Tempels in the preface to *La Philosophie bantoue* (see Diop, 1949). In this controversial book, the Belgian Franciscan expounded – in an essentializing fashion, as Hountondji (1977), the main critic of ethno-philosophy, would later argue – the major characteristics of what he called 'Bantu ontology'. In this ontological system, Tempels focused on the participatory nature of the Bantu social structure, on its purported lack of genuine individualist drives, on the omnipresent significance of 'force vitale' and the centrality of the chief, as the bearer of tribal tradition and intermediary between the world of the ancestors and the living. Although these ideas were appropriated and adapted by Senghor and Kangafu for very different reasons, their ongoing contribution to critical debates demonstrates the difficulty encountered by African intellectuals, before but also after decolonization, in developing a language of their own in which to write about Africa.

This recognition of Africa's inability to create its own conceptual tools is one of the key concerns of Mudimbe's intellectual project. It has been developed in his novels, notably in *Entre les eaux* (1973b) and *L'Écart* (1979), in his poetry, but also in all his major essays. This focus on cultural dispossession (and lack of autonomous language) is the clearest evidence of Mudimbe's postcolonial commitment and sensitivity. In *Black Skin, White Masks* (1952), Fanon explored the black Caribbean's schizophrenic entrapment in the other's language and psychosocial formations. In the preface to *The Wretched of the Earth*, Sartre described the *évolués* as 'walking lies' (1967 [1961]: 9). In *Orientalism*, Said would later deplore the fact that the orientalist tradition, although revealing more of the 'culture that produced it than [of] its putative object' (1978: 22), also provided, in the Middle East and in India, the paradigmatic grids through which local thinkers would study their own cultures.

Africanism – that is, African anthropology – is also presented in Mudimbe's writings as a language eventually internalized by indigenous thought: 'Western interpreters as well as African analysts have been using categories and conceptual systems which depend on a Western epistemological order. Even in the most explicitly "Afrocentric" descriptions, models of analysis [...] refer to the same order' (Mudimbe, 1988: x). Mudimbe acknowledges as a fait accompli African dependence on Europe and North America (Mudimbe, 1982: 118) and therefore rejects all attempts to return to illusory authentic pasts or fictitious black essence (Mudimbe, 1994a: 61), such as that proposed by Negritude, or thinkers such as Cheikh Anta Diop or Martin Bernal (1994a: 179; 1988: 78–79). Mudimbe's acknowledgement of Africa's economic and discursive reliance on the West – what he aptly called *L'Odeur du père* [the scent of the father] – can, however, also be read as an attempt to escape this 'Eur-american' (to use Mudimbe's own term) dependence. In *L'Autre face du royaume*, his first major essay, he observed that his project – in this case, the analysis of ethnology – was primarily guided by the hope and the conviction that a serious endeavour to understand this discipline (its history, limitations and shortcomings) ought to contribute to a radical transformation of social sciences in Africa and reduce the discrepancy between 'pratique de la connaissance et praxis révolutionnaire' [practice of knowledge and revolutionary praxis] (Mudimbe, 1973a: 11).

This ambition of reflecting upon anthropological language and methodological procedures is, of course, closely related to Michel Foucault's work on knowledge and social order. For Foucault, knowledge has the ability, or power, to silence and reify its subjects: for example, he declares that psychiatry is a 'monologue de la raison sur la folie' [monologue of reason on madness] (Foucault, 1994: 160). In *The Invention of Africa*, Mudimbe uses Foucault's archaeological model to account for the evolution of anthropological discourses since the end of the eighteenth century, a period that Foucault regards as characterized by an epistemological caesura and the advent of a new *Order of Things* (1970 [1966]), or 'order of knowledge' as Mudimbe would later put it. He remarks that the perception of Africa was radically transformed in the modern period. When Portuguese travellers brought back the first African *feitiços* from their expedition in the fifteenth century, these objects were considered neutral from a cultural perspective: '[b]ecause of their shapes and styles, sometimes a bit terrifying, they account[ed] for the mysterious diversity of the Same' (Mudimbe, 1988: 10). He adds, however, that '[i]t [was] not until the eighteenth century [i.e. with the emergence of a new episteme] that, as strange and "ugly" artefacts, they really enter[ed] into the frame of African art' (1988: 10). Mudimbe implies here that the epistemological shift that occurred at the time of the French Revolution produced a new language, or discourse, on alterity. Anthropology as a discipline – with its array of scientific networks and legitimizing institutions (museums, universities) – is the product of a reordering of knowledge that coincided with and echoed a remapping of national and racial perceptions. In this respect, one cannot fail to observe the concomitance, throughout the nineteenth century in Europe, of nation-building and the construction of an increasingly large body of racial(ist) theories (Affergan, 1987; Taguieff, 1998; Young, 1995a). The development of the discipline appears, therefore, to follow that of European modernity and to reflect Europe's rise to prominence.

In his analysis, Mudimbe also rejects the assumption (as Foucault did about the history of madness from the Baroque to the modern age) that modernity was predicated upon a genuine ethics of progress. Ultimately, this archaeology of anthropology reflects Foucault's ambition to study 'l'histoire de ce qui rend nécessaire une certaine forme de pensée' [the history of what makes a certain form of thought necessary] (Foucault, 1994: 786). Anthropological discourses are, according to Mudimbe, 'constrained discourses' inasmuch as they 'develop within the general system of knowledge which is in an interdependent relationship with systems of power and social control' (1988: 28). By the same token, he remarks that the theses of Durkheim, Lévy-Bruhl and Frazer 'bear witness [...] to the same epistemological space in which stories about Others, as well as commentaries on their differences, are but elements in the history of the Same and its knowledge' (1988: 28). One can therefore understand why the study of anthropology is presented as a 'pretext' (Mudimbe, 1973a: 10) to understand the 'modalités actuelles de notre intégration dans les mythes de l'Occident' [current modalities of our integration into Western myths] but also to produce the conditions 'qui nous permettraient d'être critiques face à ces "corpus"' [which would enable us to face these "corpora" critically] (Mudimbe, 1982: 13) so that social sciences do not generate '"un même" inoffensif' [an inoffensive 'same'] (1982: 14).

Mission impossible

Religion and, more generally, the (Christian) faith, is the other haunting presence in Mudimbe's writings. In the extensive discussions that he conducts on the (Roman Catholic) Church, its development since the Renaissance and its links with African (de)colonization, Mudimbe is eager to emphasize the dogged consistency of its mission. The Church, he argues, has been since the age of the great discoveries – and, equally, since Pope Alexander VI's injunction in his bull *Inter Caetera* (1493) to eradicate paganism (Mudimbe, 1982: 106; 1988: 45; 1994b: 30) – unrelenting in spreading and imposing its theses across the globe. In the analysis of this process, Mudimbe tends to discard the input of individuals such as missionaries and other ecclesiastical figures, who appear as mere spokespersons for existing discourses. Evangelization's success, in Africa and elsewhere, has been premised on what he calls 'the authority of the truth' (Mudimbe, 1988: 47), that is, an ethnocentric stance, which demands the other's 'reduction to', or 'regeneration in', the order 'that the missionary represents' (Mudimbe, 1988: 47–48).

To illustrate the consistency of this evangelical discourse in a world that has nevertheless profoundly changed since the 'pagan' domain was unilaterally declared *terra nullius* during the Renaissance (Mudimbe, 1988: 45; 1994b: 37), he establishes a complex network of relationships between the Church's prime ambition to convert at all costs and the discursive strategies and language used to achieve this goal. In this appraisal, he compares the actions and writings of three Christian clerics involved in the evangelization of Africa from the seventeenth century. These figures were, according to the author, 'neither the best of all missionaries, nor necessarily the most remarkable' (Mudimbe, 1988: 48). Mudimbe's assessment is evidently not hagiographic; he treats them as 'models' (1988: 48) in order to articulate a 'general theory' (48) and to demonstrate that, although they operated in very different periods and epistemological contexts, '[t]hese three models [...] signify the authority of the truth, its signs and discourse' (50). The missionary hegemonic posture and its underlying self-petitioned 'truth' are, therefore, measured against the background of evolving 'strategies and tactics of domestication' (Mudimbe, 1994b: 114–23) deployed by the missionaries to strengthen their African presence. Through these three figures, therefore, Mudimbe describes three epistemological moments of ecclesial praxis from the ancien régime to the period immediately before decolonization.

The first cleric is the seventeenth-century Italian missionary Giovanni Romano. Mudimbe focuses on the latter's account of his mission in the Catholic Kingdom of Kongo. He argues that Romano used a 'language of orthodoxy' (Mudimbe, 1988: 48). His stance towards the Congolese was not derogatory, but mirrored contemporary discursive practices, that is, those used by the Church in feudal Europe. In his interpretation of the African kingdom, Romano insisted not so much on racial differences – '[a]t the heart of Romano's conviction lies the desire for the universality of God's law' (1988: 49) – as on social hierarchies induced by feudalism between the ruling elite and the 'poor and pagan people' (48). Mudimbe contends, therefore, that, in spite of its African setting Romano's evangelizing action had the same basis as that of, for instance, St Boniface in Germany several centuries previously (48).

The other two missionaries need to be understood in the new epistemological and, therefore, more racialized context that emerged after the Enlightenment. The first one, Samuel Crowther, was a native of Yorubaland and became the first black Anglican bishop of West Africa in 1864. In his analysis, Mudimbe shows that Crowther, despite his skin colour and his origins, internalized the evolutionary discourse on Africa and so used a classificatory grid in which Africans were invariably associated with nakedness, paganism or cannibalism (49).

The third figure of this genealogy is Placide Tempels. As in the case of Crowther, Tempels also expressed 'signs of an episteme' (49). Whereas Crowther was the advocate of what Mudimbe calls 'the Missionary Theology of Salvation' (53), Tempels' approach bore witness to the advent of relativism in anthropological and evangelical practices and was, therefore, the expression of the so-called 'Theology of Indigenization' (57). This move towards the indigenization of the Christian message resulted, on the part of the papacy and the missionary authorities, from the very pragmatic ambition to consolidate the presence of the Church through the creation of a local (in this instance Congolese) clergy. The language used by Church officials changed and became more accommodating, less overtly derogatory towards local religious customs. Gradually, African religions were reassessed for their potential to integrate Christian values and monotheism. The focus shifted from the idea of their eradication to that of their adaptation to the Christian model. This gentler and definitely less assimilationist type of conversion did not, however, disrupt the old paternalistic hierarchy nor question the above-mentioned 'authority of the truth', of which Tempels remained a staunch defender (Mudimbe, 1997a: 155–56). What this discursive shift demonstrates, ultimately, is the ability of the Christian faith to invent new means of conversion.

In his appraisal of post-independence attempts on the part of African Christians to liberate themselves from Western intellectual models and the notion of 'conversion', Mudimbe is also very pessimistic. He has repeatedly argued that missionaries (as proselytizers but also as Africanist scholars) and anthropologists operated within the same epistemological framework. In the field of anthropological research, this framework, as mentioned above, did not disappear after 1960. An analogous (and just as insidious) dependence applies to religion: 'la "mission" [...] a [...] abandonné l'exotisme [...] mais les réseaux qui la fondent se maintiennent' [the 'mission' [...] has abandoned exoticism [...] but its founding networks have been maintained] (Mudimbe, 1982: 118).

Mudimbe shows that the idea of 'indigenization' was gradually superseded by that of 'incarnation'. With the 'theology of incarnation', African clerics have endeavoured since the 1960s to 'reconcile Christianity and africanity' (Mudimbe, 1988: 58) and to promote the 'Africanization of Christianity' (1988: 59), rather than the mere adaptation – as in the 'theology of indigenization' – of African practices to the Christian liturgy. This incarnation aims, therefore, at a much deeper level of integration, which would, however, need to be articulated not only by Africans but also, above all, by African theologians. Consequently, at the heart of this 'incarnation' lies the ambition to create an African meta-discourse on the Christian faith in order to rid sub-Saharan Africa of 'l'odeur du père' and build – Mudimbe quotes here an African prelate – 'a new African society whose identity is not conferred from outside' (62). On the other hand, Mudimbe also exposes the limits of this theologian dynamics, since it manifested itself – the author is referring to the late 1970s and early 1980s – 'in the arena that the voices of missionaries, anthropologists and colonial administrators [had] dominated so far' (62). He therefore argues, as do Eboussi-Boulaga (1981) and D. A. Masolo (1994), that this new discourse is above all a 'discourse of succession' (63). The theology of incarnation indeed developed as a religious response to Negritude (60), a movement that had not quite shed its colonial legacy, and its quest for religious authenticity became, at the time of Mobutu's attempt to 'zairianize' the former Belgian Congo, the tool of 'new political chauvinisms and idols, repeating the missionary's dream of conciliating God's glory and Caesar's power' (63).

Beyond the nineteenth century

Mudimbe's focus on the intricate relationship between power and knowledge has remained a salient feature of his reflection on sub-Saharan (de)colonization. This concern, however, is also subordinated to the exploration of the concept of race. Mudimbe argues that nationalism, as it has been culturally perceived and politically instrumentalized since the early nineteenth century, was also shaped by the new racial hierarchies that were developed in Europe (and its colonies) after the French Revolution. Decolonization and the various intellectual or spiritual movements that have supported and accompanied this political rupture – for example, Negritude, or the theology of incarnation – have not quite fulfilled their original promises. Mudimbe contends that the twentieth century 'could be seen as simply the continuation of a long nineteenth century [...]' and that apart from Heidegger 'most twentieth-century thinkers do belong to the nineteenth century in the same way that the concepts and realities of the state/nation, the bourgeoisie, and the proletariat, as well as colonization, revolution and modernity, are nineteenth-century products' (Mudimbe, 1997b: 2). Mudimbe's genealogical analysis of power and faith in sub-Saharan Africa can therefore be read as an attempt to reveal the many dynamic legacies of an over-racializing nineteenth century on to the twentieth century. His careful (and overall sympathetic) reading of Martin Bernal's controversial *Black Athena* (Mudimbe, 1994b: 92–104) is in this respect instructive of the enduring (and ironic) power of racial discourses on the critique of ethnocentrism itself.

Bernal regards himself as the heir to a critical tradition inaugurated by thinkers such as W. E. B. Dubois and Ali Mazrui (1994b: 101). Bernal's essay focuses on Hellenism and the cultural paradigms adopted throughout the history of ideas to define Greek civilization and culture, from which he identifies two conflicting models. First, the so-called 'Ancient model', which was accepted by the Ancient Greeks themselves and which, according to Bernal, was based on the assumption that cultures from the Mediterranean region (the Levant) and black Africa (Ethiopia) had significantly contributed to the construction and refinement of Hellenism. This idea prevailed until it was replaced during the *Aufklärung* by the 'Aryan model'. This paradigm resulted from an ethnocentric move on the part of influential philosophers and philologists such as Wilhelm von Humboldt, Hegel, Marx and Barthold Niebuhr (98), to promote the Indo-European roots of the 'Greek miracle' (Mudimbe, 1997a: 187). Mudimbe praises *Black Athena*'s ideological premise – the reactivation of a discourse silenced by Western cultural imperialism – but questions, although he acknowledges the essayist's impressive erudition, Bernal's ability to provide a completely impartial exegesis of his corpus (Greek, Roman, but also modern authors). What is implicitly at stake in this criticism is Bernal's paradigmatic approach. The binary opposition upon which his thesis is articulated espouses the very dualism that it also seeks to criticize. Ultimately *Black Athena,* because of its radical political agenda, results in a culturally biased account, which, in the same way as Negritude and other Afrocentric movements, does not quite escape 'l'odeur du père'. Mudimbe understands the 'political significance' of Bernal's work but, at the same time, is concerned that 'his project and usefulness might [...] be manipulated by both the oversophisticated and the least critical of his constituencies for reasons that have nothing to do with science and the search for truth' (1997a: 104).

This search for truth is, by way of conclusion, an integral part of Mudimbe's trajectory as a writer and a scholar. The emphasis on Africa is, to some extent, accidental, or a necessary (autobiographical) 'pretext' to use a term that he himself applied to his analysis of anthropology (Mudimbe, 1973a: 10). He has embraced throughout his oeuvre a method of reading that clearly situates him within the (post)structuralist realm and, more specifically, in the archaeological vein expounded and perfected by Michel Foucault, to whom he repeatedly declares himself to be intellectually and methodologically indebted (see, for example, Mudimbe 1988: 190; 1994a: iii; 1994b: 71). This dimension of his work has been explored by his commentators (Bisanswa, 2000; Kasende, 2001; Kavwahirerhi, 2006; Mouralis, 1988; Semujanga, 1998; Syrotinski, 2002) and sometimes criticized (Masolo, 1994: 179, 187–88; Mongo-Mboussa, 2001: 259) as a partly unsuccessful attempt, on the part of the former colonized elite, to bring an end to their intellectual subservience to the West (primarily to Foucault and Lévi-Strauss). This latter view does not, in my opinion, satisfactorily reflect Mudimbe's relationship to Western philosophical thought. The paternalistic world into which he was born was primarily constructed on a set of dualities, which mirrored ad nauseam the racial and – it was also postulated – the cultural divides of colonial society. Mudimbe's oeuvre is an attempt to overcome the old (textual but also 'real') dichotomies that have maintained, and are still maintaining, sub-Saharan (intellectual but also 'real') dependence on its Euramerican patrons. His method of reading is therefore put in place in order to surmount – textually and intellectually – what Sartre called an 'anti-racist racism' in 'Black Orpheus' (1988 [1948]: 296). One can thus understand why he objected to the binary ideological stance adopted by Bernal in *Black Athena*. Conversely, this explains his enthusiasm for *Culture and Imperialism* (Mudimbe, 1994c), a text in which Said approaches the colonial archive 'contrapuntally', in its 'overlapping territories' and 'intertwined histories' (Said, 1993: 1–72), that is, beyond the same vs. other opposition that had dominated *Orientalism*'s overarching discursive articulation.

Mudimbe does not re-establish the old hierarchy between Europe and Africa. His main contributions imply that the reinvention of a firmly scientific African gnosis needs to be the result of a de-racialized reading practice. This new practice must therefore generate the appraisal of ideas expressed now in Africa and in the (Francophone and Anglophone) African diasporas, but also before Mudimbe's 'long nineteenth century' by pre-modern figures such as Herodotus, Diodorus or Pliny (Mudimbe, 1988; 1994b) or, much closer, Giovanni Romano. His use of Western thinkers is anything but hagiographic. In his intellectual autobiography, *Les Corps glorieux,* he declares that he approached his first major essay as an exercise that would enable him to attack his 'maîtres aimés' [beloved masters] (1994a: 160). His attachment to structuralism (and its inherent anti-humanism) is therefore not exclusive. Mudimbe also regards himself as an existentialist, which is something of a paradox for a structuralist: indeed, Lévi-Strauss famously dismissed existentialism as a 'shop-girl metaphysics' (1976 [1955]: 58). Consequently, he positions himself as a privileged and subjective witness to a specific 'archeological' milieu (Mudimbe, 1982: 14).

This focus on subjectivity and also this effort to reconcile existential phenomenology and structuralism (Mudimbe, 1991: xi) is thus a dominant concern of Mudimbe's intellectual itinerary. He acknowledges and analyses the tyranny of discourses (how Africa was and is invented) but, at the same time, he also postulates, as Sartre and Merleau-Ponty had done, the importance of singular experiences (Kavwahirerhi, 2006: 225–53; Syrotinski, 2002). This existentialist position inflects Mudimbe's novels, which are all characterized by a tendency to create a dialectic between grand narratives, such as the Bible (Mudimbe, 1973b; 1989), Marxism (1973b; 1979), anthropological tradition (1979) and African authenticity (1973b; 1976; 1979; 1989), and individual 'heroes' attempting (and often failing) to overcome the intrinsic bad faith of their situation. Finally, this subjective dimension also informs Mudimbe's academic style, in that it is marked by a propensity to blur the demarcation line between essay and autobiography. Overall, Mudimbe-the-subject does not want to distance himself from Mudimbe-the-researcher. His writings promote self-reflexively this generic pollution and are the sites of salutary intellectual collages in which an order, that of the conventional essay (but ultimately also its underlying norms, prejudices and pretensions to synthesis or totality), is bypassed and relegated to an outdated tradition, which can no longer account for the present.[1]

---

1   This article is a reworked and expanded version of an earlier paper delivered in French

Further reading

Mudimbe, V. Y., 1971. *Déchirures, poèmes* (Kinshasa: Éditions du Mont Noir). In this collection of poems, Mudimbe questions and attempts to renew the poetical doxa established by Negritude and its major figure, Senghor.

Mudimbe, V. Y., 1979. *L'Écart* (Paris: Présence Africaine). In this phenomenological novel – a pastiche of Sartre's *La Nausée* – Mudimbe focuses on the inability of an African anthropologist to escape Western discourses.

Mudimbe, V. Y., 1988. *The Invention of Africa: Gnosis, Philosophy, and the Order of Knowledge* (Bloomington: Indiana University Press; London: James Currey). This groundbreaking essay investigates how Western history and anthropology invented, idealized (and also distorted) Africa as an object of scientific study.

Mudimbe, V. Y. (ed.), 1992. *The Surreptitious Speech: Présence Africaine and the Politics of Otherness, 1947–1987* (Chicago: University of Chicago Press). This collection of essays by African, American and European experts offers a comprehensive overview of Présence Africaine's effort to promote African literature and philosophy.

Mudimbe, V. Y., 1994a. *Les Corps glorieux des mots et des êtres: esquisse d'un jardin africain à la bénédictine* (Paris: Présence Africaine; Montreal: Humanitas). In this autobiographical essay – a pastiche of (and tribute to) Sartre's *Les Mots* – Mudimbe describes his intellectual itinerary and pays homage to Senghor, Damas and Glissant, but also Foucault and Merleau-Ponty.

(and entitled 'Le Sujet du discours chez V. Y. Mudimbe') on 1 December 2006 at the annual colloquium of the Society for Francophone Postcolonial Studies (at Florida State University). I am very grateful to the British Academy for an Overseas Conference Grant, which enabled me to attend the conference.

CHAPTER 11

Roads to Freedom: Jean-Paul Sartre and Anti-colonialism

Patrick Williams

There is, perhaps, an excessive obviousness in the decision to focus on the concept of freedom in any discussion of Jean-Paul Sartre, since if there is one pre-eminently Sartrean theme, it is arguably that of freedom. However, precisely because of the dangers inherent in the 'obviousness', in regarding the chosen subject as already known and comprehended, but also because of the inevitably changing and evolving sense of the term in the context of a lifetime's passionate engagement, we would be wrong to think that we fully understand Sartre's repeated working through – 'elaboration' in the strongest Gramscian sense – of the meanings of freedom. As he once commented: 'La liberté est une, mais elle se manifeste diversement selon les circonstances' [Freedom is indivisible, but it manifests itself differently according to the circumstances] (Sartre, 1947: 289).

The second 'obviousness' – the evocation of Sartre's great post-war trilogy *Les Chemins de la liberté* in the title of this chapter – is also deliberate, since if Sartre was keenly aware of the historical and conjunctural mutability of the character of freedom, he was no less aware of the diverse nature of the paths to its achievement. That was as true for himself as an individual as it was for the kind of collectivities that we shall be examining in the course of this chapter, and in Sartre's case we can identify, and somewhat schematically separate, three main paths. The first of these, the last to be taken fully and the one to which we will devote least attention, is the practical-activist path. This is the Sartre arrested in the events of May 1968, the Sartre of demonstrations against the Vietnam War, of the Russell Tribunal to expose American war crimes, of revolutionary speeches to workers in Renault factories, of committees in defence of political prisoners in Iran and, most famously, of mobilization of support for the Algerian War of Independence. The second is the textual-polemical path of the novels and the plays, as well as the essays, prefaces and articles – most importantly, for our concerns here, those collected in *Situations V*, translated as *Colonialism and Neocolonialism* (2001a [1964]). The final path is the philosophical-analytical one, typically seen as threading its way from *Being and Nothingness* and *Existentialism and Humanism* in the 1940s to the *Critique of Dialectical Reason* in 1960. Although this trajectory is usually read as being from existentialism to Marxism, we shall be arguing here that its philosophical endpoint, or high point, is in fact located in anti-colonialism. If, for Althusser in the 1960s, philosophy could be construed as 'class struggle in the field of theory' (1984: 67), then for Sartre in that same period philosophy was more usefully seen as anti-colonial struggle in the field of theory.

Sartre's intellectual (and activist) engagement with anti-colonialism sets him apart from most other Marxist intellectuals, especially European ones. Although, following Marx and Engels, a number of Marxists – most famously, perhaps, Lenin, Rosa Luxemburg, Andre Gunder Frank and Samir Amin – devoted varying amounts of time and effort to theorizing colonialism and imperialism, very few of them (Trotsky is one exception here) paid much attention to the question of actually existing anti-colonialism in the shape of national liberation struggles. To an extent, that is perfectly understandable: the theoretical primacy of the class struggle for Marxists, as well as its (geographical and cultural) immediacy as a lived phenomenon, combine to render other forms of struggle doubly marginalized. In the same way, although freedom could be said to be as central to Marxist thought in general as it is to Sartre's in particular, its theorization did not necessarily extend to anti-colonialism. For Marxism, the most significant form of freedom is freedom from the alienation caused by class oppression and economic exploitation, where the collective self-emancipation of the workers produces a more appropriately human relation to one another and to the natural world, creating in the process, as Marx famously expressed it in *Capital III*, 'the true realm of freedom' by breaking free from 'the realm of necessity' (Bottomore and Rubel, 1963: 260). For Sartre, on the other hand, the more Marxist he became, the more freedom came to be articulated in terms of the fight against colonial domination.

The latter is one of the ways in which we could most obviously see Sartre as postcolonial: the resistant practice, which indicates the fact of having 'gone beyond' or broken free of colonial ideologies and discourses. Others include the simple question of temporality, his writing and activism in this area continuing after the period of decolonization, as well as his relevance for contemporary postcolonial politics, ranging from questions of terrorism to anti-globalization movements. Most significantly, in terms of the argument to be put forward in the final section of this chapter, there is Sartre's instanciation of postcolonialism – as Childs and Williams argue in their *Introduction to Post-Colonial Theory* (1996) – as an 'anticipatory' discourse, less concerned with celebrating the successes of an earlier generation than looking forward to the achievement of an as-yet-unrealized condition of freedom.

Beyond this, the relationship of Sartre to postcolonialism is a matter of complete disagreement. On the one hand, it is claimed that he is absent, neglected: 'Although overlooked by critics in postcolonial studies, Sartre's contribution to the debate on colonialism is of great importance' (Haddour,

2001: 7). On the other, he is apparently far too present:

> Still the dominant conceptual frameworks of postcolonial theory [here construed as altogether unsatisfactory] remain tethered to assumptions embedded in the first form of anticolonial theory to assume a major role in Western intellectual history, that of Jean-Paul Sartre and his associates. [...] [O]nly by breaking with its Sartrean legacy can postcolonial theory nurture a literary criticism that takes seriously non-Western historicity, agency, and rationality. (Wehrs, 2003: 3, 12)

In *Jean-Paul Sartre: Philosophy in the World*, the long-time Sartre commentator Ronald Aronson argues that Sartre's 'discovery' of the Third World in the late 1950s and early 1960s represented 'a new zone of hope just as Europe was coming to appear hopelessly compromised' (1980: 175). Leaving aside the profoundly Eurocentric/colonialist connotations of 'discovery', it is clear that Sartre's engagement with 'Third World' issues predates this moment by at least a decade, and 'Black Orpheus', his preface to Léopold Sédar Senghor's 1948 *Anthologie de la nouvelle poésie nègre et malgache de langue française*, is the most obvious marker of that. The essay also marks a visible shift in Sartre's thinking about the nature of freedom. The key Sartrean texts of the 1940s in that area are *Being and Nothingness*, *Existentialism and Humanism* and the posthumously published *Notebooks for an Ethics*. In the first two in particular, freedom is construed in terms of the condition of the self and its individual relation to the Other, frequently conflictual and problematically contingent, but in contradistinction to the resolutely individualist conception of freedom in the early philosophy, 'Black Orpheus' offers something more complex.

Articulating anti-colonialism

Importantly, from the opening words of the essay, the image of freedom is a collective, not an individual one: 'When you removed the gag that was keeping these black mouths shut, what were you hoping for? That they would sing your praises?' (Sartre, 1988 [1948]: 291). As well as freed voices, black people also embody a liberated gaze. Hitherto the property of (singular) white male power, the gaze has now been collectively appropriated:

> For three thousand years, the white man has enjoyed the privilege of seeing without being seen [...]. Today, these black men are looking at us and our gaze comes back to our own eyes. [...] But there are no more domesticated eyes: there are wild and free looks that judge our world. (1988: 291–92)

Once freed, both of these faculties, the vocal and the visual, are deployed in critical, resistant, anti-white – and, by extension, anti-colonial – ways.

There is, however, a white collectivity for Sartre to set alongside the mass of colonized black people: the working class. As he realizes: 'Like the white worker, the Negro is a victim of the capitalist structure of our society. This situation reveals to him his close ties – quite apart from the colour of his skin – with certain classes of Europeans who, like him, are oppressed' (1988: 295). However, although both may constitute oppressed groups, the specific forms of their oppression, as well as the particular roads to their freedom, are very different. Since black people are colonized in and through their blackness, that is where the process of their liberation must start: '[T]he unity which will come eventually, [...] must be preceded in the colonies by what I shall call the moment of separation or negativity: this antiracist racism is the only road that will lead to the abolition of racial differences' (1988: 296). The elaboration of a black subjectivity creates the necessary starting point for the construction of a black collective consciousness, which in turn will provide the foundation for anti-racist, anti-colonial processes of liberation.

The central and defining characteristic of this black subjectivity, the subject of Sartre's analysis in the preface, is Negritude, and his discussion of it is – in what it is tempting to call a typically Sartrean manner – contradictorily torn between a celebratory mode, which embraces many of the transcendental or ahistorical categories employed by writers such as Senghor, and a desire to historicize appropriately the conditions of Negritude's emergence and growth. (For a discussion of Senghor, see Chapter 12; for a discussion of Negritude, see Chapter 18.) Thus, an historically informed discussion of the reasons why the European proletariat currently do not produce poetry while colonized black people do, sits alongside claims such as: 'Techniques have contaminated the white peasant, but the black peasant remains the great male of the earth, the world's sperm' (1988: 316). Marie-Paule Ha's broadly postcolonial reading of 'Black Orpheus' takes Sartre to task for a number of similar contradictions, but also attributes faults of which he is arguably not guilty, for example: 'The stubbornness on Sartre's part to see precolonial Africa as the pristine prelapsarian childhood paradise to which the alienated blacks should return' (1997: 96). While Sartre certainly highlights the Edenic condition evoked by Negritude poetry, the direction he sees for black people is – repeatedly and unequivocally – forward into a liberated future free of ethnic categories, not back into a past defined by them. In addition, one aspect of that forward movement offers a possible way out of the contradiction indicated at the beginning of the paragraph, as Sartre describes the ahistorical blackness itself becoming history.

A more famous criticism (and possible misreading) of 'Black Orpheus' is offered by Fanon in *Black Skin, White Masks* (1952), where he vents his anger and disappointment at Sartre describing Negritude as 'le temps faible' (variously translated as either a 'minor term', 'weak stage', or 'upbeat [unaccented beat]') in a dialectical progression. While Fanon cannot or will not see the importance of the dialectic here – where the experience of colonized black people leads them to a superior understanding of all forms of oppression, not just racial ones, and hence to fight for freedom for all – he somewhat ironically instantiates Sartre's point that moving beyond Negritude will be particularly painful for black people because it represents their profoundly embodied, lived experience. (And of course the original title of the relevant chapter in *Black Skin, White Masks* – translated as 'The Fact of Blackness' – is 'L'Expérience vécue du noir' [The lived experience of black people].) In fact, Fanon and Sartre are much more in agreement than the former's criticisms would suggest, since both look forward, in the same not-quite-yet-Marxist way, to a humanized world beyond alienation, especially the alienation produced by colonial and racial oppression. (For a discussion of Fanon, see Chapter 5.)

Whatever their differences on the categorization of Negritude, Sartre and Fanon were much more closely aligned by the time Sartre came to write the preface for *The Wretched of the Earth* (1961). In what is now his most famous anti-colonial piece, Sartre offers an analysis that Aronson sees as a 'masterpiece of self-flagellation' (1980: 176). Again, however, unless the self is a collective (white European) one, the connotations of masochistic excess hardly seem appropriate for Sartre's painstaking dissection of the forms and implications of white colonial power (which, if anything, is the locus of excess – though sadistic rather than masochistic in nature). In terms of roads to freedom, Sartre focuses on what became the most controversial aspect of Fanon's book, his discussion of violence. While Fanon's claim in the opening sentence that 'decolonisation is always a violent phenomenon' (1967 [1961]: 27) may not be universally correct, it is certainly true for the white settler colonies in Africa, of which Algeria was one of the largest examples and whose decolonization was by far the bloodiest. Sartre echoes Fanon's insistence that, firstly, in the circumstances, violence represents the only meaningful path towards the removal of colonial rule, and, secondly, that, far from demonstrating the inherent savagery of the colonized peoples, their violence is nothing other than the violence the colonizers brought and which is now being turned against them. Fanon's is the more pithy expression: 'The violence of the colonial regime and the counter-violence of the native balance each other and respond to each other in an extraordinary reciprocal homogeneity' (1967: 69). Fanon's argument that the category of 'native', as well as the identity it imposes, is both created and maintained by the colonizer, is indebted to the claim in Sartre's *Anti-Semite and Jew* that the identity of the Jew is a product of anti-Semitism, and in 'Colonialism is a system', that 'the colonist is fabricated like the native; he is made by his function and his interests' (2001a: 44). In turn, in relation to the liberatory nature of anti-colonial violence, Sartre says in the preface, in very Fanonian tones: '[T]o shoot down a European is to kill two birds with one stone, doing away with oppressor and oppressed at the same time: what remains is a dead man and a free man' (2001a: 148). Here, the act of violence has destroyed the enforced, inauthentic identity of 'native' and created a new being – liberated and transformed.

Much of what Sartre has to say in this essay is as a white European speaking unpalatable truths to others of his kind: 'You who are so liberal, so humane, and take a love of culture as far as affectation, pretend to forget that you have colonies and that people are being massacred there in your name' (2001a: 143–44). Just as these refined qualities do not prevent Europeans from being, at the very least, complicit with colonialism, so one of their most cherished values, humanism, is shown to be active in the dehumanization of non-Europeans: 'Nothing is more consistent, among us, than racist humanism, since Europeans have only been able to make themselves human beings by creating slaves and monsters' (2001a: 151). For Sartre, the 'conclusion of the dialectic' is that now Europe is being decolonized in addition to Africa, Asia and the rest of the world; indeed, that the former process of liberation is a direct consequence of the latter.

The mutual or reciprocal production of freedom in this way is not, however, something to be taken for granted. At the time of 'Colonialism is a system', in 1956, it seemed that to fight for Algerian freedom was also to fight for the freedom of France. At the moment of the ceasefire, however, after another six years of bitter struggle on the part of the Algerians – and without many French conspicuously fighting alongside them – the picture looked very different: 'the Algerians have won their freedom, the French have lost theirs' as a result of the relentless squandering by the latter of their much-vaunted values such as democracy and justice (2001a: 134). The only kind of freedom that Sartre could now envisage for the French was that of being freed from the necessity to commit more crimes in the shape of colonial oppression.

Altogether less well known than the preface to Fanon or 'Colonialism is a system', Sartre's lengthy essay on 'The Political Thought of Patrice Lumumba' is very different but certainly no less impressive in terms of its careful analysis, not so much of Lumumba's political thought, in fact, but rather of the various political paths taken and not taken, and that eventually led to the Congolese leader's downfall and murder. It is an essay of strong representative figures: for Sartre, Lumumba embodies 'Africa in its entirety'; for Lumumba, the Congo typifies the whole continent. Certainly, the relation between national and international is crucial in a way that recalls Fanon at the end of 'On National Culture' (Fanon, 1967): 'to struggle for independence was to struggle not only for national unity, but, at the same time, for a free Africa' (Sartre, 2001a: 173); not only that, but without the liberation of the continent, the newly independent nation would not be able to guarantee its own freedom. Once again, it is the reciprocal and/ or dialectical nature of both freedom and the means to achieve it that is most important. Further, within the borders of the nation state, 'independence was not an end in itself, but the beginning of a struggle to the death to win national sovereignty' (2001a: 174), and this struggle might need to be waged against those who were supposed to be allies: as Lumumba said, 'The last battle of the colonised against the colonisers will often be that of the colonised amongst themselves' (2001a: 157). In his own case, that meant facing the opposition of African nations who were hostile to Congolese independence and, more immediately, resisting those forces within the Congo – manipulated by Belgian or US interests – which would in the end unite and destroy him.

One of the lessons to be learned, slowly and painfully, by Lumumba was the pointlessness of thinking in terms of reform. As Sartre says: 'No reform was conceivable for the sole reason that colonialism maintains itself by coercion and disappears when it makes concessions. The only solution would be revolutionary: breaking away, independence' (2001a: 164–65). For someone who had, for a long time, been ensnared by colonial ideology, to abandon the gradualism that was deemed to be the only acceptable path to freedom for colonized people was a mark of dangerous radicalization, a sign that he needed to be removed from power. At the same time, the perception that freedom needed to be total, and immediate, had the effect of making Lumumba's stance appear all the more 'violent', revolutionary and threatening to some.

Becoming human

In *Sartre: The Necessity of Freedom*, Christina Howells argues against oversimplified readings of the nature and trajectory of Sartre's ideas: 'It is a critical cliché – and Sartre himself contributed to its dissemination – to view the progression of his thought as moving away from a conception of absolute freedom towards a mature position which takes into account the constraints and conditioning of the external world' (1988: 1). Arguably one such oversimplification is to see his thought merely as 'moving from the ethical to the political' (Young, 2001b: viii), when at the very least it might be better viewed as moving from the ethical to the political and back to the ethical (as the point of principal tension for the political). For Sartre, life, rather than being a linear progression, consists of a series of spiral movements, where earlier points are later passed at a higher level of complexity and integration. The same holds true for the trajectory of ideas. While this image might look like another way of conceiving the dialectic, not least in terms of the classic Hegelian *aufhebung* of an idea simultaneously being retained and improved upon, Sartre's reopening of the question of ethics two decades after the publication of *Being and Nothingness* marks a particularly important spiralling return.

Being and Nothingness had promised that a subsequent book would complete the study of ethics, but that book never materialized: *Notebooks for an Ethics*, sketched out in 1947–48, was only published posthumously in 1983. In the 1960s, therefore, Sartre returned to the question of ethics in order to produce an analysis that better suited both the temper of the times and the changes his thinking had undergone; even when it was a question of philosophy, Sartre said that his main aim was 'to write for his time'. Once again, no book was to emerge from this period of speculation, but Sartre delivered a significant lecture at the Instituto Gramsci in Rome in 1964. Provisionally entitled 'Morality and History', this text, like the series of lectures he was due to give at Cornell University the following year on the same topic, remains unpublished. It nevertheless represents perhaps the most important ethical enquiry of his entire career, since according to Stone and Bowman, it is 'better argued, conceptually richer, and philosophically more consistent than any published work on ethics by Sartre. Its radical challenge to the modern tradition of ethical theorising will, we believe, reinvigorate ethical enquiry generally' (1986: 211). Not only that, but, 'As for this work's contemporary bearing, we think Sartre's dialectical ethics might well be considered *the* theory of ethics proper to Marxism' (212; emphasis in original). The discussion that follows here necessarily offers only a truncated view of this complex Sartrean meditation.

Among the things that make Sartre's dialectical ethics significant in their own right and relevant to our purposes here are, first, their concrete and historicized nature, as opposed to the more typically abstract nature of much philosophical speculation; and secondly, the fact that this historicized analysis takes the system of colonialism as its major object of study. This double presence – of history and colonialism – is important. In his chapter on Sartre in *White Mythologies* (1990), Robert Young correctly identifies the difficulties into which Sartre's thinking on history increasingly led him in the two volumes of *Critique of Dialectical Reason*, but, rather strangely, agrees with Lévi-Strauss's dismissal of Sartre's model of history as ethnocentric and Eurocentric. It is strange, given what we have already seen of Sartre's strenuous efforts to criticize ethnocentrism and Eurocentrism, for example in the shape of an exclusionary and racist humanism, and it makes no sense at all in the context of Sartre's dialectical ethics.

One of the first benefits of the inclusion of colonialism as example is the focus it provides on the way in which human existence is increasingly dominated by powerful systems. Although he wants to distance himself as far as possible from the overemphasis on systematicity in the work of the structuralists (such as Lévi-Strauss), Sartre is nevertheless concerned to examine the way in which systems such as capitalism and colonialism, as well as producing particular forms of human behaviour are also the products of human activity. As he says, 'it is man who produces them through the objectivation of his praxis' (Stone and Bowman, 1986: 198). The human activity that produces and reproduces the system comes not only from those who are its beneficiaries (capitalists, colonizers) but also, paradoxically, from those who are oppressed and exploited by it (the working class, colonized peoples), especially insofar as it renders them unable to see, and struggle towards, a freer life and a world beyond the system. However, although the future envisaged by the 'favoured classes' (Sartre's somewhat euphemistic term) is limited to the present system, the 'unfavoured classes' in their labour – and particularly their labour as creative praxis (or transformative action, which Sartre sees as reordering the world) – embody the possibility of a radically different future.

While the construction of such a future for the colonized is a practical and political process for Sartre, it is no less a moral and ethical one, since it involves the rejection of 'sub-human' status on their part. Although capitalism produces a class of exploited workers, the artificially maintained economics of the colonialist system require a 'super-exploited' workforce, paid at a level that does not even guarantee survival. As Sartre had previously argued: 'Hunger is already a demand for freedom' (2001b: 10), and freedom is a key element in the production of full, or, in Sartre's words, integral humanity.

In the particular context of colonized Algeria, Sartre sees the combined struggle for the fulfilment of need (which he regards as the very basis of morality), the rejection of sub-humanity and the attainment of freedom as proceeding in three stages. These inevitably recall, but are fundamentally different from, the three stages that Fanon sees colonized intellectuals as going through. The first of these is a period of revolt against the initial colonial conquest in the nineteenth century, and aimed at a kind of recovery of lost 'humanity' through the restoration of cultural and political systems destroyed in the process. This, which Sartre regards as typically retrograde, is forcibly resisted by the colonizers, and failure at this level leads the colonized to attempt stage two, which is that of assimilation, where, having been prevented from pursuing their own conception of humanity, the colonized now look to adopt a more (self-proclaimed) successful one – that of the colonizer. Since, however, colonialism is premised on the fact that the 'natives' cannot be like 'us', assimilation is no more successful in producing an integral humanity. The third stage is what Sartre terms 'the dialectic of the impossible', where impossibility of life in either a pre-colonial past or an assimilated pseudo-colonialist present points the way to the construction of a liberated, humanized future through the radical praxis of the colonized people: 'The profound demand of morality is not just that needs are met but that the emancipation of subhuman agents comes autonomously from *their own* praxis' (Stone and Bowman, 1986: 210; emphasis in original). Whereas Fanon had ended *The Wretched of the Earth* with a stirring call for the emergence of a new humanity, here Sartre arguably does the harder work of articulating that humanity's process of self-production.

The question of the means used in that process returns us to the vexed issue of violence. As we saw above in relation to the preface to Fanon, Sartre asserts the right of colonized people to resort to violence as the only method of ending their oppression. As well as (unsurprisingly) attracting a lot of criticism, this apparently stands in direct contradiction to Sartre's long-held beliefs on the subject of violence. In *Notebooks for an Ethics*, for example, he points out the way in which violence involves both self-contradiction and – that most unacceptable of conditions in Sartrean terms – 'bad faith': 'In violence, one treats freedom like a thing, all the while recognising its nature as freedom' (1992: 203). Certainly, Sartre saw particular forms of violence, above all what he classed as 'Terror', as problematic or unacceptable: 'We need not see in terrorist violence, in a Hegelian manner, a passage towards liberation, but rather a dead-end' (1992: 406). Unlike the images of individual acts that dominate current perceptions of terrorism, however, Sartre's properly historicized view of the phenomenon recognized it as primarily a function of state power: 'Colonial aggression is internalised as Terror by the colonised' (2001a: 145). Nevertheless, by the 1960s violence had come to seem comprehensible, even perhaps justifiable, if it repre-sented a collective effort to bring violent oppression to an end. Even within the specifically ethical context of 'Morality and History', violence may be justified if it is a temporary expedient, expressing the will of the people, and oriented towards the production of a liberated future for an integral humanity.

For some critics, this is nothing more than Sartre trapped in self-contra-diction, a philosophical and ethical lapse compounded by his reaction to the kidnapping of Israeli athletes at the 1972 Munich Olympics by members of the

Palestinian Black September movement (and the subsequent killing of all the Israelis and most of the Palestinians by the German police). Although Sartre was a long-standing advocate of the right of Israel to exist, the occupation of Palestine and the brutal suppression of the Palestinian people created a situation that paralleled the very recently disbanded colonial empires. Once again, violence is the means to emancipation when all else fails:

> It is therefore politically accurate to say that a state of war exists between Israel and the Palestinians. In this war the Palestinians' only weapon is terrorism. It is a terrible weapon but the oppressed poor have no other [...]. This abandoned, betrayed, exiled people can show its courage and the force of its hate only by organising deadly attacks. (Sartre, 2003b [1972]: 7)

Sartre goes on to criticize those – press and politicians above all – who react with horror to the terrorism of the Palestinians, but have nothing to say about the routine killing of Palestinians by Israelis. Three decades later, as the 'deadly attacks' remain the focus of ever-more hysterical denunciations, and their daily oppression becomes more extensive, more systematic and more cruel, freedom for the Palestinians looks no nearer. In thinking about how such freedom might be prised from this last outpost of colonialism in a notionally postcolonial world, Sartre's anti-colonial ethics retain their relevance and their inspirational impact.

Further reading

Howells, Christina, 1988. *Sartre: The Necessity of Freedom* (Cambridge: Cambridge University Press). Although it does not include any mention of the important return to ethics in the 1960s, this remains the best general discussion of the question of freedom in Sartre's work, organized according to the many genres (philosophy, fiction, drama, biography, autobiography) in which he wrote.

Stone, Robert, and Elizabeth Bowman, 1986. 'Dialectical Ethics: A First Look at Sartre's Unpublished 1964 Roman Lecture Notes', *Social Text*, 13–14: 195–215. The work of Stone and Bowman (see also Bowman and Stone in the Bibliography) represents the best sustained analysis of Sartre's re-engagement with ethics in a materialist context, as well as an important consideration of its relevance for contemporary thought and politics.

Wehrs, Donald, 2003. 'Sartre's Legacy in Postcolonial Theory; or, Who's afraid of non-Western historiography and cultural studies?', *New Literary History*, 34.4, 761–89. Focusing on issues of violence and militarism in Sartre, this interesting, and variously problematic, article offers a strong challenge to the attempt to view Sartre's relationship to postcolonial thought in a positive light. (An appropriate engagement with it is unfortunately outside the scope of this chapter.)

CHAPTER 12

Léopold Sédar Senghor: Race, Language, Empire

David Murphy

Since the beginning of the new millennium there has been a remarkable turna-round in the critical appraisal of the life and work of Senegalese poet-president, Léopold Sédar Senghor, the writer most closely associated with the Francophone literary movement of Negritude. In the course of the preceding decades, Senghor had come to be seen by numerous critics (if by no means all) as an anachronistic figure, whose ideas had served their time and were no longer useful in thinking about Africa. The high point of the more recent positive reappraisal came in 2006 (the centenary of his birth), which l'Organisation Internationale de la Francophonie – an organization of which the Senegalese writer is considered by many to be the founding father – had decreed to be *L'Année Senghor* (The Year of Senghor). Major (and minor) French publishers rushed to repackage and reissue existing material on Senghor, including a new edition of his collected poetry (Senghor, 2006), updated editions of critical works (Guibert and Nimrod, 2006), and translations of work previously published in English (Vaillant, 2006); and also to commission new (and often hagiographic) studies by former colleagues and acquaintances (see, in particular, Bourges, 2006; Brunel et al. 2006; *Mémoire Senghor*, 2006; Njami, 2006; Roche, 2006). In the course of the year, this led to the publication of well over 20 volumes that dealt with his career as poet, politi-cian and theorist. (This Senghormania extended to the publication of a volume in his honour by a collective of cartoonists from Burkina Faso: see *Senghor, cent ans*, 2006).

The reappraisal (or, in many cases, pure celebration) of Senghor's work had begun in December 2001, following his death at his home in Normandy, where he had retired after stepping down from the presidency of Senegal at the end of 1980 (see Brandily, 2002; Nimrod, 2003). That Senghor's body had to be returned 'home' to Senegal for burial from his final 'home' in France is a clear illustration of his emotional and intellectual attachment to two 'patries', which represented for him two separate (but complementary) notions of the self.

From the late 1960s onwards, a young generation of radical African intellectuals had turned against Senghor and Negritude (e.g., Adotevi, 1972; Towa, 1976), precisely because they perceived them as incapable of breaking with France; his belief in an essential form of black identity was, for these critics, a smokescreen designed to hide Senegal's (and, more widely, Francophone Africa's) neocolonial dependence on France, whose language and culture informed Senghor's entire career. Equally, however, it is this 'double allegiance' to France and to Africa that Senghor's defenders view as a fundamental aspect of his desire to promote the *métissage* of the different cultures that were brought into contact by the French colonial project.

The aim of this chapter is to revisit three of Senghor's key concepts, *négritude*, *francité*, *civilisation de l'universel*, in order to explore the ambiguities at the heart of his attempt to think through notions of blackness, Frenchness, and the possibility of a new and truly diverse global culture emerging in the wake of decolonization. It will focus primarily on his voluminous essay-writing, but will also, on occasions, examine his poetry. Negritude placed a high value on the importance of poetic language as a key aspect of the expression of black thought. The examination of Negritude poetry as an example of the movement's thought is, as a result, absolutely necessary. The anthologization of his essays and speeches in the five volumes of the *Liberté* series – volumes 1, 3 and 5 are devoted to culture (1964; 1977; 1993), while volumes 2 and 4 (1971; 1983) are dedicated to politics – is part of an attempt to give his thought a sense of overall coherence and natural evolution, which belies the uneven and fragmented fashion in which it actually emerged. (See Chapter 6 on Édouard Glissant for an account of a similar anthologization of the Martiniquan theorist's ideas.) Senghor – and his many 'gatekeepers' – endlessly sought to shape his own body of work and the surrounding field in ways that fitted with his evolving understanding of race, language and empire while simultaneously situating Negritude as the privileged (and foundational) form of literary and cultural expression in Francophone Africa. Adopting a diachronic approach, in this chapter I will revisit the historical context in which his ideas emerged and also explore the ways in which both he and his critics revised and reinterpreted them subsequently. In so doing, I will attempt not only to qualify some of the excesses of Senghor's recent Francophone champions but also to underline the significance of his thought to Anglophone postcolonial scholars, many of whom remain largely unaware of his work. *L'Année Senghor* passed off relatively unnoticed in the Anglophone world, and knowledge of his ideas in postcolonial circles is often limited to an awareness of Senghor as the individual on the receiving end of Wole Soyinka's infamous jibe about Negritude that 'a tiger does not proclaim its tigritude' (cited in Ashcroft et al., 1989: 124; see Chapter 18 in this volume on Negritude and Présence Africaine).[1] This is not to say that

---

1   For instance, there are just three passing references to Senghor in *The Empire Writes Back*, the text that marked the institutionalization of postcolonial studies within the Anglophone academy (Ashcroft, et al., 1989: 21, 22, 123). Although Senghor's work is

Senghor's work is unknown to Anglophone scholars. For instance, the field of African/Black studies, particularly in North America, has on the whole continued to foster a largely positive appraisal of his work (e.g. Irele, 1981), as is revealed in the mostly glowing tributes that appeared in a special issue of the journal *Research in African Literatures* (2002) in the year following his death. (Indeed, this special issue opens with a tribute from Soyinka, which suggests that the two men had made their peace regarding their earlier differences; although, on closer inspection, Soyinka's short text is a masterpiece in the genre of the ambivalent tribute.)[2]

The reason for Anglophone postcolonialism's distrust of Negritude is succinctly summarized by Benita Parry: '[T]his body of writing is routinely disparaged as the most exorbitant manifestation of a mystified ethnic essentialism, as an undifferentiated and retrograde discourse installing notions of a foundational and fixed native self, and demagogically asserting the recovery of an immutable past' (2004: 43). Even at the height of its influence, there was a sense in some quarters that Negritude was a necessary phase through which anti-colonial expression must pass but which was in itself doomed to disappear, weighed down by the weight of its own contradictions. For instance, in the preface to one of the most important Negritude texts, Senghor's *Anthologie de la nouvelle poésie nègre et malgache de langue française*, Jean-Paul Sartre famously described it as 'an anti-racist racism' and the 'negative stage in a dialectical progression' (Sartre, 1988 [1948], 296). In the post-independence period, Negritude increasingly came to be seen as a necessary development whose time had now passed.

Parry has provocatively described this critical reception as a case of 'two cheers for nativism', although it is worth noting that her own reconsideration of Negritude focuses on Césaire and sees little worth redeeming in Senghor's writings. As with Parry's approach, this chapter will attempt to avoid 'disciplining' nativism, 'theoretical whip in hand', and will instead '[...] consider what is to be gained from an unsententious interrogation of such articulations which, if often driven by negative passion, cannot be reduced to a mere inveighing against iniquities or a repetition of the canonical terms of imperialism's conceptual framework' (Parry, 2004: 40). This study will explore the significance of Senghor's ideas in terms of their challenge to colonial authority, and their attempt to think through notions such as hybridity and *métissage*, which have been central to many of the theorists who have been deemed key proponents of both Anglophone and Francophone postcolonial thought (Bhabha and Glissant, most notably). Although fully acknowledging the ability of ideas to travel and take on new meanings in different periods and contexts, it is vital to understand the very real and pressing issues that faced Senghor as a colonized thinker in

---

included in some of the early postcolonial studies readers (see Williams and Chrisman, 1993), it gradually retreats from view as postcolonial canons and paradigms become more entrenched.

2   Somewhat ironically, given Soyinka's criticisms of Negritude, his compatriots Chinweizu, Jemie and Madubuike (1980) famously identified with Senghor as the more 'authentic' African writer.

the 1930s and 1940s. What, then, did the early development of Negritude *mean* in the context of French colonial practice and thought of the interwar period?

Negritude and colonial humanism

Born in the south-western coastal region of Sine, Senghor was the son of a wealthy Catholic trader with strong ties to powerful French merchants. Although his father's religion was an eclectic mix of Catholic and animist beliefs (he had several wives), the young Sédar Senghor was to develop a strong and devout Catholic faith that informed much of his writing. After spending the early years of his life with his mother in her home village, Senghor moved to the local town of Joal to live with his father. He excelled at Catholic missionary schools in Sine and in Dakar (at one stage, he felt he had a vocation to be a priest), and – in what was to become the classic movement of the colonized intellectual from village to town to metropolitan centre – he eventually gained a scholarship from the colonial authorities that allowed him to pursue his studies at university in Paris, where he arrived in the autumn of 1928. The string attached to this funding was that Senghor would have to serve the colonial regime for a full ten years after the end of his studies (Vaillant, 1990: 34–63). By 1935, he had become the first African to pass the prestigious and highly competitive *agrégation* exams (in grammar), and along the way he had become a French citizen. In many ways, Senghor seemed to be the model *évolué* or educated African, whose very being was proof of the benign intentions of French colonial rule. However, in the seven years between his arrival in France and his success in the *agrégation*, Senghor had undergone profound changes in his outlook. He had discovered jazz, the Harlem Renaissance, Picasso, the anti-rationalist writings of Henri Bergson and the anti-modernist work of the proto-fascist author Maurice Barrès. He had also encountered Aimé Césaire and Léon Gontran Damas, the writers with whom he gradually elaborated the ideas that would constitute Negritude. Slowly but surely during this period, two key ideas crystallized for Senghor: France's black subjects must refuse assimilation and learn to value their blackness. It was in this anti-assimilationist context that Negritude was born.

Although Senghor did not coin the term 'Negritude' – he always generously and truthfully conceded this achievement to his friend and colleague, Aimé Césaire – it has become synonymous with him due to his persistent efforts throughout his life to revisit and refine his vision of it. In the relatively short (by Senghor's standards) late volume *Ce que je crois* (1988), in which the writer was invited literally to set out 'what I believe [in]', he situates Negritude as a primary statute of faith: '[J]e crois, d'abord et par-dessus tout, à la culture négro-africaine, c'est-à-dire à la Négritude, à son expression en poésie et dans les arts' [I believe, first of all and above all else, in black African culture, that is to say, in Negritude, and in its expression through poetry and the arts] (25). Negritude is 'l'ensemble des valeurs de la civilisation noire' [the collected values of black civilization] (137), which are based on a spiritual and poetic understanding of the world; for

Senghor, blackness is defined by poetry, rhythm, nature, that is, by a sensual rather than a rational engagement with, and understanding of, the world.

Negritude was in many respects his response to the crisis of identity he underwent during his first decade in France. The sense of confusion and ambiguity felt by Senghor during the 1930s is evident in his poetry of that period, which was first published after the war in the collection *Chants d'ombre* (1945), the very title of which, 'Songs of the Shadows', indicates the interstitial space in which the young *évolué* found himself. In many of the poems, there is a restless movement between France and Africa in an attempt to find a sense of home. Senghor uses the whiteness of the snow falling on Paris, in 'Neige sur Paris' [Paris in the Snow], as an image of a temporarily restored purity bestowed upon a culture that has ravaged Africa (2006: 21–23).[3] Simultaneously, there is a nostalgic longing for the continent, which becomes associated for him with romanticized memories of his childhood in Sine. In 'Que m'accompagnent kora et balafong' [For Kora and Balafong] (28), he writes of 'paradis, mon enfance africaine' [paradise, my African childhood], while in 'Joal', the insistent repetition of 'Je me rappelle' [I remember] underlines his love for the site of his childhood, a theme that he would develop all through his career: in a later collection, *Ethiopiques* (1956), he refers to his childhood as 'Royaume d'enfance' [the Kingdom of childhood] (2006: 109) and he declares that 'je confonds toujours l'enfance et l'Eden' [I always confuse childhood with Eden] (148): this mix of nostalgia for a lost Africa and the Catholic evocation of a lost paradise sums up a key element of Senghor's vision. Although many of the poems in *Chants d'ombre* enact what would become the standard Negritude trope of celebrating traditional African culture, there is also a sense that the future lies with Europe: this is particularly evident in the final poem, 'Le Retour de l'enfant prodigue' [The Return of the Prodigal Son], which closes with the lines,

> Demain, je reprendrai le chemin de l'Europe, chemin de l'ambassade
> Dans le regret du Pays noir. (2006: 52)

> Tomorrow, I will set out once more on the road to Europe, the road to the embassy
> Homesick for my black homeland.

However, African culture will survive in this new world, and in 'Prière aux masques' [Prayer to the Masks], its spirituality and rhythm are 'le levain qui est nécessaire à la farine blanche' [the leaven that white flour needs] (23).

As the historian Gary Wilder has shown in his groundbreaking study of French colonialism in the interwar period, Negritude emerged at a moment when a form of colonial humanism had begun to modify the nature of French colonial rule in Africa (Wilder, 2005). A new wave of reforming colonial administrators such

---

3   A selection of Senghor's poetry has been translated in various volumes: see, in particular, the bilingual edition of his *Selected Poems* (Senghor, 1976). As these translations are scattered across several different publications, and their quality is sometimes slightly uneven, all translations from his poetry here are mine.

as Maurice Delafosse, Georges Hardy and Robert Delavignette (whom Senghor knew well) began to move away from the rhetoric of Africa as a blank canvas on to which France would project its civilization through a process of assimilation. These administrators were also (amateur) ethnographers, who knew and valued the cultures of the countries that they governed and, in their writings they began to elaborate a colonial policy that would move away from the stated (if largely illusory) goal of assimilation in order to create a specially adapted education system that would respect the values and address the needs of local cultures. Colonial reformers promoted a more positive view of Africa on which Negritude was able to build,[4] but this conception of blackness could not escape the 'double bind' of what Wilder terms the 'French imperial nation-state', which was simultaneously 'universalizing' in its elaboration of notions of citizenship and rights, and 'particularizing' in the way in which these rights were selectively applied in its colonies. Essentially, colonial humanism promoted a more inclusive colonial policy, but the equality towards which France was allegedly working was postponed indefinitely, for it would take a long (and unspecified) time to bring the 'natives' up to the standards of French 'civilization'. Consequently, the colonized intellectuals of what would become the Negritude movement were faced with a very specific dilemma:

> Neither republicanism nor nativism were in themselves adequate responses to a system that was simultaneously universalizing and particularizing. An antiracism that attempted to attack only one of these terms from the standpoint of the other risked reproducing rather than resolving the colonial antimony that it hoped to contest. (Wilder, 2005: 149–50)

For Wilder, Negritude, in rejecting assimilation while retaining the demand for equality, managed to divorce the notion of citizenship from an explicit and exclusive adherence to French culture: to be a French citizen and to enjoy equal rights, one did not have to renounce other elements of one's identity. (For a more negative reading of these developments, see Genova, 2004.) The fact that such debates about citizenship, culture and identity still rage in Fifth Republic France in the early twenty-first century is a clear indication of just how radical was Negritude's demand for the acceptance of difference within the framework of the interwar imperial nation-state.[5] However, to demand rights within the Republic was also to fail to imagine the possibility of independence. In this and other respects, Negritude might be considered a relatively conservative and apolitical turn in the development of 'black' thought in the interwar period. In order to explore the limitations of Senghor's Negritude, it is thus necessary to explore the exclusionary practices at work in 'official' narratives of its development.

4   Steins persuasively argues that Negritude was able to build on positive images of Africa that were circulated by a colonial literature that opposed itself to the 'false' images of exoticist literature (Steins, 1981).
5   Edwards (2003) and Thomas (2007) have both shown the complex transnational imaginary of blackness that has been developed in France since the interwar period.

The canonization of Negritude

The foundational moment of Negritude has long been considered to be the publication of the first issue of the journal, *L'Étudiant noir* (1935), with the more radically titled *Légitime Défense* (1932) usually attributed the role of 'precursor'. The key critical text in establishing a retrospective sense of the chronological and aesthetic development of Negritude is Lilyan Kesteloot's *Black Writers in French* (1963), in which she declares that we will not 'speak of black writers prior to the *Légitime Défense* manifesto' as their works are 'not sufficiently literary to be included in our study' (1991: 10). The literature on which her book will focus is the 'literature of "Negritude"', which she contrasts with the 'inauthentic' work of a century of black Antillean writing. Negritude is thus the expression of an 'authentic' communal black identity and not just an act of individual self-expression: 'it is not only himself that [the black writer] expresses but all Negro peoples in all parts of the world. He expresses an African soul' (11). Kesteloot's exclusion of work deemed insufficiently 'literary' is a common gesture of the critic seeking to establish the credentials and parameters of a favoured literary school or movement, and, in certain respects, *L'Étudiant noir* did retrospectively turn out to be something of a landmark publication. It was in this first issue that Senghor and Césaire first appeared in print together and, by the early 1960s, when Kesteloot was writing, they had established themselves as the leading lights of a by then firmly established Negritude. However, in the mid-1930s Césaire and Senghor had yet to become published poets (indeed, Senghor's contribution to *L'Étudiant noir* was his first publication of any kind). Equally, there is a highly revealing slippage in Kesteloot's terms between her relatively neutral title and the claim in her introduction that her focus is in fact the literature of Negritude, a category into which all black writing post-Senghor and Césaire is expected to fit.[6] If Negritude is the expression of an essential blackness shared by all black people, then surely the work of all 'authentic' black writers is encompassed within Negritude?

Kesteloot's 'interventionist' strategy in deciding what is included or excluded from the body of 'authentic' black writing (i.e. from Negritude) clearly builds on Senghor's own view of the literary-cultural sphere. As Richard Watts has convincingly argued, Senghor sought actively to shape the emerging field of black writing in French:

> Through his work as literary patron of novels, short stories, and collections of poetry from the late 1940s to the 1960s, Senghor was instrumental in marking out the contours of [the] literary field whose shape has changed since the mid-century but that still significantly bears his mark. (Watts, 2005: 77)

Senghor was remarkably generous with his time, contributing over 30 prefaces, generally to the work of emerging young writers, but he was often patronizing

---

6   It is interesting to note that the sub-title of Kesteloot's book in its English translation enshrines more clearly the idea that her focus is indeed the writing of 'Negritude'.

towards these works in a manner reminiscent of the colonial *préfacier* (Watts, 2005: 85). In many respects, he positioned himself as the arbiter of what constituted 'good' African writing; but whether good or bad, these works remained lesser or greater expressions of Negritude. (The significance of valorizing African writing *in French* will be analysed in the next section.)

The emphasis on the importance of a high literary culture in the writings of both Senghor and Kesteloot illustrates the specific cultural milieu from which Negritude emerged.[7] However, within the terms of this canonization of Negritude as a fundamental expression of Africanness, we are invited not only to believe that an intellectual elite had forged a vision of Africa that was shared by the masses but that it had ultimately led to independence from the European imperial powers (see Kesteloot, 1968). Critics as diverse as Steins (1976), Midiohouan (1986) and Miller (1998) have all questioned the idea that Negritude constituted a uniquely radical challenge to empire in the 1930s. Indeed, in many ways, Negritude marked a retreat from the fiery and more overtly political challenges of a 'proletarian' African community in France in the 1920s, largely constituted of demobilized soldiers who had fought for France in the First World War (Dewitte, 1985). In short-lived newspapers such as *Le Paria* and *La Race nègre*, or in Lamine Senghor's polemical anti-colonial novella *La Violation d'un pays* (1927), there was a sustained challenge to empire, often from a communist perspective, but one that was also informed by the need to develop a positive and collective sense of black identity. Explicitly challenging Kesteloot's position, Miller argues that: 'In certain of these texts, a lack of literary pretension seems to make possible a more radical critique of France than one can find for many years after; writers who were less elite and less aesthetically sophisticated were less indebted to the French system' (Miller, 1998: 10). Such interrogations of this earlier period have allowed critics to understand more precisely who the Negritude authors were and what exactly Negritude represented to them. In essence, Negritude might loosely be defined as the cultural 'revolt' of a colonized elite against the path that the colonial system had laid out for it. This revolt may at first have limited itself to the cultural sphere but it still caused great concern to the colonial regime. Official colonial reports of the 1920s and 1930s consistently voiced fears that colonial education was in fact producing a body of dissatisfied colonized *évolués* who, due to their role within the colonial system, may begin to undermine it from within.

At the same time, we must recognize that the literary musings of a colonized elite were by no means the only challenge to empire: it has been a general problem in postcolonial studies that the work of one section of society has been given an unquestioned 'representative' status (see Harrison 2003a: 92–111). To look beyond Negritude is, in Miller's terms, 'simply to contribute to a more inclusive vision of the literary and intellectual history of Francophone Africans' (1998: 10). Even when Negritude was at its zenith, Senghor's thought was

---

7   Such elitist notions survive today: see for example Nimrod's depiction of contemporary African authors as 'écrivailleurs sénégalais' (which might loosely be translated as 'scribbling foot soldiers'), compared to Senghor, the literary genius/general (2003: 13).

not wholly 'representative' of Senegalese cultural production, let alone that of Africa. To cite just one example, his compatriot the Marxist novelist and filmmaker Ousmane Sembene was an implacable enemy of Senghor both politically and culturally: in his scathing film *Xala* (1974) Sembene denounces what he sees as the hypocrisy of Senghor's 'African socialism', which veils the reality of neocolonial dependence on France; while in his novel *The Last of the Empire* (1981), he creates a vicious caricature of Senghor and derides Negritude – by then enshrined as state cultural policy of Senegal – as *authénègrafricanitus* (see Murphy, 2000). In return, Senghor's view of Sembene is telling:

> Nous souhaitons seulement que ses films soient moins superficiels, moins politiques, donc plus nègres, plus culturels – au sens de la profondeur. [...] J'aimerais qu'il y eût un cinéma fidèle aux valeurs de la Négritude. (Senghor, 1980: 231)

> We only wish that his films were less superficial, less political, and therefore more black, more cultivated – with more depth. [...] We only wish there were a cinema that was faithful to the values of Negritude.

Reconciling Negritude and *francité*: towards a 'universal civilization'?

Negritude was never conceived of by Senghor as an end in itself, a simple retreat into a self-contained and self-isolated 'blackness', which is why we also need to consider the term in relation to the concepts of *francité* and *civilisation de l'universel*. In the brief introduction to *Liberté 1*, Senghor concedes that in its early incarnations in the 1930s, Negritude may well have been the 'anti-racist racism' that Sartre identified, but it had gradually transformed itself into a 'black humanism', and it is in this context that he invites us to read the essays in the volume (1964: 8). For instance, his infamous maxim that 'L'émotion est nègre comme la raison héllène' [Emotion is black just as reason is Hellenic] (1964: 24) – perhaps the best known and least contextualized sentence from his entire oeuvre – is drawn from an essay entitled 'Ce que l'homme noir apporte', which is an exploration of 'what the black man brings' to a world that has been ruled for centuries by a rational, white Europe. Originally published in 1939, in the period of highly racialized thought that marked the interwar years in Europe, the essay seeks to carve out a space for the black voices that are beginning to demand recognition of their culture and history. As Senghor consistently claimed in later life, 'La Négritude est un Humanisme' [Negritude is a Humanism] (1964: 8): Negritude is thus as an attempt to give voice to the previously subjugated black peoples of the world within a truly universal conception of humanity.

As was argued above, Senghor's Negritude constitutes a challenge to an ethnocentric view of Frenchness as the expression of white, metropolitan, French culture. It is in the space opened up by this challenge to an exclusive notion of Frenchness that Senghor inserts the notion of *francité* as an abstract set of values and a mode of expression that is shared by all French speakers irrespective of their origins. For Senghor, the acknowledgement by educated, French-speaking Africans of their 'authentic' black nature does not entail a corresponding rejection of their French education. As he explains in an essay first published in 1945, 'Vues sur l'Afrique noire, ou assimiler, non être assimilés', educated Africans must maintain their 'authentic' African identity while benefiting from their French education: the challenge facing them is 'to assimilate' Frenchness and not themselves 'to be assimilated' by it (1964: 39–69). It is thus necessary to combine a sense of one's blackness with a sense of one's Frenchness, which he called *francité*, a term he began to define after the Second World War but whose outline is already present in the pre-war writings. For Senghor, his *francité* is as much a part of his identity as his blackness: his election to the *Académie Française* in 1983 – the first African to receive such recognition – has been seen by many commentators as emblematic of his dual identity.

Although Senghor's celebration of *francité* easily lends itself to caricature – see, for example, his absurd claims regarding the 'natural superiority' of French over other languages (1988: 188–94) – and is often cited as evidence of his neocolonial mindset, it would be inaccurate to say that Senghor's writing displays no hostility towards the French colonial enterprise. As was illustrated above, the poems of *Chants d'ombre* reveal the anger, disillusionment and confusion that he felt towards France in the 1930s. However, even at his angriest Senghor always seeks reconciliation rather than rupture. In perhaps his most complex collection of poems, *Hosties noires* (1948), he returns incessantly to the figure of the *tirailleur sénégalais* [colonial infantryman], some of whom he came to know personally during his time as a prisoner of war from 1940–42. In the opening poem, 'Poème liminaire' [Preliminary/Liminal Poem], the poet rails against an ungrateful France. The poet claims: 'Je déchirerai les rire *Banania* sur tous les murs de France' [I will tear down those *Banania* smiles from every wall in France] (see 2006: 55), referring to the iconic, racist imagery of the advertisement for a popular cocoa-based drink featuring a grinning *tirailleur*. In 'Tyaroye', Senghor reacts to current events, namely the massacre of 44 *tirailleurs* by the colonial army at a demobilization camp on the outskirts of Dakar (the massacre took place on 1 December 1944; Senghor's poem is dated 'December 1944'). At first, his dismay at this event leads to him ask 'est-ce vrai que la France n'est plus la France?' [is it true that France is no longer France?] (2006: 90); however, by the end of the poem, the murder of these *tirailleurs* has been poetically transformed into a form of martyrdom,

> Non, vous n'êtes pas morts gratuits. Vous êtes les témoins de l'Afrique immortelle
> Vous êtes les témoins du monde nouveau qui sera demain. (2006: 91)

> No, you did not die in vain. You bear witness to immortal Africa
> You bear witness to the new world that tomorrow will bring.

thereby echoing the image of the 'black host' of the collection's title, which is also used to close the poem, 'Au Gouverneur Éboué' [To Governor Éboué]:

L'Afrique s'est faite acier blanc, l'Afrique s'est faite hostie noire
Pour que vive l'espoir de l'homme. (2006: 74)

Africa has transformed itself into white steel, Africa has transformed itself
into a black host.
So that the hope of man will live on.

In what many commentators have seen as an expression of his profoundly
Catholic vision, Senghor here (and elsewhere in his work) seeks to avoid conflict
and to promote reconciliation.

For Senghor, *francité* is expressed most clearly in the cultural domain, and
he defines it as 'l'ensemble des valeurs de la langue et de la culture, partant de
la civilisation française' [the collected values of the language and culture that
emanate from French civilization] (1988: 158). The future of Francophone Africa
lies in a Franco-African cultural hybridity of which he and his fellow *évolués* will
serve as a sort of avant-garde. It is this desire to locate and define this emerging
culture that marks his prefatory contributions, which have been explored so
expertly by Richard Watts (cited above). An example of this approach to culture
is given in his introduction to a 1977 anthology of Senegalese literature, in
which Senghor praises two early Senegalese authors from the colonial era, David
Boilat and Bakary Diallo, as worthy founders of the Franco-Senegalese literary
tradition for the manner in which they represent a Franco-African hybridity:

Ce qui caractérise cette littérature sénégalaise, c'est qu'elle participe, à la fois,
de la négritude et de la francité: qu'elle est négro-africaine dans les valeurs
qu'elle exprime tout en gardant un certain sens de la mesure, où se révèle
l'influence française. (1977a: 9)

Senegalese literature is characterized by its expression of both Negritude and
francité: it is black-African in terms of the values it expresses but nonetheless
it maintains a certain sense of balance, which reveals the French influence.

For Senghor, French colonialism has produced a hybrid Senegalese culture in
which the Senegalese share 'French' and 'African' traits in equal measure, with
African 'passion' and 'rhythm' balanced by French 'logic' and 'clarity'; essentially, for Senghor, only the French language can capture the hybrid consciousness introduced by colonialism. As I have argued elsewhere (Murphy, 2008),
this attempt to imagine Senegalese/African hybridity solely in terms of the
encounter between a (generically defined) African culture and the culture of
the colonizer is to neglect much of the complexity of (post)colonial cultures.
Jocelyne Dakhlia's work on the pre-colonial Maghreb is highly instructive in this
context. For Dakhlia, it is important to destabilize 'the far-too-widely accepted
understanding that real identitary complexity, with all it brings in the way of
existential enrichment and suffering, began only with colonization' (2002: 241).
North African culture prior to European conquest was deeply hybrid and, in fact,
it was 'linguistic colonialism [that] resulted in a binary opposition, opposing an
Arabic-speaking Muslim population to an assimilating French-speaking group'

(241). Equally, to view Senegalese/black African culture and history in terms of a syncretic mix of (African) tradition and (European/Western) modernity, as certain critics have unquestioningly done, is to deny their full complexity in which Islam, race, ethnicity, class and gender, as well as the legacy of colonialism, all have a part to play (see Diouf, 1989).

The paradoxical vision of the fixed notions of Negritude and *francité* somehow combining to forge a 'Universal Civilization' is one of the most problematic, but also most inspirational and utopian aspects of Senghor's thought:

> Je crois également, pour l'avenir, à la Francophonie, plus exactement, à la Francité, mais intégrée dans la Latinité et, par-delà, dans une Civilisation de l'Universel, où la Négritude a déjà commencé de jouer un rôle, primordial. (1988: 25)

> I also believe, for the future, in *la Francophonie*, or to be more precise, in *Francité*, but it must be integrated into *Latinité* and, beyond that, into a Universal Civilization, where Negritude has already begun to play a fundamental role.

Senghor's retrospective account of the evolution of his thought in the volumes of the *Liberté* series and *Ce que je crois* stresses a movement from the particular of racial identity through the enabling power of the French language and onwards to the global rendezvous of a Universal Civilization, which emerges from a process of *métissage* in an ever-more globalized world. In a sweeping and highly complex rhetorical gesture, Senghor imagines a rapidly evolving process of global *métissage,* in which elements of blackness and Frenchness are combined but never lost entirely. It is a question of maintaining diversity within a globalized world, and it is obvious why such notions have been so important to the contemporary institutions of *la Francophonie*, which have gradually evolved from a defence of the role of 'Frenchness' in the world to a defence of all 'cultural diversity' in the face of what is perceived as a rampant Anglo-American culture.

Senghor borrows his conception of a *Civilisation de l'Universel* from the French Jesuit palaeontologist, theologian and mystic Pierre Teilhard de Chardin: this vision posits a common source of humanity as emerging from the first forms of human life in Africa. Senghor was clearly inspired by archaeological discoveries in the second half of the twentieth century that had begun to trace patterns of human evolution in which Africa was seen as the 'original' source of global cultural diversity. However, despite recurrent references in his essays to the 'brassage' [mixing] of various peoples, it is remarkable that his work never manages to develop a coherent historical narrative of change. Cultural and racial 'mixing' may have taken place throughout the history of mankind, but Senghor perceives a deep-seated and immutable foundation to culture. For instance, in *Ce que je crois*, he takes the reader on a 100-page detour through the prehistory of Africa, stressing the continuities in African cultural expression as a 'necessary' prelude to introducing the concept of Negritude. Moreover, there is an extremely dangerous biological determinism at work in his vision of the unity of black African culture, which suggests that he never fully freed himself from the legacy of 1930s racialized thought. Senghor's education in the Classics and his linguistic work on the development of African languages gave him an important 'long view' on the process of cultural evolution, but this results in a largely static view of cultures as fundamentally unchanging: his visions of Africa and Europe are remarkably monolithic for someone who believed so powerfully in the notion of *métissage*. This enables him to develop a powerful and empowering image of blackness that rejects the cold rationality of the modernist project; but its images of this blackness are all turned towards the past, with little sense of the very real engagements with Western-dominated modernity taking place throughout Africa.

This chapter has attempted to restore to Senghor's thought some of the complexity that is often absent from its interpretation by both his admirers and his detractors. Senghor's conception of Negritude is not as reductive and essentialist as his critics have made out. However, inviting scholars, particularly those hostile to Senghor's work, to reassess his career should not be seen as an acknowledgement that the criticism of his work in the 1960s and 1970s was in some way the result of its authors' 'crise de personnalité juvenile' [adolescent identity crisis], as Henri Lopes has suggested (Brandily, 2002: 36). Returning to the specific colonial context of the 1930s allows us to understand more precisely the forces that shaped Senghor's thought but it is also necessary to recognize the ways in which his ideas have 'travelled' (in Said's sense of that term). The richness of Negritude's imaginary and its utopian/Edenic vision of Africa may be deeply problematic, but they also offer the potential for new and productive readings by later generations of black people to emerge. Equally, Senghor's vision of cultural diversity in a globalized world has been a powerful rallying cry for those keen to promote a multi-polar world. At the same time, it is crucial that we remain aware of the origins of his ideas, for there is a very real danger of simply repeating the same mistakes and reaching the same intellectual impasses as Senghor did. His ideas were born within the framework of the colonial encounter with France, and the question of whether his work remains trapped inside, or manages to imagine a way beyond, empire lies at the heart of Francophone postcolonial criticism. Senghor has long enjoyed the 'officially' sanctioned status of Francophone intellectual, and his ideas are routinely used to sanction *la Francophonie* as an idealized framework grouping together the constituent elements of France's former empire. It is now time to resituate Senghor as a key Francophone *postcolonial* intellectual, whose work demonstrates the ambiguities of the French colonial legacy (Forsdick and Murphy, 2009).[8]

8   I would like to thank the Carnegie Trust for the Universities of Scotland for its financial support, which allowed me to conduct much of the research for this chapter.

Further reading

Miller, Christopher L., 1998. *Nationalists and Nomads: Essays on Francophone African Literature and Culture* (Chicago and London: University of Chicago Press). An important intervention in the history and evolution of Francophone African writing and thought. Building on the pioneering work of Martin Steins, Miller provides in the first chapter of this volume a highly nuanced account of the neglected voices of radical black thought, most notably Lamine Senghor, which pre-dated Negritude.

Senghor, Léopold Sédar, 1988. *Ce que je crois* (Paris: Grasset). A succinct late account, in Senghor's own words, of his fundamental beliefs, this volume provides a more reader-friendly introduction to concepts such as Negritude, *francité* and *civilisation de l'universel* than the encyclopaedic collections of his essays and speeches in the *Liberté* series.

Vaillant, Janet G., 1990. *Black, French and African: A Life of Léopold Sédar Senghor* (Cambridge, MA, and London: Harvard University Press). A largely sympathetic and very thorough account of Senghor's life and work, both as poet and as politician. It is particularly useful in explaining the socio-cultural context from which the writer emerged in colonial Senegal, and also in analysing the precise context in which black, colonized writers came together in 1930s Paris.

Wilder, Gary, 2005. *The French Imperial Nation-State: Negritude and Colonial Humanism between the Two World Wars* (Chicago and London: University of Chicago Press). Perhaps the best example of the recent historical scholarship that has sought to provide a more complex account of the ways in which spaces for criticism of the French colonial project were opened up in the interwar period. A brilliant account of how the thinking of Senghor, Césaire and Damas both borrowed from and went beyond the ideas of reforming colonial administrators.

Themes, Approaches, Theories

CHAPTER 13

Postcolonial Anthropology in the French-speaking World

David Richards

It is a foolish commentator indeed who would attempt to claim a precise moment in history when anthropology in the French-speaking world *became* postcolonial – that point in time when predominantly French anthropological thought turned on its own history of involvement in the imperial enterprise and began to challenge anthropological theories and practices grounded in the discourses and assumptions of colonialism. That anthropology was one of the handmaidens of colonialism, a science of empire, is indisputable and well documented. For many, the postcolonial turn has yet to occur and anthropology is still irredeemably and fatally tainted by its colonial origins.

A spectacular illustration of the origins of the relationship between the ambitions of empire and colonial anthropology is provided by Napoleon's military expedition to Egypt (1798–99). Although the expedition was intended to extend French trade and disrupt Britain's access to its eastern empire, Bonaparte also included in the occupying force 160 scientists from the Institut de France, whose task was to research the culture of both ancient and modern Egypt and to construct an archive which would be of use to France's present and future imperial ambitions (Néret, 2002). As a consequence, the model of anthropological research methods for successive generations of French anthropologists was based upon the Napoleonic expedition: a kind of scientific raid on Otherness, collecting artefacts and reporting on the strangeness of aliens while marching across exotic territory. But if anthropology's origins (in France, as elsewhere) lie in the expansion of the empire with which it is indelibly linked, the very nature of the materials anthropologists gathered and the theories of social formations and cultural practices which their contact with Otherness engendered invariably contained, at some level or other, inherent critiques of imperial projects. The sheer difference, the unimagined diversity, and the rich complexity of other cultures which anthropology revealed undermined progressively the simplistic, fixed ideas of the imperial designation of the colonized as 'primitive' and 'brutish'. Napoleon may have returned from Egypt declaring (*contra* Rousseau) that 'l'homme sauvage est un chien' [the wild man is a dog], but he had already set in train a process of discovery that would profoundly question such imperialistic sentiments and justifications while ostensibly advancing imperial ambitions.

The anthropological project and its postcolonial turns

If it is possible, therefore, to read a postcolonial subtext in even the most committed imperialist anthropological text, the question of a moment of postcolonial recantation is problematic simply because there are so many candidates. With justice, one could point to Durkheim's refusal to make any distinction between Western Christianity and Australian aboriginal spirituality when discussing the social expression of religious belief (Durkheim, 2001 [1912]). Similarly, Mauss's descriptions of the evolution of Western ideas of the self draw heavily on kindred data taken from non-European societies (Mauss, 1985 [1938]), or Van Gennep's 'rites of passage' seem equally applicable in Paris as in Papua (Gennep, 2004 [1909]). Yet none of these early twentieth-century anthropologists are *self-consciously* engaged in employing the anomalous materials of anthropological research overtly to challenge the assumptions of an anthropological community of knowledge. Their questioning happens after the fact, as a subsidiary effect of the data deployed in the main argument.

For there to be a truly postcolonial turn in the anthropological text, the challenge to the colonial construction of knowledge of the Other must expose and critique the nature of the power relationships involved in the making of cultural representations, as in the following passage which occurs in Claude Lévi-Strauss's *Tristes Tropiques*. This is a remarkable text, justly celebrated as a great literary achievement, but which is itself rather difficult to place generically. Perhaps the nearest approximation would be to the *voyage philosophique*, since it records Lévi-Strauss's experiences as an expatriate living in Brazil from 1935–39 as part of a French cultural mission, and a later anthropological expedition to the Mato Grosso and Amazonian rainforest. But although it is an account of his forays into the jungle in the time-honoured tradition of the French anthropological expedition, it is difficult to ascertain the exact routes he takes and the geography he traverses. Similarly, the text combines different expeditions – none of any great duration – over the years he spent in Brazil, so it is also impossible to have a clear sense of chronological order, or, indeed, of when any of these events happened in time. The record of these expeditions is further disrupted by frequent digressions, meditations on philosophical matters, and Romantic or Symbolist poetic interludes. The text often gives extensive ethnographic descriptions of the hidden structures and patterns of Amerindian culture: structures that he finds repeated in different combinations in the various people he encounters.

Throughout *Tristes Tropiques*, as the title suggests, is a lament for a world that is being lost, destroyed by the encroachment of Western civilization and predatory colonization. The following passage occurs towards the end of the text and here Lévi-Strauss glimpses the ultimate goal of his, and all other, anthropological expeditions:

> I had wanted to reach the extreme limits of the savage; it might be thought that my wish had been granted, now that I found myself among these charming Indians whom no other white man had ever seen before and who might never be seen again. After an enchanting trip up-river, I had certainly found my savages. Alas! they were only too savage. Since their existence had only been revealed to me at the last moment, I was unable to devote to them the time that would have been essential to get to know them. The limited resources at my disposal, the state of physical exhaustion in which my companions and I now found ourselves – and which was to be made still worse by the fevers of the rainy season – allowed me no more than a short busman's holiday instead of months of study. There they were, all ready to teach me their customs and beliefs, and I did not know their language. They were as close to me as a reflection in a mirror; I could touch them, but I could not understand them. I had been given, at one and the same time, my reward and my punishment. Was it not my mistake, and the mistake of my profession, to believe that men are not always men? that some are more deserving of interest and attention because they astonish us by the colour of their skin and their customs? I had only to succeed in guessing what they were like for them to be deprived of their strangeness: in which case, I might as well have stayed in my village. Or if, as was the case here, they retained their strangeness, I could make no use of it, since I was incapable of even grasping what it consisted of. Between these two extremes, what ambiguous instances provide us with the excuses by which we live? Who, in the last resort, is the real dupe of the confusion created in the reader's mind by observations which are carried just far enough to be intelligible and then are stopped in mid-career, because they cause surprise in human beings similar to those who take such customs as a matter of course? Is it the reader who believes in us, or we ourselves who have no right to be satisfied until we have succeeded in dissipating a residue which serves as a pretext for our vanity? (Levi-Strauss, 1976 [1955]: 436–37)

At first sight, this may seem an inauspicious place to seek a postcolonial turn in the anthropological project since, on the contrary, it appears to reproduce the essential myths of colonial anthropology. The quest for the ultimate Other waiting to be found by the heroic anthropologist in 'the extreme limits of the savage' sustained a colonial myth of absolute difference. Yet Lévi-Strauss, having evoked what Marc Augé and Jean-Paul Colleyn would later call 'the exercise of systematic astonishment' (Augé and Colleyn, 2006 [2004]: 12), then begins to deconstruct it. The ultimate Other is a chimera; if such a people ever existed, their absolute difference would render them unknowable to us, but if they were knowable they would be 'deprived of their strangeness', the whole exercise would be pointless and the anthropologist might just as well have stayed at home.

In an elegant parodic gesture, Lévi-Strauss sweeps away many of the foundational assumptions of colonial anthropology and turns his attention, not to the 'savage', but to the motives of the anthropologist and 'the excuses by which we live'. This self-reflexive turn questions the relationship of the anthropologist to his subjects, who are, when all the mythologies of colonial Otherness are stripped away, 'always [and, perhaps, "only"] men' who 'astonish us by the colour of their skin and their customs'. But, Lévi-Strauss seems to say, anthropologists are culpable not only for creating myths of the primitive, which confine their subjects to a colonial model of Otherness and 'discovery', but also of 'duping' their readers. Lévi-Strauss is here foregrounding a significant issue which will not be picked up in Anglo-American anthropological theory until 30 years later: the assumption among anthropologists that theirs is an objective, 'transparent' science when, in fact, what anthropologists actually do is write, and in writing they create complex narratives, metaphors and cultural representations for their readers, which are neither simply objective nor transparent (see Clifford and Marcus, 1986). In a poignant and revealing image, Lévi-Strauss gazes into absolute difference and sees, not the 'charming savages', but 'a reflection in a mirror'.

I do not claim that *Tristes Tropiques* marks *the* moment of postcolonial transformation of anthropology in the French-speaking world, but it is a significant and influential staging post in that still-incomplete process. It is clear from Lévi-Strauss's text that something, many things, have changed and are changing. His book is a passionate indictment of modernity and its impact upon the environment and cultures of the Amazon. In that sense, change is being forced upon anthropology because anthropology's traditional subjects are being eradicated. But other forces, intrinsic and extrinsic to anthropology, are also forcing change. The fall of France in the Second World War caused a deep rift to open in French intellectual life, as the anthropologist and ethnographic filmmaker Jean Rouch powerfully testified:

> Everything that my generation learned during the previous twenty years was revealed to be an illusion in just one month in May 1940. The army, Verdun, France, honour, dignity, money, church, work, society, family, economic man, libido, historical materialism, everything had been taken away by the winds of one of the brightest springs the world has known. [...] [W]e had nothing left, and absolutely nothing left to lose. (Rouch, 2003: 103)

These strains were particularly evident among anthropologists between those who stayed in France throughout the occupation and those who went into exile. The end of the war saw a purge of those in influential academic posts accused of collaboration with the Nazis and their replacement by a new generation of returned exiles. Almost at a stroke, the intellectual horizons of the human sciences were transformed as the older generation of colonial anthropologists was swept away. The breaking up and eventual demise of the French Empire abroad embroiled anthropologists in new debates and radical questioning of anthropological assumptions. Contact with British and American anthropologists brought about a change in research methodologies, as the 'Napoleonic expedition' was replaced by participant observation and in-depth microsociological surveys, although many of the newly independent postcolonial states (particularly in Indo-China, North and sub-Saharan Africa) viewed anthropology with suspicion as the handmaiden of empire, and refused anthropologists access to their traditional areas of fieldwork. Even the name of the discipline changed to the Anglo-American 'anthropology' from the traditional French 'ethnology'. The disciplinary boundaries of the subject became much more porous as anthropologists engaged in debates and controversies outside their traditional fields, with existentialist and poststructuralist philosophers and writers, the women's movement, and the artistic avant-garde.

Here is not the place, nor is there space to elaborate upon this historic period of transformation, but the changes presaged in Lévi-Strauss's text brought about reassessments of the fundamental nature of anthropological enquiry, which increasingly took account of postcolonial contexts: changes in terminology, methodology, the objects of study, the 'field', relations with other disciplines, with the process of writing and acts of cultural representation, and with the subject's relationship to a 'globalized' world. If it is possible, therefore, to speak with some accuracy of 'postcolonial anthropology' – a concept that would appear at least oxymoronic, if not contradictory, given the discipline's imperial history – what would such a phenomenon look like, and how would it be practised?

In search of a postcolonial anthropology

Postcolonial anthropology is not dedicated to the pursuit of 'objective scientific truth', but acknowledges that such notions of 'truth' are ideologically constructed and determined by colonial power relations, both historically and in the present. Postcolonial anthropology is, therefore, polemical, engaged and oppositional. Its goal is to make an intervention and to transform cultural representations in ways which foreground the unequal nature of global power relationships. Its subject matter reflects anthropology's traditional concerns with issues of language, economics, social formation, politics, religion and other forms of cultural production, but in ways which put the social subjects' own interpretation at the centre of the enquiry rather than subjugate those interpretations to 'authoritative' external discourses. Although the term 'postcolonial anthropology' is barely recognized in France, it is, nonetheless, deeply indebted to French-language theoretical and critical writings in poststructuralism, psychoanalysis, Marxism and feminism.

Postcolonial anthropology does not itself have a dominant discourse, but at its centre is a critique of all forms of essentialism (principally ethnocentrism, race, ethnicity and nationality), and it is centrally concerned with issues of identity, not as a unitary or fixed entity, but as a complex interaction of processes in constant evolution and change. Postcolonial anthropology, albeit by any other name, is, therefore, an inevitable product not only of the collapse of empire but also of the growth of the culture and economy of globalization, which both creates and destroys opportunities for individual and collective identity, and perpetuates some of the elements of the empires it has replaced. Perhaps the most significant contribution of postcolonial anthropology has been to a process of revision of the central anthropological notion of 'situated identities': a 'classical' anthropological subject located in an unchanging, self-perpetuating, fixed social order, which is pristine, culturally isolated, and 'pure'. Postcolonial anthropology condemns such colonial mythologies, and argues that there is not, nor has there ever been, a pure and homogeneous culture: all cultures, everywhere, have always been subject to external influence, transformation and change. The postcolonial anthropological subject is therefore marked as hybrid, combining a diverse range of 'alien' and 'indigenous' cultural influences and social practices.

The remainder of this chapter will be concerned with the practice of postcolonial anthropology: how it defines the subjects of study, where and how it conducts research in the 'field', and how an increased self-reflexive awareness of anthropologists as 'writers' and makers of cultural representations affects their work.

Transgressing borders, reframing themes

The goal of 'classical' anthropology, as has been argued, was to find and document a hitherto uncontaminated exotic culture. The archive is replete with examples, none perhaps so noteworthy as the work of Marcel Griaule and Germaine Dieterlen on the complex religious and astronomical beliefs of the Dogon of Mali in West Africa (Griaule, 1965 [1948]), which brought the Dogon from obscurity and poverty to celebrity as an anthropological people par excellence and a popular destination for exotic tourism. Yet Lévi-Strauss's insistence 'that men are [...] always men' significantly challenged the perceived 'uniqueness' of 'primitive' peoples such as the Dogon. His work in structural anthropology deployed methods derived from the linguistic analyses practised by Ferdinand de Saussure and Roman Jakobson to show that all cultures shared underlying patterns and deep structures (Lévi-Strauss, 1962; 1978 [1958]). Lévi-Strauss's structuralist method was itself challenged in turn by poststructuralist thinkers as being reductive (complexity was reduced to simplicity), repetitive (everything was always the same thing), and ahistorical (deep structures cannot change). Yet in arguing that the anthropologist's subject was not a particular exotic tribe but the underlying architecture of the human mind, shared by all and giving rise to various social and cultural forms, it therefore did not make much difference where anthropology's subjects were located, since the Dogon or the Nambikwara possessed the same deep structural capacities as factory workers in Lyon or, for that matter, anthropologists in Paris. Lévi-Strauss was in fact doing little more than reasserting a tradition in French-language anthropology which goes back to the *année sociologique* school of Durkheim and Mauss, who frequently dissolved boundaries between the 'primitive' and the 'civilized', but the effects were nonetheless significant.

Firstly, the disciplinary borders between anthropology, history and sociology were much more porous in France and, several decades before Britain and America, anthropologists in France 'repatriated' anthropology and, in Paul Rabinow's phrase, 'anthropologise[d] the West' (Rabinow, 1986: 241). Qualitative anthropological and ethnographic methods were therefore deployed in a range of deeply influential texts concerned not with 'primitive' but with 'metropolitan' societies: Michel de Certeau documented the 'tactics' by which individuals negotiated their quotidian existences in *The Practice of Everyday Life* (1974) and Pierre Nora's collective project, *Les Lieux de Mémoire* (1984–93), explored sites of collective cultural memory in key locations in France. France itself became the subject of anthropological enquiry alongside more exotic locations, with the result that French culture was 'defamiliarized'. Gérard Althabe was an early pioneer of this postcolonial self-reflexive turn, where anthropology's gaze turned inwards as he moved seamlessly from his work on African and Madagascan cities to investigations into French 'urban ethnology' (Althabe, 1969).

Secondly, although many of the old anthropological themes retained their centrality, albeit in altered forms, new terms and conceptual tools were introduced. Pierre Bourdieu was a key figure in building bridges between anthropology and sociology, bringing his insights from the 'field' (in the Kabylie of Algeria, where he conducted research during the War of Independence) to home ground in works on 'taste', academic communities and television (Bourdieu, 1984; 1996; 1998), and introducing a number of key methodological and conceptual innovations, notably *habitus* and symbolic capital (Bourdieu, 1977 [1972]; 2001). The former is a concept which evades precise definition – indeed, its imprecision is precisely the point, since it occupies the space between the antitheses of subjectivism and objectivism. *Habitus* (which Bourdieu derived from Mauss and Aristotle) is a range of 'dispositions', which the individual acquires and by which s/he thinks and acts accordingly. They are neither wholly subjective, in the sense of being independently created by the individual, nor wholly objective, in the sense of being externally imposed, but an agglomeration of attitudes, thoughts and perceptions; *habitus* connects the individual to the social structure and vice versa. Symbolic capital has a similar 'inbetween-ness' about it, as Bourdieu attempts to account for the exercise of influence by individuals and groups who may have little or no economic or political weight, but who possess 'prestige' in one form or another. Symbolic capital signifies 'wealth' or power in an 'economy' of symbolic exchange, dominance and 'violence' (the overwhelming of another by one's own prestige). Colonial regimes on the one hand, and education systems on the other, are both prime examples of the exercise of symbolic capital.

Habitus and symbolic capital testify to an important element in Bourdieu's attitude to the nature of both anthropological and sociological research: oppression operates upon the *habitus* through symbolic violence in ways which are more effective than physical violence, but an (anthropological) understanding of the workings of these structures is the surest way to combat their manipulation. The duty of the anthropologist/sociologist is not, therefore, to be neutral on such matters but to engage combatively with the public sphere. Just as Lévi-Strauss debated freedom with Jean-Paul Sartre in the 1960s, so did Bourdieu himself argue in Pierre Carles's documentary film that sociology is a 'martial art' (Carles, 2001). Loïc Wacquant, Bourdieu's most steadfast disciple, termed this interventionist role the practice of 'carnal sociology'.

Yet while innovations in the subject brought new materials and modes of analysis, the stalwart subjects of anthropology, such as kinship, politics, religion and ritual, were also subject to change. Kinship represents a fundamental research theme for anthropologists; there are a relatively small number of ways in which descent and relationship can be reckoned, so kinship provides a valuable tool for categorizing and comparing different and otherwise disparate cultures. Kinship is anthropology's equivalent to algebra's differential equation, but in its 'classical' or colonial formulation, the equation was heavily biased towards both a Eurocentric view of the family and a male-centred attitude to descent. Again, Lévi-Strauss in *The Elementary Structures of Kinship* (1949) (which Simone de Beauvoir reviewed very favourably) began a process of rethinking kinship. Louis Dumont's *Homo Hierarchicus* (1966) was centrally concerned with Indian castes, but he also reflected on the mutual relatedness of Indian and Western practices in ways which challenged a Eurocentric perspective, and Françoise Heritier's collection of essays written between 1979 and 1993, *Masculin/féminin: la pensée de la différence*, reassesses the algebra of kinship terminologies to locate 'la valence différentielle' of the sexes in the exclusion of the female terms of the equation.

Reconfiguring the anthropological field: tradition, politics and contemporaneity

It was perhaps, however, in the re-imagining of an anthropology of politics that anthropology was most directly concerned with independence and liberation movements in the dying empire. Georges Balandier contributed to a remarkable flowering of African urban studies in the 1960s, which was little short of revolutionary in proposing new models for investigating and theorizing colonial and postcolonial urban social formations. Hitherto, anthropologists had tended to be interested in colonial politics only insofar as they reflected the so-called 'origins of the state'. By contrast, Balandier's work in Senegal, Mauritania, Guinea and, above all, in the equatorial city of Brazzaville at the end of colonization, argued for a study of African cities as sites of contestation between traditional society and colonial (soon to be postcolonial) modernity (Balandier, 1955; 1966 [1957]; 1970 [1967]). His work focused on the various power relations and political dynamics of societies in the throes of change. He criticized both the colonial hierarchies, which exercised an illegitimate and violent power, and ethnographies which supported colonial systems by preferring to see the timeless and unchanging nature of a primitive Africa, while refusing to acknowledge the revolutionary processes of Africa's decolonization. Balandier prepared the ground for a new political anthropology, which saw colonialism as a 'totality' involving not only the colonized but also the colonizers in complex dialectical economic, political, and cultural confrontations and exchanges (see Abélès and Collard, 1985; Terray, 1987).

In many respects, Balandier's work was a precursor to Michel Foucault's explorations of the discourses of power (and the power of discourse) in diverse forms in Western societies. Although Foucault taught at the University of Tunis from 1965 to 1968, the focus of his work was wholly concerned with the history of systems of Western thought. Nonetheless, Foucault's approach issued a productive challenge to anthropological assumptions since his work, particularly *The Archaeology of Knowledge* (1969), was fundamentally anti-anthropological, at least as anthropology was constituted in the 1960s. Foucault simply reversed the anthropological construction of the human subject to argue that the subject is formed by discourse and discursive practices which change over time, rather than the prevailing notion of the subject as a fixed site in a set of rigid cultural coordinates. The truth-value, and even the meaning of any particular discourse is therefore not the main issue in cultural and historical analysis. What is significant is the operation of discourses which are perceived to be truthful and meaningful by subjects in a particular culture at a particular time. There are therefore no anthropological absolutes, no external measures of truth outside the cultural system which the anthropologist can lay claim to: discourse makes meaning and constitutes the subject.

Foucault's thought is more complex than this brief sketch will allow, and in many respects, in anthropological contexts, it is little other than a more sophisticated form of Boas's cultural relativism, which was so influential for Lévi-Strauss in the 1940s (Boas, 1940). But the poststructuralist influence upon postcolonial anthropology made it possible to rethink anthropology's key concepts. Ethnicity, race or nationality, for example, are not simply a matter of 'natural' consanguinity, genealogy, ancestry, territory or shared language, but are 'produced' or constructed by discourses of and about consanguinity, genealogy, ancestry, territory or shared language. Jean-Loup Amselle accordingly argued that ethnicities are 'relations of forces' of language, political power and religion in a fluid state of 'composition, decomposition and recomposition' (Amselle, 1985: 23). Lévi-Strauss had argued that the anthropological study of religion was neither a matter of proving or disproving the truth of revelation but of analysing the ways in which cultures created order from the apparent chaos of nature (Lévi-Strauss, 1978), and before that, Durkheim had seen religion as the reflection and celebration of social bonds, obligations, and functions (Durkheim, 2001). Foucault's example broadened the scope of anthropology's approach to religion by demonstrating that, as discourse, numerous different, competing and contradictory 'truths' can exist simultaneously. In all these respects, anthropology's key concepts underwent radical revision and changed, and as Marc Augé has argued, from being essentially a 'science of facts, norms and structures, it became a science of processes' (Augé and Colleyn, 2006: 62).

But poststructuralism's major contribution to postcolonial anthropology was in enabling a redefinition of human subjectivity, not as a settled or common-sense matter, but as a 'construct' realized in the 'process' of the performance of identity. In important respects, this also has precedents in an older French anthropology; Michel Leiris's interweaving of ethnography, poetics and autobiography in *L'Afrique fantôme* (1934) had explored the performative nature of identity through surrealist collages (Leiris, 1981 [1934]; 2003). From being a function in a system of structures of meaning, the anthropological subject had become transformed into an actor performing a play of self-representation on the stage of culture.

These reconfigurations of the anthropological subject have also engendered new ways of recording and transmitting ethnographic materials. From the 1950s, the pioneering filmmaker Jean Rouch experimented with *ciné-ethnography*. From his early films on Songhay religion and magic, Rouch developed ever more complex narratives of postcolonial African lives: films about migration (*Madame L'Eau*, *Les Maîtres fous* and *Jaguar*), urban slum dwellers (*Moi, un noir*), the impact of postcolonial modernity (*La Pyramide humaine*), and African migrants and racism in Paris (*La Punition* and *Rose et Landry*). Rouch was acutely aware that 'the observer's presence can never be neutral. Whether he wishes it or not, the observer is integral to the general movement of things'; 'he ethno-looks, ethno-observes, ethno-thinks' (Rouch, 2003: 97, 100). His films underscored the self-reflexive moment of the ethnographer's intervention in recording cultural practices by deploying innovative cinematic techniques (hand-held cameras, portable synchronous-sound equipment, natural light) to foreground the nature of the medium – techniques which were profoundly influential on the *nouvelle vague* of directors practising the visual aesthetic of *cinéma-vérité*. His goal was to achieve a form of ethnographic reflexivity, which he called *anthropologie partagée* or 'shared anthropology' (2003: 18), and in attempting to define *anthropologie partagée* further he offered a most lucid definition of the ambitions of postcolonial anthropology:

> It is this permanent ethno-dialogue that appears to be one of the most inter-esting angles in the current progress of ethnography. Knowledge is no longer a stolen secret, devoured in the Western temples of knowledge; it is the result of an endless quest where ethnographers and those whom they study meet on a path that some of us now call 'shared anthropology'. (Rouch, 2003: 100)

Thus far I have been concerned with the ways in which anthropology has adapted to the new conditions and innovations postcolonialism has brought about in the methodologies of research, the idea of the 'primitive' subject, situated identities, the repatriation of anthropology, transformations in anthropology's key concepts, and the difficult issue of cultural representation. The subjects of Rouch's films, however, raise significant questions about the 'field' of postcolonial anthropology; his films are not about Lévi-Strauss's pure 'savage' in the emerald forest, but the 'shared anthropology' of 'migration, refugees, cosmopolitanism, new religions, and the sociology of networks': the new anthropology of globalization which, as Marc Augé has argued, has challenged the very idea of the 'field' or 'fieldwork' (Augé and Colleyn, 2006: 79, 93–95).

In a series of short works, Augé has begun to document an anthropological field which has neither fixed location nor homogeneous culture, but where the 'human condition [is] undergoing perpetual redefinition' and, for the first time ever, has shared global references (Augé and Colleyn, 2006: 17; see also Augé, 1999a [1994]). The field of the anthropologist is therefore not bounded by geopolitical entities; anthropologists can no longer be designated Africanists or Orientalists because his anthropology of 'contemporaneity' conceives of culture as crossing traditional national and cultural borders; anthropology's subject has 'a plurality of forms'; it is a vision of 'society in fragments' and a 'collection of communities claiming truth'; this is the end of autonomous cultures. 'All the relevance and difficulty of anthropology today', he writes, 'has to do with the coexistence of the singular entity implied by the word "contemporaneous" and the multiplicity of worlds it qualifies' (Augé, 1999a: 83). In a striking example drawn from his more 'traditional' fieldwork area in West Africa, Augé describes the rise in the twentieth century of a group of religious prophets who, to be accepted by their followers, had to construct an identity which absorbed and performed a mass of external cultural influences and traces. Their example was prophetic in more than one sense of the word since, for Augé, these:

> [p]rophetic movements as such constitute an anticipation, if not a prophecy, of what is today a situation we all share – the internationalization of the planet. Colonized peoples were the first to have this experience because they were the first to suffer it. [...] I am referring, of course, to the acceleration of history, the shrinking of space, and the individualizing of destinies. [...] It seems fair to say that the colonized peoples were the first to undergo these experiences and that the prophetic movements, and more generally all political-religious movements that have been analysed as reactions to colonization, are also, even more pointedly, anticipations of the situation we all now experience as our present reality. (Augé, 1999a: 101, 102)

Far from being postcolonial in the sense of being 'after the event of colonization', the anthropology of contemporaneity discovers in the examples of postcolonial, hybrid, dislocated cultures a perpetuation and deepening of colonial processes. The postcolonial subject is strangely predictive of a future which threatens the global population:

> To put it in a nutshell, we all have the feeling that we are being colonised but we don't exactly know who by; the enemy is not easily identifiable; and one can venture to suggest that this feeling now exists all over the world, even in the United States. (Augé, 1999b [1997]: 6)

We are all subject to the same regimes of advanced global colonization. We are all postcolonial now.

Further reading

Augé, Marc, 1992. *Non-lieux* (Paris: Seuil). A meditation on contemporaneity, which Augé finds is revealed in its starkest form in the 'non places' of 'supermodernity': motorways, hotel lounges, airports. Non places are indicative of our increasing loss of a sense of a creative engagement with cultural forms, historical sites of memory, shared local culture and repositories of identity. By contrast, supermodernity gives rise to the historyless, blank place, lacking organic social identity: the cultureless zones of global modernity. A sobering account of the logic of late capitalism and of how the anthropologist must increasingly turn to devising an 'ethnography of solitude'.

Bourdieu, Pierre, 1977 [1972]. *Outline of a Theory of Practice*, tr. Richard Nice (Cambridge: Cambridge University Press). [First published as *Esquisse d'une théorie de la pratique*.] Drawing upon his ethnographic research in Kabylie, Bourdieu elaborates a provocative critique of the anthropological practices of constructing ethnocentric cultural 'maps' of other societies. As a counter argument, Bourdieu also explores the nature of 'praxis' and proposes the concept of *habitus* as a significant force in social life.

Griaule, Marcel, 1965 [1948]. *Conversations with Ogotemmêli: An Introduction to Dogon Religious Ideas* (London: Oxford University Press). [First published as *Dieu d'eau: entretiens avec Ogotemmêli*.] Griaule was the leader of the Dakar-Djibouti expedition (1931–33) and a significant later influence on the changes in post-war French fieldwork methodologies, but he is best known for his work on the Dogon of Mali, a project that lasted for more than twenty-five years. *Dieu d'eau* is remarkable in two respects: it is an elaborate exploration of Dogon religion and cosmology; and it is the record of Ogotemmêli's (Griaule's chief informant) own account of Dogon culture, and therefore pre-empts many later attempts at ethnographic dialogue by some thirty years.

Leiris, Michel, 1981 [1934]. *L'Afrique fantôme* (Paris: Gallimard). Originally written in 1934 as an unofficial record of Michel Leiris's experiences as the secretary-archivist on the Dakar–Djibouti expedition, this remarkable text is not only an ethnographic record, but also a brilliant exploration of the role of the anthropologist. Leiris had strong and lasting affiliations with the surrealists and much of the text reflects these interests, and his obsessive self-psychoanalysis.

Lévi-Strauss, Claude, 1976 [1955]. *Tristes Tropiques*, tr. John and Doreen Weightman (Harmondsworth: Penguin). In a similar vein to Leiris's text, Lévi-Strauss weaves philosophical reflections and lyrical interludes into his ethnographic accounts. An important text for the insights it gives into the human capacity to construct complex symbolic systems, its polemical stance on the destruction of other cultures, and its constant probing of the motives of anthropological enquiry.

CHAPTER 14

French Theory and the Exotic

Jennifer Yee

From the sixteenth century, the French adjective *exotique* was used to refer to the natural or cultural product of another country, but the term rapidly became marked by its current Eurocentrism, losing any reversibility. It was a virtual synonym of 'colonial' by the nineteenth century, when the noun *exotisme* appeared (1845). The newly reified concept had acquired connotations of hackneyed imagery and falsity in the representation of the Other (Moura, 1998: 19–40). This pejorative sense was not to be seriously challenged until the early years of the twentieth century, by Victor Segalen (1878–1919), who attempted to revalorize the concept in his notes towards an *Essay on Exoticism*. Since the term was so compromised, much of this project involved sweeping away the accumulated literary banalities of preceding generations. He went on to redefine exoticism as '[…] nothing other than the notion of difference, the perception of Diversity, the knowledge that something is other than one's self; and Exoticism's power is nothing other than the ability to conceive otherwise' (2002 [1978]: 19). He saw exoticism not as a fixed state but as a tension between two poles, emphasizing, for example, 'exoticism to the second degree' (15), or the effect of the subject (e.g. traveller or colonist) on the Other; he also situated the exotic in an oscillation between the realms of the real and the imaginary, the real being direct experience of the Other and the imaginary being the construction of that Other through reading, daydreaming and, in some cases, stereotyping.

Although Segalen's project was in many ways unique, the seriousness of this early attempt to engage intellectually with the literary tradition of exoticism foreshadows the attitude of much twentieth-century French theory. Its contradictory positions and fierce debates over exoticism are in themselves indicative that in France the complexities of the 'exotic' are not dismissed in quite so cavalier a manner as is often the case in English–language theory. Nor can French exoticism be easily reduced to mere self-indulgence: France's *avant-gardes* have long been attracted to the exotic, from the Impressionists' *japonisme*

185

and Gauguin's Maori inspiration to primitivism in the early twentieth century. Later *avant-garde* movements, more literary and conceptual than visual in their inspiration, can also be understood in terms of an attraction to the exotic: the counter-cultural movements of the 1960s and 1970s were drawn to the Far East, in particular, as a means to subvert Western norms and logic.

Yet Segalen's work was little known in the decades following his death, and exoticism as a concept acquired new pejorative connotations in the era of decolonization. Césaire saw Western knowledge of other cultures as dependent on the falsifications of exoticism made by amateurs (1955 [1950]); Fanon in *Toward the African Revolution* (1964) saw exoticism as a form of simplification that prevents confrontations between cultures (Forsdick, 2000: 48). Theirs has been the dominant interpretation of the exotic in postcolonial theory. It is, moreover, largely on the work of the French theorist Michel Foucault that Edward Said drew for the theoretical basis of *Orientalism* (1978), that milestone in the postcolonial denunciation of literary exoticism's role as an instrument of the West's construction of the Other. More recently, French theorists have condemned exoticism from the particularly French perspective of humanist universalism, once reflected in the colonial-era *mission civilisatrice* and the Republican ideal of assimilation, but which has reappeared in a new form. French theory in relation to exoticism could thus, at risk of simplification, be seen as oscillating between three poles: the (anti-colonialist) denunciation of the exotic as ossified tradition; the exotic as defining a counter-hegemonic position; and the assertion of universalism as overriding, but also containing, the exotic. This chapter will look at several key thinkers of the last third of the twentieth century, whose divergent paths – although they share some beginnings in the avant-garde of the 1960s–70s – contribute in extremely varied ways to debates on exoticism and, thus, indirectly to postcolonial criticism.

Tel Quel and the subversion of Western ideology

The journal *Tel Quel* (1960–82) left an enduring mark on the French intellectual scene through its association with a group of intellectuals who included Roland Barthes, Julia Kristeva, Philippe Sollers and Jacques Derrida. Disillusioned after 1968 by the French Communist Party, these left-wing intellectuals increasingly sought an alternative model of theoretical and political revolution, which they situated largely in the Chinese Cultural Revolution. Chinese culture, and Maoism in particular, were used as a means of subverting (Western) state ideology, taking on a privileged relation to the group's emergent poststructuralism (Young, 2001a: 187). Sollers used his influence to assist in the publication of Maria-Antonietta Macciocchi's volume *De la Chine* (1971), which was to trigger virulent debates in French political circles. It served the group as a weapon against the French Communist Party, its praise of Maoism being used to highlight the failings of classic Marxism. This publication initiated the peak Maoist period of

Tel Quel, with a double issue on Chinese thought in 1972. The group's fascination with China represented both a political allegiance to Maoism, and aesthetic and philosophical concerns, in particular the desire to establish links with a non-Western mode of thought. Their interest was, however, predominantly in *ancient* Chinese culture, so that the suggestion that their aesthetic concerns are politically grounded in Maoism is generally tenuous (Forest, 1995; ffrench, 1995). Many of the group travelled to China in 1974 (11 April–2 May). The delegation included Sollers, Kristeva, Marcelin Pleynet, Roland Barthes and François Wahl (Jacques Lacan was to have accompanied them, but withdrew at the last moment). A whole issue of *Tel Quel* was devoted to the trip, and following numbers also concentrated more or less on Maoist China. In 1975 Kristeva published a collective volume, *La Traversée des signes*, whose contributors look at Chinese, Sanskrit, Islamic and biblical poetry as foreshadowing modernism, a reading whose emphasis on textuality and the ancient Orient is reminiscent of much nineteenth-century exoticism.

By 1976, however, *Tel Quel* was distancing itself discreetly from its Maoist allegiance, which has since come to be seen as a source of ineffaceable shame. Yet the group's Maoism was not intended as an allegiance to totalitarianism, but as an act of subversion: China in their works operated as a means to found the possibility of a new poetic language, and to engage in an aggressive dialectic with French conservatives and staid French communism alike (Forest 1995: 484–85). Of course, such idealization of the Cultural Revolution was only possible because of the censorship of information coming from China. And ignorance as the basis for utopian politics, like the emphasis on the distant past, is in itself typical of the workings of a certain type of exoticism.

Barthes and Kristeva: shifting relations to the exotic

Roland Barthes has a double relationship to exoticism. His early work, *Mythologies* (1957), can be read as having an anti-colonialist aim: to denounce the false consciousness of white, middle-class European constructions of the world, including racist or 'orientalist' structures. Barthes's development of semiology in the 1950s and 1960s was an attempt to undermine bourgeois rhetoric in all its forms, among other things a critique of 'white' forms of consciousness in response to the decolonizing process that was going on at the time (Sandoval, 1997: 87; 95). He draws a direct parallel between colonialism and capitalist exploitation, and sees exoticism as a petit bourgeois strategy of mystification, which serves to situate the Other in nature and deny its historicity. Indeed, the French critique of humanism was from the outset not merely philosophical, but grounded in anti-colonialism (Young, 1990: 123). Yet the polemical anti-colonialist attacks made by Barthes in *Mythologies* have often been underestimated (Knight, 1993: 620–21; Sandoval, 1997: 96), partly because Barthes himself does not acknowledge the parallels between his theories and those of contemporary anti-colonialist thinkers such as Fanon.

In his later work, however, Barthes's relation to exoticism shifts significantly, moving from acerbic critique in the late 1950s to 'the dramatic practice of orientalism as a writing strategy in the mid-1970s' (Lowe, 1991: 153). Inspired by Barthes's trip to Japan in 1966, *Empire of Signs* (1970) has thus been seen as falling into the very traps that he denounced in *Mythologies*. It can be read in parallel with his brief response to the 1974 trip to China 'Well, and China?' (1975), although he was notoriously lacking in enthusiasm about the experience, projecting China as above all boring and bland, a flat surface that frustrates the Western gaze and its desire to find meaning. In China, however, pure political discourse is omnipresent, so that as for other members of *Tel Quel*, the Far East is an imagined space from which to criticize the West. Japan, similarly, is not approached as a separate nation with its own traditions and modes of thought, but as a sign system characterized by its reducibility to the void, a conclusion which itself involves a certain refusal to look into the complexities of Japanese life (Forsdick, 2000: 54–56). The volume has been dismissed as mere 'impressionism' (Todorov, 1993 [1989]: 345–46) and as typical of a 'postmodern aesthetic [that] continues to raid the "inarticulate" cultural forms of the "Third World", to "textualize" a geographically lost terrain' (see Kumkum Sangari in Ashcroft et al., 1995: 145). Yet *Empire of Signs* is extremely self-aware about its use of both the language of exoticism and of 'Japan' to project a fantasized civilization that stands as an imaginary space of the untranslatable in which the West and its symbolic system are subverted (Célestin, 1995: 144, 159, 172). This acute self-reflexivity effectively pre-empts any accusation of a possible slip into naively 'authentic' representation. Barthes' writings on Japan and China reflect an attempt 'to devise new writing practices in order to escape the reactive formation of ideology and counterideology' (Lowe, 1991: 158). They can be read as a rejection of the Western will to meaning and the orientalist metaphor of penetrative domination (Ha, 2000: 95–117), and as a challenge to the relegation of the Other to the domain of nature (Célestin, 1995: 141). In this sense, Barthes pursues Segalen's effort to 'envision a place of otherness and difference capable of putting into question the claims of the sovereign self imagined in the "West"' (Harootunian, 2002: xviii).

This defence of Barthes seems, however, problematic in the light of a much less public textual production that followed his stay in Morocco (1968–69), and in which he conflates sexuality and the Orient: *Incidents* (written in 1969 but not published until after his death, in 1987) celebrates the sexual availability of Third-World subjects in Sadeian terms. During his Moroccan stay Barthes was, moreover, working on his book about Japan, in a curious process according to which North Africa is a foil for the fantasy of another, more distant Orient that has the advantage of not being caught up in the problematics of the French language and colonialist heritage: he makes Morocco into 'the ideological reverse side of a utopian Japan' (Knight, 1993: 622; 630). The writings on Morocco reflect a slippage towards the conflation of liberated sexuality with the Orient, a traditional trope of orientalism found in Gide's writings and also in the work of earlier exoticist writers, such as Pierre Loti, whose Turkish novel Barthes helped to put back on the literary map through an essay 'Pierre Loti: *Aziyadé*' (1971), which emphasizes its play on sexual ambiguity and its homosexual subtext.

Julia Kristeva's first major engagement with the exotic was in the text *About Chinese Women* (1974), an extremely personal response to the *Tel Quel* trip to China, in which she relates to Chinese women through her own situation as a foreigner in France and as an isolated female intellectual. She begins with an emblematic moment: the discovery, in the gaze of the Chinese peasants, that the Western viewer is the Other for his/her Other. This returned gaze of the Other is, of course, an old theme, explored by French thinkers from Montaigne to Segalen. Most of all, however, the Chinese experience is of particular value for Kristeva because she associates the supposed matriarchal systems of ancient, pre-Confucian China with a pre-oedipal phase of childhood. China is thus a key to her attempt to renew the vision of gender proposed by psychoanalysis by putting to the fore the concept of a pre-oedipal phase which precedes the child's entrance into the symbolic, or language, and the social order. Kristeva's version of this phrase emphasizes the child's identification with the mother and the feminine; thus, for example, she interprets tonal language as being a remnant of the preverbal rhythms of the maternal body. She links this matriarchal theory with a utopian understanding of Chinese communism in the 1970s. In Lisa Lowe's terms, 'her figuration of Chinese otherness is part of a strategy to subvert Western ideology by positing a feminine, maternal realm outside its patriarchal system' (1991: 137). China, and its vast history, thus serve as support for Kristeva's theory of an archaic, pre-linguistic maternal space that she calls the 'chora', a concept developed in 1974 in her *Revolution in Poetic Language*. Kristeva, like Barthes, can thus be seen as using China as a utopian Other space, whose main function is to serve as a foil to the West.

More than a decade later, in *Strangers to Ourselves* (1988), Kristeva moves towards the third pole of French exoticist theory and a reaffirmation of universal values. She looks at the stranger or foreigner encountered not abroad but 'at home', and covers a wide historic range, from ancient Greek and biblical accounts through the European tradition of the Renaissance and the Enlightenment, up to the present day and recent nationalism. She sees the foreigner in the light of our projection of the stranger within, which leads towards a call in the name of Freudian psychoanalysis to accept difference, 'l'inquiétante étrangeté', the *unheimlich* or uncanny within us all, so that accepting the strangeness within the self becomes a basis for living with difference in others. This combination of psychoanalysis with a surprising reversion to humanism has not always convinced critics (e.g. Moruzzi, 1993).

In other, more specifically literary works, Kristeva developed the concept of intertextuality, a model of literary transmission that is significantly different from that put forward in Said's *Orientalism* (see, notably, her essay, 'Word, Dialogue, and Novel' [1969], and *Revolution in Poetic Language*). Intertextuality sees literature as able to transgress and transform itself and the world, though without passing through an autonomous subject (the 'author'), who was famously being declared dead around this time. Through intertextuality, writing is able to engage actively with an anterior textual corpus, whereas in Said's *Orientalism*, on the contrary, each text is bound in an overarching paradigm that sees it helplessly repeating what has been said before (ffrench, 1995: 170). Whether Kristeva's intertextuality and similar approaches could thus be used as a means of renewing our reading of the exotic literary impulse is a question that remains to be fully thought through.

Foucault and the discursive construction of the Other

Michel Foucault, who was briefly associated with the *Tel Quel* group, but rapidly distanced himself from it and, indeed, from communism in general, never directly addressed the issues of imperialism. The Eurocentrism of his approach has often been criticized by postcolonial theorists (Said, 1986; Spivak, 1987; JanMohamed, 1992; Stoler, 1995). Young (1995b; 2001a) underlines the paradoxical and perhaps deliberate nature of this silence in the context of the 1950s and 1960s, especially given Foucault's two-year residence in Tunisia (1966–68). Yet despite this, his work has had an enormous influence on postcolonial theory. His theorization of the discursive construction of Europe's *internal* Others has contributed indirectly to postcolonial theory. Moreover, certain less well-known aspects of his work, which have become widely available relatively recently, can be seen as having a more direct bearing on imperialism.

Although it was not explicitly applied to the context of imperialism, Foucault's critique of historicism and humanism as globalizing discourses is an important basis for postcolonial theory, as is his highlighting of authority and exclusion, technologies of power and apparatuses of surveillance. Said's *Orientalism* is a key example of the reliance on Foucauldian theoretical models in major works of Anglo-American postcolonial theory, referring most directly (Said, 1978: 3) to the notion of discourse in *The Archaeology of Knowledge* (1969) and *Discipline and Punish* (1975). Said applied these models to questions of colonialism, showing how orientalism developed as a conceptual structure and a language that gave authority over the 'Orient'. The idea of examining orientalism as a 'discourse' (rather than, say, a discipline) stems from a Foucauldian emphasis on discourses of power in which the interdependence of knowledge and power is fundamental, as is suggested by his use of the compound term 'power/knowledge'. For Said, as for Foucault, knowledge and scholarship are not autonomous, but are, instead, always formed through an interaction with systems of power. Thus, orientalism is complicit in imperialism and cannot be considered separately, or as a mere side-effect. For Young, however, Said's orientalism is a discursive practice that misrepresents an outside reality, which in itself 'implies an ideology-versus-reality distinction, or signifier-signified distinction, which Foucault's analyses explicitly reject' (Young, 2001a: 399). In his later work, moreover, Said distances himself from his earlier adherence to Foucauldian discourse analysis because of concerns about its theoretical 'overtotalization' that did not allow sufficient space for resistance (Said, 1983; see also Bové, 1986).

Foucault did, however, deal with the key subject of race, although this is not usually seen as a direct contribution to postcolonial theory because he considers it *within* the West. In the 1970s he moved towards a more explicit focus on power and on discursive systems of domination and exploitation, and the first volume of *The History of Sexuality* (1976) links sexuality with the construction of the concept of race (see Stoler, 1995). Here he developed the concept of 'biopouvoir' [biopower], and, in a contemporaneous series of lectures at the Collège de France in 1975–76 (which were not published until much later (1997, as *Society Must be Defended*), he applied this concept to the appearance, in England and France in the seventeenth century, of a new historical discourse that introduced the paradigm of 'racial war' (between Saxons and Normans, Gauls and Franks). This theme was used to undermine the power of the absolute monarchy and promote the role of the aristocracy, itself for the first time viewed as a racial group. This subversive use of racial theory to suggest division *within* society was rapidly appropriated by the state, so that racialization became a means of keeping the Other at a distance.

Biopower, as deployed by the state, is the technology that regulates the human – no longer considered as an individual but as a population – through birth rate, hygiene, mortality, epidemics, and the concept of race itself. Indeed, in Foucault's account, racism is a necessary consequence of the emergence of biopower. His focus on *state* racism leads him, perhaps surprisingly, to see it as emerging no earlier than the late nineteenth century; indeed, he finished his lecture series by comparing the state racism that was constitutive of Nazism with that of Stalinism, a comparison that appears to have been rather shocking in France at a time when there was considerable sympathy for the communist model.

It has been suggested that Foucault shared the utopian exoticism of other French thinkers of his generation (Schaub, 1989; Kurasawa, 1999). Cited as an example of Foucault's exoticism is his use of Borges's Chinese encyclopaedia in the preface to *The Order of Things* (1966) as a diametric opposite to European thought. Overall, however, Foucault's theory can be seen as part of a reaction against the universalism of the Enlightenment and an attempt to reinterpret the history of discourse by including the subject position of the Other, though for him that Other is, above all, within society (the madman, the prisoner), rather than without. The exotic impulse is not fundamental to this thought; rather, it is the absence of a direct approach to the problematics of imperialist racism in his work that could be seen as symptomatic of a certain Eurocentrism.

The new humanist universalism

Unlike the *Tel Quel* group, many of the French critics engaged in the study of colonial discourse and literature can most clearly be distinguished from their Anglo-American counterparts by their emphasis on universalism. Their adherence to concepts of universal, 'natural' law and political citizenship, which are seen in the French context as republican values, leads them to a rejection of cultural relativism. This new universalism is not, however, to be caricatured as a mere echo of the old colonial version; it tends to situate itself in terms of exchange or hybridity [*métissage*], while still insisting on legal equality and universal principles. The most important theorist to apply this humanist universalism to the postcolonial condition is Tzvetan Todorov.

Reacting against his own 1960s association with *Tel Quel*, Todorov published two works, *The Conquest of America* (1982) and *On Human Diversity: Nationalism, Racism, and Exoticism in French Thought* (1989), both of which attempt to rehabilitate the Enlightenment tradition of universalism in approaches to human diversity (see also Todorov, 1986). His attempt to reinvent a humanist position involves opposing political extremes both to the right and the left, as well as criticism of the more sophisticated forms of anti-humanism in theorists such as Foucault and Claude Lévi-Strauss.

Todorov is opposed to relativism, of which he considers exoticism and nationalism to be two opposite, but symmetrical, forms: exoticism positions the Other as superior, just as nationalism does the self. Both value judgements are misguided, since they are based only on where one is positioned. Moreover, 'knowledge is incompatible with exoticism, but lack of knowledge is in turn irreconcilable with praise of others; yet praise without knowledge is precisely what exoticism aspires to be' (1993 [1989]: 265). Todorov's defence of universalism also seeks to undermine its association with imperialism by distinguishing it from ethnocentrism, which, like scientism, is merely a caricature of true universalism. In true universalism humanity is one because the Other is, fundamentally, just like 'us'.

Todorov's reading of the exotic in terms of the opposed poles of universalism and relativism (1993) is weighted heavily in one direction by his association of relativism with racialists such as Ernest Renan, Arthur de Gobineau and Gustave Le Bon. It is through such an association that he condemns the relativists (e.g. Segalen and Lévi-Strauss), whose defence of the exotic leads them to reject the tendency to cultural (and racial) 'mixity'. Relativism, according to Todorov's argument, is not really a solution at all, since it leads either to inconsistency or to the denial of the unity of the human species. He calls instead for a new critical humanism that will reject the dangers of 'perverted universalism' and relativism alike, and he bases it on the idea that the universality of humanity lies in liberty and the ability to reject determinism.

Todorov's brief preface to the French translation of Said's *Orientalism* (1980), while it is globally positive, highlights Said's failure to indicate the way forward to a new, lucid, non-utopian morality of tolerance (one which, implicitly, his own universalist humanism aims to provide). In fact, he sees many of the critical positions of postcolonial theory as falling into an inverted ethnocentrism by maintaining cultural relativism. Nor does he accept the central postcolonial tenet that the colonized Other is produced by imperialist discourse. In *The Conquest of America* he attempts to base his analysis of intercultural encounters on neutral, disinterested categories such as the means of communication. This has in itself been seen as an attempt to depoliticize the debate, and indeed Todorov's supposedly neutral categories appear in many ways to echo colonialist discourse by emphasizing the absence of certain traits among the Aztecs that are defined according to a European norm, such as phonetic writing (Root, 1988: 199; 206–08). Todorov thus ascribes the Aztec defeat to an inherent inability to adapt and improvise and to give value to the individual, which he links to the use of pictograms; this is seen by some as 'essentially a racialist explanation' (Root, 1988: 215).

Yet it is perhaps too simplistic to view Todorov as a 'neocolonial wolf, dressed in the sheep's clothing of "universality"' (Gates, 1986: 408). In a way that is ironically reminiscent of Segalen, Todorov sees human identity as being constituted through exchange with the Other (1996). The presence of the Other is thus understood as a constitutive human need, not to be limited to the sexual drive or to a Hegelian struggle for power. Indeed, to avoid reducing the human search for recognition to Hegel's antagonistic pair of master and slave, Todorov substitutes it with the parent/child couple in what could equally be read as an attempt to revalorize the exotic temptation from within universalism.

In French theory, clearly, the relation to the Other is a shifting paradigm, and debates over exoticism in its various forms are far from conclusive. In an apparent paradox, while French theory is more attracted to universalism than is commonly seen as acceptable in the English-speaking world, it is also more ready to admit the attraction of the 'exotic'. The distant glow of the exotic has seemed to offer hope of a counter-hegemonic position, however fragile this might appear in retrospect. And yet French theory – the early Barthes, Foucault – has also provided inspiration for a reading of the exotic in the harsher light of our own era of suspicion. This plurality of positions, these internal contradictions of twentieth-century readings of the exotic in France, should in themselves suggest to us that the self-righteous search for the cliché to which colonial discourse analysis can so often be reduced is not in itself enough. Such a willingness to take exoticism seriously, so that the gaze turned outwards towards the Other is not automatically – or not *only* – read as exploitative, is nowhere more apparent than in the critical approach known as *imagologie*. Originating in post-war France and Germany, imagology defines itself as an anthropology of the imaginary, with particular emphasis on the representation of the foreign and the foreigner (Moura, 1998). It has close links to the venerable tradition of comparative literature, but concentrates instead on intercultural relations, understood in terms of mutual perceptions, images and self-images. Based neither in utopian counter-hegemony nor in ultimately conservative universalism, imagology offers a critical practice, if not a fully fledged theoretical approach, which suggests a more nuanced understanding of the ways in which diversity can be perceived than is common in the English-speaking world. Like French theory, in its very varied extremes, French critical practice thus suggests ways of approaching the 'Other' that include a serious and nuanced engagement with the exotic position – that is, with the European gaze turned outwards towards diversity.

Further reading

Lowe, Lisa, 1991. *Critical Terrains: French and British Orientalisms* (Ithaca, NY, and London: Cornell University Press). Lowe's landmark volume offers a significant reinterpretation of Said's *Orientalism* by situating orientalist texts in a heterogeneous tradition, both historically and in terms of class and gender differences. She looks at discourse in terms of disruption, change and even resistance, covering a range of texts from Montesquieu to Barthes.

Stoler, Ann Laura, 1996. *Race and the Education of Desire: Foucault's 'History of Sexuality' and the Colonial Order of Things* (Durham, NC: Duke University Press). This is the first major study to place Foucault's work in explicit relation to issues of postcolonial theory. It looks both at his omissions and at the significant contributions his theory has made indirectly, notably taking into account material only recently available, such as the lecture series at the Collège de France.

Todorov, Tzvetan, 1993 [1989]. *On Human Diversity: Nationalism, Racism, and Exoticism in French Thought*, tr. Catherine Porter (Cambridge, MA: Harvard University Press). [First published as *Nous et les autres: la réflexion française sur la diversité humaine.*] This is a major historical overview of French exoticism or reflection on human diversity from Montaigne to the twentieth century. Extremely thought-provoking, it contrasts various forms of universalism and relativism that are reinterpreted in the light of Todorov's humanist universalism.

CHAPTER 15

The End of the Ancien Régime French Empire

Laurent Dubois

During the last decades of the eighteenth century and the first decades of the nineteenth, the major Atlantic empires confronted, and in several cases succumbed to, movements for national independence in the Americas. The political defeats in the Americas overlapped with, and sometimes drove, the painfully slow elimination of the Atlantic slave trade, though slavery itself survived in one form or another in all the independent American republics except for one. They also overlapped with – and informed, both as sources of inspiration and as warnings – the beginnings of territorial expansion into Africa and Asia. Events in all the Atlantic empires shaped each other profoundly as well. These overlapping and interconnected historical turning points can only be understood in relation to one another, and yet one must also seek to untangle them in order to understand the various forces at work in the reconfiguration of empire during the period.

Haiti, France and the Americas

The French Atlantic empire was thriving in the late eighteenth century, chiefly through the immense productivity of its Caribbean colonies. And it was there, particularly in its most important colony of Saint-Domingue, that this empire was challenged, transformed and, ultimately, largely undone. As a result, the French presence in the Americas diminished substantially, not in territorial terms, since the land held by France in the late eighteenth century was in fact quite small, but in economic and political terms. Yet the undoing of France's eighteenth-century Atlantic empire took place in quite a different way from that of the Spanish and British. For while in the other Atlantic empires slaves played crucial roles in independence struggles, they were not its central protagonists. In the French Atlantic, however, it was slave revolutionaries who confronted, reformulated and, ultimately, expelled empire in what had been its most important location: Saint-Domingue. The creation of Haiti had multiple and in some ways contradictory effects on the long-term history of French empire, and long remained – as it remains, in some ways – a spectre that is at once everywhere and, all too often, invisible.

What from one perspective registers as a defeat of imperial designs can also be signalled as an impressive feature of the history of the French Atlantic. Alone among the American empires, France generated – and, for a time, actually embraced – a successful slave revolution. In an Atlantic world whose central pillar was the slave trade and slavery, this stands out as a curious success: one not willed, by any means, by imperial governors, and yet one that can only be understood if it is situated within the history of the French imperial system. One can argue that Haiti could have happened in other colonies, and it is undeniable that large-scale slave resistance and revolt took place essentially in all of the colonies. But Haiti did not happen in any other empire. And it is worth taking stock of that, and considering why that might be, and what it might tell us about French Atlantic colonialism. In this chapter, I consider how we might interpret the Haitian Revolution, and the broader transformations of French empire in the late eighteenth century, not just as a counterpoint and undoing of that empire but also as its product.

France's American empire has several interesting geographical features that are worth noting from the outset. While it included vast portions of North America for over a century, the areas that were geographically most significant within the empire were economically the least important. French colonization in the Americas began, roughly in parallel, in the Eastern Caribbean in St Christopher and then Guadeloupe and Martinique (Boucher, 1992), and eastern North America, in what became Quebec. Colonization in Louisiana began later, but by the early eighteenth century the French could lay claim to a vast territory that stretched through Canada, down the Mississippi and to the Gulf Coast. They could lay claim, and they did – and yet, as is often the case in frontier colonialism, this claim was largely imagined and imaginative. In fact, through most of this territory, small numbers of French traders and travellers, often married into Native American communities, participated in a world of trade and culture that they influenced but never controlled. The circulation of people, products and, often and importantly, diseases, reshaped Native American worlds in all of these regions. But to claim that the French actually controlled this territory, outside a few settlements and missions in Canada and Louisiana, would be a powerful exaggeration (White, 1991). And these settlements themselves often stagnated, their demographic history contrasting with that of the British North American colonies, which drew larger numbers of Europeans and evolved differently as a result.

Settlements throughout North America confronted similar problems, and yet French Canada and Louisiana drew far fewer voluntary migrants from Europe. The reasons for this are complex: there were demographic differences between the British Isles and France; while both countries were prey to deep and violent religious conflict during the early modern period, it took a somewhat different shape in each case; and certain aspects of imperial policy, as well as the particularities of climate, Native American response, and disease environments in the French settlements all also played a role. Of course, it is difficult to know what would have happened in Louisiana and Canada if these territories had not been surrendered by a defeated France at the end of the Seven Years' War, which played a crucial role in the history of the British, French and Spanish empires in the late eighteenth century.

Both before but especially after the Seven Years' War, the centre of France's empire was in the Caribbean, which, over the course of the seventeenth and eighteenth centuries provided the most dynamic and profitable colonies. In this French territories did not differ substantially from British North America. The wealthiest settlers in the Anglo-Atlantic were also in colonies such as Barbados and Jamaica; moreover, the Southern plantation economies, as well as the New England slave-trading, logging and rum-producing industries, were all tightly linked to the Caribbean. But because France's North American colonies were more sparsely populated and ultimately less profitable than Britain's, and because it lost its territories there in the mid-eighteenth century, the Caribbean became even more central for France than for Britain. Of course, the opposite is also true: it was in part *because* France prized its Caribbean colonies so much that it agreed to the cession of Canada. At one point during the negotiations with Britain at the end of the Seven Years' War, the major debate on both sides was: what was more valuable – the tiny Eastern Caribbean island of Guadeloupe, or Canada? On both sides, there were many who argued that the obvious answer was Guadeloupe, which, largely thanks to British investment during the occupation years had expanded into an important sugar-producing colony that seemed both more profitable and easier to control than a vast territory like Canada.

Slavery and the French Atlantic economy

The size of colonial territory mattered much less, ultimately, than what it could produce and generate for the metropole. And the Caribbean produced sugar, coffee and indigo. Sugar was especially important and especially profitable for France, which, unlike Britain, exported a large portion of its colonial sugar production to other nations of Europe, satisfying much of the continent's ever-more demanding sweet tooth. This was where the money was: in the slave trade, in the plantation commodities produced by slave labour, and in the processing and selling of these commodities to European markets. For French migrants seeking a fortune in the Americas, the Caribbean was the destination of choice, though with land relatively scarce by the mid-eighteenth century such migrants often found it hard to establish a footing in the colonies. The French government invested in the colonies through military and naval infrastructure, which were essential in an eighteenth century traversed by imperial wars, as well as through public works projects, most notably the construction of successful irrigation works in certain plains of Saint-Domingue. And the plantation colonies grew at a stunning pace. This was particularly true of Saint-Domingue, which was only settled in the mid-to-late seventeenth century, and whose plantation economy expanded significantly only at the beginning of the eighteenth. Yet, by the end of that century, it was the leading producer of sugar in the world – matching the exports of Jamaica, Cuba and Brazil combined. It also produced about half of the world's coffee. It was a stunning economic success, and one remarked upon throughout the Americas and Europe (Dubois 2004a).

Le Cap, Saint-Domingue's economic (though not political) capital, was the size of Boston. Le Cap and St Pierre in Martinique were important cultural centres of the eighteenth-century world, boasting scientific societies, as well as active and important theatres that drew actors and musicians from France. In addition to the classic plays by Voltaire and Molière, the newest works arrived quickly from the metropole, and there was also a tradition of local plays, some written in Creole and including slave characters (performed by whites in black-face). The first balloon flight in the Americas took place above a sugar planta-tion in the northern plain of Saint-Domingue in 1784. There were important jurists, the most famous of them the Martiniquan-born Moreau de St Méry, who argued for a locally generated jurisprudence based on local knowledge. From the Caribbean colonies came poets, such as Nicolas Léonard, musicians, for example the Chevalier de Saint-Georges, and a series of revolutionary generals, most notably the Guadeloupean planter Coquille Dugommier and Alexandre Dumas, the son of a slave master and a slave woman, and the father of the great nineteenth-century author of the same name.

French Caribbean political and cultural traditions would shape the horizons of many societies, notably those of Louisiana, where refugees from Saint-Domingue would double the population of New Orleans in the early nineteenth century and create a community whose descendants, among them Homer Plessy, would one day play central roles in the struggle against segregation in the United States. The impact of the French empire – specifically linked to the new cultures and politics generated in the colonies, largely by slaves and free people of African descent – would infuse and outlast the actual French territo-rial control of Louisiana.

Metropolitan France was, of course, also permanently transformed by this imperial process. The port towns of Bordeaux, Nantes and La Rochelle boomed entirely because of the trade with the colonies, primarily those of the Caribbean, and the slave trade that sustained these colonies. The Atlantic trade opened up opportunities for families to enrich themselves and gain economic and political clout. But the effects of colonial trade seeped through all of France. The ideological and cultural impacts were also enormous. The confrontation with Native American cultures, first through the Jesuit texts and ultimately through the writings of a range of philosophical thinkers, helped to shape ideas of 'natural law', and the debate about the morality of slavery, while often muted and contradictory, infused philosophical tracts, novels and many plays. Through all of this, the configuration and reconfiguration of racial ideologies created a complex terrain of thought and representation that constituted an important foundation for later forms of colonial racism and anti-racism. In Paris, slaves working with leading jurists brought masters to trial, arguing that since slavery had been abolished in France centuries before, they were free the moment they set foot in the metropole. In many cases, they won, creating in the meantime an important set of legal precedents, even as the royal government allowed for the creation of loopholes, especially in the port towns, that allowed for masters to safely keep their slaves in metropolitan France. Free men and women of African descent, as well as slaves, lived in the port towns and in Paris, as well as in smaller French towns: the future author of the Haitian Declaration of Independence, Louis Boisrond-Tonnerre, lived and was educated in the small town of Tonnerre, south of Paris (Garrigus, 2006). The integrated circuits of the French empire of the eighteenth century helped to create contacts and networks that were powerfully mobilized for change during the Haitian Revolution.

The French Atlantic, then, was a highly connected world, whose poles were Saint-Domingue and Martinique, the Atlantic port towns, and Paris, but in which other regions under French control – such as Gorée and St Louis in Senegal, Guadeloupe and French Guiana, and Louisiana and Canada – all shaped and were shaped by the broader matrix of imperial domination. And all of these regions were also deeply connected to other centres: kingdoms and polities in West and Central Africa, various political configurations among Native Americans, and the many port towns of other empires, whether Spanish, Dutch, Danish, British, and later those of the independent United States.

Slavery and revolution in the French Atlantic

Within this complex world, though, there was one central artery: the mass deportation of Africans across the Atlantic and into these Caribbean societies. Throughout the early nineteenth century, it was this crossing that brought the vast majority of peoples to the Americas: according to one recent estimate, 77 per cent of those who crossed the Atlantic before 1820 came from Africa. The Caribbean was the largest destination for these slaves, receiving 48 per cent of the total (Davis, 2006: 80; 104). Saint-Domingue alone received between 850,000 and 1 million slaves (perhaps 10 per cent of the entire volume of the slave trade) during its short existence. Africans, then, were by far the largest group of individuals to arrive in the French colonies of the Americas. And their enslaved labour was the foundation for the wealth of the French Atlantic.

It was also these enslaved people who would generate the revolution that confronted and transformed the French empire in the Americas in the last decades of the eighteenth century. Through a massive slave revolution that began in 1791, they established themselves as a political, military and ideological force that could not be circumvented. They deployed a range of discursive and symbolic forms in presenting their demands, from associations with the kings of France and Spain (and, at least at one point, Africa) to insistence that

199

the Declaration of the Rights of Man and of the Citizen applied to them and should be understood as rendering slavery effectively illegal. They won a series of compounding victories, culminating in 1793 when the French commissioner in Saint-Domingue declared slavery abolished there, and all former slaves free citizens. This decision was ratified in Paris in 1794. In its wake, emancipation was consolidated in Saint-Domingue under the leadership of Toussaint Louverture (Dubois, 2004a).

In each of the Eastern Caribbean colonies of Martinique and Guadeloupe, the events of the revolutionary period took a different course. In Martinique, where an early slave revolt in August of 1789 augured the broader process that would follow in the region, mobilization both of the enslaved and of free people of colour parallelled that in other colonies. But in early 1794 Martinique was occupied by the British, who would hold on to the island, thus 'preserving' it from the abolition of slavery, until it was returned to France at a moment when Bonaparte had decided to reverse the policies of emancipation. Guadeloupe, the theatre of several slave revolts, including a large one at Trois-Rivières in 1793, was also occupied by the British in early 1794. But a few months later a small French mission, carrying the decree of emancipation from Paris, arrived and managed to take back the island, with the support of slaves transformed into soldier-citizens. As in Saint-Domingue, emancipation was decreed and instituted through a regime that mixed liberation with new forms of labour coercion, justified both through the needs of wartime France and through a rhetoric of 'Republican racism', grounded in part in abolitionist portrayals of the degrading effects of slavery itself. Guadeloupe became the centre for a Republican campaign against nearby British possessions, which were attacked through armies composed largely of ex-slaves. St Lucia was briefly captured by the French, while conflicts in St Vincent and Grenada, in which French armies allied with local insurgents, continued through the late 1790s (Dubois, 2004b).

After 1794, then, Republican France supported and sustained the former slave insurgents of the Caribbean, and a new and radical political order took root. In Saint-Domingue, and to a lesser extent in the Eastern Caribbean, a new elite of African descent, often made up of people who were free before abolition (such as Toussaint Louverture in Saint-Domingue and Louis Delgrès in Guadeloupe), emerged in the colonies. There were also free men of African descent, notably Jean-Baptiste Belley, serving as representatives for the colonies in the parliaments in Paris. In some sense, this transformation represented the 'end' of the 'ancien régime' empire, for it eliminated many of the basic juridical structures and principles that had governed this empire. In place of a legal order that was highly differentiated between metropole and colony, with, for instance the Code Noir applicable in the colonies but not in the metropole, came a system that was based on the principle of an integrated legal order. There were many ways in which this integrated order was undermined, both by the lack of application of certain laws and the actions of metropolitan commissioners. And yet the population in the Caribbean acted on, and therefore made concrete on many levels, the idea that the laws of the French Republic were to be applied universally across the empire.

What was the ideological and political content of this new order? It represented at once an intense challenge to French empire and a layered compromise with it. On the one hand, figures like Toussaint Louverture and Jean-Baptiste Belley, both former slaves freed by the time of the Revolution, as well as the French aristocrat and general Etienne Laveaux, who was allied with them, articulated a powerful vision of a racially egalitarian Republic in which slavery was replaced by a unity between metropole and colony and between people of all colours. Their main symbol for this new order was the Republican military, but they also sought, in ways ultimately heavy with contradictions, to present the plantation workers themselves as 'new citizens' supporting the imperial order, working for fair wages in new and fair relationships with their former masters.

Although there were serious limits to the freedom experienced by former slaves, the transformations they brought about should not be underestimated. In Saint-Domingue, plantation assemblies were created, where both men and women voted on issues having to do with their work and other matters. Bureaucracies were set up to hear complaints from plantation workers, and they functioned, sometimes imprisoning or punishing whites who overstepped their bounds. Payment, in the form of a portion of plantation production, was delivered to the workers. Perhaps most importantly, the new situation seriously undermined the power of white masters, and on many plantations where they remained or that were rented out to new white landlords, former slaves clearly changed their work habits, putting more energy into their own plots and provisions grounds, and refusing to comply with demands in ways that previously would have probably earned them whippings, or worse. Louverture, especially by the late 1790s, heavily militarized plantation agriculture, convinced that it was the necessary foundation for the preservation of liberty, and black soldiers meted out punishment against plantation workers. Yet it seems clear that most understood that what had happened was an improvement, and perhaps the beginning of a larger process of gaining rights, for despite the limits placed on their freedoms they were quite ready to fight courageously against the French troops who had come to re-establish the old order.

The advantages of this new order for France were numerous and, indeed, acknowledged even by Napoleon Bonaparte, who ultimately destroyed it. Plantation productions may have dropped considerably, but they were steadily rebuilt over the course of the 1790s, notably in the area of coffee production in Saint-Domingue. At the same time, military and political gains were enormous. France, like other Atlantic empires, had always suffered major losses among its troops when they were sent to the Americas, even during peace time, because of the ravages of disease. Emancipation provided the French empire with a method for raising troops in the Caribbean itself, among individuals already acclimatized to the area. And it also provided these troops with an ideological project – they were fighting for and representing the benefits of emancipation – that energized them and allowed them to work with individuals within the colonies they were attacking, as they did to great effect in the Eastern Caribbean. The other empires, and the United States, were, of course, not ready to take the step taken by the French. Even if the British did successfully create units of slaves or former slaves to fight against the French, they had to respond to French advances largely with troops sent from England, losing up to 60,000 in the Caribbean theatre during the 1790s.

The French would, of course, find themselves facing similarly dramatic casualties when in the early 1800s they opted to reverse the emancipatory project of the previous years. This decision not only ended the brief experiment in egalitarian and republican imperial rule but it also triggered the end of much of the territorial empire itself. Bonaparte re-acquired Louisiana from the Spanish as part of a grand plan to rebuild the plantation economy in Saint-Domingue, using Louisiana to grow provisions and harvest timber to sustain this growth (thus replacing the mostly illegal trade with the US that had always provided these goods). His attempt was, in some sense, aimed at reconstructing what had been lost in 1763 after the defeat by the British. But rather than build on the emancipatory order inaugurated in 1794, he decided that it represented a crucial obstacle to his plans. This was a striking decision, for it effectively condemned his plans, something he himself later admitted, realizing that instead of attacking Toussaint he should have 'recognized' him and collaborated with him. But it seems that the major non-negotiable demand of Louverture's regime – the permanent end to racial exclusion, and the racial integration of the ruling class – was too much for the French to accept. France's decision also came at a moment of peace with Britain (negotiated through the Treaty of Amiens starting in late 1801), which meant that the military value of the black armies of the Caribbean was less crucial than it had been before.

In Saint-Domingue, Bonaparte's plans unravelled in the course of a brutal and costly war. Although the French secured the surrender of Louverture and other generals after several months of fighting, and then imprisoned Louverture and sent him to prison in France, where he died, their success was already a sign of their failure. Their mission had been to eliminate the 'colonial' army that Louverture had created, made up of former slaves and men of colour who had been free before the revolution. But, having suffered significant losses through the military campaigns against Louverture, as well as from the continuing fighting and the progress of disease, they found themselves completely dependent on these troops in order to fight against those rebels who continued to resist their presence. Paranoid about defections, they carried out increasingly indiscriminate exactions against even the black troops who were fighting with them. Eventually, they drove generals who were fighting with them, most notably Jean-Jacques Dessalines, into the revolutionary camp. The defection of these generals and their troops helped to consolidate the resistance, and over the course of late 1802 and early 1803 the French position became hopeless. The reopening of war with the British sealed their fate, and on 1 January 1804, Dessalines proclaimed the birth of a new nation called Haiti.

Legacies of the ancien régime empire

In direct response to the situation in Saint-Domingue, Bonaparte decided to sell Louisiana to the United States, quickly abandoning his projects for a reborn French empire in the Americas. In the meeting during which he took this decision, François Barbé-Marbius argued that, in effect, imperial futures were hopeless in the Americas. Arguing in favour of selling Louisiana, he noted that French efforts to create colonies on the continent of America had 'everywhere proved abortive', and that even if Louisiana became prosperous, this would only create the 'germ of independence'. He also argued that ultimately, slavery would be eliminated – that the 'general sentiment of the world is favourable to emancipation' and that this 'movement' of 'public opinion' was unstoppable. Furthermore, the old 'exclusive system' of colonial commerce was also certain to be swept away. Barbé-Marbius's account of his speech must be read with some scepticism, given that he presents himself, from the comfort of 1830, as quite a prescient observer of the doom of colonialism and slavery in the Americas. On the other hand, Barbé-Marbius had almost been killed because of colonial policy – once during the early days of the Revolution in Saint-Domingue (at the hands of whites), and later by being deported to the deadly climate of Guiana – so perhaps his feelings of hostility towards the enterprise were heartfelt. Although his prediction about the end of slavery would take some time to come true, his statements seem a fitting epitaph to the French empire in the Americas (Barbé-Marbius, 1977 [1830]: 263–74).

The ancien régime empire did not end there. Guiana, Guadeloupe, and Martinique – returned to France in 1802, although a few years later it would be reoccupied by the British for a time – remained part of the French empire. Slavery was successfully re-established in Guadeloupe, despite resistance by an army led by Louis Delgrès, and in Guiana. The population of the French Caribbean would have to wait until 1848 for a definitive abolition of slavery. In these French Caribbean colonies, there were important struggles for political and social rights during the late nineteenth and early twentieth centuries, and these culminated in 1946, when all three became fully integrated departments of France, with their colonial subjects transformed into citizens with equal political representation and equal legal rights. These colonies played an important role in the history of France's empire in Africa and Asia, for many Antilleans worked as colonial administrators across the Atlantic. Among them the most famous was Félix Éboué, born in Guiana, who as the governor of French Equatorial Africa, rallied to De Gaulle in 1940, earning himself a place in the French Panthéon in 1949. He was to be followed there decades later by Toussaint Louverture and Louis Delgrès, acknowledged with plaques in the hallway near Éboué's tomb, and by Alexandre Dumas, grandson of a Saint-Domingue slave.

Today, at least a third of French citizens of Caribbean background live in metropolitan France. As debates and struggles over the political status of these départements continue, so do debates about the way in which the history and memory of slavery should be acknowledged, monumentalized and confronted in France. And the Caribbean contribution to France has been made symbolically evident through the presence of football players such as Thierry Henry, William Gallas, Eric Abidal, Florent Malouda, and especially the Guadeloupe-born Lilian Thuram who, in addition to forming the backbone of the French defence has also positioned himself as an eloquent critic of racism and of political figures such as Jean-Marie Le Pen and Nicolas Sarkozy.

Outside the borders of France, its ancien régime empire also continues to influence political and cultural life in Quebec and in Louisiana, where descendants of Caribbean migrants shaped the political and cultural life of New Orleans and, therefore, of the United States as a whole, and where descendants of deported Acadians became 'Cajuns', who maintain ties to French and Canadian history. If the concept of 'Francophonie' can be used to describe this complicated landscape, it certainly must be applied with an understanding of the complex and politically productive history through which French empire was confronted and reformulated from within. For what we might call 'French', on both sides of the Atlantic, was, in fact, always the product of a complex and deeply transcultural process of political, social and cultural transformation, struggle and invention.

Further reading

Boucher, Philip, 1992. *Cannibal Encounters: Europeans and Island Caribs, 1492–1763* (Baltimore, MD: Johns Hopkins University Press). Through its examination of European relations with the indigenous people in the Eastern Caribbean, this book presents an excellent overview of the development of French empire in the region.

Dubois, Laurent, 2004a. *Avengers of the New World: The Story of the Haitian Revolution* (Cambridge, MA: Harvard University Press). This book presents a narrative synthesis of the history of the Haitian Revolution.

Garrigus, John, 2006. *Before Haiti: Race and Citizenship in French Saint-Domingue* (New York: Palgrave-Macmillan). A fine recent study of free people of colour in Saint-Domingue, and of their role in the social order of the pre-revolutionary colony and in the Haitian Revolution itself.

Havard, Gilles, and Cécile Vidal, 2003. *Histoire de l'Amérique française* (Paris: Flammarion). A fine synthesis of the history of French empire throughout North America, which brings together the history of Louisiana and Canada, as well as bridging political and diplomatic history with the approaches of social and cultural history.

White, Richard, 1991. *The Middle Ground: Indians, Empires, and Republics in the Great Lakes Region, 1650–1815* (Cambridge: Cambridge University Press). A classic study of the history of Native American groups and their negotiations and struggles with both the French and the British.

CHAPTER 16

The End of the Republican Empire (1918–62)

Philip Dine

The paradoxical empire

Although it spanned the long century from the Algiers Expedition of 1830 to Algerian independence in 1962, and covered an area only surpassed by the British Empire, France's modern colonial edifice was, throughout its existence, built on sand. This weakness was both structural and conceptual:

> Small islands and extensive continental land masses, the territorial possessions of France were found all around the world, yet were so scattered, so disparate in environment and culture, that they could hardly become the empire *en bloc* that imperialists urged that they be at the end of the nineteenth century. 'Empire' was a verbal convenience, perhaps a shibboleth uttered to conjure up what was not there. (Betts, 1991: 10)

This lack of territorial integrity was exacerbated by an evident failure of imperial will. For the French colonial enterprise was only ever the preoccupation of a relatively small group of activists, with the great majority of the metropolitan population disinclined to invest their savings, still less their lives, in *la France d'outre-mer* [Overseas France]. Such imperial reluctance is underlined by the emergence, even before the First World War, of significant opposition to colonialism, including the socialist leader Jean Jaurès and the celebrated novelist Anatole France. Nevertheless, between 1918 and at least 1945, a broad if essentially tacit consensus may plausibly be said to have existed in favour of France's self-appointed 'civilizing mission' – an imperial vocation celebrated in spectacular fashion by the 1930 Algerian Centenary and the 1931 Paris Colonial Exhibition. Central to this process was the denial of the pre-colonial history of the colonized territories, which, in turn, permitted the systematic suppression of the cultural, psychological and, above all, political identities of their indigenous populations. Effective opposition to the French empire would thus necessitate an extended struggle in the cultural and psychological spheres, as well as more obviously political varieties of contestation. Hence the importance of even such apparently futile demonstrations of resistance as the counter-exhibition organized in 1931 by Louis Aragon, André Breton and other surrealists, who appealed (unsuccessfully) to their compatriots not to visit that year's grandiose display of imperial self-confidence.

The ideological roots of such intellectual hostility to the empire are contained in the oxymoron 'Republican empire' (see Wilder, 2005). For in this juxtaposition of terms, many of the conflicts, as much moral as material, that would systematically undermine and ultimately undo France's colonial project are effectively prefigured. As an influential recent analysis of the French colonial experience has underlined, these terms are mutually contradictory, in that the existence of a republic (of consenting citizens) precludes the existence of a colony (of constrained subjects) (Bancel et al., 2003: 11). In what follows, this basic contradiction between republican principles and colonial practices will be explored, particularly as regards the use made by a variety of thinkers of the paradigm of the French Republic itself. The survey proposed will thus seek to combine a chronology of French decolonization and a typology of Francophone anti-colonial thought over this period, with particular emphasis on the turning against the Republic of its own system of values, together with its most prominent symbols and slogans. This mobilization of republican discourse may conveniently be subdivided into three constituent figures: the Republic of Laws, the Republic of Letters, and the Republic of Revolutions. Each of these rhetorical constructs may in turn be equated with one term of the celebrated republican triptych of *Liberté, Égalité, Fraternité*. However, in the ostensible 'process' of French decolonization, demands for national self-determination were for long overshadowed by calls for the equitable treatment of individuals and for harmony between ethnic communities. In consequence, it is with an examination of appeals to the notional equality of the Republic of Laws that we must open this survey, before going on to consider the real and imagined intellectual fraternity of the Republic of Letters, and then turning finally to the contested political liberties of the Republic of Revolutions.

Equality: the Republic of Laws

The inherent weakness of France's republican empire was exacerbated by the reactions to the recent European hostilities of colonizers and colonized. For French imperialists, the mobilization of the empire's natural and human resources underlined the advantages to be gained by its future development. For the colonized peoples, in contrast, the war not only intensified the harshness of daily life but also revealed the possibility of change. In particular, those transported to France to serve as soldiers or industrial workers were exposed to progressive political currents – especially socialism and, after 1917, communism – thus encouraging a new militancy. A characteristic feature of such Paris-based movements was their syncretism, which itself reflected the commitment to assimilation of France's republican empire. Thus, in the writings of the young Nguyên Ai Quôc (who, as Ho Chi Minh, would go on to lead Vietnam to independence), the principles of the French Revolution were combined with elements drawn from both Confucianism and Marxism-Leninism (Thobie et al., 1990: 191). In a less radical vein, the first black African to be elected to the French National Assembly, Blaise Diagne, from Senegal, who had played a leading role in the imperial war effort, used his parliamentary position to seek what the majority of such activists demanded after the sacrifices of 1914–18, namely the equal citizenship proposed, but only rarely granted, by the republican empire (Biondi, 1992: 15).

The small group actually afforded this privileged status included those, like Diagne, who were to remain committed to the cause of assimilation; however, it also included intellectuals, whose demands would evolve through varieties of reformism to both constitutional and revolutionary forms of nationalism. In consequence, these so-called *évolués* [French-educated autochthons] would constitute an elite group within colonial society and, crucially, be destined to have a disproportionate impact on the cultural and political life of their respective countries. They included pivotal figures such as Ferhat Abbas in Algeria, Aimé Césaire in Martinique, and Léopold Sédar Senghor in Senegal. In their writings and political practice, these products of assimilation all stressed the fundamental contradiction between the daily experience of colonial life and the tenets of the French Revolution, as enshrined in the Declaration of the Rights of Man and of the Citizen (1789). For in the supposedly republican empire, so general was the denial of the 'natural, inalienable, and sacred rights of man' that it was manifestly untrue to state, as did the Declaration's celebrated opening article, that 'men are born and remain free and equal in rights'. Effectively rejecting the 'fusion of imagined administrative responsibility with proclaimed revolutionary purpose [that] was the foundation of French colonial ideology' (Betts, 1991: 17), such colonized intellectuals drew attention to the republican empire's conceptual fault lines and thus mobilized France's own revolutionary legacy for anti-colonial purposes.

Colonial nationalists also found encouragement in the anti-colonial stances of the United States under Woodrow Wilson and the newly established Soviet Union. For its part, the French Communist Party (PCF), founded in 1920, provided a focus for militancy and a model for oppositional organization. The PCF notably expressed solidarity with a number of insurrectionary challenges to French rule in the interwar years, of which the most serious were the Rif wars in Morocco (1925–26) and the Yen Bay uprising in Indo-China (1930). However, if some metropolitan commentators were now motivated by the Marxist-Leninist (and later Stalinist) line of the PCF, many more were inspired by the spirit of 1789 than by that of 1917. Their interventions included the pioneering investigative journalism of Albert Londres, who uncovered the colonial prison system in French Guyana, including the notorious penal colony of Devil's Island (*Au Bagne*, 1924), before going on to expose the virtual slavery endured by African workers in France's sub-Saharan colonies (*Terres d'Ébène*, 1929). Even more influential was the denunciation of colonial abuses made by the leading novelist of the day, André Gide, in his *Voyage au Congo* (1927) and *Retour du Tchad* (1928). Gide had travelled extensively in North Africa in the mid-1890s, where he was among a number of metropolitan intellectuals to discover a personally therapeutic freedom from conventional moral (and specifically sexual) constraints. In contrast, his writings on sub-Saharan Africa were consciously inspired by, and clearly echo, Joseph Conrad's depiction of the horrors of the Belgian Congo in his much-analysed novella *Heart of Darkness* (1902). Like Conrad, Gide does not so much criticize the imperial project itself as make the case for reforms to bring colonial practice into line with the Republic's humanitarian aspirations. Nevertheless, such was the political resonance of Gide's account that questions were asked in the National Assembly; while the accompanying documentary made by his nephew Marc Allégret has been described as 'the first French "anticolonial" film' (Ukadike, 1994: 48). Other influential travel-writings published during this period included those of Paul Morand (*Paris-Tombouctou* and *Magie noire*, both 1928), while Louis-Ferdinand Céline's iconoclastic *Voyage au bout de la nuit* (1932) contained a characteristically bleak episode based on the author's experiences as the manager of a rubber plantation in Cameroon.

If the revelations of celebrated travellers were one way in which the colonies achieved a new visibility in the interwar years, another was the new metropolitan sensitivity to indigenous cultures. This built on the pre-war reappraisal of the 'primitive' art of Africa and Oceania by the French artistic avant-garde, as well as the more recent vogue for black American jazz music. Such high and popular cultural challenges to metropolitan ethnocentrism in turn combined with a rejection of the philosophical values of the supposedly 'developed' societies that had engineered the bloodbath of the Great War. Taking their lead from the cultural pessimism of Oswald Spengler's *Decline of the West* (1918), a number of French intellectuals now looked to the ancient cultures of India and China especially for insights into alternative social models. Situated at the junction of these two great civilizations, colonial Indo-China was to prove particularly appealing for such influential figures as the novelist André Malraux, who wrote extensively on (and in) the territory. Contrary to the received wisdom, his stance on the future of France's South-East Asian 'protectorates' was throughout reformist rather than revolutionary (Harris, 1996: 33–35). In contrast, radical opposition was mounting from the outlawed Indo-Chinese Communist Party, formed by Ho Chi Minh in 1930.

Elsewhere, political challenges to colonial rule were taking similarly militant forms. In Algeria, the undoubted jewel in the French imperial crown, opposition came from a combination of Marxist-inspired revolutionaries, Islamic traditionalists, and such erstwhile proponents of assimilation as the Sétif-based pharmacist, Ferhat Abbas. In 1936, Abbas stated that he was not a nationalist because he had looked for, but could not find, the Algerian nation. However, the failure that year of the leftist Popular Front's plans for significant reforms marked the beginning of a radicalization of Abbas's politics that would transform him and his fellow *évolués* into reluctant revolutionaries. It was against this backdrop, and in the broader context of global economic depression and the rise of fascism, that an important contribution to the colonial debate was made by a young reporter for the left-of-centre *Alger Républicain* newspaper. On the eve of the Second World War, and under the evocative general title 'La Misère de la Kabylie' (1958 [1939]), Albert Camus bore witness to the dreadful conditions of existence of the colonized peoples of Algeria. Although Camus would later be widely condemned (most famously by Jean-Paul Sartre) for his failure to support the goal of Algerian independence, his engagement at this time significantly preceded not only Sartre's own but also that of the great majority of metropolitan intellectuals. His revelations of the famine and chronic unemployment in Kabylia concluded with an appeal for major investment in the region, as well as for the extension of full political rights and associated Republican 'justice' to the local Berber population (1958: 72–73). However, as Algeria and the other colonial territories were caught up in a new European conflagration, the time for paternalist reform, if it had ever existed, was certainly long gone. The pressing need now was for a radical alternative to colonialism. As we shall see, this was perceived most forcefully, and would be engaged with most productively, by a group of intellectuals based in Paris that brought together influential thinkers and activists from the Caribbean and sub-Saharan Africa.

Fraternity: the Republic of Letters

The French empire was both made and unmade on the ground, and just as colonialism was fundamentally the product of the colonizer, anti-colonialism was primarily generated by the colonized (Biondi, 1992: 15). Indeed, the critical engagement of metropolitan intellectuals in the interwar period may itself be understood as a response to new expressions of the colonized's growing self-awareness, especially in the literary domain. Thus, for instance, Gide's writings on the Congo may actually have been prompted by René Maran's *Batouala* (1921) (Jack, 1996: 226). Subtitled a 'véritable roman nègre' [true black novel], this was the first literary work to receive formal recognition of the colonized's ability to speak effectively about his/her own condition when it was awarded the highly prestigious Prix Goncourt. Based on Maran's experiences in Africa with the French colonial service, the novel caused a scandal, mainly because of its author's highly critical preface. Maran's text is of particular importance in that it was subsequently hailed – by no less a figure than Léopold Sédar Senghor – as 'the precursor of negritude in francophone culture' (cited in Coundouriotis, 1999: 5) and may thus be said to mark the beginning of a process in which the French empire began to 'write back'.

René Maran was the first of a highly influential group of Martiniquan writers (Maran himself was born in Martinique of Guyanese parents), each of whom may be said to typify a distinct stage in the evolution of Francophone anti-colonial thought. For if Maran's novel of 1921 represents an early expression of 'black consciousness', Aimé Césaire's long and complex poem *Cahier d'un retour au pays natal* (1939) constitutes its mature expression in the language of Negritude, a now celebrated neologism first used in that seminal work. In turn, Césaire's two most celebrated students at the Lycée Schoelcher in Fort-de-France, Frantz Fanon and Édouard Glissant, would go on to become leading theorists of, respectively, anti-colonial struggle and postcolonial identity. Together with the Guyanese writer Léon Gontran Damas and the Senegalese poet Léopold Sédar Senghor, Césaire was the founder of the most influential colonial literary and cultural movement of the later 1930s and 1940s. A paradoxical product of the policy of assimilation, in that it was an expression of the colonized intellectuals' disaffection with the cultural values of France – and, more generally, of the 'white world' – Negritude took shape in Paris, where *évolués* from the Caribbean and Africa came into contact with black American activists, including W. E. B. Du Bois and Langston Hughes, and where important periodicals such as *L'Étudiant noir* (1935) and, later, *Présence africaine* (1947) were published. At the core of the movement was the assertion of the uniqueness and intrinsic value of African culture, including its diasporic manifestations, all of which were perceived by its advocates to be rooted in a distinctively African 'personality'. Crucially, as Benita Parry has persuasively argued with particular reference to Césaire's writing, 'Negritude is not a recovery of a pre-existent state, but a textually invented history, an identity effected through figurative operations, and a tropological construction of blackness as a sign of the colonised condition and its refusal' (Parry, 2004: 45). The 'coming home' foregrounded by Césaire in his 1939 poem thus not only denotes the personal experience of the returning exile but also offers a key metaphor for the affective reinscription of the hitherto denied individual and the community to which s/he belongs.

Influenced by surrealism and other forms of literary modernism, Césaire's seminal work was not widely read until its republication in 1947, with an important preface by André Breton. The following year, Senghor's *Anthologie de la nouvelle poésie nègre et malgache de langue française* (1948) was accompanied by an even more influential preface, Jean-Paul Sartre's 'Black Orpheus'. In what was to be the first in a series of such interventions, Sartre hailed the poets of Negritude as revolutionaries, describing the 'orphic' descent of the colonized into the darkness of subjective racial identity as a precondition for the emergence of an objectively revolutionary consciousness. While not itself an ideology of revolution, Negritude was thus an important stage in the self-affirmation of colonial intellectuals, and also in the new engagement with colonial issues of the metropolitan cultural elite. In a contemporaneous but lesser-known contribution to this process of reclaiming the hitherto denied history of the colonized, Paul Hazoumé, from Dahomey (modern Benin), published his only novel *Doguicimi* (1938), a work now 'usually identified as the first work of historical fiction from francophone Africa' (Coundouriotis, 1999: 9).

The Negritude movement's assertion of African cultural values is to be set against the French Republic's historical promotion of a unitary national culture. As the backbone of the highly centralized education system established in the

1880s by leading colonialist Jules Ferry, teachers became key figures in the inculcation of Republican values: the so-called 'black hussars' of a regime itself often described as 'the republic of schoolmasters'. Crucially, the competitive examinations used to recruit teachers were open to the colonial *évolués* who had acquired French nationality, with Césaire and Senghor among those brought to Paris as a result. The colonial state's official policies of assimilation and merit-based promotion, expressed in its key institutions of educational recognition, thus offered colonized intellectuals a privileged route to cultural legitimacy and, crucially, political influence. For both Césaire and Senghor this would involve lengthy careers in the French parliament, as well as making them pivotal figures in what became a specifically Francophone and anti-colonial version of the Republic of Letters. Césaire was the Communist parliamentary deputy for Fort-de-France from 1945 to 1956, when he resigned from the PCF; while Senghor, who also entered politics in 1945, would go on to become independent Senegal's first president in 1960, remaining in office until 1980. These iconic figures of the Negritude movement thus embodied the permanent tension between centrifugal and centripetal forces, both cultural and political, that typified nationalist movements within the republican empire. They may thus be fairly described, in the words of the eminent Trinidadian theorist C. L. R. James, as 'leading the struggle with blood, with boldness and with brilliance available to all who use the French language' (1980 [1938]: 408).

Senghor's first collection of poems, *Chants d'ombre* (written before the war, but only published in 1945), although exploring the experience of being torn between two identities, had been marked by personal lyricism; his second, *Hosties noires* (1948), marked a crucial shift towards a denunciation of the West, with specific criticism reserved for France's treatment of its colonial troops in the two world wars (Jack, 1996: 235–36). A similar political awakening in the immediate post-war period would be recorded by Algeria's most formally innovative novelist and playwright, Kateb Yacine, whose anti-colonial cultural and political engagement had its origins in his adolescent experience of the bloody repression that took place on 8 May 1945 (VE day), and in the days that followed, of the nationalist insurrection in the Sétif region. Having been brought up to identify with and even to love the French Revolution, Kateb would discover in the Sétif events the true meaning of revolutionary fraternity, as well as the flesh-and-blood reality of Algeria and his fellow Algerians (cited by Maspero, 1994: i). These and similar examples of resistance to attempts to return to business as usual in the colonies would spell disaster for the 'new deal' theoretically offered by the 1944 Brazzaville conference and the post-war French Union. In consequence, we must now consider the revolutionary movements that not only permitted a series of successful struggles for national liberation, but also overturned many of the French intellectual assumptions inherited from the Enlightenment.

Liberty: the Republic of Revolutions

France's revolutionary heritage was readily transposed to the colonies, where its model of insurrectionary violence could be expanded to include both local traditions of resistance and internationally organized action. The spontaneous uprising at Sétif in May 1945 was part of a much broader series of insurrectionary disturbances throughout an empire significantly weakened by the defeats and divisions of the war years, but to which a France desperate to re-establish its 'Great Power' status was determined to cling. Uprisings also occurred in Morocco (1944), Madagascar (1947–48) and the Ivory Coast (1949–50), all of which were ferociously suppressed by French forces. In contrast, in Indo-China, the revolutionary Vietminh was able to mobilize international communist support for a peasant-based nationalist insurgency in order to wage a successful military campaign from 1945 to 1954, which climaxed with the crushing defeat of French forces at Dien Bien Phu.

In Algeria, France's most important colony in Africa, national identity was even more obviously born of violent struggle. After a century and a quarter of French military occupation and administrative assimilation, during which armed resistance had regularly occurred, it would require eight years of often savage fighting (from 1954 to 1962) finally to persuade France to accept the inevitability of Algerian independence. This conflict would see a mobilization of metropolitan intellectuals on an unprecedented scale, particularly in opposition to the 'pacification' methods employed by the French army, including the systematic use of torture, summary executions and the large-scale displacement of the civilian population. In spite of strict censorship, news of these methods was revealed to a metropolitan and international audience through accounts such as that of the former editor of the banned *Alger Républicain* newspaper, Henri Alleg, of his illegal detention and torture by French paratroopers during the pivotal 'Battle of Algiers' (1956–57). In an important review of Alleg's book *La Question* (1958), the leading intellectual critic of empire, Jean-Paul Sartre, underlined its significance: Sartre argued that it was the first 'optimistic' book to come out of the Algerian War. It affirmed the possibility of overcoming apparently insurmountable odds and demonstrated that 'this age of shame and scorn [*le temps du mépris*] contains the promise of victory' (cited by Schalk, 2005: 66). In a related development, the Republic of Letters symbolically united at the Sorbonne in December 1957 to award a doctorate in absentia to Alleg's friend, mathematics lecturer Maurice Audin, who had 'disappeared' during the Battle of Algiers.

While the intellectual campaign against the conduct and continuation of the Algerian war drew support right across the political spectrum, few commentators were able to accept the prospect of an independent Algeria led by the revolutionary *Front de Libération Nationale* (FLN). This reticence was most clearly felt by those liberal intellectuals (such as the leading Catholic figure, François Mauriac) who saw the Algerian conflict as a second Dreyfus affair, in which France needed to be reminded of its particular obligation to respect the principles and processes of republican justice, especially as it occurred just a decade after France's own experience of the combined horrors of the Nazi occupation and the Vichy regime. In contrast, a group of intellectuals associated with the militantly anti-colonial review, *Les Temps modernes*, including Sartre and Simone de Beauvoir, together with their close collaborator Francis Jeanson, looked for new directions in both analytical and practical terms. Previously close to the PCF but never actually members, this group had rallied to the Communists' cause during the Indo-China conflict, particularly during the trial and imprisonment of anti-war activist Henri Martin (1950–53), as had such celebrated figures as Jean Cocteau, Jacques Prévert and Pablo Picasso. In Jeanson's case, political commitment to the cause of Algerian self-determination would lead him to organize a network of associates prepared to engage in illegal direct action on behalf of the FLN. While not violent in itself – typical activities included the provision of safe houses, the hiding of documents and, especially, the transport of funds for the Algerian revolutionaries by so-called *porteurs de valises* – such intellectual engagement involved genuine risk and was to result in another much-publicized prosecution.

The trial of the Jeanson network in September 1960 coincided with the publication of the most important intellectual petition against the Algerian war, the Manifesto of the 121. Sartre not only signed this extended justification of illegal action, but also published an open letter – which was read out in court and also published in *Le Monde* – restating his personal support for the actions of Jeanson and his group, and challenging the authorities, *à la* Émile Zola in his celebrated *J'Accuse* (1898), to arrest him too. Such was his prestige that Sartre was never, in fact, troubled by the French state, although his apartment and the offices of *Les Temps modernes* did become targets for terrorist attack. Undeterred, Sartre continued to engage in a highly productive dialogue with anti-colonial theorists in a series of influential prefaces, reviews, and other interventions, where he provided glosses to their analyses and documented his own evolving understanding of national liberation movements throughout the French empire and beyond. These included particularly his January 1956 argument that 'Colonialism is a System', and his prefaces to two essential analyses of the psychological mechanisms of colonial domination: Albert Memmi's *Portrait du colonisé/Portrait du colonisateur* (1957) and Frantz Fanon's *Les Damnés de la terre* (1961). As Sartre was quick to appreciate, these landmark works were truly revolutionary not simply because they made the case for national self-determination, but rather because they required a decolonization of the mind.

Both texts were, at least in part, responses to the theory of the supposed immaturity and resulting 'dependency complex' of the colonized peoples put forward by Octave Mannoni in his *Psychologie de la colonisation* (1950), an analysis that effectively ignored the constitutive violence of the 'colonial situation'. In his prefaces to the two works, Sartre stresses precisely the empire's historical origins in and systematic reliance on violence and thus the denial of the human rights elsewhere protected by the Republic (2003a: 22; 1967: 13). Given that the colonial system can never be reformed, the only solution is revolutionary violence, which is at the heart of Fanon's psychoanalytically informed account of the colonized's liberation from material constraints and mental subjugation. Grasping a nettle that many French intellectuals, including a majority on the Left, were to avoid, Sartre states not only the political necessity for armed struggle but also the psychological inevitability of often extreme acts of violence against the colonizer. Following Fanon, whom he wryly urges France's 'worthiest souls' to read, he observes, in a transparent allusion to the Republic's own brutal origins (and perhaps also to the recent French experience of Nazi occupation): 'I think we understood this truth at one time, but we have forgotten it – that no gentleness can efface the marks of violence; only violence itself can destroy them' (Sartre, 1967: 18)

The profound transformation of mentalities necessitated by decolonization was additionally encouraged by a series of important artistic interventions, particularly in the theatre. These included the ferociously iconoclastic drama of Jean Genet, as well as Sartre's own *Les Séquestrés d'Altona* (1959), in which the French use of torture during the Algerian war – not ostensibly the subject of the play nor, indeed, referred to directly in the work – is implicitly alluded to and critiqued through reference to the actions of the Nazis, allowing the author thus to circumvent the challenges of censorship at the time. A multiple and lifelong outsider to 'respectable' French society, Genet himself, long championed by Sartre, was to engage in an unremitting critique of what he saw as the racist and colonialist West in his controversial plays on racism (*Les Nègres*, 1958) and the Algerian war (*Les Paravents*, 1961) (Khélil, 2001: 149; see also Khélil, 2005). Although not widely appreciated as a significant anti-colonial work on its first appearance, Marguerite Duras's novel *Un barrage contre le Pacifique* (1950) is also now recognized as an important critique of colonialism, whose project may usefully be likened to the 'making foreign' of Frenchness that motivates Genet's writing. An early exploration of the issues of identity and alterity (in terms both of ethnicity and of gender) that Duras would go on to develop significantly in subsequent works – including particularly in *L'Amant* (1984; Prix Goncourt) and *L'Amant de la Chine du Nord* (1991) – the novel draws on her own upbringing as a poor white settler in Indo-China to explore the mutually reinforcing racial economy and sexual politics of the colony. Her scathing analysis of the colonial city is particularly to be noted: 'Decades before postcolonial studies, Duras portrays the Eden [white colonial] district as the place where whiteness is constructed and divisions are installed. Describing Eden [...], she tears off colonialism's majestic mask to reveal it as narcissistic, self-referential, self-serving' (Winston, 2001: 172).

Reclaiming the word

As the republican empire entered its terminal phase, thinkers both in France and in the newly independent nations would continue the re-imagining that had begun in the trenches and factories of the First World War. This process of reinvention would be conducted not only through radical artistic innovation, but also in a cumulative demonstration of the relativity of cultures by social scientists. Such investigations demonstrate – as Edward Said put it, following Frantz Fanon – 'that when you extend not just Freud, but all the [...] achievements of European science into the practice of colonialism, Europe ceases to occupy a normative position with regard to the native' (Said, 2003: 20). Perhaps the most imitated example of such critical interventions was the semiotic analysis of colonial systems of signification outlined by Roland Barthes in his *Mythologies* (1957). This pioneering analysis of colonial discourse, as exemplified by such signifiers of 'imperiality' as a *Paris-Match* image of an African soldier saluting the French flag and the 'African Grammar' employed by politicians and the mass media, was to provide a model for much subsequent engagement with the graphic and textual articulations of colonialism. By revealing the historic and political determinants of colonial modes of speaking (about) the world, Barthes drew attention to the vital issue of the ownership of *la parole* [speech], something that Sartre would later underline in the opening lines of his preface to Fanon's *Les Damnés de la terre*, forcefully contrasting those who do and those who do not have ownership of *le Verbe* [the Word] (Sartre, 1967: 7). Confiscated by the colonizer, reappropriated by the colonized, language was thus foregrounded as part of a broader critique of the naturalized value systems of the 'one and indivisible' Republic. In the process, France was compelled finally to abandon its phantasmatic empire, being summoned instead to adapt to the multicultural challenges of a postcolonial society, and thus a plurality of real and imagined 'republics'.

Further reading

Le Sueur, James D., 2001. *Uncivil War: Intellectuals and Identity Politics during the Decolonization of Algeria* (Philadelphia: University of Pennsylvania Press). An incisive intellectual history of the most traumatic war of French decolonization.

Ross, Kristin, 1995. *Fast Cars, Clean Bodies: Decolonization and the Reordering of French Culture* (Cambridge, MA: MIT Press). A fascinating essay that combines the generally separated narratives of decolonization and modernization in France.

Schalk, David L., 2005 [1991]. *War and the Ivory Tower* (Lincoln, NE: University of Nebraska Press). A readily accessible, but always challenging, comparative study of the role of intellectuals and political engagement in the Franco-Algerian conflict and America's Vietnam War.

CHAPTER 17

Postcolonialism and Deconstruction: The Francophone Connection

Michael Syrotinski

One of the most significant recent developments within postcolonial theory has been its belated engagement with the Francophone world, after a decade or more of sustained critical attention to Anglophone texts and contexts. Indeed, one might have expected the dialogues that are now taking place to have begun much earlier, given that so much of the writing of the three figures most associated with the emergence of postcolonial theory – Homi Bhabha, Edward Said and Gayatri Spivak – owes a clear intellectual debt to an earlier generation of French theorists. A number of genealogical lines of influence are now beginning to be drawn, and within this narrative, one more or less accepted view is that postcolonialism cut its theoretical teeth in the wake of 'poststructuralism' (a category that seems to include any French theorist writing from about 1968 onwards, and certainly Michel Foucault, Roland Barthes, Jacques Derrida, Gilles Deleuze, Félix Guattari, Hélène Cixous, Louis Althusser among others). This relay seems to provide an easy linkage of postcolonialism and poststructuralism, via Bhabha's reference to, and reappropriation of, a number of Derrida's 'key concepts', such as *différance*. Thus Ashcroft, Griffiths and Tiffin, for example, in their *Key Concepts in Post-Colonial Studies*, describe the 'third space' of Bhabha's 'ambivalence' as 'something like the idea of deferral in poststructuralism' (Ashcroft et al., 1998: 61). While the work of many of these thinkers has often been quite brilliantly adapted and redeployed (for example, Lacan by Bhabha, Foucault by Said, Foucault and Lévi-Strauss by Mudimbe, Deleuze and Guattari by Édouard Glissant and others), the uncertain status of Derrida's work within this configuration, and of deconstruction generally, makes this at once a particularly compelling narrative, and one that needs to be teased out quite carefully, since its assumptions underpin many of the recent debates in postcolonial theory.

One effect of this uncertainty seems to have been a certain polarization of the field of postcolonial studies, which is divided between on the one hand critics inspired by the theories of what is loosely referred to as French poststructuralism, and on the other those who are sceptical about what they perceive as a textualist emphasis, and who advocate the necessity of attending to the material conditions of life in postcolonial cultures. Responding to these 'materialist' critics (e.g. Ella Shohat, Arif Dirlik and Benita Parry), the cultural theorist Stuart Hall has talked of this polarization as 'a certain nostalgia [...] for a return to a clear-cut politics of binary oppositions' (Hall, 1996: 244). For him, the term 'post-colonial' only has meaning if it is taken both as a *chronological* marker that has generated a critical reflection on the grand histories of European colonialism, imperialism and globalization, and also as an *epistemological* opening that retrospectively re-reads these narratives (what V. Y. Mudimbe terms the 'colonial library'), and that unsettles the authority these texts claim for themselves. As Hall says: 'It is in this reconstitution of the epistemic and power/knowledge fields around the relations of globalization, through its various historical forms, that the "periodization" of the "post-colonial" is really challenging' (1996: 250). Within the array of different reading practices one might broadly term poststructuralist, deconstruction is for Hall the most rigorously attentive to this epistemological reassessment. Furthermore, he goes on to argue, a deconstructive reading allows both senses of the 'post-colonial' to be kept in play at once, such that 'the tension between the epistemological and the chronological is not disabling but productive' (1996: 254). This would suggest that the relationship between deconstruction and postcolonialism could indeed be one of mutual interdependence, and some critics have even talked of the Francophone African *roots* of deconstruction (Ahluwalia, 2005).

Deconstruction and decolonization (Young)

Robert Young made this very case in *White Mythologies* (1990), arguing that Jacques Derrida has always, beginning with *Of Grammatology* (1967) challenged the founding assumptions of colonialist ideology, insofar as his meticulous analysis of the historical privileging of speech over writing (Derrida's celebrated 'logocentrism') in the Western metaphysical tradition is relayed through a critique of *ethnocentrism*. In a more recent article, 'Deconstruction and the Postcolonial' (2000), Young has gone further, and has recontextualized Derrida's work within a postcolonial (and, from the outset, anti-colonial) theoretical framework. The unacknowledged shared interests of deconstruction and postcolonial theory are made explicit, according to Young, by Derrida's publication in the 1990s of texts that are both more autobiographical (*Monolingualism of the Other*, *Circumfession*, and *Archive Fever*, among others) and more overtly ethico-political in terms of their themes (*Specters of Marx*, *Of Hospitality*, and *On Cosmopolitanism and Forgiveness*, for example). Once this 'Francophone connection' has been uncovered, it seems logical enough in Young's view that Derrida's notion of *écriture* would go hand in hand with his persistent and enduring condemnation of forms of *actual* violence, starting with his own experiences of racism and exclusion as a Francophone Maghrebian Jew in colonial Algeria.

Thus, contrary to a materialist postcolonial view that Derrida, for all his radicalism, is ultimately a representative of the Western philosophical tradition he is deconstructing, Young recasts Derrida within another, more militant Francophone anti-colonial genealogy, placing him alongside other French writers and theorists who have or had close biographical or intellectual ties with Algeria (Hélène Cixous, Jean-François Lyotard, Pierre Bourdieu), a list he extends to include the more familiar figures of Frantz Fanon, Abdelkébir Khatibi, Albert Memmi and Jean-Paul Sartre. (See Chapters 5, 8, 9 and 11 of this volume for discussion of these writers.) Derrida playfully inscribes himself into this genealogy in his quasi-autobiographical text, *Monolingualism of the Other* (1996), and Young thus suggests that deconstruction has 'itself been a form of cultural decolonization' (2000: 199). Furthermore, Derrida's reference to Sartre's critique of totalitarian politics, in North Africa and elsewhere, is generalized according to Young into a conceptual critique of *all* forms of 'totalization'. Pursuing this intellectual genealogy, Young argues that once Derrida moved to metropolitan France from Algeria, his early experiences were translated into a permanent and continuous political subversiveness, and his ideas were subsequently taken up by minority, migrant and immigrant groups, and applied to their own political situations (2000: 208). Young has been criticized for downplaying the historical fact of Derrida's lack of involvement in any actual struggle for independence, armed or otherwise, and one might suspect that, in his eagerness to prove materialist critics and their version of intellectual history wrong, Young is constructing an *alternative* grand narrative, which produces the sort of thematic coherence that might be the very object of critique of a deconstructive reading. Whichever narrative one favours, we still seem to be caught epistemologically within a form of binaristic oppositional thinking, since whether deconstruction and postcolonial theory are seen as antagonistic modes of thinking and analysis, or as partner theories (where the claim is that this complicity has simply been misrecognized), both do so on the assumption of a shared heritage or interdependent history. In an effort to move beyond this impasse, we have, over the past decade or so, witnessed a number of alliances between postcolonial theory and theories of globalization, subaltern studies, or transnational cultural studies, for example, as different ways of moving on with the times, and addressing the socio-political concerns of our age (Apter, 1999; Spivak, 2000; Bongie, 2003a). However this concern to 'move on' may, as Hall points out (1996: 255), and as Mudimbe did before him (1982: 44), simply be another ruse of (Western) dialectical thinking, and thus subsumed and assimilated by the genealogical historical narrative it appears to be challenging. Several postcolonial theorists have sought, in different ways, to write according to the different logic that deconstruction offers, and a brief analysis of several of those who might be considered among the most important – Homi K. Bhabha, Gayatri Spivak, V. Y. Mudimbe and Achille Mbembe – allows for a more nuanced understanding of the broader narrative of postcolonialism's 'Francophone connections'.

Dislocating the hybrid (Bhabha)

Bhabha's *The Location of Culture* has become a key point of reference for thinking about the relationship of deconstruction to postcolonial theory, and he describes the book as an attempt to 'give poststructuralism a specifically postcolonial provenance' (1994: 64). Many of Derrida's familiar early concepts, or quasi-concepts (such as *supplementarity*, *différance* with an 'a', and *translation*, as a kind of linguistic defamiliarization) are re-inscribed by Bhabha in a postcolonial context, but perhaps the most highly charged and misunderstood of all the terms he deploys is *hybridity*. Readers of Bhabha's work sometimes overlook the fact that he is constantly and simultaneously working with, and reworking, *two* concepts of hybridity, so that the word itself is always marked by an internal splitting, and structured according to the logic of *différance*. For Bhabha, this takes the form of a crucial distinction between cultural *diversity* and cultural *difference*. Cultural diversity refers to forms of hybridity that would typically include multiculturalism, transnationalism, transculturation (Pratt, 1992), multiple ethnic, cultural or religious affiliations (such as African-American, Pakistani-English, Palestinian-Jew, and so on), and creole identities, or *métissage* (see Amselle, 1990; Lionnet, 1995). The analysis of narrative and artistic mixing of genres and styles that give expressive form to this notion of hybridity are a major feature of much postcolonial criticism.

Cultural difference, however, is different, since it does not to refer to any determinate object of culture, however fluid, complex and multiply referenced it may be. Perhaps the clearest and most direct transposition of a deconstructive logic of hybridity within Bhabha's work is his theorization of the 'contact zone' of relations between colonizer and colonized. As he puts it, there is in fact an irreducible ambivalence built in to the very enterprise of colonialism, and the discursive modalities by which it represents and enacts its mission. According to him, colonialism *has* to exist in a state of self-difference, since it is inevitably split between its view of itself as culturally whole (with an apparently inexhaustible capacity to incorporate or assimilate culturally diverse Others into this whole), and the distortion and fracturing of this whole that occurs in the very act of colonization itself. To this extent, Bhabha's work does come out of anti-humanist critiques of the confident claims of the sovereign subject, of universalism, of human agency and of intentionality, and so it has important implications for the traditional political philosophy of revolutionary anti-colonial movements, for example. What Bhabha is attempting to do is to find a critical language that can prise open the traditional political and philosophical categories that have determined colonial discourse (and which might be shown to derive ultimately from a strong European humanist tradition). At the same time, he is seeking to describe the 'psychodynamics' of colonizer-colonized relations. Lacanian psychoanalysis provides much of the conceptual underpinning of the psychic operations of the very context-specific mode of ambivalence that constitute hybridity, but this is more than a psychologizing of the political, or a theoretical abstraction of the lived reality of the violence and traumas of colonial history, which is how critics of Bhabha often describe his form of postcolonial analysis.

In order to underline the crucial political implications of his theory, he turns to Frantz Fanon, whose work enacts this necessary correlation of the psycho-analytical and the political. This ambivalent hybridity is elsewhere figured as a disjunction between the 'pedagogical' and the 'performative'. 'Pedagogical' in Bhabha's terms refers to the objective contemplation and analysis of a culture, its texts and its history. The 'performative', by contrast, looks at the movement or act of colonization itself, but also – in a postcolonial context – at the various counterhegemonic acts of resistance by which formerly colonized individuals or peoples reclaim their culture. For Bhabha, these two modes are not discrete or separable, but coexist as a kind of permanent internal tension, one effect of which is to disrupt normative conceptions of the causal flow of history, and of temporality. This is what Bhabha calls 'the post-colonial time-lag' (1994: 252), and he explicitly compares it to the logic of the *supplement* in Derrida.

Bhabha's postcolonial hybridity could thus be called deconstructive to the extent that it demonstrates how the explicit (thematized) meaning in a given discourse (its 'pedagogy') stands in a problematic, but productive, relationship to the very act of its enunciation (its 'performance'). Bhabha himself is a careful enough reader of Derrida to understand that his own reading is necessarily caught within the same logic, and the same critical self-awareness character-izes Spivak's relation to deconstruction. Both Bhabha and Spivak engage, in different ways, in a conscious repetition, and distortion-within-repetition, alert to the fact that, unlike other methodologies ('poststructuralist' or not), decon-struction is not a set of analytical tools that could help unlock the meaning of a given cultural object. Indeed, such a misunderstanding often informs the work of critics such as Arif Dirlik, Aijaz Ahmad or Benita Parry, for whom deconstruc-tion's obsession with the textual to the exclusion of the material is conclusive proof of its inability to engage with 'actual' politics.

Postcolonial reason and its critique (Spivak)

Although she is often closely associated with postcolonial theory, Gayatri Spivak has consistently refused any allegiance to this label. *A Critique of Postcolonial Reason* (1999) contains her most comprehensive panoply of arguments against the use of the category 'postcolonial' as a catchall term for contemporary· cultural, historical and literary studies that take the Third World as their object of analysis. Weaving together the multifarious strands of much of her work, what Spivak does in this book is to track the complicity connecting several of the 'grand narratives' of contemporary Western humanism (specifically, certain texts by Kant, Hegel and Marx), to the epistemological assumptions upon which not only imperialist ideology but also contemporary colonial discourse and postcolonial studies are founded. She leaves this well-trodden path, however, when she goes on to claim that this complicity – for which 'postcolonial reason' is her shorthand term – is itself necessarily constituted by 'foreclosing' (in the strong psychoanalytical sense of the term) the inassimilable 'Other' of Western humanist discourse. Reading the impossible but necessary position of this inassimilable Other becomes the primary labour of her project.

Her celebrated essay 'Can the Subaltern Speak?' (1988) looks at the case of Bhubaneswari Bhaduri, who was active in the Indian independence movement, and who committed suicide, but disguised it as a traditional Hindu widow sacrifice (sati) in order to prevent capture by the British colonial authorities. For Spivak, this is not only an exemplary instance of a historical discursive silencing but it also figures the silencing of contemporary subaltern women in general. She expands the question of subalternity into a problematic of the 'Native Informant' (those foreclosed and barely recognizable cultural outsiders), and in this text it is deconstruction that provides her, again and again, with the most effective critical language and conceptual structures with which to articulate her paradoxical theoretical position, in particular the mode of rhetorical reading Spivak learned from Paul de Man as his student at Cornell University during the 1960s (indeed, *A Critique of Postcolonial Reason* is dedicated in part to de Man). If literature is for her the focal point of Third World activist reading, this is not because of an uncritical faith in the political benefits of literary representation (or self-representation) of so-called emergent or re-emergent cultures and voices, which are for Spivak all too readily co-opted by the prevailing hegemonies, but because literature offers the most far-reaching examples of the kinds of critical reading practices that allow colonial and postcolonial studies to question and problematize accepted historical records. Literature provides, in other words, insights into the strategies we can use to tease out and lay bare the underlying rhetorical and political tensions of imperial historiography, and the philosophical foundations that underpin Western hegemony. This is often Spivak's own starting point and the site of some of her richest interventions.

Her early readings of literary texts and (post)colonial historiography bear the hallmark of a typical de Manian manoeuvre of reading a text's performance over and against its explicit assertions. Across the entire range of her work, in fact, deconstruction serves as a kind of ethical safeguard, a constant awareness and need to take account of one's own positionality and complicity, or, as she will later put it, to 'unlearn one's own privilege' (Spivak, 1990: 30). Spivak generally, and quite refreshingly, bypasses the more familiar and well-worn of Derridean terms 'under erasure', and is drawn instead to some of his composite neologisms, or more complex tropes, such as 'teleopoesis'. This is a term formed by grafting two etymologies suggesting an imaginative 'making at a distance', and is described by Derrida in *Politics of Friendship* as the 'generation by a joint and simultaneous grafting, without a proper body, of the performative and the constative' (Derrida, 1997a [1994]: 32).

In her essay 'Deconstruction and Cultural Studies' (2000), Spivak brings into play a number of important motifs of a deconstructive approach to postcolonialism: the logic of undecidability, the double inscription (here the simultaneity of the performative and constative, but with an added twist), the notion of constitutive impropriety (that is, the absence of a pure, proper origin), and a rethinking of agency (redefining the political and philosophical lines of force of imperialism, colonialism and postcolonialism by activating the 'impossible' figure of the Native Informant). The constitutively undecidable moment in any reading of the past, and therefore in any calculation of the future, will thus necessarily pass through a process of 'teleopoesis', or imaginative grafting, and this will be exemplified later on by Spivak's reading of Assia Djebar's *Far From Medina* in her article 'Ghostwriting' (1995), a long and polemical response to Derrida's *Specters of Marx* (1993). Although she often criticizes Derrida for blurring precise distinctions between labour-value and exchange-value, and failing to address industrial capital as well as the increasing feminization of the global workforce, Spivak uses 'teleopoesis' to read Djebar's story as a kind of spectralized version of what she thinks Derrida ought to have been doing in *Specters of Marx*. She does so, however, by re-inscribing herself into a line of genealogical succession (that is, as deconstruction's rightful heir), and is at the same time marking her difference from Derrida in affirming a certain critical autonomy (and making a strong claim that it is around the question of sexual difference that their readings diverge), while using the techniques and terminological resources of deconstruction in order to do so.

Spivak's work thus plays out a rather ambivalent 'debt' to deconstruction, moving as it does between repetition and reinvention, fidelity and disrespect, thematization and performance, continuity and disruption. It also addresses important questions about whom or on whose behalf the postcolonial critic can claim to speak or write, since her disruption or interruption of cognitive logic, and what looks like political common sense, is the mode in which she affirms the need to challenge unquestioned assumptions about the very nature of representation.

Deconstructing Africa (Mudimbe)

One writer and thinker who raises similar questions about how truly 'representative' African intellectuals can be is V.Y. Mudimbe (see Chapter 10 of this volume), who has also been accused of a certain methodological dependence on French poststructuralism. As the title of his best-known work *The Invention of Africa* suggests, Mudimbe is concerned with deconstructing and reconstructing the 'archaeology' of representations, or misrepresentations, of Africa and its culture, going back to the Ancient Greeks, but primarily in relation to the French and Belgian colonial missions in Africa. His work is explicitly Foucauldian in its inspiration, and is for this reason often described as 'deconstructionist' (Masolo, 1994: 179). Indeed, the issue of his adaptation of Foucault goes to the heart of this question, since it occasions a double misreading: firstly, that Mudimbe simply borrows Foucault's genealogical model (thus mimicking the 'Western' critical theorist and his tools); and, secondly, that one could equate

Foucault's critical methodology with deconstruction. In actual fact, Mudimbe in his writing takes up a critical position with respect to Foucault (as well as to other French thinkers with whom he claims a strong affiliation, such as Sartre and Lévi-Strauss), since they are ultimately, as he says, part of the heritage from which an African discourse would wish to liberate itself. He emphasizes the need for many African writers and thinkers to adopt a similar critical distance, for their acceptance of the epistemological ground rules of colonialism means they 'belong to the signs of the same power' (Mudimbe, 1988: 43).

Some critics, such as Masolo, nonetheless consider Mudimbe's reliance on theorists such as Foucault and Lévi-Strauss as symptomatic of an inability to ground his 'elegant deconstructionist method' in the 'idioms of everyday life' (Masolo, 1994: 186). As Masolo puts it, 'he lamentably fails to emancipate himself from the vicious circle inherent in the deconstructionist stance' (1994: 188). This would seem to imply that there is a readily available consensus on what Mudimbe's 'deconstruction' consists of, which is certainly not the case, and far from being blind to the risks of his own discursive dependence, Mudimbe states the necessity of a critical vigilance at the heart of any reaffirmation of subjectivity. In this regard, Mudimbe often cites Frantz Fanon, one of the most radical and profound thinkers of African colonial subjectivity, as an important influence on his own work.

Mudimbe's subjective re-inscription of Foucault and Lévi-Strauss can be read productively in the light of Derrida's early critique of these same thinkers, and particularly in relation to Foucault's interpretation of Descartes' *cogito* in *The History of Madness*. Mudimbe recognizes that one cannot simply step outside the canon to which Lévi-Strauss and Foucault belong, and his adaptation of their respective projects effectively displaces the *cogito* from its historically determinate context through the performative act of reaffirming African subjectivity, an act that itself would, in Derrida's terms, be closer to the *cogito*, or to the irreducible madness at its very heart. The African *cogito* – which Mudimbe promotes enthusiastically at the end of *The Idea of Africa* (1994) – involves *in its very affirmation* both a disarticulation of Western discursive objectification, and a claim to a new form of subjective agency founded on a radically different mode of invention, and a certain a-rationalism (which would not be an *irrationalism*). So Mudimbe in fact does exactly what Masolo says he fails to do, since his 'reaffirmed subjectivity' does not fall into the discursive trap of believing it can 'step outside' of essentializing categories, but it is both an inventive enunciation and the strategic dismantling of the discourses through which it is objectified. Mudimbe thus affirms African subjectivity in its necessary doubleness, a doubleness that is again something *other* than hybridity, and closer in this respect to Bhabha's cultural difference than his cultural diversity.

The African postcolony (Mbembe)

Another major Francophone voice in postcolonial Africa is the social theorist Achille Mbembe, who also confesses a strong political and philosophical debt to Frantz Fanon. One might even say that if Fanon took on the mantle of spokesperson and principal theorist of the anti-colonialist cause in Africa, Mbembe has similarly assumed the role of the most articulate commentator of the African postcolonial period. Mbembe sees African political and social history, and African subjectivity, as in many ways still trapped within an internalized Hegelian master-slave dialectic of European colonizer and African colonized, with all the attendant structures of fantasy and desire that persist to this day in postcolonial Africa. His best-known book, *On the Postcolony* (2000), originally published in French, describes the interlocking dynamics of economic interests, the violent exercise of power, and structures of desire in contemporary Africa. Like Mudimbe, he critiques discourses of Africanism – whether in the work of Africans or non-Africans – that continue to be informed by colonialist ideologies of Africa and its social formations, and also those that are characterized by an appeal to authenticity and tradition. Mbembe is sceptical of the 'representational' bias of much contemporary theory, and criticizes postcolonial theory, as well as theorists of rationality and modernism, for not attending sufficiently to the lived, existential experience of the African subject, or the economic conditions underlying the various symbolic and discursive theories they might bring to bear upon the analysis of contemporary Africa.

For Mbembe, most present-day political and economic theories that are applied to Africa and its problems are little more than neo-liberal ideologies that have their eyes firmly set on the global market economy; for example, policies of deregulation end up financing the ongoing relations of subordination of the people to autocratic regimes. He recognizes that postcolonial theory in general has made a decisive contribution to understanding the operations of Western discursive hegemony in relation to its colonial ventures, and it has also, as he says in a recent interview, 'revealed the violence of Western epistemologies and the dehumanizing impulse at the heart of their definition of the human' (Mbembe, 2005: 2). If it is to retain its critical edge, however, Mbembe argues that postcolonial theory will need to respond with greater urgency to the shifting priorities of contemporary global politics, as well as the complexity of everyday life in the 'African postcolony', and for him 'postcolonial theory would gain a lot by reframing its foundational interrogations' (2005: 2). He makes it clear, therefore, that his use of the term 'postcolony' takes him beyond the range of concerns that have typically been the domain of postcolonial studies of the 1980s and 1990s, and that he is heading in different directions politically and philosophically.

One of the major concepts of *On the Postcolony* is that of *commandement*, which describes the relations of power in much of postcolonial Africa. What Mbembe terms 'colonial sovereignty' is, for him, at the source of the brutal relationships that characterize the postcolony in Africa. This is more than just the well-worn theme of the ways in which post-independence neo-colonial regimes adopted, to a large degree, the colonial framework they inherited from their former masters. For Mbembe, this colonial sovereignty fundamentally determines the relationship of the governing class to the people within many African nation-states, and he traces back to the 'founding violence' of the act of colonial conquest the corruption and violence that is at the heart of many African postcolonial regimes. Postcolonial regimes have by and large inherited the same unwritten laws of impunity and violence, and sustained them by representing their native populations as less than human (Mbembe talks of 'animality' in this regard). The forms of 'citizenship' which this has produced in postcolonial Africa have thus been grotesquely distorted, since the ruling elites have put in place technologies of domination that deny individuals many of the basic rights of citizens. This domination is economic in its many corrupt and repressive forms, to be sure, and these are detailed at great length (Mbembe, 2001 [2000]: 66–101), but Mbembe stresses that *commandement* works perhaps even more powerfully at both a sensual and an imaginary level.

The typically prosaic quality of this sensualized coercion is elsewhere described by Mbembe, in the chapter 'The Aesthetics of Vulgarity', as the 'banality of power' (102–41). He takes as his point of reference Bakhtin's analysis of the 'carnivalesque', that is, the popular satirical use of the grotesque and the obscene as an extravagant aesthetic means of undermining the authority of the dominant social class. While such modes of contestation may be prevalent in everyday Africa, they function according to a very different dynamic, which may bear a structural resemblance to Bhabha's double split subjectivity of colonial relations, but are very different in tenor and in affirmative potential. Mbembe describes the relationship of interdependence between the dominant class and the dominated as one of 'conviviality', and the use of the term is clearly a long way from its usual connotations of mutual respect. It does capture, though, the notion of a certain bond of co-dependence, in a shared living space, such that even the most extreme acts of aesthetic subversion are not only tolerated but also actively encouraged, since they ultimately confirm the status and power of the potentate. Thus 'conviviality' is what, for Mbembe, distinguishes the *colonial* relationship of domination (which was merely geared towards the creation of obedient subjects, with economic productivity as the underlying raison d'être) from the *commandement* of the postcolonial (which relies upon the dominated to sustain it through an imaginary investment in its 'vulgar aesthetics'). Mbembe thus refutes the common dismissal of his work that it indulges in a (very sophisticated and, some might say, poststructuralist) form of Afro-Pessimism, by making it clear that his critical project is to find an alternative language to the 'miserabilism' of the victim-syndrome, and by also proposing a strong, positive, and materially grounded vision of a future for Africa that can truly lay claim to subjective and political autonomy.

While a specifically Francophone perspective on postcolonial theory seems to corroborate the emerging genealogy of its 'poststructuralist' links, and even origins, an attentive reading of a number of the texts concerned leads to more complex, nuanced and challenging versions of this narrative, particularly with critics such as Bhabha and Spivak, who are keenly attuned to the ambivalent place that deconstruction occupies within this configuration. The work of a number of Francophone African intellectuals such as Mudimbe and Mbembe, who are in no small measure indebted to a certain French poststructuralism, opens up yet further lines of thinking. Their particular brand of philosophical and political engagement emphasizes the need to resist easy critical binarisms (opposing, for example, 'materialist' and 'textualist' theories) and the overly coherent postcolonial narratives that are sustained by such criticism. As deconstruction teaches us, whatever the term 'postcolonial' may *denote*, it seems also to *connote* most productively an infinite capacity to keep on the move, to transform itself, to refuse to settle down. It is, in short, perhaps the exemplary instance of what Charles Forsdick, echoing Said, has recently foregrounded as a *travelling* concept (Forsdick, 2003).

Further reading

Bhabha, Homi K., 1994. *The Location of Culture* (London and New York: Routledge). A seminal text of postcolonial theory. Bhabha engages in a series of dazzling 'relocations' of culture from a postcolonial perspective. A key point of reference in any discussion of the relationship of deconstruction to postcolonial theory.

Mbembe, Achille, 2001 [2000]. *On the Postcolony* (Berkeley, CA: University of California Press). Originally published in French as *De la postcolonie*, a series of essays describing the interlocking dynamics of economic interests, the violent exercise of power, and structures of desire in contemporary postcolonial Africa.

Mudimbe, V. Y., 1988. *The Invention of Africa: Gnosis, Philosophy and the Order of Knowledge* (Bloomington and London: Indiana University Press). A Foucauldian 'archaeology' of representations, or misrepresentations, of Africa and its culture, as far back as the Ancient Greek mapping of the continent, but primarily in relation to the French and Belgian colonial missions in Africa.

Spivak, Gayatri Chakravorty, 1999. *A Critique of Postcolonial Reason: Towards a History of the Vanishing Present* (Cambridge, MA: Harvard University Press). A rich and challenging volume that reworks much of Spivak's earlier writings on deconstruction, globalization, cultural studies, colonial historiography, and subalternity (including a revision of her famous 'Can the Subaltern Speak?' essay).

Young, Robert, 1990. *White Mythologies: Writing History and the West* (New York and London: Routledge). One of the earliest and most influential studies of the major figures of postcolonial theory (including Said, Bhabha and Spivak) from a poststructuralist perspective.

CHAPTER 18

Negritude, Présence Africaine, Race

Richard Watts

When Wole Soyinka famously pronounced at a conference in Berlin in 1964 that 'a tiger does not proclaim his tigritude, he pounces' (quoted in Jahn, 1968: 266), he was suggesting that Negritude, the literary and cultural movement initiated in the 1930s by young writers from the French colonies in Africa (Léopold Senghor of Senegal), the Caribbean (Aimé Césaire of Martinique), and South America (Léon Damas of Guyana) who were studying in Paris, was unnecessary, even redundant. (See Chapters 1 and 12 on Césaire and Senghor respectively.) In Soyinka's view, Negritude, with all its talk of racial identity and pride, was long on discourse and short on action. Soyinka took the position that dialogue with white, colonizing Europe was, in effect, pointless and that black Africa had to forge a separate path (1976: 126–39). Inasmuch as Negritude can be considered a coherent movement with a clear set of principles, its position was indeed different from Soyinka's on this point, and avowedly so. Negritude was always explicitly dialogical, locked as it was at its origins in a forced embrace with a continent and a country that had theretofore determined the terms of the relationship between black and white, master and slave, colonizer and colonized, dominator and subaltern. That the Negritude movement first began to take form in French educational institutions in the mid-1930s, and that the publishing house Présence Africaine was established and still has its headquarters in the heart of the Latin Quarter in Paris, are ample proof of this will to dialogue and of the conditions that necessitated it. The form and content of so much of what the Negritude writers produced and Présence Africaine published testify to the desire and necessity to engage in an argument with Europe that would take place among equals who were, nonetheless, different. In this 'argument', which was really about culture, but that in the colonial era was perforce coded racially, the meaning of race and the questioning of racial hierarchies were the issues at hand. Negritude was the concept that federated Africa and the diaspora and allowed discussion with hegemonic white culture to

227

take place, and Présence Africaine – through its eponymous journal, the novels, essays, and poetry printed by the publishing house, and the cultural events it organized – was one of the primary conduits for the voices of black intellectuals and those who supported them in the Francophone world and beyond from the 1940s to the 1980s.

While it is difficult to cast 'dialogue' as such in a negative light, Soyinka's widely cited aphorism points to a certain ambiguity at the heart of the Negritude movement and the Présence Africaine publishing project: which part of Negritude's dialogue with the Western world that it inhabited was a function of political necessity and which part of it an expression of quiescence? V. Y. Mudimbe has argued that the intellectual space that Negritude and Présence Africaine carved out in Paris is 'not the other side of […] Western space. In fact, it belongs to it, though it is true that from the beginning *Présence* defines itself on the margins of the center it challenges' (1992: 435). Negritude sought to transform the lot of the colonized by challenging France on its own terms and, perhaps just as significantly, on its own turf, since that is where the African diaspora was first able to come together. Yet this very positioning is the source of an ambivalence that adhered to Negritude from its origins and that it was never quite able to shake off. How, critics asked, could Présence Africaine, located in Paris, lead Africa and the diaspora to independence? Surely the work of racial revalorization needed to happen in Africa and the Caribbean, not in the French capital? Further complicating Negritude's status is the fact that it was an internally contested signifier from its very origins, torn between Césaire's vision of 'a complex historical process where the forces of violence and exploitation weigh in against the author's utopian project' (Nesbitt, 2003: 78) and the essentialism and 'comfortable accommodationism' of Senghor (Miller, 1998: 40). Since they are apparent from the beginning, these tensions cannot be considered the source of Negritude's lapse into obscurity in the 1980s. They are, in fact, constitutive of Negritude. Perhaps it is more appropriate to state, then, that it is because of these fractures and divisions, and not in spite of them, that Negritude was the movement that made race the locus of political contestation in France and its former colonies over the course of the twentieth century.

While Negritude, Présence Africaine and race intersect in a number of places, the three terms around which this chapter is organized do not overlap perfectly. Much of the cultural history of the Negritude movement lies beyond the reach of Présence Africaine. Contrary to Elisabeth Mudimbe-Boyi's assertion that Présence Africaine 'was practically the only French publisher of African and Caribbean writers' until the 1970s (2006: 737), it only began publishing contemporary novels and collections of poetry in 1955, by which point many of the foundational Negritude texts were already in circulation: Aimé Césaire's *Cahier d'un retour au pays natal* originally published in 1939, was first released in book form in France by Bordas in 1947 (and reprinted by Présence Africaine in 1956); Léopold Senghor's major collections of poetry (*Chants d'ombre*, *Hosties noires*, *Éthiopiques*), were all with the French publisher, Seuil; and Léon Damas's *Pigments* (1937), *Graffiti* (1952) and *Black-Label* (1956), were published by a variety of mainstream French publishers. Likewise, Présence Africaine published a number of works that could be considered to fall outside Negritude's purview (it would be tendentious to place under the Negritude rubric a work so openly mocking of the archetypal black postcolonial dictator and his complacent black people as Henri Lopes's *Le Pleurer-rire*, published by Présence Africaine in 1982; notably, this is the only one of Lopes's many novels that Présence Africaine would publish). There is also the problem of sequencing: race-consciousness movements in the Francophone world existed, of course, prior to the appearance of Negritude as a concept, and Negritude as a self-conscious movement or practice itself preceded, by the better part of a decade, the founding in 1947 of the journal *Présence Africaine* by the Senegalese Alioune Diop. Still, it is in the years immediately following the Second World War that Negritude passed from a minor and mostly artistic challenge to European cultural dominance to an institution on the French cultural scene, with its aforementioned internal contradictions intact, and this is in large part the result of the work of Présence Africaine in all its manifestations. While this chapter will devote some space to Negritude's pre-history and its afterlives, it is centrally concerned with that period of institutionalization from the founding of Présence Africaine in 1947 until the 1970s, when Negritude's influence began to wane.

Black internationalism and the origins of Negritude

In Lilyan Kesteloot's groundbreaking study, *Black Writers in French* (her 1961 doctoral dissertation), first published in French in 1963 (translated into English in 1991), the appearance in the 1930s of the anti-racist cultural movement, Negritude, is characterized as nothing less than an epistemic shift, a kind of reordering of race relations in the colonial world that had no significant antecedents. Recent years have witnessed an outpouring of scholarship that challenges that assertion. Christopher Miller's *Nationalists and Nomads* (1998) does not so much shift this chronology back in time, as show that there is a continuum of anti-racist and anti-colonial writing (not all of it properly 'literary', one of the self-imposed limits of Kesteloot's study) by African authors that flows from the 1920s to the 1960s, much of it more radical than the works produced by the Negritude writers who followed them. In a similar way, T. Denean Sharpley-Whiting's *Negritude Women* (2002) seeks to highlight the role that writers such as the Nardal sisters and Suzanne Césaire played in laying the groundwork for Negritude. Perhaps the most significant intervention in the recasting of the early history of racially inflected anti-colonialism is Brent Hayes Edwards' *The Practice of Diaspora* (2003). By showing the extensive exchanges that took place between writers from the Harlem Renaissance and their counterparts from Francophone Africa and the Caribbean who were gathered in Paris, Edwards makes a compelling case for the existence of a fully fledged Black Internationalism as early as the 1920s. Although often subject to the vagaries of translation, one of the tropes Edwards exploits to good effect, these exchanges allowed nuanced perspectives on race and racism to develop on both sides of the Atlantic. Most crucially, as it concerns the history of Negritude, Edwards argues that it is only in Paris that these exchanges could have taken place:

> It is important to recognize that the significance of Paris in this period is not a question of sheer population size. […] [T]he European metropole after the war provided a special sort of vibrant, cosmopolitan space for interaction that was available neither in the United States nor in the colonies. […] Paris is crucial because it allowed boundary crossing, conversations, and collaborations that were available nowhere else to the same degree. (2003: 4)

It is near the end of the period of transatlantic cultural ferment described by Edwards that the three writers associated with the origins of Negritude met in Paris. Aimé Césaire arrived in Paris from Martinique in 1931, Léon Damas (who had taken philosophy classes in high school with Césaire at the Lycée Schoelcher in Martinique in the 1920s) from French Guyana in 1929, and Léopold Senghor from Senegal in 1928. Their first cultural project together (which also included the Senegalese writer Birago Diop) was the student journal *L'Étudiant noir*, published briefly in 1935. It was modelled, but only in part, on *Légitime Défense*, a journal edited by the Francophone Caribbean writers René Ménil, Jules Monnerot and Etienne Léro that appeared just once in 1932: contrary to their predecessors on *Légitime Défense*, whose anti-colonialism was explicit (leading to the censure of the journal), the editors of *L'Étudiant noir* produced a journal that tended to pursue political goals by other – which is to say, literary or cultural – means. It is in this journal that the word *négreries*, a clear precursor to 'Negritude', appears for the first time in an article by Césaire. Cultural work substituting for explicitly political activism would become one of the hallmarks of Negritude and the source, not coincidentally, of the accusations of quietism that would dog the movement. In the tense political climate of Paris in 1934, as war with Nazi Germany began to seem inevitable and all forms of open dissent, especially by the colonized, were subject to swift repression – one has only to think of the arrest and deportation of Vietnamese students and workers who had staged a peaceful demonstration in front of the Élysée Palace in May 1930 (Marr, 1981: 40) – pursuing political ends by cultural means does not seem an unreasonable strategy to adopt.

Césaire, Damas and Senghor continued their studies in Paris throughout the mid-to-late 1930s, all working toward earning their teaching certificates (the *agrégation*). Two of them also began their literary careers as published poets during this period. Damas saw two poems appear in *Esprit* in 1934, and a first volume of poetry, *Pigments*, was published in 1937. The French Government would retroactively ban this work in 1939 for 'atteinte à la sûreté de l'État' [risk to the security of the State]; a translation of the volume into Baoulè had purportedly inspired young men in Ivory Coast to refuse conscription into the French colonial army. Césaire published a first version of his epic poem, *Cahier d'un retour au pays natal*, in 1939 in the surrealist journal *Volontés*, edited by Henry Miller and Raymond Queneau. Césaire used the term 'Negritude' for the first time in this poem, defining it almost as much by what it is not (i.e., capitalist and imperialist) than by what it is: 'My Negritude is neither tower nor cathedral' (2000: 67). The choice of poetry by Césaire and Damas (and, later, by Senghor, who began publishing in earnest in the post-war period) is not insignificant, nor is it coincidental. Poetry, which had at the turn of the twentieth century the status of the highest literary form, had become (under the influence of both Parnassian and Symbolist poets) a genre turned largely inward. However, there were currents in the early part of the century that sought, on the one hand, to return poetry to its popular roots and, on the other, to make it an instrument of psychological revolution. While Damas plugged into the former current, Césaire aligned himself with the latter, making a lateral connection with the surrealist poets who were seeking to transform alienated modern consciousness. What he added to the surrealist project is, of course, the dimension of race. Yet this first call for a revolution in racial consciousness went largely unheeded. As Abiola Irele notes, 'Césaire left Paris for Martinique shortly after the publication of the poem, which went unnoticed in the tense situation that prevailed in Paris on the eve of the Second World War' (see Césaire, 2000: xxviii).

Institutionalizing Negritude

What changed, then, in the years immediately following the Second World War that allowed race and anti-colonialism to move from the margins to the centre of public discourse? Part of this shift can be accounted for by the succinctness of the term coined by Césaire, which would allow Negritude to become a meme of sorts for a complex of interests (race, anti-colonial struggle, poetic innovation). In more concrete terms, though, the opening in post-war French society to questions of race and colonialism was created by broader political realities that were the legacy of the war. The prevailing sentiment that the colonies had saved the Republic, both as a base of operations for de Gaulle's *Comité Français de Libération Nationale* (French Committee for National Liberation), formed in Algiers in 1943, and as a source of soldiers for the Resistance, embodied by the *tirailleurs sénégalais* (Senegalese riflemen), led to a greater visibility of the colonized in the post-war years. Likewise, France's grip on its colonies had loosened considerably during the war, and its efforts to reassert control in parts of the empire were met with scattered but tenacious resistance. The uprising in Sétif, Algeria, in May of 1945 and the general strike in Douala, Cameroon, part of French Equatorial Africa, in September of the same year represented just the earliest symptoms of the forthcoming dissolution of the empire. Accommodation of some of the demands of the colonized seemed the only path to avoid the total loss of the empire, and it is in that spirit that the political structure known as the Union française, which was meant to register a shift from France's domination of the colonies to association with them, was created in 1946.

Negritude capitalized on the more receptive political climate by publishing what would become its central texts and launching important cultural initiatives in the years following the war. In addition to their individual poetic production, both Damas and Senghor published popular anthologies of colonized literature. In 1947, Damas edited *Poètes d'expression française*, a collection of poems from Africa and the diaspora, and Senghor co-edited *Les Plus Beaux Écrits de l'Union française*, an anthology of primarily pre- or early-colonial texts from French colonies in Asia, Africa, and the Caribbean, which, in many instances were being translated into French for the first time. The choice of anthologies as a means of establishing a cultural presence was in no way arbitrary. Anthologies exist to perform a simple function; they establish or re-establish the contours of a literary field, giving it coherence and providing a set of texts that serve as a baseline of comparison for inclusion or exclusion from the field. It is easy to understand, then, why anthologizing would have seemed an important task to the Negritude poets. In the interwar years in the French publishing context, novels and poetry by black writers were largely discredited, when they were not simply ignored (with the notable exception of René Maran's 1921 *Prix Goncourt*-winning novel *Batouala*). Establishing a canon of past and present production by black writers gave Negritude a certain amount of cultural capital and a place in the French literary world.

Another important factor in cultural institutionalization is the patronage of one's forebears or leaders. The flurry of publications that explicitly or implicitly endorsed the Negritude project in the years from 1945 to 1950 significantly benefited from the interventions of French intellectuals. The most important anthology of Negritude writing of the post-war years (and, arguably, all the way into the twenty-first century, when it was reissued for the ninth time in 2005) is Senghor's 1948 *Anthologie de la nouvelle poésie nègre et malgache*. The wide dissemination of this anthology can be credited in large measure to Jean-Paul Sartre, whose magisterial, 50-page preface 'Orphée noir' (Sartre, 1988 [1948]) became, for a time, the definitive statement on Negritude. (See Chapter 11 on Sartre.) For Sartre, Negritude was the poetic manifestation of the assumption of subjecthood by black people, who previously had been confined by white people to the category of object. It therefore constituted an 'anti-racist racism' (1988: 296), which is to say, a discourse that focuses on race in order to disrupt racist discourse. Still, given Sartre's position as the pre-eminent public intellectual of the post-war years, it seems likely that Senghor's anthology would have been read far and wide, even if Sartre had written something less than the totalizing statement on Negritude that 'Orphée noir' constitutes.

Another major post-war cultural event was the publication in 1947 of the first issue of the journal *Présence africaine*. Launched by Alioune Diop and backed by a prestigious *Comité de patronage* that included the metropolitan French intellectuals Sartre, André Gide, Théodore Monod and Emmanuel Mounier, and black writers such as Richard Wright, Césaire and Senghor, *Présence africaine* sought to represent African values to Africa and the diaspora, as well as to Europe. Here, too, the 'borrowed symbolic capital' (Nesbitt, 2003: 106) of French intellectuals who lent their support to the journal was determinant. Most notable is the Introduction by Gide, which called for Europe to view Africa not just as a site of material riches to be exploited, but of cultural wealth to be appreciated. However, this support came at a price. In the course of his Introduction, Gide reinforced the emerging divisions within Negritude by underscoring what he saw as essential differences between Europe and Africa. For Gide, the European had lost contact with the body, with sensuality, and he proposed that Africa could help him reunite with his neglected corporality. Taking the example of music, Gide writes that: '[L]a musique nègre fit irruption dans notre savante culture et bouscula soudain nos clefs de sol, nos modes, nos subtils et délicats moyens d'expression de l'âme par les sons. Triomphante sensualité' [Black music erupted into our intellectual culture and destabilized our scales, our modes, our subtle and delicate means of expressing the soul through sound. Triumphant sensuality] (1947: 5). Gide's comments on the 'élémentaire et sauvage énergie' [elementary and savage energy] of the African writer have a similar ring. He quotes at length, in fact, from Arthur de Gobineau's infamous *Essai sur l'inégalité des races humaines* (1854) to make this point. Gide is clearly uncomfortable with Gobineau's explicitly racist pronouncements. But as Aliko Songolo points out, Gide 'retains [Gobineau's] central thesis that the black race is intellectually inferior and sensually superior to the white race' (1988: 29). From its origins, then, the journal *Présence africaine* was marked by its association with a dubious ethnographic perspective, the same perspective that would become central to Senghor's version of Negritude, where reason, analytical thought, and dispassionate discourse were European and intuition, passion, and sensuality were African.

Perhaps the most important cultural event from this period as it concerns the development of Negritude was the re-publication in 1947 of Aimé Césaire's *Cahier d'un retour au pays natal* with a preface by André Breton. Just as Sartre's preface to Senghor's anthology propelled that text towards a profound cultural impact, so Breton's preface, 'Un Grand poète noir' [A Great Black Poet], gave Césaire's poem a reach it may otherwise not have had. For Breton, the *Cahier*'s singularity lies in its ability to challenge the pessimism of the war years (the preface was written while Breton was in exile in Martinique in 1941): 'Défiant à lui seul une époque où l'on croit assister à l'abdication générale de l'esprit [...] le premier souffle nouveau, revivifiant, apte à redonner toute confiance est l'apport d'un Noir' [Single-handedly defying an era in which we appear to be witnessing the general abdication of the mind [...] the first revivifying new breath capable of restoring confidence comes from a black man] (Breton in Césaire, 1947: xii). Like Sartre, Breton suggests that the force and vitality of Césaire's poetry is not so much a function of race as it is a function of the oppression to which black people have been subjected. Césaire's poem itself articulates the values and practices that are associated with blackness, but there is an emphasis on Negritude's contingent status. Negritude is not a fixed essence, 'no longer a cephalic index, or plasma, or soma, but measured by the compass of suffering' (Césaire, 1956 [1939]: 77). This contingent status of Césaire's Negritude allows for transformation and even a transcendence of sorts. The fixed, essentialist vision of race increasingly propounded by Senghor and Césaire's contingent understanding became the poles of dispute within Negritude in the 1940s, 1950s and beyond.

The Premier Congrès International des Écrivains et Artistes Noirs (First International Conference of Black Writers and Artists), organized by Présence Africaine and held at the Sorbonne in September 1956, was a symbol, among many others, of the increasing cultural (and, shortly thereafter, political) independence of black people, but it also underscored the diverging perspectives on Negritude represented by Césaire on one side and Senghor on the other. Senghor devoted much of his speech at the conference to the essential 'physiopsychology' of black people, with few references to current events (Premier Congrès, 1956: 51–65). In spite of the organizers' insistence on 'l'unanimité qui s'est dégagée' [the unanimity that emerged] (Premier Congrès, 1956: 3) from the conference, Richard Wright, for one, castigated Senghor for privileging the very version of African identity – intellectual inferiority to Europe, countered by Africa's emotional superiority – that had allowed Europe to justify slavery and colonialism (Premier Congrès, 1956: 67–69). Césaire, for his part, pushed questions of race consciousness to the background in order to foreground anti-colonial struggle:

> [Q]uelque désireux que l'on soit de garder aux débats de ce Congrès toute leur sérénité, on ne peut pas, si l'on veut serrer de près la réalité, ne pas aborder le problème de ce qui [...] conditionne au plus près le développement des cultures noires: la situation coloniale. (Premier Congrès, 1956: 190)

> [as much as we may wish for the debates during this Conference to remain measured, we cannot, if we want to hew close to reality, avoid discussing the problem that [...] most directly affects the development of black cultures: the colonial situation].

Césaire rightly foresaw that, as the years of decolonization drew to a close and most of the former colonies gained their independence from France, Negritude would become less relevant, and it did indeed start to be displaced in the cultural landscape of the 1960s by concepts such as 'pan-Africanism' and 'Third-Worldism', terms with which it overlapped, but only imperfectly. Yet a certain version of Negritude, one that was not historically contingent, survived, for better or for worse, the political changes of the late-1950s and early 1960s.

The decline and persistence of Negritude

In its 1981 edition, the principal French encyclopedic dictionary, *Le Petit Larousse*, defined the term 'Negritude' as follows: 'Ensemble des caractères, des manières de penser, de sentir propres à la race noire' [the collection of characteristics and modes of thinking and feeling specific to the black race]. Beyond the obvious problem of this definition's suggestion that personality and psychology are biologically determined, there is the further problem of its belatedness: by 1981, this notion of a unified field of blackness, even simply in the Francophone world, had run its course. As I have shown, Negritude, in its mid-century guise, was already somewhat less than a perfectly unified field, but Senghor's psychologizing and universalizing version of the concept proved to be durable in the popular imagination. The definition in *Le Petit Larousse* is proof enough of this. In the dominant critical discourse, Negritude had been historicized and effectively taken out of circulation well before 1981. Whether it was being pilloried or praised, Negritude was largely confined in critical narratives of the 1970s to a particular cultural and political moment stretching from the interwar years to the early years of independence, even if some writers and thinkers kept the torch burning a bit longer.

More often than not, Negritude was being pilloried in these narratives. The ideas that Negritude embodied had been under serious pressure since Frantz Fanon's *The Wretched of the Earth* (1961), which did not dismiss the concept of race entirely but which privileged the collective of the colonized, of the oppressed, over a racially defined grouping in anti-colonial struggles. In any case, for Fanon, who was working and writing from Algeria, Negritude was not a capacious enough term to include the Arab and Berber anti-colonial revolutionaries crucial to his essay. (This is why the sub-title to the original English translation is potentially misleading: on the cover, it touts *The Wretched of the Earth* as 'the handbook for the Black revolution that is changing the shape of the world'.) Stanislas Adotevi, in his 1972 essay *Négritude et négrologues* continued the questioning of Negritude's assumption of a fundamental difference between black and white. Adotevi saw in Senghor's conviction that whiteness was linked to reason, and blackness to emotion, a form of voluntary apartheid. Black people in such a scenario are a race apart, forever confined to the margins of modernity. Not coincidentally, Adotevi cited Fanon frequently in his critiques of Senghor, then president of Senegal, whom he portrayed as a sort of philosopher king manqué, whose people have only a vague notion of what Negritude constitutes and do not see in it any concrete plan of action (1972: 104). Like many critics of his generation, Adotevi saw the solution to Africa's problems in a Marxist humanism that largely evacuated the question of race.

The most recent critiques of Negritude have come from the writers and critics who have proffered the concepts of hybridity, *métissage* or creolization as ways out of the black-white binary that, in their view, structured and limited the debate regarding the role of race in culture and politics. In their critiques, race and, more specifically, Negritude, the discursive form that race takes in the Francophone African diaspora, is a singular configuration, a dangerous attachment to one origin, namely black Africa. In language that, in its use of botanical metaphors evokes or directly invokes Gilles Deleuze and Félix Guattari's *A Thousand Plateaus*, writers and theorists such as Édouard Glissant, Raphaël Confiant and Patrick Chamoiseau have replaced the discourse of the single root or origin with the discourse of the multiply determined rhizome, whose racialized figuration is the *métis*. Not surprisingly, this discourse has its greatest number of exponents in the Americas and, more specifically, in the Caribbean. Although the three particular writers cited above abandon the concept of specificity to varying degrees, they all present Negritude as the counter-example to the ontological freedom enabled by creolization. Raphaël Confiant goes furthest in this regard, devoting an entire book, *Aimé Césaire: une traversée paradoxale du siècle* (1993), to cataloguing the ideological failings of Césaire, the result, he argues, of the latter's continued investment in Negritude.

By the mid-1990s, word of the death of Negritude as a movement had reached even the lexicographers at *Le Petit Larousse*, who revised their definition of the term in the 1994 edition to read as follows: 'Ensemble des valeurs culturelles et spirituelles des Noirs' [the collective cultural and spiritual values of black people]. This, of course, eliminates the vexing biological determinism evident in the earlier definition. Furthermore, a parenthetical note is added indicating that the term first appeared around 1935, producing a distancing and historicizing effect: Negritude now belongs to the past, their new definition suggests, as does, by extension, the problem of race.

The genealogy of the demise of Negritude up to this point is a familiar story. And often, this story is told in triumphant tones. Contemporary criticism scoffs at the naïveté of previous generations of writers who were overly invested in the concept of race. As Christopher Miller has recently shown, characterizing writers (even Césaire) as essentialist has become an expedient means of dismissing their work and of trumpeting one's poststructuralist and postcolonialist credentials: 'Essentialism, with its deterministic identitarianism, is of course the cardinal sin of postcolonial studies, the kryptonite, the poison pill. And the essentialist, *c'est toujours l'autre*' (2008: 329). Ours is ostensibly a post-racial, post-national, fully globalized moment where spasms of racism and nationalism are deemed simple aberrations, so many outlying phenomena in the inevitable march toward Glissant's creolized utopia.

Yet whereas many critiques of Negritude fall into the trap of retrospective wisdom, several recent interventions in the debate on the place of race and race consciousness in the Francophone world manage to avoid it and, in the process, force us to consider the historical necessity of Negritude. Roger Toumson's largely neglected *Mythologie du métissage* (1998) constitutes an argument with the proponents of *métissage* in all its forms and centres on the question of memory. Whereas Negritude, at least as articulated by Aimé Césaire, constitutes the remembering of an erased past in order to more effectively confront the present, hybridity is for Toumson a voluntary amnesia (1998: 28). By this, he means that *métissage*, whether of races, languages or of cultures, places disparate cultural elements together in such a way that the precise hierarchical relations that obtained between them begin to be forgotten or written over, as in a palimpsest. The logical conclusion reached by this type of discourse is that the Caribbean now maintains only the most tenuous connection to Africa, the place that for Toumson is the single most important source of difference in the Americas. In Toumson's account, the prophets of hybridity enact, then, the end of history, which implies, of course, the end of the type of resistance that Negritude rendered possible (65–66). Mongo Beti, who had spent much of his career as a writer attacking Negritude as vehemently as he had coloni-

alism, challenges writers from the black world to reinvigorate the term in his
Dictionnaire de la Négritude:

> La Négritude, c'est l'image que le Noir se construit de lui-même en réplique
> de l'image qui s'est édifiée de lui [...] – image de lui-même sans cesse recon-
> quise, quotidiennement réhabilitée contre les souillures et les préjugés de
> l'esclavage, de la domination coloniale et néo-coloniale. (Beti and Tobner,
> 1989: 6)

> [Negritude is the image that Black people create for themselves in response to
> the image others had created of them [...] – an image of themselves constantly
> fought for, rehabilitated on a daily basis against the stains and prejudices of
> slavery, colonialism and neocolonialism].

These seemingly belated attempts to rescue Negritude from historical irrele-
vancy suggest its value as an ongoing political project, the very value with which
Césaire had sought to invest it from the beginning. Viewed from the present,
the work of the Negritude writers and of the journal and publishing house
Présence Africaine in acknowledging racial difference as an arbitrary justification for oppression played a crucial role in modifying race consciousness, both
in Europe and in Africa and the diaspora, which was a necessary predicate to
the end of colonialism. Soyinka's bon mot should, then, perhaps be modified
to read as follows: 'A tiger does not always need to proclaim his tigritude, but
doing so can sometimes be enough to make the hunter think twice'.

Further reading

Beti, Mongo, and Odile Tobner, 1989. *Dictionnaire de la Négritude* (Paris: L'Harmattan).
    Co-written by the iconoclastic Cameroonian novelist and essayist Mongo Beti and his
    wife, the classical scholar Odile Tobner, this dictionary of the key terms of Negritude
    is, by turns, a scathing indictment of the essentialism of Senghorian Negritude and a
    passionate rehabilitation of the term as an open, historically contingent specificity.
Mudimbe, V. Y. (ed.), 1992. *The Surreptitious Speech: Présence Africaine and the Politics of
    Otherness, 1947–1987* (Chicago and London: University of Chicago Press). A collection
    of essays that takes the measure of the journal *Présence africaine* on its 40th anniver-
    sary, with a particular focus on its contributions to African historiography and philos-
    ophy and the dissemination of African literatures and literary criticism. Regrettably,
    the role of the Caribbean in the *Présence africaine* project is under-represented in this
    collection.
Sartre, Jean-Paul, 1988 [1948]. 'Black Orpheus', in *'What is Literature?' and other essays*
    (Cambridge, MA: Harvard University Press), pp. 289–330. This essay, which served
    as the preface to the 1948 collection of poems by writers from sub-Saharan Africa,
    Madagascar and the African diaspora, edited by Léopold Senghor, helped define
    Negritude as a cultural and a political movement. Sartre called the texts he introduced
    the only revolutionary literature of its time. However, in arguing that Negritude was
    a phase in the passage toward a raceless universalism of the proletariat, the preface
    came to be viewed as a betrayal by many of the self-identified black writers it was
    meant to support.

CHAPTER 19

Francophone Island Cultures: Comparing Discourses of Identity in 'Is-land' Literatures

Pascale De Souza

> The act of writing can unveil the infinite that the colonial domination tends to make us call *île* (or *petit pays,* or *pays périphérique*).
>
> (Chamoiseau, 1997: 245; translated in Perret, 2006: 123)

The general lack of scholarly interest in the contribution of island cultures to postcolonial debate, as underlined by the Caribbean/South Pacific scholar Elizabeth Deloughrey (2001a: 22), takes on specific dimensions within Francophone postcolonial studies. While Caribbean authors have elicited much interest, literature from the Mascarenes and the South Pacific remains to a large extent excluded both from Francophone research conducted in Europe or North America and from Anglophone postcolonial discussions of regional identity. Comparative readings have the potential, however, to reveal rifts and commonalities.

The identification of an appropriate terminology emerges as the first challenge facing such readings across cultural boundaries. French-speaking islands range in status from independent states, such as Haiti, Mauritius or ni-Vanuatu, to France's 'far-flung extra-continental territories' (Brown, 2005b: 42). Though the latter are still often referred to as 'Départements and Territoires d'Outre-Mer' (DOM-TOM), most were assigned a new status in 2003, when French Guyana, Guadeloupe, Martinique and Réunion became 'Départements and Régions d'Outre-Mer' (DOM-ROM), Saint-Pierre-and-Miquelon, Mayotte, French Polynesia and Wallis-and-Futuna 'Collectivités d'outre-mer' (CT), while the uninhabited 'Terres Australes et Antarctiques Françaises' (TAAF) retained its appellation. New Caledonia's status is more ambiguous. The labels 'Pays d'Outre-Mer' (POM) and 'Collectivité Sui Generis' are both used, but the status of Pays d'Outre-Mer does not appear in the 1998 Noumea Agreements. As a result, New Caledonia is referred to locally as a Collectivité Territoriale de la République. This complex framework reflects France's attempt to keep colonies within the nation while providing opportunities for a delegation of powers.

Given the political diversity of these French-speaking island spaces, the term 'postcolonial' appears to be simultaneously emblematic and problematical. Postcolonialism has come under criticism for privileging the 'role of colonialism as the principle of structuration in [the colonized's] history' (Ahmad, 1995: 7). Such an emphasis leads to a disregarding of indigenous traditions, notably at a time when they enjoy a renewal of interest (exemplified by the inclusion of 'la coutume kanak' in the Noumea agreement), and to a situating of 'colonialism in the remote past rather than responding to more recent US occupations such as Puerto Rico, Grenada and Haiti' (Deloughrey, 2001b: 35). In addition, the term 'island' presents its own set of challenges and opportunities. Loxley illustrates the ways in which European discourses about islands can provide a framework for an idealized, sanitized European colonial history, suggesting that the central impulse of such discourses is 'to create a *tabula rasa* upon which [colonizers] can erect their own story' (1990: 102). (Hence the tendency to assign new names for colonized archipelagoes, such as New Britain, New Hebrides, New Ireland or New Caledonia, the final of which was named after Scotland by James Cook.)

Given that 'island history has [often] been recorded by occupants of larger, continental landscapes without the presence of the "I-lander"' (Deloughrey, 2001a: 39), some island narratives emerge as what Trinidadian writer Marlene Nourbese Philip calls an exploration of 'Islandness and its transformation into *I-landness*' (Nourbese Philip, 1995: 41). The sub-title of this chapter is inspired by another islander's autobiography, New Zealander Janet Frame's *To the Is-land*. Frame's spelling allows the island to emerge 'as the space where identity ('I'), place ('land'), and being in time ('is') coincide' (Blowers, 2000: 52). In *Une tempête* (1969), Aimé Césaire provides an island narrative which re-inscribes local subjectivities on to the tabula rasa, thereby allowing the island to emerge as a locale where identity, place and being in time can coincide. The search for a dialogue between the Caribbean, the Mascarenes and the South Pacific echoes such a quest for alternative discourses. It emerges as an attempt to bridge islands which share not only a common colonial heritage and geographical identity but also a present, wherein the 's' in 'island' can be read as a silent letter and as the marker for the plural in French, thereby pointing to the silencing of voices and to the plurality of identities feeding into the 'I'.

Within the South Pacific, a more specific labelling issue emerges. As Peter Brown underlines:

> 'French' is indicative of a colonial situation of fact, while 'Polynesian' is a term created by nineteenth-century European taxonomy, one of the triumvirate of Greek-inspired words coined by the French navigator and sometime anthropologist Dumont d'Urville to classify the peoples of the Pacific according to geographic (Polynesia, Micronesia) or supposed racial features (Melanesia). (2006: 246)

More recently, the terms 'néo-polynésien' and 'polynésien' have been used to refer not only to first settlers but also to more recent immigrants, in an attempt by the anti-independence Gaullist leaders in power from 1982 to 2004 to promote their political agenda (Saura, 2004: 169). As for Tahiti, it has emerged as a 'synecdoche', a 'telescoped western generic label for anyone coming from "French Polynesia"' (Brown, 2006: 246), thereby erasing the identity of writers such as Chantal Spitz (Huahine) or Taaria Walker (Rurutu). As Spitz concludes:

> Drôle de pays où l'on se définit sans porter le nom du pays qui nous porte. Drôle de pays où l'on s'origine dans un pays étranger. Drôle de pays où l'on ne parle pas la langue du pays. Drôle de pays où l'on folklorise son peuple. Drôle de pays où l'on exotise son peuple. Drôle de pays, ce pays, le nôtre qui n'est même pas un pays. (Spitz, 2002a: 110)

> [This is an odd country where one defines oneself without using the name of the country which bears us. An odd country where one traces one's origins to a foreign country. An odd country where one does not speak the language of the country. An odd country where people become part of folklore. An odd country where people are exoticized. An odd country, this country, ours which is not even a country].

Beyond terminology

A review of courses offered in European and North American universities (and of scholarly essays produced by those working in them) illustrates that '[j]ust as (Anglophone) Postcolonial studies has been dominated by certain theoretical or regional paradigms, so might the fully diverse potential of Francophone Postcolonial Studies be eclipsed by prominent trends in scholarship' (Forsdick and Murphy, 2003: 12). Indeed, 'Francophone' trends tend to favour African, Caribbean, North African/Beur and Quebecois subjects, while authors from the Mascarenes and the South Pacific remain un(der)explored. More survey and comparative courses could help address this under-representation in university courses. However, the offering of such courses calls for scholars to be willing to explore multiple regions in their own research, along the lines of the approach adopted by Elizabeth Deloughrey, who has explored literatures from the Antilles and from the South Pacific in *Routes and Roots: Navigating Caribbean and Pacific Island Literatures* (2007). As for scholarship within the French-speaking world, Forsdick and Murphy regret the absence of a chapter on 'Francophone island cultures' in *Francophone Postcolonial Studies* (2003: 12). While the Caribbean is given extensive coverage, the Mascarenes and the South Pacific are absent, both in name and representation. This omission might be ascribed to a dearth of European- or North American-based scholars whose research focuses on these regions.[1]

---

1 As guest editors of 'Oceanic Dialogues: From the Black Atlantic to the Indo-Pacific' for the *International Journal of Francophone Studies*, Adlai Murdoch and I experienced first hand a similar challenge. While Caribbean scholars promptly answered our call for contributions, more probing was required to locate specialists in Mauritian, Réunionese and South Pacific studies, most of whom were from and/or based in their region of interest (De Souza and Murdoch, 2005).

Comparative regional essays could offer opportunities to inscribe the South Pacific and the Mascarenes on both the Anglophone and Francophone literary maps. However, the following conclusion holds true beyond Caribbean shores:

> Until recently, much scholarship on the Caribbean archipelago – with some notable exceptions – has tended to be produced according to the dominant languages spoken within the region, with the result that a polyglossic, pan-Caribbean space is fragmented into smaller spaces still defined along transatlantic axes in relation to their former colonial occupiers. (Forsdick and Murphy, 2003: 12)

'Notable exceptions' would include Michael Dash's *The Other America: Caribbean Literature in a New World Context* (1998), as well as recent editorial initiatives such as Gordon Collier and Ulrich Fleishman's *A Pepper-Pot of Cultures, Aspects of Creolization in the Caribbean* (2004), Elizabeth Deloughrey, Renée Gosson and George B. Handley's *Caribbean Literature and the Environment: Between Nature and Culture* (2005), and special issues of the *Journal of Caribbean Literatures* edited by Anna Malena and myself.[2] Margaret Heady (2006) addresses another manifestation of Caribbean fragmentation, namely the tendency among French-speaking scholars to specialize either in Haiti or the French Caribbean. As she demonstrates, Jacques-Stephen Alexis's use of magic realism to transcend European literary influences and question truth and authenticity can, for instance, shed light on the postmodernist approach adopted by Guadeloupean writer Simone Schwarz-Bart.

In studies of the Mascarenes and the South Pacific, recent publications include the proceedings of the numerous CORAIL conferences held at the University of New Caledonia, *Littératures d'émergence et mondialisation* (2005), and *Correspondances Océanes,* a thematic bi-annual journal promoting Oceanic cultures. Several recent initiatives also aim to make Francophone postcolonial authors more accessible to an Anglophone audience. In Mauritius, historian Marina Carter and poet Khal Torabully have edited *Coolitude: An Anthology of the Indian Labor Diaspora* (2002), and Danielle Tranquille has translated *Toufann* (1991), a play by Dev Virahsawmy, and *Roses are Ashes, Ashes are Roses* (2005), an anthology of poems by Shakuntala Hawoldar. In New Caledonia, playwrights Déwé Gorodé and Nicolas Kurtovitch have co-published a series of dialogues *Dire le vrai/To Tell the Truth* (2000), local historian Frédéric Angleviel has launched a collection entitled 'Portes Océanes', with a view to translating Pacific writers into French, English and Italian, while Australian scholar Peter Brown has edited *Living Heritage: Kanak Culture Today* (2000) and a series of translations and presentations of New Caledonian authors.[3] In ni-Vanuatu, Josué Célestin is translating tradi-

---

2   'The Caribbean that isn't? Exploring rifts and disjunctions', in the *Journal of Caribbean Literatures,* 2001, 3.1, focuses on ethnic, social and cultural divisions within and among Caribbean literatures in French, English, Spanish and Dutch; 'The Caribbean that is? Exploring intertextualities', in the *Journal of Caribbean Literatures,* 2002, 3.2, examines how Caribbean authors borrow from each other across linguistic lines.

3   The first two volumes, *The Kanak Apple Season* (Brown, 2004) and *Sharing as Custom Provides*

tional stories into Bislama, English and French, and in French Polynesia, Kareva Mateata-Allain, Alexander Mawyer and Frank Stewart have co-edited *Varua Tupu* (2005), the first anthology of Tahitian/Ma'ohi literature in English.[4]

Negritude, *créolité*, *Indianité*: echoes of vertical integration

Both commonalities and disjunctions characterize links between the Caribbean and the Mascarenes. If 'the most authentic meaning of the word Caribbean is the organization of labour within the region by people particularly from Asia and Africa, and the responses of their labour to imperial rule' (Lamming, 1996: 3), several other 'African diasporic island cultures' are 'Caribbean' (Deloughrey, 2001a: 33).[5] A shared history of plantation-based economies fuelled by slavery and indenture should not, however, mask demographic divergences. Unlike the Caribbean, the Mascarenes were uninhabited when the first European explorers arrived and they have since experienced much higher levels of Asian migration. The political evolution of Mauritius from colony to independence has undoubtedly better positioned it to forge its own identity than its sister island of Réunion, which still grapples with 'a hegemonic or dominant symbolic system – metropolitan French culture' (Lionnet, 1993: 105). However, while Mauritian multiculturalism has indeed allowed 'minorities the right to their own language, their own religion, and their own cultural practices' (1993: 106), Afro-Mauritian voices often remain unheard (Prabhu, 2005). Prabhu provides an interesting point of departure for a concurrent analysis of the under-representation of Indo-Caribbean minorities in the French Caribbean, of which Indo-Mauritian poet Khal Torabully is clearly aware in his comments on 'la profonde attente des indo-antillais, qui ont besoin de rassembler les fragments de leur être pétri de silences et d'acculturation' [the deep yearning among the Indo-Antilleans, who need to gather the fragments of their being full of silences and loss of cultural markers] (Couassi, 1998: 69). Jacqueline Manicom, Maryse Condé and Raphaël Confiant have partly met such expectations by introducing Indo-Caribbean characters in some of their novels. More recently, Confiant has situated the Indo-Caribbean experience at the centre of *La Panse du Chacal* (Prix des Amériques insulaires et de la Guyane 2004; see Bragard, 2006 for a comparative analysis of Confiant's novel and Mauritian Nathacha Appanah-Mouriquand's *Les*

(Brown, 2005a), focused respectively on short fiction and poetry by Déwé Gorodé. The third will deal with New Caledonian playwrights.

4   Australia-based Celestine Hitiura Vaite has also published several Tahitian novels in English (see ht tp: // w ww . Celestine vaite . com).

5   The islands of the South Pacific never relied on plantation systems fuelled by slavery and indentureship. In New Caledonia, however, the Code de l'Indigénat (1887–1946) obliged the Kanak to provide free labour and pay taxes, and denied them any civil rights, while some Asian ethnic migrants were brought in as indentured labour (see Angleviel, 2005). In French Polynesia, Chinese immigrants came to work in mines and plantations. Emigration included the coerced or forced drafting of some islanders to work on Queensland plantations, in Peruvian mines or on whale ships.

Rochers de poudre d'or). Such initiatives augur well, but the French Caribbean still awaits the rise of a major Indo-Caribbean author who can explore this diasporic experience in the way V. S. Naipaul has done for the Indo-Trinidadians or David Dabydeen for the Indo-Guyanese.

Further exploration of Réunionese and Mauritian literatures reveal fragmentation and the emergence of a complex theoretical dialogue with the French Caribbean. The emergence in the Caribbean of 'a specific form of oppositional consciousness via the medium of negritude, and then of *antillanité*' (Lionnet, 1993: 102) did not occur in Réunion, which has instead fostered two identity discourses: *Créolie*, and a form of *créolité*. Proponents of the former, such as Gilbert Aubry, argue that the Creole language is fast disappearing, eroded by modernity, triggering the need to record folk tales and other expressions of Creole identity for posterity, while proponents of the latter, such as poet Axel Gauvin, suggest that a *créolité* based on the defence of Creole is alive and well, and 'can account for the constitution of a hybrid cultural specificity, of a true *réunionité*' (1993: 111).

Mauritius has seen the emergence of another discourse on identity through poet Khal Torabully's *coolitude*. Since the publication of *Éloge de la créolité* (Bernabé et al., 1989), no new Caribbean discourse has pursued or challenged the tenets of the preceding Negritude and *antillanité* movements, or addressed the criticisms levelled at the *Éloge* for its French-Caribbean centricity. In *Cale d'Étoiles-Coolitude* (published in Réunion in 1992) and *Chair Corail, Fragments Coolies* (written after a meeting with Aimé Césaire and published in Guadeloupe in 1999), Torabully provides, however, a fascinating new 'trace'. *Coolitude* thus builds on several discursive strategies, including Negritude, *créolité* and *Indianité*, in order to explore the experience of 'indenture and coolietization' (Henry, 2003), but also denounces all three as too centred, respectively, on Africa, the French Caribbean and India. That is why Torabully could 'not do for India what [Césaire] did for Africa' (Carter and Torabully, 2002: 147).

The very terms *réunionité* and *coolitude* suggest that the attempts by the authors of *Éloge de la créolité* to subsume the Mascarenes into their own version of *créolité* may reflect a Caribbeano-centric view of the Creole world. The elogists argue that '[w]e, the Caribbean Creoles, enjoy […] a Creole solidarity with all African, Mascarin, Asian, and Polynesian peoples' (Bernabé et al., 1993: 94). (New Caledonia and ni-Vanuatu would be excluded here as they are part of Melanesia.) Such premises led Confiant to conclude, in his preface to *Chair Corail, Fragments Coolies*, that

> [l]a Coolitude vient, aux côtés de la Négritude, de la Békénitude, de la Sinitude et de la Syro-Libanitude, apporter son indispensable pierre à l'édifice que nous sommes tous en train de construire depuis des siècles: la créolité. (Confiant, 1999: 9)

> [*Coolitude*, along with Negritude, Bekenitude, Sinitude and Syro-Lebanonitude, provides its own brick to the edifice we have all been building for centuries: *créolité*.]

Coolitude is not, however, a facet of *créolité*, but a much wider 'cadre de réflexion' [frame for reflection] for a 'diversification de l'imaginaire de la relation' [diversification of the imaginary of relation] (Boni, 1999: 32).

The word 'Creole' appears in and of itself problematical as the basis for a common definition of identity. South Pacific authors rarely use it to refer to their region, while Mascarene writers would find the following French Caribbean definition ill-fitting:

> Tous ces termes [chabin, Nègre, griffe, Mulâtre, câpresse, échappé Couli, Couli blanc, couli béké et consorts] sont saturés de connotations raciales souvent péjoratives alors que le terme 'Créole' n'en comporte aucune, rigoureusement aucune. Il permet enfin de dépasser le seul cadre géographique des Antilles et d'établir une parenté, un cousinage avec d'autres aires créoles du globe telles que les Mascareignes. (Confiant, 1993: 224)

> [All these terms (chabin, black, griffe, mulatto, câpresse, échappé Couli, Couli blanc, couli béké and so forth) are loaded with racial, often pejorative connotations, whereas the term 'créole' implies none, absolutely none. It allows one finally to go beyond the geographical framework of the Antilles and establish a common bond with other Creole areas of the world such as the Mascarenes.]

In Mauritius, 'créole', however, refers specifically to the population of 'African ancestry, identified by dark skin and "African appearance"' (Prabhu, 2005: 185) and, in Réunion, to any person whose blood has been so mixed that it is difficult to trace his/her origins.

While *coolitude* establishes links with *Indianité*, it does not imply an ethnocentric approach but focuses instead on the *kala pani*, the crossing itself as the matrix of a new identity. As Torabully writes: 'En disant "coolie", je dis aussi tout navigateur sans registre de bord: je dis tout homme parti vers l'horizon de son rêve, quel que soit le bateau qu'il accosta ou dût accoster' [When I say 'coolie', I also mean any navigator without a set destination: I say any man who left towards the horizon of his dream, whichever boat he may have boarded or had to board] (Torabully, 1992: 89). Such 'de-centeredness and hence openness to other cultures and identities' (Henry, 2003) echoes Glissant's rhizomatic networks and his *Poétique de la Relation*. By 'making the crossing central' (Carter and Torabully, 2002: 15), it also evokes Benítez-Rojo's *Repeating Island* (1996) and Gilroy's *Black Atlantic* (1993) insofar as they become 'a trope that foregrounds the fluidity of water as a channel for a circuitous series of migrations' (Deloughrey, 2001b: 41). As Bragard concludes, *coolitude* emerges as a poetics that focuses on the transoceanic crossing of coolies, establishing it as a central metaphor for identities characterized by '*multiple* crossings: crossings between cultures, heritages, places, generations, gender, historical assertions, and mythical references' (2005: 219).

Island links

In the French South Pacific, distance from other French-speaking countries is compounded by limited regional migration (except from Wallis and Futuna to New Caledonia), a tendency which contrasts sharply with pre-colonial times and current trends within the Anglophone Pacific. As a result, 'rather than a history of forced (or induced) migration', the region 'continues to experience imposed silence' (Mateata-Allain, 2005: 270). The exploration of multi-ethnicity in New Caledonian and French Polynesian socio-literary discourses echoes Gilroy's desire to transcend 'the constraints of ethnicity and national particularity' (Gilroy, 1993, 19), and Torabully's search for plural identities. The prism of convict deportation could also offer opportunities for comparative studies and for the emergence of another *coolitude* discourse, while an exploration of the construction of the self in island narratives could help (re)create links among and between 'broken archipelago[s] subject to militourism and in danger of being sold to continents as a "Chain store of islands"' (Walcott, cited in Deloughrey, 2001a: 46).

In 'Dream-country', Delphine Perret (2006) reveals how Chamoiseau's perception of Martinique in *Écrire en pays dominé* (1997) shifts from island to country to place. Such an evolution echoes Tongan Epeli Hau'ofa's visions of the South Pacific. Chamoiseau concludes that under the colonizer's gaze, the island becomes the place of a confined isolation and insularity, epitomized by 'this lost man in the bitter ocean', and 'insularity, his spirit, the narrow way to see the world in the celestial sea-chains of blue' (Chamoiseau, 1997: 234; translated in Perret, 2006: 121). Likewise, Hau'ofa argues that '[n]ineteenth-century imperialism erected boundaries that led to the contraction of Oceania, transforming a once boundless world into the Pacific islands, states and territories that we know today. People were confined to their tiny spaces isolated from each other' (1999: 33). Both Glissant and Chamoiseau have denounced such balkanization of the Caribbean islands (Glissant, 1989: 248), which were viewed in pre-colonial times as 'the poles of an Archipelagic sojourn' (Chamoiseau, 1997: 241; translated in Perret, 2006: 122).

Chamoiseau's contrastive analysis leads him to reject the word 'île' [lilèt], which in Creole designates only some 'almost uninhabitable concretions' (1997: 244; translated in Perret, 2006: 122). Likewise, Hau'ofa suggests that the phrase 'Pacific Islands' denotes 'small areas of land sitting atop submerged reefs or seamounts', and that 'focusing in this way stresses the smallness and remoteness of the islands' (1999, 31). Seeking to deorientalize that view of the South Pacific, he suggests adopting the term 'Oceania' to reflect a universe which once comprised '[n]ot only land surfaces but also the surrounding ocean as far as [Pacific islanders] could traverse and exploit it, the underworld with its fire-controlling and earth-shaking denizens, and the heavens above' (1999: 33). Hau'ofa's quote finds echoes in New Caledonia and Martinique. Jean Mariotti sees his island as a ship, 'que l'on pouvait chevaucher dans l'infini' [which could be sailed to infinity] (1996: 57), while for Chamoiseau, in Creole, '[l]'île n'existe pas, c'est un inépuisable pays, une terre inscrite au monde par le derme de la mer. Là règne l'ouverture: la merveille marine, la ruée de vents voyous, la flèche céleste de gibiers migrateurs' [the island does not exist; it is an inexhaustible country, a land inscribed in the world by the skin of the sea. There reigns the opening: the marvel of the sea, the rush of vagabond winds, the celestial flesh of migrating game] (1997: 244; translated in Perret, 2006: 122).

If 'every archipelagic thought is a thought of trembling, of non-presumption, but also of opening up and sharing' (Glissant, 1997b: 231; translated in Perret, 2006: 130), such thought may be seen to lead to a confluence of roots and routes, a rhizomatic island network. Glissant claims, for instance: 'The single root is grounded in a land that becomes a territory. A "real" notion today, in every composite culture, of identity as a rhizome' (1997b: 195–96; translated in Perret, 2006: 129), whereas Turo a Raapoto states that: '"Ohi" [in *Ma'ohinété*] refers to a sprout which has already taken root, while being linked to the mother stem' (cited in Nicole, 2000: 183). These converging views expressed by a Martiniquan and a Tahitian author are not limited to networks within their respective regions but extend beyond the Caribbean and Oceania to include any region which has experienced diasporic trends. Such 'submarine unity' (Brathwaite, 1974: 67) or 'Oceanic Dialogue' (De Souza and Murdoch, 2005) remains, however, mostly silenced within and between Francophone and Anglophone island studies.

In October 2005, New Caledonia invited several writers from France and the South Pacific to its second Salon International du Livre Océanien.[6] While some participants, such as New Caledonian Déwé Gorodé, expressed their weariness at writing *for* outsiders: 'on ne veut pas être perçu dans le miroir de l'autre' [we do not want to be seen in the other's mirror] (Brown, 2006: 253), others, such as New Zealander Patricia Grace or New Caledonian Arlette Peirano, welcomed being read by the outside world. Their views echo previous comments made by ni-Vanuatuan Jacques Gédéon and Huahinian Chantal Spitz. Gédéon sees publishing as a cultural imperative 'afin qu'un jour nous ayons notre propre littérature' [so that one day we may have our own literature] (cited in Angleviel and Laux, 2006: 82), and Spitz grasps it as an opportunity to break the silence imposed by the colonizer, and 'calibanize' his discourse:

> Publier pour prendre-dire parole d'une histoire dérobée déformée défigurée par tous les autres d'hier et d'aujourd'hui s'installant pensants disants de tous pour nous. Publier pour mettre le doigt sur les plaies les purulences et ronger avec le suprême outil la suffisance des mystificateurs qui nous affirment que notre peuple est toujours enfant notre pays toujours paradis notre ciel toujours bleu notre océan toujours vierge. (Spitz, 2002b: 109)

> [Let's publish to grasp-say words of a history which has been stolen deformed disfigured by all the others from the past and today settling down thinking

6 Including Geoff Cush, whose novel *Son of France* (2002; French version, *Graine de France*) questions the notion of (colonial) progress in New Zealand portrayed as a French colony.

saying all for us. Let's publish to put our fingers on the oozing wounds and use the supreme tool to nibble at the self-satisfaction of those who mystify us when they assert that our people is still in its infancy our country a paradise our skies always blue our ocean always pure.]

Publication is a first step prior to translation and to (comparative) scholarly essays, both of which subsequently ensure that such discourse does not remain limited to regional salons or to French-language readers. In this vein, the aim of this chapter has been to contribute to putting an end to 'l'antique combat contre la perfide Albion modernisé en lutte pour la francophonie contre l'anglophonie' [the age-old fight against the perfidious Albion modernized into a struggle between francophonia and anglophonia] (Spitz, 2002a: 110).[7]

Further reading

Bragard, Véronique, 2005. 'Transoceanic Echoes: coolitude and the work of the Mauritian poet Khal Torabully', *International Journal of Francophone Studies,* 8.3: 219–33. Bragard analyses how Torabully maps 'Indian identity', shifting the emphasis from a fossilizing nostalgia for a fixed India to the ocean space that mediates numerous cultural (ex)changes.

Carter, Marina, and Khal Torabully (eds), 2002. *Coolitude: An Anthology of the Indian Labour Diaspora* (London: Anthem Press). This anthology combines history and poetry to bring into focus the Indian diasporic experience and explore Torabully's poetics of *coolitude.*

Deloughrey, Elizabeth, 2001a. '"The litany of islands, the rosary of archipelagoes"': Caribbean and Pacific Heterotopias', *Ariel,* 32.1: 21–51. [Special issue: 'Small Cultures: The Literature of Micro-States'.] Deloughrey analyses the contrast between, on the one hand, the Anglo-American mystification of Caribbean and Pacific islands presented as remote isolated entities to be subdued and, on the other, postcolonial discourses which locate the island within an archipelagic system and seek out the I-lander's voice.

De Souza, Pascale, and Adlai Murdoch, 2005. 'Introduction', *International Journal of Francophone Studies,* 8.2: 255–68. [Special issue: 'Oceanic Dialogues: from the Black Atlantic to the Indo-Pacific'.] This introduction examines to what extent Gilroy's 'Black Atlantic' may emerge as an analytical tool for island literatures beyond Atlantic shores.

Mateata-Allain, Kareva, Frank Stewart and Alexander Mawyer (eds), 2005. *Varua Tupu: New Writing and Art from French Polynesia* (Honolulu: University of Hawaii Press). This anthology makes French Polynesian authors' exploration of issues such as the shifting political scene, French cultural domination and nuclear testing available to an Anglophone audience.

Finally, the 'Ile en île' website provides an excellent introduction to island cultures in the French-speaking world: http://www.lehman.cuny.edu/ile/en.

7   The author would like to thank Frédéric Angleviel, Véronique Bragard, Peter Brown, Kareva Mateata-Allain and Priscilla Maunier, for their editorial suggestions.

CHAPTER 20

Locating Quebec on the Postcolonial Map

Mary Jean Green

Quebec and postcolonial studies

In his introduction to a 2003 issue of *Québec Studies*, Vincent Desroches poses the question, for the first time in the context of a serious theoretical discussion: 'En quoi la littérature québécoise est-elle postcoloniale?' [In what sense can Quebec literature be deemed postcolonial?] (2003b). It is not surprising that this question, framed in French by a *Québécois* scholar, is given serious consideration in a journal published in the United States: in US academic circles Quebec literature had, for at least a decade, been associated with the postcolonial, however loosely defined. Yet within Quebec itself the term 'postcolonial' is still largely ignored, and the theoretical approach it evokes often rejected as a new attempt to impose Anglophone critical hegemony on a Francophone literature. The question posed by Desroches and the responses it has inspired have done much to clarify the terms of the debate, launching critical discussion of the complex ways in which Quebec can be considered postcolonial in a historical sense, as well as a reflection on the ways in which postcolonial readings of Quebec literature can be useful, although not without their dangers.

Since postcolonial studies, and especially the work of Gayatri Chakravorty Spivak, teaches us the importance of situating the critic, I must confess my own involvement in locating Quebec within the postcolonial. In 1996, as Desroches mentions, I was part of an editorial group that included women writers from Quebec in an essay collection entitled *Postcolonial Subjects: Francophone Women Writers*, a title that juxtaposes the terms 'postcolonial' and 'Francophone'. Almost inadvertently, we had entered the now hotly contested terrain of Francophone postcolonial studies, at the same time placing Quebec within it. *Postcolonial Subjects* was, of course, embedded in an American academic world where, as David Murphy commented in 2003, 'the term Francophone Studies has for over a decade now been used as a synonym for Postcolonial Studies' (74). In fact, the use of 'postcolonial' came as a last-minute substitute for the collection's original title, *Beyond the Hexagon*, which our editor had rightly deemed incomprehensible to American readers. In combination with the term 'Francophone', 'postcolonial' seemed to perform the same desirable task of 'decentring' a Francophone world too often centred in Paris.

Moreover, with its emphasis on domination and resistance, the term 'postcolonial' seemed appropriate for the feminist project of recognizing the importance of Francophone women writers. In fact, theorists like Spivak and Chandra Talpade Mohanty, referenced in our 1996 introduction as 'feminist', later found themselves included in postcolonial anthologies, and several articles in the collection explicitly employed concepts of postcoloniality in discussing texts written by Francophone women writers. This was especially true of the concluding essay by Françoise Lionnet, who has been credited by H. Adlai Murdoch and Anne Donadey as one of the first to make the connection between 'postcolonial' and 'Francophone' (2005: 8). In her 1995 book, *Postcolonial Representations*, Lionnet had defined 'postcoloniality' as 'a condition that exists within, and thus contests and resists, the colonial moment itself with its ideology of domination' (4).

Several years after the publication of *Postcolonial Subjects*, I began to confront the theoretical complexity of this early venture in naming when I was forced by tragic circumstances to assume responsibility for a course on postcolonial theory that had been designed by my late colleague, Susanne Zantop. Although, with one exception, the postcolonial theorists included in the course had little interest in Quebec, Susanne Zantop's own expansion of the purview of Edward Said's conception of Orientalism to include German colonial fantasies and Spanish colonization in the New World showed me the importance of expanding the boundaries of a postcolonial 'canon' largely focused on India and the Arab world. In this context, further expanding the postcolonial to include Quebec seemed not only reasonable but also potentially fruitful.

One theorist on the postcolonial syllabus had considered the postcoloniality of Quebec: Albert Memmi, whose *The Colonizer and the Colonized* (1957) had been an important influence on Quebec intellectuals of the 1960s. As recorded in an essay in *Dominated Man* (1968), Memmi had been confronted in 1967 by a group of students who sought his response to the question, 'Are French Canadians colonized?' Memmi's response was not an unqualified 'yes': although he recognized Quebec's specific situation of economic and cultural domination by English Canadians and 'Anglo-Americans', he chose to qualify French Canadians as 'dominés', a concept that was at the centre of his work in the 1960s as he expanded the analysis of colonial domination to include groups such as black people, Jews, workers and women. Yet Memmi went on to identify specific features of the colonial situation that French Canadians clearly shared, especially the condition he had identified as 'colonial diglossia', in which the language of the colonizer, participating in the functioning of economic and political power, reduced the native language to impotence and inferiority. This was the situation in which he saw French in Quebec. In a second parallel, Memmi evoked the tendency of colonized peoples to retreat to traditional sources of value, like religion and the family, as a refuge from colonial oppression. In the case of French Canadians, Memmi identified these 'refuge-values' with the Catholic Church.

With this single exception, Quebec has not, until very recently, been considered within the field of the postcolonial. One reason so little has been written on the subject is that intellectuals in Quebec (as opposed to Québécois academics working in US or Anglophone Canadian settings) have not, in the main, felt themselves to be included in the debates on postcolonial studies going on around them. Often, they have reacted against both the 'postcolonial literatures' approach set forth by Bill Ashcroft, Gareth Griffiths and Helen Tiffin in *The Empire Writes Back* (1989), and the enterprise of 'postcolonial theory' focused on what has been called the 'holy trinity' of Edward Said, Homi Bhabha and Gayatri Spivak.

As used in *The Empire Writes Back,* the term 'postcolonial' includes 'settler cultures' like Canada and Australia, implicitly including Quebec – which is then immediately excluded by the effective limitation of the study to literatures written in English. It is no wonder that a work of this nature proved unappealing to Francophone Québécois, even as it was embraced by English departments in Anglophone Canada, Britain and the US. On the other hand, the 'postcolonial theory' approach, generally posited as dating from the publication of Said's *Orientalism* in 1978, tends to focus on the work of Said, Bhabha and Spivak, which is written in English and is grounded in models of colonization originating in India and the Middle East. Not surprisingly, these three Anglophone theorists, whose work has only recently been translated into French, have largely been ignored by Francophone intellectual circles in Quebec. Yet, even more than Ashcroft, Griffiths and Tiffin, these theorists have been eagerly received in US and British French departments, because of their explicit references to French colonialism and their evident grounding in the work of French thinkers such as Foucault, Lacan and Derrida.

Thanks to the proliferation of postcolonial readers and anthologies, the domain of what is now called postcolonial studies has included the work of many theorists of decolonization, notably Aimé Césaire, Frantz Fanon and Albert Memmi (see Chapters 1, 5 and 9 respectively) – now clearly identified as Francophone – just as it has also included the work of 'international' feminist theorists such as Trinh Minh-ha. Even in France, where the reception of postcolonial studies has also been hesitant, Jean-Marc Moura's groundbreaking *Littératures francophones et théorie postcoloniale* (2007 [1999]) has been able to demonstrate the usefulness of postcolonial theory in the study of Francophone literatures. Yet, even in its expanded form, the field of postcolonial studies has seemed to attract few disciples in Quebec, especially as no Quebec intellectual manages to gain a place in the postcolonial anthologies, even in the impressive five-volume reader compiled by Canadian-based scholar Diana Brydon (2000).

Post/colonial Quebec?

Yet, only a few decades ago, Quebec intellectuals and writers rushed to define themselves as 'colonized'. As they took part in their own 'Quiet Revolution' on the political front, they were eager to affiliate themselves with the process of decolonization then occurring around the world, which was especially marked for Francophones by the Algerian War. The Francophone 'discourse of decolonization,' as Robert Schwartzwald (1985) has termed it, became an important element in a new process of cultural self-definition, which included the adoption of the term *Québécois* as a replacement for the doubly colonizing identitary marker of *Canadien français*. Quebec nationalist poets such as Gaston Miron and Paul Chamberland were influenced by the anti-colonial texts of Martiniquan Aimé Césaire. Identifying with the racial oppression denounced in the work of Césaire and Fanon, Pierre Vallières entitled his autobiography *Nègres blancs d'Amérique* (1969) while Michèle Lalonde publicly declaimed her contestatory poem 'Speak White' (1974), in which she associates the oppression of *Québécois* with the blood being shed in the streets of Algiers and Little Rock. Identifying with the struggle of the Algerian people, the FLQ (Front de Libération du Québec), with which writer Hubert Aquin was famously associated, named itself in homage to the Algerian FLN. André d'Allemagne developed the concept of *Le Colonialisme au Québec* in his 1966 book, and the group of independence-minded intellectuals clustered around the journal *Parti pris* devoted entire issues to the construction of a *Portrait du colonisé québécois* [Portrait of the Colonized *Québecois*], in which they adapted Memmi's description to their own situation.

In fact, the historical relationship of Quebec to colonization has been complex. As Marilyn Randall has observed,

> [T]he French in Canada have been at times united against a common enemy and at others divided among themselves, occupying a confusing variety of subject positions within the range of colonial possibilities: colonizer and colonized; victim and political partner; collaborator in their own oppression and active rebel. (2003: 86–87)

However, once we get beyond the clear, binary distinctions made by nationalist independence movements, a similar complexity can be found in the history of many areas to which the adjective 'postcolonial' is commonly applied. As the 'postcolonial' writer Assia Djebar reminds us, even Algeria, considered by many to be an iconic Francophone postcolonial space, has a complex history of multi-layered colonization, in which Arabs and other Muslims have, like *Québécois*, been both colonizer and colonized. Even Memmi, who wrote so convincingly about a world neatly divided between colonizer and colonized, was himself, as a member of the indigenous Tunisian Jewish community, ambivalently situated between the two, as his autobiographical work reveals. It is perhaps for this reason that Memmi was able to respond so sympathetically to the particular ambivalence of Quebec.

The 'colonization' of Quebec to which the 1960s intellectuals were referring began in 1763, when, following the French defeat on the Plains of Abraham, Quebec (then New France) became a colony of Britain. The Treaty of Paris initiated a period of domination begun by London and continued by English Canadians in Ottawa as Canada itself progressively gained its autonomy. Before *la Conquête*, as the event is commonly known in Quebec, New France arguably fitted into the category of 'white settler colony', as used by the authors of *The Empire Writes Back* to define the status of other parts of Canada, Australia and the United States. Because of their early displacement and their 'colonization' of indigenous peoples under the *régime français*, some Canadian critics – most famously, Linda Hutcheon in her 1990 article, 'Circling the Downspout of Empire' – would deny French Canadians any claim to the status of 'colonized', an exclusion from the postcolonial that Marie Vautier has chosen to contest in her 1998 comparative study, *New World Myth: Postmodernism and Postcolonialism in Canadian Fiction*. Other critics – for example Sylvia Söderlind, in her 1991 *Margin/Alias: Language and Colonization in Canadian and Québécois Fiction* – would place Quebec in the same category as Canada as a whole, including it within the sphere of 'colonization' but ignoring the historical specificity of a Francophone population dominated by the British.

In the early decades of post-1763 British rule in Quebec, Francophone parliamentary leaders contested the power of colonial authorities, a resistance that in 1837–38 culminated in scattered episodes of armed rebellion that were crushed by the British army. This event, known as the Patriots Rebellion, crystallized the French Canadian response to British rule, as Marilyn Randall (2003) rightly points out, and it took on particular historical significance for the Quebec intellectuals and writers of the 1960s. In a special issue of the journal *Liberté* in 1965, the contributors saw this nineteenth-century rebellion as an early example of popular resistance to British colonial rule and as a humbling defeat that initiated the 'colonized' mentality they sought to contest: as André Major expressed it, 'This image of our defeat haunted me [ ]. Never will I be able to accept our reality, never will I resign myself to our daily defeat' (1965: 94–95). Even as recently as 1978 – in the years leading up to the 1980 referendum on Quebec's sovereignty – playwright Roland Lepage was able to call forth tears of rage from Quebec theatre audiences as he evoked the Patriots Rebellion in his play, *La Complainte des Hivers Rouges*, depicting the burning of Quebec farms, the destitution of widows and children in the freezing Quebec winter, and the martyrdom of the twelve Patriots condemned to the gallows.

The failure of the Patriots Rebellion ushered in a period of increased British domination, in which Quebec (then known as Lower Canada) was combined with Upper Canada in a nation where it was relegated to perpetual minority status. The new situation was defined by Lord Durham in his 1838 report to the Crown, in terms that resonate with the nineteenth-century discourse of colonization. Analysing the problems of Canada as 'a struggle, not of principles, but of races' (Durham, 1963 [1838]: 23), Lord Durham describes the French settlers as 'a nationality [...] destitute of all that can invigorate and elevate a people,' as demonstrated by the fact that '[t]hey are a people with no history and no literature' (150) – a pithy put-down that would fan the flames of Quebec resistance for years to come. In language Edward Said would no doubt have found familiar, Durham aspired to come to the aid of these culturally deprived Frenchmen by encouraging them to take on 'our English character' (149). Yet, despite this enunciation of a sort of British *mission civilisatrice,* French Canadians (much like the indigenous Algerians who insisted on retaining their Muslim religion and native languages) were, in reality, excluded from the sites of political and economic power by their Catholic religion and French language – or, as Lord Durham had put it, their persistence in 'retaining their peculiar language and manners' (150).

In response to the colonial domination that ensued after 1840, French Canadians turned to what they considered traditional values of the pre-Conquest period (which Memmi would call 'refuge-values'), notably the large rural family (termed 'the revenge of the cradle') and the intellectual and spiritual leadership of the Catholic Church, creating an ideology of *survivance* that maintained its hold over Quebec's culture for the following century. As if in direct response to Lord Durham's memorable condemnation of them as 'a people with no history and no literature', French Canadians after 1840 set out to prove him wrong by writing both historical and literary texts that emphasized the values of the French settlement period. Published two decades after the Durham Report, Philippe Aubert de Gaspé's revealingly titled *Les Anciens Canadiens* (1863) situated itself at the moment of the Conquest and ended with its heroine symbolically rejecting a proffered marriage with a British officer, albeit a Scottish Catholic. By the very act of writing themselves into literature and history *in French*, nineteenth-century French Canadians were effectively 'writing back to the centre' of British colonial domination. Yet they were also writing back to the former metropolitan centre of France, which had compounded the abandonment of its North American colonies by overthrowing the pre-Revolutionary values of New France. In contrast to the secular literature predominant in nineteenth-century France, the new literature of French Canada was to ground itself in the Canadian natural setting and preserve its traditional Catholic values: in the words of the influential Abbé Casgrain: 'If […] literature is the reflection of the customs, character, aptitudes and genius of a nation, if it retains the imprint of the places that gave it birth, the various aspects of nature, sites, perspectives, horizons – ours will be solemn, meditative, spiritual, religious' (1866: 25–26). For Jean-Marc Moura, it is this 'emergent' literature of nineteenth-century Quebec, in its resistance to the hegemony of metropolitan France, that seems most parallel to the twentieth-century Francophone literatures of sub-Saharan Africa and the Maghreb (2007: 159).

But this was the literature of only one of Quebec's 'colonial moments'. Another would be initiated following the Second World War, a literature whose resistance was no longer directed against London or Paris, but rather against the very ideology of *survivance* and the literature it had inspired. If Quebec protest in the political arena was directed primarily against *Anglo* domination, in the literary domain Quebec writers targeted the 'colonized' mentality that had developed as a consequence of the effort to resist assimilation – which, as Marilyn Randall has observed, 'implied submission to a subaltern role within the larger economic and political context of Canada and North America' (2003: 86). If Quebec intellectuals made frequent reference to Fanon's *Les Damnés de la terre* (1961), they seemed to have absorbed and analysed his earlier study of the pernicious effects of internalizing colonizing attitudes, *Peau noire, masques blancs* (1952), a text later foregrounded by Homi Bhabha. Such a colonized identity is at the centre of Anne Hébert's powerful short story, 'Le Torrent', written in 1945, which begins with the words: 'J'étais un enfant dépossédé du monde' [I was a child dispossessed of the world], a statement later uncannily echoed in the title of the influential 1963 book by French decolonization theorist Jacques Berque, *La Dépossession du monde*.

Resistance to the perceived suffocating effects of a rigidly enforced traditional ideology, of which Hébert's text is an early expression, is at the centre of many now-classic texts of the 1960s. Numerous novels, such as Jacques Godbout's *Salut Galarneau!* (1967), construct the typical *Québécois* as an oppressed working-class male, a man of the *peuple*: Godbout's Galarneau is a hot-dog vendor determined to express himself in an exuberant spoken *québécois*. As poets such as Césaire and Léopold Sédar Senghor had affirmed their Negritude in order to oppose racist denigration, some writers consciously adopted the often-denigrated Montreal working-class dialect of *joual*. While, for some, *joual* was a literary language invented to support a political stance, for playwright Michel Tremblay it was the language of his own Montreal childhood. When he brought it to the stage in his 1967 play, *Les Belles-Sœurs*, he shocked Quebec audiences – and transformed Quebec theatre. A work that fits readily within a postcolonial frame, *Les Belles-Sœurs* presents a Fanonian vision of colonized subjects taking out their frustration on each other. At the same time, the play makes brilliant use of an evidently 'colonized' language to give expression to what Gayatri Spivak would identify as a subaltern voice, in this case, the voice of lower-class Montreal housewives trapped in the large-family ideology of pre-1960 Quebec. Producing a similar linguistic shock by the first words spoken on screen, Claude Jutra introduced an analogous Quebec dialect in his 1970 feature film on the asbestos-mining region, *Mon Oncle Antoine*.

Beyond the Quiet Revolution

Quebec's Quiet Revolution has generally been seen as marking a sharp break between tradition and modernity. Recently, however, Quebec historians Linda Cardinal, Claude Couture and Claude Denis, applying what they call an 'approche post-coloniale', have questioned this interpretation, pointing out that this labelling may have been the effect of a dominant Anglo-American discourse that claimed the status of 'modernity' for itself. From a similar perspective, readings of the 1960s as a period of 'revolution' may, equally well, be an effect of the discourse constructed by Quebec intellectuals of the time, eager to represent a Quebec being 'liberated' from the 'colonized' mentality of the past. As political scientist Daniel Latouche has suggested (1985), the Quiet Revolution itself may be less a political phenomenon than a literary construction.

The concern with defining a new, decolonized *Québécois* identity that dominated the literary institutions of the 1960s tended to privilege texts by writers such as Jacques Godbout, Hubert Aquin and other contributors to *Liberté* and *Parti pris*. Only a few women's texts of the period were able to attain wide recognition in this context, among them Marie-Claire Blais's *Une saison dans la vie d'Emmanuel* (1965) and Anne Hébert's *Kamouraska* (1970). Yet writers like Blais, Hébert and Michel Tremblay were already opening the binary discourse of decolonization to more complex analyses of domination, in a progression that had been suggested by the work of Memmi. By seeking the voice of a nineteenth-century 'gendered subaltern' through family memory and the legal records of a murder trial, Hébert's *Kamouraska* participates in the project described by Gayatri Spivak in her much-reprinted article, 'Can the Subaltern Speak?' (1988), which has become a matrix for feminist postcolonial readings. And in the work of Blais and Tremblay, the paradigm of colonization is extended to explore the effects of domination by heterosexual norms.

The contestatory discourse of the 1960s was taken up in the political arena of the 1970s by René Lévesque's Parti Québécois, which succeeded in making French the official language of Quebec while failing to attain the announced goal of independence from Canada. Freed from the need to articulate issues now being attended to by politicians, many Quebec writers of the 1980s continued to explore more complex forms of domination in texts that can fruitfully be read in terms established by postcolonial theorists like Spivak and Bhabha. Enmeshed in a love-hate relationship with France, Quebec's writers of the 1980s also displayed a profoundly ambivalent attitude towards the United States, seen as a fascinating New World neighbour and, at the same time, a neo-imperial Anglophone oppressor. They also began to analyse the effects of domination produced by Quebec's own project of cultural self-definition, including the displacement of indigenous peoples begun in the early settlement period and exacerbated by a perceived takeover of their lands in the course of Quebec's important new hydroelectric development of the 1960s, often viewed as a national project.

Jacques Poulin's *Volkswagen Blues* (1988), an emblematic text of the 1980s that is frequently characterized as 'postcolonial', engages these multiple strands of domination, as his writer-protagonist and a mixed-blood Amerindian woman companion travel across the North American continent from Quebec to San Francisco. Beginning on the Gaspé peninsula, site of Jacques Cartier's arrival in New France, the two travellers re-read the history of French presence in the Americas from their divergent viewpoints, undermining dominant narratives at every turn in the road. Undoing stereotypes of gender and ethnicity, their couple provides a complexly doubled perspective on the history of the land they traverse, in which *Québécois* are shown to be both colonizers and colonized, by France, Canada, and a neo-imperialist United States as well as by stereotypes of race and gender. Even the dominant 'American' narrative in which writer-protagonist Jack Waterman's road-trip is framed – Jack Kerouac's *On the Road* – is revealed to be the work of a Franco-American, a beat generation leader who contested dominant American values.

As Quebec literature became less preoccupied with its 'colonized' status vis-à-vis Canada and more conscious of the converging forces in which Quebec was enmeshed, it also began a struggle to redefine Quebec's cultural identity in the wake of a recent wave of immigration by Francophones and others who, like Brazilian-born writer Sergio Kokis or Chinese-born Ying Chen, readily adopted the French language. Now accepted as a Quebec literary classic, the 1983 novel *La Québécoite* by Parisian-born Quebec resident Régine Robin was among the first to express the way in which the newly constructed identity of *Québécois* nationalism was itself experienced as a form of domination by Quebec's multi-ethnic immigrants. As Alec Hargreaves and Mark McKinney have said of immigrant writing in France, placing it within Stuart Hall's definition of the postcolonial perspective, Quebec's immigrants have also begun to produce 'a decentred diasporic or "global" rewriting of earlier, nation-centred imperial grand narratives' (1997: 5).

Particularly articulate among Quebec's immigrant communities are Haitians, who fled the political turmoil of their native island to a neighbouring country of the Americas where they could continue to use French. While some writers, such as Gérard Étienne, have sympathized with Quebec's own identitary struggle, others, for example Marie-Célie Agnant, have framed a bipolar diasporic identity oscillating between Haiti and Montreal. Still others, notably Dany Laferrière, have chosen to situate themselves in the expanded context of the Americas. As Laferrière has said:

> Qui choisir? Mon ancien colonisateur: le Français. Ou le colonisateur de mon ancien colonisateur: l'Anglais. […] Finalement, je pris une decision mitoyenne. Je choisis de devenir un écrivain américain écrivant directement en français. (Quoted in Brière, 2005: 164)

> [Which one should I choose? My former colonial master, French, or the colonial master of my former colonizer, English? [...] Finally I opted for the middle of the road. I decided to become an American writer who would write directly in French.]

It is the phenomenon of immigrant writing that some critics are most disposed to include within the postcolonial frame, in an effort to locate Quebec's specific experience in a global perspective. Detaching the 'postcolonial' label from its frequent association with the now outdated Quebec discourse of the 1960s, Amaryll Chanady welcomes a postcolonial criticism defined by Arif Dirlik as the 'globalization of cultural discourses' (2003: 33). In the same vein, Marie Vautier (2003) would divide recent Quebec fiction into two periods: the 'roman québécois contestataire' of the 1960s and 1970s and a 'roman postcolonial contemporain' which she dates as beginning in 1985, concerned with the question of cultural hybridity and related to other literatures of the New World.

Recent critics who have placed Quebec literature within postcolonial studies have done so with attention to Quebec's historical specificity, avoiding the pitfalls of assimilating Quebec to an undifferentiated Canadian 'settler colony' or setting it adrift on an alien Third World sea. Postcolonial scholarship on Quebec has focused on exploring what might be called particular 'postcolonial moments'. While Moura would view Quebec literature of the nineteenth century as entering most easily within the paradigm of 'writing back to the centre', other critics, such as Marilyn Randall, Sandra Hobbs, and myself, would emphasize the analysis of 'colonization' that is evident in the contestatory literature of the 1960s; while still others, such as Chanady, Vautier and Brière, would focus on the multilayered critiques of forms of subalternity and hybridity that characterize Quebec texts of the 1980s and beyond.

When applying postcolonial theory to Quebec, these critics are careful to define the concept of the postcolonial, often expanding its domain or emphasizing theorists such as Memmi or Glissant, who have made specific reference to Quebec. The postcolonial studies perspective, broadly defined, has been particularly welcomed by critics – many of them working in academic institutions outside of Quebec itself – who have sought to include Quebec within a broader context. Like other theorists within Quebec, most notably historian Gérard Bouchard, both Marie Vautier and Amaryll Chanady would locate Quebec in a postcolonial New World, a gesture that has been reciprocated by a growing interest in Quebec literature from Mexico, Brazil and other New World countries. Scholars located in US and British universities, and, to a limited extent, in France, have already moved to include Quebec within Francophone studies, which, as we have seen, has integrated many elements of postcolonial theory.

Already minoritized within the field of 'Canadian studies' and largely neglected by contemporary French literary theory, Quebec has more recently been sidelined by dominant models of Francophone studies in the US and Britain, a situation further complicated by the addition of the postcolonial, with its implicit Third World focus. Those who would include Quebec in the postcolonial world have been motivated in part by institutional concerns, as observers such as Schwartzwald (2003) and Desroches have pointed out, but they have also been grounded in the desire to locate Quebec's vibrant Francophone culture on larger maps from which it has too often been erased.

Further reading

Desroches, Vincent (ed.), 2003a. *Québec Studies*, 35. [Special issue: 'Quebec and Postcolonial Theory'.] Prefaced by an insightful introduction by Desroches, this issue includes important articles on Quebec's postcolonial status by scholars based in Quebec, Canada, the US and Britain. Authors include Marie Vautier, Amaryll Chanady, Rosemary Chapman, Obed Nkuzimana, Mary Jean Green, Sandra Hobbs, Robert Schwartzwald, Marvin Richards, and Katherine Roberts.

Durham, John George, Earl of Lambton, 1963 [1838]. *Lord Durham's Report: An Abridgement of Report on the Affairs of British North America*, ed. G. M. Craig (Toronto: McClelland & Stewart). Lord Durham recommended institutional reform in Canada. At the same time, however, he characterized French Canadians as an 'inferior' people – 'a people with no history and no literature' – and urged them to adopt 'our English character'.

Memmi, Albert, 1968. 'Les Canadiens-Français sont-ils des colonisés?', in *L'Homme dominé* (Paris: Gallimard), 86–95. In answer to a direct question about the colonized status of French Canadians, Memmi defined them, in 1967, as *dominés,* a people dominated by Anglophone Canadians and Americans. He did, however, see them as participating in the situation of 'colonial diglossia', in which the French language was dominated by English, as well as sharing the tendency of colonized peoples to find cultural definition in traditional 'refuge-values'.

Randall, Marilyn, 2003. 'Resistance, submission and oppositionality: national identity in French Canada', In Forsdick and Murphy (eds), *Francophone Postcolonial Studies*, 77–87. Randall chooses the Patriots Rebellion of 1837–38 as the crucial moment in Quebec's complex relationship to concepts of colonization and the postcolonial. Especially as interpreted by Quebec intellectuals of the 1960s, this nineteenth-century uprising, in Randall's reading, reveals a 'subjectivity of oppositionality' that marks the postcolonial condition.

CHAPTER 21

Diversity and Difference in Postcolonial France

Tyler Stovall

Questions of immigration, diversity and race have dominated the social, cultural and political life of France since the late twentieth century. Even before the widespread uprisings in the *banlieues* (France's deprived suburbs) in the autumn of 2005, the question of how the French might conceive of themselves as a nation that could (or could not) embrace peoples of different origins and traditions fuelled seemingly endless debates among intellectuals, politicians and people of all walks of life. The riots themselves focused attention as never before upon the fact that large numbers of French citizens not only resented police harassment and lack of job opportunities but also felt fundamentally alienated from traditional ideas of what it meant to be French. At the same time, increasing questions about France's colonial past – about the Algerian War, or the history of Caribbean slavery – have forced reappraisals of the nation's treatment of peoples of colour in its empire. For few other countries in the contemporary world has the question of postcolonialism and national identity been so agonizing.

At the heart of debates about postcolonialism in France lies the contrast many have drawn between republican universalism and multiculturalism. Frequently (and at least in part erroneously) conceptualized as French universalism versus Anglo-Saxon multiculturalism, this dichotomy posits the following opposition. On the one hand, some argue that all citizens of the Republic should be treated as individuals only, without regard to or even knowledge of community traditions or differences based upon race, religion, gender, or other factors (Finkielkraut, 1987). On the other hand, many believe that such an approach ignores the very real differences between citizens in France, and that only state policies that consciously take difference into consideration can hope to create a nation in which all citizens are truly equal (Wieviorka, 1996). As many commentators noted during the disturbances of the autumn of 2005, the riots resulted in large part from the failures of the republican model of social integration, and those who participated were at least implicitly attacking the contradiction between that model's theoretical emphasis on equality and the very real discrimination they suffered at the hands of the French state because of their race or religion.

Behind this contradiction exists another, even more fundamental one that shapes much of the history and contemporary condition of postcolonial France. The relationship between republic and empire has not only prefigured many current postcolonial conflicts but has also been a key factor in the modern history of France as a whole. As Gary Wilder has pointed out, France under the Third Republic presented the curious contradiction of an imperial republic, a state that represented both universal citizenship and colonial dominion over millions of non-European subjects (Wilder, 2005). An empire without emperor or empress, Third Republic France embodied the idea of colonialism as both oppressive and emancipatory at the same time. More generally, each of France's five republican regimes has had a specific relationship to empire, from the anti-imperialism of the French Revolution to the postcolonialism (some would say neo-colonialism) of the Fifth Republic. The difficulties colonial administrators experienced in trying (or not trying) to transform native subjects into French citizens lie at the root of today's concerns about republican models of national integration.

This chapter will consider the relationship between this paradox of republican imperialism and questions of difference in contemporary France. Not only does a direct relationship exist between the failures of French colonialism, in particular its policy of assimilation, and conflicts over immigration, religion, and race today, but both issues highlight certain fundamental inconsistencies in the republican project as a whole. As Joan Scott has demonstrated with regard to gender and feminism, the very issue of difference is both uncomfortable for and central to republican discourse in modern France (Scott, 1996). Moreover, the exclusion of the empire and its natives from the rich cultural and political ideas of French national identity that developed during the nineteenth century has made it extremely difficult to integrate their contemporary descendants into the French nation: if mosques did not belong in France in 1856 then they do not belong there in 2006 either.

At the same time, I would reject a portrait of postcolonial France as the straightforward descendant of the nation's imperial history. The sea change from colony to metropole brought about interactions with aspects of French life much less evident (or evident in different ways) in France's overseas possessions. The social explosion that rocked France's suburbs in November 2005 had as much to do with working class as with colonial legacies, and its significantly gendered nature intertwined historically metropolitan and imperial concerns. Ultimately, the French republics arose from both French and colonial histories, and one should view postcolonial France not as the melding of two distinct trajectories, but rather as an expression of the continuity of this deeply interconnected past (Peabody and Stovall, 2003).

From the anti-imperial republic to the republican empire

One cannot easily overstate the centrality of republicanism to the history of modern France. The nation has had five republican regimes since 1792, and since the late nineteenth century, this form of government has constituted the standard against which all others (notably the Vichy state of the 1940s) have been found wanting. During the nineteenth century, republicanism grew from a small and often distrusted theory to become not just politically dominant but a centrepiece of French national identity as a whole (Nord, 1995). During the same period, the relationship between republicanism and empire underwent a sea change. Whereas the first two republics, both short-lived creations of revolution, resisted but ultimately were overthrown by empire, the Third Republic managed to blend republican ideology with the creation of the second largest formal empire in world history. It is this transition, as well as the history of imperial republicanism, that underlies postcolonial conflicts over the possibilities of a multicultural France.

In order to understand how this transition could occur, one must delve a bit into the paradoxical history of empire in nineteenth-century France. The century opened with Napoleon Bonaparte's proclamation of a new French empire, which, among other things finally destroyed the First Republic. Although historians have generally paid little attention to the relationship between Napoleon's empire and the history of French colonialism (with the exception of his attempts to suppress the Saint-Domingue revolution), the Napoleonic era, nonetheless, was seminal in the development of republican imperialism. The fact that any on-line library search using the terms 'France' and 'empire' will generally yield references to Napoleon is not just linguistic slippage. One of the classic debates in French historiography concerns Napoleon Bonaparte's relationship to the French Revolution: was he ultimately its gravedigger or did he give it its global significance (Kafker and Laux, 1989)? As far as colonialism is concerned, Napoleon left a paradoxical legacy. Not only did he bring the First Republic to an end but also his heir, Napoleon III, did the same for the Second Republic. In contrast to this opposition between Bonapartism and Republicanism, however, one can also point to the Napoleonic emphasis on spreading the ideals of the French Revolution abroad, by force if necessary. Napoleon's creation of the civilizing mission became a central aspect of French colonialism in the modern era, distinguishing it from the ancien régime's empire.

The Third Republic created its own imperial mission by blending republican ideology with Bonapartist expansionism. The creation of a new colonial empire began well before 1870, starting with the annexation of Algeria in 1830, followed by substantial expansion in sub-Saharan Africa and the Pacific. But the republican governments of the late nineteenth century created the greatest empire that France had ever known. Humanitarianism and uplifting the natives from barbarism to civilization constituted key justifications for imperial expansion.

As Jules Ferry, the liberal prime minister whose passion for empire earned him the sobriquet *le Tonkinois*, put it:

> Can you deny, can anyone deny that there is more justice, more material and moral order, more equity, more social virtue in North Africa since France carried out its conquest? Is it possible to deny that it is the good fortune of the miserable population of equatorial Africa to come under the protection of the French nation or the English nation? (Cited in Aldrich, 1996: 98–99)

Republican imperialism represented a kind of secular missionary project, bent upon saving the natives from themselves.

Such good intentions aside, the contradiction of a republican regime based upon citizenship ruling millions of imperial subjects had to be addressed, and the most systematic attempt to do so was the ideology of assimilation. This policy, based upon the assumption of native inferiority, aimed at gradually giving the colonized all the rights of French citizens after a process of education and uplift. It held, in effect, that Africans and Asians could become French by learning the French language and embracing French culture. The requirement of accepting French law meant, for example, that Muslims effectively had to renounce Islam in order to qualify. Very few colonial subjects ever became citizens under this policy, due both to its demands for cultural alienation and to the failure of colonial administrations to provide more than token educational resources. A successor policy, association, which emphasized the differences between French and native cultures, also became popular. Both policies projected a sense of French cultural and racial superiority, the idea that to be free meant to be French (Betts, 1961).

This linking of political and national culture also operated within the metropole itself under the Third Republic. The second half of the nineteenth century witnessed the imposition of an increasingly standardized French national culture throughout the country. The development of efficient national transportation and communications networks, the increased hegemony of standard French over local dialects and, in particular, the rise of mandatory primary education created a national culture that became the basis of modern French identity. At the end of his celebrated study *Peasants into Frenchmen*, the historian Eugen Weber compared this process of national integration to the cultural imperialism of overseas France, arguing for the difference between the two processes (1976: 485–96). However, it is worth mentioning that these two phenomena occurred not only at roughly the same time but also in relation to each other, so that a central part of the cultural construction of the modern French nation was the emphasis on the difference between France and its colonies. Conscripts who served in colonial regiments learned to treat the natives as Other, for example, and republican schools viewed colonial conquest as the victory of the French over foreign peoples. During the twentieth century, the suppressed local cultures within the metropole often reappeared as cultural and political regionalist movements in areas like Brittany, Provence and Corsica, and struggles for greater regional autonomy, even independence, at times paralleled colonial movements for self-determination (Chartier and Larvor, 2004).

The idea of popular republicanism as central to French national identity thus developed concurrently with the unprecedented expansion of overseas France. The complex relationship between Bonapartism and republicanism proved fertile ground for the creation of a nation, which claimed a mission of maintaining millions of people as subjects in order to make them free and French, and the development of a national political culture by the end of the nineteenth century underscored the link between freedom and French identity. As the empire became more of a factor in the life of the metropole during the twentieth century, these conflicts would become central to the creation of a new, postcolonial France.

Postcolonial prelude: the First World War

Although scholars generally consider the postcolonial era in Europe as something that happened after 1945 and the mid-twentieth century wave of decolonization, the First World War provides our first significant glimpse of the future new relationship between Europe and its empires. In part, this was simply a matter of massive population movements. During the years between 1914 and 1918, the French state imported several hundred thousand natives from its colonies to metropolitan France to serve as soldiers in its armed forces and as labourers in its factories and farms. For the first time in the modern era, one could meet large numbers of non-whites from Asia and Africa in cities and towns throughout France, giving the empire a direct physical presence in the metropole it had never before enjoyed. More generally, during the First World War the French came face to face with the importance of the empire to their national existence. The idea of the 'nation of 100 million Frenchmen' was born during the war, as a response to the numerical superiority of Germany over metropolitan France. This assertion of imperial unity was certainly disingenuous, yet it also illustrated the fact that for many French policymakers France could only achieve and retain its world power status as an imperial nation-state. Finally, the integration of colonial troops and labourers into a war fought ostensibly for freedom and democracy and against barbarism highlighted the contradiction between the nation's imperial mission and its resistance to the Central Powers. The fact that the war ultimately destroyed every empire within Europe, yet reaffirmed the overseas colonial possessions of victorious powers such as France, in effect made the French notion of republican imperialism a European, even a global, phenomenon.

In wartime France itself the treatment of its colonial subjects illustrated how the nation sought to keep them within a strictly colonial context, and how this context kept breaking down, subverted by interactions with life in the metropole that would become central to postcolonial life in France generations later. The French government generally kept colonial troops in separate regiments and tried to isolate them from the civilian population. It followed the same tactic with colonial workers, isolating them in segregated labour battalions from other workers in war plants and other settings. Public authorities feared bringing an unprecedented level of racial diversity to the metropole; they also worried about the lessons these people from Africa and Asia would learn in France and bring back home. Yet in spite of these attempts to limit contacts with the metropole, these imperial subjects did develop relationships with French civilians and gained a different view of France from that available in the colonies. In particular, the authorities worried incessantly about sexual relations between colonial men and French women. Not only did they harshly penalize those colonial subjects engaged in such relationships but they also tried to prevent them from sending pornographic postcards to friends and relatives back home, which would, they believed, undermine the natives' respect for white womanhood. Once the war ended, the French authorities quickly repatriated soldiers and labourers alike, judging that France was not ready for such an experiment in multiracial society (Stovall, 1998).

However, one can never put the genie back into the bottle. France's brief flirtation with postcolonialism during the First World War made it clear that the colonies constituted an integral part of the nation, and that one could not indefinitely maintain hard and fast boundaries between republican liberty and colonial servitude under the same flag. This insight was not lost on the colonial veterans of the First World War, many of whom went home to demand greater political representation and even independence (Mann, 2006). As with French women, colonial subjects would have to wait for another world war to achieve real progress on their desires for citizenship. But the impact and disappointments of the First World War ensured that this question would remain a live one both in France and its empire.

The blurring of boundaries between European and overseas France during the war also reshaped post-war metropolitan culture and society. The famous vogue for exoticism that so marked French culture during the 1920s attempted to restore the division between France and its colonies by casting the latter as the racialized Other, and at the same time underscored the importance of the nation's overseas possessions to metropolitan society and culture. The most prominent example of this, the *Exposition Coloniale* of 1931, graphically illustrated the power and diversity of the 'nation of 100 million Frenchmen', and emphasized the European supremacy that lay at its heart. The increased prominence of racial thinking in interwar France also illustrated a new consciousness of empire, suggesting one way of conceptualizing the relationship between republic and colonies. In a very different vein, avant-garde artistic and literary movements such as surrealism and Negritude placed questions of race and colonialism at the centre of a new vision of French culture. Like it or not, the mobilization of imperial resources and peoples during the First World War not only revealed the multiracial aspects of French national identity but also indicated the difficulties France faced in coming to terms with this view of itself (Ezra, 2000; Wilder, 2005).

The empire comes home

The period from the end of the Second World War to the mid-1970s, often called *les trente glorieuses* in acknowledgment of the economic dynamism of the era, laid the bases for the postcolonial France of the late twentieth and early twenty-first century. Two broad social and political processes fundamentally reshaped the nature of republican empire into a new French reality. One was decolonization, the traumatic transition away from formal empire that shook overseas France from the late 1940s until the early 1960s. The granting of political independence to most French colonies did not completely end France's imperial hegemony overseas, but it did create new relationships between centre and periphery, and more concretely defined France as a European nation, without significant colonial appendages.

The other major process, immigration, in many ways ran counter to the first. If decolonization reaffirmed national boundaries, both of France and its former colonies, immigration called them into question. Whereas decolonization constituted a move away from the nation's colonial past, immigration redeployed it in a new, postcolonial framework. Like colonialism, immigration is a subject that many French have found extremely difficult to reconcile with traditional republican conceptions of national identity. As Gérard Noiriel has made clear, even though in the modern era France has been one of the world's chief recipients of immigrants, their contribution to French history has rarely been acknowledged, because republican ideology has generally refused to recognize the different national and cultural origins of its citizens (Noiriel, 1998).

The millions of immigrants who settled in post-war France came from a variety of places, both European and non-European. They fundamentally transformed the nation; France's unprecedented material prosperity after 1945 would have been unimaginable without them. During the 1950s and 1960s the majority of immigrants came from elsewhere in Europe: the Portuguese constituted the largest single foreign nationality in France well into the 1970s. Gradually, however, those coming from former colonies, especially those of North Africa, increased in number, so that 'immigrant' more and more meant non-European, non-white. By the late 1970s the processes of decolonization and immigration had converged, transforming the former colonial native into the new postcolonial immigrant. As a result, the contradiction that lay at the heart of republican empire, the idea that all men deserved freedom as long as they accepted civilization, metamorphosed into the effective marginalization of those whose racial and religious traits did not conform to traditional expectations of what it meant to be French.

At the same time, the post-war era brought about major changes in the nature of republican ideology in France. The successful struggle against Vichy and the reactionary forces it represented made republicanism more dominant in French political culture than ever before. Both the near-annihilation of the antirepublican right and the integration of the Communist party into the national political consensus made republicanism more than ever a key ingredient of French national identity. Moreover, the pernicious legacy of Vichy's racism reaffirmed for many the necessity of universalism: if the state could distinguish between citizens on the basis of religion, race or other differences, it could also persecute them for those differences. Thus, post-war republicanism both symbolized and championed the unity of all French peoples.

This took place, of course, in the context of a basic redefinition of the relationship between republic and empire. While republicanism was more popular than ever in the metropole, its obstinate resistance to demands for independence in its colonies revealed the failure of republican imperialism as never before. Not only did this create an exceptionally violent process of decolonization in Indo-China and Algeria but it also gave empire an unprecedented importance in metropolitan affairs. The French empire never had a greater presence in French life than when it was about to disappear. The Fourth Republic became the only regime in modern French history to collapse as a result of a colonial conflict, and the semi-authoritarian creation of the Fifth Republic by Charles de Gaulle demonstrated the essential inability of republican politics to resolve the contradictions of republican empire. By granting either independence (and, thus, formal separation from France) to its colonies, or departmental status to the *vieilles colonies* of the Caribbean and the Indian Ocean, France made it clear that if it was to survive, the republic had to get out of the empire business altogether (Ageron, 1991).

And yet, ultimately, France could not simply leave its colonial past behind. The increasingly postcolonial nature of immigration after the 1960s made that impossible. More generally, the retreat from formal empire represented not only the triumph of national independence movements but also the failure of French republicanism to create a truly egalitarian and multicultural vision of Greater France. Some, including some scholars, have considered the trauma of decolonization in general, and the Algerian war in particular, to be a key reason for France's difficulties in accepting postcolonial immigrants, especially from North Africa (Weil, 1995). I would argue that the relationship between these two phenomena is not so much causal as propinquitous; both arose from the same failure of republican discourse. The same failure lies at the heart of the difficulties of postcolonial society in France, and stoked the fires that raged through the suburbs of France in the autumn of 2005.

Towards a new France?

The advent of the Fifth Republic, born of the trauma of decolonization, marked not only a new phase in the history of French colonialism but also of republicanism in general. Far more than earlier republics, it centred on a strong executive, a president elected for a renewable seven-year term. Charles de Gaulle and François Mitterrand in particular came to symbolize a kind of elected monarchy or imperial presidency, presiding over a regime in which democratic parliamentarianism marched hand in hand with powerful leadership. This represented a new twist on the old nineteenth-century paradox of Bonapartist republicanism, a transformation of the Napoleonic model that re-emphasized a combination of liberalism and authority. The fact that such a regime arose in response to imperial crisis and collapse constituted an example of how colonial legacies could shape postcolonial republican politics in France.

As Jacques Marseille and Kristin Ross have both noted, French society after the Second World War was transformed by a combination of decolonization and modernization (Marseille, 2005 [1984]; Ross, 1995). One must also note that modernity in France often displayed traits inherited from empire. The most notable example of this was the rise of massive new suburban belts around Paris and other French cities during the post-war era. Ever since the mid-nineteenth century, French suburbs have symbolized not semi-pastoral luxury, but rather poverty and exclusion from the benefits of urban civilization. During much of the modern era they have constituted working-class ghettos, areas to which society consigned those with the least skills or resources (Bastié, 1964). After 1945 they became strongholds of the PCF, whose political marginality perfectly expressed their inhabitants' social exclusion. The rise of prosperity and consumerism in the post-war era led not to greater integration of French workers into mainstream society, which would have called into question the division of urban France into cities and suburbs. Instead, the new affluence reinforced the character of the suburbs as a world apart, resulting in the building of huge new public housing estates that combined an increased level of material comfort with physical ugliness and a lack of urban sociability. By the 1980s, the towers of Sarcelles and other *HLMs* had lost whatever appeal they possessed when new, reviving instead the traditional image of the suburbs as the place beyond the walls of civilization (Brunet, 1995).

By the 1980s, the new public housing estates also came to symbolize postcolonial immigration. An important parallel has long existed between France's suburbs and France's colonies: both represent places where the French flag flies outside the limits of French culture, or, at their most threatening, the barbarians lurking outside the gates. As Eugen Weber noted in relation to the French peasantry, nineteenth-century urban observers often used colonial imagery to describe French suburbia (Stovall, 2003). By the late twentieth century, however, the image of the suburbs as internal colonies achieved a new level of significance with the rise of a large new non-white population there. Many of the post-war public housing estates had been built for populations displaced by decolonization in general and the Algerian War in particular. In 1974 France largely terminated legal foreign immigration into its territory, a reaction to the end of post-war prosperity and to the increasingly postcolonial character of the immigrants. At the same time, however, it allowed a select number of immigrants to bring their families to live with them in France, in part to guard against the social danger posed to French society by single foreign men. The result was the creation of a new category of non-French family in France. Many of these families came from former colonies and many abandoned urban slum areas where male immigrants had traditionally lived, moving to the *HLMs* of the suburbs instead.

By the 1980s, in consequence, the suburbs of Paris and other French cities had, in effect, replicated colonial society on the soil of metropolitan France. Young people of non-European descent born in France, the so-called 'second-generation immigrants', came to symbolize this new face of suburban marginality. The very phrase 'second-generation immigrant', an oxymoronic term if there ever was one, illustrated the limits of republican universalism when confronted with differences based on race and religion. The widespread rioting between adolescent suburban males and French police graphically demonstrated the depths of alienation among France's new postcolonial population. If young men posed a problem for public order, young women challenged public education and republican culture. The nationwide furore that erupted in 1989 after a state school in Creil expelled four Muslim girls for wearing the veil in class pitted the tradition of republican secularism against ideas of multiculturalism and of militant Islam. All this took place against the backdrop of economic stagnation and endemic unemployment, especially for minority youth, the insurgent political racism of the National Front and, in general, a renewed challenge to the welfare state. The crumbling housing projects in the suburbs thus exemplified the decay of *l'état providence*, the idea that the republic served as the best guarantor of French freedom and prosperity. Just as the imperial republic had failed to implement its ideal of assimilating the natives, so did the postcolonial republic (in particular, republican institutions such as the schools and the police) seem to abandon the natives' descendants on metropolitan soil (Kepel, 1991; Jazouli, 1992).

The rise of a substantial non-white population in France and the difficulty of integrating it into mainstream French life provoked a series of debates about race and the role of racial difference in the national experience. Before the late twentieth century, race was something that, for the most part, the French had relegated to their colonies, so that even though imperial France combined a metropole of mostly white citizens with overseas territories of mostly non-white subjects, racial difference seemed to play no role in national life. In contrast, postcolonialism in France meant, above all, the erasure of this geographical separation, bringing African, Asian and Caribbean populations to live in the metropole itself. In coming to terms with the new visibility of racial difference on French soil, many reasserted the value of republican universalism, arguing that to recognize publicly distinctions between citizens was to risk adopting state racism or fragmenting France among many different ethnic communities (Finkielkraut, 1987). Others, notably Michel Wieviorka, Harlem Désir, Julia Kristeva and Tzvetan Todorov, criticized the failure of abstract universalism to recognize, let alone provide any solution for, racial discrimination and inequality in French society (Todorov, 1993 [1989]; Wieviorka, 1996). Yet those who make such arguments have up to the present been a minority in France, and the nation as a whole has generally stuck to a colour-blind approach in terms of race. Even attempts to address racial inequality, such as the affirmative action programme launched at the Fondation nationale des sciences politiques, have often tried to cope with the problem without explicitly recognizing race as a factor (Sabbagh, 2004). In general, the positing of an opposition between republican ideology and multiculturalism implies that the very idea of the postcolonial republic, like that of the imperial republic before it, is fundamentally contradictory and unstable.

The failure of republican discourse to cope with the legacies of colonial France left a vacuum that was in part filled by the riots of the autumn of 2005. If the republican school, for example, could not adequately treat and reflect France's imperial and racial past (and present), then it would and did become a target for the inarticulate rage of those whose history it denied. The suburban uprisings represented not only a reaction to the inability of republican France to integrate peoples of diverse backgrounds and cultures but also a new kind of working-class insurgency, one that showcased the wide cleavages between rich and poor in contemporary French society. The ubiquitous burnings of cars represented not only an attack on a consumer product most suburban youth could not afford but also an assault against a symbol of mobility (both spatial and social) denied them. The very racialization of the concept of immigration in France points to another mode of social conflict and politics, one that blends class and race into a new synthesis of societal marginalization. Similarly, the emphasis on young suburban men as a danger to society replicated both colonial fears of insurgent masculinity and republican traditions that tended to relegate women to the political sidelines. The portrayal of the movement as a kind of fundamentalist Islamic revolt against the secular republic, even as a new front in the West's war against 'terror' (itself a kind of neo-imperialist crusade), recalled colonial legacies that barred practising Muslims from becoming French citizens. The suburban disturbances of the autumn of 2005 thus both showed the extent to which non-white youth had become integrated into French traditions of political protest and class insurgency, and at the same time underscored the inability of republican universalism to recognize such integration and to accept the idea that the republic must itself change in order to create a place for the descendants of empire in France.

In conclusion, the history of interaction between republic and empire in modern France has created a situation that opposes republican tradition and racial multiculturalism, one that replicates colonial conflicts on metropolitan soil and at the same time blends them with other social fissures to create the kind of potent mixture that exploded in the suburban uprisings of 2005. In order to find its way out of this impasse, France will have to rethink its conception of the republic. Let no one read this chapter as an obituary for French republicanism: it is a broad and malleable political culture, one that has changed over time and will continue to do so. Certain encouraging trends, like the public engagement with the legacies of colonialism and slavery over the last ten years, point the way forward (Hargreaves, 2005). Ultimately, those who believe in the genius of French republicanism will have to renounce the imperial dimensions of this ideology, accepting the fact that republicanism is not something one simply gives to others, but also a political culture that grows by accepting ideas from outsiders. This alternative view of social integration, as a two-way street rather than the imposition of 'French' values, will and must be the basis of a truly postcolonial France.

Further reading

Hargreaves, Alec G., 1995. *Immigration, 'race' and ethnicity in contemporary France* (New York and London: Routledge). [An updated and expanded version of this text was published as *Multi-Ethnic France: Immigration, Politics, Culture and Society* in 2007.] Hargreaves' study is a foundational text in postcolonial analysis of contemporary France. Hargreaves focuses upon non-white immigrants, especially the young people who became labelled 'second-generation immigrants'. He explores this phrase and the argument behind it, namely that postcolonial immigrants ultimately cannot assimilate into French life and culture. Hargreaves rejects this argument, and instead makes the case that the major difference between the experience of contemporary postcolonial immigrants and earlier migrants from within Europe lies primarily in the stagnant French economy of the late twentieth century and its impact upon youth in particular. He makes this argument while considering issues ranging from Islam, gender and language to republican traditions and state policies.

Silverman, Maxim, 1992. *Deconstructing the Nation: Immigration, Racism and Citizenship in Modern France* (New York and London: Routledge). Silverman's *Deconstructing the Nation* was, like the text by Hargreaves cited above, one of the first major texts to analyse critically the relationship between immigration, racism and republican tradition in modern France. He considers the ways in which immigration has shaped modern France, and how it became racialized at the end of the twentieth century. He also describes in detail the conflict between defenders of republican universalism and of multiculturalism, especially concerning the wearing of the Islamic veil in public schools. In general, Silverman argues against viewing these two models as polar opposites, suggesting instead that one should see them as tensions within all Western nations.

Wilder, Gary, 2005. *The French Imperial Nation-State: Negritude and Colonial Humanism between the Two World Wars* (Chicago: University of Chicago Press). *The French Imperial Nation-State* is a leading example of the turn towards colonialism by the younger generation of historians of France. In this text Wilder creates the concept of republican imperialism, underscoring the contradictory nature of such an historical phenomenon and at the same time emphasizing that the contradiction existed in both the metropole and the empire. In creating this concept, Wilder argues for the fundamental unity of France and its colonies, perceiving them as one internally variegated unit. He concentrates specifically on two cultural and discursive movements in interwar France: Negritude in Paris, and colonial humanism in French West Africa. His focus on colonial subjects in the metropole and French administrators in the colonies gives his work an imperial scope, and he demonstrates how both movements illustrated the crisis of the French imperial nation-state.

CHAPTER 22

Colonialism, Postcolonialism and the Cultures of Commemoration

Charles Forsdick

The Bicentenary of the French Revolution in 1989 heralded the series of com-memorations by which late twentieth-century France now appears to have been increasingly characterized. In the 1990s, literature, cinema and intellectual debate all began to reflect an increasing focus on memory, a tendency also apparent in popular culture and public life. The historian Pierre Nora, inaugurating in 1984 *Les Lieux de mémoire*, a monumental collection of essays on key 'sites' of the French historical experience understood as having had an impact on national self-identity, presented the lack of shared post-war national memory as a rationale for alternative manifestations of the past. By the time his seventh and final volume appeared in 1992, Nora would comment with surprise on how this situation had changed radically, as France entered a comprehensive 'ère de la commémoration' [era of commemoration] (Nora, 1997, III: 4687–719) in which considerations of history were eclipsed by a near-obsession with memory (Revel, 2000).

In reflecting such an engagement with the past, the celebrations of 1989 provided an opportunity for national introspection at a time when France was facing a series of new challenges: a progressively expanding Europe; the erosion of the country's influence as a world power, and the associated steady decline of French as a global language; the increasing acknowledgement within France itself of a range of minority groups, who were seen to challenge the universalist assumptions of a supposedly all-inclusive French republican ideology. In such a context of doubt and instability, it was unsurprising that the then president, François Mitterrand, exploited the symbolic potential of these commemorative events in a series of rituals reflecting the 'unity of the nation' (Northcutt, 1991: 153), which had itself been one of the central themes in his second successful presidential campaign the previous year. Although there was some debate among historians concerning what and who should constitute the focus of the bicentennial celebrations (Kaplan, 1995), there was wide consensus across the political spectrum regarding the importance to these events of the 'universal' revolutionary slogan: 'Liberty, Equality, Fraternity'. Subsequent analyses of 1989 have centred on questions of this purported universalism, exploring the ways in which the Bicentenary may instead be read as a staging of late twentieth-century 'Frenchness', i.e., as an illustration of the continued domestication of the core values of the French Revolution, and of their deployment for restrict-edly national strategic purposes within a Francocentric frame of reference (Northcutt, 1991: 157).

One of the cultural high points of the year, Jean-Paul Goude's 'opera-ballet' or 'Marseillaise procession' on Bastille Day 1989, aimed to stage-manage what was projected as the forward-looking multiculturalism of contemporary France. The coincidence of this event with that year's G7 summit, hosted by France, provided precisely this type of performance of national identity – this 'spectacle of French power' (Leruth, 1998: 57) – with the international dimension and wide media attention on which its more general success would depend. Based on the theme of the 'Rights of Man', and performed to a range of world music, the procession culminated symbolically in a rendition of the French national anthem by the US-born opera singer, Jessye Norman. The aim was to recon-cile a persistent French exceptionalism with the realities of a late twentieth-century globalized world, accordingly attempting to stage the extremes of universalism and diversity, modernity and memory. The flamboyant and provocative procession became a neo-exoticist spectacle, reminiscent in places of the French tradition of the colonial exhibition (1998: 71–72). It presented a 'palatable pluralism' (1998: 63), which, it could be argued, failed to pose searching questions about the durability and appropriateness of revolutionary and republican values in a France whose 'postcolonial' status was becoming increasingly apparent. Goude's meticulously choreographed event ultimately sidestepped the challenges and tensions inherent in what Laurent Dubois has dubbed the 'république métissée' [hybridized republic] that France had by then become: in Dubois's terms, the procession 'placed the "multiculturalism" of France's own history on display in a way that did not confront the broader structural contradictions of a system that has long celebrated its universalism and tolerance while maintaining structures of racial and economic exclusion' (2000: 20).

Remembering slavery

Dubois's discussion of the 1989 celebrations appears in an article exploring the continuing ideological impact of the Haitian Revolution on discussions of race and ethnicity in contemporary France. His central argument is that a 'better understanding of French colonial history is a vital foundation for an engage-ment with contemporary debates about race, immigration and national identity in France' (2000: 18). Thus, he builds on the work of several critics already vocal in 1989, whose discordant analyses of the then unfolding events saw in the

Bicentenary celebrations evidence of the hijacking, on the one hand, of the past mentioned above and, on the other, of the instrumentalization – conscious or otherwise – of the legacies of the Revolution for the ideological purposes of the present. Jean Rouch, the veteran ethnographic filmmaker, was commissioned by the Bicentenary's organizing committee to make a documentary reflecting the year. The opening scenes of the resultant film, *Liberté, égalité, fraternité, et puis après...* (1990), focuses not on the more prominent Parisian events of 1989, such as Goude's procession, but on the planting of a Tree of Liberty at Courtomer, one of the 'myriad of micro-events' (Gerson, 2003: 545) by which the Bicentenary was marked locally. Rouch's film provocatively presents two black African actors, Brice Ahounou and Tam Sir Doueb, dispatched in costume to mingle with the official pageant and to interact with other actors portraying figures from French history. The result is a progressive decentring of the French Revolution, and a parallel privileging of phenomena traditionally 'silenced' (Trouillot, 1995) by French revolutionary historiography, both the Haitian Revolution, and one of its key actors, Toussaint Louverture.

Although in the closing sections of the film the action returns to Paris, this manoeuvre permits a further disruption of the Bicentenary's celebratory rhetoric: the Abbé Grégoire is released from the crypt of the Panthéon, to where the concluding rituals of 1989 had confined him, and Toussaint is reconciled, in a *vodou* ceremony performed in front of Les Invalides, with Napoléon (responsible for the latter's death in the fort at Joux in 1803). The dual strands of Rouch's conclusion not only explore the potential implications of a radical thinker, such as the abolitionist Grégoire, for contemporary discussions of ethnicity and French identity (implications that his Pantheonization is seen to tame), but also gesture towards a reintegration of Toussaint – as well as of what Nesbitt (2005) has dubbed the 'idea of 1804' that the Haitian revolutionary himself embodies – into the French republican narrative, universalizing this narrative in ways unimaginable if memories of France's colonial empire are persistently excluded (see Chapters 21 and 24 for further discussion of these ideas).

Rouch's film suggests that remembering the French Revolution as an exclusively national event risks restricting its more comprehensive, and in many ways more complex, interpretation as part of a wider international, transatlantic movement. By foregrounding questions of slavery and its resistance, it shows how one of the most important poles in this movement – located in the French colony of Saint-Domingue, but evident throughout the wider French Caribbean – serves to illuminate the blind spots of memories of the revolutionary events in France itself. The implication is that factoring Haiti out of discussions of French national history only permits a partial narrative of republicanism to emerge, thereby ignoring the ways in which the universal pretensions of the French Revolution were compromised from the outset by the reluctant and principally pragmatic decision to abolish slavery in 1794, by the reimposition of slavery in 1802, and by the continued failure to interpret the 'rights of man' in the ethnically inclusive sense that figures such as Toussaint understood them. Historian Marcel Dorigny (2005) presents the French 'loss' of Haiti in 1804 as a traumatic event, and as one of the foundations of the 'colonial fracture' that has shaped culture and society in contemporary France; and French neocolonial involvement in the February 2004 ousting of the democratically elected Haitian president, Jean-Bertrand Aristide, may be seen as further evidence of this legacy (Hallward, 2008). The refusal, in the light of such an interpretation, to present the Haitian Revolution as an exotic parody of its French counterpart – as well as the acknowledgement that, at various points of the 1790s, the hub of French revolutionary activity was not Paris but Saint-Domingue – permits the reading of the 1989 Bicentenary in a wider context of colonial memory, extending this commemoration beyond the national frame to which its is often reduced. Such an extension of memorial implications can be applied to other late twentieth-century anniversaries celebrated in France: the European dimensions of the 50th anniversary of VE day (8 May 1945), for instance, tended to eclipse the other events that occurred on the same date, most notably the massacres by French troops of pro-independence demonstrators in several cities in eastern Algeria, particularly Sétif and Guelma (Planche, 2006).

Such tensions between the national and the international, between competing narratives of the past, became particularly apparent in 1998, during the 150th anniversary of the (second) abolition of slavery in the French colonial empire (on memories of slavery, see Vergès, 2006). Édouard Glissant stated a fear that this sesquicentenary would become an 'affaire franco-française' [exclusively French matter] (Catinchi, 1998), encapsulating the clash of divergent memories that the remembrance of slavery invariably implies: the French remember abolition, whereas the descendants of enslaved people tend to remember enslavement itself (and the constant resistance to/against slavery). In the light of the eulogies of the abolitionists and of the self-congratulatory accounts of republican philanthropy, these fears were, on that occasion, well grounded. The reappearance in 1998 of what C. L. R. James had described in *The Black Jacobins* as 'prose-poetry and flowers' (1980 [1938]: 63), i.e., the commemorative phenomena that disguise in retrospect the confusion of historical process, ignores the fact that abolition was extracted from a largely reluctant French parliament. Morever, abolition was primarily a question of the humanization, as opposed to the absolute liberation, of enslaved people, a process that was gradualist as opposed to immediatist (Jennings, 2000), and – particularly in the case of the French Caribbean – only conceivable to many within the frame of a continued colonial domination culminating in the departmentalization process of 1946.

The French privilege largely celebratory memories of the second abolition of slavery (1848), to the detriment of any recognition of the almost entirely ignored first abolition (1794). Such amnesia tends conveniently to obscure the fact that, despite a long tradition of French philosophical debates regarding (a reimposed) slavery, France accepted the inevitability of abolition later than Britain and Holland. Such debates concerning historiographic emphases are, of course, replicated in a range of postcolonial arenas, where competing versions of the colonial past lead to often radically divergent interpretations, emphases and memorial practices. The practical and general implications of symbolic dates become apparent in the choice of 10 May for the French national commemoration of slavery. The now officially sanctioned date overrides historically symbolic alternatives, such as 23 August (the beginning of the Haitian Revolution, and UNESCO's Slavery Remembrance Day); instead, alluding to recent legislative activity (namely, the passing of the 2001 'loi Taubira', designating transatlantic slavery a crime against humanity), this choice risks a further evacuation of the past, becoming the site of a self-referential commemoration of a commemoration.

Rethinking colonial memories

It is to such complexities of recollection and memorialization, problematizing legacies of empire and its various manifestations, that this chapter responds. It focuses in particular on the competing, often contradictory, traditions (personal, group and collective; intra-cultural, inter-cultural and trans-cultural) that characterize postcolonial memory. The field of reference is complex and deliberately wide: differing modulations and manifestations of memory reveal not only the often uneasy relationships existing between France and its former colonies but also the residual, unresolved conflicts concerning empire that persist among the 'French' themselves, fissuring any pretensions to singularity that such a marker of national identity may be seen to imply. After a prolonged period of apparent colonial amnesia (following, it is often argued, the end of the Algerian War of Independence), the current prominence of memory debates in France means that this context is very much a 'live' one, triggering a series of questions that relate to the workings of memory in a wider Francophone space.

This chapter thus serves several functions: it endeavours to map the debates among those who have, in recent years, begun to explore the rich resources relating to colonial memory in France and elsewhere, in concrete archives, or in the often more ephemeral traces of recollections by individuals and groups. At the same time, it speculates on the possible contribution of postcolonial thought to understandings of memory. This body of thought is characterized by what may be seen as two essential, guiding principles: the benefits of elaborating a common field of reflection, without imposing any artificial commonality; the need to acknowledge the rootedness of apparently divergent memories in shared historical experiences, without blunting the stark differences and asymmetries that these experiences imply. Three distinct (even divergent) examples, drawn from a much wider range of possible examples, crystalize the various intersecting questions central to this chapter.

October 2001: In the aftermath of the Maurice Papon trial (and of Papon's unsuccessful counter-suit, against the historian Jean-Luc Einaudi, for the use of the term 'massacre' to describe the then Prefect of Police's brutal suppression of the FLN demonstration of 17 October 1961), Bertrand Delanoë, Mayor of Paris, inaugurated a municipal – and, significantly, not national – memorial to the victims of these events. Speaking at the unveiling of the plaque on the Pont

Saint-Michel, Delanoë called for integration and reconciliation through acts of commemoration:

> Cette plaque [...] est dédiée aux victimes de ce moment douleureux et à leurs descendants. Je veux que leurs descendants sachent qu'ils sont membres de la communauté des Parisiens et que leur histoire est notre histoire. (cited in Jelen, 2002: 32)

> [This plaque is dedicated to the victims of that painful moment and to their descendants. I want their descendants to know that they are members of the Parisian community and that their history is our history].

The loaded tensions between possessive adjectives – '*leur* histoire est *notre* histoire' – reflect not only dislocated memorial practices but also a will to forge a shared relationship to the past in which divergent experiences coexist, permitting a shift from memorializing the past to engaging with the present. The immediate context of Delanoë's speech had been indicated shortly before, on 6 October. The first international football match between France and Algeria since 1962, styled the 'match de la réconciliation' [reconciliation match], had been marked by the disruption of *La Marseillaise* and an eventual pitch invasion. The Algerian ambassador to France, Mohamed Ghoualmi, cited the encounter's historical resonances, and identified (perhaps in an overly simplistic fashion) those who forced an early end to the match as the descendants of the victims of 17 October 1961, to whom Delanoë would himself allude. This debate begs the question of where, for certain members of the French population, there are spaces available – shared or otherwise – in which to carry out their own *travail de mémoire*.

March 2003: The French *ministre délégué aux anciens combattants*, Hamlaoui Mekachera, visited Hanoi to propose to the Vietnamese government a joint commemoration of Dien Bien Phu the following year, planning accordingly to 'construire un hommage *ensemble*, qui serait un témoin à transmettre aux nouvelles générations' [build *together* a tribute, which would be a warning to pass on to subsequent generations] (cited in Cooper, 2004: 453). Hanoi seemed uninspired by this vision of a shared memory, and the two governments planned their own separate commemorations, which eventually produced contrasting visions of, on the one hand, 'le Verdun des colonies' [the colonial Verdun] and, on the other, a glorious 'victoire nationale' [national victory]: neither participated in the other's ceremonies. Largely eclipsed by celebrations of the 60th anniversary of the Normandy landings (whose 50th anniversary had equally detracted from the already minor attention given to the bicentenary of the first abolition of slavery a decade previously) official French remembrance of Dien Bien Phu was subdued. In Vietnam, however, 2004 was celebrated as an 'année touristique de Dien Bien Phu', with events including a cycling tournament that commemorates the role played by *coolies-vélos* in the winning of the battle (see Cooper, 2004; Logan, 2006).

December 2005: As public and professional pressure mounted in opposition to the now infamous fourth clause of the *loi du 23 février 2005* (on this legislation, see Bertrand, 2006), Nicolas Sarkozy prepared to leave mainland France for a visit to Martinique. Édouard Glissant and Patrick Chamoiseau wrote an open letter to the then Minister of the Interior, underlining the indelicacy, in the current circumstances, of his planned trip to their 'terre d'esclavage, de colonisation, et de néo-colonisation' [land of slavery, colonization and neo-colonization].[1] Martinique, they claimed, has taught them the benefits of 'l'échange et le partage' [exchange and sharing]; it had fostered an understanding of 'les sociétés multi-trans-culturelles' [multi-trans-cultural societies], rooted in a desire to 'partager les vérités de tout passé commun' [share the truths of every common past]. Shortly afterwards, Sarkozy cancelled his journey. The following day Chamoiseau called in *Libération* for 'une solidarité des mémoires' [a solidarity of memories] (Thibaudat, 2005), adding that memory exists in common and potentially provides a means of rethinking the coexistence of France and its overseas territories.

What these three examples illustrate is the complex process of reflecting on, and intervening in, debates about the relationality of multiple *colonial* memories in a period that considers itself historically *post*colonial. The unevenness of such memories is patent, dependent as they are on the different locations of those remembering, on the actions of lobbies and other interest groups, on often quixotic attempts at memorial legislation, on the activities of groups of historians, and on the unstable relationship between the individual and the group, the group and the collectivity, the collectivity and the nation. The three examples above, each in its own way, reflect efforts to reconcile divergent memories of empire, within or across cultures, efforts rooted in a variety of motivations, both intellectual and ideological. At the same time, each example reveals the continued frustration of such endeavours, a frustration that reflects the incomplete nature of decolonization and the ways in which the legacies of empire persist in shaping memories of colonialism in contemporary societies.

Realms of colonial memory

A common starting point in any discussion of these processes, as is made clear by reference in the introduction to this chapter, is Pierre Nora's *Lieux de mémoire*. The now widely remarked exclusion from this collection of any sustained reference to the memorial legacy of empire has been described by historian Gregory Mann as 'nothing short of fantastic' (Mann, 2005: para 4; see also Tai, 2001). It is a commonplace, now even predictable observation that the essay on the 1931 exhibition remains Nora's only concession to the colonial past (1997, I: 493–515), yet it is important to note that for its author, Charles-Robert

---

1 The full text is available on the website of the Toulon branch of the Ligue des Droits de l'Homme. See http://www.ldh-toulon.net/spip.php?article1067 [consulted 28 January 2008].

Ageron, the *Exposition coloniale* is essentially a metropolitan event, figuring in the memories of its French visitors (statistics relating to whom are provided). Critiqued by *L'Humanité* and the surrealists, the 1931 event nevertheless remains in this account of it seemingly absent from the memories of those living colonial exhibits who brought its displays to life, i.e. more a thematic gesture than a genuinely direct challenge to the exceptionalist rationale of Nora's primarily national project. The collection permits, of course, the notion of a hexagonal space subject to fluctuation (e.g. the addition of Corsica in 1768) and even to temporary amputation of certain regions (e.g. the loss of Alsace-Lorraine in 1870); but the tendency towards a relative stability nevertheless remains. The ancien régime territories – in India and the Caribbean, appropriated long before the acquisition of Corsica – are absent, as are, despite the project's privileging of the Third Republic, the vast swathes of Asia and Africa, absorbed into Greater France during that period. The porosity of 'Frenchness', the progressive hybridization of any such notion, its ability to be displaced and transculturated: all of these are absent (on the difficulties of reconciling French republicanism and empire, see Bancel, Blanchard and Vergès, 2003, and Wilder, 2005).

It is possible to imagine a reconfiguration or rewriting of the collection in the light of such a postcolonial critique. Antoine Prost's contribution on war memorials, for instance, focused primarily on a French national narrative, fails to account for the complex situation of similar monuments *outre-mer* (Nora, 1997, I: 199–223). However, such memorials have been studied elsewhere, for instance in Eric Jennings' account (1998) of Guadeloupean 'monuments to Frenchness', erected in the interwar period as a response to the progressive erosion of any post-abolitionist republican project in the French Caribbean, or in Gregory Mann's work on the Malian memory of the *tirailleurs*, monuments to whom he studies in Bamako, Reims and Fréjus (2005). Neither does Prost, unlike Bertrand Tavernier, in his 1989 film *La Vie et rien d'autre*, reflect on the prescribed ethnicity of the *soldat inconnu* (explicitly, according to Tavernier, not a black *tirailleur*); and he pays no attention to the presence, on French memorials themselves, of thousands of names of colonial troops, patently disruptive of any discourse of national coherence. Jennings, again, has studied the *temple du souvenir indochinois*, one of the few remaining traces of the 1931 *Exposition*, a hybrid metropolitan space in which French commemorative genres are grafted on to their Indochinese equivalents (2003); and David Schalk reminds us that the more recent Fréjus memorial, to those killed in the Indo-Chinese war, indicates that French was not the nationality of many of the combatants there (2002). In an essay on the *tricoleur*, to take another example, Raoul Girardet, despite his status as a colonial historian (albeit with marked pro-colonial tendencies), pays little if any attention to the flag's travels and to the resulting instabilities of the *francité* it embodies (Nora 1997, I: 49–66). These are aspects that Roland Barthes (1972 [1957]), for instance, had previously and famously explored. And, to focus on the pre-republican Empire, or at least on the shift from an ancien régime colonialism to its republican descendant, Mona Ozouf analyses 'Liberté, égalité, fraternité' (Nora, 1997, III: 4353–88) without reflecting on the implications, for such ideals, of French amnesia regarding Saint-Domingue already discussed above.

On the one hand, there is a risk that analyses such as these reflect an (at worst) facile and (at best) superficially partisan reading of Nora's collection, undeniably monumental in its own right, which might, of course, like any collective project, have been produced with different emphases. This is criticism that Nora himself anticipates, accepting in the opening presentation of the collection its inherent 'échantillonage' [sampling], and acknowledging the 'part d'arbitaire' [element of arbitrariness] that this entails (1997, I: 19). On the other hand, however, it is possible to argue that these apparent blind spots reflect a series of more generalized phenomena relating to late twentieth-century memory in France. The 'lecture innocente' [innocent reading] solicited by the editor in his initial comments is not one in which any rigorous postcolonial scholar may indulge. Nora's collection permits certain counter-memories, or the existence of alternative, competing memory traditions – Jean-Clément Martin's study of the Vendée is a clear case in point (Nora, 1997, I: 519–34) – but the contestatory (yet in many ways conciliatory) potential of colonial memories is not permitted to emerge.

There is little denying the fact that Nora's project, when launched in 1984, was methodologically provocative as well as conceptually innovative, not least in its deliberate separation of 'history' from 'memory'. It aimed to deconstruct the remains of an official, elitist history, and to replace this with a series of salvaged focal points around which collective memories seem to have coalesced: i.e., it was not so much concerned with what actually happened as with the ways in which the past is transferred, reused, abused and offered some form of afterlife in the present. Some of the assumptions underpinning this provocation require close scrutiny. Not only is the choice of a national frame explained through references to 'l'originalité, la spécificité et l'exceptionalité françaises' [French originality, specificity and exceptionality] (1997, II: 2235), but also this national frame is constructed in relation to a decidedly Hegelian notion of extra-Hexagonal, pre-colonial history associated with a 'sommeil ethnologique' [ethnological slumber] from which (according to the introduction to the first volume) newly independent postcolonial nations had, through colonial contact, been forced to emerge (Nora, 1997, I: 23). *Les Lieux de mémoire*, as critics such as Steven Englund (1992) have made clear, is an 'autumnal' collection, emerging from a fin-de-siècle anxiety over France in crisis, from a sense of painful social dislocation exemplified both in the increasing alienation of a sizeable number of young French people of immigrant origin and in the associated re-emergence of the Far Right. Nora, ever the good republican historian, seems to suggest that the secular republic – subject of the inaugural volumes of his collection – remains the only frame(work) within which modern France is imaginable, with other possible perspectives (monarchist, Catholic, Muslim) largely ignored: as an explanatory framework, the *lieux de mémoire* project fails then to answer a series of questions triggered by the more general notions of 'identity' and 'national memory'.

There remains a risk, however, that the often ad hominem overtones of any such critique obscure the wider methodological richness of Nora's collection, while failing at the same time to situate it in a wider context of reluctance, in France *and elsewhere*, to confront the colonial past. It may therefore be possible to move away from the often reductive identification of gaps in this work in order to investigate and develop more fully the enabling implications, for the study of post/colonial memory, of Nora's methodology and his overarching narrative relating to the situatedness of memory. For despite its blind spots, Nora's collection invites us more generally to direct our attention to the critical relationship between memory and space. The prising open of such an approach – not least to include what Catherine Reinhardt, in the context of the French Caribbean, has dubbed 'sites of forgetting' and 'silent sites of memory' (2006) – may even permit a response to evolving attitudes towards empire, moving from an initial recovery of traces of the past (often fulfilling predominantly metro-politan agendas) towards the elaboration of more complex, intersecting fields of memory (in which former colonizer and former colonized are precariously, often unwillingly, but unavoidably linked).

Such a manoeuvre is, in part, associated with the export of the concept of the *lieu de mémoire* to other national, or even continental, contexts, seen for instance in the efforts of Henri Moniot (1999) to 'faire du Nora sous les tropiques' [apply Nora's approach to the Tropics] (see also Konaté, 2006). At the same time, however, there is a need for a substantial departure from such a persistently monocultural approach, drawing instead on the increas-ingly comparatist dimensions of postcolonial critique to analyse pairs or sets of related sites in a wider Francophone space, and using such analysis to illuminate the ties by which parts of that space have been historically 'assembled', and according to which, often in reconfigured relationships, they remain intercon-nected. The cemetery in which are buried victims of the 1944 massacre of *tirail-leurs indigènes* [indigenous infantrymen] at Thiaroye in Senegal, as well as the complex national commemorative practices that are associated with that space, exists in a contrapuntal relationship with French memorials to colonial troops alluded to above. Equally, commemorative sites in North America, both Acadian and Cajun, may be related to memorial traces on the French Atlantic coast of seventeenth-century emigrations.

Reframing memories of empire

To illustrate the complexities of such a manoeuvre, the example of the October 1961 massacres in Paris (dubbed euphemistically by Maurice Papon, the police chief under whose authority they occurred, as the 'Bataille de Paris') is telling. The killings are often cited as an example of French postcolonial amnesia and of its progressive erosion through acts of resistant remembrance. Recent historical enquiry (especially House and MacMaster, 2006) challenges this linear account of repression and recovery in two ways. First, it suggests that the forensic and statistical dimensions of subsequent memorialization may have obscured any acknowledgement of the ways in which the massacre was the culmination of a much longer process of violent oppression, related to the progressive racialization of North African immigrants in the final years of the Algerian War of Independence. Second, by engaging with a field of memory covering France and Algeria, it reveals a more complex process of amnesia and instrumentalization on *both sides* of the Mediterranean.

The work of House and MacMaster reflects increasing attention to the contrasting memories of the massacre, which remains for the 'French' the most public of the crimes perpetuated during this period, but for the 'Algerians', one of the more distant and remote of their many traumas. The crudity of any such binary interpretation is highlighted by the genuine complexities of remembering and forgetting in this case: the systematic orchestration of French amnesia was, for instance, matched by parallel attitudes of ambivalence in Algeria, where the Fédération de France du FLN, the organizer of the 1961 demonstration, was progressively distanced from the post-independence government. It was as if the demonstrators, reminders of splits in the FLN and of de Gaulle's inability to control his internal forces, disrupted straightforward narratives of the Algerian conflict and were accordingly denied a place in the postcolonial memories of both countries. The massacre almost immediately became obscured, but apparent silence was, of course, not forgetting. The now almost five decades since the events are characterized by multi-layered processes of remembrance and recollection, both in France and Algeria, in which the private and domestic progressively yielded to more public manifestations.

The complexity of these processes contextualizes and even relativizes key memorial interventions, such as Didier Daeninckx's *Meurtres pour mémoire* (1984). Without wanting to lessen the importance or impact of such a text, it is important to see Daeninckx's *polar* [thriller] as part of a manoeuvre whereby the massacre, invariably related to Vichy, plays a metonymic function for French anti-fascist activists. Algerians are presented as victims of oppression, rather than as political agents in their own right, with the result that questions of Algerian independence (and post-independence) are eclipsed by a critique of French *national* memory. The more recent work of novelists from Algeria (or of Algerian origin), e.g. Mehdi Lallaoui and Leila Sebbar, has engaged more openly with Algerian memories of the events, and there has been a more coherent and sustained effort on the part of historians to collect accounts of the victims' experience (see Forsdick, 2007). This has permitted a more complex and sensitive understanding of Franco-Algerian memories of the massacre, moving away from earlier dislocations inherent in binary, national interpretations.

Illustrating the various ways in which recollection of the past permits discussion of the relationships between France and the wider Francophone world, this chapter has asked to what extent any shared memories of empire are either possible or desirable. In talking of sharing – of histories, of narratives, of memories – there is a need to reflect vigilantly on the nature of the common ownership of the past this implies, to ask whether it is latent or engineered, existing or fantasized. The emphasis in the preliminary report of the Comité pour la mémoire de l'esclavage (2005) is on the fostering, from the multiple memories of slavery, of a 'mémoire partagée' [shared memory], which would itself permit the elaboration of what Paul Ricoeur dubbed a 'récit partagé' [shared narrative]. The possibility of such shared phenomena, linking France and its overseas departments in a reflection on slavery and its aftermath, is, as the report makes clear, greatly facilitated by the existence of common structures, educational and cultural, whereby such connections may be forged. In most other cases, including a number of those alluded to above, where the institutional and diplomatic dislocation between former colonizer and former colonized is more stark, any common ownership may prove much less consensual.

What is clear, however, from the range of cases on which the chapter has drawn, in which memories appear divergent or convergent, antagonistic or complementary, is that a self-sufficiently national memory of empire remains inevitably partial and increasingly unsustainable. Any such memory ignores, on the one hand, the emergence of more complex spaces, underpinned by the dynamics of memory, and, on the other, the often contrastive, contrapuntal existence of competing alternative memories. What models or approaches might then reflect, and permit the exploration of, these spaces of remembering and forgetting, which are themselves often dependent on spatial connections that, in reality, bypass national boundaries? How might one identify connections that ignore the at times arbitrary chronological moments at which the colonial past is supposedly eclipsed, through collective amnesia and its judicial support of amnesty, by the (would-be) postcolonial present? To what extent do such connections evolve according to complex itineraries in which decades of forgetting can be unpredictably disrupted by the resurgence of the past (see Cole, 2001)?

In answering such questions about possible models and approaches, the aim must be to move towards a more inclusive awareness of the plural, multi-directional nature of colonial memory. This would challenge reductively national accounts of memory's workings, while avoiding any tendency to reduce *lieux de mémoire* in postcolonial locations to the status of little more than a continued means of interrogating the metropole itself. There is a clear need for constant vigilance in the elucidation of distinctions between history and memory (see Cubitt, 2007), all the more so because the sudden emergence of the memorial legacies of empire in twenty-first-century France might usefully be read in the light of Patrick Weil's observation that 'too little history is compensated for by an excess of memory' (cited in Thomas, 2007: 37). In reflecting on the spatial dynamics and complex interconnections of colonial memories, a lead is offered by Frederick Cooper and Ann Stoler. They call, in 'Between Metropole and Colony', for a comparatist postcolonial approach to the history (as opposed to the memory) of empire, encouraging the treatment of 'metropole and colony, colonizer and colonized' in 'one analytic field' (1997: 15). The methodological and pedagogical implications of such a suggestion have been addressed by Alice Conklin (2000) in her explorations of the ways in which we might teach 'French history as colonial history and colonial history as French history'. This is a suggestion further illustrated by the work of a range of scholars, including Yves Benot, Laurent Dubois and John Garrigus, who have all followed C. L. R. James's example in reading the shortcomings of the French Revolution in the light of its Haitian counterpart (and not, as is customary, vice versa). Such approaches, in their various ways, negotiate the pitfalls identified by historian Gregory Mann in relation not only to memory itself but also to the wider historiography with which it is often closely associated. Mann warns against:

> [t]he new colonial history [that] risks ending where it began, in a national history of a different nation – one that takes the imperial archive into account but does not go beyond it – rather than in a post-national history that might better help historians understand the world in which they and others live. (2005: para 42)

Any understanding of memory informed by this 'post-national history' must not, however, become a homogenizing practice, whose globalizing ambitions grind down the singularities that national histories and memories tend to (over)privilege. Genuine tensions remain. Paul Silverstein (2004) describes France and Algeria as a 'transpolitical' space of shared memories, a concept manifest in the crowd disturbance at the 2001 France-Algeria match alluded to above; he focuses on a century of migrations across the Mediterranean, describing the emergence within France of political loyalties that ignore national boundaries. Such tensions – between communality and dislocation, between convergence and divergence, between theory and practice, between policy and the context on which this is imposed – deny the existence, and even the possibility, of any monolithic model of transnational, or perhaps more accurately transcultural, memory; but the challenge remains to identify sites that resonate for both (former) 'colonizer' and (former) 'colonized'. It is such sites that bear multiple, competing and at times conflicting memories, perpetuated in often refracted forms in the postcolonial present.

Further reading

Aldrich, Robert, 2005. *Vestiges of the Colonial Empire in France: Monuments, Museums and Colonial Memories* (Basingstoke: Palgrave Macmillan). A comprehensive study of sites of colonial memory in France itself, focused in particular on its architectural and institutional traces, by one of the foremost historians of the French empire in the Anglophone world. The author situates such vestiges in their contemporary, early twenty-first-century context. It can be usefully read in relation to the work of historians such as Eric Jennings and Gregory Mann on colonial memory in former colonial sites.

Hargreaves, Alec (ed.), 2005. *Memory, Empire, and Postcolonialism: Legacies of French Colonialism* (Lanham, MD: Lexington Books). A broadly focused collection of essays, edited by one of the leading international specialists on postcolonial France, covering questions of colonial memory in North America, the Caribbean, Africa, Asia and Europe. There is an emphasis on the wars of decolonization in Algeria and Indochina, with notable additional essays on slavery and the Haitian Revolution by Catherine Reinhardt and Nick Nesbitt.

Outre-Mers, 2006, 350–51. [Special issue: 'Sites et monuments de mémoire'.] A special issue of the journal of the Société française d'histoire d'outre-mer, guest editor Robert Aldrich. The issue is devoted to discussion of current debates surrounding colonial history and memory. Contributors include some of the leading scholars active in the field, including Laurent Dubois and Lawrence Brown on the French Caribbean, and Eric Jennings on Madagascar.

CHAPTER 23

Gender and Empire in the World of Film

Winifred Woodhull

France in film

Insofar as film scholarship followed literary studies, in the 1980s and 1990s, in taking up Benedict Anderson's work on the construction of national identity through imagined communities, much attention has been devoted to looking at French films that participate in that process by construing colonized peoples as primitive and frequently feminized 'Others', in opposition to whom the French define themselves as rational, enlightened and civilized. Like the films themselves, the analyses vary in the degree to which they see colonizer/colonized relations in terms of stark binaries or in terms of ambiguous hybrid identities on both sides. Yet whatever the emphasis, it is French national identity that takes centre stage. The chapter will consider the ways in which gender and empire figure in films concerned mainly with Africa and other formerly colonized spaces. The initial intention, however, is to assess some of the more interesting film scholarship on questions of gender, empire and French national identity, especially with respect to colonial films of the interwar period, as well as postcolonial films looking back at the French empire, usually in a nostalgic way.

Ginette Vincendeau's *Pépé le Moko* (1998) is the most sustained analysis of a single classic film and the historical context of its production and reception. Like many studies of the past two decades, it highlights cinematic masculinity as a problem that warrants as much scrutiny as its feminine counterpart. It shows, for example, how Julien Duvivier's 1937 film, set in the casbah of Algiers, eroticizes the working-class French thief played by Jean Gabin in ways that are quite distinct from Hollywood representations of mob bosses. Duvivier uses high-key lighting and close-ups to emphasize the beauty of Pépé's blue eyes and his elegant dress in ways that are usually reserved for female stars: the spectator's gaze is continually drawn to his impeccable suits, silk scarves, fedora and spats, in the same way that it is drawn to the eyes, sparkling jewels and designer dresses and hats of Gaby (Mireille Balin), the French femme fatale with whom the hero falls in love. Both male and female beauty and fashion evoke the sophistication of Paris, although Pépé's seductive masculinity is associated as well with the thrilling French underworld.

In her assessment of the film's treatment of female identity in a colonial context, Vincendeau demonstrates that Gaby is contrasted with Pépé's unrefined, gypsy-like, dark-skinned mistress (Line Noro) and with the fleshy, repellent prostitutes of the casbah. The contrasting representations of femininity encode the colony as an exotic refuge from the French police and a stifling prison in its own right, while simultaneously encoding Paris as an infinitely desirable yet unattainable ideal, an elusive 'elsewhere' for Pépé and other members of the 'dangerous classes'. Even though Pépé's exit from the casbah will cost him his life, he is unable to resist the allure of the French capital, associated not only with his nostalgia for the metro and the Place Blanche but also with the glamorous Gaby (who grew up in Les Gobelins, the same working-class neighbourhood as Pépé), as well as the wealth and social status of her sugar daddy, the Champagne magnate.

It is interesting to note the interrelation of gender and ethnicity in *Pépé le Moko*, where the colony is presented not only in terms of dangerous femininity but also in terms of uncontrolled racial and ethnic interaction. As many critics have noted, the chaotic ethnic mixing evoked in the film's opening sequence – a rapid montage of shots taken from widely disparate angles and distances, narrated in voice-over by an alarmed French police inspector – goes hand in hand with the excessive, unruly, destructive sexuality attributed to women of the casbah. In their cinematic presentation, the labyrinthine streets, dark doorways and secluded rooms of Duvivier's casbah seem to foster shady relations between members of myriad groups, including sub-Saharan Africans, various Mediterranean peoples and Asians, while at the same time, quite remarkably, excluding Arabs – the very people who have the greatest stake in resistance to French colonialism in North Africa. At once ethnically erased and feminized (and thus symbolically stripped of their oppositional force), the Arabs who constitute a threat to the French empire are effectively neutralized in Duvivier's film.

As David Slavin has shown in *Colonial Cinema and Imperial France* (2001), the Arab threat is handily contained in many other interwar films set in North Africa, such as Jacques Feyder's *Le Grand Jeu* (1934) and Marcel L'Herbier's *Les Hommes nouveaux* (1936), where 'natives' are usually played by European actors and are either demonized or idealized, if, indeed, they appear on-screen at all. And as Martin O'Shaughnessy has argued (2001), critics who adopt a national rather than a transnational framework in the analysis of French interwar cinema, particularly of colonial films like *Pépé le Moko*, unwittingly reproduce the colonial logic of the films themselves by locating cultural and ethnic 'Otherness' exclusively within a distant colony, rather than acknowledging the multi-ethnic character of France, which, in this period, was home to many North Africans. Elizabeth Ezra's analysis of Josephine Baker's films in *The Colonial Unconscious* (2000) is noteworthy for its attention to the presence and the cultural production of non-European people living in France in this period. Similarly, her critical look at the Miss France d'Outre-Mer beauty contest (held in France in the same year as the 1937 World's Fair) offers an exemplary interpretation of France's national obsession with race, one that deconstructs the apparent opposition between separatist eugenicists and advocates of *métissage*.

Ironically, the nearly exclusive focus on French national identity continues unabated in French postcolonial films dealing with French imperial ventures in Africa and Indo-China, even though these films necessarily grapple with the insurgencies that eventually led to the political sovereignty and cultural self-affirmation of formerly colonized peoples, whose aim was precisely to challenge France's preoccupation with its own interests at the expense of others' needs and desires. Relevant films in this category, directed by women and focused on women's experience in the colonies, include Claire Denis's look at colonial Cameroon in *Chocolat* (1988), and Brigitte Roüan's depiction of revolutionary Algeria in *Outremer* (1990). One could also cite Régis Wargnier's heritage film *Indochine* (1992), centred on the Catherine Deneuve character, a tough French plantation owner, who has grown up in Indo-China but is ultimately forced to leave. Some of the more interesting studies of French heritage films, such as Brigitte Rollet's 'Identity and Alterity in Wargnier's *Indochine*' (1999), note the preponderance of female figures whose function is to take the rap for colonialism (a bad idea, as the female leads' male counterparts sagely observe), while simultaneously dazzling audiences with their beauty, their star power, their period costumes, and their association with gorgeous landscapes that evoke nostalgia and admiration for the empire of yore. Another much-discussed postcolonial film, Jean-Jacques Annaud's *L'Amant* (1992), based on Marguerite Duras's autobiographical novel set in the Indo-China of her youth, follows a similar pattern, as Panivong Norindr shows in *Phantasmatic Indochina* (1996). Unfortunately, the narrow national perspective deployed in these films often passes unnoticed by the films' critics, who express unbounded sympathy for the French people's sense of defeat, loss or guilt in the face of the empire's collapse, while turning a blind eye to its significance for colonized peoples, as in certain essays in *Cinema, Colonialism, Postcolonialism* (Sherzer, 1996).

Other cinematic worlds

Countering the works that privilege France's experience of colonization and loss of empire are those centred on Africans' experiences. In the wake of the African independences, Ousmane Sembene's *Black Girl* or *La Noire de…* (Senegal, 1966), for example, uses new wave filmmaking techniques in a cinematic critique of the myth of decolonization. The film shows how impoverished Africans, far from being 'free', are forced to seek employment in France under conditions that are as demoralizing as they are economically exploitative. At the centre of Sembene's narrative is a young Senegalese maid who is taken to the Riviera by her French employers. Having rebuffed a suitor's proposal of marriage, Diouana (Mbissine Thérèse Diop) goes off to France in hopes of seeing the world while earning a living and achieving a degree of independence – goals she has set for herself as a modern woman. Yet her employers' racist condescension and her enforced social isolation drive her to suicide, the only act of defiance open to her in these circumstances. When her French employer returns to Dakar with Diouana's personal effects, adding insult to injury by offering money to Diouana's mother in compensation for her daughter's life, Diouana's entire Dakar community condemns his moral bankruptcy.

The post-independence years also saw the production of many films that were critical of Africa's new leaders. Sembene's *Xala* (Senegal, 1974), Jean-Marie Teno's *Afrique, je te plumerai* (France/Cameroon, 1991) and Cheick Oumar Sissoko's *Guimba, un tyran, une époque* (Mali/Burkina Faso, 1999) are emblematic of such films, which deliver scathing critiques of the most egregious aspects of African politics: dictatorships; widespread corruption and greed among government officials, military officers and police; and the ruthless exploitation of the urban and rural poor. Gender relations are a key issue in *Xala* and in many later African films, such as Adama Drabo's *Taafe Fanga* (Mali/Germany, 1997) and Fanta Régina Nacro's *Le Truc de Konaté* (Burkina Faso, 1998), a comedy dealing with a married woman's insistence on her husband's condom use to prevent the spread of HIV. These films have been widely discussed in terms of their denunciation of the cynical invocation of 'tradition' as a means of justifying male privilege and the ongoing institutionalized subordination of women in the family, in education, and in local and national decision-making processes. African films have long promoted an idea that NGOs and international organizations are at last taking seriously, namely, that African women are the most likely candidates to create a viable economy and to develop social networks capable of ensuring the well-being of all members of African societies.

Although a significant number of films and a fair amount of film criticism adopt a national perspective on African cultural politics, many films simultaneously speak, in a broader sense, to issues that are common to most nations south of the Sahara. This is particularly true of the work of Senegalese director Djibril Diop Mambéty, for whom Africa's self-destructive reliance on European and North American models of 'modernization', as well as Africa's forced reliance on Western-controlled economic institutions such as the International Monetary Fund and the World Bank, are key concerns. Mambéty's *Hyènes* (Senegal, 1994), *Le Franc* (Senegal, 1994) and *La Petite Vendeuse de Soleil* (Senegal, 1999) provide examples of films that are set in Senegal (and spoken mainly in Wolof), yet clearly address matters that are of vital importance to much of Africa. While many critics have analysed the far-reaching scope of Mambéty's films, Ellie Higgins is the only one to have approached them systematically in terms of gender and transnational economies (Higgins, 2002). Even as she underscores the female characters' potency as public actors and makers of social meanings, Higgins points to the significance, both in the films and in African societies, of internal migrations from the countryside to the cities and the power of local markets to defy the disastrous structural adjustment programmes imposed by the dispensers of 'aid'.

In Higgins's reading of *La Petite Vendeuse de Soleil*, the disabled protagonist Sili (Lissa Balera) refuses to accept her 'place' as defined by a gender hierarchy that is violently enforced, whenever possible, by boys in Dakar who see newspaper sales as a male province. Sili perseveres in selling the national newspaper in order to earn money for her family. Yet at the same time, she takes an active role in interpreting and altering the meaning of 'zones of influence' in and around local markets where rural and urban populations converge. Higgins cites Manthia Diawara's analysis of these zones in order to demonstrate their importance in the global economy, as figured in Mambéty's film. Diawara writes: 'traditionally centers of international consumption and cross-fertilisation', these sites of exchange make it 'impossible for nation-states to control the flow of goods, currency exchange rates, the net worth of markets' (Diawara, 1998: 42). One might well take issue with Higgins's sunny view of the film's articulation of possibilities for national solidarity based on the goodwill of all concerned, especially the police and the wealthy male entrepreneur who steps in to support Sili's industriousness; *La Petite Vendeuse de Soleil* can legitimately be read as sentimental and paternalistic in this regard. Nonetheless, Higgins's essay is exemplary in its sustained attention to gender, not just in the tired old terms of 'images of women' and their 'roles' but as a category of analysis in the local/global economic nexus.

As for the much-discussed figure of Linguère Ramatou (played by Ami Diakhate) in Mambéty's best film, *Hyènes*, she has frequently been interpreted in transnational terms. The wealthy old woman who returns to her home town in Senegal after a decades-long absence is typically seen as an emblem of Western economic and cultural imperialism. However, too little attention has been paid to her iconic status as a prostitute, a negative (and clearly gendered) incarnation of modernity, which has figured centrally in cinema from the silent period on, for example in Jean Renoir's films *Nana* (1926) and *La Chienne* (1931). Impregnated and betrayed by her young lover at the age of 17, Ramatou is forced to leave her village and to live abroad as a prostitute. When she returns home thirty years later, 'richer than the World Bank', she promises to bestow her wealth on the residents of the dying village of Colobane. However, she imposes the condition that the townspeople kill her former lover – a condition that they ultimately accept, ostensibly in the name of 'justice'. Linguère Ramatou succeeds in her mission of 'turning the world into a brothel' and forcing her fellow villagers to acknowledge the truth about themselves, that is, that they are self-interested 'hyenas', who prey on others in order to advance themselves in the 'modern' consumer economy, represented in the film principally by modern appliances such as washing machines and electric fans, and by flashy cars, fine cigars and cognac. True, the film draws attention to the lover's and the villagers' guilt in betraying Ramatou and avoids simplistic moral condemnation of the woman who had no choice but to earn her living as a prostitute. Yet Ramatou inspires far more dread in the spectators than her lover, or the acquisitive, murderous villagers. By means of low-angle shots emphasizing Ramatou's excessive wealth, power and cruelty, and close-ups of her hard, unfeeling stare, she is portrayed as a monstrous 'distortion' of femininity, which is conceived in terms of emotional attachment, devotion to others and selflessness.

As they are rendered in *Hyènes*, Ramatou's autonomy and power are appalling, just as her artificial limbs, a leg and a hand 'all made of iron' signify her monstrosity and inhumanity. Mambéty, who is rightly praised for his avant-garde filmmaking, reinscribes in Ramatou the quintessential avant-garde figure of the monstrous female prostitute, the emblem of all that is wrong with modernity, and the screen on to which the fear and loathing it inspires may be projected. The figure of the African female prostitute as the icon of Western-inspired modernity should be seen as the obverse of the idealized, equally feminized figure of 'Mother Africa', whether in her maternal guise, celebrated by the Negritude poets, or in her aspect as a warrior of epic proportions, as in Med Hondo's *Sarraounia* (Mauritania, 1986). In Hondo's film, the almost super-human female leader of the revolt against European colonization embodies the embryonic nation or even the African continent, but has almost nothing to do with flesh-and-blood women; rather, much like Marianne, the figure of the French Republic, she supplies an unconvincing symbolic alibi for a 'modern' nation that continues to subordinate women.

Cinema's focus on transnational relations has nowhere been more apparent than in films by black women. Prior to the emergence of global economies, Sarah Maldoror, who was raised in France yet identified as Guadeloupean, is widely recognized as a trailblazer in black women's film, particularly in *Sambizanga* (Angola, 1972), in which she provides a gendered account of the Angolan struggle for independence from the Portuguese: a resistance fighter is arrested and the film follows his wife's quest to find him and secure his freedom. In her position as a woman from the African diaspora, Maldoror empathizes with her heroine's plight while simultaneously registering the specificity of Angolan women's experience of war, dispossession and dislocation.

Melissa Thackway's first-rate examination of women directors and gender issues in Francophone African film in *Africa Shoots Back* (2003) – unique in its careful, historically grounded analyses of film form and style – productively relates Maldoror's work of the 1970s to that of Togolese director Anne-Laure Folly two decades later. Thackway shows how Folly's *Les Oubliées* (France, 1996) takes up Maldoror's concern with Angolan women and war, using a close-up technique in interviews '[t]o encourage the spectator literally to look the women in the eye in an attempt to reduce the distance between the subject and the director/spectator, and thus to lessen the divide' (2003: 158). Thackway demonstrates that '[t]his closeness is accentuated in *Les Oubliées* by Anne-Laure Folly's direct voice and actual presence in the film, which subsequently becomes the record of her own personal journey' (159).

Thackway's discussion of *Les Oubliées* and of Folly's other documentary, *Femmes aux yeux ouverts* (France, 1993), enjoins spectators and critics to take seriously the agendas African women activists set for themselves in addressing issues such as HIV/AIDS, excision and forced marriage, as well as war and dislocation. It urges us to try to *hear* what African women are saying, whether in fiction films such as Fanta Régina Nacro's *Bintou* (Burkina Faso, 2001), on a woman's determination to pay for her daughter's education against her husband's wishes, or in documentaries such as those cited above. Looking African women in the eye and making a serious attempt to hear what they are saying can help to counter the long history of erasure of African women in films the world over, and the equally long history of sensationalist, objectifying media accounts of their situations – 'coverage' that plays a key role in thwarting women's struggles for economic empowerment and social equality.

Alternative masculinities

What of the disruptive potentialities of alternative masculinities in African cinema? To date, they have remained largely unexplored. I want to suggest, however, that Abderrahmane Sissako's *Sabriya* (Tunisia, 1997) is a compelling exception in this regard. One of several short African films on the topic of love, commissioned for a television mini-series entitled *Africa Dreaming*, *Sabriya* resembles Sissako's better-known, feature-length film, *La Vie sur terre* (Mali, 1998) in its incorporation of poetic language, its use of filters to evoke the intense light of the desert and of ochre-coloured interior settings, its long takes and abrupt cuts at unexpected moments, its use of still shots and leisurely tracking shots and pans, and its slow yet deliberate rhythm, which conveys 'African time', as opposed to the frenetic pace of life in the West. A native of Mali, who attended film school in Moscow before the collapse of the Soviet Union, Sissako has a unique sensibility that speaks to relatively broad audiences without resorting to colonialist clichés.

Set in the remote village of Sabriya in southern Tunisia, Sissako's film is structured by a twist on the narrative convention of the love triangle. A young man named Youssef (Chawki Bouglia) becomes intrigued with a young woman, Zarah (Rim Turkhi), whom he meets at a desolate train stop on the outskirts of Sabriya. Youssef is returning home after going to a neighbouring town to buy water. Zarah, on the other hand, is just arriving in Sabriya as a visitor. In terms of the film's fiction, at least, Zarah speaks perfect Tunisian Arabic although she looks rather 'foreign': she is very light-skinned, is travelling alone, addresses strange men with confidence, and wears revealing clothing, notably a short, tight skirt with a slit in the back, which Youssef naively mistakes for a tear. Zarah explains that the reason for her visit is that one of her parents is a native of Sabriya, 'only my mother, not my father'. As Youssef becomes increasingly infatuated with Zarah, his close friend Said (Nabil Chahed) also becomes intrigued, less with Zarah herself than with Youssef's desire for her.

During her stay in Sabriya, Zarah seems quite happy to spend time with Youssef whenever he finds a pretext to seek her out. Indeed, at one point she goes to the town tavern looking for him, a move that is so shocking to the tavern-keeper that he is reduced to a state of near paralysis. Yet the film makes clear that Zarah and Youssef are not lovers, other than in Youssef's imagination, and that they are, in fact, on quite different wavelengths. Zarah's interest in Youssef is merely friendly; she gently chides him for fantasizing about their future together as a couple selling palm wine in Genoa, where Zarah presumably lives – an Italian city that recalls Tunisia's ancient ties with the northern rim of the Mediterranean. Zarah also chides Youssef for disregarding the need for a passport and other papers in today's world. At the film's conclusion she is shown leaving Sabriya by train, looking calm and displaying no regret about her departure.

Indeed, one of the film's central concerns is Youssef's obliviousness to Zarah's benign indifference: he is in love with love, not with Zarah. We last see him at the tavern, alone, mimicking the gestures he might make if he were Zarah's partner, putting his arm around her shoulders and so on. Moreover, the shots that present Zarah as an erotic object, for example, when she basks in the desert sun in a bathing suit, or narcissistically sways and caresses herself in the cool waters of a cascade, seem to do so in a deliberately clichéd manner: Zarah resembles nothing so much as a model in a televised commercial for sunscreen or shampoo. Significantly, these shots are not clearly shown to represent Youssef's point of view as a 'real' observer of Zarah near the cascade. Indeed, the clichéd images of Zarah under the waterfall recall the glossy colour photos in the illustrated magazine that Youssef is reading in an earlier scene, photos depicting beautiful, elegant, wealthy Westerners, with whom he has no social contact. In short, in a gently humorous way, Sissako's film calls attention to the repertoire of images from 'elsewhere' that shape Youssef's fantasies about Zarah.

More intriguing than Youssef's fascination with Zarah as an embodiment of his 'own' desire, necessarily mediated by Western cultural images, is Said's fascination with Youssef's desire. Until Youssef's preoccupation with love begins to irritate and unsettle Said, the two friends play chess together at the tavern with other men of the village, who gather to smoke, drink and talk. Interestingly, Youssef and Said also live together. Apart from their small, separate bedrooms, we are shown only a dimly lit hallway in their dwelling, where Said stands as he looks in on Youssef thumbing through the glossy magazine or mumbling in his sleep about the shop he wants to open with Zarah in Genoa. In contrast to Youssef's idleness, the film initially emphasizes Said's engagement in down-to-earth domestic tasks such as making his bed, shaking sand from his pillow and using his hands to pile up the sand that has accumulated on the floor during his night's sleep. Only later does Youssef's infectious dreaminess affect Said, sending him off into a sandstorm in search of Youssef (who, he imagines, is in search of Zarah) and ultimately prompting him to board the train that Youssef had recently ridden, the very train that Zarah is taking as she leaves Sabriya. Indeed, Said sits next to Zarah in the car, but neither one seems to know the other. Strangers on a train, they are as oblivious to each other as Youssef had unwittingly been to Zarah. In a sense, Said has taken Youssef's place in a fantasy that only superficially involves love for a woman, or even the idea of love for a woman. Sissako's cinematic images compellingly convey Said's identification with Youssef and with the latter's desire.

Yet there is more. Unlike any other African film I have seen – including films such as Laurent Bocahut's and Phillip Brooks's *Woubi chéri* (France/Ivory Coast, 1998), whose theme is the homosexual and transgender community of Abidjan – Sissako's *Sabriya* subtly explores homosocial identifications and affective relations between men. In the tavern, an affectively charged and mildly erotic atmosphere is established through the warm, dim lighting; the slow, fluid tracking shots and pans that seem to allow the spectator's gaze to float dreamily from one group of men to another; and the hushed atmosphere that is only occasionally disturbed by music or words coming from the old radio on the bar. These effects are reinforced by the circulation of a man with matches, who moves silently from table to table lighting men's cigarettes; by the tavern-keeper's recitation of love poetry that he has just penned; and by one patron's mockery of the tavern-keeper's idealized evocations of love: holding up his glass and cursing his betrayal by a lover, he declares that drink is all he has left.

The warm lighting, the fluid camera movements and the hushed atmosphere of the tavern reappear in the shots of the domestic space shared by Youssef and Said. In one scene in Youssef's bedroom, Said sits next to him on the bed, holding Youssef's head with one hand and applying salve to his eyelids with the other – this in the wake of Youssef's train trip, in the course of which his eyes were apparently irritated by sand, despite the traditional white cloth he had wrapped around his head and neck as a means of protection. The narrative justification for the 'innocent' yet intimate physical contact between the men is tenuous at best. Said's shirtless torso is bathed in ochre light, and his face is almost touching Youssef's as he gently applies the soothing ointment to his eyelids. The film's rendering of Said's ministrations suggests an alteration of vision; it provides new images that channel spectators' yearnings in new directions.

In a later scene Youssef and Said wrestle, shirtless, in the dark hallway between their rooms, breathing heavily, then laughing and joking. Next, there is a cut to a shot of Said attending to Youssef, this time by massaging his shoulders. Here, too, Sissako provides only feeble narrative motivation for the physical contact between the two shirtless men. And in this instance, the erotic charge of the contact is unmistakable. Initially we see the two young men in a medium shot showing Youssef lying on his stomach in bed; the shot contrasts Youssef's peaceful immobility with the movement of Said's arms and hands as he massages his friend's shoulders. Then the camera pulls back and lingers for several seconds on the rhythmic back-and-forth movement of Said's torso and hips. My point is not that *Sabriya* depicts a homosexual relationship between Tunisian men; in my view it does no such thing. Rather, it deftly explores the shifting psychic, erotic and social dynamics between men in a largely sex-segregated society. (Other than Zahra, we see only one female in Sabriya, a young girl who watches in amazement from her doorstep as Zarah breezes into town.) *Sabriya* shows us how modes of identification are shaped by heteronormativity on the one hand and by the power and prestige of former colonizing forces on the other (Zahra, Genoa, and Western advertising).

Yet *Sabriya* – a film about a remote village in southern Tunisia, made by a Soviet-trained director from Mali – also exemplifies a mode of transnational identification that unsettles the opposition between the global north and the global south. Its visual rhetoric opens spaces of pleasure and fantasy that may enable spectators, whose point of identification in the last shot is Said, to go in a different direction from Youssef and to imagine a future that is not defined in advance by the current Western norms of heterosexual romance and consumer culture, embodied by Zahra and Genoa. Certainly, Sissako's *Sabriya* is unique among African films in its exploration of male homosocial relations from a transnational perspective. At the same time, its affectionate yet critical take on men's experience in a remote Tunisian village effectively counters the ethnocentrism and unwitting self-absorption of most French directors who have made films dealing with questions of gender and empire.

Further reading

Armes, Roy, 2005. *Postcolonial Images: Studies in North African Film* (Bloomington: Indiana University Press). Armes provides an overview of North African cinema from its beginnings in the 1960s, as well as giving careful readings of individual films with attention to issues of gender and decolonization.

Harrow, Kenneth (ed.), 1994. *With Open Eyes: Women and African Cinema* (Amsterdam: Rodopi). This volume contains interesting essays on Western filmmakers' representations of African difference; on women in films from Algeria, Mali, Nigeria, Tanzania and Togo; and on the interpretation of African women's films from the standpoint of French feminist theories of subject formation and representation. It also includes a helpful (though now dated) filmography of work by sub-Saharan African women and an annotated bibliography on women in African cinema, including information about actresses, festivals, filmmakers and film criticism.

Tarr, Carrie, 2005. *Reframing Difference: 'Beur' and 'Banlieue' Filmmaking in France* (Manchester: Manchester University Press). Tarr's twelve lively essays focus on a large number of films by and about immigrant communities in France. They offer compelling interpretations of the films' gender politics, considered in relation to other concerns such as ethnicity and cross-cultural social protest. The book shows how France's imperial past informs the present.

CHAPTER 24

From Colonial to Postcolonial: Reflections on the Colonial Debate in France

Nicolas Bancel and Pascal Blanchard

Over the past two decades, postcolonial studies – or postcolonial theory – has firmly established itself within the Anglophone academy. In France, however, the perception of this critical body of thought labours under a certain number of misconceptions that have rendered the development of an equivalent 'hexagonal' movement deeply problematic, and have given rise instead to a determined opposition in the general 'intellectual field'. By 'intellectual field' we mean the broad domain constituted by publications and debates in the social sciences, particularly sociology, history, political sciences and, more marginally, anthropology. This 'intellectual field' includes academic publications, but also essays by public intellectuals who are not part of the academic community. In this chapter, we will specify the term 'academic field' when the questions raised relate more specifically to debates between university scholars. Within these French academic contexts, reaction to postcolonial theory has been characterized by a conservatism underpinned by a relative lack of awareness of key critical works and thinkers, a problem that is compounded by the unavailability of translations.[1]

To be sure, various recent publications, such as the translations of work by Stuart Hall and Neil Lazarus, published by Les Éditions Amsterdam, have provided readers with better knowledge of 'des concepts clés, des méthodes, des sources intellectuelles, des théories et des débats qui se sont développés au sein des études postcoloniales' [key concepts, methods, intellectual sources, theories and debates that have been developed within postcolonial studies] (Lazarus, 2006: 446). Similarly, several special issues of journals have encouraged a more sustained engagement with postcolonial criticism. The pioneering volume in this context is the special issue of *Dédale*, entitled 'Postcolonialisme:

---

1   For instance, pioneering works of postcolonial studies such as *The Empire Writes Back* (Ashcroft et al., 1989) have yet to be translated into French.

Décentrement, Déplacement, Dissémination', which was edited by Abdelwahab Meddeb (1997); others include: *Labyrinthe*, 'Faut-il être postcolonial?' (2006); *Multitudes*, 'Postcolonial et politique de l'histoire' (2006); *Vingtième siècle*, 'Mémoires Europe-Asie' (2007).

Equally, it should be noted that over the past few years a number of French researchers have borrowed from postcolonial theory to broach particular postcolonial issues: in the historical field alone, there has been a wide range of postcolonial work in the past few years (see Bancel et al., 2003; Dozon, 2003; Ferro, 2003; Manceron, 2003; Hajjat, 2005; Vidal and Bourtel, 2005). The precarious institutional status of these researchers, however, is revelatory of the position of postcolonial studies within the wider French academy: these researchers work within a broad range of disciplinary contexts and remain isolated not only within their discipline's theoretical boundaries but also from their immediate colleagues, for there is currently no research cluster in France working on specifically postcolonial issues. Alongside the postcolonial historical work cited above, there are also isolated researchers working in other fields such as sociology, political science and comparative literature (see Boubeker, 1999; 2003; Bouamama, 2004; Guénif-Souilamas, 2000; 2006; Mbembe, 2001 [2000]; Moura, 2007 [1999]; Weil, 2005). The publication of our edited volume (with Sandrine Lemaire) *La Fracture coloniale* (Blanchard et al., 2005) thus allowed for a timely, cross-disciplinary critical dialogue between institutionally isolated researchers from these disparate fields. Although these various publications have sought to bring postcolonial research in France progressively up to date, postcolonial studies nonetheless remains in its infancy, a victim of academic and, arguably, editorial marginalization.

Carving a space for postcolonial studies in the French academy

A range of factors explains the antipathy within the French university system towards postcolonial studies. The undeniable heterogeneity of postcolonial research and the multiple interpretations to which it gives rise offers one explanation. Contrary to the widespread belief in certain quarters that postcolonialism merely constitutes a reconfiguration of 'Third Worldism' or an 'anachronistic' resurgence of anti-colonialism, postcolonial thought is resolutely anti-teleological. Furthermore, it has developed across different disciplinary spaces and represents a constantly evolving critical practice rather than a specific 'theory' or 'system'. Within the French academy there has often appeared to be a compulsion to reduce this diversity to a highly debatable binary opposition between, on the one hand, nostalgics and reactionaries and, on the other hand, postcolonialists and anti-colonialists (for a discussion of these polarized debates, see Lebovics, 2004). This perception is not entirely erroneous: in effect, recent debates on the past and colonial memory in France have given rise to a marked polarization of intellectual positions. Certain contributions to these debates, often aimed at wide non-specialist audiences, have taken the form of publications aiming to restore a 'classical' colonial history, which notably evades the question of the effects of colonization on the metropole, both during and after the colonial period (see Bruckner, 2006; Lefeuvre, 2006).[2] In the academic context, there has often been a straightforward refusal of postcolonial research, and, on occasions, attempts to suppress the questions posed by it (Chrétien, 2006). Needless to say, the polarization of these positions does not favour the emergence of French-based postcolonial research wishing to dissociate itself from such jaded thinking.

It bears repeating that, from a disciplinary point of view, postcolonial studies has diverse 'homes', which include literary studies, political science, anthropology and history. However, from a French perspective, this disciplinary 'wandering' and the multiple connections highlighted by postcolonial researchers are often seen as a form of 'homelessness'; this explains the field's isolation within a research context where interdisciplinary communication and research are more often the exception than the rule. The importance of the institutional context is reinforced by the opposition of several French Africanists, as well as scholars of the 'fait colonial' [the fact of colonialism] or of immigration. In our view, such hostility is a result of the hierarchical nature of French higher-level institutions: in this context, postcolonial research is often perceived as an institutional threat from younger researchers working on issues that an older generation has never addressed and has no interest in promoting.

If postcolonial thought has inherited theoretical and analytical models of thought from anti-colonial intellectuals, it also draws on Western philosophy and on the disciplinary paradigms of the social sciences as elaborated in Europe. The diverse disciplinary and theoretical origins of postcolonial theory have led to a fragmented body of thought that nonetheless proposes a coherent critical understanding of how blinkered Western reasoning and narrow conceptions of universalism and humanism operate within colonial discourse. However, within the French academic context, this critical perspective, which has been central to postcolonial studies, was very quickly understood as a broader questioning of the role of 'traditional' academic thought in the study of the 'fait colonial'. In this regard, some of the works cited above have been seen to constitute a form of transgression that is both chronological and methodological: chronological in their radical revision of the 'break' between the colonial and the postcolonial eras; methodological in the way they understand the colonial period as a system of dialectical exchanges between the colonized and the colonizer, the consequences of which can be evinced both in the colonial territories *and* in the metropole.

French academic opposition to postcolonial research emerges from two distinct theoretical traditions. The first, relatively classical one is based on the notion of inviolable interpretative concepts. Thus, for example, the primary

2   For a very well-documented critique of Lefeuvre's text, see Catherine Coquery-Vidrovitch's review article. Available athttp://cvuh.free.fr/spip.php?article73 (consulted on 27 February 2008).

importance accorded to economic factors entails the subjugation of cultural phenomena to the struggle between social classes; this struggle is, in turn, over-determined by the violence of market capitalism. Thus, the 'reemergence of the colonial' within the metropole is deemed 'marginal': phenomena such as the emergence of hybrid identities or of complex forms of historical memory are cast as insignificant, and they are, in any case, products of the 'superstructure' (see Bertrand, 2006; Chrétien, 2006). Behind these approaches hangs the immense shadow of Marxism, and the critical approaches to which it has given rise, which encourage, on occasion, not only a teleological link between 'infrastructure' and 'superstructure' but also a restrictive conception of the perspectives opened up by the *École des Annales* (that is, the 'supremacy' of economic and social history, and the development of a long-term historical frame).

The second theoretical position informing resistance to postcolonial theory posits a radical break between the metropole and its colonies. It is possible to discern in this position the weight of several decades of critical practice, which have cast France and its former colonies in Africa as completely distinct entities: intellectual tools were forged almost 40 years ago in order specifically to analyse African societies, and these were, consequently, considered inapplicable to the metropolitan context: as early as 1992, Daniel Rivet argued in a pioneering article that 'le phénomène colonial souffre de rester sous-analysé et gommé dans le territoire de l'historien' [the phenomenon of colonialism remains under-analysed and erased in historical debate] (Rivet, 1992: 127–38). We are not referring here to questions of power, although the colonial situation offers a striking example of a completely asymmetrical power relationship between colonizer and colonized, even if strategies of resistance, indifference, temporization, or alliances with the colonial powers have been widely studied. Rather, we are concerned with the specific nature of those colonial and postcolonial migrations mentioned above, and with cross-community relationships such as those in the *banlieues* [France's deprived suburbs]. France is a republic and it is thus inconceivable for society to be seen in terms of 'communities', despite the fact that communities exist and, increasingly, people see themselves, and are thought of as, belonging to one. While some may regret this historical development, one cannot deny its existence, which has grown more pronounced over recent years and has become the focus of a significant number of sociological studies.[3]

The *conservative* reaction to the presence of any postcolonial element in interpretations of the colonial past and, moreover, of its legacy in the present, is exemplified in a recent article by Emmanuelle Sibeud (2004), in which the author sets out a systematic – albeit very academic – critique of postcolonial thought by 'listing' all of the 'French' received ideas concerning this approach (indeed, this is what makes the text instructive!). However, this carefully reasoned catalogue of criticisms also reveals the main barriers to the development of postcolonial

---

3   On the situation in French *banlieues*, see Vieillard-Baron, 1994; Costa-Lacoux, 2001; Bui-Trong, 2003; Richard, 2004; Maurin, 2005.

studies in France; these were set in place as early as 2004 and still function today. Thus, according to her analysis, postcolonial studies lies somewhere between a 'theoretical project' and a 'political' position, and it is subject to an unquestionable 'gauchissement' [left-wing tendency]. For Sibeud, these developments remain 'very exotic' and also 'mysterious' (2004: 87); postcolonialism's theoretical references are heterogeneous and especially 'jargonnantes' [jargonistic] (87); its vision is restricted to a 'binary' logic that privileges the confrontation between 'them' and 'us' (87), and encourages 'une interprétation assez manichéenne de l'histoire et du présent' [a quite Manichean interpretation of history and the present] (91). In conclusion, Sibeud explains that postcolonial studies 'voient du colonialisme partout' [sees colonialism everywhere] (93), whereas the academic study of colonial history (colonial studies) 's'efforce de mesurer avec précision [les] incidences [du fait colonial] dans les sociétés colonisées et colonisatrices' [endeavours to measure accurately [the] influence [of the 'fait colonial'] on colonized and colonizing societies] (93). In short, postcolonial studies is a 'globalisation militante de l'histoire contemporaine' [militant globalization of contemporary history] in the service of an anti-colonialist 'rearguard' that is clearly 'mystificateur' [delights in obfuscation] (94).[4]

The accusation is clear, the criticism virulent and the fault line conspicuous. It is obvious that the problem facing a large number of French researchers working in this area is that while in essence it is permissible to speak of 'postcolonial societies' when dealing with the formerly colonized territories, the term is not deemed apposite when dealing with the 'ex-metropole'. (Scholars such as Sibeud are products of a younger generation of French scholars, which suggests that the problem here is not a generational one.) In other words, postcolonial studies is deemed to serve an ideological purpose, rather than purely to develop the field of 'objective' knowledge. Indeed Sibeud's pithy accusation that this critical field 'sees colonialism everywhere' compels postcolonial studies researchers to prove constantly that this is not their aim. Clearly, such a task goes beyond the ability of the individual researcher, but it has, nonetheless, become a necessary process in combating the prevailing conservatism regarding postcolonial theory.

Another strong criticism of the postcolonial approach concerns its lack of attention to the social context. For instance, Alexandre Mamarbachi writes in relation to *La Fracture coloniale* that 'ce livre révèle aussi les limites d'une démarche qui, se focalisant sur la postcolonialité, détache celle-ci des processus sociaux dans lesquels elle s'inscrit' [this book also reveals the limits of an approach, which, in focusing on postcoloniality, removes this very issue from the social processes that frame it] (2006: 145). Mamarbachi does recognize that *La Fracture coloniale* 'fournit un ensemble assez riche d'analyses qui rendent intelligibles des phénomènes qui nous concernent dans leur actualité' [provides quite a rich collection of analyses that provide an insight into phenomena that still concern

---

4 For an analysis of this same question but from an opposing point of view, see Gilbert (1997).

us today] (143), yet argues that these legacies of the colonial era are presented in a manner that dissociates them too neatly from their social context, and he concludes by arguing that it is precisely 'les conditions matérielles dans lesquelles ces phénomènes s'inscrivent' [the material conditions that frame these phenomena] (148) that must be taken into account. This critical standpoint claims that the postcolonial approach ignores the social and economic dimensions of the issues it raises. However, such a criticism is completely unfounded, given that postcolonial theory endeavours to take account of a range of historical factors (social, economic, political, cultural) without, it is true, privileging any of them.

Finally, opposition to postcolonial studies takes a more virulent form in another strand of French thought, for example in the journal *Politique africaine* or in Romain Bertrand's *Mémoires d'empire* (2006). In this work, there is a constant anxiety that new approaches such as postcolonial studies posit a profound threat to established academic structures. This institutional apprehensiveness concerning the questions raised by postcolonial studies, and the crisis of 'legitimacy' that is posed by this rival approach to the 'colonial field', can take various forms; the persistent defence of long-term historical perspectives that are deemed inviolable (i.e., the 'longue durée' approach); resorting to social explanation as the ultimate goal of historical analysis. In turn, postcolonial studies is critiqued for the alleged absence of social issues, and the erroneous accusation that the postcolonial has no interest in such questions; the postcolonial induces a confusion between the goal and its predicted political consequences (certain historical objectives are potentially dangerous and are therefore better left unexplored). These arguments constitute a type of 'Atlantic wall' around the 'fait colonial', as if the postcolonial approach has as its goal to call into question the validity of all historical work in relation to the 'fait colonial'.

What this evidence suggests is that a significant number of French researchers working on the 'fait colonial' or immigration have failed to grasp that the 'shift' implied by postcolonial studies is not temporal – coming after ('post') the colonial era – but instead marks the aim of reflecting upon colonial history beyond both the limits of established chronologies and the usual intellectual paradigms concerning the North/South divide. In the process, postcolonial studies suggests that there is only 'one world' in which the relationship between the dominant and the dominated evolves and transforms itself, and in which multicultural diasporas create links and bridges not only between the West's present and the formerly colonized worlds, but also between the colonial past and the contemporary world. This constellation of ideas and approaches gives rise to an intense 'translation of cultures' or movement towards cultures that underlies our multicultural and hybrid world (see Dirks, 1992).

Rethinking the republican and inviolable 'nation'

French academic resistance to postcolonial theory does not rest solely on these 'scientific' conflicts of opinion, but equally, and more implicitly, on notions of the nation and the republic. Following deconstructive practices, postcolonial thought highlights on the one hand the violence resulting from a hegemonic use of reason, of which colonialism is one manifestation, and on the other, the disjuncture between a particular form of European ethics and the implementation of a set of colonial and postcolonial politics and practices characterized by extreme violence, both real and symbolic. In the French context, this requires an examination of hexagonal discourses of the past, or the 'national narrative'. A postcolonial approach permits us to question the dual nature of French discourse concerning its own identity and the wider world, and also to identify the gap between avowed republican humanism and the ease with which the lives, work, cultures and subjectivity of colonized peoples were repeatedly sacrificed.

Furthermore, at the heart of this deconstructive task, the notions of 'race' and 'identity' are shown to be omnipresent in colonial discourse as explanatory tools, as a method for controlling the colonized, and as everyday social practices (see Bayart, 1996; Dupin, 2004). They serve an explanatory purpose across a range of literary, philosophical and dramatic discursive fields/formations. Equally, they serve as a means of control made manifest within the legal, political and administrative apparatus of colonialism, within everyday practices of exploitation, and they are mainstays of the systematic debasement and denial of the Other that flourished in the colonized world. In order to understand how humanism can so easily coincide with the succession of humiliations and crimes that characterize the colonial situation, and form the framework for the denial of the colonized's subjectivity, postcolonial thought suggests that humanism is underwritten by something akin to 'self-hatred'. In this context, racism becomes a transference of this self-hatred on to the colonized, a means for the colonizer to affirm his/her own life through the power s/he exercises over the lives of the inferior colonized.

This thesis regarding the colonial situation has met with strong resistance in France (see Raybaud, 1997). If a large majority of public opinion, including the intellectual elite, does not go quite as far as defending a 'positive' view of colonization, over the last decade there has, nonetheless, been a desire to 'rehabilitate' the colonial project, to deny the link between colonialism and racial hierarchies by proposing a humanist vision of France's colonial activity. This denial has formed the basis for the reactivation of a discourse regarding France's 'civilizing mission', demonstrated most prominently by the law of 23 February, 2005, but also by several museum projects aiming to present the colonial past in a 'positive' light. To be sure, the relaunching of this discourse is a less frequent feature of the academic world than it is of controversial publications within the wider 'intellectual field'. In this latter category, one finds successful authors such as Max Gallo, a member of the Académie Française, whose hastily written pamphlet *Fier d'être Français* [Proud to be French] (Gallo, 2006) describes itself as a scathing polemic in defence of a 'France' that must not 'hang its head' in shame. Similarly, the essayist Pascal Bruckner (2006) predicts – through a series of systematically spurious amalgamations – that wallowing in 'colonial guilt' will lead to France's inevitable decline (and also, for good measure, to that of the entire West). These, and numerous other works in the same vein, such as Paul-François Paoli's *Nous ne sommes pas coupables* [We are not guilty] (2006), constitute the most visible aspect of this intellectual resistance, which objects to the development of postcolonial research in France by labelling it as 'destructive' of national and republican cohesion.

In *Orientalism* (1978), Edward Said deconstructs colonial discourse by analysing the imaginary, representative and symbolic forms that underpinned the imperial project and legitimized its domination of the colonies. From this same perspective, postcolonial researchers reveal the power of this discourse to distort, and the impact of its lies and myth-making strategies, without which colonialism, as a historical configuration of power, would have failed. In this way postcolonial theory seeks to elucidate the manner in which the transposition of so-called European humanism to the colonies is consistently marked by duplicity, doublespeak and the distortion of 'reality'. In other words, postcolonial approaches propose the deconstruction of French colonial thought in the shape of its republican 'civilizing mission'. Work on the 'colonial republic' touches upon a veritable taboo by appearing to question both the 'republican pact' and the fundamental values on which modern French democracy rests. Consequently, the rejection of a historical perspective seeking to understand the simultaneous development of republican principles and colonial practices since the Third Republic galvanizes not just reactionary intellectuals, but also academics, in particular certain historians (e.g. Lefeuvre, 2006; Rioux, 2006).

An exchange on the notion of 'Fraternity' published in a recent special issue of *Télérama* (2007: 58–62), in which the contributors explore the boundaries of a nationalist, republican history, offers a more enlightened vision of these debates. Dominique Schnapper reminds us that there was clearly a contradiction 'entre le projet républicain et le projet colonial, qui aboutissait à créer deux catégories de citoyens' [between the republican and the colonial projects that led to the creation of two categories of citizen]. However, Schnapper goes on to reaffirm the essential principle: 'L'utopie républicaine est en tant que telle la seule idée dont nous disposions pour créer une société humaine convenable' [The republican utopia is the only idea we had at our disposal in order to create a decent human society.] Similarly Denis Sieffert states that the 'republican idea' was 'pervertie par le colonialisme, par le mythe d'un universalisme que l'on pourrait imposer' [perverted by colonialism, by the myth of a universalism it was believed could be imposed] and Christophe Prochassen speaks of 'cette monstruosité juridique' [legal monstrosity] constituted by the 'code indigène'. In essence, these analyses differ little from works on the 'colonial republic'. For example Denis Sieffert also analyses the intellectual impasse produced by the controversy surrounding the 'colonial republic': 'L'argument républicain, avec une définition jamais énoncée, [est] juste une manière de clore la discussion en excluant tout contradicteur' [the republican argument, which remains undefined, [is] simply a means to silence debate by excluding those who contradict it]. And finally, Schnapper submits that 'ceux qui s'affirment républicains ne le sont pas plus que les autres, et ceux qui les attaquent ne le sont pas moins qu'eux [those who declare themselves to be republicans are no more so than others, and those who attack them are no less so].

Intellectual obstacles

There can be no doubt that the barriers facing postcolonial studies are embedded within the wider context of French society, and accusations of anti-republicanism are symptomatic of the specific form that opposition to the postcolonial is taking. This is not to reduce the Republic to a purely colonial status; however, alongside its humanist and anti-colonialist actions, the Republic was quite clearly a colonial one. Indeed, if the Republic has at times appeared out of tune with its own principles, this does not mean that the values established by the French Revolution are somehow obsolete. However, this is an ethical question and not a historical one. To brandish the republican flag each time the colonial question is raised is symptomatic of the deliberately muddled thinking that attempts to shut down debate. In this regard, the principle of self-defence – as employed by Romain Bertrand, for example – prevents any understanding of postcolonialism and reveals a blind spot rather than a genuinely republican critical stance.

Admittedly, our own position within this debate is not entirely neutral, given that our aim throughout various projects has been to influence positively French perceptions of postcolonial thought. Publications such as *La République coloniale* (Bancel et al., 2003), the trilogy *Culture coloniale* (Blanchard and Lemaire, 2003), *Culture impériale* (Blanchard and Lemaire, 2004), *Culture post-coloniale* (Blanchard and Bancel, 2006), and works on the migration of colonial diasporas to France have all sought to clear a space for this critical approach within French research culture. *La Fracture coloniale* (Blanchard et al., 2005) undoubtedly represents our most successful attempt to achieve this, and its publication gave rise in France to criticism of an unprecedented virulence. Certain of these criticisms have prompted us to reflect upon our own work but, more significantly, they explicitly reveal the intellectual and institutional issues surrounding the debates highlighted by the various analyses in the volume. The situation in France – its 'exceptionalism' perhaps – appears all the more surprising, given that postcolonial studies borrows heavily from those French thinkers, such as Levinas, Merleau-Ponty, Sartre, de Certeau and, more recently, Foucault or Derrida, who have explored the notion of alterity; they also borrow from Francophone thinkers such as Fanon, Memmi and, more marginally, Sayad. And yet institutional and intellectual resistance to postcolonial perspectives within France indicates indirectly that the legacy of these key players in post-war critical thought has been denied as though it were irrelevant to the analysis of colonial and postcolonial situations. However the difficulties currently faced by postcolonial studies in France is more complex than a simple retreat into itself by a section of the French academy, even if such a move cannot be neglected. Rather, the problem is located in a jealously guarded cultural isolationism that is characterized by a form of suspicion that sometimes tips over into an arrogant rejection of the new critical perspectives that feed – often in highly contested fashion – into contemporary patterns of global thought.

As we have illustrated throughout this chapter, conservative attitudes towards postcolonial studies in France are consolidated by presenting this new field as being too simplistic (Bertrand, 2006; Chrétien, 2006), overly theoretical, or insufficiently empirical (Sibeud, 2004), criticisms that simply cannot be supported when the wide range of critical work within the field is taken into account. Postcolonial theory has also been presented as 'ideological' (Lefeuvre, 2006), as being in the service of political thought (Keslassy and Rosenbaum, 2007), and as fundamentally opposed to 'la pensée historique française' [French historical thought] (Bruckner, 2006; Gallo, 2006). The colonial past and the slave trade are, therefore, relegated to an historical limbo, and the impact of colonial realities on French culture is deemed an aberrant hypothesis.

And yet, if we were to apply the premises of postcolonial theory to a French context, it could be ventured that since the periods of the slave trade and of colonization all notions of French identity and French 'lieux de mémoire' [sites of memory] involve the simultaneous consideration of 'here' and 'elsewhere'. In other words, elsewhere is constitutive of here, and vice versa. There is no longer an 'inside' that exists in isolation from an 'outside', a past that is not linked to the present. Contemporary French critical thought no longer knows how to speak *of* the Other, much less *to* the Other. It generally prefers, in the 'good, old-fashioned colonial way', to speak *for* the Other, with well-documented catastrophic results, such as the surreal debate on the positive effects of colonization (as in the law of 23 February 2005, cited above).

In conclusion, it would seem that postcolonial studies has only managed to gain legitimacy in English-language contexts, for France has refused, over the past two decades, to contemplate the insights it offers. In addition to the above-mentioned conservatism in French universities, the rejection of this critical approach could also be seen as an act of defiance in the face of a current of thought that proposes a critical interpretation of universalism, and a profound questioning of the 'national narrative' and republican history. Once this obstacle has been overcome, it is to be hoped that the situation will change.

In the field of intellectual and scholarly debate, it is difficult to imagine just how deep is the incomprehension, and sometimes indignation, that this conservatism has sparked on the part of certain researchers, often from the 'South', in relation to research in France; equally, our backwardness in comparison to the world of English-language research is only barely beginning to be realized. This withdrawal from the world, this inability to look outside France, to accept and to open up to other approaches – which does not prevent us from adopting a healthy scepticism towards these ideas – is forcing France to turn ever more firmly inwards, to idealize its past and to view the postcolonial perspective as potentially destabilizing for the nation itself. Consequently, there is no doubt that France is ripe for the postcolonial approach.[5]

Further reading

Bancel, Nicolas, Pascal Blanchard and Françoise Vergès, 2003. *La République coloniale: essai sur une utopie* (Paris: Albin Michel). This volume analyses the complex relationship between modern republican ideology – informed by a discourse of rationality, progress and emancipation – and the colonial framework. The encounter between republicanism and colonialism in the late nineteenth century led republicans to rally to the colonial project, and to create a colonial-republican discourse, which legitimized colonization as the accomplishment of France's 'civilizing mission'. *La République coloniale* explores the gaps between this discourse and specific colonial practices, while also attempting to understand the legacy of this encounter for the postcolonial period.

Blanchard, Pascal, Nicolas Bancel and Sandrine Lemaire (eds), 2005. *La Fracture coloniale: la société française au prisme de l'héritage colonial* (Paris: La Découverte). Using diverse forms of analysis, the essays in this volume explore the relationship between the colonial and postcolonial periods in France, and examine the ways in which colonial memory is avoided or erased. This was the first text in the social sciences in France to adopt an explicitly postcolonial perspective, and it gave rise to extremely polemical reactions, which reveal the tensions and the blockages surrounding the memory of colonialism.

Boubeker, Ahmed, 1999. *Familles de l'intégration: les ritournelles de l'ethnicité en pays jacobin* (Paris: Stock). Boubeker's book is the result of a sustained period of fieldwork, which permitted the author to address some of the most pressing issues facing second- and third-generation members of postcolonial immigrant minorities. Boubeker analyses with great incisiveness the construction of immigrant social identities within the context of a markedly 'Jacobin' France.

Lefeuvre, Daniel, 2006. *Pour en finir avec la repentance coloniale* (Paris: Flammarion). In this polemical volume, Lefeuvre uses incomplete statistics, hasty generalizations, outrageous simplifications and the 'liberal' interpretation of various 'facts' to denounce a 'hypothetical' group of 'penitents', whose alleged aim is to destroy the French republican social model. He also challenges what he sees as the exaggeration that characterizes certain historical accounts of some of the most tragic colonial episodes, and he downplays the social and economic importance of colonial and postcolonial immigration to France. Lefeuvre's position is representative of the extreme hostility towards postcolonial and subaltern studies that exists among certain members of the French intelligentsia.

---

5   Sections of this chapter are based on Nicolas Bancel's introduction to the dossier 'Retours sur la question coloniale' published by the journal *Cultures Sud* (Bancel, 2007) and on Pascal Blanchard's contribution to this same volume (Blanchard, 2007).

Notes on Contributors

Nicolas Bancel is currently Professor of History at the Universities of Strasbourg 2 and Lausanne. He is also a researcher in three pan-European research networks, and is vice-president of the research group ACHAC. He is a specialist on colonial and postcolonial history, and in particular on the representation of the body within these contexts. In works such as *Images et Colonies* (1993) and *La République coloniale* (2003), he has worked on the construction of colonial ideology and the colonial imaginary through the elaboration of discourses and systems of representation. Equally, in *Zoos humains* (2002) and *De l'Indochine à l'Algérie* (2003) he has examined various cultural formations that have contributed to the development of a 'colonial culture' in France. He has also studied the complex relationship between the colonial and postcolonial periods, in order to trace the legacy of imperialism in contemporary France: *De l'indigène à l'immigré* (1998), *La Fracture coloniale* (2005), *Culture post-coloniale* (2006), *Retours sur la question coloniale* (2007).

Pascal Blanchard is an historian, an associate member of the research groups on the Anthropology of Representations of the Body (GDR 2322, CNRS, Marseille) and the Laboratoire de Communication et Politique (UPR 3255, CNRS, Paris) and is also president of ACHAC (Paris). He works primarily on the ideology of colonial representation, as well as on the presence of the 'South' in the former metropolitan centre. He is the author and co-author of several volumes analysing these issues: *Images et Colonies* (1993); *De l'indigène à l'immigré* (1998; new edition, 2007); *Zoos humains* (2002; new edition 2004), an updated English version of which appeared in 2008 from Liverpool University Press; *La République coloniale* (2003); *La Colonisation française* (2007). He has co-edited a series of three volumes for the publisher Autrement – *Culture coloniale* (2003), *Culture impériale* (2004) and *Culture post-coloniale* (2006); these three works were republished in a single, updated volume by CNRS Éditions in 2008 under the title

Culture coloniale en France – and he also co-edited the highly influential volumes, *La Fracture coloniale* (2005) and *Les Guerres de mémoire* (La Découverte, 2008). Finally, he has made several documentary films, including *Zoos humains* (Arte, 2002), *Paris couleurs: un siècle d'immigration dans la capitale* (France 3, 2006) and, most recently, *Des Noirs en couleur: la saga des joueurs afro-caribéens et calédoniens en équipe de France de football* (1930–2008) (Canal+, 2008).

Chris Bongie is Full Professor and Queen's National Scholar in the English Department at Queen's University in Canada. He is the author of two monographs published with Stanford University Press: *Literature, Colonialism and the Fin de siècle* (1991) and *Islands and Exiles: The Creole Identities of Post/Colonial Literature* (1998). He has translated Victor Hugo's novel *Bug-Jargal* into English (Broadview Press, 2004), and produced an edition of the first two novels about the Haitian Revolution, Jean-Baptiste Picquenard's *Adonis* and *Zoflora* (L'Harmattan, 2006). His latest book is *Friends and Enemies: The Scribal Politics of Post/Colonial Literature* (Liverpool University Press, 2008).

Patrick Crowley is Lecturer in French at University College Cork. His teaching and research concentrates on contemporary writing and thought addressing issues such as identity, form and the legacies of colonialism. He is the author of *Pierre Michon: The Afterlife of Names* (2007) and co-editor of *Formless: Ways In and Out of Form* (2005). He has written articles on writers such as Eugène Savitzkaya, Kateb Yacine, Patrick Chamoiseau and Édouard Glissant, as well as on contemporary Algerian cinema.

Pascale De Souza is currently leading the French Programme at SAIS-Johns Hopkins University. She has published essays in journals such as *Comparative Literature Studies*, *French Studies*, *MaComère*, *Oeuvres et Critiques*, *Romantic Review*, and *Studies in Twentieth-Century Literature*, as well as chapters in *Penser la créolité*, *A Pepper-pot of Cultures*, *Maryse Condé: une nomade inconvenante* and *Emerging Perspectives on Maryse Condé*. She has co-edited three special issues for the *Journal of Caribbean Literatures*, focusing on comparative Caribbean literatures and French Caribbean literature, and two issues of the *International Journal of Francophone Studies* focusing respectively on the Black Atlantic in French overseas literatures and on the representation of migration and *métissage* in South Pacific literatures. Her current research explores links and dissonances between various island literatures, with a focus on the Caribbean, the Mascarenes and the South Pacific.

Philip Dine is a Senior Lecturer in French at the National University of Ireland, Galway. He is the author of *Images of the Algerian War: French Fiction and Film, 1954–1992* (Clarendon Press; Oxford University Press, 1994). He has published widely on representations of the French colonial empire, including, particularly, decolonization, in fields ranging from children's literature to professional sport. Other published research includes *French Rugby Football: A Cultural History* (Berg, 2001), as part of a broader reflection on leisure and popular culture in France. He is currently working on a survey of sport and identity in France funded by the Irish Research Council for the Humanities and Social Sciences (2006–09).

Laurent Dubois, a specialist in the history and culture of France and the Caribbean, is Professor of History and Romance Studies at Duke University. He is the author of *Avengers of the New World: The Story of the Haitian Revolution* and *A Colony of Citizens: Revolution and Slave Emancipation in the French Caribbean, 1787–1804*, which won four book awards, including the Frederick Douglass Prize. With Richard Turits, he is currently working on a general history of the Caribbean (under contract with University of North Carolina Press). He is also writing a history of the banjo (under contract with Harvard University Press), and a book on soccer, race and the legacies of empire and in contemporary France (under contract with University of California Press).

Charles Forsdick is James Barrow Professor of French at the University of Liverpool. His publications include *Victor Segalen and the Aesthetics of Diversity* (Oxford University Press, 2000) and *Travel in Twentieth-Century French and Francophone Cultures* (Oxford University Press, 2005). He is co-editor (with David Murphy) of *Francophone Postcolonial Studies: A Critical Introduction* (Arnold, 2003).

Pierre-Philippe Fraiture is Associate Professor of French at the University of Warwick, where he teaches French and Francophone literatures. His research focuses on sub-Saharan Africa, modernity and (post)colonialism. His main publications are: *Le Congo belge et son récit francophone à la veille des indépendances: sous l'empire du royaume* (2003); *La Mesure de l'autre: Afrique subsaharienne et roman ethnographique de Belgique et de France (1918–1940)* (2007). He has also co-edited volumes of essays on the Belgian fin de siècle and modernity. He is currently writing a monograph on Valentin Yves Mudimbe, and is co-editor of the journal *Francophone Postcolonial Studies*.

Mary Gallagher is Associate Professor of French and Francophone Studies at University College Dublin. She is the author of *La Créolité de Saint-John Perse* (Gallimard, 1998) and *Soundings in French Caribbean Writing since 1950* (Oxford University Press, 2002). Her critical editions of the French translations of Lafcadio Hearn's *Two Years in the French West Indies* appeared with L'Harmattan: *Esquisses martiniquaises* I and II (2003) and *Un voyage d'été aux tropiques* (2004). She is the editor of *Ici-Là: Place and Displacement in Caribbean Writing in French* (Rodopi, 2003) and of *World Writing: Poetics, Ethics, Globalization* (University of Toronto Press, 2008), and is co-editor (with Michael Brophy) of *Sens et présence du sujet poétique: la poésie de la France et du monde francophone depuis 1980* (Rodopi, 2006) and (with Phyllis Gaffney and Michael Brophy) of *Reverberations: Staging Relations in French since 1500* (University College Dublin Press, 2008). She is currently writing a monograph on Lafcadio Hearn's Creole odyssey.

Mary Jean Green is the Edward Tuck Professor of French at Dartmouth College (New Hampshire), where she also teaches in Women's and Gender Studies and Comparative Literature. The author of a number of articles on Quebec fiction and film, she has published on the tradition of Quebec women's writing in her book, *Women and Narrative Identity: Rewriting the Quebec National Text*. Her earlier book,

Marie-Claire Blais, was an overview of the work of one of Quebec's most prominent women novelists. Green was active in the creation of the American Council
for Quebec Studies, an interdisciplinary association that brings together US
academics whose work is focused on Quebec, and she was the founding editor
of the Council's journal, *Québec Studies*. In addition to her work on Québec literature, she has published on contemporary writers and filmmakers in France and
other French-speaking regions. She is currently working on a study of women
and the writing of history in the Francophone world, which will focus on Maryse
Condé, Assia Djebar, Anne Hébert and Régine Robin.

Nicholas Harrison is Professor of French Studies and Postcolonial Literature at
King's College London. He studied at the University of Cambridge, worked as
a lecteur in Tunis, Quebec and Paris, and held lectureships at Cambridge and
UCL before moving to King's. His publications include two books, *Circles of
Censorship: Censorship and its Metaphors in French History, Literature, and Theory*
(Oxford University Press, 1995) and *Postcolonial Criticism: History, Theory and the
Work of Fiction* (Polity Press, 2003), and, as editor, two collections of essays,
The Idea of the Literary, a special issue of *Paragraph* (Edinburgh University Press,
2005), and a special issue of *Interventions: International Journal of Postcolonial
Studies* (November 2007), entitled *Pontecorvo's Battle of Algiers, 40 Years On*. His
next project is on secularism and colonial education in North Africa.

Jane Hiddleston is a CUF Lecturer at the University of Oxford, and Fellow of
Exeter College. She has published two books, *Reinventing Community: Identity and
Difference in Late Twentieth Century Philosophy and Literature in French* (Legenda,
2005) and *Assia Djebar: Out of Algeria* (Liverpool University Press, 2006). She is
currently working on a study of the relation between poststructuralism and
postcolonial thought.

Typhaine Leservot is Assistant Professor in the Romance Languages and
Literatures Department (French) and College of Letters at Wesleyan University in
Middletown, Connecticut. She specializes in the intersection of globalization and
Francophone postcolonial studies. Her book *Le Corps mondialisé: Marie Redonnet,
Maryse Condé, Assia Djebar* was published in December 2007 by L'Harmattan.
Her latest article on Maryse Condé, 'Accident and the Postcolonial Subject in
Condé's Detective Fiction', appeared in *Women in French Studies* in 2008 and is
part of a larger project on the impact of globalization on postcolonial theory.

David Murphy is Professor of French and Postcolonial Studies at the University
of Stirling. He has published widely on African literature and cinema, as well
as on the relationship between Francophone studies and postcolonial theory,
in journals such as *French Cultural Studies*, *New Left Review*, *L'Esprit Créateur*,
New Formations and *Research in African Literatures*. He is the author of *Sembene:
Imagining Alternatives in Film and Fiction* (James Currey, 2000), and is co-author
(with Patrick Williams) of *Postcolonial African Cinema: Ten Directors* (Manchester
University Press, 2007). He is also co-editor (with Aedín Ní Loingsigh) of

Thresholds of Otherness (Grant & Cutler, 2002), and (with Charles Forsdick) *Francophone Postcolonial Studies: A Critical Introduction* (Arnold, 2003). He is currently preparing a critical edition of Lamine Senghor's *La Violation d'un pays* for L'Harmattan's 'Autrement Mêmes' series.

Panivong Norindr teaches French and Comparative Literature and chairs the Department of French and Italian at the University of Southern California. He is the author of *Phantasmatic Indochina: French Colonial Ideology in Architecture, Film, and Literature* (Duke University Press, 1996). His most recent essays are entitled: 'Angkor filmée: de l'exotisme à l'identité nationale', in Hughes Tertrais's edited volume, *Angkor VIII–XXIe siècle* (Autrement, 2008), and 'On Photography, History, and Affect: Re-Narrating the Political Life of a Laotian Subject', in *Historical Reflections* 34.1 (2008).

Alison Rice teaches twentieth- and twenty-first-century French and Francophone literature and film at the University of Notre Dame. She has research interests in autobiography, critical theory, postcolonial studies, immigrant and second-generation literature, translation theory, contemporary women's writing, music in literature and 'Francophonie' in its widest sense. Her publications include articles in *PMLA*, *Expressions maghrébines*, *Contemporary French and Francophone Studies* and the *International Journal of Francophone Studies*. Her essay 'The Improper Name: Ownership and Authorship in the Literary Production of Assia Djebar', in *Assia Djebar: Studien zur Literatur und Geschichte des Maghreb* (Verlag Königshausen & Neumann, 2001), was awarded the 2002 Florence Howe Award for Feminist Scholarship. Her recent book, *Time Signatures: Contextualizing Contemporary Francophone Autobiographical Writing from the Maghreb* (Lexington Books, 2006), closely examines the writing of Hélène Cixous, Assia Djebar and Abdelkébir Khatibi. Her current project, 'Metronomes: Francophone Women Writers in Paris. A Series of Filmed Interviews', is an in-depth study of women writers of French from around the world.

David Richards is Professor of English Studies and Director of the Centre of Commonwealth Studies at the University of Stirling. His chief research interests are in the areas of colonial and postcolonial literature, anthropology, art history and cultural theory. His published work includes studies of individual writers, the representation of other cultures in literature, anthropology and art, and cultural production in postcolonial cities. He is also a member of the editorial boards of several journals. He is currently completing a monograph on the cultural history of the archaic, which will examine the role of anthropology and (more centrally) archaeology in modernism and postcolonialism over the period from 1875 to the present. He is also developing an interdisciplinary collaborative project on the politics of memory.

Max Silverman is Professor of Modern French Studies at the University of Leeds. He is a specialist in the areas of: post-Holocaust culture; colonial and postcolonial theory and cultures; cultural theory and debates; and immigration, race, nation and citizenship. He has written two monographs, *Deconstructing the*

Nation: Immigration, Racism and Citizenship in Modern France (Routledge, 1992) and *Facing Postmodernity: Contemporary French Thought on Culture and Society* (Routledge, 1999), has edited two collections of essays, *Race, Discourse and Power in France* (Avebury, 1991) and *Frantz Fanon's 'Black Skin, White Masks'* (Manchester University Press, 2005), and has published numerous chapters in books and journal articles on the above topics. At present he is working on connections between the Holocaust and colonialism in the French cultural imaginary, and a four-year, AHRC-funded project (in collaboration with Griselda Pollock) entitled 'Concentrationary memories and the politics of representation'.

Tyler Stovall is a professor of French history at the University of California, Berkeley. He gained his PhD from the University of Wisconsin-Madison, and has taught at Ohio State University, the University of California, Santa Cruz, and the Université française du Pacifique. He is the author and editor of several books and articles on French history and Francophone studies, including *Paris Noir: African Americans in the City of Light* (1996), and *The Color of Liberty: Histories of Race in France* (2003; co-edited with Sue Peabody). He is currently working on a study of Caribbean migration to metropolitan France.

Michael Syrotinski is Professor of French and Francophone Studies at the University of Aberdeen, and he has published widely on Francophone Africa and twentieth-century French literature and theory. He is co-founder, and until recently Associate Director, of the Centre for Modern Thought at Aberdeen. His previous books include *Defying Gravity: Jean Paulhan's Interventions in Twentieth Century French Intellectual History* (SUNY Press, 1998), *Singular Performances: Reinscribing the Subject in Francophone African Writing* (University of Virginia Press, 2002), *The Flowers of Tarbes, or Terror in Literature* (translation and critical edition of Jean Paulhan's *Les Fleurs de Tarbes, ou la Terreur dans les Lettres*, University of Illinois Press, 2006), and *Deconstruction and the Postcolonial: At the Limits of Theory* (Liverpool University Press, 2007). He has also published translations from the French of texts by, among others, Maurice Blanchot, Roger Caillois, Jacques Derrida, Jean-Luc Nancy, Jean Paulhan and Henri Thomas.

Richard Watts, Associate Professor of French and Francophone studies at the University of Washington, Seattle, studies the cultural artefacts that constitute *la francophonie* in its various guises. He is the author of *Packaging Post/Coloniality: The Manufacture of Literary Identity in the Francophone World* (Lexington Books, 2005), which considers how the packaging of a book – its cover, illustrations, dedications, and, most significantly, prefaces – allows it to pass from the post/colonial space of its production to the largely metropolitan space of its consumption, creating in the process the differentiated field now known as Francophone literature. His current project, *Water Narratives: Post/Colonial Representations of a Global Commodity,* considers the cultural meaning of water in the Francophone world. Written at the intersection of postcolonial studies and ecocriticism, this study aims to show how the pollution, privatization, and manufactured scarcity of water, experienced in the post/colonies as a legacy of colonialism, are rapidly

311

altering its previously stable symbolic value in literature, cinema and other forms of cultural production. He has published on these and other subjects in *Atlantic Studies*, *Modern Language Notes*, *Research in African Literatures*, *Traduction-Terminologie-Rédaction*, *French Forum* and *Sites*.

Patrick Williams is Professor of Literary and Cultural Studies at Nottingham Trent University, where he teaches courses on postcolonial theory and culture, diaspora, and race and nation in twentieth-century Britain. His publications include *Colonial Discourse and Post-Colonial Theory* (Columbia University Press, 1993); (with Peter Childs) *Introduction to Post-Colonial Theory* (Longman/Pearson, 1996); *Ngugi wa Thiong'o* (Manchester University Press, 1999); *Edward Said* (Sage, 2000); (with David Murphy) *Postcolonial African Cinema* (Manchester University Press, 2007).

Winifred Woodhull is Associate Professor of French and Cultural Studies at the University of California, San Diego, where she teaches literatures in French, Third World studies, critical gender studies, film, and diaspora studies. She has published widely on the literature, film, and cultures of Africa, the Caribbean and France.

Jennifer Yee is Tutor in French at the University of Oxford and Fellow of Christ Church. Her publications include *Clichés de la femme exotique: un regard sur la littérature coloniale française entre 1871 et 1914* (L'Harmattan, 2000); *Barnavaux aux colonies*, a re-edition of selected works by Pierre Mille (L'Harmattan, 2002); and edited volumes on nineteenth-century French literature and on France and 'Indochina'. Her most recent book is *Exotic Subversions in Nineteenth-Century French Literature* (Legenda, 2008). She has also published numerous articles on colonial literature, with a particular interest in the intersections of gender and racial difference, and in *métissage* in the literature of the nineteenth century. She is currently working on race and empire in the nineteenth-century realist novel.

Bibliography

Abélès, Marc, and Chantal Collard, 1985. *Âge, pouvoir et société en Afrique noire* (Paris: Karthala).

Adotevi, Stanislas, 1972. *Négritude et négrologues* (Paris: UGÉ).

Affergan, Francis, 1987. *Exotisme et altérité: essai sur les fondements d'une critique de l'anthropologie* (Paris: PUF).

Ageron, Charles-Robert, 1991. *La Décolonisation française* (Paris: Armand Colin).

Ahluwalia, Pal, 2005. 'Out of Africa: poststructuralism's colonial roots', *Postcolonial Studies*, 8.2: 137–54.

Ahmad, Aijaz, 1992. *In Theory: Classes, Nations, Literatures* (London: Verso).

——, 1995. 'The Politics of Literary Postcoloniality', *Race and Class*, 36.3: 1–20.

Aldrich, Robert, 1996. *Greater France: A History of French Overseas Expansion* (London: Macmillan).

——, 2005. *Vestiges of the Colonial Empire in France: Monuments, Museums and Colonial Memories* (Houndmills: Palgrave Macmillan).

Althabe, Gérard, 1969. *Oppression et libération dans l'imaginaire: les communautés villageoises de la côte orientale de Madagascar* (Paris: Maspero).

Althusser, Louis, 1984. *Essays on Ideology* (London: Verso).

Amselle, Jean-Loup, 1985. 'Ethnies et espaces: pour une anthropologie topologique', in Jean-Loup Amselle and Elikia M'Bokolo (eds), *Au cœur de l'ethnie: ethnies, tribalisme et état en Afrique* (Paris: La Découverte), 11–48

——, 1990. *Logiques métisses: anthropologie de l'identité en Afrique et ailleurs* (Paris: Payot).

Anderson, Benedict, 1983. *Imagined Communities: Reflections on the Origin and Spread of Nationalism* (London: Verso).

Angleviel, Frédéric, 2005. 'De l'engagement comme "esclavage volontaire", le cas des Océaniens, Kanaks et Asiatiques en Nouvelle-Calédonie (1853–1963)', *Journal de la Société des Océanistes*, 110.5: 65–81.

——, and Claire Laux, 2006. 'Le réseau associatif francophone en Océanie:

faiblesses en terres françaises, dynamisme en terres anglophones', in *Les Associations dans la Francophonie* (Bordeaux: Maison des sciences de l'homme d'Aquitaine), 75–89.

Apter, Emily, 1995. 'French Colonial Studies and Postcolonial Theory', *SubStance* 76–77: 169–80.

——, 1999. *Continental Drift: From National Characters to Virtual Subjects* (Chicago: University of Chicago Press).

——, 2006. '"Je ne crois pas beaucoup à la littérature comparée": universal poetics and postcolonial comparatism', in Saussy, 2006: 54–62.

Araujo, Nara (ed.), 1996. *L'Oeuvre de Maryse Condé: à propos d'une écrivaine politiquement incorrecte* (Paris: L'Harmattan).

Armes, Roy, 2005. *Postcolonial Images: Studies in North African Film* (Bloomington, IN: Indiana University Press).

Arnold, A. James, 1981. *Modernism and Négritude: The Poetry and Poetics of Aimé Césaire* (Cambridge, MA: Harvard University Press).

Aronson, Ronald, 1980. *Jean-Paul Sartre: Philosophy in the World* (London: New Left Books).

Ashcroft, Bill, Gareth Griffiths and Helen Tiffin, 1989. *The Empire Writes Back: Theory and Practice in Post-colonial Literatures* (London and New York: Routledge).

——, Gareth Griffiths and Helen Tiffin, 1995. *The Post-Colonial Studies Reader* (London and New York: Routledge).

——, Gareth Griffiths and Helen Tiffin (eds), 1998. *Key Concepts in Post-Colonial Studies* (London: Routledge).

Aubert de Gaspé, Philippe, 1979 [1863]. *Les Anciens Canadiens* (Montreal: Fides).

Augé, Marc, 1992. *Non-lieux* (Paris: Seuil).

——, 1999a [1994]. *An Anthropology for Contemporaneous Worlds*, tr. Amy Jacobs (Stanford, CA: Stanford University Press). [First published as *Pour une anthropologie des mondes contemporains*.]

——, 1999b [1997]. *The War of Dreams: Exercises in Ethno-fiction*, tr. Liz Heron (London: Pluto). [First published as *La Guerre des rêves: exercices d'ethno-fiction*.]

——, and Jean-Paul Colleyn, 2006 [2004]. *The World of the Anthropologist*, tr. John Howe (Oxford: Berg). [First published as *L'Anthropologie*.]

Balandier, Georges, 1955. *Sociologie des Brazzavilles noires* (Paris: Armand Colin).

——, 1966 [1957]. *Ambiguous Africa: Cultures in Collision*, tr. Helen Weaver (London: Chatto and Windus). [First published as *Afrique ambiguë*.]

——, 1970 [1967]. *Political Anthropology*, tr. A. M. Sheridan Smith (London: Penguin). [First published as *Anthropologie politique*.]

Bancel, Nicolas (ed.), 2007. *Cultures Sud*, 165. [Special issue: 'Retours sur la question coloniale'.]

——, and Pascal Blanchard, 2007. '*La Fracture coloniale*: retour sur une réaction', *Mouvements*, 51: 40–51.

——, Léla Bencharif and Pascal Blanchard, 2007. *Lyon, capitale des outre-mers* (Paris: La Découverte).

——, Pascal Blanchard and Françoise Vergès, 2003. *La République coloniale: essai sur une utopie* (Paris: Armand Colin).

——, Pascal Blanchard, Gilles Boëtsch, Éric Deroo and Sandrine Lemaire (eds), 2002. *Zoos humains: de la Vénus hottentote aux reality shows* (Paris: La Découverte).

Barbé-Marbius, François, 1977 [1830]. *The History of Louisiana* (Baton Rouge, LO: Louisiana State University Press).

Barbour, Sarah, and Gerise Herndon (eds.), 2006. *Emerging Perspectives on Maryse Condé: A Writer of Her Own*. (Trenton, NJ: Africa World Press).

Bardolph, Jacqueline, 2002. *Études postcoloniales et littérature* (Paris: Champion).

Barthes, Roland, 1972 [1957]. *Mythologies*, tr. Annette Lavers (London: Cape). [First published as *Mythologies*.]

——, 1977 [1975]. *Roland Barthes*, tr. Richard Howard (New York: Farrar, Strauss and Giroux). [First published as *Roland Barthes par Roland Barthes*.]

——, 1980 [1971]. 'Pierre Loti: *Aziyadé*', in *New Critical Essays*, tr. Richard Howard (New York: Hill and Wang), 105–21.

——, 1982 [1970]. *Empire of Signs*, tr. Richard Howard (London: Cape). [First published as *L'Empire des signes*.]

——, 1986–87 [1975]. 'Well, and China?', *Discourse* 8: 116–21. [First published as *Alors la Chine?*]

——, 1992 [1987]. *Incidents*, tr. Richard Howard (Berkeley, CA: University of California Press). [First published as *Incidents*.]

Bastié, Jean, 1964. *La Croissance de la banlieue parisienne* (Paris: PUF).

Bayart, Jean-Francois, 1996. *L'Illusion identitaire* (Paris: Fayard).

Beckett, Samuel, 1979 [1953]. *The Unnamable*, in *The Beckett Trilogy* (London: Picador). [First published as *L'Innommable*.]

Beniamino, Michel, and Lise Gauvin (eds), 2005. *Vocabulaire des études francophones: les concepts de base* (Limoges: PULIM).

Benítez-Rojo, Antonio, 1996. *The Repeating Island: The Caribbean and the Post-Modern Perspective* (Durham, NC: Duke University Press).

Bennington, Geoffrey, and Jacques Derrida, 1993 [1991]. *Jacques Derrida*, tr. Geoffrey Bennington (Chicago: University of Chicago Press). [First published as *Jacques Derrida*.]

Benot, Yves, 1992. *La Démence coloniale sous Napoléon: essai* (Paris: La Découverte).

——, 1994. *Massacres coloniaux, 1944–1950: la IVe République et la mise au pas des colonies françaises* (Paris: La Découverte).

Bensmaïa, Réda, 2003. *Experimental Nations: Or, the Invention of the Maghreb* (Princeton, NJ, and Oxford: Princeton University Press).

Bergner, Gwen, 1995. 'Who is that masked woman? or, the role of gender in Fanon's *Black Skin, White Masks*', *PMLA*, 110.1: 75–88.

Bernabé, Jean, Patrick Chamoiseau and Raphaël Confiant, 1993 [1989]. *Éloge de la créolité/In Praise of Creoleness*, tr. M. B. Taleb-Khyar (Paris: Gallimard).

Bernal, Martin, 1987–91. *Black Athena: The Afroasiatic Roots of Classical Civilization*, 2 vols. (New Brunswick, NJ: Rutgers University Press).

Bernasconi, Robert, 2005. 'The European knows and does not know: Fanon's response to Sartre', in Silverman, 2005: 100–11.

Bertrand, Romain, 2006. *Mémoires d'empire: la controverse autour du 'fait colonial'* (Broissieux: Éditions du Croquant).

Beti, Mongo, 1972. *Main basse sur le Cameroun: autopsie d'une décolonisation* (Paris: Maspero).

——, and Odile Tobner, 1989. *Dictionnaire de la Négritude* (Paris: L'Harmattan).

Betts, Raymond F., 1961. *Assimilation and Association in French Colonial Theory* (New York: Columbia University Press).

——, 1991. *France and Decolonisation, 1900–1960* (London: Macmillan).

Bhabha, Homi K., 1986. 'Remembering Fanon: self, psyche and the colonial condition', in Fanon, 1986: vii–xxvi.

——, 1994. *The Location of Culture* (London and New York: Routledge).

——, 2003. 'Democracy De-realized', *Diogenes*, 50.1: 27–35.

——, 2007. *Les Lieux de la culture: une théorie postcoloniale*, tr. Françoise Bouillot (Paris: Payot).

Biondi, Carminella, and Elena Pessini, 2004. *Rêver le monde, écrire le monde: théorie et narrations d'Édouard Glissant* (Bologna: CLUEB).

Biondi, Jean-Pierre, 1992. *Les Anticolonialistes (1881–1962)* (Paris: Robert Laffont).

Birnbaum, Jean, 2004. '1930–2004, Jacques Derrida', *Le Monde*, 11 October.

Bisanswa, Justin K., 2000. *Conflit de mémoires: V. Y. Mudimbe et la traversée des signes* (Frankfurt: IKO).

Blais, Marie-Claire, 1965. *Une saison dans la vie d'Emmanuel* (Montreal: Éditions Quinze).

Blanchard, Pascal, 2007. 'Histoire coloniale: la nouvelle guerre des mémoires', *Cultures sud,* 165: 30–35.

——, and Nicolas Bancel (eds), 2006. *Culture post-coloniale, 1961–2006: traces et mémoires coloniales en France* (Paris: Autrement).

——, and Éric Deroo, 2004. *Le Paris Asie: 150 ans de présence asiatique dans la capitale* (Paris: La Découverte).

——, and Sandrine Lemaire (eds), 2003. *Culture coloniale, 1871–1931: la France conquise par son empire* (Paris: Autrement).

——, and Sandrine Lemaire (eds), 2004. *Culture impériale, 1931–1961: les colonies au cœur de la République* (Paris: Autrement).

——, Nicolas Bancel and Sandrine Lemaire (eds), 2005. *La Fracture coloniale: la société francaise au prisme de l'héritage colonial* (Paris: La Découverte).

Blanchot, Maurice, 1980. *L'Écriture du désastre* (Paris: Gallimard).

Blowers, Tanya, 2000. 'To the is-land: self and place in autobiography', *Australian-Canadian Studies*, 18.1–2: 51–64.

Boas, Franz, 1940. *Race, Language and Culture* (New York: Macmillan).

Boehmer, Elleke, and Frances Gouda, 2009. 'Postcolonial Studies in the context of the "diasporic" Netherlands', in Keown et al., 2009: 37–55.

Bongie, Chris, 1998. *Islands and Exiles: The Creole Identities of Post/Colonial Literature* (Stanford, CA: Stanford University Press).

——, 2003a. 'Belated Liaisons', *Francophone Postcolonial Studies*, 1.2: 11–24.

——, 2003b. 'Exiles on Main Stream: Valuing the Popularity of Postcolonial

Literature', *Postmodern Culture*, 14.1: 64 paragraphs.

Boni, Tanella, 1999. 'Entretien avec Khal Torabully', *Africultures*, 24: 28–32.

Bottomore, Tom, and Maximilien Rubel (eds), 1963. *Karl Marx: Selected Writings in Sociology and Social Philosophy* (Harmondsworth: Penguin).

Bouamama, Said, 2004. *L'Affaire du foulard islamique: la production d'un racisme respectable* (Roubaix: Geai bleu).

Boubeker, Ahmed, 1999. *Familles de l'intégration: les ritournelles de l'ethnicité en pays jacobin* (Paris: Stock).

——, 2003. *Les Mondes de l'ethnicité: la communaute d'expérience des héritiers de l'immigration maghrébine*. Paris: Balland.

Boucher, Philip, 1992. *Cannibal Encounters: Europeans and Island Caribs, 1492–1763* (Baltimore, MD: Johns Hopkins University Press).

Bourdieu, Pierre, 1977 [1972]. *Outline of a Theory of Practice*, tr. Richard Nice (Cambridge: Cambridge University Press). [First published as *Esquisse d'une théorie de la pratique*.]

——, 1984. *Homo academicus* (Paris: Minuit).

——, 1996 [1992]. *The Rules of Art: Genesis and Structure of the Literary Field*, tr. Susan Emmanuel (Cambridge: Polity Press). [First published as *Les Règles de l'art: genèse et structure du champ littéraire*.]

——, 1998 [1996]. *On Television and Journalism*, tr. Priscilla Parkhurst Ferguson (London: Pluto). [First published as *Sur la télévision*.]

——, 2001. *Langage et pouvoir symbolique* (Paris: Seuil).

Bourges, Hervé, 2006. *Léopold Sédar Senghor: lumière noire* (Paris: Mengès).

Bové, Paul A., 1986. 'Intellectuals at War: Michel Foucault and the Analytics of Power'. *SubStance*, 37–38: 36–55.

Bowman, Betsy, and Bob Stone, 2004. 'The End as Present in the Means in Sartre's *Morality and History*', *Sartre Studies International*, 10.2: 1–27.

——, 2005. 'The Alter-Globalisation Movement and Sartre's *Morality and History*', *Sartre Studies International*, 11.1–2: 265–85.

Bragard, Véronique, 2005. 'Transoceanic Echoes: coolitude and the work of the Mauritian poet Khal Torabully', *International Journal of Francophone Studies*, 8.3: 219–33.

——, 2006. 'Regards croisés sur la mémoire coolie des Antilles aux Mascareignes', *Nouvelles Études Francophones*, 21.2: 163–80.

Brandily, Max Yves (ed.), 2002. *Hommage à Léopold Sédar Senghor* (Paris: Éditions du Photophore; Maisonneuve et Larose).

Brathwaite, Kamau (1974). *Contradictory Omens: Cultural Diversity and Integration in the Caribbean* (Mona, Jamaica: Savacou Publications).

Breton, André, 1948. *Martinique, charmeuse de serpents* (Paris: Sagittaire).

Brière, Eloïse A., 2005. 'Quebec and France: *La Francophonie* in a Comparative Postcolonial Frame', in Murdoch and Donadey, 2005: 151–74.

Britton, Celia, 1999. *Édouard Glissant and Postcolonial Theory: Strategies of Language and Resistance* (Charlottesville, VA: University of Virginia Press).

——, 2003. 'New Approaches to Francophone Literature', *Francophone Postcolonial Studies*, 1.1: 29–32.

——, 2008. *The Sense of Community in French Caribbean Fiction* (Liverpool: Liverpool University Press).

——, and Michael Syrotinski (eds), 2001. *Paragraph*, 24.3. [Special issue: 'Francophone Texts and Postcolonial Theory'.]

Brocheux, Pierre, 2000. *Ho Chi Minh* (Paris: Presses de Science-Po).

Brown, Peter (ed.), 2000. *Mwà Véé: revue culturelle kanak*, October. [Special issue: 'Living Heritage: Kanak Culture Today'.]

—— (ed.), 2004. *The Kanak Apple Season* (Canberra: Pandanus Books).

—— (ed.), 2005a: *Sharing as Custom Provides* (Canberra: Pandanus Books).

——, 2005b. 'The geopolitics of French language and culture and "La Francophonie"', *CESAA Review*, 33: 42–57.

——, 2006. 'Books, Writing, and Cultural Politics in the Pacific, The New Caledonian *Salon du Livre*, October 2003–October 2005', *International Journal of Francophone Studies*, 9.2: 239–56.

Bruckner, Pascal, 2006. *La Tyrannie de la pénitence* (Paris: Grasset).

Brunel, Pierre, Jean-René Bourrel and Frédéric Giguet, 2006. *Léopold Sédar Senghor* (Paris: adpf).

Brunet, Jean-Paul (ed.), 1995. *Immigration, vie politique et populisme en banlieue parisienne: fin XIXe–XXe siècles* (Paris: L'Harmattan).

Brydon, Diana (ed.), 2000. *Postcolonialism: Critical Concepts in Literary and Cultural studies*, 5 vols. (London and New York: Routledge).

Bui Trong, Lucienne, 2003. *Les Racines de la violence* (Paris: Louis Audibert).

Burton, Richard D. E., 1997. *Le Roman marron: études sur la littérature martiniquaise contemporaine* (Paris: L'Harmattan).

Busca, Joëlle, 2000. *L'Art contemporain africain: du colonialisme au postcolonialisme* (Paris: L'Harmattan).

Cailler, Bernadette, 1976. *Proposition poétique: une lecture de l'oeuvre d'Aimé Césaire* (Sherbrooke, QC: Naaman).

Camus, Albert, 1958 [1939]. 'La Misère de la Kabylie (1939)', in *Chroniques algériennes, 1939–1958* (Paris: Gallimard), 31–90.

Cardinal, Linda, Claude Couture and Claude Denis, 1999. 'La Révolution tranquille à l'épreuve de la "nouvelle" historiographie et de l'approche postcoloniale', *Globe*, 2.1: 75–95.

Carles, Pierre, 2001. *La Sociologie est un sport de combat* (France: C-P Productions [video]).

Carter, Marina, and Khal Torabully (eds), 2002. *Coolitude: An Anthology of the Indian Labour Diaspora* (London: Anthem Press).

Casgrain, Henri-Raymond, 1866. 'Le Mouvement littéraire au Canada', *Le Foyer Canadien*, January: 1–31.

Catinchi, Philippe-Jean, 1998. 'Penser l'abolition', *Le Monde des Livres*, 24 April: viii.

Célestin, Roger, 1995. *From Cannibals to Radicals: Figures and Limits of Exoticism* (Minneapolis, MN: University of Minnesota Press).

——, Eliane DalMolin and Isabelle de Courtivron (eds), 2002. *French Feminisms Debates on Women, Politics, and Culture in France, 1981–2001* (New York: Palgrave).

Certeau, Michel de, 1984 [1974]. *The Practice of Everyday Life*, tr. Steven Rendell (Berkeley, CA: University of California Press). [First published as *L'Invention du quotidien: arts de faire*.]

Cesaire, Aimé, 1943. 'Maintenir la poésie', *Tropiques*, 8: 7–8.

——, 1946. *Les Armes miraculeuses* (Paris: Gallimard).

——, 1947 [1939]. *Cahier d'un retour au pays natal* (Paris: Bordas).

——, 1948a. *Esclavage et colonisation* (Paris: PUF).

——, 1948b. *Soleil cou coupé* (Paris: Éditions K).

——, 1949. *Corps perdu* (Paris: Éditions Fragrance).

——, 1955 [1950]. *Discours sur le colonialisme* (Paris: Présence Africaine).

——, 1956a [1939]. *Cahier d'un retour au pays natal* (Paris: Présence Africaine).

——, 1956b [1946]. *Et les Chiens se taisaient* (Paris: Présence Africaine).

——, 1961a. *Ferrements* (Paris: Seuil).

——, 1961b. *Cadastre* (Paris: Seuil).

——, 1961c [1960]. *Toussaint Louverture: la Révolution française et le problème colonial* (Paris: Présence Africaine).

——, 1963. *La Tragédie du Roi Christophe* (Paris: Présence Africaine).

——, 1966. *Une saison au Congo* (Paris: Seuil).

——, 1969. *Une tempête* (Paris: Seuil).

——, 1978. 'Entretien avec Aimé Césaire par Jacqueline Leiner', in *Tropiques*, 2 vols (Paris: Jean-Michel Laplace), I: v–xxiv.

——, 1982. *Moi, laminaire* (Paris. Seuil).

——, 2000 [1939]. *Cahier d'un retour au pays natal*, ed. Abiola Irele (Columbus, OH: Ohio State University Press).

——, 2005. *Nègre je suis, nègre je resterai: entretiens avec Françoise Vergès* (Paris: Albin Michel.)

——, and René Ménil,1942. 'Introduction au folklore martiniquais', *Tropiques*, 4: 7–11.

Chafer, Tony, 2002. *The End of Empire in French West Africa: France's Successful Decolonization?* (Oxford and New York: Berg).

Chamoiseau, Patrick, 1991. 'Reflections on Maryse Condé's *Traversée de la mangrove* [*Crossing the Mangrove*]', tr. Kathleen M. Balutansky, *Callaloo*, 14.2: 389–95.

——, 1997. *Écrire en pays dominé* (Paris: Gallimard).

Chanady, Amaryll, 2003. 'Rereading Québécois Literature in a Postcolonial Context', *Québec Studies*, 35: 31–44.

Chartier, Erwan, and Ronan Larvor, 2004. *La France éclatée? Enquête sur les mouvements régionalistes, autonomistes, et indépendantistes en France* (Spezet: Coop Breizh).

Chaulet-Achour, Christiane, and Romuald-Blaise Fonkoua (eds), 2001. *Esclavage: libérations, abolitions, commémorations* (Paris: Séguier).

Cherki, Alice, 2000. *Frantz Fanon, portrait* (Paris: Seuil).

Chevrier, Jacques (ed.), 1999. *Poétiques d'Édouard Glissant* (Paris: Presses de l'Université de Paris-Sorbonne).

Cheyette, Bryan, 2005. 'Frantz Fanon and the Black-Jewish Imaginary', in Silverman, 2005: 74–99.

Childs, Peter, and Patrick Williams, 1996. *Introduction to Post-Colonial Theory* (Harlow: Pearson).

Chinweizu, Onwuchekwa Jemie, and Ihechukwu Madubuike, 1980. *Toward the Decolonization of African Literature* (London: Kegan Paul).

Chrétien, Jean-Pierre, 2006. 'Autour d'un livre: *La Fracture coloniale. La société française au prisme de l'héritage colonial,* dirigé par Pascal Blanchard, Nicolas Bancel et Sandrine Lemaire', *Politique africaine,* 102: 89–108.

——, (ed.), 2008. *L'Afrique de Sarkozy: un déni d'histoire* (Paris: Karthala).

Clancy-Smith, Julia A., and Frances Gouda (eds), 1998. *Domesticating the Empire: Gender and Family Life in French and Dutch Colonialism* (Charlottesville, VA, and London: University of Virginia Press).

Clifford, James, 1988. *The Predicament of Culture: Twentieth-Century Ethnography, Literature, and Art* (Cambridge, MA: Harvard University Press).

——, 1989. 'Notes on Travel and Theory', *Inscriptions,* 5: 177–88.

——, 1997. *Routes: Travel and Translation in the Late Twentieth Century* (Cambridge, MA, and London: Harvard University Press).

——, and George E. Marcus, 1986. *Writing Culture: The Poetics and Politics of Ethnography: A School of American Research Advanced Seminar* (Berkeley, CA: University of California Press).

Cole, Jennifer, 2001. *Forget Colonialism? Sacrifice and the Art of Memory in Madagascar* (Berkeley, CA: University of California Press).

Cole, Joshua, 2007. 'Understanding the French Riots of 2005: What Historical Context for the "Crise des banlieues"', *Francophone Postcolonial Studies,* 5.2: 69–100.

Colette, Élise, 2007. 'Quand Sarko "découvre" l'Afrique…', *Jeune Afrique,* 5–11 August: 40–47.

Collier, Gordon, and Ulrich Fleishman (eds), 2004. *A Pepper-Pot of Cultures: Aspects of Creolization in the Caribbean* (Amsterdam: Rodopi).

Conan, Éric, and Henry Rousso, 1994. *Vichy, un passé qui ne passe pas* (Paris: Fayard).

Condé, Maryse, 1982 [1976]. *Heremakhonon,* tr. Richard Philcox (Washington, DC: Three Continents Press). [First published as *Heremakhonon.*]

——, 1987 [1984]. *Segu,* tr. Barbara Bray (New York: Viking Penguin). [First published as *Ségou: les murailles de terre.*]

——, 1988 [1981]. *A Season in Rihata,* tr. Richard Philcox (London: Heinemann). [First published as *Une saison à Rihata.*]

——, 1990 [1985]. *The Children of Segu,* tr. Linda Coverdale (New York: Viking and Ballantine). [First published as *Ségou: la terre en miettes.*]

——, 1992a [1985]. 'Three Women in Manhattan', tr. Thomas C. Spear, in Lisa Paravisini Gebert and Carmen Esteves (eds), *Green Cane and Juicy Flotsam: Short Stories by Caribbean Women* (New Brunswick, NJ: Rutgers University Press), 56–68. [First published as 'Trois femmes à Manhattan', in *Pays-mêlé.*]

——, 1992b [1986]. *I, Tituba, Black Witch of Salem,* tr. Richard Philcox (Charlottesville, VA: University of Virginia Press). [First published as *Moi, Tituba, sorcière noire de Salem.*]

——, 1992c [1987]. *Tree of Life*, tr. Victoria Reiter (New York: Ballantine). [First published as *La Vie scélérate*.]

——, 1993a. *La Colonie du Nouveau Monde* (Paris: Robert Laffont).

——, 1993b. 'Order, Disorder, Freedom, and the West Indian Writer', *Yale French Studies*, 83.2: 121–35.

——, 1995a. 'Chercher nos vérités', in Maryse Condé and Madeleine Cottenet-Hage (eds), *Penser la créolité* (Paris: Karthala), 305–10.

——, 1995b [1989]. *Crossing the Mangrove*, tr. Richard Philcox (New York: Anchor-Doubleday). [First published as *Traversée de la mangrove*.]

——, 1997 [1992]. *The Last of the African Kings*, tr. Richard Philcox (Lincoln, NE: University of Nebraska Press). [First published as *Les Derniers Rois Mages*.]

——, 1998a [1995]. *Windward Heights*, tr. Richard Philcox (London: Faber & Faber). [First published as *La Migration des cœurs*.]

——, 1998b. '*Créolité* without the Creole Language?', in Kathleen M. Balutansky and Marie-Agnès Sourieau (eds), *Caribbean Creolization: Reflections on the Cultural Dynamics of Language, Literature, and Identity* (Gainesville, FL: University Press of Florida), 101–09.

——, 2000 [1997]. *Desirada*, tr. Richard Philcox (New York: Soho Press). [First published as *Desirada*.]

——, 2001a [1999]. *Tales from the Heart*, tr. Richard Philcox (New York: Soho Press). [First published as *Le Cœur à rire et à pleurer, contes vrais de mon enfance*.]

——, 2001b. *La Belle Créole* (Paris: Mercure de France).

——, 2002. 'Autobiographical Essay'. *Contemporary Authors Online* (Gale Database).

——, 2004 [2000]. *Who Slashed Célanire's Throat?* tr. Richard Philcox (New York: Atria Books). [First published as *Célanire cou-coupé*.]

——, 2006a [2003]. *The Story of the Cannibal Woman*, tr. Richard Philcox (New York: Atria Books). [First published as *Histoire de la femme cannibale*.]

——, 2006b. *Victoire, des saveurs et des mots* (Paris: Mercure de France).

Confiant, Raphaël, 1993. *Aimé Césaire: une traversée paradoxale du siècle* (Paris: Stock).

——, 1999. 'Préface', in Khal Torabully, *Chair Corail, Fragments Coolies* (Guadeloupe: Ibis Rouge), 7–9.

Conklin, Alice, 2000. 'Boundaries Unbound: Teaching French History as Colonial History and Colonial History as French History', *French Historical Studies*, 23.2: 215–38.

Cooper, Frederick, 2005. *Colonialism in Question: Theory, Knowledge, History* (Berkeley, CA: University of California Press).

——, and Ann Laura Stoler, 1997. 'Between Metropole and Colony: Rethinking a Research Agenda', in Cooper and Stoler (eds), *Tensions of Empire: Colonial Cultures in a Bourgeois World* (Berkeley and Los Angeles: University of California Press), 1–56.

Cooper, Nicola, 2004. 'Dien Bien Phu: 50 Years On', *Modern and Contemporary France*, 12.4: 445–57.

Costa-Lacoux, Jacqueline, 2001. 'L'ethnicisation du lien social dans les banlieues françaises', *Revue européenne des migrations internationales*, 2: 123–38.

Cottenet-Hage, Madeleine, and Lydie Moudileno (eds), 2002. *Maryse Condé: une nomade inconvenante* (Guadeloupe: Ibis Rouge).

Couassi, Ana, 1998. 'Rencontre avec Khal Torabully', *Jeune Afrique*, 8–14 September: 68–69.

Coulon, Virginia, 2003. 'Étude bibliographique de l'oeuvre de V. Y. Mudimbe', in Mukala Kadima-Nzuji and Sélom Komlan Gbanou (eds), *L'Afrique au miroir des littératures, des sciences de l'homme et de la société: mélanges offerts à V. Y. Mudimbe* (Paris: L'Harmattan), 557–89.

Coundouriotis, Eleni, 1999. *Claiming History: Colonialism, Ethnography, and the Novel* (New York: Columbia University Press).

Coursil, Jacques, and Dominique Perret, 2005. 'The Francophone Postcolonial Field', in Murdoch and Donadey, 2005: 193–207.

Crowley, Patrick, 2003. 'Postcolonial Theories and Colonial Microhistories', *Francophone Postcolonial Studies* 1.2: 33–40.

Cubitt, Geoffrey, 2007. *History and Memory* (Manchester: Manchester University Press).

Cush, Geoff, 2002. *Son of France* (Auckland, NZ: Vintage).

Daeninckx, Didier, 1984. *Meurtres pour mémoire* (Paris: Gallimard).

Dakhlia, Jocelyne, 2002. 'Lingua Franca: A Non-Memory', in Elisabeth Mudimbe-Boyi (ed.), *Remembering Africa* (Portsmouth, NH: Heinemann), 234–44.

D'Allemagne, André, 1966. *Le Colonialisme au Québec* (Montreal: Éditions RB).

D'Almeida, Irène Assiba, 2003. 'A Necessary Uneasiness', *Francophone Postcolonial Studies*, 1.1: 25–28.

Damas, Léon Gontran, 1937. *Pigments* (Paris: Guy Lévis Mano).

—— (ed.), 1947. *Poètes d'expression française, 1900–1945* (Paris: Seuil).

——, 1952. *Graffiti* (Paris: Seghers).

——, 1956. *Black-Label: poèmes* (Paris: Gallimard).

Dash, J. Michael, 1992. 'Writing the Body: Édouard Glissant's Poetics of Re-Membering', in Maryse Condé (ed.), *L'Héritage de Caliban* (Pointe-à-Pitre: Jasor), 75–83.

——, 1995. *Édouard Glissant* (Cambridge: Cambridge University Press).

——, 1998. *The Other America: Caribbean Literature in a New World Context* (Charlottesville, VA: University of Virginia Press).

Davis, David Brion, 2006. *Inhuman Bondage: The Rise and Fall of Slavery in the New World* (Oxford: Oxford University Press).

Debray, Régis, 2004. *Haïti et la France* (Paris: La Table Ronde).

Delas, Daniel, 2003. 'Francophone Literary Studies in France: Analyses and Reflections', *Yale French Studies,* 103: 43–54.

Deleuze, Gilles, and Félix Guattari, 1986 [1975]. *Kafka: Toward a Minor Literature*, tr. Dana Polan (Minneapolis, MN: University of Minnesota Press). [First published as *Kafka: Pour une littérature mineure*.]

Deloughrey, Elizabeth, 2001a. '"The litany of islands, the rosary of archipelagoes": Caribbean and Pacific Heterotopias', *Ariel*, 32.1: 21–51.

——, 2001b. 'Some pitfalls of Caribbean regionalism, colonial roots and migratory routes', *Journal of Caribbean Literatures*, 3.1: 35–55.

——, 2007. *Routes and Roots: Navigating Caribbean and Pacific Island Literature* (Honolulu: University of Hawaii Press).

——, Renée Gosson and George B. Handley (eds), 2005. *Caribbean Literature and the Environment: Between Nature and Culture* (Charlottesville, VA: University of Virginia Press).

Derrida, Jacques, 1976 [1967]. *Of Grammatology*, tr. Gayatri Chakravorty Spivak (Baltimore, MD: Johns Hopkins University Press). [First published as *De la Grammatologie*.]

——, 1978 [1967]. *Writing and Difference*, tr. Alan Bass (London: Routledge and Kegan Paul). [First published as *L'Écriture et la différence*.]

——, 1982 [1972]. *Margins of Philosophy*, tr. Alan Bass (Brighton: Harvester). [First published as *Marges de la philosophie*.]

——, 1985. 'Racism's Last Word', tr. Peggy Kamuf, in Henry Louis Gates, Jr. (ed.), *'Race', Writing, and Difference* (Chicago: University of Chicago Press), 329–38.

——, 1990. *Du Droit à la philosophie* (Paris: Galilée).

——, 1991 [1987]. *Cinders*, tr. Ned Lukacher (Lincoln, NE: University of Nebraska Press). [First published as *Feu la cendre*.]

——, 1992a [1991]. *The Other Heading: Reflections on Today's Europe*, tr. Michael Naas (Bloomington, IN: Indiana University Press). [First published as *L'Autre Cap*.]

——, 1992b. *Acts of Literature*, ed. Derek Attridge (New York and London: Routledge).

——, 1994 [1993]. *Specters of Marx: The State of Debt, the Work of Mourning, and the New International*, tr. Peggy Kamuf (London: Routledge). [First published as *Spectres de Marx: l'état de la dette, le travail du deuil, et la Nouvelle Internationale*.]

——, 1997a [1994]. *Politics of Friendship*, tr. George Collins (London: Verso). [First published as *Politiques de l'amitié*.]

——, 1997b. *Du Droit à la philosophie du point de vue cosmopolitique* (Paris: Verdier).

——, 1998 [1996]. *The Monolingualism of the Other, or the Prosthesis of Origin*, tr. Patrick Mensah (Stanford, CA: Stanford University Press). [First published as *Le Monolinguisme de l'autre, ou, le prothèse de l'origine*.]

——, 2000 [1997]. *Of Hospitality: Anne Dufourmentelle invites Jacques Derrida to Respond*, tr. Rachel Bowlby (Stanford, CA: Stanford University Press). [First published as *De l'hospitalité: Anne Dufourmentelle invite Jacques Derrida à répondre*.]

——, 2001 [1997]. *On Cosmopolitanism and Forgiveness*, tr. Mark Dooley and Michael Hughes (London: Routledge). [First published as *Cosmopolites de tous les pays, encore un effort!*]

De Souza, Pascale, and Anne Malena (eds), 2001. *Journal of Caribbean Literatures*, 3.1. [Special issue: 'The Caribbean that isn't? exploring rifts and disjunctions'.]

——, and Anne Malena (eds), 2002. *Journal of Caribbean Literatures*, 3.2. [Special issue: 'The Caribbean that is? exploring intertextualities'.]

——, and H. Adlai Murdoch (eds), 2005. *International Journal of Francophone Studies*, 8.2–3. [Special issue: 'Oceanic Dialogues: from the Black Atlantic to the Indo-Pacific'.]

Desroches, Vincent (ed.), 2003a: *Québec Studies*, 35. [Special issue: 'Quebec and Postcolonial Theory'.]

——, 2003b: 'Présentation: en quoi la literature québécoise est-elle postcoloniale?', *Québec Studies*, 35: 3–12.

De Witte, Ludo, 2002 [1999]. *The Assassination of Lumumba*, tr. Ann Wright and Renée Fenby (London and New York: Verso).

Dewitte, Philippe, 1985. *Les Mouvements nègres en France, 1919–1939* (Paris: L'Harmattan).

D'Haen, Theo, 1998. *(Un)writing Empire* (Amsterdam: Rodopi).

Diawara, Manthia, 1998. *In Search of Africa* (Cambridge, MA: Harvard University Press).

Dinh, Pierre Do, Mohamed el Kholti, Léopold Senghor, A. Rakoto Ratsimamanga and E. Ralajmihiatra (eds), 1947. *Les Plus Beaux Écrits de l'Union française et du Maghreb* (Paris: La Colombe).

Diop, Alioune, 1949. 'Niam M'Paya, ou de la fin que dévorent les moyens', in Tempels, 1949: 7–12.

Diop, Samba (ed.), 2002. *Fictions africaines et postcolonialisme* (Paris: L'Harmattan).

Diouf, Mamadou, 1989. 'Représentations historiques et légitimités politiques au Sénégal (1960–1987)', *Revue de la Bibliothèque Nationale*, 34: 14–23.

Dirks, Nicholas, 1992. *Colonialism and Culture* (Ann Arbor, MI: Michigan University Press).

Dirlik, Arif, 1994. 'The Postcolonial Aura: Third World Criticism in the Age of Global Capitalism', *Critical Inquiry*, 20: 328–56.

Djebar, Assia, 1958 [1957]. *The Mischief*, tr. Frances Frenaye (London: Elek). [First published as *La Soif*.]

——, 1961 [1961]. *Women of Islam*, tr. Jean MacGibbon (London: Deutsch). [First published as *Femmes d'Islam*.]

——, 1989 [1985]. *Fantasia, An Algerian Cavalcade*, tr. Dorothy Blair (London: Quartet). [First published as *L'Amour, la fantasia*.]

——, 1992 [1980]. *Women of Algiers in Their Apartment*, tr. Marjolijn de Jager (Charlottesville, VA, and London: Caraf Books). [First published as *Femmes d'Alger dans leur appartement*; expanded edition 2002].

——, 1993. 'Solitude et soleil. Soleil noir', in *Pour Rushdie: cent intellectuels arabes et musulmans pour la liberté d'expression*. (Paris: La Découverte; Carrefour des littératures; Colibri), 124–25.

——, 1994 [1991]. *Far from Madina* (London: Quartet). [First published as *Loin de Médine*.]

——, 1999a [1995]. *So Vast the Prison*, tr. Betsy Wing (New York: Seven Stories Press). [First published as *Vaste est la prison*.]

——, 1999b. *Ces voix qui m'assiègent ... en marge de ma francophonie* (Paris: Albin Michel).

——, 2000 [1995]. *Algerian White*, tr. David Kelley and Marjolijn de Jager (New

York: Seven Stories Press). [First published as *Le Blanc de l'Algérie*.]

——, 2003. *La Disparition de la langue française* (Paris: Albin Michel).

——, 2006. 'Discours de réception'. Available at http://www.academie-francaise. fr/immortels/index.html (consulted on 31 January 2008).

——, 2007. *Nulle part dans la maison de mon père* (Paris: Fayard).

Documentation Française, 2003. 'Vers des Statuts sur mesure: la persistence de la diversité statutaire après 2003'. Available at http://www.ladocumenta-tionfrancaise.fr/dossiers/outre-mer/statuts-sur-mesure.shtml (consulted on 8 January 2008).

Donadey, Anne, 1996. '"Une certaine idée de la France": The Algeria Syndrome and Struggles over "French" Identity', in Steven Ungar and Tom Conley (eds), *Identity Papers: Contested Nationhood in Twentieth-Century France* (Minneapolis, MN: University of Minnesota Press), 215–32.

Dorigny, Marcel, 2005. 'Aux origines: l'indépendance d'Haïti et son occultation', in Blanchard et al., 2005: 45–53.

Dozon, Jean-Pierre, 2003. *Frères et sujets: la France et l'Afrique en perspective* (Paris: Flammarion).

Droz, Bernard (ed.), 2007. *L'Histoire*, 318. [Special dossier: 'Colonisation: les massacres oubliés.']

Dubois, Laurent, 2000. '*La République métisée*: citizenship, colonialism, and the borders of French history', *Cultural Studies*, 14.1: 15–34.

——, 2004a. *Avengers of the New World: The Story of the Haitian Revolution* (Cambridge, MA: Harvard University Press).

——, 2004b. *A Colony of Citizens: Revolution and Slave Emancipation in the French Caribbean, 1787–1804* (Chapel Hill, NC: University of North Carolina Press).

Dugas, Guy, 2001. *Albert Memmi: du malheur d'être juif au bonheur sépharade* (Paris: Nadir).

Duiker, William, 2000. *Ho Chi Minh: A Life* (New York: Hyperion).

Dumont, Louis, 1970 [1966]. *Homo Hierarchicus: The Caste System and its Implications*, tr. Mark Sainsbury (London: Weidenfeld & Nicolson). [First published as *Homo hierarchicus: essai sur le système des castes*.]

Dupin, Eric, 2004. *L'Hystérie identitaire* (Paris: Le Cherche-Midi).

Durham, John George, Earl of Lambton, 1963 [1838]. *Lord Durham's Report: An Abridgement of Report on the Affairs of British North America*, ed. G. M. Craig (Toronto: McClelland & Stewart).

Durkheim, Émile, 2001 [1912]. *The Elementary Forms of Religious Life*, tr. Carol Cossman (Oxford: Oxford University Press). [First published as *Les Formes élémentaires de la vie religieuse*.]

Eboussi-Boulaga, Fabien, 1981. *Christianisme sans fétiche: révélation et domination* (Paris: Présence Africaine).

Edwards, Brent Hayes, 2003. *The Practice of Diaspora: Literature, Translation, and the Rise of Black Internationalism* (Cambridge, MA, and London: Harvard University Press).

Englund, Stephen, 1992. 'The Ghost of Nation Past', *The Journal of Modern History*, 64.2: 299–320.

Erickson, John, 1998. *Islam and the Postcolonial Narrative* (Cambridge: Cambridge University Press).

Ezra, Elizabeth (2000): *The Colonial Unconscious: Race and Culture in Interwar France* (Ithaca, NY: Cornell University Press).

——, 2008. *Jean-Pierre Jeunet* (Urbana and Chicago: University of Illinois Press).

Faessel, Sonia, and Michel Ferez (eds), 2004. *Littératures d'émergence et mondialisation: théorie, société et politique* (Paris: In Press).

Fanon, Frantz, 1967 [1961]. *The Wretched of the Earth*, tr. Constance Farrington (New York: Grove Press). [First published as *Les Damnés de la terre*.]

——, 1970a [1959]. *A Dying Colonialism*, tr. Haakon Chevalier (London: Penguin Books). [First published as *L'An V de la révolution algérienne*.]

——, 1970b [1964]. *Toward the African Revolution*, tr. Haakon Chevalier (London: Penguin Books). [First published as *Pour la Révolution africaine*.]

——, 1986 [1952]. *Black Skin, White Masks*, tr. Charles Lam Markmann (London: Pluto Press). [First published as *Peau noire, masques blancs*.]

Ferguson, Niall, 2003. *Empire: How Britain made the Modern World* (London: Allen Lane).

Ferro, Marc, 2003. *Le Livre noir du colonialisme* (Paris: Robert Laffont).

ffrench, Patrick, 1995. *The Time of Theory: A History of 'Tel Quel' (1960–1983)* (Oxford: Clarendon Press).

Finkielkraut, Alain, 1987. *La Défaite de la pensée* (Paris: Gallimard).

Fonkoua, Romuald, 2002. *Essai sur la mesure du monde au XXe siècle: Édouard Glissant* (Paris: Honoré Champion).

Forest, Philippe, 1995. *Histoire de 'Tel Quel', 1960–1982* (Paris: Seuil).

Forsdick, Charles, 2000. *Victor Segalen and the Aesthetics of Diversity: Journeys between Cultures* (Oxford: Oxford University Press).

——, 2003. 'Challenging the monolingual, subverting the monocultural: the strategic purposes of Francophone Postcolonial Studies', *Francophone Postcolonial Studies*, 1.1: 33–41.

——, 2005. 'Between "French" and "Francophone": French Studies and the postcolonial turn', *French Studies*, 59.4: 523–30.

——, 2007. '*Ceci n'est pas un conte, mais une histoire de chair et de sang*: representing the colonial massacre in Francophone literature and culture', in Lorna Milne (ed.), *Postcolonial Violence, Culture and Identity in Francophone Africa and the Antilles* (Oxford and Bern: Peter Lang), 31–57.

——, and David Murphy (eds), 2003. *Francophone Postcolonial Studies: A Critical Introduction* (London: Arnold).

——, and David Murphy (eds), 2007. *Francophone Postcolonial Studies*, 5.2. [Special issue: 'France in a Postcolonial Europe: Identity, History, Memory'.]

——, and David Murphy, 2009. 'The Rise of the Francophone Postcolonial Intellectual: the emergence of a tradition', *Modern and Contemporary France*, 17.2: 163–75.

Foucault, Michel, 1970 [1966]. *The Order of Things: An Archaeology of the Human Sciences* (London: Tavistock). [First published as *Les Mots et les choses: une archéologie des sciences humaines*.]

——, 1977 [1975]. *Discipline and Punish*, tr. Alan Sheridan (New York: Pantheon). [First published as *Surveiller et Punir*.]

——, 1979 [1976]. *The History of Sexuality, Vol. 1: The Will to Knowledge*, tr. Robert Hurley (London: Allen Lane) [First published as *Histoire de la Sexualité 1: la Volonté de savoir*.]

——, 1994. *Dits et écrits, 1954–1988*, ed. Daniel Defert, François Ewald and Jacques Lagrange (Paris: Gallimard).

——, 2002 [1969]. *Archaeology of Knowledge*, tr. A. M. Sheridan Smith (London: Routledge). [First published as *L'Archéologie du savoir*.]

——, 2003 [1997]. *Society Must be Defended*, tr. David Macey (London: Penguin). [First published as *Il faut défendre la société*.]

Fraiture, Pierre-Philippe, 2007. *La Mesure de l'autre: Afrique subsaharienne et roman ethnographique de Belgique et de France (1918–1940)* (Paris: Honoré Champion).

Fuss, Diana, 1999. 'Interior colonies: Frantz Fanon and the politics of identification', in Nigel C. Gibson (ed.), *Rethinking Fanon: The Continuing Dialogue* (New York: Humanity Books), 294–328.

Gallagher, Mary, 2003. 'ASCALF R.I.P.: Some (Mischievous) Thoughts on Postcolonial Studies', *Francophone Postcolonial Studies*, 1.2: 51–54.

——, 2007. 'Genre and the Self: Some Reflections on the Poetics and Politics of the "fils de Césaire"', *International Journal of Francophone Studies*, 10.1–2: 51–56.

Gallo, Max, 2006. *Fier d'être français* (Paris: Fayard).

Garrigus, John, 2006. *Before Haiti: Race and Citizenship in French Saint-Domingue* (New York: Palgrave-Macmillan).

Gaspard, Thu Trang, 1992. *Ho Chi Minh à Paris* (Paris: L'Harmattan).

Gassama, Makhily (ed.), 2008. *L'Afrique répond à Sarkozy: contre le discours de Dakar* (Paris: Éditions Philippe Rey).

Gates, Henry Louis, Jr., 1986. 'Talkin' that talk', in Henry Louis Gates, Jr. (ed.), *'Race', Writing, and Difference* (Chicago and London: University of Chicago Press), 402–09.

Gearhart, Suzanne, 1998. 'Colonialism, Psychoanalysis, and Cultural Criticism: The Problem of Interiorization in the Work of Albert Memmi', in John Carlos Rowe (ed.), *Culture and the Problem of the Disciplines* (New York and Chichester: Columbia University Press), 171–97.

Gehrmann, Susanne, and Claudia Gronemann (eds), 2006. *Les Enjeux de l'autobiographique dans les littératures de langue française: du genre à l'espace, l'autobiographie postcoloniale, l'hybridité* (Paris: L'Harmattan).

Geismar, Peter, 1971. *Fanon* (New York: Dial Press).

Gendzier, Irene L., 1973. *Frantz Fanon: A Critical Study* (London: Wildwood House).

Gennep, Arnold van, 2004 [1909]. *The Rites of Passage*, tr. S. J. Leinbach (London: Routledge). [First published as *Les Rites de passage*.]

Genova, James E., 2004. *Colonial Ambivalence, Cultural Authenticity, and the Limitations of Mimicry in French-Ruled West Africa, 1914–1956* (New York: Peter Lang).

Gerson, Stéphane, 2003. '*Une France locale*: The Local Past in Recent French Scholarship', *French Historical Studies*, 26.3: 539–59.

Gibson, Nigel C., 1999a. 'Radical mutations: Fanon's untidy dialectic of history', in Nigel C. Gibson (ed.), *Rethinking Fanon: The Continuing Dialogue* (New York: Humanity Books), 408–46.

——, 1999b. 'Fanon and the pitfalls of cultural studies', in Anthony C. Alessandrini (ed.), *Frantz Fanon: Critical Perspectives* (London and New York: Routledge), 99–125.

——, 2003. *Fanon: The Postcolonial Imagination* (Cambridge: Polity).

Giddens, Anthony, 1996. 'Living in a post-traditional society', in *In Defence of Sociology: Essays, Interpretations and Rejoinders* (Cambridge: Polity), 8–64.

Gide, André, 1947. 'Avant-propos', *Présence Africaine*, 1.1: 3–6.

Gilbert, Bart Moore, 1997. *Postcolonial Theory: Contexts, Practices, Politics* (London and New York: Verso).

Gilroy, Paul, 1993. *The Black Atlantic: Modernity and Double Consciousness* (Cambridge, MA: Harvard University Press).

——, 2000. *Between Camps: Nations, Cultures and the Allure of Race* (London and New York: Routledge).

Glissant, Édouard, 1981. *Le Discours antillais* (Paris: Seuil).

——, 1989 [1981]. *Caribbean Discourse: Selected Essays*, tr. J. Michael Dash (Charlottesville, VA: University of Virginia Press).

——, 1996. *Introduction à une Poétique du Divers* (Paris: Gallimard).

——, 1997a [1990]. *Poetics of Relation*, tr. Betsy Wing (Ann Arbor, MI: University of Michigan Press). [First published as *Poétique de la Relation*.]

——, 1997b. *Traité du Tout-Monde: Poétique IV* (Paris: Gallimard).

——, 2005. *La Cohée du Lamentin: Poétique V* (Paris: Gallimard).

——, 2007. *Mémoires des esclavages: la fondation d'un centre national pour la mémoire des esclavages et de leurs abolitions* (Paris: Gallimard).

——, and Patrick Chamoiseau, 2007. *Quand les Murs tombent: l'identité nationale hors-la-loi?* (Paris: Éditions Galaade; Institut du Tout-Monde).

Godbout, Jacques, 1967. *Salut Galarneau!* (Paris: Seuil).

Golsan, Richard (ed.), 2000. *The Papon Affair: Memory and Justice on Trial* (New York and London: Routledge).

Gopal, Priyamvada, and Neil Lazarus (eds), 2006. *New Formations*, 59. [Special issue: 'After Iraq: Reframing Postcolonial Studies'.]

Gordon, Lewis R., 1995. *Fanon and the Crisis of European Man: An Essay on Philosophy and the Human Sciences* (New York and London: Routledge).

Gorodé, Déwé, and Nicolas Kurtovitch, 2000. *Dire le Vrai/Tell the Truth* (Nouméa: Grain de sable).

Gough, Kathleen, 2002 [1967]. 'New Proposals for Anthropologists', in Joan Vincent (ed.), *The Anthropology of Politics: A Reader in Ethnography, Theory and Critique* (Malden, MA, and Oxford: Blackwell), 110–19.

Green, Mary Jean, 2003. 'Toward Defining a Postcolonial Quebec Cinema: The Films of Claude Jutra', *Québec Studies*, 35: 89–98.

Green, Mary Jean, 2006. 'Albert Memmi', in Lawrence D. Kritzman (ed.), *The*

Columbia History of Twentieth-Century French Thought (New York: Columbia University Press), 617–20.

Green, Mary Jean, Karen Gould, Micheline Rice-Maximin, Keith L. Walker and Jack A. Yeager (eds), 1996. *Postcolonial Subjects: Francophone Women Writers* (Minneapolis, MN, and London: University of Minnesota Press).

Griaule, Marcel, 1965 [1948]. *Conversations with Ogotemmêli: An Introduction to Dogon Religious Ideas* (Oxford: Oxford University Press). [First published as *Dieu d'eau: entretiens avec Ogotemmêli.*]

Guénif-Souilamas, Nacira (ed.), 2000. *Des Beurettes aux descendantes d'immigrants nord-africains* (Paris: Grasset).

—— (ed.), 2006. *La République mise à nu par son immigration* (Paris: La Fabrique).

Guérin, Jeanyves (ed.), 1990. *Albert Memmi: écrivain et socioloque* (Paris: L'Harmattan).

Guibert, Armand, and Nimrod, 2006 [1969]. *Léopold Sédar Senghor* (Paris: Seghers).

Gyssels, Kathleen, Isabel Hoving and Maggie Ann Bowers (eds), 2002. *Convergences and Interferences: Newness in Intercultural Practices* (Amsterdam: Rodopi).

Ha, Marie-Paule, 1997. 'The Narrative of Return in "Orphée Noir"', in Jean-Francois Fourny and Charles Minahen (eds), *Situating Sartre in Twentieth-Century Thought and Culture* (New York: St Martin's Press), 93–110.

——, 2000. *Figuring the East: Segalen, Malraux, Duras, and Barthes* (New York: State University of New York Press).

Haddour, Azzedine, 2000. *Colonial Myths: History and Narrative* (Manchester: Manchester University Press).

——, 2001. 'Introduction', in Sartre, 2001a: 1–16.

Hajjat, Abdellali, 2005. *Immigration postcoloniale et mémoire* (Paris: L'Harmattan).

Hall, Stuart, 1996. 'When Was "The Post-Colonial"? Thinking at the Limit', in Iain Chambers and Lidia Curtis (eds), *The Post-Colonial Question: Common Skies, Divided Horizons* (London and New York: Routledge), 242–59.

——, 2007. *Identités et cultures: politiques des cultural studies*, tr. Christophe Jacquet (Paris: Les Éditions Amsterdam).

Hallward, Peter, 2001. *Absolutely Postcolonial: Writing Between the Singular and the Specific* (Manchester: Manchester University Press).

——, 2008. *Damming the Flood: Haiti, Aristide and the Politics of Containment* (London: Verso).

Hargreaves, Alec G., 1995. *Immigration, 'Race' and Ethnicity in Contemporary France* (New York and London: Routledge).

——, 2003. 'Ships Passing in the Night? France, Postcolonialism and the Globalization of Literature', *Francophone Postcolonial Studies*, 1.2: 64–69.

—— (ed.), 2005. *Memory, Empire, and Postcolonialism: Legacies of French Colonialism* (Lanham, MD: Lexington Books).

——, and Mark McKinney (eds), 1997. *Post-Colonial Cultures in France* (London and New York: Routledge).

Harootunian, Harry, 2002. 'Foreword: The Exotics of Nowhere', in Segalen, 2002: vii–xx.

Harris, Geoffrey T., 1996. *André Malraux: A Reassessment* (London: Macmillan).

Harrison, Nicholas, 2003a. *Postcolonial Criticism: History, Theory and the Work of Fiction* (Cambridge: Polity).

——2003b. 'Postcolonialism and the Object of French Studies', *Francophone Postcolonial Studies*, 1.1: 42–48.

—— (ed.), 2005. *Paragraph*, 28.2. [Special issue: 'The Idea of the Literary'.]

Harrow, Kenneth (ed.), 1994. *With Open Eyes: Women and African Cinema* (Amsterdam: Rodopi).

Haubert, Maxime, and Pierre-Philippe Rey (eds), 2000. *Les Sociétés civiles face au marché: le changement social dans le monde postcolonial* (Paris: Karthala).

Hau'ofa, Epeli, 1999. 'Our Sea of Islands', in Vilsoni Hereniko and Rob Wilson (eds), *Inside Out: Literature, Cultural Politics, and Identity in the New Pacific* (Lanham, MD: Rowman & Littlefield), 27–38.

Havard, Gilles, and Cécile Vidal, 2003. *Histoire de l'Amérique française* (Paris: Flammarion).

Hawkins, Peter, 2003. 'How appropriate is the term "post-colonial" to the cultural production of Réunion?', in Kamal Salhi (ed.), *Francophone Post-colonial Cultures: Critical Essays* (Lanham, MD: Lexington Books), 311–20.

Hayes, Jarrod, 2007. 'Circumcising Zionism, Queering Diaspora: Reviving Albert Memmi's Penis', *Wasafiri*, 22.1: 6–11.

Heady, Margaret, 2006. 'From roots to routes: double consciousness in the francophone Caribbean novel', *International Journal of Francophone Studies*, 8.2: 147–64.

Hébert, Anne, 1970. *Kamouraska* (Paris: Seuil).

——, 1976 [1945]. 'Le Torrent', in *Le Torrent* (Montreal: HMH), 1–65.

Hélie-Lucas, Marie-Aimée, 1987. 'Bound and gagged by the family code', in Miranda Davies (ed.), *Third World, Second Sex: Volume 2* (London: Zed), 3–15.

Hémery, Daniel, 1990. *Ho Chi Minh: de l'Indochine au Vietnam* (Paris: Gallimard).

Henry, Paget, 2003. 'Coolitude, Openness and Poststructuralism', *International Association of Labour History Institutions*. Available at http://www.ialhi.org/news/i0306_8.php (consulted on 15 January 2008).

Héritier, Françoise, 1996. *Masculin/féminin: la pensée de la différence* (Paris: Odile Jacob).

Herndon, Gerise, 1993. 'Gender Construction and Neocolonialism', *World Literature Today*, 67.4: 731–36.

Hewitt, Leah, 1995. 'Condé's Critical Seesaw', *Callaloo*, 18.3: 641–51.

Hiddleston, Jane, 2005. 'Derrida, Autobiography, and Postcoloniality', *French Cultural Studies*, 16.3: 291–304.

——, 2006. *Assia Djebar: Out of Algeria* (Liverpool: Liverpool University Press).

Higgins, Ellie, 2002. 'Urban Apprenticeships and Senegalese Narratives of Development: Mansour Sora Wade's *Picc Mi* and Djibril Diop Mambéty's *La Petite Vendeuse de Soleil*', *Research in African Literatures*, 33.3: 54–68.

Hitchcott, Nicki, 2006. *Calixthe Beyala: Performances of Migration* (Liverpool: Liverpool University Press).

Hobbs, Sandra, 2003. 'De l'opposition à l'ambivalence: la théorie postcoloniale et l'écriture de la résistance au Québec', *Québec Studies*, 35: 99–111.

Hornung, Alfred, and Ernstpeter Ruhe (eds), 1998. *Postcolonialisme et autobiographie: Albert Memmi, Assia Djebar, Daniel Maximin* (Amsterdam: Rodopi).

Hountondji, Paulin J., 1977. *Sur la philosophie africaine* (Paris: Maspero).

House, Jim, 2003. 'Francophone Postcolonial Studies and New Historiographies of the Colonial and Postcolonial Encounters', *Francophone Postcolonial Studies* 1.2: 72–78.

———, and Neil MacMaster, 2006. *Paris 1961: Algerians, State Terror, and Memory* (Oxford: Oxford University Press).

Howells, Christina, 1988. *Sartre: The Necessity of Freedom* (Cambridge: Cambridge University Press).

Huggan, Graham, 2001. *The Postcolonial Exotic: Marketing the Margins* (London and New York: Routledge).

———, 2002. 'Postcolonial Studies and the Anxiety of Interdisciplinarity', *Postcolonial Studies* 5.3: 245–75.

———, 2008. 'Perspectives on Postcolonial Europe', *Journal of Postcolonial Writing* 44.3: 241–49.

Hutcheon, Linda, 1990. 'Circling the Downspout of Empire', in Ian Adam and Helen Tiffin (eds), *Past the Last Post: Theorizing post-colonialism and post-modernism* (Calgary, AB: University of Calgary Press), 167–89.

Irele, Abiola, 1981. *The African Experience in Literature and Ideology* (London: Heinemann).

Jack, Belinda, 1996. *Francophone Literatures: An Introductory Survey* (Oxford: Oxford University Press).

Jahn, Jahnheinz, Oliver Coburn and Ursula Lehrburger, 1968. *Neo-African Literature* (New York: Grove).

James, C. L. R., 1980 [1938]. *The Black Jacobins: Toussaint L'Ouverture and the San Domingo Revolution* (London: Allison and Busby).

JanMohamed, Abdul R., 1992. 'Sexuality on/of the Racial Border: Foucault, Wright, and the Articulation of "Racialized Sexuality"', in Donna C. Stanton (ed.), *Discourses of Sexuality: From Aristotle to AIDS* (Ann Arbor, MI: University of Michigan Press), 94–116.

Jaulin, Robert, 1970. *La Paix blanche: introduction à l'ethnocide* (Paris: Seuil).

Jazouli, Adil, 1992. *Les Années banlieues* (Paris: Seuil).

Jelen, Brigitte, 2002. '17 octobre 1961–17 octobre 2001: une commémoration ambiguë', *French Politics, Culture and Society,* 20.1: 30–43.

Jennings, Eric, 1998. 'Monuments to Frenchness? The Memory of the Great War and the Politics of Guadeloupe's Identity, 1914–1945', *French Historical Studies*, 21.4: 561–92.

———, 2003. 'Remembering "Other" Losses: The *Temple du Souvenir Indochinois* of Nogent-sur-Marne', *History and Memory*, 15.1: 5–48.

Jennings, Laurence, 2000. *French Anti-Slavery: The Movement for the Abolition of Slavery in France, 1802–1848* (Cambridge: Cambridge University Press).

Jonaissant, Jean, 2003. 'Sur un champ miné de bonnes intentions: Francophone

Postcolonial Studies', *Francophone Postcolonial Studies*, 1.2: 83–93.

Kafker, Frank, and James Laux (eds), 1989. *Napoleon and his Times: Selected Interpretations* (Malibar, FL: R. E. Krieger).

Kangafu, Kutumbagana, 1973. *Essai sur la problématique idéologique du 'recours à l'authenticité'* (Kinshasa: Presses Africaines).

Kaplan, Stephen L., 1995. *Farewell, Revolution: Disputed Legacies, France, 1789/1989* (Ithaca, NY: Cornell University Press).

Kasende, Jean-Christophe Luhaka, 2001. *Le Roman africain face aux discours hégémoniques: études sur l'énonciation et l'idéologie dans l'oeuvre de V. Y. Mudimbe* (Paris: L'Harmattan).

Kaup, Monika, and Debra J. Rosenthal (eds), 2002. *Mixing Race, Mixing Culture: Inter-American Literary Dialogues* (Austin, TX: University of Texas Press).

Kavwahirehi, Kasereka, 2006. *V. Y. Mudimbe et la ré-invention de l'Afrique: poétique et politique de la décolonisation des sciences humaines* (Amsterdam: Rodopi).

Kelly, Debra, 2005. *Autobiography and Independence: Selfhood and Creativity in Postcolonial African Writing in French* (Liverpool: Liverpool University Press).

Keown, Michelle, David Murphy and James Procter (eds), 2009. *Comparing Postcolonial Diasporas* (Basingstoke: Palgrave).

Kepel, Gilles, 1991. *Les Banlieues d'Islam* (Paris: Seuil).

Keslassy, Eric, and Alexis Rosenbaum, 2007. *Mémoires vives: pourquoi les communautés instrumentalisent l'histoire* (Paris: Bourin).

Kesteloot, Lilyan, 1968. *Négritude et situation coloniale* (Yaoundé: CLÉ).

——, 1979. *Aimé Césaire* (Paris: Seghers).

——, 1991 [1963]. *Black Writers in French: A Literary History of Negritude*, tr. Ellen Conroy Kennedy (Washington, DC: Howard UP). [First published as *Les Écrivains noirs d'expression française: naissance d'une littérature*.]

Khalfa, Jean (ed.), 2005–06. *Les Temps Modernes*, 635–36. [Special issue: 'Pour Frantz Fanon'.]

Khatibi, Abdelkébir, 1969. *Le Roman maghrébin* (Paris: Maspero).

——, 1971. *La Mémoire tatouée: autobiographie d'un décolonisé* (Paris: Denoël).

——, 1974. *La Blessure du nom propre* (Paris: Denoël).

——, 1976. *Le Lutteur de classe à la manière taoïste* (Paris: Sindbad).

——, 1979a. *Le Livre du sang* (Paris: Gallimard).

——, 1979b. *Le Prophète voilé* (Paris: L'Harmattan).

——, 1983. *Maghreb pluriel* (Paris: Denoël).

——, 1985. *Le Même Livre* (Paris: Éditions de l'Éclat).

——, 1986. *Dédicace à l'année qui vient* (Paris: Fata Morgana).

——, 1987. *Figures de l'étranger dans la littérature française* (Paris: Denoël).

——, 1988. *Par-dessus l'épaule* (Paris: Aubier).

——, 1990a [1983]. *Love in Two Languages,* tr. Richard Howard (Minneapolis, MN: University of Minnesota Press). [First published as *Amour bilingue*.]

——, 1990b. *Un été à Stockholm* (Paris: Flammarion).

——, 1995. *Du Signe à l'image* (Casablanca: Lak).

——, 1996. *La Civilisation marocaine* (Arles: Actes Sud).

——, 1999. *La Langue de l'Autre* (New York: Les Mains secrètes).

——, 2001. *L'Art contemporain arabe* (Paris: Al Manar).

——, 2002. *Le Corps oriental* (Paris: Hazan).

——, 2003. *Pèlerinage d'un artiste amoureux* (Paris: Éditions du Rocher).

——, 2005. *Féerie d'un mutant* (Paris: Le Serpent à plumes).

Khélil, Hédi, 2001. *Figures de l'altérité dans le théâtre de Jean Genet: lecture des 'Nègres' et des 'Paravents'* (Paris: L'Harmattan).

——, 2005. *Jean Genet: arabes, noirs et Palestiniens dans son oeuvre* (Paris: L'Harmattan).

Knight, Diana, 1993. 'Barthes and Orientalism', *New Literary History*, 24.3: 617–33.

——, 1997. *Barthes and Utopia: Space, Travel, Writing* (Oxford: Clarendon Press).

Konate, Doulaye, 2006. 'Une relecture des *Lieux de mémoire* au regard du vécu africain', *Notre Librairie*, 161: 9–15.

Kristeva, Julia, 1977 [1974]. *About Chinese Women*, tr. Anita Barrows (London: Boyars). [First published as *Des Chinoises*.]

——, 1984 [1974]. *Revolution in Poetic Language*, tr. Margaret Waller (New York: Columbia University Press). [First published as *Révolution du langage poétique*.]

——, 1986 [1969]. 'Word, Dialogue, and Novel', in Toril Moi (ed.), *The Kristeva Reader* (Oxford: Blackwell), 35–61. [First published as part of *Séméiôtikè: recherches pour une sémanalyse*.]

——, 1991 [1988]. *Strangers to Ourselves*, tr. Leon S. Roudiez (New York and London: Harvester Wheatsheaf). [First published as *Étrangers à nous-mêmes*.]

Kritzman, Lawrence D., 2003. 'A Certain Idea of French: Cultural Studies, Literature and Theory', *Yale French Studies*, 103: 146–60.

Kruks, Sonya, 1996. 'Fanon, Sartre, and identity politics', in Lewis R. Gordon, T. Denean Sharpley-Whiting and Renee T. White (eds), *Fanon: A Critical Reader* (Oxford: Blackwell), 122–33.

Kurasawa, Fuyuki, 1999. 'The Exotic Effect: Foucault and the Question of Cultural Alterity', *European Journal of Social Theory*, 2.2: 147–65.

Labyrinthe, 2006: 24. [Special issue: 'Faut-il être postcolonial?'.]

Lacan, Jacques, 1981 [1973]. *The Four Fundamental Concepts of Psycho-Analysis* (New York: W. W. Norton). [First published as *Les Quatre Concepts fondamentaux de la psychanalyse*.]

Lacouture, Jean, 1968 [1967]. *Ho Chi Minh: A Political Biography*, tr. Peter Wiles (New York: Random House). [First published as *Ho Chi Minh*.]

Lalonde, Michèle, 1974. *Speak White* (Ottawa, ON: L'Hexagone).

Lamming, George, 1996. 'Concepts of the Caribbean', in Frank Birbalsingh (ed.), *Frontiers of Caribbean Literature in English* (London: Macmillan Education), 1–14.

Laroui, Fouad, 2007. 'Sommes-nous des "primitifs"?' *Jeune Afrique*, 21–27 January: 92.

Laroussi, Farid, and Christopher L. Miller (eds), 2003. *Yale French Studies*, 103. [Special issue: 'French and Francophone: The Challenge of Expanding Horizons'.]

Latouche, Daniel, 1985. 'The Power of Words: The State as a Literary Creation', *Québec Studies*, 3: 12–31.

Lazarus, Neil, 1999. *Nationalism and Cultural Practice in the Postcolonial World* (Cambridge: Cambridge University Press).

——, 2004. *The Cambridge Companion to Postcolonial Literary Studies* (Cambridge: Cambridge University Press).

——, 2006. *Penser le postcolonial: une introduction critique*, tr. Marianne Groulez, Christophe Jaquet and Hélène Quiniou (Paris: Les Éditions Amsterdam).

Lebeau, Vicky, 2005. 'Children of violence', in Silverman, 2005: 128–45.

Lebovics, Herman, 2004. *Bringing the Empire Back Home: France in the Global Age* (Durham, NC: Duke University Press).

Lebrun, Annie, 1996. *Statue cou coupé* (Paris: Jean-Michel Place).

Leclerc, Gérard, 1972. *Anthropologie et colonialisme: essai sur l'histoire de l'africanisme* (Paris: Fayard).

Le Cour Grandmaison, Olivier, 2005. *Coloniser, exterminer: sur la guerre et l'état colonial* (Paris: Fayard, 2005).

Lefeuvre, Daniel, 2006. *Pour en finir avec la repentance coloniale* (Paris: Flammarion).

Leiner, Jacqueline, 1993. *Aimé Césaire: le terreau primordial* (Tübingen: G. Narr).

Leiris, Michel, 1981 [1934]. *L'Afrique fantôme* (Paris: Gallimard).

——, 2003. *La Règle du jeu* (Paris: Gallimard).

Lepage, Roland, 1974. *La Complainte des hivers rouges* (Ottawa: Leméac).

Leruth, Michael F., 1998. 'François Mitterrand's "Festival of the World's Tribes": the logic of exoticism in the French Revolution bicentennial parade', *French Cultural Studies*, 9.1: 51–80.

Le Sueur, James D., 2001. *Uncivil War: Intellectuals and Identity Politics During the Decolonization of Algeria* (Philadelphia, PA: University of Pennsylvania Press).

Lévi-Strauss, Claude, 1962. *La Pensée Sauvage* (Paris: Plon).

——, 1969 [1949]. *The Elementary Structures of Kinship*, tr. J. H. Bell, J. R. von Sturmer and R. Needham (Boston: Beacon Press). [First published as *Les Structures élémentaires de la parenté*.]

——, 1976 [1955]. *Tristes Tropiques*, tr. John and Doreen Weightman (Harmondsworth: Penguin). [First published as *Tristes Tropiques*.]

——, 1978 [1958]. *Structural Anthropology*, tr. Claire Jacobson and Brooke Grundfest Schoepf (Harmondsworth: Penguin). [First published as *Anthropologie structurale*.]

Lewis, Barbara, 1995. 'No Silence: An Interview with Maryse Condé', *Callaloo*, 18.3: 543–50.

Lewis, Shireen K., 2006. *Race, Culture, and Identity: Francophone West African and Caribbean Literature and Theory from Négritude to Créolité* (Lanham, MD: Lexington Books).

Liauzu, Claude, 2007a. 'Ministère de l'hostilité', *Le Monde diplomatique*, July: 28.

——, 2007b. 'Retour à l'histoire', *L'Histoire*, 318: 54–55.

——, and Gilles Manceron (eds), 2006. *La Colonisation, la loi et l'histoire* (Paris: Syllepse).

Lionnet, Françoise, 1993. '*Créolité* in the Indian Ocean: two models of cultural diversity', *Yale French Studies*, 82.1: 101–12.

——, 1995. *Postcolonial Representations: Women, Literature, Identity* (Ithaca, NY, and London: Cornell University Press).

——, 2003. 'Introduction', *Modern Language Notes,* 118.4: 783–86.

——, 2005. 'Francophonie, Postcolonial Studies, and Transnational Feminisms', in Murdoch and Donadey, 2005: 258–69.

——, and Ronnie Scharfman (eds), 1993. *Yale French Studies,* 82–83. [Special issues: 'Post/Colonial Conditions: Exiles, Migrations and Nomadisms'.]

——, and Shuh-Mei Shih (eds), 2005. *Minor Transnationalism* (Durham, NC: Duke University Press).

——, and Dominic Thomas (eds), 2003. *Modern Language Notes,* 118.4. [Special issue: 'Francophone Studies: New Landscapes'.]

Logan, William S., 2006. 'Dien Bien Phu, Vietnam: Managing a Battle Site, Metaphoric and Actual', *Outre-Mers,* 350–51: 175–92.

Loomba, Ania, 1998. *Colonialism/Postcolonialism* (London and New York: Routledge).

Lopes, Henri, 1982. *Le Pleurer-rire* (Paris: Présence Africaine).

Lowe, Lisa, 1991. *Critical Terrains: French and British Orientalisms* (Ithaca, NY, and London: Cornell University Press).

Loxley, Diana, 1990. *Problematic Shores: The Literature of Islands* (London: Macmillan).

Macey, David, 2000. *Frantz Fanon: A Life* (London: Granta).

MacGaffey, Wyatt, 1983. *Modern Kongo Prophets: Religion in a Plural Society* (Bloomington, IN: Indiana University Press).

MacMaster, Neil, 2002. 'The torture controversy (1998–2002): towards a "new history" of the Algerian war?', *Modern and Contemporary France,* 10.4: 449–59.

McClintock, Anne, 1999. 'Fanon and gender agency', in Nigel C. Gibson (ed.), *Rethinking Fanon: The Continuing Dialogue* (New York: Humanity Books), 283–93.

McCormack, Jo, 2007. *Collective Memory: France and the Algerian War (1954–1962)* (Lanham, MD: Lexington Books).

McCusker, Maeve, 2007. *Patrick Chamoiseau: Recovering Memory* (Liverpool: Liverpool University Press).

McLeod, John, 2003. 'Contesting contexts: Francophone thought and Anglophone postcolonialism', in Forsdick and Murphy, 2003: 192–201.

—— (ed.), 2007. *The Routledge Companion to Postcolonial Studies* (London and New York: Routledge).

Major, André, 1965. 'Chénier, mon ancêtre', *Liberté,* 7.1–2: 94–95.

Majumdar, Margaret, 2007. *Postcoloniality: The French Dimension* (Oxford and New York: Berghahn).

Mamarbachi, Alexandre, 2006. 'Quand la fracture coloniale fait disparaître les rapports de classe', *Contretemps,* 16: 143–49.

Manceron, Gilles, 2003. *Marianne et les colonies: une introduction à l'histoire coloniale de la France* (Paris: La Découverte; Ligue des droits de l'homme).

Mann, Gregory, 2005. 'Locating Colonial Histories: Between France and West

Africa', *American Historical Review*, 110.2: 42 paragraphs. Available at http://www.historycooperative.org/journals/ahr/110.2/mann.html (consulted on 28 January 2008).

——, 2006. *Native Sons: West African Veterans and France in the Twentieth Century* (Durham, NC: Duke University Press).

Manzor-Coats, Lillian, 1993. 'Of Witches and Other Things: Maryse Condé's Challenges to Feminist Discourse', *World Literature Today*, 67.4: 737–44.

Maran, René, 1921. *Batouala, véritable roman nègre* (Paris: Albin Michel).

Mariotti, Jean, 1996. *À bord de l'Incertaine* (Nouméa: Grain de Sable).

Marr, David G., 1981. *Vietnamese Tradition on Trial, 1920–1945* (Berkeley, CA: University of California Press).

Marriott, David, 2005. 'En moi: Frantz Fanon and René Maran', in Silverman, 2005: 146–79.

Marseille, Jacques, 2005 [1984]. *Empire colonial et capitalisme français: histoire d'un divorce* (Paris: Albin Michel).

Marshall, Bill, 2009. *The French Atlantic: Travels in Culture and History* (Liverpool: Liverpool University Press).

Masolo, Dismas A., 1994. *African Philosophy in Search of Identity* (Bloomington, IN: Indiana University Press).

Maspero, François, 1994. 'Préface', in Benot, 1944: i–xvi.

Mateata-Allain, Kareva, 2003. 'Ma'ohi Women Writers of Colonial French Polynesia: Passive Resistance toward a *Post*(-)colonial Literature', *Jouvert*, 7.2. Available at http://social.chass.ncsu.edu/jouvert/v7i2/mateat.htm (consulted on 23 January 2008).

——, 2005. 'Oceanic people in dialogue: French Polynesian literature as transnational link', *International Journal of Francophone Studies*, 8.3: 269–88.

——, Frank Stewart and Alexander Mawyer (eds), 2005. *Varua Tupu: New Writing and Art from French Polynesia* (Honolulu: University of Hawaii Press).

Maucorps, Paul H., Albert Memmi and Jean-François Held, 1965. *Les Français et le racisme* (Paris: Payot).

Maurin, Eric, 2005. *Le Ghetto français: enquête sur le séparatisme social* (Paris: Seuil).

Mauss, Marcel, 1985 [1938]. 'A category of the human mind: the notion of person, the notion of self', in Michael Carrithers, Steven Collins and Steven Lukes (eds), *The Category of the Person: Anthropology, Philosophy, History* (Cambridge: Cambridge University Press), 1–25. [First published as 'Une catégorie de l'esprit humain: la notion de personne, celle de "Moi", un plan de travail'.]

Mbem, André Julien, 2007. *Nicolas Sarkozy à Dakar: débats et enjeux autour d'un discours* (Paris: L'Harmattan).

Mbembe, Achille, 2001 [2000]. *On the Postcolony* (Berkeley, CA: University of California Press). [First published as *De la postcolonie: essai sur l'imagination politique dans l'Afrique contemporaine*.]

——, 2005. 'Interview with Christian Hoeller', *Springerin Magazine*. Available at http://www.springerin.at (consulted on 31 January 2008).

——, 2007. 'L'insolence de l'ignorance', *Jeune Afrique*, 12–25 August: 156.

Mbom, Clément, 1979. *Le Théâtre d'Aimé Césaire ou la primauté de l'universalité humaine* (Paris: Nathan).

Meddeb, Abdelwahab (ed.), 1997. *Dédale*, 5–6. [Special issue: 'Postcolonialisme: Décentrement, Déplacement, Dissémination'.]

Memmi, Albert, 1960 [1955]. *Strangers*, tr. Brian Rhys (New York: Orion). [First published as *Agar*.]

——, 1962 [1962]. *Portrait of a Jew*, tr. Elizabeth Abbot (New York: Orion). [First published as *Portrait d'un juif*.]

——, 1966 [1966]. *The Liberation of the Jew*, tr. Judy Hyun (New York: Orion). [First published as *La Libération du Juif*.]

——, 1968 [1968]. *Dominated Man: Notes Towards a Portrait*, tr. Eleanor Levieux (New York: Orion). [First published as *L'Homme dominé*.]

——, 1971a [1969]. *The Scorpion or The Imaginary Confession*, tr. Eleanor Levieux (Chicago: J. Philip O'Hara). [First published as *Le Scorpion ou la confession imaginaire*.]

——, 1971b. 'La Vie impossible de Frantz Fanon', *Esprit*, 406: 248–73.

——, 1975 [1974]. *Jews and Arabs*, tr. Eleanor Levieux (Chicago: J. Philip O'Hara). [First published as *Juifs et Arabes*.]

——, 1977. *Le Désert ou la vie et les aventures de Jubaïr Ouali El-Mammi* (Paris: Gallimard).

——, 1988. *Le Pharaon* (Paris: Julliard).

——, 2000a [1982]. *Racism*, tr. Steve Martinot (Minneapolis, MN: University of Minnesota Press). [First published as *Le Racisme*.]

——, 2000b. *Le Nomade immobile* (Paris: Arléa).

——, 2001 [1953]. *The Pillar of Salt*, tr. Édouard Roditi (Boston: Beacon Press). [First published as *La Statue de sel*.]

——, 2003 [1957]. *The Colonizer and the Colonized*, tr. Howard Greenfeld (London: Earthscan). [First published as *Portrait du colonisé précédé du Portrait du colonisateur*.]

——, 2006 [2004]. *Decolonization and the Decolonized*, tr. Robert Bononno (Minneapolis and London: University of Minnesota Press). [First published as *Portrait du décolonisé arabo-musulman et de quelques autres*.]

Mémoire Senghor: 50 écrits en hommage aux 100 ans du poète-président, 2006. (Paris: UNESCO).

Midiohouan, Guy Ossito, 1986: *L'Idéologie dans la littérature négro-africaine de langue française* (Paris: L'Harmattan).

Miller, Christopher L., 1998. *Nationalists and Nomads: Essays on Francophone African Literature and Culture* (Chicago: University of Chicago Press).

——, 2008. *The French Atlantic Triangle: Literature and Culture of the Slave Trade* (Durham, NC: Duke University Press).

Milne, Lorna, 2003. 'Gare au gauffrier! Literature and Francophone Postcolonial Studies', *Francophone Postcolonial Studies*, 1.1: 60–63.

Mongo Mboussa, Boniface (ed.), 2000. *Africultures*, 28. [Special issue: 'Postcolonialisme: inventaire et débats'.]

——, 2001. *Désir d'Afrique* (Paris: Gallimard).

Moniot, Henri, 1999. 'Faire du Nora sous les tropiques', in Jean-Pierre Chrétien and Jean-Louis Triaud (eds), *Histoire d'Afrique: les enjeux de mémoire* (Paris: Karthala), 13–26.

Morris, Keidra T., and Sydney Reece, 1998. 'Interview with Maryse Condé, September, 1998, Petit Bourg, Guadeloupe'. Available at http://www.bunchecenter.ucla.edu/diaspora/research_topics/Caribbean_literature.htm (consulted on 28 January 2008).

Moruzzi, Norma Claire, 1993. 'National Abjects: Julia Kristeva on the Process of Political Self-Identification', in Kelly Oliver (ed.), *Ethics, Politics, and Difference in Julia Kristeva's Writing* (London and New York: Routledge), 135–49.

Moura, Jean-Marc, 1998. *La Littérature des lointains: histoire de l'exotisme européen au XXe siècle* (Paris: Champion).

——, 2007 [1999]. *Littératures francophones et théorie postcoloniale* (Paris: PUF).

Mouralis, Bernard, 1988. *V. Y. Mudimbe ou le discours, l'écart et l'écriture* (Paris: Présence Africaine).

——, 2006. 'Prise en compte du fait colonial et notion de postcolonial: la question de l'auteur', *Francophone Postcolonial Studies*, 4.2: 42–57.

Mudimbe, Valentin Yves, 1971. *Déchirures, poèmes* (Kinshasa: Éditions du Mont Noir).

——, 1973a. *L'Autre face du royaume: une introduction à la critique des langages en folie* (Lausanne: L'âge d'homme).

——, 1973b. *Entre les eaux: Dieu, un prêtre, la révolution* (Paris: Présence Africaine).

——, 1976. *Le Bel immonde* (Paris: Présence Africaine).

——, 1979. *L'Écart* (Paris: Présence Africaine).

——, 1982. *L'Odeur du père: essai sur les limites de la science et de la vie en Afrique noire* (Paris: Présence Africaine).

——, 1988. *The Invention of Africa: Gnosis, Philosophy, and the Order of Knowledge* (Bloomington and Indianapolis, IN: Indiana University Press; London: James Currey).

——, 1989. *Shaba deux: les carnets de mère Marie-Gertrude* (Paris: Présence Africaine).

——, 1991. *Parables and Fables: Exegesis, Textuality, and Politics in Central Africa* (Madison, WI: University of Wisconsin Press).

—— (ed.), 1992. *The Surreptitious Speech: Présence Africaine and the Politics of Otherness* (Chicago: University of Chicago Press).

——, 1994a. *Les Corps glorieux des mots et des êtres: esquisse d'un jardin africain à la bénédictine* (Paris: Présence Africaine; Montreal: Humanitas).

——, 1994b. *The Idea of Africa* (Bloomington and Indianapolis, IN: Indiana University Press; London: James Currey).

——, 1994c. 'La Diaspora et l'héritage culturel de l'impérialisme comme lieu de discours critique et de représentation du monde', *Revue Canadienne des Études Africaines*, 28.1: 89–100.

——, 1997a. *Tales of Faith: Religion as Political Performance in Central Africa* (London and Atlantic Highlands, NJ: The Athlone Press).

—— (ed.), 1997b: *Nations, Identities, Culture* (Durham, NC: Duke University Press).

Mudimbe-Boyi, Elisabeth, 2006. 'Présence Africaine', in Lawrence D. Kritzman (ed.), *The Columbia History of Twentieth-Century French Thought* (New York: Columbia University Press), 736–38.

Multitudes, 2006: 26. [Special issue: 'Postcolonial et politique de l'histoire'.]

Munro, Martin, 2007. *Exile and Post-1946 Haitian Literature* (Liverpool: Liverpool University Press).

Murdoch, H. Adlai, 2001. *Creole Identity in the French Caribbean Novel* (Gainesville, FL: University Press of Florida).

——, and Anne Donadey (eds), 2005. *Postcolonial Theory and Francophone Literary Studies* (Gainesville, FL: University Press of Florida).

Murphy, David, 2000. *Sembene: Imagining Alternatives in Film and Fiction* (Oxford: James Currey; Trenton, NJ: Africa World Press).

——, 2003. 'Choosing a Framework: The Limits of French Studies/Francophone Studies/Postcolonial Studies', *Francophone Postcolonial Studies*, 1.1: 72–80.

——, 2006. 'Beyond Anglophone Imperialism?', *New Formations*, 59: 132–43.

——, 2008. 'Birth of a Nation? The Origins of Senegalese Literature in French', *Research in African Literatures*, 39.1: 48–69.

Mwayila, Tshiyembe, 1990. *L'État postcolonial, facteur d'insécurité en Afrique* (Paris: Présence Africaine).

Ndaywel è Nziem, Isidore, 1998. *Histoire générale du Congo: de l'héritage ancien à la République Démocratique* (Paris and Brussels: Duculot).

Néret, Gilles (ed.), 2002. *Description de l'Égypte*, tr. Chris Miller (Cologne: Taschen).

Nesbitt, Nick, 2003. *Voicing Memory: History and Subjectivity in French Caribbean Literature* (Charlottesville, VA: University of Virginia Press).

——, 2005. 'The Idea of 1804', *Yale French Studies*, 107: 6–38.

Ngal, Georges, 1994. *Aimé Césaire: un homme à la recherche d'une patrie* (Paris: Présence Africaine).

Nicole, Robert, 2000. *The Word, the Pen, and the Pistol: Literature and Power in Tahiti* (New York: State University of New York Press).

Nimrod, 2003. *Tombeau de Léopold Sédar Senghor* (Cognac: Le Temps qu'il fait).

Njami, Simon, 2006. *C'était Senghor* (Paris: Fayard).

Noiriel, Gérard, 1988. *Le Creuset français: histoire de l'immigration, XIX–XXe siècle* (Paris: Seuil).

——, 2007. 'Non au ministère de l'immigration et de l'identité nationale!', *Jeune Afrique*, 5–11 August: 103.

Nora, Pierre, 1997 [1984–93]. *Les Lieux de mémoire*, 3 vols (Paris: Gallimard).

Nord, Philip, 1995. *The Republican Moment: Struggles for Democracy in Nineteenth-Century France* (Cambridge, MA: Harvard University Press).

Norindr, Panivong, 1996. *Phantasmatic Indochina: French Colonial Ideology in Architecture, Film, and Literature* (Durham, NC: Duke University Press).

Northcutt, Wayne, 1991. 'François Mitterrand and the Political Use of Symbols: The Construction of a Centrist Republic', *French Historical Studies*, 17.1: 141–58.

Nourbese Philip, Marlene, 1995. 'A Piece of Land Surrounded', *Orion*, 14.2: 41–47.

O'Shaughnessy, Martin, 2001. 'The Parisian popular as reactionary modernization', *Studies in French Cinema*, 1.2: 80–88.

Ostler, Nicholas, 2005. *Empires of the Word: A Language History of the World* (London: HarperCollins).

Outre-Mers, 2006: 350–51. [Special issue: 'Sites et monuments de mémoire'.]

Paoli, Paul-François, 2006. *Nous ne sommes pas coupables: assez de repentances* (Paris: La Table Ronde).

Parry, Benita, 1994. 'Signs of our Times: A Discussion of Homi Bhabha's *The Location of Culture*', *Third Text*, 28–29: 5–24.

——, 2004. *Postcolonial Studies: A Materialist Critique* (London: Routledge).

Peabody, Sue, and Tyler Stovall (eds.), 2003. *The Color of Liberty: Histories of Race in France* (Durham, NC: Duke University Press).

Perret, Delphine, 2006. 'Dream-Country', tr. Susan Guillory, *Journal of Caribbean Literatures*, 4.2: 117–33.

——, and Marie-Denise Shelton (eds), 1995. *Callaloo,* 18.3. [Special Issue: 'Maryse Condé'.]

Petit Larousse Illustré 1981, 1980. (Paris: Librairie Larousse).

Petit Larousse Illustré 1994, 1993. (Paris: Librairie Larousse).

Petrey, Sandy, 2003. 'Language without Meaning', *Yale French Studies*, 103: 133–45.

Pfaff, Françoise, 1996 [1993]. *Conversations with Maryse Condé*, tr. Françoise Pfaff (Lincoln, NE, and London: University of Nebraska Press). [First published as *Entretiens avec Maryse Condé*.]

Planche, Jean-Louis, 2006. *Sétif 1945: histoire d'un massacre annoncé* (Paris: Perrin).

Poddar, Prem, Rajeev Patke and Lars Jensen (eds), 2008. *A Historical Companion to Postcolonial Literatures: Continental Europe and its Empires* (Edinburgh: Edinburgh University Press).

Poulin, Jacques, 1988. *Volkswagen Blues* (Montreal: Leméac).

Prabhu, Anjali, 2005. 'Representation in Mauritian politics: who speaks for African pasts?', *International Journal of Francophone Literatures*, 8.2: 183–97.

Pratt, Mary Louise, 1992. *Imperial Eyes: Travel Writing and Transculturation* (London and New York: Routledge).

Premier Congrès Des Écrivains et Artistes Noirs, 1956. (Paris: Présence Africaine).

Price, Sally, 2007. *Paris Primitive: Jacques Chirac's Museum on the Quai Branly* (Chicago: University of Chicago Press).

Puri, Shalini, 2004. *The Caribbean Postcolonial: Social Equality, Post-Nationalism, and Cultural Hybridity* (New York: Palgrave Macmillan).

Quinn-Judge, Sophie, 1993. 'Hô Chi Minh: New Perspectives from the Comintern Files', *Viet Nam Forum,* 14: 61–81.

——, 2002. *Ho Chi Minh: The Missing Years, 1919–1941* (Berkeley, CA: University of California Press).

Rabinow, Paul, 1986. 'Representations are social facts: modernity and post-modernity in anthropology', in Clifford and Marcus (eds), 1986: 234–61.

Randall, Marilyn, 2003. 'Resistance, submission and oppositionality: national identity in French Canada', in Forsdick and Murphy, 2003: 77–87.

Raybaud, Antoine, 1997. 'Deuil sans travail, travail sans deuil: la France a-t-elle une mémoire coloniale?', *Dédale*, 5–6: 85–93.

Reinhardt, Catherine A., 2006. *Claims to Memory: Beyond Slavery and Emancipation in the French Caribbean* (New York: Berghahn).

Research in African Literatures, 2002. 33.4. [Special issue: 'Léopold Sédar Senghor, 1906–2001'.]

Revel, Jacques, 2000. 'Histoire *vs* mémoire en France aujourd'hui', *French Politics, Culture and Society*, 18.1: 1–12.

Ribbe, Claude, 2005. *Le Crime de Napoléon* (Paris: Éditions Privé).

Rice, Alison, 2006. *Time Signatures: Contextualizing Contemporary Francophone Autobiographical Writing from the Maghreb* (Lanham, MD: Lexington Books).

Richard, Jean-Luc, 2004. *Partir ou rester? Destinées des jeunes issus de l'immigration* (Paris: PUF).

Rioux, Jean-Pierre, 2006. *La France perd la mémoire: comment un pays démissionne de son histoire* (Paris: Perrin).

Rivet, Daniel, 1992. 'Le fait colonial et nous: histoire d'un éloignement', *Vingtième Siècle*, 33: 127–38.

Robin, Régine, 1993 [1983]. *La Québécoite* (Montreal: XYZ).

Roche, Christian, 2006. *Léopold Sédar Senghor: le président humaniste* (Toulouse: Privat).

Rollet, Brigitte, 1999. 'Identity and Alterity in Wargnier's *Indochine*', in Phil Powrie (ed.), *Contemporary French Cinema: Continuity and Difference* (Oxford: Oxford University Press), 37–46.

Root, Deborah, 1988. 'The Imperial Signifier: Todorov and the Conquest of Mexico', *Cultural Critique*, 9: 197–219.

Rosello, Mireille, 2003. 'Unhoming Francophone Studies: A House in the Middle of the Current', *Yale French Studies*, 103: 123–32.

——, 2005. *France and the Maghreb: Performative Encounters* (Gainesville, FL: University Press of Florida).

Ross, Kristin, 1995. *Fast Cars, Clean Bodies: Decolonization and the Reordering of French Culture* (Cambridge, MA: MIT Press).

Rouch, Jean, 2003. *Ciné-ethnography* (Minneapolis, MN: University of Minnesota Press).

Roumani, Judith, 1987. *Albert Memmi* (Philadelphia, PA: Celfan Edition Monographs).

Rousso, Henry, 1986. *Le Syndrome de Vichy* (Paris: Seuil).

Royle, Nicholas (ed.), 2000. *Deconstructions: A User's Guide* (Basingstoke: Palgrave Macmillan).

Ruedy, John (ed.), 1994. *Islamism and Secularism in North Africa* (New York: St Martin's Press).

Ruscio, Alain (ed.), 1990. *Ho Chi Minh: textes, 1914–1969* (Paris: L'Harmattan).

Sabbagh, Daniel, 2004. 'Affirmative Action at Sciences Po', in Herrick Chapman and Laura Frader (eds), *Race in France: Interdisciplinary Perspectives on the Politics of Difference* (New York: Berghahn), 246–58.

Said, Edward W., 1978. *Orientalism: Western Conceptions of the Orient* (London: Routledge and Kegan Paul).

——, 1980. *Orientalisme: l'Orient créé par l'Occident*, tr. Catherine Malamoud (Paris: Seuil).

——, 1983. 'Traveling Theory', in *The World, the Text, and the Critic* (Cambridge, MA: Harvard University Press), 226–47.

——, 1986. 'Foucault and the Imagination of Power', in David C. Hoys (ed.), *Foucault: A Critical Reader* (London: Basil Blackwell), 149–55.

——, 1993. *Culture and Imperialism* (London: Vintage).

——, 2000. *Culture et impérialisme*, tr. Paul Chemla (Paris: Fayard; Le Monde diplomatique).

——, 2003. *Freud and the Non-European* (London: Verso).

——, 2004. *Humanism and Democratic Criticism* (New York: Columbia).

Sandoval, Chéla, 1997. 'Theorizing White Consciousness for a Post-Empire World: Barthes, Fanon, and the Rhetoric of Love', in Ruth Frankenberg (ed.), *Displacing Whiteness: Essays in Social and Cultural Criticism* (Durham, NC: Duke University Press), 86–106.

Sarkozy, Nicolas, 2007. 'Allocution de M. Nicolas Sarkozy, Président de la République, prononcée à l'Université de Dakar. Available at http://www.elysee.fr/elysee/elysee.fr/francais/interventions/2007/juillet/allocutionaluni-versitededakar.79184.html (consulted 3 October 2008).

Sartre, Jean-Paul, 1947. *Situations 1* (Paris: Gallimard).

——, 1948 [1946]. *Anti-Semite and Jew*, tr. G. J. Becker (New York: Schocken Books). [First published as *Réflexions sur la question juive*.]

——, 1967 [1961], 'Preface', in Fanon, 1967: 7–26.

——, 1988 [1948]. 'Black Orpheus', in *'What is Literature?' and other essays* (Cambridge, MA: Harvard University Press), 289–330. [Originally published as 'Orphée Noir'.]

——, 1992 [1983]. *Notebooks for an Ethics,* tr. David Pellauer (Chicago: University of Chicago Press). [Originally published as *Cahiers pour une morale*.]

——, 2001a [1964]. *Colonialism and Neocolonialism*, tr. Azzedine Haddour, Steve Brewer and Terry McWilliams (London: Routledge). [Originally published as *Situations V.*]

——, 2001b [1948]. 'To be hungry already means that you want to be free', tr. Adrian van den Hoven, *Sartre Studies International*, 7.2: 8–11. [First published in *Caliban* 20, October.]

——, 2003a [1957]. 'Preface', in Memmi, 2003.

——, 2003b [1972]. 'About Munich', tr. Elizabeth Bowman, *Sartre Studies International*, 9.2: 7–8. [First published in *La Cause du people,* 29, 15 October.]

Saura, Bruno, 2004. 'Tahiti (Polynésie Française) est métissée; mais est-elle métisse?', in Frédéric Angleviel (ed.), *La Nouvelle-Calédonie, terre de métissages* (Paris: Les Indes savants), 161–77.

Saussy, Haun (ed.), 2006. *Comparative Literature in an Age of Globalization* (Baltimore, MD: Johns Hopkins University Press).

Schalk, David L., 2002. 'Of Memories and Monuments: Paris and Algeria, Fréjus and Indochina', *Historical Reflections/Réflexions historiques*, 28.2: 241–53.

——, 2005 [1991]. *War and the Ivory Tower* (Lincoln, NE: University of Nebraska Press).

Scharfman, Ronnie, 1987. *Engagement and the Language of the Subject in the Poetry of Aimé Césaire* (Gainesville, FL: University Press of Florida).

Schaub, Uta Liebmann, 1989. 'Foucault's Oriental Subtext', *PMLA*, 104.3: 306–16.

Schehr, Laurence R., 2003. 'Albert Memmi's Tricultural *Tikkun*: Renewal and Transformation through Writing', *French Forum*, 28.3: 59–83.

Schwartzwald, Robert, 1985. 'Literature and Intellectual Realignments in Québec', *Québec Studies*, 3: 32–56.

——, 2003. 'Rush to Judgment? Postcolonial Criticism and Quebec', *Québec Studies*, 35: 113–32.

Scott, David, 1999. *Refashioning Futures: Criticism after Postcoloniality* (Princeton, NJ: Princeton University Press).

——, 2004. *Conscripts of Modernity: The Tragedy of Colonial Enlightenment* (Durham, NC: Duke University Press).

Scott, Joan, 1996. *Only Paradoxes to Offer: French Feminists and the Rights of Man* (Cambridge, MA: Harvard University Press).

Segalen, Victor, 2002 [1978]. *Essay on Exoticism: An Aesthetics of Diversity*, tr. and ed. Yaël Rachel Schlick (Durham, NC: Duke University Press). [First published as *Essai sur l'exotisme: une esthétique du divers*.]

Sekyi-Otu, Ato, 1996. *Fanon's Dialectic of Experience* (Cambridge, MA, and London: Harvard University Press).

Semujanga, Josias, 1998. 'De l'autobiographie intellectuelle chez V. Y. Mudimbe', in Suzanne Crosta, (ed.), *Récits de la vie de l'Afrique et des Antilles* (Quebec-Laval: Grecla), 53–99.

Senghor, cent ans: la BD burkinabè célèbre le poète-président, 2006. (Bobo-Dioulasso: Atelier de Sya).

Senghor, Lamine, 1927. *La Violation d'un pays* (Paris: Bureau d'éditions de diffusion et de publicité).

Senghor, Léopold Sédar (ed.), 1948. *Anthologie de la nouvelle poésie nègre et malgache de langue française* (Paris: PUF).

——, 1964. *Liberté 1: Négritude et humanisme* (Paris: Seuil).

——, 1971. *Liberté 2: Nation et voie africaine du socialisme* (Paris: Seuil).

——, 1976. *Selected poems/Poésies choisies*, tr. Craig Williamson (London: Rex Collings).

——, 1977a. 'Avant-Propos ou Comment être nègre en français?', in Gisela Bonn (ed.), *Le Sénégal écrit: anthologie de la littérature sénégalaise d'expression française* (Tübingen: Horst Erdmann; Dakar: NÉA), 7–10.

——, 1977b. *Liberté 3: Négritude et civilisation de l'universel* (Paris: Seuil).

——, 1980. *La Poésie de l'action* (Paris: Stock).

——, 1983. *Liberté 4: Socialisme et planification* (Paris: Seuil).

——, 1988. *Ce que je crois* (Paris: Grasset).

——, 1993. *Liberté 5: Le Dialogue des cultures* (Paris: Seuil).

——, 2006. *Oeuvre poétique* (Paris: Seuil).

Serrano, Richard, 2005. *Against the Postcolonial: 'Francophone' Writers at the Ends of French Empire* (Lanham, MD: Lexington Books).

Sharpley-Whiting, T. Denean, 1998. *Frantz Fanon: Conflicts and Feminisms* (Lanham, MD: Rowman & Littlefield).

——, 2002. *Negritude Women* (Minneapolis, MN: University of Minnesota Press).

Sharrad, Paul, 1998. 'Pathways in the sea: a pelagic post-colonialism', in Jean-Pierre Dutrix (ed.), *Literary Archipelagoes* (Dijon: Presses Universitaires de Dijon), 95–108.

Sheller, Mimi, 2003. *Consuming the Caribbean: From Arawaks to Zombies* (London: Routledge).

Shelton, Marie-Denise, 1993. 'Condé: The Politics of Gender and Identity', *World Literature Today*, 67.4: 717–22.

Shepard, Todd, 2006. *The Invention of Decolonization: The Algerian War and the Remaking of France* (Ithaca, NY: Cornell University Press).

Sherzer, Dina (ed.), 1996. *Cinema, Colonialism, Postcolonialism: Perspectives from the French and Francophone Worlds* (Austin, TX: University of Texas Press).

Sibeud, Emmanuelle, 2004. '*Post-colonial* et *Colonial Studies*: enjeux et débat', *Revue d'Histoire Moderne et Contemporaine*, 51: 87–95.

Silverman, Maxim, 1992. *Deconstructing the Nation: Immigration, Racism and Citizenship in Modern France* (New York and London: Routledge).

—— (ed.), 2005. *Frantz Fanon's 'Black Skin, White Masks'* (Manchester: Manchester University Press).

——, 2007. 'The empire looks back', *Screen*, 48.2: 245–49.

Silverstein, Paul, 2004. *Algeria in France: Transpolitics, Race, and Nation* (Bloomington and Indianapolis, IN: Indiana University Press).

Slavin, David, 2001. *Colonial Cinema and Imperial France, 1919–1939: White Blind Spots, Male Fantasies, Settler Myths* (Baltimore, MD: Johns Hopkins University Press).

Smouts, Marie-Claude (ed.), 2007. *La Situation postcoloniale* (Paris: Les Presses Sciences Po).

Söderlind, Sylvia, 1991. *Margin/Alias: Language and Colonization in Canadian and Québécois Fiction* (Toronto: University of Toronto Press).

Songolo, Aliko, 1988. 'Early PA: Muffled Discourse', *ALA Bulletin*, 14.3: 25–29.

Soyinka, Wole, 1976. *Myth, Literature and the African World* (Cambridge: Cambridge University Press).

——, 2002. 'Senghor: Lessons in Power', *Research in African Literatures*, 33.4: 1–2.

Spaas, Lieve, 2007. 'France's postcolonialism: an English debate?', *Journal of Romance Studies*, 7.3: 133–42.

——, 2008. *How Belgium Colonized the Mind of the Congo: Seeking the Memory of an African People* (Ceredigion: Edwin Mellen).

Spitz, Chantal, 2002a. Untitled. *Revue LittéraMa'ohi: ramées de littérature polynésienne*, 1: 108–09.

——, 2002b. 'Identité Comment', *Revue LittéraMa'ohi: ramées de littérature polynésienne*, 1: 110–13.

Spivak, Gayatri Chakravorty, 1987. *In Other Worlds: Essays in Cultural Politics* (London and New York: Routledge).

——, 1988. 'Can the Subaltern Speak?', in Cary Nelson and Lawrence Grossberg (eds), *Marxism and the Interpretation of Culture* (Basingstoke: Macmillan), 271–313.

——, 1990. *The Post-colonial Critic: Interviews, Strategies, Dialogues*, ed. Sarah Harasym (London and New York: Routledge).

——, 1993. *Outside in the Teaching Machine* (London: Routledge).

——, 1995. 'Ghostwriting', *Diacritics*, 25.2: 65–84.

——, 1999. *A Critique of Postcolonial Reason: Towards a History of the Vanishing Present* (Cambridge, MA: Harvard University Press).

——, 2000. 'Deconstruction and Cultural Studies', in Royle, 2000: 14–43.

——, 2006. 'World Systems and The Creole', *Narrative*, 14.1: 102–12.

Steins, Martin, 1976. 'Jeunesse nègre', *Neohelicon*, 4.1–2: 91–121.

——, 1981. 'Entre l'exotisme et la négritude: la littérature coloniale', *L'Afrique littéraire et artistique*, 58: 71–82.

Stevens, Mary, 2008. 'Re-membering the Nation: the Project for the Cité nationale de l'histoire de l'immigration', unpublished PhD dissertation, University College London.

Stoler, Ann Laura, 1995. *Race and the Education of Desire: Foucault's 'History of Sexuality' and the Colonial Order of Things* (Durham, NC: Duke University Press).

——, Carole McGranahan and Peter C. Purdue (eds), 2007. *Imperial Formations* (Sante Fe, NM: School for Advanced Research Press; Oxford: James Currey).

Stone, Robert, and Elizabeth Bowman, 1986. 'Dialectical Ethics: A First Look at Sartre's Unpublished 1964 Roman Lecture Notes', *Social Text*, 13–14: 195–215.

Stovall, Tyler, 1998. 'The Color Line Behind the Lines: Racial Violence in France during the Great War', *American Historical Review*, 103.3: 737–69.

——, 2003. 'From Red Belt to Black Belt: Race, Class, and Urban Marginality in Twentieth-Century Paris', in Peabody and Stovall, 2003: 351–69.

——, and Georges Van Den Abbeele (eds), 2003. *French Civilization and its Discontents: Nationalism, Colonialism, Race* (Lanham, MD: Lexington Books).

Strenski, Ivan, 2004. '*Nous et les Autres*: The Politics of Tzvetan Todorov's "Critical Humanism"', *French Politics*, 2.1: 97–109.

Strike, Joëlle, 2003. *Albert Memmi: autobiographie et autographie* (Paris: L'Harmattan).

Suk, Jeannie, 2001. *Postcolonial Paradoxes in French Caribbean Writing: Césaire, Glissant, Condé* (Oxford: Clarendon Press).

Syrotinski, Michael, 2002. *Singular Performances: Reinscribing the Subject in Francophone African Writing* (Charlottesville, VA, and London: University of Virginia Press).

——, 2007. *Deconstruction and the Postcolonial: At the Limits of Theory* (Liverpool: Liverpool University Press).

Taguieff, Pierre-André, 1998. *La Couleur et le sang: doctrines racistes à la française* (Paris: Mille et une nuits).

Tai, Hue-Tam Ho, 2001. 'Remembered Realms: Pierre Nora and French National Memory', *American Historical Review*, 106.3: 38 paragraphs. Available at http://www.historycooperative.org/journals/ahr/106.3/ah000906.html (consulted on 28 January 2008).

Tarr, Carrie, 2005. *Reframing Difference: 'Beur' and 'Banlieue' Filmmaking in France* (Manchester: Manchester University Press).

Télérama, 2007. April. [Special issue: 'Fraternité'.]

Tempels, Placide R., 1949 [1945]. *La Philosophie bantoue*, trad. A. Rubbens (Paris: Présence Africaine).

Terray, Emmanuel, 1987. *L'État contemporain en Afrique* (Paris: L'Harmattan).

Thackway, Melissa, 2003. *Africa Shoots Back: Alternative Perspectives in Sub-Saharan Francophone African Film* (Bloomington, IN: Indiana University Press; Oxford: James Currey).

Thibaudat, Jean-Pierre, 2005. 'Édouard Glissant et Patrick Chamoiseau, écrivains, détaillent leur refus de la loi de février: "Il faut une solidarité des mémoires"'. *Libération*, 8 December. Available at http://www.liberation.fr/page.php?Article=343424 (consulted on 9 December 2007).

Thobie, Jacques, Gilbert Meynier, Catherine Coquery-Vidrovitch and Charles-Robert Agéron, 1990. *Histoire de la France coloniale, 1914–1990* (Paris: Armand Colin).

Thomas, Dominic, 2005. 'Intersections and Trajectories: Francophone Studies and Postcolonial Theory', in Murdoch and Donadey, 2005: 235–57.

——, 2007. *Black France: Colonialism, Immigration, and Transnationalism* (Bloomington and Indianapolis, IN: Indiana University Press).

Todorov, Tzvetan, 1980. 'Préface', in Said, 1980: vii–x.

——, 1984 [1982]. *The Conquest of America: The Question of the Other*, tr. Richard Howard (New York and London: Harper and Row). [First published as *La Conquête de l'Amérique*.]

——, 1986. '"Race", Writing, and Culture', tr. Loulou Mack, in Henry Louis Gates, Jr. (ed.), *'Race', Writing, and Difference* (Chicago and London: University of Chicago Press), 370–80.

——, 1993 [1989]. *On Human Diversity: Nationalism, Racism, and Exoticism in French Thought*, tr. Catherine Porter (Cambridge, MA: Harvard University Press). [First published as *Nous et les autres: la réflexion française sur la diversité humaine*.]

——, 1996. 'Living Alone Together', *New Literary History*, 27: 1–14.

——, 2007. 'Un ministère indésirable dans une démocratie libérale'. *Le Monde*, 17 mars.

Torabully, Khal, 1992. *Cale d'étoile, coolitude* (Île de la Réunion: Azalées éditions).

——, 1999. *Chair corail, fragments coolies* (Guadeloupe: Ibis Rouge).

Toumson, Roger, 1998. *Mythologie du métissage* (Paris: PUF).

Towa, Marcien, 1976. *Léopold Sédar Senghor: négritude ou servitude?* (Yaoundé: CLÉ).

Tran Dan Tien, 1967. *Souvenirs sur Ho Chi Minh* (Hanoi: Foreign Languages Press).

Tremblay, Michel, 1972 [1967]. *Les Belles-Soeurs* (Montreal: Leméac).

Trivedi, Harish, 1999. 'The Postcolonial or the transcolonial? Location and language', *Interventions*, 1.2: 269–72.

Trouillet, Michel-Rolph, 1995. *Silencing the Past: Power and the Production of History* (Boston: Beacon Press).

Tshitenge Lubabu, Muitubile K. (ed.), 2004. *Césaire et nous: une rencontre entre l'Afrique et les Amériques au XXIe siècle* (Bamako: Cauris).

Turner, Lou, 1996. 'On the difference between the Hegelian and Fanonian dialectic of lordship and bondage', in Lewis R. Gordon, T. Denean Sharpley-Whiting and Renee T. White (eds), *Fanon: A Critical Reader* (Oxford: Blackwell), 134–51.

Ukadike, Nwachukwu Frank, 1994. *Black African Cinema* (Berkeley, CA: University of California Press).

Vaillant, Janet G., 1990. *Black, French and African: A Life of Léopold Sédar Senghor* (Cambridge, MA: Harvard University Press).

——, 2006. *Vie de Léopold Sédar Senghor: noir, français et africain*, tr. Roger Meunier (Paris: Karthala).

Vallières, Pierre, 1969. *Nègres blancs d'Amérique* (Montreal: Parti pris).

Vautier, Marie, 1998. *New World Myth: Postmodernism and Postcolonialism in Canadian Fiction* (Montreal and London: McGill-Queen's University Press).

——, 2003. 'Les Pays du nouveau monde, le post-colonialisme de consensus, et le catholicisme québécois', *Québec Studies*, 35: 13–30.

Vergès, Françoise, 2005. 'Where to begin? "Le commencement" in *Peau noire, masques blancs* and in creolisation', in Silverman, 2005: 32–45.

——, 2006. *La Mémoire enchaînée: questions sur l'esclavage* (Paris: Albin Michel).

Verschave, Xavier, 2003. *La Françafrique: le plus long scandale de la République* (Paris: Stock).

Vidal, Dominique, and Karim Bourtel, 2005. *Le Mal-être arabe: enfants de la colonisation* (Paris: Agone).

Vieillard-Baron, Hervé, 1994. *Les Banlieues françaises ou le ghetto impossible* (La Tour d'Aigue: L'Aube).

Villepin, Dominique de, 2004. *Le Requin et la Mouette* (Paris: Albin Michel).

Vincendeau, Ginette, 1998. *Pépé le Moko* (London: British Film Institute).

Vingtième Siècle, 2007. 94. [Special issue: 'Mémoires Europe-Asie'.]

Watts, Richard, 2005. *Packaging Post/Coloniality: The Manufacture of Literary Identity in the Francophone World* (Lanham, MD: Lexington Books).

Wauters, Alphonse-Jules, 1895. *Bibliographie du Congo 1880–1895: catalogue méthodique de 3.800 ouvrages, brochures, notices et cartes relatifs à l'histoire, à la géographie et à la colonisation du Congo* (Brussels: Administration du Mouvement Géographique).

Weber, Eugen, 1976. *Peasants into Frenchmen: The Modernization of Rural France, 1870–1914* (Stanford, CA: Stanford University Press).

Wehrs, Donald, 2003. 'Sartre's Legacy in Postcolonial Theory; or, Who's afraid of non-Western historiography and cultural studies?', *New Literary History*, 34.4: 761–89.

Weil, Patrick, 1995. *La France et ses étrangers: l'aventure d'une politique de l'immigration de 1938 à nos jours* (Paris: Gallimard).

——, 2005. *La République et sa diversité: immigration, intégration, discrimination* (Paris: Seuil).

White, Richard, 1991. *The Middle Ground: Indians, Empires, and Republics in the Great Lakes Region, 1650–1815* (Cambridge: Cambridge University Press).

Wievorka, Michel (ed.), 1996. *Une société fragmentée? Le multiculturalisme en débat* (Paris: La Découverte).

Wilder, Gary, 1996. 'Irreconcilable Differences: A conversation with Albert Memmi', *Transition*, 71: 158–77.

——, 2005. *The French Imperial Nation-State: Negritude and Colonial Humanism between the Two World Wars* (Chicago: University of Chicago Press).

Williams, Emily Allen, and Melvin Rahming (eds), 2006. *Changing Currents: Transnational Caribbean Literary and Cultural Criticism* (Trenton, NJ, and Asmara, Eritrea: Africa World Press).

Williams, Patrick, and Laura Chrisman (eds), 1993. *Colonial Discourse and Post-colonial Theory: A Reader* (London: Harvester Wheatsheaf).

Winston, Jane Bradley, 2001. *Postcolonial Duras: Cultural Memory in Postwar France* (New York: Palgrave).

Woodhull, Winifred, 1993. *Transfigurations of the Maghreb: Feminism, Decolonization, and Literatures* (Minneapolis, MN: University of Minnesota Press).

——, 2004. 'Deterritorializing Francophone Studies', *Francophone Postcolonial Studies*, 2.1: 83–86.

Yacine, Kateb, 1970. *L'Homme aux sandales de caoutchouc* (Paris: Seuil).

Yaeger, Patricia, 2007. 'Editor's column: The End of Postcolonial Theory? A Roundtable with Sunil Agnani, Fernando Coronil, Gaurav Desai, Mamadou Diouf, Simon Gikandi, Susie Tharu and Jennifer Wenzel', *PMLA*, 122.3: 633–51.

Young, Robert J. C., 1990. *White Mythologies: Writing History and the West* (London and New York: Routledge).

——, 1995a. *Colonial Desire: Hybridity in Theory, Culture and Race* (London and New York: Routledge).

——, 1995b. 'Foucault on Race and Colonialism', *New Formations*, 25: 57–65.

——, 2000. 'Deconstruction and the Postcolonial', in Royle, 2000: 187–210.

——, 2001a. *Postcolonialism: An Historical Introduction* (Oxford: Blackwell).

——, 2001b. 'Preface', in Sartre, 2001a: vii–xxiv.

Zantop, Susanne, 1997. *Colonial Fantasies: Conquest, Family, and Nation in Precolonial Germany, 1770–1870* (Durham, NC, and London: Duke University Press).

——, 2002. 'Europe's Occidentalisms', in Bill Ashcroft and Hussein Kadhim (eds), *Edward Said and the Post-Colonial* (Huntington, NY: Nova Science Publishers), 107–26.

Žižek, Slavoj, 2004. *Iraq: The Borrowed Kettle* (London: Verso).

Index

Printed and bound by CPI Group (UK) Ltd, Croydon, CR0 4YY

13/04/2025

14656555-0005